JANE FONDA

MY LIFE SO FAR

Published in the United States of America by
Random House Large Print in association with
Random House, New York.
Distributed by Random House, Inc., New York.

Library of Congress Cataloging-in-Publication Data

Fonda, Jane, 1937-
My life so far/Jane Fonda.
p. cm.
ISBN 0-375-43502-6
1. Fonda, Jane, 1937– 2. Motion picture actors and
actresses—United States—Biography. 3. Large type
books. I. Title.

PN2287.F56A3 2005b
791.4302'8'092—dc22
[B]
2005042771

www.randomlargeprint.com

FIRST LARGE PRINT EDITION

10 9 8 7 6 5 4 3 2 1

This Large Print edition published in accord with the
standards of the N.A.V.H.

PREFACE

If we do not know our own history, we are doomed
to live it as though it were our private fate.
—HANNAH ARENDT

The past empowers the present,
and the groping footsteps leading to this present
mark the pathways to the future.
—MARY CATHERINE BATESON

I was born December 21, the shortest day of the year.
I've always seen a year as a circle, with December settled down at the bottom, like 6 on a clock. Then,
when the new year starts up again, I see myself moving upward, counterclockwise, till, twelve months
later, I've come full circle, back to the bottom again,
to that shortest of days. On the day in 1996 when I
turned fifty-nine, I realized that, assuming I live to
be ninety, give or take, the next full circle would raise
the curtain on my third act.

I've had a career both in film and theater for more than forty years, and I know something about third acts. Haven't you ever been to a play where the first two acts seemed confused, then along came the third act and pulled it all together? Ah-ha, you said to yourself. So **that's** what that scene in the first act was leading to! Or, conversely, the first two acts can be brilliant, and then in the third, things disintegrate. However, the third act is definitely key, the payoff that pulls the seemingly random bits and pieces of the first two acts into a coherent whole.

The big difference between life and acting, though, is that in life there's no rehearsal and no "take two." This is it; better get it right before it's over.

To have a good third act, you need to understand what the first two have been about. To know where you're going, you must know where you've been. Call me a control freak, but I don't want to be like Christopher Columbus, who didn't know where he was headed when he left, didn't know where he was when he got there, and didn't know where he'd been when he got back. So on my fifty-ninth birthday, I knew I had some serious thinking to do.

In **Bird by Bird,** Anne Lamott writes, "If you want to make God laugh, tell her your plans." Quite right. But when I talk about figuring out my third act, I'm not talking about making plans. I'm talking about being disciplined enough to learn what my past has to teach me, brave enough to take those lessons into my heart—to own them—and to commit myself to doing what is necessary to make them a part of my future. This is hard.

I once saw a quote from dancer/choreographer Martha Graham framed and hung on a wall in a ballet studio. It said DISCIPLINE IS LIBERATION. At first that seemed like an oxymoron—isn't liberation the opposite of discipline? But discipline here doesn't mean tightness and rigidity, or punishment for wrongdoing. It means being so committed and so fully contained that you can let go; so deeply connected that you can detach; so strong that you can be gentle. Liberation takes intentionality, deliberation, courage, and—yes—discipline.

I think of the tremendous discipline it took the great ballet dancer Rudolf Nureyev to be temporarily liberated from gravity and soar through the air. I think of Greg Maddux, for many years the Atlanta Braves' outstanding pitcher, and the discipline that went into his ability to stand on the mound at the bottom of the ninth inning of the World Series and be physically and mentally relaxed.

For me, discipline, liberation, means acknowledging my demons, banishing them to the corner, seeing my past and excising the old patterns and baggage to make room for stillness. It is within stillness that I will hear the small voice and know where it is leading me. Call that voice what you will, but it has always been there, although during my second act—and in much of my first, for that matter—it was too risky for me to hear it.

It is taking discipline to liberate myself into a quieter third act, discipline in order to live with the awareness of my death.

I don't want to die without knowing who I am.

Remember those toys where you'd drop some hard, dry kernel thing into a glass of water and it would expand into an underwater landscape of mystery and color? Well, for me, to be disciplined and to live with the awareness of death means taking every minute and dropping it into a glass of water and having it swell into something fuller, more complete.

To understand why I decided to prepare this way for my third act, I have to take you back a few years, to my forties. My father was dying. I would sit by his bedside in silence for long periods of time hoping that he would talk to me, say something about what he was thinking and feeling as he was being rocked away from us to that eternal place. He never did.

If he couldn't come to me, I would go to him. I would focus on his face and try to put myself inside his body, become him. I remember feeling so profoundly sad for him—not that he was dying, but that he had never really been able to get close to me or to my brother, Peter. I felt sure he must regret that. I would if I were him.

This experience taught me that I was not afraid of dying. What I am terrified of, however, is getting to that place right at the edge of life when there's no time left, being filled with regrets, and having no time to set things right.

Of course we always have regrets—things we've done that we wish we could take back or erase. I have significant ones that will haunt me forever, which I hope I have been brave enough to confront in this book. But it's what you **didn't** do that you know you **should** have done, rather than what you **did** do that you **shouldn't** have done, that's the worst: the if-onlys and what-ifs.

"Why didn't I tell her how much I love her?"

"If only I'd been brave enough to address that old fear of mine."

I began thinking a great deal about these things in my late fifties. I had begun to go through deep inner changes—changes that I didn't fully understand until I began writing this book. I realized then that to avoid regrets, I would have to start, while I was still healthy and strong, to name what those might be—and to do something about them. I needed to live consciously, and I knew it would mean facing things that frightened me—like intimacy.

All this washed over me on my fifty-ninth birthday, in 1996. It was now or never. Fish or cut bait. In a year I would be sixty. One friend of mine said she slept through her sixtieth; another said he "went into hiding." Now, don't get me wrong. I hate getting old—it's a vanity and joints thing. But I knew that I would have to do what I usually do when I'm scared of something: sidle up to it, get to know it, and make it my friend. I have made the truism "Know thine enemy" work for me many times over the years. For instance, when I was in my forties, knowing that I was approaching menopause and the inevitable changes that would bring, I spent two years research-ing and writing a book with my friend Mignon Mc-Carthy, called **Women Coming of Age**, about how women can prepare for menopause and the aging process. When the changes did begin (much later than I had anticipated), I was prepared. I knew what was negotiable and what wasn't.

With all this in mind, I decided to fully embrace my upcoming sixtieth birthday by exploring what my life had been about up until then. Doing this changed me in ways I would never have foreseen. Coming to see my various individual struggles within a broader societal context enabled me to understand that much of my journey was a universal one for women—played out in different ways and with different outcomes, perhaps, but with common core experiences. This is what liberated me to write this book.

I also realized that it was time to talk about my personal experiences during the last five years of the Vietnam War. I want to do this partly to set the record straight but mostly because of what my experiences during those years taught me—about myself, about courage, about redemption. The most important of these lessons came from U.S. servicemen, from whom I learned that although we may enter the heart of darkness, if we are brave enough to face and then speak our truth, we can change and be set free.

Much has been said (not always in a friendly way) about the many variations of my life and how they have played themselves out in public; about the varied personas I seem to have taken on, the new faces that seemed to come with each new man in my life. I understand—now—what that was all about, and I explore it in this book. I hope that other women might see something of their own experiences in what I have to say about how a girl can lose touch with herself, her body, and have to struggle—hard—to get herself, her voice, back. Also, I believe that change can be a good thing, **if** you are fully **in** each phase and **if** the changes represent growth. For better or worse, I have been fully invested in each phase of my life, and I'm glad, because it enabled me to learn and grow. I hope this book will infuse the saying "Life is the journey, not the destination" with flesh and blood, because I believe that it is more joyful to embrace and be in the journey than to assume you'll ever "arrive."

My life has been marked not only by change but by discontinuity. Bucking social, familial, and professional expectations, I never focused on a pot at the end of my rainbow, and I now think this **lack** of early focus is one of the things that saved me. Had I, out of fear or laziness or "normalcy," done a freeze-frame on my earlier self, the self that wanted approval, well, I can tell you with certainty that I'd be sleeping through this third act . . . probably with the help of pills.

I feel that the very changing nature of my life helps to make my story relevant to other people and also to this modern era. Everything about our world today speaks to the need for flexibility and improvisation, yet young people still feel pressure to do life the way their parents did: deciding early on what they want to be when they grow up and committing to it. They feel there must be something wrong with them when it doesn't work out that way. We're brought up waiting for closure (when I graduate, when I get married, when I know what I want to do and become a grown-up), and we expect contentment to follow. Youthful dreams then give way to "reality" and we succumb to what **is** rather than striving for **what if.** Consistency can be a trap, especially if it leads to being consistently wrong rather than to stopping, admitting your mistake, and changing course.

One thing is for sure—the genie of "continual flux" is out of the bottle. Tectonic shifts in our global socio-psycho-economic realities have made constant change the norm—consistently! I believe in the words of the Sufi poet Rumi: "The alchemy of a changing life is the only truth." Certainly, my own life is proof that flux is often creative, enlivening.

I have structured this book into three acts. The first act I call "Gathering," because it was in those first thirty years of my life that I took in all that had made me **me**—the tools, the experiences, and the scars that I would spend the next two acts recovering from, and also building upon. The first act is also when I gathered resilience.

The second act I call "Seeking," because that is when I turned my eyes outward and began a search in the world, for meaning beyond the narrow confines of myself and my immediate life, asking, What am I here for? What are other people's lives like? Can I make it better?

The final act is called "Beginning," because—well, that's what it feels like.

While the high visibility of my public life has not always brought personal peace and happiness, it has lent a certain universal quality to my various metamorphoses. In the course of my writing, I have realized that perhaps I can use this to advantage: I can peel back the surface layers of events with which you, the reader, already have an association and invite you to see them through a new lens, with new eyes.

I moved "out of myself"—my body—early on and have spent much of my life searching to come home . . . to be embodied. I didn't understand this until I was in my sixties and had started writing this book. I have come to believe that perhaps my purpose in life is to show you—through my own journey—how and why this "disembodiment" happens, especially to women, and how, by moving back inside ourselves, we can restore balance—not just within ourselves but on the planet. I discovered that being disembodied rendered me incapable of intimacy, and so halfway through my second act, I went on a search for that.

I have dedicated this book to my mother. For me, this is a big deal—a way for me to begin to restore my own balance. You see, I have spent most of my life feeling and acting like an Immaculate Conception in reverse: born of a man, without aid of woman. For reasons you will come to understand, I have spent far too much energy obliterating all in my life that represented my mother. This has taken a profound toll. Dedicating this book to her marks another turning point in my attempt to live a full, conscious life.

So here's to you, dear reader. And here's to you, Frances Ford Seymour, my mother—you did the best you could. You gave me life; you gave me wounds; you also gave me part of what I needed to grow stronger at the broken places.

CONTENTS

PREFACE

ACT ONE GATHERING

CHAPTER ONE BUTTERFLY 7
CHAPTER TWO MY BLUE GENES 28
CHAPTER THREE LADY JAYNE 56
CHAPTER FOUR TIGERTAIL 69
CHAPTER FIVE WHERE'D I GO? 86
CHAPTER SIX SUSAN 107
CHAPTER SEVEN HUNGER 118
CHAPTER EIGHT WAITING FOR
MEANING 139
CHAPTER NINE TURNING POINT 163
CHAPTER TEN DOUBLE
EXPOSURE 185
CHAPTER ELEVEN VADIM 200
CHAPTER TWELVE THE MAGICIAN'S
ASSISTANT 222

CHAPTER THIRTEEN   PUTTING DOWN
                    ROOTS   248
CHAPTER FOURTEEN   **BARBARELLA**   261

ACT TWO   SEEKING

CHAPTER ONE   1968   281
CHAPTER TWO   **THEY SHOOT
                    HORSES,
                    DON'T THEY?**   307
CHAPTER THREE   COMING HOME   322
CHAPTER FOUR   SNAPSHOTS FROM
                    THE ROAD   342
CHAPTER FIVE   **KLUTE**   368
CHAPTER SIX   REDEMPTION   387
CHAPTER SEVEN   INSURRECTION
                    AND SEXUALITY   401
CHAPTER EIGHT   TOM   421
CHAPTER NINE   HANOI   437
CHAPTER TEN   BAMBOO   456
CHAPTER ELEVEN   FRAMED   489
CHAPTER TWELVE   ADIEU, LONE
                    RANGER   505
CHAPTER THIRTEEN   THE FINAL PUSH   517
CHAPTER FOURTEEN   I'M **BAAAAAACK!!!**   546
CHAPTER FIFTEEN   THE WORKOUT   587
CHAPTER SIXTEEN   GHOST   609
CHAPTER SEVENTEEN   SYNCHRONICITY   619
CHAPTER EIGHTEEN   **ON GOLDEN POND**   638

CHAPTER NINETEEN	CLOSURE	670
CHAPTER TWENTY	MAKING MOVIES	681
CHAPTER TWENTY-ONE	THE GIFT OF PAIN	701
CHAPTER TWENTY-TWO	PHOENIX ON HOLD	711
CHAPTER TWENTY-THREE	TED	741
CHAPTER TWENTY-FOUR	A CALLING	777
CHAPTER TWENTY-FIVE	YEARNINGS	794

ACT THREE BEGINNING

CHAPTER ONE	SIXTY	817
CHAPTER TWO	MOVING ON	836
CHAPTER THREE	LEAVING MY FATHER'S HOUSE	850
	EPILOGUE	861
	FILMOGRAPHY	873
	ACKNOWLEDGMENTS	875
	INDEX	879
	CREDITS AND PERMISSIONS	903

ACT ONE

GATHERING

Everything is gestation and then birthing.
—RAINER MARIA RILKE,
Letters to a Young Poet

At age two, totally
focused.

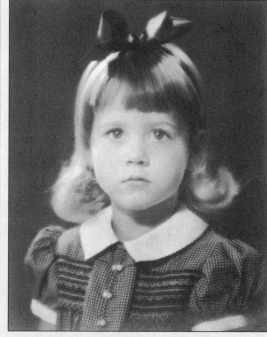

Already the dead-
serious Lone Ranger.

My photograph for **Harper's Bazaar**
by Richard Avedon, 1960.

Plain Jane with bad hair.

A brief stint with the jet set
at about nineteen.
(Yale Joel/Time & Life Pictures
Getty Images)

With Dean Jones in **Any
Wednesday.**
(Photofest)

Barbarella between takes.

CHAPTER ONE

BUTTERFLY

Stay near me—do not take thy flight!
A little longer stay in sight!
Much converse do I find in thee,
Historian of my infancy!
—WILLIAM WORDSWORTH,
"To a Butterfly"

I SAT CROSS-LEGGED on the floor of the tiny home I'd created out of cardboard boxes. The walls were so high that all I could see if I looked up was the white-painted tongue-and-groove ceiling of the glassed-in porch so common in Connecticut in the 1940s. The porch ran the entire length of the house and smelled of mildew. Light from the windows bounced off the ceiling down to where I sat, so I didn't need a lamp as I worked on the saddle. I was eleven years old.

It was an English saddle, my half sister Pan's, from the time before she'd gotten married, sold her horse, and moved to New York City—from the time when we still believed things would work out all right.

I held the saddle on my lap, rubbing saddle soap into the beautiful, rich leather, over and over. . . . Make it better. I know I can make it better. The smell of saddle soap was comforting. So was the smallness of my home. This was a place where I could be sure of things. No one was allowed in here but me—not my brother, Peter, not anyone. Everything was always arranged just so—the saddle, the soap, the soft rags folded carefully, and my book of John Masefield poems. Neatness was important . . . something to count on.

Mother was home for a while and if I leaned forward ever so slightly, I could look out my "door" down the length of the porch, to where she sat at an oilcloth-covered table on which stood a Mason jar. A butterfly would be beating its wings frantically against the glass walls of the jar, and I could see my mother pick up a cotton ball with tweezers, dip it into a bottle of ether, unscrew the top of the jar, and carefully drop in the ether-soaked ball. After a minute, I could see the butterfly's wings begin to slow their mad fluttering, until gradually they would stop moving altogether. Peace. A whiff of ether drifted down to where I sat, making me think of the dentist. I knew just what the butterfly felt, because whenever I went to have my braces tightened, the nurse would put a mask over my nose and tell me to breathe deeply. In no time the edges of my body would begin to disappear. Sound would come to me from far away and I would feel a wonderful, cosmic abandon as I fell backward down a dark hole, like Alice to Wonderland. Oh, I wished that I could make that sensation last forever. I didn't feel sorry at all for the butterfly.

After a while, mother would unscrew the lid; gently remove the butterfly with the long tweezers; carefully, lovingly, pierce its body with a pin; and mount it on a white board on the wall above the table. There were at least a dozen of them up there, different kinds of swallowtails, a southern dogface, a red admiral, a clouded sulphur, and a monarch. I never could decide which one was my favorite.

Once she took me with her to a meadow full of wildflowers and tall grasses where she went to catch her butterflies. There was still an abundance of wild places—swamps, unexplored forests, and meadows— in Greenwich, Connecticut, in the 1940s. I watched as she moved through the grass—her blond, sun-blushed hair blowing in the wind—swooping down with her green net, then flipping the net quickly to close off the butterfly's escape route. I would help her get it safely into a jar and quickly screw the top on.

It puzzled me a little why Mother had decided to take up butterfly collecting. I don't remember her ever doing this when we lived in California. I was the one fascinated with butterflies. I was always painting pictures of them. When I was ten, right be-fore we'd moved from California, I gave my father a drawing for his birthday. "Butterflies by Jane Fonda" was written up in the right-hand corner, and then

two rows of them with their names written underneath in my tight, straight-up-and-down-careful-not-
to-reveal-anything handwriting. My letter said:

> May 19, 1948.
> Dear Dad,
>   I did not trace these drawings of but-
> terflies. I hope you had a happy birthday. I
> heard you on the Bing Crosby program.
> Every two days I will send you another
> picture of butterflies.
>   Love, Jane.

By the time Mother took up the butterfly
hobby, I had turned eleven, Peter was nine, and we
were living in our second rented house in Connecticut. It was a rambling two-story wood house perched
atop a steep hill overlooking a tollgate on the Merritt
Parkway. I could look out my bedroom window and
count the cars. Prior to the move east, we'd grown up
in California's Santa Monica Mountains and, instead
of a tollgate, we looked out onto the vast, shimmering Pacific Ocean. Maybe that is why my childhood
fantasies of conquering all the enemies of the world
were so expansive. Had I grown up overlooking the
tollgate, I might have seen myself as an accountant.

    This new house was on a large piece of property
bordered to the west by an immense hardwood forest
that, in the winter, became a leafless gray fortress.
Then in the spring, dogwood would bloom, hopeful
and white through the layered forest gray, and red-
bud would add slashes of magenta. By May, an array

of greens would transform the woods once again. For someone who had spent the first ten years of her life seasonless in California, this ever-changing palette seemed miraculous.

The house had an uncomfortable Charles Addams–y quality about it, always too dark and chilly, and it had far more rooms than there were people living there, which added a sense of impermanence and awkwardness to its hilltop perch. There was Grandma Seymour (Mother's mother), Peter, me, and a Japanese-American maid named Katie. Peter says Katie's familiar presence with us after three years was comforting to him. I, on the other hand, barely remember her. But then Peter got more attached to people than I did. I was the Lone Ranger.

Mother wasn't with us much anymore, though I didn't know why. It was during one of the periods when she was back from wherever it was she went that the butterfly collection was started. Maybe someone had suggested that she get herself a hobby. Peter and I had stopped paying much attention to her being away, or at least I had. It had simply become a fact of our lives: Mother would be there, and then she wouldn't. When she wasn't there, and even when she was, Grandma Seymour would be in charge of us. Grandma was a strong woman, a constant presence in our early lives. But though I loved her, I don't remember ever running joyfully into her arms the way my own grandchildren do with me. I don't remember her ever imparting grandmotherly wisdom or even being fun to be with. She was a more

formal, stalwart presence. But she was always there
to meet our external needs.

Around the house there'd be an occasional mur-
mured mention of a hospital or of an illness, and
right after we'd moved to Greenwich, Mother had
been in Johns Hopkins Hospital for a long time, for
an operation on a dropped kidney. Grandma took
Peter and me to visit her there once, and I remember
Mother telling me they'd almost cut her in half. But
she'd been "ill" and in hospitals so much that it had
lost any real meaning. Hospitals were supposed to
make you well so you could come home and **stay.**

Ever since we had moved to Greenwich I had
spent a lot of time in hospitals myself—me, the
healthy one. I'd developed blood poisoning, then
chronic ear infections; then I started breaking bones.
My arm was broken the first time during a wrestling
match with a boy, Teddy Wahl, the son of the man
who ran the nearby Round Hill Stables and Riding
Club. Teddy threw me against a stall door. It hurt,
but I walked home and didn't say anything—between Peter and Mother, we had enough hypochon-
driacs in the house. I was not going to complain.
Instead, I sat in front of the black-and-white TV to
watch **The Howdy Doody Show,** my favorite because it regularly included a short **Lone Ranger** film.

I sat carefully on my hands, as I always did when
Dad was home, because I was scared he would see
that I was still biting my fingernails. As we sat down
to eat, Dad asked me if I'd washed my hands, and
when I told him I hadn't, he exploded in anger,

pulled me out of my seat and into the bathroom, turned on the faucet, took the broken arm (which I'd been holding limply by my side), and thrust it under the water. I passed out. He'd no idea that I was hurt and was very apologetic as he rushed me to the hospital, where my arm was X-rayed and put into a cast. The worst part was that all this happened right before school started, my first year at the all-girls Greenwich Academy—just at the time when everybody would be checking out who was cool (we called it "neat" back then), who was good at field hockey, and whom they wanted to be friends with, I had to show up with my arm in a cast.

At the time, Dad was starring in the Broadway smash hit **Mister Roberts.** I now realize that I must have sensed that something was very wrong between my parents. Palpable tension was in the air: Dad's anger and black moods; Mother's increasing absences. Even if I had had the words to express what I "knew," I'd already learned that no one would listen to words that spoke about feelings. So instead, my body was sending out distress signals.

There's a set of photos of us taken around that time. Just after we left California, **Harper's Bazaar** had come out to interview Dad and take pictures of the family "picnicking"—one of those setup jobs that make the children of movie stars feel like props. The pictures show us sitting on the lawn: Dad, Mother, Peter, me, and Pan (my half sister, the one with the saddle), who at sixteen was beautiful and remarkably voluptuous.

There is one photograph in particular that says it all. I discovered it in a scrapbook many years of therapy later, when I was able to see it with more perception and compassion. Dad is in the foreground leaning back on his elbows, looking as if he's got something really good going on in his head that has nothing to do with all of us. I am kneeling next to him, looking intently at him, as I often did in our family pictures, showing clearly whose side I was on. Behind me Peter is playing with the cat, and Pan is lounging glamorously. And then, in the background, almost like an outsider, there's Mother, leaning forward toward us with an expression of pain and anxiety on her face. I feel so sad when I look at that face, which I've done often with a magnifying glass.

Why couldn't I have known? Why wasn't I nicer? I was ten years old.

Dad had come out of the navy at the end of World War II and (what felt like) the very next day had gone off to New York to start rehearsals for **Mister Roberts** while we stayed in California. When it became clear that the play was in for a long run, Mother decided to put our home up for sale and move east. She settled on Greenwich, thinking that the thirty-five-minute train or car ride from New York City would make weekend commutes easy for Dad. Plus, in that well-heeled Connecticut enclave, there would be homes to rent on large enough pieces of property so that Peter and I could continue our habit of roaming the outdoors. My parents were at least right about that part.

A faux family picnic in Greenwich
for **Harper's Bazaar** magazine.
That's Mother in the background.
(Genevieve Naylor/Corbis)

I don't remember Dad being around much after we moved to Greenwich. When he was there, I could almost feel his energy pulling him back toward New York, though I didn't really know why. I supposed it was just that Mother, Peter, and I weren't all that interesting. When he'd visit us I could sense that he didn't really want to be there. But Dad had been an Eagle Scout, and the commitment to doing one's duty was embedded in his DNA. I wish the Scouts had taught him how to make it seem less like a duty.

Sometimes Dad would come out on a Sunday and take Peter and me fishing for flounder in nearby Long Island Sound. Dad was usually in a bad mood, which meant these excursions weren't exactly "fun times," but I enjoyed them anyway—all of us together in the little rented motorboat, the salty smells mixed with engine fumes, the anticipation as we'd pull out of the harbor, round the buoy, and head to sea. Because flounder are bottom feeders, we'd never go out very far before Dad would turn off the motor and tell us to bait our hooks. This was always the moment of reckoning.

Baiting the hook meant reaching into a bucket filled with reddish brown kelp, among which writhed long reddish brown bloodworms with what appeared to be claws in their heads. Peter didn't like them at all. Peter, in fact, would refuse to touch them—which in itself took guts. Dad wouldn't even try to disguise the disgust he felt about Peter's squeamishness, and his moods would get blacker and blacker. Whereupon I, the Lone Ranger, would ride to the rescue and be man enough for both of us. I'd pick up that worm and stick the hook right through its squirmy head without even a shudder. I didn't do this to make Peter look bad. I loved my brother. I just wanted to prove my toughness to Dad and make the tension go away.

Peter was who he was. When he was scared he showed it; if he was sick, he'd complain about it—damn the consequences. I often wished he'd pretend like I did, just to make things easier. But, no, Peter was himself. And I, well, I'd gotten into the habit of leaving myself behind someplace in order to win Dad's approval. **Make things better. I know I can make things better.**

Once, Dad had us come into the city and took us to the circus. A New York columnist, Radie Harris, who knew our family, was also there and was quoted as saying:

> **I remember sitting in a box at the circus a few months after Mister Roberts opened. Hank sat just to my right. With him were Jane and Peter, and not once during the entire performance did he say a word to either child. And either the children knew enough to say nothing, or they might have been too intimidated to speak. He didn't buy them hot dogs, cotton candy, or treat them to souvenirs. When the circus was over, they simply stood up and walked out. I felt sorry for all three of them.**

Then one day, when I'd just finished breakfast and was heading out the door to school, I saw that Mother was standing at the entrance to the living room. She motioned me to come to her. "Jane," she said, "if anyone tells you that your father and I are getting divorced, tell them you already know."

That was it. And off to school I went.

I had realized the year before that parents getting divorced didn't mean that you, the child, would fall through a crack in the floor and no one would ever look for you again. Some of my friends had divorced parents and seemed to have survived just fine. I do remember that day at school feeling a little out of body, as if I'd had some of the dentist's ether, but I also felt oddly important and deserving of special attention. Divorces were fairly uncommon in those days.

A few days after "divorce" had been uttered (only to me, not to Peter) I was lying on Mother's bed with her and she asked if I wanted to see her scar from her recent kidney operation. I didn't really want to. But since she'd asked, I felt she needed to show it to me and that I shouldn't say no. She pulled up her satin pajama top and lowered the pants and there . . . oh, horror—**that's** why they were getting divorced! Who would want to live with someone who'd been cut in half and had a thick, wide pink scar that ran all around her waist? It was terrifying.

"I've lost all my stomach muscle," she said sadly. "Doesn't that look awful?" What did she want me to say, that it wasn't bad? Or did she want me to agree with her?

"And look at this," she said, showing me one of

her breasts. The nipple was all distorted. I felt so bad for her—it must have hurt so much—but I also didn't want to be her daughter. I wanted to wake up and discover I was adopted. I wanted a mother who looked healthy and beautiful, at whom a father would want to look when she had no clothes on. Maybe then he'd want to stay at home. This was all her fault.

I think it was around that time, maybe right there on that bed, that I vowed I would do whatever it took to be perfect so that a man would love me. Fifty-three years later, Pan told me that Mother had had a botched breast implant. I guess Mother had tried to be perfect, too. I will return to the sad topic of breast implants in act two.

Howard Teichmann, who wrote my father's authorized biography, **My Life,** wrote that when Dad told my mother he wanted a divorce, she said, "Well, all right, Hank. Good luck, Hank."

> **In retrospect, Fonda says, "I've got to tell you she was absolutely wonderful. . . . She accepted it. She was sympathetic. She couldn't have been more understanding."**

Yeah, sure. Mother was acting by the rules. If she could love the **right** way—selflessly, with understanding and no anger—perhaps Dad would come back to her. In private, though, she was disintegrating. She hacked off her hair with nail scissors and, while staying in a friend's New York apartment, walked the neighborhood in her nightgown.

In those days, I too walked in my nightgown,

but in my sleep, always propelled by the same nightmare: I was in the wrong room and desperately needed to get out, get back to where I was supposed to be. It was dark and cold and I never could find the door. In my sleep I would actually move large pieces of furniture around my bedroom trying to find the way out, and then, because it was futile, I would give up and get back in bed. The next morning the furniture would have to be moved back into place. It was a nightmare that stayed with me—albeit with variations on where I was trying to get to—until I married Ted Turner, when I was fifty-four.

One of my most vivid memories of that time was sitting in silence at the dinner table in that spooky house on the hill—Peter, Grandma, Mother, and me. Through the window I could see the gray March landscape. Mother, at the head of the table, was crying silently into her food. It was spinach and Spam. We ate a lot of canned food in those days, as though the war and food rationing were still going on. I used to wonder about this, but now I know that Mother was terrified of running out of money and not receiving anything from Dad in the divorce.

No one said anything about the fact that Mother was crying. Maybe we feared that if one of us put words to what we saw and heard, life would implode into an unfathomable sadness so heavy the air wouldn't bear it. Not even after we left the table was anything said. Grandma never took us aside to explain what was happening. Perhaps if "it" was not named, "it" would not exist. Peter and I went to our rooms as always, to do our homework. The dinner scene got buried in a graveyard somewhere next door to my heart, and the habit of not dealing with feelings became embedded in another generation.

But life goes on, as life does—until it doesn't, especially when you're in the discovery mode of an eleven-year-old. That year I managed to take a horse over a four-foot jump for the first time and became obsessed with the card game canasta. And Brooke Hayward and I began a successful writing partnership that won us "Best Short Story" awards at Greenwich Academy.

Within walking distance of the house was a riding stable—not the big one where Teddy Wahl broke my arm, but a small one with only an outdoor riding ring, where I often took jumping lessons on a borrowed white horse named Silver. My best friend, Diana Dunn, took lessons there, too. We both adored the teacher, a cozy Irishman named Mike Carroll. Next to being inside my cardboard "home" with my sister's saddle, this was where I most liked to be. Horses were my passion, my escape.

Grandma told me many years later that it was around this time that Mother had been moved, on the advice of her doctors, from the Austen Riggs Center, a more open residence for the affluent "mentally afflicted" in Stockbridge, Massachusetts, to the Craig House sanitarium in Beacon, New York. The doctors said that her emotional deterioration and suicidal tendencies required she be under constant guard. Grandma was with her for the move and told me that Mother was in a straitjacket and didn't recognize her. I can't manage to wrap my mind around that image of Mother in a straitjacket, or what Grandma's anguish must have been.

One day Mother came home accompanied by a uniformed nurse. I refused to see her. I was playing jacks with Peter on the hardwood floor upstairs when she arrived in a limousine. Grandma called for us to come down.

"Peter." I grabbed his arm. "Don't go down. I'm not going to. Let's just stay up here and play jacks. I'll let you win. Okay?"

"No, I'm going," Peter said, and he went downstairs.

Why didn't I go down? Was I so angry with her for not being there for us? Was it I'll-show-you-I-don't-need-you-either?

I never saw her again.

She must have known it would be her last time home. She'd come, I guess, to say good-bye—but also to get the small razor that she kept in a black enamel box given to her years before by her friend Eulalia Chapin. Apparently, she had rushed upstairs and just managed to slip the razor into her purse when the nurse, who'd been sent to make sure such a thing didn't happen, caught up to her.

A month later, in April, on her forty-second birthday, Mother wrote six notes—one each to Peter, Pan, and me; one to her mother; one to her nurse, telling her not to go into the bathroom but to call the doctor; and one to the doctor, her psychiatrist:

"Dr. Bennett, you've done everything possible for me. I'm sorry, but this is the best way out."

Then she went into her bathroom in the Craig House sanitarium, carefully withdrew the razor she'd managed to keep hidden, and cut her throat. She was still alive when Dr. Bennett arrived, but she died a few minutes later.

The fluttering slowed; the wings grew still. Then peace.

I came home from school that afternoon, and as I walked through the front door, Grandma called down to me from her bedroom at the top of the stairs.

"Jane, something's happened to your mother. She's had a heart attack. Your father is on his way here right now. Please stay in the house and wait for him. Don't go out."

I turned right around, ran out the door, and ran all the way to the stables, where I was to have a riding lesson. I don't remember feeling anything at all, though I must have known something serious was happening, because Dad didn't just travel out from the city unexpectedly on a weekday.

In the middle of my lesson the phone in the stable rang. It was Dad telling whoever answered to make me come home immediately. But I took my time. There were so many dead bugs and interesting rocks in the dirt driveway that I needed to stop and examine. Eventually, when I could find no more ways to stall, I trudged up the hill. A strange car was parked at the bottom of the steps. Must be Dad's rental, I thought with a shudder. In some deep part of me that wasn't my mind, some part that could keep secrets from the rest of me, I knew what was coming. My **conscious** mind knew this was all a dream, that I was about to wake up. I opened the heavy front door and walked into the living room. Nobody had turned on any lights, and the room seemed grayer than usual. Dad and Grandmother were sitting up very straight, each on a different couch, facing each other. Dad took me on his lap and told me that my mother had had a heart attack and was dead.

Dead. Now, there's a word. Short, heavy. I felt myself holding it in my hands, like a brick. **Dead, like the butterflies mounted on that board on the other side of the living room wall. Her jars and tweezers were lying spread around on the table out there. I'd seen them only yesterday when I'd gone to polish the saddle. She couldn't be dead. She hadn't put her things away. Maybe I** was **dreaming.** Then I was outside my body looking back at myself, waiting for myself to react. Everything was familiar, yet nothing was the same. From another room came the loud ticking of a clock—jarring, wrong. Didn't it know that time no longer mattered? I noticed wrinkles in the chintz slipcovers and tried to smooth them out. **Make it better. I know I can make it better.**

Peter came home a few minutes later. Dad got up and switched seats with Grandma, taking Peter on his lap and repeating the story to him. I had to get away from all of them, to be by myself, try to get myself back into my body, figure out how I felt.

"Excuse me, please. I'm going to my room."

I could hear Peter crying as I followed myself upstairs. Sitting on the edge of my bed, **I wondered why I couldn't cry, like Peter.** "Mother's dead. I will never see her again." I said it over and over to myself, trying to bring up some tears. But I felt nothing.

I remembered that I had stayed upstairs the day she'd come home for the last time. **Why hadn't I gone down to see her?** I felt something begin to stir in my chest. **Ah, here it comes. I'm normal.** But the feeling skittered away and I went outside myself again, and again I went numb.

When I was in my forties and the tears for Mother did finally come—unexpectedly and for no apparent reason—they were unstoppable. They came from so deep within me that I feared I wouldn't survive them, that my heart would crack open, and like Humpty-Dumpty, I'd never be able to be put back together again.

Grandmother and Dad arranged to have Mother cremated, and then Dad drove back into the city in time for his performance of **Mister Roberts.** Didn't miss a beat. I don't think this implied he didn't feel anything; it's just that Dad didn't know how to deal with feelings or to process pain. He knew only how to cover it up. Or maybe he'd grown numb, like me. Maybe I learned it from him.

As soon as Dad left the house, I went into

Mother's room and found a favorite purse of hers, with its special lipstick smell. On the bedside table lay her dog-eared copy of Dale Carnegie's **How to Win Friends and Influence People.** Everywhere—on the floor of her closet, in her coat pocket—there were pieces of her unfinished—never to be finished—life. In the medicine cabinet all the little bottles were lined up: FRANCES FONDA, with dates of expiration—**but she'd expired first**—lined up like orphans. Like me. Would they be thrown out now? Would I?

My girlhood friend Diana Dunn told me recently that her father said to her, "Jane's mother has just died and we have to go to her house and bring her here." Dad or Grandmother must have called and told him. Diana says I stayed with them for several days, but **not one word** was ever spoken about Mother's death. "You never cried," she said. "I felt fear then. Your mother had just died and I didn't understand why no one said anything to you. You were my best friend. I loved you and I didn't know what to do for you."

Never in all the subsequent years, all the way to his own death, did Dad and I ever mention Mother. I was afraid it would upset him. I was sure he felt guilty because he'd asked for the divorce. **Make it better.** I don't even know if he knew that I knew the heart attack story wasn't true. Don't ask, don't tell. Peter, on the other hand, wore it all on both sleeves. The following Christmas, eight months after her death, Dad came up from New York City to open presents with us in Greenwich, where we were being looked after by Grandma and Katie, the maid. Peter had filled an entire wingback chair with presents for Mother and a letter he'd written to her. Looking back, it is so terribly sad and poignant, an eleven-year-old boy needing to let his mother know he loved her and missed her and wanted people to acknowledge her. But, oh God, nothing he could have done could have made that Christmas Day any worse. I was furious with Peter and sided with Dad, who seemed to see Peter's behavior as a play for sympathy. What a thought!

In the week that followed Mother's death, my seventh-grade teachers seemed to go out of their way to be kind and understanding. I became aware that the rap on me was just what I had hoped: that I was remarkably brave and took everything in stride. What was really happening, though, was that I was getting psychic perks for shutting down! What had been a tendency for most of my young life was now being praised, and I began to hone this into a fine art: **You don't really feel what you feel; you didn't really hear what you heard.** It's not that I **consciously** did these things—buried them. It's just that I'd been doing it for so long that I had begun to **live** that way. I simply didn't know anymore what I knew or wanted or thought or felt—or even who I was in an embodied way. I would become whatever I felt the people whose love and attention I needed wanted me to be. I would try to be perfect. It was safer there. It was a survival mechanism that served me well—back then.

CHAPTER TWO

MY BLUE GENES

And yet they, who passed away long ago,
still exist in us, as predisposition,
as burden upon our fate, as murmuring blood,
and as gesture that rises up from the depths of time.
—RAINER MARIA RILKE,
Letters to a Young Poet

The past is never dead. It's not even past.
—WILLIAM FAULKNER,
Requiem for a Nun

MOTHER

SHE WAS AN ICON, always at the center of things, and, boy, did she love life!" Listening to the voice at the other end of the line, I thought this woman must be a little batty to have seen Mother as an icon! The woman speaking was Laura Clark. She had worked for Elizabeth Arden in New York in the mid-1930s, modeling tea gowns for Arden clients while they were getting their beauty treatments. One day she walked into the room where my mother, a regular at Arden's, had just finished getting a facial. Mother took one look at the beautiful young girl and, instead of asking about the tea gown, offered her a cup of tea.

"My goodness," said Mother. "You look exhausted. Come over here and sit down." Whereupon they struck up a conversation that led to a lifelong friendship.

Laura Clark had been trying to reach me for more than twenty years, to talk to me about my mother, it turned out. In the seventies she had even gone backstage after my father's Broadway play **First Monday in October** to ask him how she could contact me. "Try the police!" he'd told her brusquely, referring to my controversial activism.

I vaguely remembered getting letters from a Laura Clark, but when I'd come to the sentence where she'd say she had been a friend of my mother's, I'd toss the letter away. Mother, as far as I was concerned, had no place in my life. Now, after many years, another letter had arrived from Laura, giving me a number to call if I wanted to talk. She had no way of knowing that I had decided to write this book, that I had reached a point when I knew I would need, at last, to understand my mother. I was sitting at my desk writing when I made the decision to pick up the phone and call her. I was ready. Or so I thought.

Laura's soft voice was describing a woman I don't remember knowing.

"Your mother took me under her wing and invited me to the wonderful parties she gave at her Long Island estate and at the club El Morocco. Men just fell over themselves when they saw her. She'd cast those slanted eyes at a man across the room and he couldn't resist."

"Wasn't she married?" I asked. "Was her daughter, Pan, already born?"

"She was a widow when we met. Her first husband, George Brokaw, had just died and their daughter must have been a couple of years old."

Laura went on to describe how later, during World War II, Laura had moved to Los Angeles with her young son, Danny, to find work.

"Of course, by then your mother and father had married and you and Peter were young children. Your mother found me an apartment, took me to parties like she had in New York, and helped me meet people. My name then was Laura Pyzel. Do you remember?"

"You're **that** Laura! Of course I remember you and Danny. He was Peter's age and was at our house a lot. Tell me more about my mother. Did you ever see her depressed?"

"Never. She was always 'up,' the most lively one of all, like a butterfly. Her suicide shocked me. Oddly enough, I was wearing a black lace dress she'd given me when I heard the news on the radio."

I'd always wondered if it had been difficult for Mother to adjust to a much less social life with my father in California, and I asked Laura about this.

"Yes, they were so different, and it was hard on her." Laura went on for a while, reminiscing about life in Los Angeles in the forties, and then she said, "You know, Jane, your mother was a very sexy woman with a modern outlook on life."

"What do you mean?" I sat up, alert, in my desk chair.

"Your father was overseas in the navy during the war. Frances was lonely, and while he was away she fell madly in love with a young man named Joe Wade. He was divinely attractive, a real party boy! She was crazy about him. All the women were."

My heart began to race and I had to stop taking notes. "Can you describe him to me?"

"He drank a lot and was very wild," Laura said. "We were scared for her because he was such a loose cannon. We worried what would happen when your father came home."

Suddenly a thought flashed into my mind. "Was he by any chance a musician?"

Laura was silent for a moment, then, "Why, yes, I believe he was."

Oh, my God! There it was. The puzzle was starting to come together.

When I was about seven and Dad was overseas, Mother and I were walking up the driveway of our house in California and out of the blue, she said to me, "Never marry a musician." I remember it vividly—not just because it is such an odd thing to

say to a seven-year-old, but because I can't remember
Mother ever giving me any other advice about life. I
would wonder about those words over the years. I
vaguely remembered hearing that when Dad was
away she had taken a fledgling musician under her
wing and was trying to manage his career. I saw so
clearly now: She'd fallen in love with Joe Wade and
he'd left her.

"Do you know if Joe Wade ever came to our
house?" I asked Laura. By now I was shaking and
hoping Laura couldn't tell from my voice.

"Yes, he was there often. Like I said, he was wild,
like an animal. In fact, he carried a gun and once he
shot a hole in the ceiling."

"In her bedroom ceiling?" I asked, trying to
imagine what had been going on. Wow! Mother was
beginning to take on a Mae West cachet.

"Yes," Laura answered. "Your mother was so
worried about that hole in the ceiling." I shouldn't
wonder! What could she possibly say to my father
when he came home: "Oh, Hank, it's nothing really.
I was just trying out a new pistol and . . ."

I felt a tectonic shifting of plates deep within me, an
owning of my mother. For the first time I was seeing
her not as a victim but as a woman who had claimed
her own pleasure. I hung up the phone and began to
sob uncontrollably.

The previous fall, another coincidence had made
me aware that a Dr. Peggy Miller, a psychologist from

Pacific Palisades, California, knew about my mother. Peggy had been the daughter-in-law of Mother's best friend, Eulalia Chapin. Sitting with Peggy in her living room, I felt like an archeologist on a manic dig for clues from the past that could illuminate the present.

"Talk to me about my mother, Peggy. Everything you know."

She, like Laura, spoke of Mother as someone who was always at the center of things, an adventurer.

"Dick, my late husband, even though he was a good deal younger than your mother, told me that he loved being with her because she was the most fun, amusing person he'd ever seen. He told me men were drawn to her like moths to a flame." I asked about Mother's affair with Joe Wade and she confirmed the story, saying that her mother-in-law played the role of Mother's "beard," pretending to be the one Joe was having an affair with and letting them use her home for their liaisons.

Paul Peralta-Ramos, a son of the socialite and artist Millicent Rogers and a cousin of Mother's, said:

> **The thing about Frances was that she was the person we'd go to if we had a problem. Nothing shocked her. If you knocked up a girl, your mother'd be the one to go to. She was the one who'd find a doctor. She was a rock, a problem solver.**

I was stunned. Mother? **A rock!**

Was I crazy never to have seen my mother as three people had now described her to me: a lively, pleasure-loving, iconic rock of a woman? Why have I remembered her only as a sad, nervous victim to whom I would no more turn for help than try to walk on quicksand, whom I desperately did not want to be like? I discovered the answer a year later when, with the help of lawyers, I was able to obtain Mother's medical records from the Austen Riggs Center.

I was alone in a hotel room one evening when I opened the thick envelope. When I saw the title, "Medical Records of Frances Ford Seymour Fonda," I couldn't breathe. I flung off my clothes and crawled into bed. As I began reading, my body started shaking, my teeth chattering.

In the midst of the nurses' daily accounts of Mother's deteriorating condition and the medications they were giving her, I found eight single-spaced pages that Mother had typed herself on admission to the institution, with numerous additions and corrections in her hand.

It was beyond belief. I had longed to know her early story. Now I was holding it in my hands. I'm going to share here those parts of it that have helped me understand her—and hence myself. Added to what she wrote herself are things that I have learned from others, including my half sister, Pan Brokaw.

Mother's father, Ford Seymour, was a thirty-five-year-old lawyer with a large New York firm when, while visiting his hometown, he saw a photograph in the window of a local photography store of nineteen-year-old Sophie Bower. She lived in Morrisburg, on the Canadian side of the St. Lawrence River. He was immediately smitten, which is not surprising given the fetching twinkle in my grandmother's eyes and her slightly open mouth with upturned lips. My grandfather was an exceedingly charming, devilish gentleman from a wealthy, well-connected family. He had, as my half sister, Pan, says, "a touch of madness, which was appreciated by the ladies." Madness indeed! Based on what Mother told them, the Austen Riggs doctors identified him as a paranoid schizophrenic.

He was determined to marry the young Sophie, and she was too young to have seen the warning signs. After the wedding he moved her to New York City. He would come home after work at the law firm complaining of terrible headaches and have Grandma put cold cloths on his head to soothe him. When her mother came to visit them, she saw right away what was up and said to her daughter, "Darling, the reason his head aches is because he's drunk!" Yes, it turns out Grandpa was a ladies' man, a poetry-writing philanderer with mental health problems, **and** an alcoholic. Alcoholism, according to a cousin, ran in his family. His paranoia led him to become pathologically jealous of any attention that his male colleagues paid to his beautiful young wife, and in 1906, shortly after the birth of their first child (my uncle Ford), Grandpa left his New York job and bought a farm just outside of Morrisburg on the St. Lawrence River. Within a year, Grandma found herself right back in Canada whence she'd come, and that is where my mother was born, in April 1908. When Mother was a year old, her mother gave birth to a third child, Jane, but there was something wrong with the little girl from the very beginning. She was later diagnosed as epileptic and needed constant attention.

Life was not easy for the Seymours. Mother described how her father "spanked" the children so often and so hard that Grandma would beg him to stop. Today we call that child abuse. He also kept bars on the doors to keep out anyone who knew Grandma, put towels over the windows, and wired himself into his room. The only outsider allowed to come in was the man who tuned their piano. Mother wrote that when she was eight years old this piano tuner sexually molested her.

I believe this trauma colored her life, and mine—which I will get to in a moment.

Grandpa no longer worked, and the Seymour family received financial help from wealthy relatives, supplementing this by raising chickens and selling eggs and apples. There were no machines to do the washing and no electric irons (although Grandpa expected everything to be ironed all the time); everything had to be made from scratch—including bread, soap, and butter. The only way Grandma could do all the housework and look after her ill daughter Jane was to train the young child to hang on to her skirts at all times. Wherever Grandma went, Jane would be tagging along. How, then, did the other children get the attention they needed? My heart breaks when I imagine my mother, scared of her father's spankings, hiding the dark secret of her sexual abuse by the piano tuner, and seeing this little Jane take whatever attention her mother had left to give. Mother wrote of her anger at her father for having so many children that he could neither support nor educate.

Grandfather's sister, Jane Seymour Benjamin, had a daughter, Mary, who was married to Colonel H. H. Rogers, a professional military man and the son and heir of Henry Huttleston Rogers, vice president of Standard Oil. Over the years, Mary Benjamin Rogers, who was a kind, generous matriarch, must have grown aware that her troubled uncle's family was having a hard time of it up on their farm in Canada. Fifteen years had passed, and by now Grandma had five children to take care of. Mary decided to bring her cousins to Fairhaven, Massachusetts. Before leaving, Grandma put her fifteen-year-old daughter, Jane, into an institution, where she later died of pneumonia.

Mother spent the two final years of high school in Fairhaven and was doted on by her cousin Mary and Mary's daughter Millicent Rogers, six years my mother's senior. Millicent was to become a strikingly beautiful and fashionable socialite, jewelry designer, and humanitarian. The Millicent Rogers Museum in Taos, New Mexico, which houses part of her art collection and the heavy gold and silver jewelry she de-

Mother in the 1930s.

The photo of nineteen-year-old Grandma that brought thirty-five-year-old Grandpa a-courting.

Mother in the South of France, 1935.

signed, is testimony to her talent and taste. These relatives of Mother's were interesting, gracious, strong women—the glue that held things together—and they must have been powerful role models. But Mother makes clear in the history she wrote that she was shy and intimidated by them. In her medical records, her doctor wrote, "Always she felt painfully inadequate and inferior socially and intellectually as the poor cousin."

At their home, Mother met Miss Harris, a secretary on Wall Street who earned $10,000 a year, a startlingly high salary at the time. Maybe this is what gave Mother the idea of becoming a secretary. Mother once told her friend Eulalia Chapin that she "would go to secretarial school, become the fastest typist and best secretary anyone could hire. Then I'd descend on Wall Street and marry a millionaire," she said. And that is exactly what she did.

With some financial assistance from Mary Rogers, Mother attended Katharine Gibbs secretarial school, pulled a few strings with her family's banking connections, and landed a job at the Guaranty Trust Company bank, where she learned the business world firsthand. Then, at twenty, she met multimillionaire George Brokaw, whose family fortune had come from factories that made uniforms for Yankee soldiers during the Civil War. Brokaw had recently been divorced from Clare Booth, author and future wife of Time, Inc.'s Henry Luce. In January 1931, Mother and Mr. Brokaw were married and moved into an elaborate stone mansion with a moat around it on the corner of Seventy-ninth Street and Fifth Avenue in New York City.

Mother, like her mother before her, married a man nearly thirty years her senior who was a serious alcoholic. Brokaw died in a sanitarium a few years later, leaving my mother with a three-year-old daughter (my half-sister, Frances—nicknamed Pan—Brokaw) and a share of his wealth. No longer dependent on the kindness of cousins, she now assumed the role of dispenser of largesse and immediately moved her mother, sister Marjory, and brother Rogers from Fairhaven to New York City to live with her and help look after Pan. This was when my mother met and befriended the beautiful young Arden model Laura Clark.

I closed Mother's medical records and lay in bed feeling indescribably sad for her and at the same time utterly relieved. I wished I could fold her in my arms, rock her, and tell her everything was all right, that I loved her and forgave her because now I understood. Finally, I understood the nature of one of the shadows I inherited from her that has incubated in my body for so long—the shadow of guilt that an abused girl like Mother carries. Why, you may ask, would a child feel guilty for abuse over which she had no control?

For the last decade—not knowing why until now—I have been drawn to studying the effects of sexual abuse on children. What I have learned is that a child, developmentally unable to blame the adult perpetrator, internalizes the trauma as her own fault. Carrying this guilt can make her blame herself for anything that goes wrong and hate her body and feel the need to make it perfect in order to compensate— a feeling that she can pass on to her daughter. (In her history, I was astonished to read of my mother's shame at having had plastic surgery on her nose and breasts.)

A sexually abused child will feel that her sexuality is the only thing about her that has value, and this frequently results in adolescent promiscuity. Several times in the history she wrote, Mother used the words **boys, boys, boys** to describe her school days. Often, victims of sexual abuse seem to carry a strange luminosity because of the sexual energy that was forced into their lives far too early. I have recognized this in women I know who have been abused and subjected to incest and have seen how men are drawn to it . . . proverbial moths to a flame. Learning this has given new poignancy to my father's early description of my mother: "She was as . . . bright as the beam from a follow-spot."

I can now understand that my mother was all the things that people have described—the icon, the flame, the follow-spot—and also all that I had felt as a child—a victim, a beautiful but damaged butterfly, unable to give me what I needed—to be loved, seen—because she could not give it to herself. As a bright, resilient child, I had sensed, with the animal instinct children have, deep wounds that had been inflicted on her early in her life. I had caught the doomed scent of her fragility, which was probably only intensified by the men she chose. As a child, this scared me, and I moved away from it. Now, as an adult, I can see it as **her** story, not mine, and begin to move into my own—which is the story this book aims to tell.

FATHER

My father's people, the Fondas, were originally from a valley in the Apennines, about twelve miles outside of Genoa, Italy. The valley was deep, and the town cradled in it was named Fonda, which means "bottom." In the fourteenth century, one of my Italian ancestors, the Marquis de Fonda of the Republic of Genoa, attempted to overturn the aristocratic government in order to allow ordinary citizens to elect the doge and the senate. My kind of guy. His efforts failed. He was branded a traitor to his class and fled the country, taking refuge in Amsterdam, Holland. I assume it was during this time that Dutch Calvinism seeped into the Fonda genes. Over the generations, the Fondas became more Dutch than Italian, though there remained, as my brother says, "just enough Italian to put some music into the mix."

The first Fonda to cross the ocean was Jellis Douw, a member of the Dutch Reform Church, who came to the New World in the mid-1600s, fleeing re-

Dad as Tom Joad.
(Photofest)

Tina Fonda, Troy, and me in Fonda, New York, by the graves of our namesakes.
(Montgomery County Department of History & Archives)

The last Fonda family reunion, in Denver. Dad is fourth from left in the front row next to Shirlee, then Aunt Harriet and her daughter Prudence. Back row, left to right: Peter, Amy, Becky, Bridget, and a cousin, Lisa Walker Duke.

ligious persecution. He canoed up the Mohawk River and stopped at an Indian village called Caughnawaga in the middle of Mohawk Indian territory. Within a few generations after my Dutch-Italian ancestors arrived in the Mohawk Valley, there were no more Indians—the town became known as Fonda, New York.

It is still there, not far from Albany. You get to it by riding north along the Hudson River for a while and then west, a train ride I took from Grand Central Terminal for six years—while attending the Emma Willard boarding school in Troy, New York, and then Vassar College in Poughkeepsie.

In the seventies, I visited the town of Fonda with my children and my cousin Tina, daughter of Douw Fonda, direct descendant of the original Jellis Douw. We spent most of our time in the town's graveyard, where, on lichen-covered gravestones, some almost toppled over, we could read the old Italian name Fonda, preceded by Dutch names such as Pieter, Ten Eyck, and Douw. But there, among them, was a Henry and a Jayne—our long-dead namesakes.

Mother's ancestors were Tories, loyal to the British. The Fondas were staunch Whigs who actively supported the colonial cause. After the Civil War, Ten Eyck Fonda, my great-grandfather from Fonda, New York, brought the Fondas to Omaha, Nebraska, where my father was raised. Ten Eyck went there as a telegrapher with the railroad, a skill he'd gained in the army. Omaha at that time was a hub of the new railway network.

I never knew my father's parents, who died before I was born. William Brace Fonda, my grandfather, ran a printing plant in Omaha, and my grandmother Herberta, whom I apparently favor, was a housewife who raised three children—my dad and his sisters, Harriet and Jayne. Dad's parents and many of their relatives were Christian Scientists, Readers, and Practitioners. If one can judge from the photos, they were a close, happy, smiling family.

I have often pored over shoeboxes full of family memorabilia looking for clues to my father's dark moods. I am not alone in this quest. Several years ago, when it became clear that Dad's remaining sister, Aunt Harriet, hadn't long to live, I went to visit her at her home outside of Phoenix to ask my questions.

"Was Dad close to his mother? Were there problems in the family?"

"No, absolutely not!" she answered. "And I just don't understand all you girls coming down here to look at the pictures and ask me questions about our family!"

This took me by surprise. "What do you mean, Aunt Harriet? Who else has come?"

Aunt Harriet named various cousins and their daughters. Ah-ha, thought I. Perhaps the Fonda malaise has crept into other corners of the family. Now, it seemed, some of the younger generation were seeking answers, too.

My visit with Aunt Harriet served to remind me how little the people of my father's generation were accustomed to introspection. Her memory held no nuances, no shades of gray. As far as she was concerned, theirs had been an idyllic life, and perhaps it had been.

I knew that my father had great admiration for his father, William Brace Fonda—like him, a man of few words. There are two stories my father told, and they are revealing.

One evening after dinner, William Brace drove his son down to the printing plant. From a second-story window, he had Dad look down onto the courthouse square below, where a crowd of shouting men brandished burning torches, clubs, and guns. Inside the courthouse, in a temporary jail, a young black man was being held for alleged rape. There had been no trial, not even any charges filed. The mayor and sheriff were there on horseback trying to quiet the mob. Eventually the man was brought out into the square and, in the presence of the mayor and sheriff, hanged from a lamppost. Then the mob riddled his body with bullets.

Fourteen years old, Dad watched all this in shock and terror. His father never said a word—not then, not on the drive home, not ever. Silence. The experience would forever be a part of my father's psyche. It played itself out in his **12 Angry Men,** in **The Ox-Bow Incident, Young Mr. Lincoln,** and **Clarence Darrow,** and in unspoken words that I heard plainly throughout my life: Racism and injustice are evil and must not be tolerated.

The second story has to do with his father's attitude about acting. Dad had a $30-a-week job as a clerk at the Retail Credit Company in Omaha, but Marlon Brando's mother, a friend of my grandmother's, got him involved with the Omaha Community Playhouse, where Dad was offered the part of Merton in the play **Merton of the Movies.** When Dad began talking about acting as a career, his father said it was not appropriate for his son to earn his living in "some make-believe world" when there were good steady jobs available like the one he had. Dad argued, and his father refused to speak to him—**for six weeks.**

Still, the play opened with Dad as Merton. And the whole family, including his father, went to see it. When Dad got home after the show, the family was sitting around the living room. His father had his face buried in a newspaper and still had not spoken to Dad. The mother and sisters began a very complimentary discussion of Dad's performance, but at one point his sister Harriet mentioned something she thought he could have done differently. Suddenly, from across the room his father lowered his newspaper and said to her, "Shut up. He was perfect!"

Dad said that was the best review he ever got, and every time he told the story tears would well in his eyes.

These are among the very few clues I have about my father. I think that the repressed, withholding nature of his early environment colluded with a biological vulnerability to depression to make Dad the brooding, remote, sometimes frightening figure he became. I was stunned to discover in talks with my cousins that undiagnosed depression ran in the

Fonda family. Dad's cousin Douw suffered from it, and I suspect Dad's father did as well.

Dad was a study in contradictions. Author John Steinbeck wrote this about him:

> **My impressions of Hank are of a man reaching but unreachable, gentle but capable of sudden wild and dangerous violence, sharply critical of others but equally self-critical, caged and fighting the bars but timid of the light, viciously opposed to external restraint, imposing an iron slavery on himself. His face is a picture of opposites in conflict.**

Dad could spend hours stitching a needlepoint pattern he had designed or doing macramé baskets. He painted beautifully, and there was a softness in many of his acting performances, with nary a trace of the macho ethic. But to me, Dad was not a gentle person. He could be gentle with people he didn't know, utter strangers. Often I run into people who describe finding themselves sitting next to him on transatlantic flights and go on about what an open person he was, how they drank and talked with him "for eight hours nonstop." It makes me angry. I never talked to him for thirty minutes nonstop! But I have learned that it is not unusual for otherwise closed-off men to reveal a softer side of themselves in the company of total strangers, or with animals or their gardens or other hobbies. In the confines of our home, Dad's darker side would emerge. We, his intimates, lived in constant awareness of the minefield we had to tread so as not to trigger his rage. This environment of perpetual tension sent me a message that danger lies in intimacy, that far away is where it is safe.

In his early twenties, and with his father's permission, Dad hitched a ride to Cape Cod with a family friend and soon hooked up with the University Players, a summer stock repertory company in Falmouth, Massachusetts. Among them was Joshua Logan, one of my future godfathers. Dad was the only non–Ivy Leaguer among them.

When Margaret Sullavan, a petite, talented, flirtatious, temperamental, Scarlett O'Hara–style southern belle from Virginia, was invited to join the University Players the following summer in Falmouth, she stole his shy Nebraska heart. Their romance bloomed, until Sullavan went off to star in a Broadway play.

They carried on what was reported to be a fiery, argumentative courtship. After a year and a half, Dad proposed, she accepted, and they married and moved into a flat in Greenwich Village. Less than four months later it was all over. Dad moved into a cockroach-infested hotel on Forty-second Street, and Sullavan took up with the Broadway producer Jed Harris. Dad would stand outside her apartment building at night looking up at her window, knowing Harris was inside with her. "That just destroyed me," he said a lifetime later to Howard Teichmann. "Never in my life have I felt so betrayed, so rejected, so alone."

After the breakup, Dad describes going into a Christian Science Reading Room and finding a man to whom he bared his soul. "I don't know what it was," he said to Teichmann. "I must have had faith that day. I don't even know who the man was, but he helped me to leave my pain in the little reading room. When I went out, I was Henry Fonda again. An unemployed actor but a man." Oh yes, Dad, I want to cry out when I read that, but why didn't you let that experience teach you that talking to someone who listens with an understanding ear can be healing, not a sign of weakness. If faith brought you a sort of miracle on that one day, why didn't you allow yourself to be more open to it and why did you scorn us—Peter and me—each time we turned to these supports—therapy or faith—for help in our own lives?

Dad apparently withdrew into himself after that, working odd jobs here and there. A lot of people, including Dad, didn't have enough to eat. For a while he shared a two-room apartment on the West Side with Josh Logan, Jimmy Stewart, and radio actor Myron McCormick. The four of them lived on rice and applejack. The other tenants in the building were prostitutes, and two doors down the notorious Legs Diamond had his headquarters.

While my mother, the woman who would become his second wife, was living in splendor as Mrs. Brokaw, in a mansion with a moat on Fifth Avenue, Dad was barely hanging on.

In 1933, Franklin Delano Roosevelt was inaugurated president, and within a year Dad got his first big break, doing funny skits in the Broadway review **New Faces** with Imogene Coca. His reviews were terrific and his career started to take off. Around that time, Leland Hayward, who was on the brink of becoming the top talent agent in the country, signed him up and convinced a reluctant Fonda to go to Hollywood for $1,000 a week. He was on his way.

Two years later, in 1936, my mother, complete with chaperone and her own Buick touring car, sailed to Europe. In London, while visiting a friend on the set of the film **Wings of the Morning,** in which Dad was starring with French actress Annabella, my mother met my father. By now, Dad had become something of a star, with six movies and the lead in a Broadway play under his belt.

"I've always gotten every man I've ever wanted," Mother once told a friend. My father was divinely handsome, appealingly shy, and she wanted him. He admitted that, though too shy to make a move himself, he was easily seduced if a woman set her mind to it. Well, as I learned from Laura Clark, mother was nothing if not seductive.

Soon after their return to New York, Mother and Father were married, and a year later, from that interesting and troubled genetic amalgam: **me voilà.**

They were very different people. His heart was with Roosevelt and the New Deal, hers was with the elite, many of whom were her relatives and who worried about "that man in the White House." His tastes were spartan; hers, glamorous. He wanted to go to clubs in Greenwich Village and Harlem to hear Ella Fitzgerald and Louis Armstrong. She wanted to dine with New York's high society. Not that very different people can't laminate successfully, but . . .

It's been easy for me to see Father in myself. I look like him, went into his profession, and have many recognizable characteristics of his—including, unfortunately, a tendency to withdraw and be abrupt (traits I have worked hard to rid myself of). But Dad's genes also gave me his midwestern staunchness, a respect for integrity, an identification with the underdog, and a dislike of bullies. I credit him with my feelings for the land. Though he grew up in the city of Omaha, you can't live in Nebraska—at least you couldn't back in his time—without an awareness of the land. The Midwest is our farm belt, its economy tied to the rolling grasslands of the Great Plains that seem to stretch to infinity and shimmy in the wind. I believe Dad carried a land-based morality within him till the day he died, and I inherited it— as have my children.

Partly because of my resemblance to him and partly because I wanted to distance myself from my mother, I never bothered to explore what her genes contributed to my makeup. But I have learned that there are traits of hers for which I am very grateful. Her genes provided the leavening in Father's Calvinist mix: the need to reach out to people and nurture them—and also to love a good party. My ability to organize a complex home environment comes from her, as does my generosity.

In an ideal world, people would take classes to learn how to parent. I wish I had. After all, we are required to take lessons before we can drive a car or fly a plane. Does it make sense to embark on the most complex and important task we can undertake in our lives and not be required to demonstrate even a modicum of understanding? I have learned to forgive my parents their shortcomings. I hope my children will forgive me mine.

But forgiving before you've faced why forgiveness is needed is like sewing up a wound and leaving the bullet inside. Forgiveness can't happen until we have gone back to the dark place and experienced the feelings that have been unacknowledged since childhood, named them for what they are, and then separated from them. Taking this journey back in time requires courage. When possible, it helps to have the guidance of a gifted and empathetic professional.

In **Breaking Down the Wall of Silence,** psychologist Alice Miller says, "Emotional access to the truth is the indispensable precondition of healing." Only then can we see that it wasn't **about** us. Parents were cruel, perhaps, or neglectful, but it wasn't because **we** weren't lovable. It's because they knew no other way or because they weren't mentally well.

There are, of course, those lucky few who grew

up in homes with parents who loved and respected each other; where raising children was a shared responsibility, not one left solely to the woman; where being a man meant nurturing and cuddling; where the child saw her parents work out their differences in a loving and respectful way; where the parents, when they were there, were really, wholly, fully there.

CHAPTER THREE

LADY JAYNE

In childhood dream-play I was always
the knight or squire, not
the lady:
quester, petitioner, win or lose, not
she who was sought.
—DENISE LEVERTOV,
"Relearning the Alphabet"

I LIKE THAT I WAS BORN on the shortest day—winter solstice. It makes me feel connected by some primordial energy to Stonehenge and Machu Picchu, where the solstice was celebrated and revered by the Celts and Incas. I also like that I am able to look back over my span of history to a time before plastic, before smog and sprawling suburbs and fast-food restaurants. Before television, even! I like that I can remember in my bones what it felt like to have a lot fewer people in the world than there are today. Four billion fewer, to be exact. Four billion fewer **feels** different, trust me. Life was very different then, just **because** of the fact of four billion fewer people, seven million fewer just in Greater Los Angeles alone when I was born. It's a feeling of space, more space between people, between houses, between tempers and cars, more open spaces with grass where a girl could explore and hear birdsongs. More birds.

By 1938, the year after I was born, people had picked themselves up and were dusting themselves off from the Depression. The New Deal had put in place the Social Security system, farm subsidies, a minimum wage, and public housing, in an attempt to level the playing field, to protect ordinary people from those Roosevelt, in his speech accepting the nomination, called "economic royalists." In spite of the rise of Fascism in other parts of the world, in the United States there was a sense of hope in the air.

Hope may still have reigned in my parents' marriage when I was born. Near her due date, my mother took the train to New York and checked in to the swank Doctors Hospital, where the socially prominent came to be sick, have babies, and be treated royally.

My father was filming **Jezebel** with Bette Davis at the time, and his contract stipulated that if his wife went into labor during the shooting, he could fly to New York to be with her. When the time came, Bette Davis was left to play some of their love scenes to the script supervisor. Later, she would feign anger at me about it: "You're the one who robbed me of my leading man, damn you!" she would bark in that clipped, staccato voice of hers.

They named me Lady Jayne Seymour Fonda. "Lady"! That was actually what they **called** me! Later, when I went to school, the cloth name tapes that had to be sewn onto my collar read LADY FONDA. Apparently I was related to Lady Jane Seymour, third wife of Henry VIII, on my mother's side. (But who cares about royalty; the poor woman died shortly after giving birth to the king's long-awaited son.) Not to mention the fact that I didn't want to be anything resembling a lady, nor did I want in any way to stand out. To make things worse, there was that "y" in the Jayne. (That was a Fonda family thing: My father's middle name was Jaynes.)

It appears my father was very excited about my arrival. In his biography, he is quoted as saying, "That was a great day! I took dozens of snapshots with my Leica. Every night the floor nurses had to kick me out." I liked reading that. I've saved those photos. They show me either alone in a crib or being held by a nurse with a white mask over the lower half of her face. Not one shows me in Mother's arms.

Not that my mother wasn't happy about my arrival, but if I am to believe Grandma Seymour, Mother really wanted a boy. In those days women were cautioned against having more than two cesareans and she'd already had my half sister, Pan, so as far as she was concerned, this was her last birth and it better have a penis.

Ah, how deliciously simple it would be to blame **that** for my lifelong feeling of not being good enough.

Two years later, in spite of her doctor's warnings,

mother took a final stab at having a son. Grandma Seymour told me that in the event this third child was a girl, a baby boy had been lined up to adopt— that's how much it mattered to her. Mother flew back to New York to the same hospital she'd delivered me in, but when Peter was born, instead of expressing jubilation, Mother moved into the Pierre Hotel **for seven weeks** instead of coming home with him. What was that about?

To find out, I asked Susan Blumenthal, M.D., M.P.A. Dr. Blumenthal has served as U.S. Assistant Surgeon General and the country's first Deputy Assistant Secretary for Women's Health. A national expert and leading authority on suicide and depression in women, Dr. Blumenthal is also a Clinical Professor of Psychiatry at Georgetown University and Tufts University Schools of Medicine. Dr. Blumenthal told me that Mother's behavior suggests that she may have been suffering from post-partum depression (PPD), a mood disorder that can have serious health consequences for mothers and their children. Even today, PPD often goes undiagnosed, and back then it is probable that Mother's doctors were unaware of it as a problem that needed urgent attention. In addition, Dr. Blumenthal said that bipolar disorder (manic-depressive illness) often has its initial onset in women after the birth of a baby. After years of suffering, Mother was eventually diagnosed with bipolar disorder at the end of her life.

Dr. Blumenthal also underscored that mood disorders (including manic-depressive illness) often run in families. Some research suggests that there may be a genetic vulnerability in certain families for alcoholism in the male relatives and depression in the females. Dr. Blumenthal emphasized that alcoholism can co-occur with bipolar disorder and clinical depression and that there is a higher incidence of alcoholism in people with bipolar disorder as compared to the general population. Therefore, my grandfather's possible undiagnosed mood disorder and alcoholism might have increased Mother's genetic vulnerability for bipolar disorder. Apparently, there can be a link between a father's mood changes and alcoholism and his daughter's depression, both biologically and psychologically.

So at the time of our entry into the world, Peter's and mine, everyone was hidden behind something: Mother was hidden behind depression, Dad behind his camera—capturing the moment but never **in** the moment—and the nurses behind their masks.

For Peter's birth Dad had graduated from a Leica to a home movie camera, and as soon as he got back home to California he showed Pan and me the movies he'd taken right before Mother moved into the Pierre. I remember exactly where I was sitting in the living room, close to the whirring 16-millimeter projector, when the image appeared of Peter in Mother's arms. This is my first clear memory. The bottom of life dropped out, I was falling down a dark hole. In a letter I found recently from Grandma Seymour, she wrote, "I shall never forget your reaction to seeing Peter in your Mother's arms. The tears streamed down your cheeks, but you didn't cry out loud." I believe it was right then that I sent some soft part of myself down into a vault someplace for safekeeping. I would begin to learn the combination only some sixty years later, at the start of my third act.

I remember the day, almost two months after Peter's birth, when Mother at last came back to our California home. I can see her standing in the doorway of our nursery with Peter in her arms. She was wearing a navy blue skirt and a navy blue short-sleeved pullover sweater with two little nautical flags embroidered on it. I've never been fond of navy blue.

My grandmother told me that she remembered I wouldn't let Mother touch me for a long time after she came home from the hospital with Peter, and if she did, I would cry. "You couldn't forgive your Mother," Grandma wrote me. "You thought that she had rejected you for Peter." I'm sure that her being away for so long after the birth contributed to my feeling of being abandoned, but it was deeper than that. Mother's beautiful aquamarine blue eyes were like mirrors covered with duct tape . . . they could not see me and mirror me back lovingly to myself as a mother's eyes are meant to do. Instead, I became frozen in her sightless gaze. She didn't love me. Real love means seeing the other as she truly is, fully, not just some parts that coincide with what you want to see.

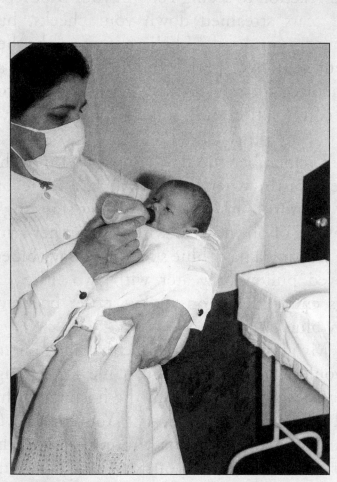

Me right after birth, in the arms of the
masked nurse.

Peter's come home and I am definitely skeptical.
That's Pan standing behind Mother.

I know he loved me when I was little.

Dad liked me, though. I knew that, especially in the earliest years. I was his firstborn, I had the Fonda look, and I was a tomboy. In the summer, he would take me into his arms, walk down the steps into the swimming pool, and play with me in the water. I would bury my nose in his shoulder on the way down the steps and smell his skin. He always had a delicious musky smell that I loved . . . the smell of Man. Yes, he was happy with me when I was little— and deep down I knew his was the winning team, the one I'd do anything to join.

My first four years were spent living in a spacious house in California, sandwiched between Beverly Hills and the coastal city of Santa Monica. Margaret O'Brien lived down the street in a big white plantation-style house. Producer Dore Schary, whose two daughters, Jody and Jill, would become schoolmates, lived around the corner. Mother had purchased a home for Grandma Seymour a few doors down from ours.

Today, the house we lived in belongs to actor/director Rob Reiner and his wife, Michelle. In the nineties, with my third husband, Ted Turner, I attended one of their Oscar-viewing parties in a new wing of the house that was the projection room. During a break in the ceremonies, I got Rob Reiner's permission to wander around the house, seeing how much of it I could remember. I walked into the first-floor master bedroom. I knew exactly where I was because the nicest memories I have of being with my mother took place right there at around age four. She would sometimes take me into her bed in the mornings and read me Grimms' Fairy Tales and the Oz stories.

Mother spent a lot of time in bed even then, and she had one of those rolling hospital tables that would swing over the bed, tilt to hold reading material, and flatten to receive a breakfast tray. She always had beautiful lacy bed jackets and peignoirs, and soft, silky sheets. Her bed was a nice place to be, and by then I guess I had forgiven her for preferring my brother. The fairy tales and children's poems she read were illustrated by Maxfield Parrish: colored plates of princesses, sorcerers, fairies, and knights brandishing swords to slay fire-breathing dragons. There was a dreamy, haunting quality about the illustrations, equally romantic and frightening. Even though the illustrated plates appeared only once every chapter, the images were so evocative that they would draw me into their dark, languorous world. Mother's voice would disappear and I would **become** the story, like a movie inside my head.

Why, I wonder, have these stories, filled with sadness, loss, and danger, lasted through the ages? Why did the writers put in things that can frighten children? But if I put myself back then, back into my four-year-old mind, I think that I, like all children, already had an existential understanding that life is dangerous and there is sadness—and rather than lying about these realities, these stories and images externalize them so that we can see and acknowledge them but not die from them.

This is how Dad looked when he'd take me
into the pool.
(John Swope, Courtesy the John Swope Trust)

Starting in the final years of the thirties, right at the end of our block lived the Hayward family. What was rather extraordinary about this was that Mrs. Hayward was none other than Margaret Sullavan, my father's first wife—the woman who had broken his heart. Mr. Hayward was Leland, my father's agent. The Haywards had three children, Brooke, Bridget, and Bill. By now, Sullavan had become a big star of both stage and screen, but her role as mother to her three children took precedence. Leland's client list included not just my father but every major star in Hollywood: Greta Garbo, Jimmy Stewart, Cary Grant, Judy Garland, Fred Astaire, Ginger Rogers— and on it went. Inevitably, the Hayward kids were over at our place or we were over at theirs. But during all those years my parents were invited only **once** to the Haywards' for a dinner party, an invitation my mother never reciprocated. I intuited that something in Dad became more alive when Sullavan was around, and if I picked it up, Mother must have.

I have a vivid image of Margaret Sullavan, from the way she looked to the deep, husky quality of her voice. But what impressed me most about her was how athletic and tomboyish she was. Dad had taught her how to walk on her hands during their courtship, and she could still suddenly turn herself upside down—and there she'd be, walking along on her hands. At the Hayward house there were always lots of games and laughter. Mother laughed in those days, too, and had many friends, but she tired easily and was not at all athletic. She would dress me up in frills and pinafores, which I hated, but Mrs. Hayward let her kids wear comfortable clothes and she herself wore old slacks and sandals.

The other major factor in my life after Peter's birth was the impending war. I remember Mother and Father leaving home to go watch the night sky for enemy bombers. This was something patriotic civilians volunteered to do: "keep our skies safe." The governess would get me all dressed for bed and then let me go downstairs to say good-bye as they walked out the door. I was filled with dread. What if they got bombed and didn't come back? The fact that the adults would try to reassure me by explaining that we weren't actually at war yet and certainly weren't being bombed made no difference. If there were no bombs, what were they scanning the sky for? It made about as much sense as the "finish your plate, think of all the starving children in China" routine. If they're hungry, send **them** the food, right? I mean, where's the logic? Adults!

CHAPTER FOUR

TIGERTAIL

I am much too alone in the world, and not alone
enough to truly consecrate the hour. . . .
   I want my own will,
   And I want to simply be with my will,
   As it goes toward action . . .

   I want to be with those who know secret things
   Or else alone.
   —RAINER MARIA RILKE,
   "I Am Much Too Alone in This World,
   Yet Not Alone"

MOTHER AND DAD decided around 1940 to
buy nine acres of land on the end of a dirt
road called Tigertail because of the way it wound
around the mountain. That part of the Santa Monica
Mountain range was all beige undulations like a
woman's body, the curves blanketed in native grasses
and tattooed with occasional scrub oaks and sturdy
California oak trees. On the steeper slopes, red-
barked manzanita, chaparral, and sage grew thick,

and from the canyon bottoms arose the California sycamores, their thick, gnarled trunks and mottled bark looking like Maxfield Parrish's trees where gremlins live. You won't see this today—those rolling hills are covered with houses now, and the exotic, imported landscaping that surrounds them has all but obliterated the beige California of my girlhood.

My parents built a home there that was as close to a Pennsylvania Dutch farmhouse as was possible, given that this was Hollywood and Mother was, well, Mother.

It is conceivable that their marriage was fairly happy, although the abrupt change in lifestyle must have been hard on Mother. She went from being a lively New York City society widow, in charge of her own life, to being, at least at first, the stay-at-home wife of a constantly working movie star who left her alone a lot and wasn't very good company when he was there.

After several years, my father began having affairs. Mother seems to have known nothing of this until one of the women filed a paternity suit against him. Mother used her own money to buy the woman's silence. Pan recalls, "I remember vividly the heavy atmosphere and anguish in Mummy's bedroom . . . her talking with Grandmother."

I am quite sure that this crisis was only the most dramatic of the problems in their marriage. Dad was so emotionally distant, with a coldness Mother was not equipped to breach. Grandma Seymour told several family friends how her daughter would beg him, "Talk to me, Hank, tell me what I've done wrong. Say something, anything.' But he would never say a word." I don't believe he meant to be cruel. Perhaps it was the chronic depression that ran in the Fonda family.

Then there were his rages. They were not the Mediterranean, get-it-all-out-and-over-with variety. They were cold, shut-you-down, hard-to-come-back-from Protestant rages. Except for Peter, who didn't seem to pay attention, we all took great care to avoid his trip wire.

His movie work frequently took him away from home, and even when he was there, he was often studying scripts and preparing his roles. He would sit for hours in our presence and never speak. It was a deafening silence. Mother must have been so lonely, and I think, like me, she blamed herself for his moods. She was outgoing and emotional, and this was surely what had originally drawn Dad to her. But he also saw emotional needs as a weakness. I think he felt that a strong, mature adult was someone who did not need others, except perhaps to satisfy needs like sex or work (although even in his career he seemed to disavow relational needs), or to keep you from feeling lonely. But the needs were what mattered most: The people themselves were more or less fungible.

One of the lessons I internalized from my parents, when I was no taller than the fashionable hems of Mother's Valentina dresses, was that a woman has to answer her husband's emotional and physical needs. She has to twist herself into a pretzel: not let him see who she really is. She should let her more fulsome self express itself **outside** the relationship— in the house, in her work, with girlfriends, affairs, whatever. Like so many wives, Mother did this, I think, not because Dad specifically **asked** her to but because that's what disembodied women do in order to be "good" wives. One thing this does **not** do is promote intimacy.

Then came the fateful day, December 7, 1941, the day, as Roosevelt said, "that will live in infamy." The radio broadcast news of the bombing of Pearl Harbor. Eight months later, Dad joined the navy. He didn't have to go, since at age thirty-seven he was over draft age and had three dependents. But he told Mother, "This is my country and I want to be where it's happening. I don't want to be in a fake war in a studio. . . . I want to be with real sailors, not extras." He was genuinely patriotic and hated Fascism, but I think it was also about him wanting to get away . . . **anchors aweigh!** Mother must have known this, and it must have created a deep sense of abandonment.

Dad graduated at the top of his naval officer candidate school class, selected air combat intelligence duty, and came home for one last week before shipping out to the Pacific. He was wearing an impressive officer's uniform with brass buttons, insignias, and cap. I remember the evening he came to say good-bye. I couldn't remember him ever sitting on my bed to say good night before. Then he sang me a song! When he was done, I sang him one, too. Then he hugged me and was gone.

I'm supposed to be this unemotional, immovable character, but after I kissed Jane and left her room, I stood outside her door, pulled out a handkerchief, and wiped my eyes. Isn't that a crazy thing to react to? I listened to her singing that song and suddenly, I didn't want to leave my family.

I was so happy to read that in his biography. I only wish he could have let himself cry in front of me so we could have shared our tears and I could have seen him vulnerable and human.

During the Tigertail years, the bad news was that I was pretty much left on my own. The good news was that I was pretty much left on my own. I became increasingly independent and found solace in the dry, pungent, natural world of Southern California.

I was still called Lady, but now I could wear blue jeans and baggy shirts and I was always full of splinters, burrs, and ticks from roaming the mountains and climbing the oak trees. I would get way up to the top of one particular oak and look out over the Pacific Ocean; triumphant martial music would ring in my head, and I would imagine myself leading an army up

A photo taken of Mother, Peter, and me to send to Dad during World War II.

Mother, Pan, Dad, Peter, and me (in the tree, in the hat), and our Dalmatian, Buzz, after the war. This was my favorite oak tree to climb.
(John Engstead/ MPTV.net)

the hill to conquer the enemy. Peter wasn't fascinated with Indians the way I was and wasn't quite as adventuresome, so I created a fantasy brother who was Native American. I used to pray: Dear God, please ask Santa Claus to bring me an Indian brother for Christmas.

We were required to take hour-long naps every afternoon when we weren't in school. I hated it, because I was never tired. Lying there for that endless hour, I would create a family out of my fingers. The middle finger, the biggest, was the father, the index finger was the mother, Peter was the pinky, and so forth. I would dress them up in robes made of tissues, and if I'd thought to sneak a pen into bed with me, I'd give them faces. When I was through, I'd wad up the Kleenex into tiny balls, as small as I could make them. Then I would try to smooth the pieces out on the bed so that they'd be just like new, with no wrinkles. While I did this, I'd say to myself, **I can make it better. I can make it all better.** That's when that personal mantra began.

My very best friend was Sue Sally Jones, the best athlete in school. I always felt I could never be as brave and strong, but maybe I could copy how she did things. I remember once asking Peter in all seriousness, "Who do you think could round up buffalo better, Sue Sally or me?"

Without hesitation he said, "You, sis."

That's my bro! Of course he probably thought that if he said Sue Sally, I'd push him off the roof.

The only time I can remember ever being sat

Sue Sally at age ten, just before we moved east. This is how we both looked at that time. Later, Sue Sally played professional polo for twenty years disguised as a man, because women weren't allowed to play. She became the first woman to break that gender barrier. I keep this photo on my desk to remind me of her courage.

At Tigertail: me on Pancho, Peter with Pedro, then Dad, Pan, and Mother.
(Motion Picture TV archive)

down on an adult's lap and told how to behave was by Sue Sally's mother, Mrs. Jones. I had said thc f-word to a boy in the playground. I was spending the night with Sue Sally, and Mrs. Jones took me aside, sat me on her lap, looked straight at me with her pale blue eyes, and said, "Lady, you know the other day on the playground you used a bad word when you were talking with one of the boys? Do you remember?"

"Yes, Mrs. Jones." I felt even worse because she wasn't yelling.

"It is not right for you, or anyone, to use dirty words. It makes you seem like you're not a nice girl. But you are a nice girl. Do you understand what I am telling you?"

"Yes, Mrs. Jones."

"Will you promise never to do it again, Lady?"

"Yes, Mrs. Jones." It is a vivid memory, I think, because of its uniqueness in my life.

In third grade, I decided to take my destiny into my own hands and announced to all that from now on I wanted to be called Jane, with no "y." My third-grade report card says, under the heading "Personality":

Jane is well adjusted, dramatic, has self-confidence and assurance. She is well liked by the children because she is interesting and vital in her responses. Jane has the ability of telling experiences in a very interesting and graphic manner. I think she has

dramatic ability and a talent for making the common place have life and interest.

I treasure this evidence that I once possessed self-confidence and self-assurance. They would soon be gone.

As for sex, my first encounter was traumatic. We had two donkeys, Pancho and Pedro, and one afternoon I took them both out, riding Pancho and leading Pedro. I was seven years old, it was a hot day, and I had on shorts. I was on the top of a nearby hill, in an oak forest, when all of a sudden two hooves clamped themselves over my bare thighs from behind and all hell broke loose: Pedro, I later realized, had decided to hump Pancho—with me astride! There was a lot of thrashing about, with bucking and with hooves digging into my legs from behind. Eventually I fell off, onto my back, and found myself staring up at—well, it was about two or three feet long, almost touching the ground, and it was all nasty and scabby.

I knew it was about sex. I don't know how, but I just knew. I looked over at Pancho's underbelly. This was the first time I'd been face-up with Pancho almost on top of me. Pancho was different down there from Pedro. Then it dawned on me: Pancho was really Panchita! A girl! She'd arrived with that boy's name and nobody told me to check it out. See what happens when you don't teach kids the facts of life? I'm not absolutely sure I've ever recovered. Stunned, in pain, and shaking with fear, I picked myself up, saw that I was bleeding where Pedro's hooves had dug into my thighs, and limped back home. I led **both** of them this time, making sure to glance constantly over my shoulder in case there was any more hanky-panky.

This was the time in my life when sex first reared its head, an unfortunate but apt pun. One day shortly after the donkey incident, I was playing catch with some friends in the school playground. There was this boy I had a crush on, and I noticed that he kept throwing the ball to this one girl over and over again but never to me. Then I heard him say to her, "I'm trying to sex you up." My heart skipped a beat. I didn't really know what that meant, but I knew that him saying it to her and not to me didn't augur well for me.

When I got home that afternoon I found Mother in her bedroom and asked, "Mom, what does 'sex you up' mean?" I'm not certain it happened this way, but what I remember was that before my eyes, she seemed to go into a sort of slow-motion meltdown. Mouth open, she stammered. But I don't think she actually said anything. Maybe she said, "Later, Lady," or, "Go ask your sister." I know I left her room as uneducated as I went in, and even more curious as to the meaning of those words. Up I went to Pan's room. She didn't seem surprised at all and proceeded to go into scatological detail about who puts what into which hole, followed by, "And then the boy goes pee pee," and so on—followed by a description of how babies come out. What I was seeing in my mind, though, was the image of what had been hanging down underneath Pedro that day on the hill and somehow trying to put that together with my own "down there" and pee pee and . . . well, I was horrified. I had to go sit in my room for a long time and take deep breaths just to settle down from this terrifying but titillating revelation. I don't remember much else about that year of my life, but I remember every single word Pan said that afternoon.

Within days our governess appeared with a book about where babies come from. It had drawings of the fallopian tubes, uterus, and penis. My mother, like so many mothers and fathers still today, was so out of touch with where I was emotionally and developmentally that she thought a mere mention of the word **sex** meant I needed to know all about the plumbing and mechanics. What I really needed was for her to sit me down, put her arm around me, and ask about where I had heard the expression **sex you up.** Then she would have realized that I needed to know about **feelings,** not mechanics; that I was jealous and hurt and thinking that I wasn't good enough to be the one that the boy wanted to "sex up." An understanding hug from her right then would have helped. And then she might have said, "He probably doesn't know what it means, either. He probably heard some man say it and thought it sounded grown-up. It doesn't mean he loves that girl and doesn't like you. It's just that this is a time when you begin to have new feelings kind of all stirred up inside when you're around a boy or girl you really like. Have you had feelings like that?" Then I would have felt safe to say, "Yes, I have those feelings around **that** boy and that's why it felt bad when he said that to the other girl," and she and I would have talked about those feelings and how beautiful and how natural they are—a part of growing up.

But though others may have seen Mother as "the one you'd go to if you had a problem," that's not the mother I knew. If it had gone down that way, I would have been able to come to her the following year, when **really** scary things began to happen. But as it was, I never asked her another sensitive question again.

It seemed there'd be a new nanny every few months; none were helpful in the sex-and-feelings department. On the contrary, one of them was very religious. Every morning she would come into my room before I was out of bed and smell my fingers to see if I'd had my hands "down there." She made it clear that pleasuring oneself was a mortal sin.

The next nanny was young and pretty and had a boyfriend in the army. One afternoon when he was home on leave, she brought him into the bathroom when I was taking a bath. She asked me to get out of the tub, and when I did, I remember her turning me around. I felt scared. But I have no memory beyond that. I do not know if he molested me, but something bad must have happened around that time, be-

In fifth grade with my braids.

cause that was when I began to behave differently and have recurring fantasies in which I either watched or participated in sexually disturbing, even violent, acts. This was also when I began to feel terrible anxiety whenever I saw public displays of sexuality—people necking in movies or smooching on the beach. This anxiety lasted into my fifties, and I do not know why. Could it be that as a child I saw something I shouldn't have? Did something happen with that nanny's boyfriend? I also began getting into trouble at school. I was caught getting a girl to pull down her pants and show me her wee-wee. I was sent to the principal's office for a "good talking-to." This was about the time when I said the f-word, the same period that Mother was having her affair with Joe Wade. I mention these experiences because during much of my life, issues of sexuality and gender have been a source of trouble and anxiety (as they are for many women and girls). That is why today I help young girls and boys work on these same things.

On August 6, 1945, the United States dropped the atomic bomb on Hiroshima. Dad was ordered back to the States the same day that Japan surrendered and was subsequently awarded a Bronze Star. Like a lot of men, he came back from the war changed. He had been living a man's life with his war buddies, unencumbered by family responsibilities. I think he liked the sense of mission, the male bonding, being a success at something real instead of just a screen hero.

After he came home, I sensed that Dad was not attracted to Mother anymore. She seemed not to be conscious of it, however, and would walk around naked in front of him. I wanted her to put her clothes on. Didn't she know? She was probably still very beautiful, but—oh, I hate myself for this betrayal of her—I saw her through my father's judgmental eyes. As an adolescent, I would recognize Dad's eyes sizing me up unfavorably. I blamed Mother for the growing distance that I sensed between her and Dad. She wasn't doing the right things to make him love her. And what it said to me was that unless you were perfect and very careful, it was not safe being a woman. **Side with the man if you want to be a survivor.** Go out there and listen to jazz with them and pour them their whiskey and even bring them women, if that's what they want, and learn to find that exciting. Be better than perfect if you want to be loved. And don't walk around naked.

A sad memory from those postwar days was the afternoon I decided to get a book and read next to Dad. Like his father before him, Dad was an avid reader and would sit reading for hours in a big overstuffed chair. My own reading skills had been honed during the years he was away, and I thought reading would be something we could share that didn't require talking. I got the novel **Black Beauty** and sat in a chair opposite him. He hadn't acknowledged my presence, but when I came to a passage that made me want to laugh, instead of stifling the laughter I encouraged it, hoping he'd ask me to share with him what was so funny. But he never looked up or said anything. It was as though I weren't even there. I'd known he loved me when I was little, but now, at nine, I wasn't so sure.

In 1947 Dad left for New York to begin rehearsals for a Broadway play called **Mister Roberts,** directed by Joshua Logan and produced by Leland Hayward, Brooke's father. Right after that, Brooke came to Tigertail to tell me that her parents were getting divorced. It was the most frightening thing I'd ever heard. If it could happen to that family, where everyone was always laughing and having fun, then . . . No, too frightening to think about.

That was in the beginning of my tenth year. By the time we rounded the circle to the bottom of that year, the end of my first decade, we'd be living in Greenwich, Connecticut—and life as I'd known it would never be the same.

CHAPTER FIVE

WHERE'D I GO?

I was doing research in a an elementary, middle,
and high school and sometimes we would thank the
students by getting them pizza for lunch. When I
would ask the girls what they wanted on their pizzas,
the ten-year-olds would say, "Extra cheese with
pepperoni," the thirteen-year-olds would
say, "I don't know," and the fifteen-year-olds
would say, "Whatever."
—CATHERINE STEINER-ADAIR, ED.D.,
**Full of Ourselves: Advancing Girl Power,
Health and Leadership.**

PEOPLE MADE A FUSS over us as we waited
backstage in the darkened theater where my father was starring in **Mister Roberts.** We had just
landed in New York that night in early June 1948,
and Mother, Peter, and I had been driven directly to
the Alvin Theater.

Standing next to the stage manager, Peter and I
waited for intermission to release our father to us. As

I peered around the curtains I saw—was it a stage or a sliver of heaven? It was so close yet far away, bathed in light, awash in an electric energy that crackled back and forth between an unseen audience and Dad in his khaki lieutenant's uniform. But he wasn't "Dad." He was a funny, talkative Mr. Roberts. Even the gunmetal gray of the set, the decks, antiaircraft guns, and turrets of the navy destroyer, seemed to glow from within. No wonder he'd left us to come to this place: Here he was more alive than life, the eye in the center of a hurricane of love and laughter.

Suddenly there was thunderous applause. People began running around backstage, and before I knew it, Dad was next to me giving me a big hug and I could feel some of the energy he'd picked up out there coming through his uniform right into me, along with a heady wave of his musk smell. I didn't want to leave, ever. But he and Mother said it was late and that we had to go to bed. So we hugged again and made the thirty-five-minute drive to Greenwich, Connecticut, our new hometown.

Peter was disconsolate at having to leave Tigertail, and rancor fairly oozed from his every pore. While I knew that the days of buckskin and bareback with Sue Sally were over, to me, it felt—at least initially—rather like an adventure. Besides, pragmatist that I am, I always meet necessity with enthusiasm. What was I to do, beg Sue Sally's mother to adopt me? No, my connection to Dad, fragile though it sometimes felt, was still my lifeline, and I wasn't about to put it to a test. I was forever amazed at

Peter's willingness to test everybody all the time. How was he so sure the bonds wouldn't fray and break?

I slept late that first morning and the sun was fully up when I jumped out of bed and threw open my window. Below me was an apple orchard that stretched farther than I could see. On either side was what appeared to be a jungle. I realized that the astounding array of greens in my colored-pencil case weren't invented by the pencil company; they were right there below me. I never got dressed so fast, and I was downstairs and out the door. The sound of the door slamming behind me made me do a double take: my first screen door—there were no mosquitoes in California. New too was the heaviness of the air that made my skin wet before I'd even had a chance to sweat—humidity. Whoa, this new place was going to be great!

The grounds seemed enormous, probably because there were no fences to mark the property. Dense hardwood forests and swamps surrounded us on three sides. By the end of the day, I had explored what seemed to be miles of steamy forest. Along the front of the property, separating the orchard from the road, was an old wall made from stacked, lichen-covered rocks without any mortar. Here and there granite boulders poked up through the lush green grasses. I had never seen rocks like these. In my California mountains, the boulders were sandstone—which could be dramatic, like a herd of elephants huddled together—but didn't have shiny grains of mica and veins of quartz and didn't seem to carry the history of the earth itself, the way these Greenwich rocks did. I fell in love with rocks that summer. Even today, the sight of an old Connecticut stone wall makes me happy.

A whole new environment suddenly became mine that first Greenwich summer and was like a salve on the wounds of the various illnesses and broken bones that began to manifest themselves as the tensions between my father and mother became more and more palpable. That was also when I started to bite my fingernails down to the bleeding quick. Mother made me sleep wearing white cotton gloves. She put bitter-tasting stuff on the ends of my fingers. She got neighbors to talk to me about how, like hairballs in cats, the chewed nails would create a ball in my stomach and make me sick. But nothing could get me to stop the nail biting, since nothing spoke to the **reasons** I was doing it. Same reasons I was getting sick so much.

One day, while walking down one of the narrow country roads that had no sidewalks, I encountered a tall, skinny, freckled-faced girl with short dark hair. Diana Dunn. It didn't take long to discover that we shared a passion for horses and would both be in the same class that fall at the all-girls Greenwich Academy.

She introduced me to the Round Hill Stables and Riding Club. I learned to take a horse over a jump there, and it was there that Teddy, the stable boy, broke my arm in a wrestling match. Another boy would find his way over to our house to play with me that summer. I don't remember his name, but he was the son of the gardener on a nearby estate.

He, Teddy, Diana, and I would roam for miles like a pack of wild dogs, noses to the ground, sniffing, snooping, rolling about, wrestling. They knew I was a girl because my name was Jane, but aside from that, it was hard to tell me from the boys. I don't think that Mother was terribly pleased that my friends were the sons of gardeners and stable hands, but she was slowly sinking into a state of painful desperation and I was left to choose the company I kept.

Diana had her own horse, a black-and-white paint named Pie. Her mother, a tall, slim woman, very much a part of the "horsey" set, was kind to me during the almost four years we lived in Greenwich. Someone, perhaps Mother, must have asked the Dunns if I could stay with them during some of her protracted absences, because I spent an inordinate amount of time there. In the fall of that first Greenwich year Dad told Mother he wanted a divorce, and then she began to disappear to what I now know was the Austen Riggs Center. That's when Grandma came from California to take care of us and run the house.

The Dunns filled the void that had opened when we left Sue Sally Jones and her mother behind in California. While Sue Sally had represented cowboys, Indians, and buckskin, Diana was about fox-hunting, canary yellow jodhpurs, patent-leather-topped boots, and hard velvet caps.

A good thing about starting a new school is that it's a chance to try on a new personality. One day I did something in study hall that made the class laugh. I don't remember what it was, but I remember how good it made me feel to be found funny. Being a clown and a cutup gave me an identity.

My first fall was a revelation to see the leaves turn vivid orange and red. It was also when I started fox-hunting at the urging of Diana Dunn. I don't remember a time when I wasn't scared while hunting. I was scared when we'd come to a jump, and I was terrified every time we'd gallop around a sharp corner when the ground was wet, for fear the horse would slip and fall on me. I was used to being scared, but I always felt that courage is the manifestation of character, so I pretended not to be. No one ever knew, especially Diana. Being scared was absolutely the worst thing a girl could be. Being scared meant you were a sissy.

Then winter came. I'd seen snow before but had never **lived** with it, where you have to shovel it to get to the car to go to school, where you can go sledding in your backyard. I was furious that Peter could whip out his little penis and write his name in the snow, so I tried to do the same by taking off my panties and running as fast as I could with my legs wide apart, trying to spell "Jane" as I peed. Needless to say, it was indecipherable—and I got very cold.

That first Christmas in Greenwich, Dad gave me a Mohawk Indian costume made out of buckskin, complete with beaded moccasins and a strip of fake hair that stood up straight when I pinned it on my head, a real Mohawk hairdo. At that point, I was only six months out of California, still had my long blond braids, and the Lone Ranger was still my role model, so this was about the most perfect thing Dad could have given me. That very afternoon I put on the outfit and Dad made a home movie of me. Out of the thick underbrush I ran on silent, agile feet to the top of a knoll, where I stopped and, just like an Indian scout, put my hand above my eyes and scanned the horizon for the enemy. Dad even shot a close-up of my serious little face, looking slowly from right to left before slipping silently back into the forest—my film acting debut. When I look at the footage now, I remember it was about that time that I started to hate the way I looked, especially my round, chubby face. I thought I looked like a chipmunk with nuts stored in my cheeks.

Performing for Dad that Christmas afternoon would mark the end of my cowboy and Indian fantasy life. I never dressed up as a Mohawk again. I was entering the period when social acceptance becomes more important to an adolescent girl than almost anything else. Shortly after that is when I had my beautiful braids cut off. Nobody else at school wore braids and they made me feel nerdy. I don't remember who cut them, Mother or a professional, but whoever did it wasn't doing me any favors. The way it was cut, my hair hung to just below my ears as straight and stubborn as a mule's tail, no style, no shape, and my cowlick made my bangs stand up as if they'd been electrocuted. Hair matters just about more than anything when you're that age, right? Girls with good hair were always more popular. I was in every sense just "plain Jane," the cutup—with bad hair.

Sometimes in the evenings I would walk down the road, peer inside houses, and watch a family at the dinner table. I was fascinated by the differences between our home and other people's. Later, when I made friends and was invited to their homes, I would sit at the dinner table feeling like a Martian as I watched parents, guests, and kids interact. The experience of being asked what I thought about a particular subject was new to me. This didn't happen in our house. Witnessing adults having multilayered exchanges, full of lively opinions and disagreements, allowed me to understand that beyond the sliver of reality that was my ten-year-old life there lay a vast world of ideas that I would one day grow into.

I lived in Greenwich through two elections—when Truman beat Dewey and when Eisenhower beat Adlai Stevenson. I remember lively discussions about the elections during dinners at my (Republican) friends' homes. Even though my father was a "yellow dog Democrat" (he'd sooner vote for a yellow dog than for a Republican) and cared passionately about his politics, he rarely engaged us children in political discussion. It was around this time that a rupture occurred in Dad's friendships with his old pals John Ford and John Wayne and his best friend, Jimmy Stewart (though this last would be patched up over time).

The rupture centered around Senator Joe McCarthy and the House Un-American Activities Committee (HUAC). "McCarthyism" became synonymous with baseless mudslinging and the manipulation of the American public through fear. Every

Riding in Greenwich meant jodhpurs, boots, and a velvet cap.

Summer camp right after Mother died, with my bunk-mates, Brooke Hayward (foreground, upper bunk) and Susan Turbell. We painted the horses.

organization associated with Roosevelt and the New Deal was labeled subversive. Thousands of innocent people who had done nothing more than join liberal organizations were criminalized. McCarthy and HUAC, which included a young congressman from California, Richard Nixon, interpreted any dissent whatsoever as subversive. Dad saw this as a "red-baiting witch hunt," and he once kicked in a television set while the HUAC hearings were being broadcast. Looking back on those times, I find it interesting that Dad never joined Humphrey Bogart, Lauren Bacall, John Huston, Lucille Ball, John Garfield, and Danny Kaye, who flew to Washington where the HUAC hearings were taking place and held a press conference in support of the Hollywood Ten, as they were called: producers and directors accused of being Communists. Some in Hollywood, like Ronald Reagan (then president of the Screen Actors Guild, who had been an FBI informant since 1946), Gary Cooper, George Murphy, Walt Disney, and Robert Taylor, cooperated with the committee and agreed to name those they believed were Communists. These "friendly" witnesses were given prepared statements and as much time as they wanted to speak, whereas "unfriendly" witnesses were cut off and their lawyers were never allowed to cross-examine. Jimmy Stewart and John Wayne, though they didn't testify, were staunch McCarthy supporters. I didn't understand what it all meant at the time, except that the careers of many people who worked in Hollywood were being destroyed because the big studios agreed to break their contracts with the Hollywood Ten and never hire them again unless they swore an oath that they weren't Communists. Charlie Chaplin, for instance, was labeled subversive and was not allowed to reenter the United States until 1972, when the Academy of Motion Picture Arts and Sciences presented him with an honorary award. I was there at the Oscars, onstage with him, that year. Little did I know that almost twenty years later I would be called before the later version of HUAC, or that at age fifty-four I would marry a man who had been brought up by his father to believe that Roosevelt and the New Deal were Communistic.

In the fall of 1948, as if it had been ordained, we were once again reunited with Brooke, Bridget, and Bill Hayward. It was amazing to all of us Fonda-Hayward children that once again our families, though slightly reconfigured, found ourselves together on the opposite side of the country from California—with all of us going to the same schools, Bill to Brunswick with Peter, Brooke and Bridget to the Greenwich Academy with me.

It helped having another Hollywood family there, because soon I realized that people were gossiping about the Fondas. In Hollywood, no one had paid much attention to the fact that Dad was a movie star and delaminating families caused little stir, but in Greenwich it shook things up. It was thought, probably correctly, that divorce and scandal were more common among entertainment folk, and perhaps there was fear that it would become contagious.

I also first heard the word **nigger** in Greenwich. One day, while riding in the backseat of the car, which Dad was driving, I said the n-word. Dad stopped the car, turned around, and smacked me (lightly) across my face, saying, "Don't you ever, ever use that word again!" You better believe I never did. It was the only time Dad ever hit me.

I have often wondered about my interest in people regardless of fame, fortune, or race. I can't help but feel that the answer lies in my father's films. Dad himself was never verbal about race or class, yet the characters he played were the kinds of men he admired: Abraham Lincoln, Tom Joad (the Okie union organizer in **The Grapes of Wrath**), Dad's character in **The Ox-Bow Incident** (who deplores the lynching of a Mexican), Clarence Darrow, Mr. Roberts. I once asked Martin Luther King Jr.'s daughter, Yolanda, if her father had talked to her much when she was little about life and values and spirituality.

"No," she said. "He never did that."

"Neither did my father," I said, "but they taught us through their films and sermons, didn't they?"

Part of the school gossip was that my father was dating a "tomato." I asked a friend what a tomato was and was told it meant a luscious, ripe young thing. The thought made me feel sort of nauseated. But like my mother, I didn't allow myself to get angry at Dad.

In seventh and eighth grades, I began my love affair with Broadway show tunes. Brooke and I learned every word to every song in the Broadway hits **South Pacific** and **The King and I.** Little did I know that the "tomato" Dad was dating was the twenty-one-year-old stepdaughter of Oscar Hammerstein—the man who wrote all the words to the show tunes I loved to sing.

As we rounded the circle to the bottom of my eleventh year, sexual feelings and being twitter-pated around certain boys had become a major facet of my life. If I felt a boy was cute, he'd be the one I'd beat up. I already mentioned Teddy, the stable boy who broke my arm. What I didn't say, though, was that he was blond and very cute and I had kicked him in the balls several weeks prior to our wrestling match, causing him to collapse and turn white. Seemed to me like a perfectly reasonable way to flirt.

I used to think I really wanted to be a boy because that's where the action was, and for a while I looked so androgynous that I'd be asked whether I was a boy or a girl. That was the biggest compliment I could get. Looking back, I think I just wanted to be exempt from what was required of girlness. I could do tomboy, but I didn't know how to do girl—except in my active fantasy life.

I remember getting sick at school once and being sent to the infirmary, where I was told to lie down till someone could come get me. As I was lying there, I looked up and saw, on a bookshelf above me, a pamphlet titled **Masturbation.** I couldn't have been all that sick, because I wasted no time getting it down and reading as much of it as I could before the school nurse came back. It said that masturbation gave you acne and made you go insane. I bet it was planted there just for girls like me. Needless to say, it shook me up, much more so than the governess who would smell my fingers. Today I believe it should be criminal for adults to try to make children feel guilty for things that are natural and perfectly healthy. It's probably because so many of them were tormented themselves by their parents and teachers when they were children, so they're taking it out on the next generation!

I was in seventh grade when we moved out of that house and into the spooky house on the hill overlooking the Merritt Parkway—where I built my little cardboard house-within-a-house and Mother began to collect butterflies.

My roaming soon ended. The Lone Ranger had become obsolete as a role model. I watched some of my friends becoming flirtatious and felt they were in on something I just didn't get. I was so earnest (like my father) that I thought if I flirted, it meant I had to be ready to follow through, go all the way. "Going all the way" seemed less sinful than being accused of "cock teasing." If you started, you were supposed to finish, sort of like cleaning your plate.

In June 1950, two months after Mother's death, I was sent to a camp in New Hampshire with Brooke and another friend, Susan Turbell. It was a complex summer for me. Outwardly I showed no effects of Mother's death, but Brooke said I would wake up in the middle of the night screaming about my mother: "I mean screaming so that the entire staff had to appear to calm her down," she wrote in her memoirs.

I got sick with a flu that was going around camp. But in addition I developed some sort of "down there" issue and it wasn't menstruation. I spent a lot of time in the infirmary for whatever diagnosable sickness I had, but I was too scared or embarrassed to ask the nurses to see what was wrong with me. It hurt, it itched, it was scary, and I told no one. I began to think that my **down there** was made wrong, that when God was passing them out, I got a defective one. It was a fear that stayed with me for years. That's one of the problems with not having a mother to talk to.

Mother had killed herself ten months before a new house she'd been building for us was finished. It was April and I guess she couldn't wait. It didn't help that April was also the month of her birthday. Dr. Susan Blumenthal reminded me of this line from a poem by T. S. Elliot, "April is the cruelest month." She said that of all the months of the year, April has the highest suicide rate, followed by October. "Spring is coming, seasons are changing, it should be a time of hope, coming out of winter, but it's also a time of changes."

Dr. Blumenthal explained that the peaks in suicide rates during the spring and fall may be linked to seasonal changes, disruptions in the sleep/wake cycle, and/or alterations in circadian rhythms—the body's biological clock—that can affect mood and behavior. She said, "Some researchers hypothesize that these seasonal changes with accompanying alterations in sleep and/or circadian rhythms and brain neurotransmitters may trigger the cycling phenomenon from depression to mania and mania to depression in certain people with bipolar disorder. Following the long winter of depression, a person's mood may seem to be improving, but in fact the individual is becoming agitated and is acquiring more energy during this cycling phase to plan and carry out a suicidal act. Additionally, there is usually some precipitating, humiliating event or loss that occurs (in the absence of protective factors) that triggers the event."

But I didn't know yet that Mother had killed herself. I learned it that fall in study hall, when a classmate passed me a movie magazine with a story about my father. I started reading it and came to this sentence: "His wife, Frances Fonda, cut her throat with a razor while in the sanitarium." I knew instantly this was the truth, that they had lied to me about the heart attack.

Following study hall was art class. We were all painting things onto black tin trays—mine were white dogwood blossoms and two yellow butterflies. Brooke was sitting next to me and I made her lean under the table, where I whispered, "Brooke, did my mother commit suicide?"

"Well, I . . . gosh, Jane . . . I don't know. I . . . ,"
she stammered, managing to avoid an answer. Later,
in her memoirs, **Haywire**, she wrote that when my
mother died:

> the entire student body at the Greenwich
> Academy was warned at the assembly by
> Miss Campbell that it was to respect that
> story [that Frances Fonda had died of heart
> failure] for an indefinite period of time.

As soon as school got out that day, I ran all the
way home and right up to Mrs. Wallace's room. Mrs.
Wallace was a governess who'd been hired to help
Grandma with us after Mother's death. She was an
attractive, kind lady with gray hair pulled back into a
soft bun.

"Mrs. Wallace," I asked breathlessly, "did my
mother commit suicide?" If Mrs. Wallace was surprised by my question, she didn't show it. Instead she
took me onto her lap and said gently, "Yes, Jane, she
did. I'm sorry to be the one to tell you."

"But is it true that she cut her throat with a
razor?"

Mrs. Wallace hesitated for a second. Right then
and there she must have made the decision to tell
me as much of the truth as a twelve-year-old could
handle.

"Yes, she did. For a few months she'd managed
to convince her doctors in the sanitarium that she
was doing better. They wrote your father and grandmother that she didn't seem 'to be behind the eight

ball anymore.' That's how they put it . . . 'not behind the eight ball.' They were hopeful that she'd be coming home for good soon and so they relaxed their guard and that's how she did it. She wrote notes to each of you before she died."

"Does Peter know?"

"No, he doesn't, and I really think it would be best if we didn't tell him just now. He's so fragile."

"Do you think I could see the note she wrote me?"

"Your grandma told me that she doesn't have the notes anymore. I'm sorry."

That would give me plenty to think about.

I wasn't angry, but I would have liked to have read her note to me. Was she mad that I hadn't seen her on her last visit home? Maybe if I **had** seen her, I could have said something really nice to her and she would have changed her mind. Maybe she knew I didn't love her and that's why she did it. But did I love her or didn't I? I couldn't answer that, because some part of my heart had been tumbled into numbness.

A few months later, in December 1950, Dad married the girl he'd fallen in love with—the tomato—Susan Blanchard, Oscar Hammerstein's stepdaughter. They flew to the Virgin Islands for the honeymoon.

One evening I was over at Diana Dunn's house when the phone rang. Mrs. Dunn answered it and her face sort of collapsed as she listened and the "Oh" that came out of her was about two octaves lower, the way voices get when there's bad news. She glanced quickly at me, then dropped her eyes and covered the mouthpiece.

"Jane, your brother has had an accident. He's shot himself and is in a hospital in Ossining. Your grandmother wants me to bring you there right away."

Peter's shot himself.

I went outside myself again.

The hospital was near Sing Sing prison. When I got there Grandma explained that Peter had been declared dead on arrival but at that very moment, miraculously, the prison doctor, who was a leading surgeon for puncture and bullet wounds, had walked into the hospital from a hunting trip. He discovered Peter's heart was still beating, though faintly, and he had worked fast to stop the bleeding. The bullet had gone into Peter's belly, hit his rib cage, pierced his stomach and kidney, and lodged just under the skin next to his spine. I sat with Grandma in the waiting room. After a while, the doctor came out of the operating room and called Grandma into the hallway. I heard him tell her that in spite of his efforts, Peter's heart had stopped beating, and while they'd managed to start it up again, he didn't know if Peter was going to make it. That was the first time I remember seriously praying. I said, "Dear God, if you let him live, I'll never be mean to him again. Amen."

Dad cut short his honeymoon, managed to get a plane from the islands (no mean feat back then), and arrived within hours at the hospital, where the three of us kept vigil into the night. Then we went home to get some sleep and came back again the next day. We did that every day for five days. I was allowed into Peter's room once to see him lying there, so small that he was barely a bump under the sheets, with all the tubes going in and out of him. On the fifth day, the doctors announced that Peter appeared to be coming out of the crisis zone. Several days later his condition was said to be stable. He was going to make it.

I returned to school in a zone of somnambulance. My routines were done, my homework turned in. But my body always felt tense, my breathing shallow. Nothing seemed to have a reason. "Isn't she something?" the teachers said. "The worse things are, the stronger she gets." The kudos I received for appearing strong satisfied a need for approval and locked me into a modus vivendi: Jane, the strong one. The shell that formed around my heart served a purpose by keeping me on my feet, but it solidified both my superficiality and my independence.

Peter stayed in the hospital for a month. He became a brat almost immediately and I began to backpedal on my promise to God.

The shooting accident had happened when Peter was visiting friends, one of whom persuaded the family chauffeur to drive them to a skeet range near Sing Sing to practice shooting an antique .22-caliber pistol. While Peter was reloading, the pistol discharged into his stomach. Fortunately, the chauffeur knew where the hospital was and acted fast to get him there. Given the timing, however, I can't help but wonder if unconscious forces weren't at work in a boy who was very hurt and angry that his father had remarried and that everyone seemed to have so quickly forgotten his mother.

It had been a rough couple of years, starting with Mother's illness and death. The following year, my classmates started having parties at their homes when their parents were away, where games like post office and spin-the-bottle were de rigueur. I wanted to be popular and fit in, but while Brooke and other girls seemed to have things under control, I dreaded these games. I don't remember if I was more scared that someone would "get" me and try "to go too far" or that no one would want to. As other girls became more and more "feminine," I seemed more and more out in limbo, a lump of androgyny, always behind, scrambling to catch up. What happened to the girl who was described in her third-grade report card as adjusted, self-confident, and assured—the girl who saw herself as heroic? She had slipped away so quietly that I never even said, "Good-bye, see you again in fifty years."

CHAPTER SIX

SUSAN

Ah, as we prayed for human help: angels soundlessly,
with single strides, climbed over
our prostrate hearts
—Rainer Maria Rilke

O<small>NE AFTERNOON</small>, Grandma took me to a
New York hospital to visit Dad, who was recovering from knee surgery. I walked into his room,
and sitting next to his bedside was the most beautiful
woman I'd ever seen. She seemed to be in her early
twenties and had light brown hair pulled back tightly
into a large chignon that accentuated her pale blue,
slanted eyes, not unlike Mother's. She wore a rather
old-fashioned high-necked white blouse trimmed
with lace. Around her wrist was a watch on a black
velvet band. Dad introduced us.

"Jane, this is Susan."

She was only nine years older than me. Still, I
so desperately needed a woman to show me how to
be that it must have been the angels who climbed

**Susan on the beach at
Ocean House.**

over our prostrate hearts to bring Susan to us. If she was a "tomato," it was definitely the sweet, sun-ripened kind.

In the summer of 1951, a little over a year after Mother's death, was when I got to know her. I was going on fourteen. Dad was finishing the national road tour of **Mister Roberts** and would be performing in Los Angeles all summer, so he had arranged for Peter and me to spend the vacation with them there.

We were ensconced in a magnificent mansion built years earlier by William Randolph Hearst for his paramour, actress Marion Davies. It had been converted into a hotel with marble columns, mosaic tile floors, gold-leafed mirrors, an Olympic-size tile swimming pool, and a beach club. We spent that entire summer at the beach, partly because it was a fun place to hang out and partly because Susan, a New Yorker, didn't know how to drive. Other wives might have demanded that Dad get a chauffeur in order to spend a lot of time in Beverly Hills engaging in "cash therapy." Not Susan. She hung in there with us. I don't understand it, given what might be my own callowness at her age, but somehow her twenty-two-year-old soul had the generosity and know-how to wrap itself around Peter and me and be a mother. Peter liked to call her Mom Two.

One perfect California evening, when the sun was setting red and the breeze was velvet and smelled of salt and kelp, she and I were sitting on the marble steps leading down to the pool when she asked me how I was feeling about Mother's death.

I stopped breathing. In all that time—more than a year—no one had raised the subject of Mother with me, much less asked how I **felt.** It was a germinal moment. The problem was that I had no words to offer her. I was so unused to expressing my feelings that I'd become emotionally illiterate. I did tell her that I hadn't been able to cry at the time and that I had learned it was a suicide from a movie magazine. She was quiet for what seemed a long time. I don't think she knew what to say. I certainly wouldn't have at her age, but I remember her suggesting that perhaps Mother's death had been a blessing in disguise. It seems strange to me now that I could have found those glib and potentially insensitive words comforting, but my thinking about Mother was so utterly confused that "blessing in disguise" provided me with a handle, a way to explain the event to myself. Maybe Susan knew I needed a handle.

She was lithe, with tiny, well-turned ankles and long, El Greco knees. She'd studied dancing with the fabled Katherine Dunham, and dancing was important to her. She was superb, often twirling or cha-cha-ing around rooms with pretend partners, her waist-length hair flying, while singing Broadway show tunes. Sometimes she'd doo-wop to a jazz record, fingers snapping, head shaking, eyes closed, while she'd dance a cool little jitterbug in place. I would go to my room afterward and try to imitate what I'd seen her do. I imitated her a lot. If I could be like her, maybe Dad would love me more.

Laughter, which had been an unfamiliar sound in our family for a long time, was a gift from Susan to us. She had a repertoire of jokes, some long, elaborate ones that would crack her up when she finally got to the punch line; some Jewish jokes that required my learning Yiddish words; some from the dark, smoky world of jazz musicians, a world with which she was familiar. Susan was a wonderful combination of goofy and sophisticated, with a little pioneer thrown in for ballast. Her joie de vivre washed over us that summer.

Mother's younger sister and her alcoholic husband had joined Grandma as our caretakers in Greenwich and were reportedly trying to get legal custody of us. Susan told Dad that it was unconscionable for us to be adopted by relatives and that he absolutely had to take us to live with them in New York. I guess he was thinking of leaving us in Greenwich and just visiting from time to time. If the wife who followed Mother had been someone other than Susan—say, like wife number four, the Italian one—I honestly don't know what would have become of us. I would have survived, maybe, but not as a productive citizen. During her brief five years with my father, Susan taught me by example how to be a stepmother. Little did I know how well that would serve me later when, between one husband or another, I would have six stepchildren of my own.

I was too smitten and immature to notice (though I probably saw but quickly forgot what I'd seen) that Susan wasn't quite the same when Dad was around. Of course, nobody was the same when Dad was around, except Peter. Her ebullience would dim a little. If she got too rambunctious, Dad would rein her in, perhaps embarrassed that her spontaneity and exuberance accentuated their age difference— twenty-three years. She once said it was as though Yente the matchmaker from **Fiddler on the Roof** lived with Ibsen's uncompromising Minister Brand. When she was interviewed by Howard Teichmann, she said, "I was your typical Japanese wife. I wanted to do everything to please him." Again, I was seeing woman-as-pleaser as the way to "do" relationship. Unbeknownst to me as well was that she was bulimic, which I would soon become.

These things don't take away from the fact that Susan wanted to be in a real relationship with me and I was ready to meet her there. She found in me not damaged adolescent goods but a responsive partner. As I look back, I see that my girlhood retreat into the Lone Ranger persona was my way of holding out for a real relationship: If it wasn't real, I'd just as soon be by myself, thank you. But like a heat-seeking infrared laser beam, I could scan the horizon and pick up the presence of anyone warm and real I could learn from and go there. But by late puberty (by which time Susan and Dad had divorced), I'd turned off the laser beam and settled for whatever relationships were out there, real or not. Being alone didn't feel like a postpuberty option!

In California that first summer, Dad and Susan would often take Peter and me with them when they went out to dinner in swank Hollywood restaurants like the Brown Derby and Chasen's, one of Dad's favorites. We had never been with him in these kinds of social situations before, so while I knew in an abstract sort of way that he was famous, I didn't know how fame manifested itself in his life. I was struck by how, when he entered a restaurant, there would be a shift in energy, as though he were a magnet. Restaurant owners like Mr. Chasen would call him by name, and as we'd be ushered to Dad's "special" table or, in the case of Chasen's, the red leather booth, heads would turn and I'd hear, "Why, that's . . . ?" being whispered at other tables. Having waiters know your name and what to bring you to drink without your even having to say anything became a sign of celebrity for me. Sometimes his agent from MCA (the Music Corporation of America) or Lew Wasserman and Jules Stein, who ran MCA, and their wives would join us.

Being invited to share Dad's grown-up world was a chance for me to see how it all worked. I noted with interest how Dad behaved differently in a social setting, how he was warmer and funnier with people who were not intimates, especially after a couple of Jack Daniel's. But it was Susan I watched most closely, logging in the details of her social moves, how she became very prim with certain older (important) people and riotous with chums like Johnny Swope and Dorothy McGuire from Dad's early days. Once, driving back to Ocean House, she reached into her dress and pulled out a falsie from her bra, laughing loudly at herself. I wondered if I could ever be that open in front of others. If there was something not perfect about myself, like the size of my breasts or bottom, I always tried to hide it as best I could and hoped no one would notice. I had a tiny waist, about nineteen inches around, and a full, high bottom that seemed to me way too big in proportion to my waist. Worse, I had overheard Dad say that my legs were too heavy. When I heard him say that, I went to bed and slept for two days, the only way I knew to escape those words that haunted me for the rest of my life.

This was a summer when I was closer to Peter than usual, literally and figuratively. Because our bedrooms adjoined and we shared a bathroom, we had ample opportunity to nurse each other's sunburns and hang together. We'd left our Greenwich friends behind, and all we had was each other as we accommodated ourselves to what was clearly a new chapter of our lives. On weekends at the hotel there would be dances for adults in the grand ballroom on the ground floor, complete with live orchestra. Under Susan's spell, I had decided dancing was something to be cultivated, so Peter and I would sneak downstairs and waltz madly together in an empty room next to the party. Sometimes we'd slow-dance real close. It was nice to have a brother to practice on safely. That summer I learned how much I cared for my brother, and I also saw more clearly how very different we were.

We have different rhythms, different life views, and different ways of handling situations. A lot of this has to do with Mother's preferring him, or at least trying to make him hers, while I was more my father's child. Recently Susan described for me how the differences manifested: "You were watchful, taking everything in. Peter was frenetic, acting out."

Though it wasn't intentional, Dad was often cruel to Peter. I use the word **cruel** because, though not deliberate, the effects were the same as cruelty. He often tried to be a good father, doing things he must have done with his father: fishing, flying kites, building model airplanes—the male bonding rituals. But if a parent doesn't like herself or himself very much, it is the child of the same sex as that parent who has the hardest time. Multiply the impact severalfold if the parent is a celebrity. It's not just your father who is making you feel like a sissy; it's an icon, adored by millions as someone of integrity. I don't think Dad liked himself very much, and perhaps he saw reflected in Peter the sensitivity and emotionalism that he had somehow buried. As Susan once said, "There's a scream in your dad that's never been screamed and a laugh that's never been laughed."

Dad hated any displays of emotion. "You disgust me," he would say to at least two wives if they cried. Perhaps it scared him; perhaps he sensed that if he ever allowed his own emotions to surface, they would swallow him up. I believe that early on Dad was taught that to be a "man" you had to disconnect from emotions like tenderness, intimate connection, and need—qualities associated with women. We have all seen how almost universal this is among men and at what price they forfeit these qualities. In my father's case, the masculine ethic may have been exacerbated by the example set by his father and rugged midwestern stoicism. Like the Ogallala Aquifer that lies beneath the surface of the Sand Hills of his native Nebraska and occasionally pops through the topsoil to create lakes, Dad's buried "other self" surfaced in his gardening and his artistry: the painting, the needlepoint, his deeply sensitive portrayal of Tom Joad.

As a girl, I intuited the tensions playing themselves out inside him, like opposing forces on a battlefield. It was his underground softness that I loved, that I needed. In **I Don't Want to Talk About It**, psychologist Terrence Real says, "Sons don't want their fathers' 'balls'; they want their hearts." Daughters, too. If Dad could have embraced the sensitive part of himself full-time, he would have been happier, and so would several subsequent generations of us, for the belief system that undergirds the old notion of masculinity is a poison that runs deep. Dad learned the steps to the relational dance of patriarchy at his father's knee, as his father likely learned it from his father (though sometimes it's learned on mothers' knees), and its toxic legacy has continued across generations, until now.

I am determined before I die to try to help change the steps of that dance—for myself, for my children, and for others.

Peter is all deep sweetness, kind and sensitive to his core. He would never intentionally harm anything or anyone. In fact, he once argued with me that vegetables had souls (it was the sixties). He has a strange, complex mind that grasps and hangs on to details ranging from the minutiae of his childhood to cosmic matters, with a staggering amount in between. Dad couldn't appreciate and nurture Peter's sensitivity, couldn't see him as he was. Instead he tried to shame Peter into his own image of stoic independence. Peter gets attached to people and animals. That summer at Ocean House he was always sifting through the sand underneath the beach club dressing rooms looking for money that might have dropped between the wooden slats. When he'd get enough coins he'd add it to his allowance and make a long-distance call back to the house in Greenwich to ask Katie about our family's six-year-old Dalmatian, Buzz. During one of those calls, he learned that Buzz had been put down without anyone asking us how we felt about it. Peter was deeply affected by this. I could hear him crying himself to sleep in his room next door. I, on the other hand, felt nothing much. Greenwich was, to all intents and purposes, a chapter about to be closed. We were going to be living in the city with Dad and Susan and . . . well, dogs in the city weren't practical.

Peter, throughout much of his school years, was faced with the taunting of schoolmates, the cruelty of boys toward peers who show signs of vulnerability as a means of proving their own unchallengeable entry into the world of "real men." It is to Peter's credit that he rarely caved. I marveled at the extent to which he would, in the face of Dad's anger, remain himself, exposing his heart, challenging Dad: "See me for who I am. I will not change in order to make you comfortable." I, on the other hand, was loath to be anything that would bring on my father's disapproval—until, at a later age, I realized that if I wanted his attention, disapproval was the best I could hope for.

CHAPTER SEVEN

HUNGER

I had been hungry, all the Years—
    My Noon had Come—to dine—
    I trembling drew the Table near—
    And touched the Curious Wine—
    'Twas this on Tables I had seen—
    When turning, hungry, Home
    I looked in Windows, for the Wealth
    I could not hope—for Mine— . . .
                . . . .
    Nor was I hungry—so I found
    That Hunger—was a way
    Of persons outside Windows—
    The Entering—takes away—
    —EMILY DICKINSON, 1862

THE HUNGER BEGAN that beach summer with Susan. That's when I moved "outside" myself full-time, and a perpetual, low-grade anxiety took up residence in the newly empty inside space. I didn't know where the anxiety came from, I just thought that was how life felt for a girl once she'd hit the you're-supposed-to-be-feminine age—feeling like an outsider, nose pressed against windows, hungry to get in, not knowing that it was myself I was outside of; but then, how could I be **inside** myself when I had discovered I was not perfect? Who'd want to be inside something imperfect? Before that summer, at age thirteen, the concept of "perfect" hadn't yet begun to darken my horizon—I was too busy climbing trees and wrestling. Now, on it came.

My feelings of imperfection centered on my body. It became my personal Armageddon, the outward proof of my badness: I wasn't thin enough. Thinking back, I am sure my mother's suicide had a role to play; after all, being superthin is a way to postpone womanliness, to put off victimhood: freedom through androgyny. Then, too, Mother had had ample obsessions of her own with body image. Certainly the fashion industry has a role to play in glorifying the emaciated-as-chic look, pushing **thin** down the throats of young girls just starting to work out their identities. But my father was implicated as well. Dad had an obsession with women being thin. The Fonda cousins have told me that this was true of all the men in the family, going back generations. On his deathbed, Douw Fonda asked his daughter Cindy, "Have you lost weight yet?" (She wasn't fat.) Eating disorders abound in Fonda women, and at least two of Dad's five wives suffered from bulimia. Once I hit adolescence, the only time my father ever referred to how I looked was when he thought I was too fat. Then it was always his wife who would be sent to let me know he was displeased, that he

wanted me to wear a different, less revealing bathing
suit, a looser belt, or a longer dress.

The truth is that I was never fat. But that wasn't
what mattered. For a girl trying to please others, what
mattered was how I saw myself—how I'd **learned**
to see myself: through others' judgmental, objectify-
ing eyes.

Maria Cooper Janis, a friend from childhood,
told me once that when she was around age sixteen,
she and her parents, Rocky and Gary Cooper, had
come to our Malibu beach house for lunch. Apparently, while we were sitting on the beach, my father
said to Rocky, "Jane's got the body, but Maria's got the
face." I was stunned when Maria told me this, partly
because her mother had repeated it to her, but mostly
because it showed how judgmental Dad was—and
willing to objectify me—even to other people.

Obviously the trouble is that wanting to be perfect is to want the impossible. We're mortal, after all;
we're not meant to be perfect. Perfect is for God:
Completion, as Carl Jung said, is what we humans
should strive for. But completion (wholeness) isn't
possible until we stop trying to be perfect. The tyranny of perfection forced me to confuse spiritual
hunger with physical hunger.* This toxic striving for

---

*I don't mean to suggest that all girls who strive for perfec-
tion and feel inadequate end up with an eating disorder, but too
many do. Every decade 5.6 percent of people with anorexia/bu-
limia die, which is about twelve times higher than the annual
death rate due to all causes of death among females ages fifteen

perfection is a female thing. How many men obsess about being perfect? For men, generally, good enough is good enough.

Dad had decided that Peter and I should go to boarding school, as was common at the time for families who could afford it. Peter was enrolled at the Fay School for boys in Massachusetts and I at the Emma Willard School in Troy, New York. Starting my freshman year at Emma Willard, being very thin assumed dominance over good hair in the hierarchy of what really mattered.

I remember cutting out a magazine ad that said with $2 and some box tops they would send you a special kind of gum that had tapeworm eggs in it and when you chewed it the worms would hatch and eat up all the food you consumed. It sounded like a splendid idea to me—a way to have your cake and eat it, too, so to speak. I sent in my $2 and the box tops, but the gum never materialized. When I told this story to a friend recently, she said, "You're a smart girl, Jane. How did you get duped into believing this and sending in the money?" Because I was

_____

to twenty-four in the general population. The deaths are usually due to complications related to the disease, such as cardiac arrest, electrolyte imbalance, or suicide (Melissa Spearing, "Eating Disorders: Facts About Eating Disorders and the Search for Solutions," National Institutes of Mental Health, NIH Publication No. 01-4901, [2001]). Feeling unwhole leads to other addictions besides those related to food. Psychologist Marion Woodman says, "An addiction is anything we do to avoid hearing the messages that body and soul are trying to send us."

thirteen (hence immortal) and health wasn't a factor if it meant getting thin. I knew tapeworms weren't fatal. If it had been a bubonic virus I was sending away for, I'd have thought twice—maybe. But anything that would allow me to get thin without having to do something active seemed attractive. Mind you, I wasn't as extreme as a few other girls, who had to be hospitalized because they refused to eat, but I prided myself on being one of the thinnest in the class.

Then, in sophomore year, Carol Bentley, a wet-eyed brunette from Toledo, Ohio, entered Emma Willard and became my best friend. I remember first seeing her as I was stepping out of the dorm shower. She was naked and took my breath away. I had never seen a body like hers: fully developed breasts that stood straight out over a tiny waist, and narrow hips with long, chiseled legs like Susan's. I felt certain right then that she would end up running the world and that if I hung around long enough, some of her power would rub off on me. Already I had learned to equate the perfection of a woman's body with power and success.

Perfect body notwithstanding, Carol joined me in having major body-image issues. It was she who introduced me to bingeing and purging, what we now know as bulimia. She said the idea came to her in a class on the history of the Roman Empire. She read that the Romans would gorge themselves on food during orgiastic feasts and then put their fingers down their throats to make themselves throw it all

Carol Bentley and me on graduation day
at Emma Willard, 1955.

back up and start over again. The idea of being able to eat the most fattening foods and never having to pay the consequences was very appealing.

We would binge and purge only before school dances or just before we were going home for the holidays, and then we would ferret away all the chocolate brownies and ice cream we could get and gobble it up until our stomachs were swollen as though we were five months pregnant. Then we would put our fingers down our throats and make ourselves throw it all up. We assumed that we were the first people since the Romans to do this; it was our secret, and it created a titillating bond between us.

Later it became ritualistic, with specific requirements: I had to be alone (it is a disease of aloneness) and dressed in loose, comfortable clothing. In a catatonic state, I would enter a grocery store to buy the requisite comfort foods, starting with ice cream and moving to breads and pastries—**just this one last time.** My breathing would become rapid (as in sex) and shallow (as in fear). Before eating, I would drink milk, because if that went into me first, it would help bring up all the rest later. The eating itself was exciting and my heart would pound. But once the food had been devoured, I would be overcome with an urgent need to separate myself from it before it took up residence inside me. Nothing could have stood in the way of my getting rid of it, differentiating myself from it—from the toxic bulk that had seemed so like a mother's nurture in the beginning—because if it remained within me, I knew that my life would be snuffed out. Afterward I would collapse into bed and sink into a numbed sleep. **Tomorrow will be different.** It never was.

What an illusion that there were no consequences to be paid! It was years before I allowed myself to acknowledge the addictive, damaging nature of what I was doing. Like alcoholism, anorexia and bulimia are diseases of denial. You fool yourself into believing you are on top of it and can stop anytime you want. Even when I discovered I couldn't stop, I still didn't think of it as an addiction; rather, it was proof that I was weak and worthless. This seems utterly preposterous to me now, but self-blame is part of the sickness. For me the disease lasted, in one form or another, from sophomore year in boarding school through two marriages and two children, until I was in my early forties. My husbands never knew, nor did my children or any of my friends and colleagues.

Unlike alcoholism, bulimia is easy to hide (except from mothers or friends who have also suffered from the disease). Like most people with eating disorders, I was adept at keeping my disease hidden, because I didn't want anyone to stop me. I was convinced that I was in control anyway and could stop tomorrow if I really wanted to. I was often tired, irritable, hostile, and sick from this, but my willpower to maintain appearances was such that most of the time no one knew the true reasons behind it.

In college I also became addicted to Dexedrine, which I began to take when I was cramming for exams and discovered that it killed my appetite. When I began modeling to earn money for acting classes and to pay the rent, I was easily able to get prescriptions from an infamous New York "diet" doctor—along with diuretics to rid myself of swelling-inducing fluids (and probably doing permanent damage to my kidneys). The Dexedrine made me hyper and emotional, and I began to feel that without it I couldn't act.

There were years when I was actively bulimic and periods of time during those years when the bulimia would be replaced by anorexia (starvation), which Jungian analyst Marion Woodman refers to as the equivalent of an alcoholic's dry drunk. At those times I would hardly eat at all, perhaps an apple core (never a whole apple) or a hard-boiled egg in the course of a day. My skin against my bones became proof of my moral worthiness. The disease would be particularly severe when there was a lot of pressure to be thin, like when I was a fashion model in my early twenties or when I was on the Broadway stage or in a movie where I had to show a lot of my body. I can look at some of my movies and see the disease in my eyes and on my face—a blank, sunken sadness—or the Dexedrine-induced hyperness in some of my television interviews, or the drawn, false thinness that comes with the use of diuretics. How much better I might have been back in those early movies had I been able to show up fully in the roles rather than work half-crippled by a disease that no one knew I suffered from!

My disease would invariably overcome me whenever I was being inauthentic in a relationship, pretending something that I didn't really feel, betraying myself on some level. Earlier, before adolescence, I could simply absent myself from false relationships— as the Lone Ranger. But as I grew into womanhood, in order to not be alone I assumed a façade so as to be loved by my father or boyfriends. It was always men I was concerned about pleasing. Sustaining inauthentic relationships and the self-abandonment it required placed me in a state of perpetual anxiety. But I chose to "stuff" my real feelings, to split off from them, rather than risk being alone.

Being around food, sitting down at the table for a meal, would cause me terrible anxiety, so I would find ways to avoid food-related social situations. I went through what should have been my most beautiful, sensual, fun-loving years in a cocoon, hiding within my numbness. I reserved what intimacy I had for the scruffy floors of the dorm john and, later, the elegant tiles of the bathrooms in Beverly Hills' best restaurants; I became expert at throwing up everything I'd eaten and returning to the table all cheery and fixed up.

I stopped my food addictions in my forties, but it was not until my third act (my sixties!) that I began to accept myself, imperfections and all, and to reinhabit my body, finding, as Emily Dickinson's poem ends, "That Hunger—was a way / Of persons outside Windows— / The Entering—takes away—"

Emma Willard was founded in 1814 as a female seminary by Emma Hart Willard, a pioneer in education for women. Prior to her advocacy, women's education had been at the mercy of private funding and student tuition, while men's education received state and federal aid.

Did you ever see the movie **Scent of a Woman** starring Al Pacino? The school in that movie is Emma Willard. It sits in Gothic splendor overlooking the wooded hills of upstate New York. It has turrets, gargoyles, leaded windows, and carved wooden balustrades curving up the impressively wide staircases. It is a classy place, and I was miserable a lot of the time I was there. Isn't it the thing to do, be miserable and complain about no boys and strict rules? Actually, I would do it all again in a heartbeat. The teachers were wonderful, the classes stimulating.

Attendance at chapel, replete with hat and gloves, was required every Sunday. The only time I remember being deeply stirred by a sermon was when Reverend Dr. Howard Thurman, the first African-American dean of chapel at Boston University, preached for us. Because my father was an agnostic, religiosity had been out of the question for me. But I loved Protestant hymns—loved singing them and loved hearing them. Today I often find myself singing those hymns when I'm fly-fishing or pulling weeds. There is an improvised scene in **Klute** when, as Bree Daniel, alone in her apartment, sitting at a table, smoking a [pretend] joint, I started singing softly to myself, "God our Father, Christ our brother, all who live in love are thine. . . ." I don't know why I did that—it just came out—and the director, Alan Pakula, always one to appreciate contradictions, left it in.

Freshman year, a group of us would gather after dinner in a small dorm room, flop down on couches, and talk. That's when I realized I was one of the few remaining girls in the class who hadn't gotten her period. There was lots of talk about which were the preferred brands of pads (Kotex), who used Tampax (very few girls), did it hurt to put a tampon in (no), who had cramps, and how long everyone's periods lasted. I was very quiet during these sessions. I didn't want anyone to know I had a faulty "down there." Actually, by then we called it vagina. I had a faulty vagina. About this time, in sophomore year, a man from the Bronx named George Jorgensen Jr. had gone to Denmark and become Christine Jorgensen, with the world's first publicized sex change operation. "Nature made a mistake, which I have corrected," wrote Christine to her parents. "I am now your daughter." The sex transformation scandalized America and made news for months, pushing the Korean War and hydrogen bomb tests on Eniwetok off the front page.

I was obsessed by the story, feeling, like Jorgensen, that a mistake had been made with me: Perhaps I was a boy inside a girl's body. Haunted by this, I would lie on the floor with my legs up on a chair, holding a mirror to see if there were any signs of a penis. It's not easy to study your vagina. It takes commitment. You have to maneuver yourself into the perfect position to catch the light and not cast shadows (or find a flashlight—but either way, positioning the mirror is never easy). I was both fascinated and scared by what I might find in all that confusion of colors and folds. (At least I didn't have to contend with pubic hair. There wasn't a hint of that, nor would there be for years to come.) I found my clitoris, of course, and for a good year was sure it was a penis waiting to be liberated, and I felt sad that Mother wouldn't even be around to learn that her daughter was really her longed-for son. I never told anyone about my concerns, just as I had never told anyone about my unusual childhood fantasies, the possible molestation by the nanny's boyfriend, or my "down there" sickness at camp. They all stayed inside me, my secret evilness.

I write about my vagina and my vagina-related fears because of the work I have chosen (and sometimes I feel I was "called") to do in my third act. I work with young people on issues surrounding gender, sexuality, early pregnancy, and parenting. It is said that you teach what you need to learn, and through this work I have learned that the traumas and anxieties I experienced as a girl are not unique to me. If I am able to write about my vagina at all, it's thanks to Eve Ensler, author of **The Vagina Monologues.** While some of you are probably wishing that was one epiphany I hadn't had, it's important for women and girls to be able to talk about that most complex part of themselves. It can represent an important owning of ourselves. Vaginas are, after all, very talented and versatile. They can stretch, shrink, give birth, feel and give pleasure. In 2001, just before coming briefly out of retirement to perform in **The Vagina Monologues** at Madison Square Garden, I said to Barbara Walters on **20/20,** "If penises could do half of what vaginas can do, there'd be postage stamps honoring them and a twelve-foot-tall bronze statue of a penis in the Rotunda of our nation's Capitol." Instead, because vaginas belong to the other gender, they have been raped, pried, cut, sewn up, objectified, and generally denigrated down through the centuries—the sorts of things one does to (apparent) objects of fear that men have so often needed to dominate.

My personal vagina was nothing but a pain in the ass till my late teens. The rest of me had succeeded in blending in rather well, but my vagina was a determined holdout. By sophomore year I took to buying Kotex (very publicly) and pretending that I too had a period. My interest in health and fitness, which surfaced midlife, was anything but evident early on. I hated physical education class and team sports, so since I was faking it anyway, I gave myself the most frequent, longest-lasting, crampiest periods in school as a way of getting excused from gym. I lived month to month, horrified I might be discovered. Scientific studies have shown us that girls who are scared of becoming women sometimes will their hormones into remaining inactive, thereby postponing puberty. Perhaps that was happening with me, because God knows I was scared of what being a woman might lead to—becoming my mother!

On vacations I'd go home to New York City, where Peter and I each had a bedroom in Dad and Susan's snug brownstone. At Christmas 1951, I went out on my first real date. Danny Selznick, son of David O. Selznick, fabled producer of **Gone with the Wind,** had invited me to go with him, his father, and his stepmother, Jennifer Jones, to see the Broadway play **Dial M for Murder.** I had known Danny off and on since childhood and would sometimes go to his house to play, but dating was something else again. I was excited and nervous, knowing that Danny was more worldly than I was and that he had also dated Brooke several times. Brooke, by the way, was still living in Greenwich and would soon appear on the cover of **Life** magazine as the debutante of the year.

For my date with Danny, Susan got me a gray shantung party dress that had a low scooped neck, and she showed me how to wear falsies. Under the dress I wore a stiff crinoline underskirt, as was the fashion in those days: tiny waist with full skirt to accentuate it, a style that played to my assets. Then, just as in the movies: The doorbell rang, Susan answered, I came down the staircase to greet Danny, we went out and got into a limousine with Mr. Selznick and Jennifer Jones, and the four of us went to have a pretheater dinner at some fancy restaurant. I remember ordering a small steak. As I was cutting it, the piece slipped off the plate and down the front of my dress, where my falsies stopped it from sliding all the way down to my waist. I pretended nothing had happened and hoped no one would notice. But after a while grease began to darken the front of the gray shantung. I excused myself and went into the ladies' room, covering my greasy chest with my purse and cursing my bad luck at being the clumsiest girl in the world. Just as the bathroom door closed behind me and I was reaching down the front of my dress, Jennifer Jones walked in and saw me. Jennifer **Song-of-Bernadette, Duel-in-the-Sun** Jones caught me as I was pulling a steak out of my dress! Totally mortified, I tried to disguise what I was doing, but Jennifer saw right away and laughed so sweetly. "Oh, Jane, you poor thing," she said, "let me help you!" And she stuffed some paper towels down my dress (**Oh please, God, don't let her feel the falsies**) and mopped up the grease, rubbed the outside with a warm, wet towel (so it wouldn't stain), gave me her shawl to cover the wet mark, and with a loving hug walked with me back to the table. From then on Jennifer topped my list of mensches—a well-known Yiddish word for all-around decent human being.

The second summer we were all together—Dad, Susan, Peter, and me—we rented a small house in the woods at the very end of Lloyd Neck, Long Island, so that Dad could commute into the city for his play **Point of No Return.**

That summer I battled bouts of depression, though no one thought of it as such, least of all me. I just saw it as "life." Some days I would sleep twelve or thirteen hours and be scolded by Dad for being lazy and moody. This was my first experience of feeling as if a party were going on somewhere else and I was left out and always would be. I could see no future ahead of me. Even the woods didn't beckon anymore. Just as adolescence marked the beginning of my rejection of my body, so it saw me moving away from the natural world I had depended on as a child.

On nearby estates, debutantes threw elaborate parties and danced with boys from elite prep schools like Phillips Andover and Phillips Exeter. I wanted so much to be included, but I didn't know how to go about it and Dad wasn't part of that ritzy Long Island scene.

Then, to make matters worse, I was invited to Syracuse, New York, to visit a girl from Emma Willard who had been my "big sister" freshman year and who desperately wanted to be my friend, though we had little in common. I didn't really want to go, but I didn't know how to say no (a problem that would plague me for longer than I'd like to admit). I was shocked when I arrived in the Syracuse station to find two reporters waiting to interview me: HENRY FONDA'S DAUGHTER COMES TO SYRACUSE TO VISIT SCHOOL MATE was the angle, with the local family's name prominently displayed, of course. I felt uncomfortable being interviewed, since I was not famous and had nothing to say, and I resented being put in this position by my friend—though of course I said nothing to her.

On the second day of my visit, we went to Lake Ontario. I decided to try out a new dive I had recently seen in a movie, where you run and fling yourself across the low waves in an effort to skim their surface. But I misjudged, and instead of skimming I hit the top of my head on the lake floor. Right away I felt something bad had happened and quickly pushed myself off the bottom, but when I surfaced and opened my mouth to scream for help, no sounds came out. My inability to make any noise frightened me. I managed to crawl out of the surf and up onto the sand, where I lay very still. I couldn't move or speak, and there was a dull pain in my back. My friend and her mother came over to see what was wrong, and I motioned for them to let me just lie there for a while. In time I was able to talk and slowly get myself up, into their car, back to their house, and into bed. The next morning I told them I needed to go back to the city. I felt strange, but mostly I thought I was exaggerating as a way to go home early. On the train ride back, I told the conductor that I needed to lie down on a full seat because my back was broken—and then felt guilty for lying to him.

I hung around our house in the city for four or five days and then went backstage at the theater to see my father. "Dad," I said, trying not to sound whiny, "I think there is something wrong with my back. I think maybe I should get an X-ray." Dad called Susan, who came and took me to the hospital. The X-rays showed that I had fractured five vertebrae between my shoulder blades. The doctors said it was a miracle that I wasn't paralyzed. One false move over the last five days, they said, could have done it for life.

Nowadays broken backs are treated very differently, but this was the fifties. The doctors put me in a plaster cast that reached from my collarbone to my pubic bone, a thick, heavy straitjacket. They didn't even bother to give me the semblance of a waist. A few weeks earlier I had received my first invitation to one of the big, formal dances I had so coveted. **Now** what was to become of me? My life was surely over. Not so, said Susan, and she took me to a maternity store, where I got an evening dress for pregnant women. When the big night came she paid special attention to my hair, gave me a little makeup, and hovered over me till I had pinned on the orchid corsage my date brought me and was safely in the backseat with him.

I was mysteriously popular at the dance. Lots of boys cut in, probably because they wanted to see what the body cast felt like up against their chests and bellies. I, on the other hand, wanted to feel their chests and bellies against mine, but the titillation of those first swelling, through-your-clothing body contacts would have to wait.

Fall came and it was time to return to Emma Willard, this time wearing maternity clothes because of the cast. The good news was that I didn't have to take phys ed. The bad news had to do with breasts. It seemed everyone had them by now except me. Of course, I hadn't had them two months earlier, when the doctors had put the cast on, but they'd left me no growing room and there was no **give** to the plaster. If my breasts **were** trying to grow, I was sure they'd be stunted permanently. Now it wasn't just a faulty vagina I would have to deal with but breasts that grew inward!

I finally got my period the summer of 1954, when I was sixteen and a half. After all my concerns about it, when it finally came I assumed it was a terrifying sign that I was bleeding to death from a wound in my faulty vagina. Susan woke me to the reality that I was menstruating. She held a towel for me to wrap myself in, handed me a Kotex pad to stick between my legs, and as I stepped out of the shower threw her arms around me, saying, "Oh, Jane, congratulations. You're a woman now!" **A woman?** While her words eased my fear of imminent death from blood loss, I felt another anxiety rise.

Woman? But I don't want to be a woman. Women are destroyed.

That afternoon Susan told me that I needed to establish a relationship with a gynecologist—she knew a very good one. She also told me that since I was now able to become pregnant, I ought to discuss birth control with the doctor and I should consider my relationship with him totally confidential. "I hope you will not have sex, Jane," she added. "You're still too young. But you need to know about contraception." What a smart stepmother! She did what every mother or stepmother should do when their daughters begin to menstruate.

His name was Dr. Lazar Margulies and he would be the pioneer of the now-famous spiral-shaped, plastic IUD. I burst into tears the moment I sat down in his office and began to describe to him all my fears about my down there, all the years of pent-up anxiety, the "Christine Jorgensen, I think I'm meant to be a man" worry—all of it came sobbing out of me. Clearly, he was used to seeing adolescents with fears and questions and listened to me with great patience. It was wonderful to have someone professional who wouldn't judge me, someone to whom I could address these difficult questions. Every child should be so lucky. When the time came for my examination, I squeezed my eyes tight and held my breath while he did what gynecologists do. And when he pronounced me 100 percent normal I burst into tears again—this time out of relief.

We discussed the available contraceptive choices: The pill hadn't yet arrived, but there were diaphragms and copper IUDs. I liked the idea of an IUD, because I didn't have to worry about putting a diaphragm in correctly. The decision was made then and there.

I remember times at Emma Willard when someone would pass around a list of every sexual act we could imagine, and we'd check off what we'd done. Carol Bentley could check off just about everything: French kissing, intercourse, oral sex, and all sorts of other things that made my breathing change just talking about them. I was in awe of her. All I'd done was kiss (no tongue) and pet, so I'd check off things I hadn't done, like French kissing and intercourse. Junior and senior year I had two boyfriends (one after the other), and with each one I tried to have intercourse. But in spite of all the huffing and puffing and rug burns, it didn't work. My body didn't seem receptive, it wouldn't let them in. Despite my doctor's assurances, this gave me a new reason to think something was wrong with me.

CHAPTER EIGHT

WAITING FOR MEANING

> They use wise discretion in disguising themselves with the caricatures we design for them. And unfortunately for us, as for them, too often adolescents retain the caricatured personalities they had merely meant to try on for size.
>
> —LOUISE J. KAPLAN,
> psychologist

DURING THE YEARS after Emma Willard and before becoming an actor, I was basically just treading water—waiting for meaning. I'm rumored to have done some wild things: ridden a motorcycle into a bar, danced on a table while stripping, setting a fire in the dorm. At Vassar, where we supposedly had to wear gloves and pearls to dinner (untrue), I'm said to have flouted the rules by coming

downstairs in gloves and pearls and nothing else.
Moi! I confess to having harbored a fondness for
shocking, but frankly I never had that kind of chutz-
pah. My life outside of school was very different
from the other girls'. They could just call up and meet
friends at the local drive-in; they had boyfriends they
jitterbugged with at sock hops in their basements. I
didn't do any of those things. The reflected glamour
of being Henry Fonda's daughter, who lived in New
York City and could put on a good façade, made
people think I was more experienced and sophisticated than I was.

To make up for what I lacked, I borrowed bits
and pieces of other people's personae and wove them
together into large enough patches of personality to
get by on dates or at parties. Only when I was comfortable with someone would I garnish this carefully
constructed persona with my uniqueness, but generally I looked and behaved as conventionally as
seersucker, blending perfectly into the flat, Ozzie-
and-Harriet-Kelvinator-Wonder-Bread, predigested
world of the fifties.

Acting never beckoned. I was too self-conscious
and never heard anyone—certainly not my father—
talk about getting emotional fulfillment from acting.
I never connected acting with **joy.** In fact, I had developed a philosophy: "Actors are too egotistical. I
have problems enough. I don't want to encourage
my self-centeredness—it's not for me." In truth I
thought of myself as fat and boring, and I was scared
to death of failure.

The summer after my last year at Emma Willard, the family went to Europe, where my father was filming **War and Peace** in Rome with Audrey Hepburn. That summer Susan decided she'd had enough of the lonely marriage, and she told Dad she wanted a divorce.

"I couldn't be myself," she told Howard Teichmann. "I wanted to discuss problems with him, and he'd turn a deaf ear. He had an ability to avoid confrontations with me. . . . [But when] his anger broke out it was terrifying. Slowly it dawned on me that I had always been afraid of this man." And slowly she had come to realize that what she had taken in the beginning for charming shyness was a more clinical rigidity that, try as she might, she could not break through. She told me that Dad would go all day without speaking to her and then, buoyed by male entitlement, hop into bed at night and expect her to make love with him.

"I'm not a machine, Jane," she said sadly. She had begged him to go into therapy with her and he'd refused. When she went to a therapist on her own (to address her bulimia), Dad told her she'd have to pay for it herself.

Susan was helping me see that what I had witnessed in my father for so long was neither imagined nor my fault. Here was a woman who, unlike my mother, was able to walk away rather than continue to live in a superficial relationship—walk away not to another man but to **herself**. She was his third wife, but introspection and professional help weren't Dad's way or his generation's way. As a result, he was married again in less than two years, to an Italian woman he met during the filming in Rome. That marriage, his fourth, would last not even four years.

Susan had come into our lives, and now she was going. But Peter and I would be forever grateful for what she had brought us.

In 1955 I was accepted at Vassar College (I had applied because Carol Bentley was going there) and went with Peter, Dad, and Aunt Harriet to spend the next summer in Hyannis Port, on Cape Cod. Dad had just completed filming **12 Angry Men,** Sidney Lumet's first time directing a feature film (Sidney would go on to direct such greats as **Serpico** and **Dog Day Afternoon**). The rental house was located just behind the Kennedy compound. Since Dad knew the Kennedys, we saw them from time to time. To say they were like royalty is a cliché, but it's the truth.

The Dennis Playhouse was in easy driving distance from our house and had a summer apprentice-ship program that Dad felt might interest me, at least the backstage, scenery-making part of it. While some acting classes were involved and the apprentices were sometimes given the opportunity to play small roles in the professional summer stock productions that came through on tour, the decision to enroll me in the program was in no way meant as encouragement for me to become an actress. Dad made that clear to both Peter and me: Acting was a very difficult profession to succeed in. He had too many friends who'd ended up performing at auto shows.

On the first day of the program, we were introduced to the stage manager, James Franciscus, whom everyone called Goey, and the moment I saw him the complexion of the summer changed. He was blond, blue-eyed, and movie-star handsome; in fact, he later became something of a star, playing the lead in such television series as **Naked City** and **Mr. Novak** and in thirty-some movies. As it happened, he was also a sophomore at Yale. I was smitten. My previous inarticulate philanderings had not prepared me for true romance, and I was very shy with him. Goey, I would soon discover, may have looked like a playboy, but he was shy, too.

Goey supervised the apprentices, so there was ample opportunity for us to be together. It soon became apparent that my interest in him was reciprocated. We talked a lot. I discovered there were things about Goey to like beyond his looks and the fact that he went to Yale: He was smart and literate; he had a sense of humor, lived in New York City, and was a preppy (only by virtue of Yale), but didn't belong to a fraternity. His family wasn't rich, he had to work, he didn't love football, and he had a passion. Other boys I'd liked had hobbies but no passion. Goey's passion was an epic drama he was writing in iambic pentameter. When he read me what he'd written so far, about a third of the entire piece, it seemed heroic and profound.

Finally, one Saturday before I went home, he

asked if he could take me to dinner the next evening, since there were no performances to stage-manage on Sunday nights. He picked me up in his old red Ford convertible, I remember that part, but nothing of the dinner or what we talked about. It's what happened afterward that still reverberates in my body when I think about it. Goey and I drove to the pier at the end of the Kennedy compound right near our house, walked out to the very end of it, and stood looking out at the setting sun. I didn't know what to say, so I just stood still. Hoping. Heart racing so loud I was sure he could hear it. Then he put his hands on my shoulders, turned me to him, and looked deeply into my eyes. His look was so long and intense that I felt embarrassed and started to pull away, but he wouldn't let me. He held me firm and then, with his eyes still looking into mine, slowly pulled me into him. My body swooned against him, my knees buckled, and he had to hold me to keep me from falling, which made him laugh while he was kissing me, a laugh of pleasure. When our lips parted I stepped back and had to sit down, **plunk.** Everything was swirling: the sea, the sky. **The sky!** I will never forget the sky, the way it looked right then. It was a different color from what it had been two minutes before, all covered with a shimmering haze. Hemingway's line "And the earth moved" came to me. This is what he meant! I thought. The earth is moving.

It was my first swoon, and while it wouldn't be my last, there's something about that first swoon—and the boy who caused it. Goey and I became an item. We were together every spare minute for the rest of that summer. I was eighteen, he was twenty, and we seemed so much younger than most kids that age seem today. Though we kissed endlessly and exchanged furtive caresses in the moonlight, we never made love, and I relished the sweet pleasure of postponement. It was the best summer of my so-far life.

Dad brought his new woman friend up to Hyannis Port. She was a Venetian woman in her thirties, with green eyes, red hair, and a certain hard-sell charm that Peter and I mistrusted instantly. "Phony" was the word that came to both our minds. We figured he intended to marry her, since he never exposed us to girlfriends unless marriage was at hand. We sensed immediately that this was no Susan, no cozy, openhearted stepmother, but we were just enough older that it didn't matter as much as it would have earlier. In some ways my relationship with my father seemed to grow even more distant the closer to womanhood I got, and his choosing to bring this Italian woman into his life created further distance. But I loved him dearly, and his long shadow was still the defining factor of my life.

I had been trying (sequentially) to lose my virginity for at least a year and a half with three different boyfriends, but it hadn't worked in the total-penetration sense—almost, but not quite. It fell in the "but I didn't inhale" category. (This technicality matters if you're trying to prove to yourself that your "down there" is normal.) My persistent virginity just sort of sloughed away incrementally and—as Carrie

Peter, Susan holding Amy
(the daughter Susan and
Dad had adopted at birth),
me, and Dad en route
to Rome, where he filmed
War and Peace.
(Bettmann/Corbis)

Goey and me at the pool by
our house in Villefranche.

Fisher wrote in **Surrender the Pink**—"not because it was so large that it took three times to knock it out." It was more that my body simply said, **Sorry, not ready.** (I couldn't call what we did making love because it wasn't, and I didn't know then that the love part would be important to me. After all, it hadn't been important to Carol Bentley, or so she said.) Later on I remember listening (sequentially) rapt and envious as two of my husbands told me of their own first times.

Vadim had lost his virginity rapturously in a haystack in France during World War II. As he wrote later in **Memoirs of the Devil,** when he climaxed, the ceiling of the barn "began to move. The ground trembled. . . . An apocalyptic rumbling filled the air." Vadim assumed at first this was the result of his orgasm (the Hemingway factor again). What had happened, however, was that he had chosen to lose his cherry "at one of the great moments of history: zero hour, 6 June 1944—the first wave of the Allied landings in Normandy"—and the barn was only a few kilometers from the coast.

Ted Turner, on the other hand, didn't make love until he was nineteen years old, but when it happened it was such an epiphany he "did it again ten minutes later" (a story he told me on our second date and often thereafter for ten years, if there was someone around who hadn't heard it before).

I can make no such life-altering claims. I simply don't remember. I know that it happened with Goey that fall at Yale. I do have an acute memory of how it felt the first time we spent an entire weekend alone together during a blizzard at a small farm his family had in upstate New York: having a whole house to ourselves, not having to worry about noise, waking up in the same bed, taking baths together, him teaching me to make whiskey sours. That part I remember. Just not the sex.

Having a steady boyfriend who was writing a classical drama validated me. I decided to ask for a dorm room of my own at Vassar, preferably a tiny garret where I could appropriately wallow in existential angst, recite speeches from Shakespeare, listen to Mozart and Gregorian chants, and read Kant into the night.

In the mid-1950s, most of the girls I knew didn't go to college to learn where their interests and talents lay in order to prepare for a profession. It was what they did until they got hitched. And they were dropping like flies. Carol Bentley left Vassar in our second year to get married, and so did Brooke Hayward. Most Americans then believed that there was something wrong with a girl if she wasn't at least engaged by the time she left college. Not me. Much as I enjoyed my relationship with Goey, I was never tempted to consider marriage. In this one area, at least, I had the good sense to know that if I got hooked to one man at that point in my life, I'd get stuck someplace I didn't belong.

One day during sophomore year I got a call from the headmaster of Westminster, the boarding school

Peter had graduated to, telling me that Peter had flipped out and I should come get him.

When I arrived I found him hiding in some bushes, his hair bleached light blond. He asked me to call him Holden Caulfield, the antihero in J. D. Salinger's **Catcher in the Rye;** Holden is kicked out of his prep school because he refuses to adjust to the phoniness he finds there. I bundled Peter up to take him—where could I take him? "Home," Dad's house in New York, wouldn't do because Dad was away working someplace and we weren't allowed to stay there alone. I couldn't keep him with me at Vassar. So I called Aunt Harriet in Omaha. Peter ended up living with her and Uncle Jack for four years.

When he first arrived they had him tested to see if he was crazy; the answer was that he needed help. They also tested whether or not he should repeat a grade; it turned out he had an IQ of over 160—in the genius category. So he began psychoanalysis (with financier Warren Buffett's father-in-law) and entered the University of Omaha. Peter was the non-conformist who "acted out." Psychotherapist Terrence Real writes in **I Don't Want to Talk About It** that acting-out boys are "little protesters, sit-down strikers refusing to march off into the state of alienation we call manhood. . . . We usually call these boys delinquents." People would say about Peter, "Well, he's just looking for attention," and I'd nod in agreement, thinking, Why can't Peter just grow up? Today, if I heard adults saying that about a kid like Peter, I'd shout, "So why don't you give him some of the attention he's looking for **before** he starts acting out, some **loving** attention!"

I acted out, too, in my way. But I was much more ready to buy into the system than Peter ever was. I never ventured too close to the edge. I knew how to play both sides—almost getting into big trouble but never really.

Aside from my relationship with Goey, nothing much remains from the two years I spent at Vassar. I drank too much, didn't study enough in spite of my good intentions, "experimented among the passions," became hooked on Dexedrine, got better grades than I deserved, and wasn't inspired by my teachers. I've learned over the years that for me to want to study, it can't be the generic liberal arts approach. I have to understand **why** I am learning, what I'm learning **for,** have to feel the **need** to learn because it relates in a palpable way to my life, to what I am **doing.** For the last twelve years or so, because of my nonprofit work with youth and families, I have needed to know why people behave as they do and what causes them to change. So I devour books on psychology, relational theory, behavioral sciences, early child development, international development, and women's biographies. But at Vassar I didn't know what I was learning **for.**

In my final music-history exam, I used my exam book to draw pictures of women screaming. A few days later, when I was called into the dean's office, I fully expected to be told I had flunked out. Instead I was told that they understood I was going through a difficult emotional time because my father had just married again (the Italian), so I would be allowed to take the music exam over. This seemed preposterous. I didn't feel emotionally upset over Dad's marriage— I was inured by then—and I found it disturbing to be let off the hook that way. I wanted and needed to be held accountable for my actions, to be challenged. That's when I decided I was wasting my time and Dad's money and that I should leave.

I told Dad that I hadn't finished my exams and didn't want to go back to college in the fall, and then I found myself telling him that I wanted to go to Paris to study painting. The truth is I wasn't entirely sure that was what I wanted, and I secretly hoped Dad would save me from myself and say no. Maybe he was distracted by his new wife. Maybe the two of them wanted me out of their hair. Whatever the reason, he agreed to let me go.

The summer of 1957 Dad rented a villa on the French Riviera near the town of Villefranche, which still retained the charm of a small fishing village. The villa was large, with a generous front yard, a pool, and a lawn rolling straight out to the edge of the rocky cliffs that rose at least one hundred feet above the Mediterranean. They did a lot of entertaining all summer long—or rather Afdera, his wife, entertained. Dad had never been part of the international jet set. It was touching to watch him try to disguise his discomfort and fit in, usually by hiding behind his camera. I loved that about him.

The luminaries of the international elite would

come and go: Gianni and Marella Agnelli; Jacqueline de Ribes; Princess Marina Cicconia and her brother, Bino; Count and Countess Volpi and their son, Giovanni; Senator Kennedy and Jackie. Elsa Maxwell, the internationally known "hostess with the mostest," had rented the adjacent villa. We visited Greek shipping magnate Aristotle Onassis on his enormous yacht, the **Christina**—which had a Picasso hanging in the living room, gold-leafed faucets in the bathrooms, a mosaic swimming pool, and always many pretty girls with secrets in their eyes who talked easily with men who owned Picassos. We paid a visit to Picasso in his nearby studio. We met Jean Cocteau, Ernest Hemingway, and Charlie Chaplin. I was continually speechless.

One afternoon when Dad and Afdera were entertaining, Greta Garbo came over with a female companion. After a perfunctory drink with the guests, she and her friend went into the house and came out wearing terry-cloth robes and white rubber swimming caps, the serious kind worn by professional swimmers. Garbo asked if I wanted to go swimming in the sea with her. You could have fanned me with a brick. Greta Garbo! By the way, she was the only guest all summer who expressed interest in leaving the social scene and walking down the steep steps carved into the cliffs to swim in the sea. I had done it myself only a few times—it was a long way down and the water was cold. But down we went—Garbo, her companion, and me. When we got to where the waves broke over the rocks, Garbo threw off her robe to reveal her **naked** athletic body, stepped out to the farthest rock, and did a perfect dive into the water—none of the dipping toes in first, then knees, the "let's get used to it gradually" approach I preferred. I reminded myself that she was Scandinavian, after all, held my breath, and threw myself in after her (wearing a bathing suit, of course). She swam vigorously for quite a ways without stopping, then turned and swam back, meeting up with me as I was trying to catch up. We bobbed about, treading water and looking at each other. Garbo's face was luminous and utterly pure, not a trace of makeup.

Then, in that throaty **Ninotchka** voice, she asked me, "Are you going to be an actress?"

I was stunned that she had asked me about myself.

"No," I said, "I don't have talent."

"Well," said Garbo, "I bet you do, and you're pretty enough to be one." **Oh my God!**

"Thank you," I said, swallowing a mouthful of salty water while my thoughts careened about: **She's just being polite. But wait a minute—someone who leaves the party to go swimming nude doesn't say things just to be polite. But how could Garbo think I'm pretty?**

We crawled out onto the rocks to dry in the sun, and I noticed that her body was healthy and athletic but not pinup beautiful. This made me feel good: Maybe you could be adored even if you didn't have a perfect figure. I remember climbing up the steps to the house behind Garbo and trying to hide the Cheshire Cat grin I could feel spreading across my face.

The village of Villefranche is just to the west of Monaco, the small independent kingdom then ruled by Prince Rainier and his wife, Grace Kelly. On the curve of the Monte Carlo harbor was the resort and casino where the rich and famous gambled. Every Saturday night in the summer there would be a gala ball where the jet set would dine, drink champagne, and dance under the stars. At the evening's close there would be an astonishing display of fireworks. Afdera arranged blind dates for me with the sons of rich counts or industrialists; I think she was hoping I would marry one—probably to get me out of the New York house but also because it would add to her cachet. I was never tempted to get serious with any of the men I met at the time—the upper-crust idle rich—any more than with the Ivy Leaguers I had met in school. I needed someone who could take me into other worlds—not of wealth but of passion and intensity. I needed a rebel, an adventurer, an outsider.

Goey and a friend of his from Yale, José de Vicuna, came to visit for a week. José, a sophisticated Spaniard, knew his way around the area and had friends to stay with, but Goey stayed in one of the many guest rooms in our villa. We would manage to meet in my room while the adults were taking afternoon siestas. I developed a fondness for lovemaking in the afternoon, lying languidly under a gently whirring ceiling fan. The roll-down canvas awnings outside the large Mediterranean windows cast long shadows on the bedroom's cool tiled floor, and the noise of the fan became synonymous with pleasure.

One afternoon Goey, José, and I drove along the coast to the small sepia-colored old fishing town of Saint Tropez. We got there just as the sun was setting, and I was awestruck by its beauty and charm. Tourists had just discovered it thanks to the recently released film . . . **And God Created Woman**, directed by a young first-time director, Roger Vadim, and starring his then wife, Brigitte Bardot.

It was sometime that summer that I realized the love affair with Goey was beginning to dim. I was getting bored. He seemed stuck, and I realized that his classic drama in iambic pentameter was emblematic— he could never get past the first act. I felt this like a cold whisper in my body but avoided talking to him about it, because I didn't want to hurt him. I am ashamed that while I no longer felt the same, I pretended nothing had changed. In doing so, I set him up for real pain when the time to turn him down finally came, and I set myself up for what was to become a familiar sense of self-betrayal. The following year, when Goey proposed and I declined, it became impossible for us to continue seeing each other as friends, and my first real love affair came to a whimpering end after a year and a half.

When the summer of 1957 came to an end, Dad and Afdera went with me to Paris, where they had arranged for me to be a **pensionnaire** in an apartment on the tree-lined avenue d'Iéna, on the

Right Bank. The daughter of one of Afdera's friends had stayed there while at finishing school. Afdera wanted me to attend finishing school as well, where young ladies from wealthy families learned manners. But I balked and enrolled instead in the Académie de la Grande Chaumière, an art school on the more bohemian Left Bank, where I intended to study painting and drawing.

Susan, my ex-stepmother, had been living in Paris for almost a year, and having her there was a comfort. But Susan had her own life now and probably assumed that at nineteen I was as mature as she had been at that age. Part of me carried the aura of maturity, but inside I was still immature and in serious need of imposed structure and boundaries. Yet I was unable to impose them on my own. I felt porous, like a colander—things just poured into me and seeped out: No there there. I had gotten in over my head and was lonely and scared. Here I was, living in a foreign city where I knew no one but Susan, spoke only halting, academic French, and didn't know my way around.

The apartment where I was staying belonged to a gray-haired woman who had once been of the haute bourgeoisie (the fine furnishings, silver, and porcelains testified to that), but there was a penurious quality about her. She wore only black and was exceedingly dour, as was her adult daughter who lived there with her. They never turned on the lights or opened the draperies, and all the living room furniture was perpetually covered in plastic sheets. Had it not been for the faint sour odor of boiling turnips, which seemed embedded in the drapes and carpet, the place could have been mistaken for a morgue.

I'm ashamed to say I attended only three classes during the two and a half months I was in Paris. Saying that I wanted to take art classes turned out to have been simply a way of getting myself out of college. Mostly I sat in sidewalk cafés and read books and newspapers.

I was smitten by Paris: Hector Guimard's art nouveau entrances to the Métro, fanciful and enchanting as Maxfield Parrish's paintings; the weeping willows and plane trees bordering the Seine; the **bateaux-mouches** carrying tourists up and down the river under the ornate, low-spanning iron bridges; the doe-colored stone buildings along the Seine with sloping, slate-tiled mansard roofs, separated into blocks by narrow cobblestone streets. I liked the sense of history evident everywhere. It reminded me how young my own country was.

One night I was at Maxim's for dinner and dancing with a group of people that included the French actress Marie-José Nat and actor Christian Marquand. A tall, dark man with exotic eyes and an erotic aura joined our group. With him was a beautiful woman who looked to be nine months pregnant. The way the energy in Maxim's shifted when he made his entrance reminded me of entering public places with my father. This was my first encounter with Roger Vadim.

He had become an overnight celebrity with the

release of . . . **And God Created Woman,** which, because of his youth (he was not even thirty) and its irreverent, iconoclastic style, came to be seen as the film that launched the **nouvelle vague** (new wave) of French cinema. But above all, it was the presence of the phenomenal Bardot that had audiences, especially in the United States, flocking to see it.

I had not realized that Vadim and Brigitte were no longer together. Apparently she had fallen in love with her leading man in the film, and Vadim had promptly hooked up with this blond Danish woman, Annette Stroyberg, who would soon bear his firstborn and would, like Bardot, become a star in one of his movies. They weren't married at the time, which somewhat shocked me. I wasn't used to this French "custom" of having babies first and then, perhaps, getting married. Vadim's presence at the table felt predatory, and I was uncomfortable, feeling square, white-bread American. I know from what he later told me that this was just how he saw me. I could never have imagined that one day these people would be a central part of my life.

From time to time Susan would invite me out to dinner with her friends, and occasionally we'd go dancing afterward at l'Éléphant Blanc, a nightclub that was the rage. Several times she was escorted by a man she considered the best dancer she knew, and it was a joy to watch them dip and glide around the dance floor like Astaire and Rogers. I've always had a weakness for people who are beautiful dancers. He was an Italian count in his thirties, a playboy whose family had lost much of its money, making it necessary for him to go to work at an American brokerage firm in Paris. He seemed to know everyone in the Parisian party world and loved to have a good time. So when he asked me out, I accepted. I think because he was a friend of Susan's, I imbued him with qualities he did not possess. Besides, I was lonely and he made me feel I was part of the scene. I wasn't especially attracted to him, but when he asked me to spend the weekend at his country estate, I didn't know how to say no. Phrases like "I am having fun with you, but I have no intention of having an affair with you so I will have to say no to your invitation" never occurred to me. I just went along, whatever he wanted.

What he wanted, besides having an affair, was to take nude photos of me. I find it hard to explain to myself that I didn't think I could say no even though I didn't want to do what he asked. This is painful to write about, but I do so because I want readers—especially women—to know that even an essentially smart and good girl, if she lacks self-esteem and believes a woman is supposed to "go along," will allow herself to get into some inexplicable situations. I wish I could say this was the last one for me. I had a brief affair with him, every moment of which I hated. Mostly I hated myself for my betrayal of my body, and I felt terrible confusion about why I was letting this happen. The nude pictures he took weren't porn photos by any means; in fact, they were rather arty and demure. I think the kick he got was from the fact that he'd managed to get Henry Fonda's nineteen-year-old daughter to pose nude for him. He wasted no time making sure the story of his wretched conquest made the rounds. Afdera, with her pointy, gossip-ferreting nose, snitched to Dad, and when I went home to New York for Christmas, he had her inform me that I would not be returning to Paris. I was mortified, horrified, and also relieved. I didn't want to go back. I felt my life was spinning out of control.

For the following six months I lived at my father's house in New York. He was doing **Two for the Seesaw** on Broadway and not happy about it. He never mentioned the photos to me, thank God. I think he was too embarrassed, and surely he thought I'd turned into a "bad" girl. But it wasn't that.

I was at a loss as to what to do with my life. I was deeply depressed, sleeping again for twelve or thirteen hours a day, and even then I'd fall asleep on dates, in theaters—a sort of adult-onset narcolepsy. I think part of it was an existential mourning for the lack of meaning in my life, a yearning for the emergence of an authentic self I wasn't sure existed.

Then came the summer, and Dad moved us all to a house on Santa Monica beach, about a mile or so from Ocean House, where Peter and I had spent summers with Susan. It was made clear to me via Afdera that come fall I had to find my own apartment and begin to support myself. I was twenty and it was a reasonable request, but I had no idea what I would do and I was in a panic.

Several years ago José (Goey's Spanish friend, who had become my lover) sent me the letters I wrote him that summer (in French) from Malibu, which reveal something of my state of mind:

> **Darling,**
>
> **I'm terribly depressed, don't really see any point in going on; after all, why try to fight when life invariably puts its foot in the door and separates us from the people we love and makes us miserable in so many ways. It's times like these I get so discouraged for no particular reason and I know I will never be very happy or make a success out of life. I don't know what I can do. I'm empty, like a vegetable. Afdera (my father's fourth wife) always uses the same words as my father does: I am a great "disappointment," "lazy," "frivolous," "weak," etc. I don't think I'm as terrible as that, but maybe she's right. I have everything and do nothing. There's a piano and I can't play. There are books in Italian and I cannot read. I cannot draw. I have not "one ounce" of interest, and I'll be like that all my life, I know it!**

And later in the letter:

> **Afdera has all but told me she has no intention of staying married to my father, says there's "no future": and thinks he**

**would go well with Lauren Bacall. I agree
and think she should leave immediately so
Miss Bacall could move in.**

Many young people feel just as I did, hopeless
and empty, not knowing what to do with their lives.
All of us want to feel we have a purpose that gives our
lives meaning. In the absence of that, we blame ourselves and feel like refuse that might just as well be
discarded. My alienation took the form of sleeping
all the time, bulimia, and deep conventionality.
Drugs, acting out, drinking, and driving too fast are
escapes other young people turn to in order to feel
they actually exist, in the absence of a sense of self.

But long about midsummer, just when all
seemed hopeless, a coincidence set me on a path to
meaning. You have to be ready for coincidences—as
Bill Moyers says, "Coincidences are God's way of remaining anonymous."

CHAPTER NINE

TURNING POINT

Our greatest gift, the closest thing to divinity, is our ability for creation. When you're creating, you start living for something outside yourself and colors vivify and sounds deepen and you feel alive and that is the intoxicating factor in performing.

—TROY GARITY,
my actor son

A SUMMER STORM was building to the west as I walked the short distance down Santa Monica beach to his rented house, shoes in hand, jaw set, leaning stalwart into the wind, and telling myself I didn't really care if he accepted me or not. I didn't want to be an actress anyway. All the same, my heart was pounding in my throat when I arrived at his back door, brushed the sand from my feet, and slipped on my high-heeled shoes, chosen carefully to match my dress and flatter my legs.

Taking a deep breath, I knocked at the back door and waited, listening to my pounding heart. Finally the door was opened by a short, bespectacled man with an exceedingly high forehead rimmed with silver hair. In a clipped, nasal voice, without looking at me or introducing himself, as though he had other pressing things awaiting him, he asked me to come in and showed me to a seat in the living room. His accent was unfamiliar, that of a Jewish man of a certain age from New York's Lower East Side, though I didn't recognize it as such at the time. It dawned on me that this was Lee Strasberg, the man I'd come to be interviewed by. He seemed more like a rabbi or a dentist than a famed acting teacher. He was dour, I thought he was angry. I wasn't used to people who didn't bother with social niceties, though in time I would come to appreciate this about him: no frills. You could trust him. If he said it, he meant it.

He sat down, looked at me, and said, "Well." The silence that followed was broken only by an odd clicking sound he was making by forcing a quick breath from his throat out his nose. (He would use this tic to great effect in his scene with Al Pacino in **Godfather II**. I was paralyzed as he stared at me, his cold eyes made eerily larger by the thickness of his glasses. Then I felt something deep inside him relax and grow gentle. Perhaps he saw how scared I was. He told me months later that I had seemed shut down, trying so hard to be a proper, conventional young woman. I asked why, then, he had accepted me into his classes, and he said, "It was your eyes. I saw something else in your eyes."

I had gotten to know his daughter, Susan, earlier in the summer. She and her brother, Johnny, who was around Peter's age, and a directorial protégé of Lee's named Marty Fried would come over and hang out at the beach house Dad had rented. Susan Strasberg, with her tiny, perfect face and skin that shone like a magnolia blossom, had created a sensation in the Broadway play **The Diary of Anne Frank,** and earlier that year she had starred opposite my father in Sidney Lumet's film **Stage Struck.** She seemed to me to be wildly confident and mature.

Day after day for more than a month as I played chess with Susan and Marty, I resisted their efforts to get me to join her father's private acting classes. "Why not give it a try?" they'd say over and over. I insisted repeatedly that I didn't want to be an actress, but the problem of what to do in the fall was looming. So in time I reluctantly gave in. I became an actress by default!

Lee Strasberg was associated with the acting style called the Method. It was not really a set of rules but a quintessentially American adaptation of an amalgam of techniques developed by the Moscow Art Theater's director Konstantin Stanislavsky— with ample contributions from Lee himself, who prior to becoming a teacher had been a stage actor and director. In 1949, two years after Elia Kazan,

Cheryl Crawford, and Robert Lewis had founded the Actors Studio, Lee was asked to join and soon after became the Studio's artistic director and sole teacher of actors. His students included most of the great actors and actresses of the time: James Dean, Paul Newman, Joanne Woodward, Anne Bancroft, Geraldine Page, Al Pacino, Julie Harris, Rip Torn, Ben Gazzara, Sally Field. They brought a new, edgy realism to their work, more internal and personal than the standard theatrical fare audiences were accustomed to. They didn't **show;** they **were.**

It was into Lee's private classes that I had been accepted—a step down from the Studio but nonetheless a step into the inner circle of the man who was considered one of the great teachers in this country. It had all come about because Marilyn Monroe was filming **Some Like It Hot** in Hollywood and Lee's wife, Paula Strasberg, was her acting coach. That's what had brought the Strasberg family to Los Angeles, living a few houses down from us on the beach. And that's the coincidence that changed my life.

I remember going with Susan Strasberg to visit her mother on the set of **Some Like It Hot.** I had been on many of my father's movie sets, but this was my first time visiting a set as a young adult, and I was paying close attention. As the heavy padded double doors that led onto sound stages thudded closed behind us and I stepped inside, I felt myself in a foreign land, a dark and secret world, what my son (who is an actor) calls "a civilization within a civilization." A movie set is not an easy place to be if you are not part of the filming. Inevitably you feel like an interloper, left out of the secret that has brought everyone else to this dark, cavernous place with padded walls and a ceiling so high you have to tilt your head all the way back to try to see it. In the center there is a circle of light where all the energy is being sucked, where the secret lies. Thick electric cables snake across the black floor and up into huge boxes on poles, the klieg lights, which, like sentinels with their backs turned, are silhouetted in a glow. Everyone but you has a task connected to that light. People talk in hushed voices that hang, muffled, in front of their faces. They're polite, but you feel an invisible cord drawing them away from you to that place. A siren shrieks. You jump and turn to see a red light swirling above the double doors, like the light on a police car. "**Silence!**" someone shouts. Then all you hear are murmurs. Then another shout: "**Camera rolling!**" Then: "**Action!**" and all sound and energy are sucked into the vacuum of light.

There was an overabundance of tension as well as excitement on the set that day, partly because of the extraordinary assemblage of star power (Marilyn, Tony Curtis, Jack Lemmon, and the director, Billy Wilder), but also because Marilyn was having problems with her lines and they had been shooting the same scene many times over. It was a scene early in the movie when she's in the train's sleeping car with Tony and Jack, who are in drag.

Susan Strasberg silently pointed out her mother to me. Paula was sitting in a canvas chair behind the camera, all her attention focused on what was going on inside the circle of light. She was a wide woman. Everything about her was wide—her eyes; her face, with high cheekbones; her body, draped in layers of black, covered by an earth-toned shawl and ethnic jewelry. Hers was a lap and bosom you'd want to be taken into. Thick glasses made her eyes large as an owl's, and her pale red hair was pulled back in a braided chignon. She had clearly been a beauty once, like her daughter, Susan.

An eternity of held breath elapsed before a voice yelled, "**Cut!**" Suddenly people sprang into action, moving out of the darkness, doing their precise, union-prescribed tasks inside that circle of light. Then into the darkness stepped Marilyn Monroe, bringing the light with her, shimmering, in her hair and on her skin. She walked with Paula toward where Susan and I were standing while someone draped a pink chenille bathrobe over her shoulders to cover her revealing nightgown. Her body seemed to precede her, and it was hard to keep my eyes from camping out there. But when I looked up at her face, I saw a scared, wide-eyed child. I was dizzy. It was hard to believe she was right there in front of me, all golden iridescence, saying hello in that breathy, little-girl voice. There was a vulnerability that radiated from her and allowed me to love her right there and feel glad that she had someone wide and soft, like Paula, to mama her. She was very sweet to Susan and me, but I could tell she wanted Paula's undivided attention, to give her what she needed so that she could go back and do the scene one more time. I wondered how it could be that she seemed so frightened when she was probably the most famous woman in the world. We lingered a few moments, said hello to Billy Wilder, whom I'd known since childhood, and to Jack Lemmon, whom I'd met at this very studio when he filmed scenes for **Mister Roberts** with my father. Then we left, stepping out of the darkness and into the blinding sunlight, into that other civilization that was real life. But for the first time a part of me felt drawn to the light within the darkness behind those heavy padded double doors.

That episode took place just weeks before my meeting with Lee, and long before the time I myself would be inside the circle of light and would have to find my own ways of dealing with the fears that celebrity cannot assuage.

A few weeks later my father brought me to the Warner Bros. Studio back lot to meet with Jimmy Stewart about the possibility of my playing his daughter in the film **The FBI Story**. Director Mervyn LeRoy had come up with the idea, and I suppose my father saw it as a harmless, all-in-the-family sort of lark, Jimmy being his best friend. For just these reasons, I didn't cotton to it in the least: It smacked too much of a "Daddy's little girl" setup, and I communicated my lack of enthusiasm strongly enough to sweet Jimmy that things never got further than that first meeting. But in light of my subsequent relationship with the Federal Bureau of Investigation, wouldn't it have been ironic if my first role had been in **The FBI Story**?

So Lee Strasberg had accepted me into his private classes in New York, and my problem of what to do in the fall was taken care of. Where exactly to live and how to pay for it all were the remaining issues. As luck would have it, Susan Stein, youngest daughter of MCA's Jules and Doris Stein and sister of Jean (Stein) Vanden Heuvel, had graduated from Vassar and was looking for an apartment and roommate in New York.

Susan Stein suggested that I meet with Eileen Ford, head of the famous Ford Modeling Agency. Maybe I could get work as a fashion model to pay my share of the rent, as well as the acting classes. Within two months of my return to the city I had started Lee's class, taken my first modeling assignments, found a duplex on East Seventy-sixth Street for Susan and me, and moved out of my father's house (to the great relief of Afdera). I was on my way, a leaf in the river's current—not in control of my destiny, perhaps, but at least on the move.

The modeling work I was doing to pay for the acting classes was difficult for me. I didn't like the incessant focus on my looks, and I never felt I was very photogenic (those round cheeks), but I had no trouble finding a doctor to prescribe Dexedrine, which kept me hyper, and diuretics, which made me urinate incessantly, thus draining my body of fluids. On my five-foot-eight-inch frame, my weight dropped from the low 120s to under 110. My face, which in those years (1959, 1960), was prominently featured in many major magazines—**Life, Esquire, Harper's Bazaar, Look, Vogue,** and **Ladies' Home Journal**—

The King Who Fell in Love With His Bride ... the story of Queen Mary and George V

FUEL FOR THE FLAME BY THE AUTHOR OF ISLAND IN THE SUN

The Marriage That Could <u>Not</u> Be Saved

THE BIBLE AND THE WORLD OF DR. KINSEY

Livable, Lovable, Wearable Fashions — 8 PAGES

Modeling to pay the rent and for acting classes.
(October 1959 **Ladies' Home Journal,** courtesy of
Meredith Corporation, photo by Roger Prigent)

looked drawn, my eyes empty. But the modeling work kept coming. I would hang around the magazine stands when one of my covers had come out, an anonymous bystander, to see how people reacted to my photo. Eileen Ford, whose agency I worked for, once said of me, "She was something. She was terribly insecure about her looks and the impact she had on people. She was astonished to learn that people would be interested in using her and paying her well."

Acting classes were held in a nondescript building in midtown, on Broadway. We'd take a cramped, musty elevator up to the sixth floor to a small theater with a proscenium stage and seats for about forty people. Do you remember the feeling of entering a new school when you were a kid, looking around and picking up clues as to where you fit in and where you were different? Well, it was clear to me from the outset that I was different: I felt uncomfortably upper-class, an elite dilettante, as though I carried a sign that read, "I'm not really sure I want to be here, I'm just trying it out." Everyone else had a scruffier, bohemian look about them that said, "I am an intense, serious New York actor. Deal with it!" My clothes were verging on preppy and my voice, with its Ivy League accent, seemed to come out of my ear. The other students knew I was Henry Fonda's daughter and, whether it was real or imagined, I felt resentment.

There were a few famous faces in the class from time to time—France Nuyen, for instance, who was starring on Broadway in **The World of Suzie Wong;** Salome Jens; Carroll Baker, who was considered a major discovery after her sexy performance in Elia Kazan's **Baby Doll.**

Then there was Marilyn Monroe, Lee's most famous student, who sat quietly and earnestly in the back of the room in a trench coat, a scarf on her head, and no makeup. Twice a week for one month I sat right behind her, trying to understand what was going on, praying Lee wouldn't call on me. I had definitely not committed myself to a career in acting and wasn't at all sure I'd even stay in the class. Marilyn, I was told, had never been able to do a scene there. Each time she'd try, fear would make her sick to her stomach. I remember following her out into the street after class one day. I stood behind her as she hailed a cab, and I watched her ride away unrecognized. I had seen her in newsreels, in the spotlight, being stormed by fans and paparazzi, and had wondered how a person could handle the extreme swing from being the center of fanatical attention to being all alone on a New York sidewalk, unrecognized and scared.

A few years later her press agent (who represented me as well) told me that once Marilyn had been so scared to come down from her hotel room to a press conference that she couldn't stop throwing up. He said she vacillated between thinking she was not just a star but a "celestial body" and the fear that "this is the day they'll find out I'm a fraud." I wish I'd gone to her and held her hand.

The first of the two weekly classes was devoted to what was called a "sense-memory" exercise. One or two students would be called on to re-create the sensations of a particular activity, its smells, feelings, sounds—actually experiencing them. Unlike pantomime, which requires you to mimic an activity exactly but without props, sense-memory involves taking minutes to really feel the heat and weight of a cup of coffee in your hand, for instance, then many more minutes to feel the heat as the cup approaches your lips. It's the difference between reenacting and **reexperiencing.** The purpose is to expand your sensory awareness and concentration. Following the exercise, Lee would do a critique of your work, and then the class could make comments as well.

Next would be the "song" exercise, where the student would stand center stage and belt out a song all on one note, each word drawn out as long as possible. Something about the note being extended on that long breath caused emotions to surface and play across the voice as though it were a harp string. The voice might begin to quaver or crack, faces and bodies would tremble, and Lee would, in his calm, nasal voice, encourage the student to keep going and to relax different parts of the face or body. This exercise was to teach actors how to use focused relaxation to enable them to go on with a scene even when powerful emotions threatened to overcome them.

After that part of the exercise, students would

continue the song while flinging themselves about the stage like limp bean bags: jumping, leaping, and swinging their arms.

It was fascinating, but at the time I didn't understand the point of it. I knew that my father felt nothing but disdain for acting classes in general and Strasberg's Method in particular. He didn't believe acting could be taught, and to him the Method was self-indulgent rubbish that allowed untalented actors to feel they were interesting and deep. As I sat there in class, I wondered if maybe he was right. It was all so easy to ridicule.

The second (and last) class of the week was scene day, when students would perform a two-person scene they had chosen, after which Lee would make his comments. I watched actors and actresses I thought were extremely talented, like Lane Bradbury, Ellie Wood, Lou Antonio, and others whose names I don't remember. Many had had small parts off Broadway or on live television shows. Some waited tables; others modeled, like me. I was struck by Lee's ability to home in on whatever it was they needed to work on. Sometimes he was easy on the actors, especially the prettier women. Sometimes he was harsh and impatient. Clearly he'd had some of the students in his classes for years, knew their strengths and weaknesses, and was frustrated when they weren't able to move forward with the work. For me, the most frightening aspect of the class was the thought of being critiqued by Lee in front of the other students. Even worse, he sometimes asked students to comment on the work of their fellow students.

I decided that before I quit the class I should at least try to do a sense-memory, and I chose drinking a glass of fresh orange juice as my exercise. I was still living in my father's house at that point. Early every evening when I'd get home from a photo shoot, I'd squeeze oranges and sit in the library with a glass, focusing as hard as I could on every aspect of the sensory experience.

One day Dad came home, found me working on this, and said, "What the hell are you doing, Jane?"

"Practicing a sense-memory exercise for class," I answered, wincing at what I knew was coming.

He looked at me with pure derision, shook his head, and walked off muttering, "Jesus Christ."

But I persevered. "Persevere" happens to be our family motto.

A whole month and a half after entering his class, I finally told Lee that I was ready to do my first exercise. The following week he called on me. Sitting on a chair center stage, I was as nervous as I'd ever been in my life. It seemed to me there were many more people than usual in the class that day, and I figured they were there to see me fail. But I launched in, placing my fingers around the imaginary glass of chilled orange juice. I closed my eyes and before long felt myself alone in a world of sensation; the nerves in my fingertips felt the cold. I opened my eyes and lifted the glass slowly, testing its weight until I could feel it in my hand, and as I brought the glass to my mouth, the taste buds on my tongue woke up in anticipation of the sweet, acidy wetness. For the first time I was experiencing something unique to actors: I knew I was on a stage before an audience, pretending—yet at the same time I was all alone and totally in the moment.

What happened next was the most important moment in my life up until then.

Lee was quiet, looking at me. Then in a low voice he said, "I see a lot of people go through here, Jane, but you have real talent."

The top of my head came off, birds flew out, and the room was bathed in light. **Lee Strasberg told me I was talented. He isn't my father or an employee of my father's. He sees actors all day long every day. He didn't have to say this. I know he's not one to "make nice."**

In that moment my life did a flip-flop, though I didn't understand at the time why it had such a powerful effect on me. When I walked outside after the class, the city felt different, as if I now owned a piece of it. I went to bed that night with my heart racing, and when I woke up the next morning, I knew why I was alive, what I wanted to do. There is nothing more exquisite in life than being able to earn your living doing what you love (that, and being capable of love). All I'd needed was for someone who was a professional—and who didn't have to—to tell me I was good.

Characteristically, I went at it full-throttle. Instead of the usual two classes a week that everyone took, I took four. Instead of one scene every few months, I'd do double. I don't think I fully understood the Method, nor do I think I really knew how to apply it in my professional work when that time came. What the classes did for me, however, was provide the confidence I so sorely needed. I knew there'd be those who'd say I'd gotten my breaks because I was Henry Fonda's daughter. At those times I needed to be able to say to myself, **I'm studying hard to develop a modicum of technique. I'm not a dilettante. I don't take this for granted.**

Before Dad ever got to Broadway or starred in a film, he'd played in hundreds of summer stock productions and road shows. They had served as his classes, where he could develop his craft. In the late fifties, when I came along, the business was far more competitive; there were many more actors looking for work, and because I was Henry Fonda's daughter, there was more attention paid to me and fewer opportunities to fumble and make mistakes incognito. For my niece, Bridget Fonda, and now for my son, Troy Garity, the field is even more competitive and challenging. Perhaps you can't teach acting **talent,** but you can learn the tools to bring that talent out in the face of what are often challenging circumstances. Dad was wrong to have thought the classes were a mistake—not for me they weren't. Years later, Troy studied acting at New York's American Academy of Dramatic Arts, and he says it saved him just as Lee Strasberg saved me.

As a girl who had grown up denying my feelings, with a father who thought emotions "disgusting," I was unaccustomed to people fully expressing themselves even to the point of looking ridiculous. So the work in Lee's classes was revelatory, a balm to my soul. Sally Field captured what acting did for girls like us who grew up in the fifties when she said, "I guess it was a way for me to release all the feelings that I had in some acceptable terms, so that I wasn't responsible for them." Through acting I could probe new parts of myself—sorrow, anger, joy—and feel safe exposing them. I felt I was appreciated for the fullness of my self rather than for some "good girl's" proper façade. I had never been so happy.

There was another element Lee brought to his classes and to the Actors Studio (for which I auditioned and to which I was accepted the following year), and that was the sense of theater as great art. The Actors Studio had grown out of the Group Theatre to carry on the tradition of actors working together to achieve a high level of truth and reality. Those of us privileged to study with Lee could feel this sense of history and commitment to an ideal, and it was inspiring.

Lee was a voracious reader, and the walls of his spacious but unassuming apartment on Central Park West were ceiling-to-floor books. That apartment became a haven for many of us, a place to sit in the kitchen, drink tea in Russian glass cups, and discuss theater. I was unaccustomed to sitting in kitchens engaged in endless discussion, being asked for and giving opinions. Another stray that seemed to find her place in that culture-laden apartment was Marilyn.

The need for Lee's method of teaching actors seemed very clear to me, and the clearer it became, the more I understood why my father put it down. Musicians use instruments to express themselves through sound. Painters, with time and solitude on their side, use paints and brushes to express themselves on canvas. For actors, their canvas, their instrument, is their **very being,** and for theater actors in particular, instead of in solitude, they are creating before an audience. It's not easy to ensure that your very being is on call, ready, willing, and able to perform to its utmost. The only thing analogous (which I would become conscious of later, during all those years of watching Atlanta Braves baseball games with Ted Turner) is the athlete up at bat, say, with the bases loaded at the bottom of the ninth. The world is watching and either he comes through or he doesn't; it's all him up there. There is another critical element the athlete and the actor share: the essential need to be relaxed.

Lee once said, "Tension is the occupational disease of the actor." I have watched carefully the not-quite-great baseball players when they strike out and walk back to the dugout, shaking their heads, swearing, and sometimes pounding their bats on the ground. The great players, on the other hand (I'm thinking particularly of Chipper Jones and Greg Maddux), take that walk as cool as a cucumber, as though nothing had gone wrong. They have found a technique to maintain physical and mental calm. You can't do most things well without being relaxed, not in sports, not in lovemaking, not in acting. Where it differs for actors is that relaxation is needed, not to swing a bat well or run swiftly, but so that the body's energetic flow is unimpeded and inspiration can rise and express itself through the actor's spirit: in eyes, voice, and movement . . . the body as instrument. But it's not as though you can get up in front of an audience and say to yourself, Relax, dammit! You can **pretend** to be relaxed, but pretending isn't going to address self-doubts and hangups, often unconscious, that block the creative process and keep you from doing what you want to do in a scene.

Some actors become famous right away and go from role to role, often being asked to play the same qualities that made them famous, over and over, until they are imitating themselves. In fact, stardom can be the death knell of an actor's best talent. Lee would sometimes say that actors develop their careers in public, but their art develops in private. It is a terrible feeling to be famous but have lost the fire in the belly and not know where it went or why. Something's wrong, but you don't know how to fix it. That's where class comes in. It is in the private sanctuary of a class, not on the job, that an actor can try things, take chances, fall on his or her face, learn how to make his or her instrument perform wholly and fully in all the ways needed, **when** needed. To achieve this goal, we must become conscious of what makes us respond the way we do in real life, in certain relationships and situations. We must confront inhibitions, fears, all of our emotional processes and what triggers them, all the things that can cause us problems without our knowing what is happening. The techniques Lee used were aimed at enabling the actor to become aware of and remove these internal barriers. He had no rigid set of rules that applied to all actors. On the contrary, he made comments and suggestions based on each actor's individual issues—and one of mine was the need always to be perfect. That made me tense, wanting constantly to prove my talent by being very emotional (something that has always come easily for me). So Lee would have me do scenes where I'd play rather dull, slow-speaking, slow-moving characters. Doing nothing was what I needed to learn.

The other big challenge for an actor is how to find inspiration. You know how some days every nerve in your body is alive and vibrating, while other days you're dull and sluggish? That's not great in civilian life, but if an actor has a critical scene to play (often, in filming, at impossible hours like 6:00 A.M. or midnight) and is "dead" inside, what to do? That's where technique is critical. By working with a variety of exercises, from the sense-memory kind to private moments, and by trying different scenes that you may never be asked to do professionally but that work on the psychic places you tend to block, you can develop an arsenal of tools to use when the need arises.

Of **course** my father would have hated the Method: It was all about being able to plumb your depths and expose yourself spontaneously on a personal level, especially in class, so as to become conscious of how your instrument functions. He lumped it together with all the other things he disdained: religion, therapy, anything that expressed need, the antithesis of the rugged individual. "Crutches, all crutches!" he would say.

Decades later we were filming a scene in **On Golden Pond** when, standing in the water next to his boat, I tell him I want to be his friend. We had rehearsed many times, and I had stifled the urge to touch his arm, wanting to save it for when it would matter most: his close-up. Dad very rarely had tears on camera, and I wanted him to have tears in this scene, which meant so much to me on a personal level. When the moment came and the camera was rolling for that close-up, I reached out and placed my hand on his arm as I said, "I want to be your friend."

What I saw amazed me: For a millisecond he was caught off guard. He seemed angry, even: **This isn't what we rehearsed.** Then the emotions hit him, tears came to his eyes, then anger again as he tensed up and looked away. All this, though barely visible to the camera, was palpably clear to me, and my heart went out to him. I loved him so much just then. It amazes me what a great actor he was in spite of his fear of spontaneity and real emotions. I remembered reading something that Leora Dana, who starred with him in the play **Point of No Return,** once said:

His acting was fantastic. His precision was so perfect it made me want to be perfect. His relaxation was tremendous. I liked that. . . . And then, one day, I touched him at a time when I wasn't supposed to be touching him. I just put my hand on his arm, and instead of that relaxed human being I felt steel. His arm was made up of bands of steel.

Of **course** he would hate the Method! But I'd found a home.*

*For more information on Lee's theories and practices, read the transcriptions of tape-recorded sessions at the Studio in **Strasberg: At the Actors Studio,** ed. Robert Hethmon, Viking Press, 1965.

CHAPTER TEN

DOUBLE EXPOSURE

When you're a nobody, the only way to be anybody
is to be somebody else.
—ANONYMOUS PATIENT,
Your Inner Child of the Past

IN THE SPRING OF 1959, Josh Logan, after
making a screen test with me, decided to put me
under contract for $10,000 a year and launch my ca-
reer with a movie version of a Broadway play called
Tall Story, co-starring Anthony Perkins. It was to be
shot at the Warner Bros. Studio in Burbank. What
fascinated me most on the lot was the wardrobe
department—two floors of a building, room after
room of costumes from different periods, each
tagged with the name of the movie and the star who
had worn it. There were the muslin-covered body
dummies of all the Warner Bros. stars: stout, thin,

buxom, they had been created to the exact measurements of the stars' bodies, ready for the seamstresses to pin their patterns to the forms. The dummies were headless, so if a particular shape intrigued you because of its dramatic curves (Marilyn's) or its petite size (Natalie Wood's), you'd have to ask one of the fifteen or so seamstresses whose it was. In the wardrobe department more than anywhere else, I felt awed in the presence of Hollywood history and realized I was about to step into that history myself. My measurements had been taken before I'd left New York and my dummy was right there next to the others, looking disappointingly straight up and down—with none of the eye-catching ins and outs that distinguished so many others.

Then came the day for makeup tests. The Warner Bros. makeup department was run by the highly regarded Gordon Bau. Down the hall I could see Angie Dickinson getting hers done; Sandra Dee was next door. I lay back and presented my face to Mr. Bau, confident that he would make me look like a movie star. When he'd finished I sat up and . . . **Oh, my God! Who is that in the mirror! Is that how he thinks I should look?** I was horrified, dumbstruck. Who was I to tell him I didn't want to be that person in the mirror? But this wasn't me. My lips had a new shape and my eyebrows were dark and enormous, like eagle's wings.

I hated the way I looked but didn't dare say so. Then I was sent to get body makeup, done by a different person (union requirements) in a different

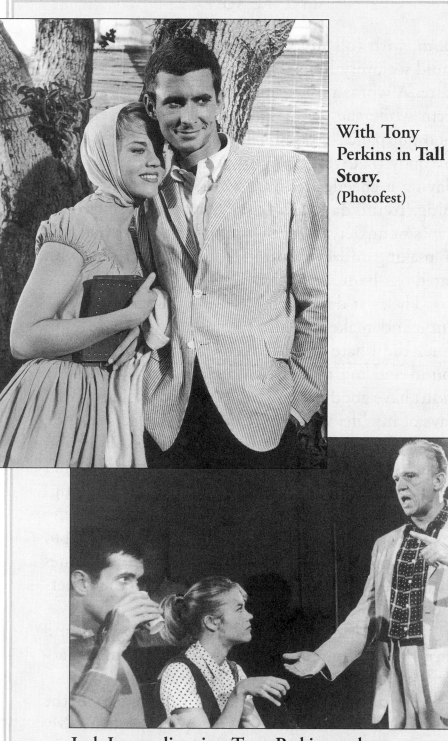

With Tony Perkins in **Tall Story.**
(Photofest)

Josh Logan directing Tony Perkins and me in **Tall Story.**

room, with (**oh my God!**) mirrors all around. You could see everything. This was turning into a nightmare. A woman asked me to stand on a small platform while she wet a sponge with Sea Breeze and then put pancake body makeup over all the parts of my body that were going to be exposed. Since I was playing a cheerleader, that meant just about everything. To this day the smell of Sea Breeze brings back waves of anxiety. I began to think that this business of making movies wasn't for people like me, who hated our bodies and faces.

The next day, when I saw the results of the costume and makeup tests, I wanted to disappear, so much did I hate how I looked onscreen—my face so round and my makeup so unreal. And I definitely didn't have good hair. To top it off as one of the worst days of my life, word came down from Jack Warner, who had also seen the tests in his private projection room, that I must wear falsies. At the same time that he notified me of Mr. Warner's demand, Josh suggested that after the filming I might consider having my jaw broken and reset and my back teeth pulled to create a more chiseled look, the sunken cheekbones that were the hallmarks of Suzy Parker, the supermodel of the time.

"Of course," said Josh, touching my chin and turning me to profile, "you'll never be a dramatic actress with that nose, too cute for drama."

From that moment on, my experience on the film **Tall Story** became a Kafkaesque nightmare. My bulimia soared out of control and I began sleepwalking again as I had as a child, but in a different context. I would dream I was in bed, waiting for a love scene to be shot, and gradually I would realize that I'd made a terrible mistake. I was in the wrong bed, in the wrong room, and everyone was waiting for me to start the scene somewhere else, though I didn't know where.

It was summertime and hot, so I often slept nude. On one occasion I woke up on the sidewalk in front of my apartment building: cold, naked, searching in vain for where (and who) I was supposed to be.

I was unable to rediscover the excitement I had experienced acting in Strasberg's classes. I didn't know how to use what I had learned there to make my cheerleader character more than one-dimensional. And the camera felt like my enemy. Standing before it, I felt as though I were falling off a cliff with no net under me. There was so much focus on externals, and there seemed no shortage of people who let me know that my externals could use some improvement— with one exception.

During a day off, I found a plastic surgeon who did reconstructive surgery, and I made an appointment to see him. In his office, I showed him my breasts and told him I needed to have them enlarged. To my amazement (and his credit), he got mad at me.

"You're out of your mind to consider doing such a thing," he said. "Go home and forget about it."

But his validation wasn't enough to put Humpty-Dumpty together again. All the things I feared most in myself—that I was boring, untalented, and plain—

came to the fore during the filming of **Tall Story**. When it was done I returned to New York, vowing I would never go back to moviemaking.

I was twenty-two, on my way to celebrity, earning my own living, and independent.

So why, when it was time for me to write about this period for my book, did I develop writer's block that lasted six months? Oh, I had lots of excuses: There was all that thistle to spray at my ranch in New Mexico. There were rocks to move and trees to cut down to make horse trails, and then my kids were visiting. . . . You know, life. But after six months I had to face the fact that I was having difficulty confronting those years following the turning point with Strasberg. Why did the ensuing years feel so sad, so false, after things had started off so well? Not that there weren't happy times, but pain engraves a deeper memory.

Does it seem strange that Strasberg's classes allowed me to discover a place of truth, an authenticity, for the first time since childhood? The moment when I did my first exercise for him I felt he "saw" me. He was, after all, a master at sensing what was real and at naming it. All my life I had been encouraged **not** to probe my depths, **not** to identify and name my emotions. But Lee encouraged me to dig deep and to come out—and I did, all raw and vulnerable, reborn. Then, **wham!** My career began, and everything that had started to happen with Lee was pushed aside and it all became about hair and big cheeks and small breasts, and I couldn't handle it, coming as it did on the heels of an emerging selfhood. I went into a three-year tailspin of private self-destruction, depression, and passivity. I don't mean this by way of self-pity. There are a lot worse things in life than having your body critiqued, and stardom is a whole lot better than a kick in the ass. But my **Tall Story** experience pushed all my insecurity buttons. I **seemed** to be doing fine. Friends who were with me during that period may be shocked to read what I was really feeling. But then I always **seem** to be fine. I know how to get by.

For one thing, when I returned to New York from Hollywood I was bingeing and purging sometimes eight times a day. It was out of control, and as a consequence I was always tired, angry, and depressed. I briefly sought help from a Freudian psychiatrist, who sat behind me as I lay on a couch, where I was convinced that he was either sleeping or masturbating. I soon realized that talking to the ceiling about my dreams wasn't what I needed. I needed immediate, look-me-in-the-eyes help—first to stop my bingeing and purging, then to help me understand why I was doing it. But I didn't know where to go.

During this period I also developed a fear of men, and my sensuality took a long hiatus. I sought safety in the company of gay or bisexual men. This is also when ballet came into my life. With its rigidly prescribed moves and required slimness, ballet is the dance style of preference for women with eating disorders. Like anorexia and bulimia, ballet is about control. This was a time when women were not supposed to sweat; it was considered unseemly. The health clubs for women that existed featured saunas, vibrating belts that made your fanny wiggle, and other forms of passive exercise. Dumbbells and machines were strictly the domain of men. Consequently ballet was my first experience with hard, sweat-producing exercise that could actually change the shape of my body, and from 1959 until I began the Jane Fonda Workout in 1978, through all those early films, including **Barbarella** and **Klute**, wherever I was working, whether in France, Italy, the United States, or the USSR—ballet was my sole form of exercise.

Within a month of my return to New York after **Tall Story,** I began rehearsals with Josh for a play he'd purchased called **There Was a Little Girl,** written by Daniel Taradash. It dealt with rape. My father begged me not to do it, fearing that critics would find it too risqué. I saw it as a way to stretch myself beyond what I'd been asked to do in **Tall Story,** and although the script was flawed, it had an interesting, quasi-feminist-before-its-time premise: A young virgin is celebrating her eighteenth birthday with her boyfriend and hoping he will make love to her. He makes it clear he is not ready, they get into a fight, and she runs out into the parking lot, where a man rapes her, aided by a gang of his friends. She returns home in a state of shock and confusion to discover that, while they don't say so overtly, her parents and sister (played wickedly by a fifteen-year-old, Joey Heatherton) assume it must have been her fault—the old you-must-have-wanted-it, blame-the-victim response. Knowing that she had wanted to have sex that night; believing that she may in fact have brought it on herself; and on the verge of a nervous breakdown, the girl goes in search of her rapist, hoping to find out directly from him where the truth lies.

Barely a year had passed since I'd begun to study acting, and a portion of that year had been spent on **Tall Story.** This was my first time in professional theater. It was a highly charged, emotional role, and I was onstage the entire time, making lightning-fast costume changes in the dark on a revolving stage while trying to get into various stages of emotional meltdown. During rehearsals in New York, it became clear to everyone that the play had major flaws, and every morning Dan Taradash would bring in new script changes. I've always liked challenges, but this went a little beyond what I was prepared for.

On New Year's Day 1960, one week before we were to begin out-of-town tryouts in Boston, we received news that Brooke Hayward's mother, Margaret Sullavan, had been found dead in a hotel room in New Haven, an apparent suicide. The news hit me like a punch to the solar plexus. Her death also hit Josh very hard, since their friendship went back to the earliest days of the University Players.

Two nights before our out-of-town opening at the Colonial Theater in Boston, Josh fired my leading man and replaced him with Dean Jones, who

In **There Was a Little Girl,** my first Broadway play. (Leonard McCombe/ Time & Life Pictures/ Getty Images)

As Kitty Twist with Laurence Harvey in **Walk on the Wild Side.** (William Read Woodfield/CPi)

barely had time to learn his lines. Two nights later, at the top of the second act, Louis Jean Heydt, who played my father, died of a massive heart attack right before his entrance. Two nights after that, Josh himself, who unbeknownst to me had long suffered from severe manic depression, had a nervous breakdown and disappeared for more than ten days, leaving us in the hands of the writer, who had never directed in his life.

Our final week of out-of-town tryouts was spent in Philadelphia. Three days in, Josh returned to us as though nothing had happened, though the way in which his wife, Nedda, clung to his side made it plain to me that something was wrong. My hotel room was next to theirs, and one night when I was getting ready for bed, I heard murmuring and decided I wanted to listen in. So I borrowed a trick I'd learned from a boyfriend: If you turn a glass upside down against a wall, it acts like a megaphone and you can hear what's being said on the other side. That first night I was astonished to hear Nedda singing "Rock-a-Bye, Baby" to Josh. I was too frightened of what lay in store for me when we opened in New York to feel compassion for Josh's illness. It only underscored how out on a limb by myself I was. The following night I again used the glass trick to eavesdrop, and this time I heard something that disturbed me far more than the lullaby: Josh was talking to someone about the necessity of keeping the play going for at least twenty-one days no matter how bad the New York reviews were, so that he could declare a tax write-off.

He knows that the play is going to be crucified, and he cares more about a tax write-off than he does about protecting our professional reputations!

My heart sank. While the Boston and Philadelphia reviews hadn't been encouraging, to say the least, I had personally received some good notices and had, in desperate hope, managed to convince myself that Josh and Dan Taradash would come through with the right script changes. Now I knew they weren't even going to try. **A tax write-off**! What about Lee Strasberg's vision of theater as high art? What about idealism?

There Was a Little Girl limped onto Broadway. I got through an embarrassing opening night and learned how to make it through Sardi's without falling apart when reviews are crucifying, though some reviews were good to me. Brooks Atkinson, in **The New York Times**, wrote, "As the wretched heroine of an unsavory melodrama, she gives an alert, many-sided performance that is professionally mature and suggests that she has found a career that suits her." John Chapman, in the New York **Daily News,** wrote, "With the budding talent that she displayed last evening, she might become the Sarah Bernhardt of 1990. But she'd better find herself a more genuine play than this one between now and then."

The play lasted sixteen performances. Josh got his tax write-off, and I emerged with the New York Drama Critics' Circle award for "the most promising actress of the year for drama."

I felt like a double exposure: There was the me people could see—my mouth opened and closed and words came out. I'll never forget an audition I did for Elia Kazan for the female lead in **Splendor in the Grass.** Kazan, who'd done **On the Waterfront** and **East of Eden,** called me down to the edge of the stage, introduced himself, reached up to shake my hand, and asked, "Do you consider yourself ambitious?" I responded immediately with a resounding, "No!" This passive voice flew automatically out of my mouth, muffling my real passions and creativity. The moment the word left my lips I knew I'd made a mistake, I could read it on Kazan's face. If I wasn't ambitious, I must not have any fire inside, I must be a dilettante. **But good girls aren't supposed to be ambitious.** I went through the motions of an audition but knew I'd already lost out. Natalie Wood got the role, starring opposite Warren Beatty. Neither of them would have hesitated in answering "Yes!" to Kazan's question.

I was utterly disembodied. Even my voice, both professionally and in my personal life, was high in the top of my head. The other, **not** high-voiced, double-exposed me was almost a stranger, someone I was with when I was alone and had nothing to prove, but not someone I could bring to the party. Like an unused muscle, that other me began to atrophy over time so that I almost forgot she was there and was bewildered when someone seemed to see her and expect more from me than I was giving or that I thought myself capable of. Not taking myself seriously, I gave myself away—to films that weren't very good and to people I didn't really care about.

In the fall of 1960, just as I opened in my second Broadway play, Arthur Laurents's **Invitation to a March,** Brooke Hayward's sister, Bridget, was found dead, an apparent suicide, in her New York apartment. The darkness that had overtaken Brooke's golden, laughing family was frightening. It meant that no one was safe; anything could reach in and pluck you from the light.

Around the same time, I discovered that Josh was about to sell my contract to producer Ray Stark for $250,000. I didn't want to be "owned" anymore, so I offered to buy back my contract for the same price he was asking from Stark. While $250,000 may not seem like much in today's show business, for me (back then) it meant having to work constantly just to be able to turn over a chunk of my paychecks to Josh for five years. But I committed to it without hesitation. Freedom was worth it to me.

Though I had vowed never to make another Hollywood film, I now needed to work to pay Josh, and when I was offered the role of Kitty Twist in the movie adaptation of Nelson Algren's dark, Depression-era novel **Walk on the Wild Side,** I grabbed it. It wasn't just for the money, however. I wanted to play the brash, train-hopping, petty thief who had just escaped from reform school and ends up a high-class prostitute in a New Orleans brothel. Kitty was about as far a cry from my role in **Tall Story** as I could get. What's more, there were other stars to take major responsibility for the film's success or failure: Barbara Stanwyck, Laurence Harvey, Anne Baxter, and Capucine.

This time out I had decided to borrow a page from Marilyn Monroe's book and bring an acting coach to Hollywood with me so I wouldn't feel so vulnerable. He was a flamboyant Greek actor and coach named Andréas Voutsinas, and we had gotten to know each other when he helped me with the scene that got me into the Actors Studio. After **Walk on the Wild Side,** he worked with me on the films **Period of Adjustment** and **In the Cool of the Day,** and directed me in a Broadway play, **The Fun Couple.**

CHAPTER ELEVEN

VADIM

Twenty years from now you will be
more disappointed by the things
you didn't do than by the ones you
did do. So throw off the bowlines.
Sail away from the safe harbor.
Catch the trade winds in your sails.
Explore. Dream. Discover.
—MARK TWAIN

"**Qui ne risque rien n'a rien**," observed the devil,
lapsing into French, as is his wont.
—MARY McCARTHY,
Memories of a Catholic Girlhood

IT WAS 1963. I was in Hollywood filming **Sunday in New York,** my sixth movie, when I got a call from my agent telling me that Roger Vadim wanted me to come to France to do a remake of **La Ronde,** the minor movie classic from the fifties. I had my agent fire back a telegram saying that I "would never work with Vadim!" I had seen his ... **And God Created Woman,** and—while I found Brigitte Bardot a fascinating force of nature and recognized that the film represented a new, iconoclastic style of filmmaking— I wasn't all that impressed with it. Besides, I remembered feeling endangered when we'd met several years earlier at Maxim's in Paris.

But France seemed to be in the cards, because shortly thereafter French director René Clément flew to Los Angeles to pitch me a film idea that would co-star Alain Delon, one of the top male box-office stars in Europe at the time. I agreed. I liked the idea of putting an ocean's distance between me, Hollywood, and my father's long shadow. Moreover, France was then at the apex of the **nouvelle vague,** with young directors like Truffaut, Godard, Chabrol, and Malle, and Vadim. Clément was up in years and wasn't part of this new wave, but he had directed the brilliant **Forbidden Games.**

On my second trip to Paris in the fall of 1963, it was love at first sight all over again. But this time the city felt like a friend ready to teach me the art of living rather than a big party from which I was excluded. You'd have thought I was a long-lost daughter coming home, so effusive was the French press. The person who took me under her wing and made me feel at home in Paris was the reknowned French actor Simone Signoret: Simone, with her charming lisp, sensual bee-stung lips, and heavy-lidded blue eyes—tough, opinionated, always insisting on being

Dad and Peter
visiting me on the set of
Sunday in New York.
(Photofest)

Paris, 1963.
(Everett Collection)

a human first, a star second. She lived with her actor-singer husband, Yves Montand, in an apartment above Restaurant Paul on Ile de la Cité, the little triangle of an island in the Seine right across from my hotel. They were good friends with the director Costa-Gavras, who coincidentally was the assistant director on **Les Félins**, my Clément film. He would later direct the great political thrillers **Z, State of Siege,** and **Missing,** and was often there among Simone and Yves's friends when they ordered up meals from Restaurant Paul and talked heatedly into the night. The stimulating, we're-not-in-a-hurry-to-get-anywhere, what-could-be-more-perfect-than-talking atmosphere was reminiscent of the Strasberg home in New York, where both Yves and Simone had often visited. Besides good food and wine, the French love all things cerebral. After all, "I think, therefore I am" was said by French philosopher René Descartes.

I had met Simone in 1959, when she'd accompanied Yves to New York, where his one-man show, **An Evening with Yves Montand,** was a smash hit on Broadway. My father, Afdera, and I had had dinner together with them at the Algonquin Hotel. I remember watching Simone stare adoringly across the table at my father, and now, in Paris, she talked to me about the films he'd made—**Blockade, The Grapes of Wrath, Young Mr. Lincoln,** and **12 Angry Men.** She said it was the values those films represented, the quality of the characters he played, that moved her so much, and I began to appreciate him in new ways. While he didn't always bring the qualities she admired **home** with him, I was old enough now to understand that there are many kinds of needs: Children need loving parents, and people need heroes they can aspire to. Perhaps it's hard to be a hero **and** a father. For the world, Dad **was** Tom Joad.

I began to realize that the enthusiasm with which France embraced me wasn't only because I was an American actress, or even because I was the daughter of an American movie star, but because I was the child of **Henry Fonda,** who embodied the best of America to them—the same America President Kennedy represented. I had come to France hoping to shed the "father's daughter" identity, only to discover that there was a lot of his identity I was proud of and wanted to be associated with.

Until coming to France, I had never been exposed to people who took an intellectual approach to filmmaking, nor had I really appreciated the effect American films had on European filmmakers, from the physical antics of Jerry Lewis's comedies to the works of John Ford, Alfred Hitchcock, and Preston Sturges.

It was in France that I made an acquaintance with small-c communism, and since over the years I have been accused of being a Communist by those who want to discredit me, I want to say something about this. As I got to know Simone and Yves, I learned that they were among France's intellectual Left, which included the other Simone (de Beauvoir), and her longtime companion, Jean-Paul Sartre, and of course Albert Camus, who had died in 1960. All of them were **engagé,** committed to activism, and in sympathy with the French Communist Party (PCF)—some joining it, then leaving; others never actually becoming party members. Simone and Yves had never joined, although they agreed with many of the party's opinions. What they and other French artists abhorred was the party's doctrinaire cultural policies, which held that artistic freedom was a petit bourgeois crime. Still, there was a long history of close ties between the French intellectual and artistic community and the PCF. They viewed the PCF as the party of change, and since the time of the French Revolution, when they had played a powerful role in toppling the monarchy, French intellectuals had always seen themselves as agents of progressive social change. They also tended to be distrustful of NATO, nuclear armament, and the new war that the United States was pretending not to be involved with—in Vietnam. Many of the French intelligentsia had been at the forefront of the movement against their own country's colonial war in Vietnam, had been active in the underground Resistance during the Nazi occupation of France, and had seen the Communist Party as the only viable way to counteract Fascism.

Having grown up with our two-party system in America, I was stunned as I learned about the many French political parties, some large and powerful, some small, many coming into being in response to a particular crisis and then disappearing or morphing into some new party. The Communist Party was one among about six other legal political parties represented in the French parliament. I remember reading somewhere that during the time I lived in France, in the fifties and sixties, nearly 40 percent of the French people voted Communist. Communists were simply part of the complex French scene and didn't seem especially threatening. I was not politically active then and especially not interested in theory or ideology (still not, to this day), and no one suggested I should be; no one proselytized. But I think this long, up-close-and-personal (nontoxic) brush with European communism is why, later, when I did become **engagé,** as Simone called it, I didn't view it with the same phobic dread as did many other Americans. As I saw it, when given a choice, people tended to keep a balance between a free market capitalist system and one that had more centralized control—"choice" being the operative word.

Oddly enough, living in Paris, I felt more American than ever before. I needed to get outside my own country to fully appreciate how different we are and what it means to be a citizen of the United States. In France (and, as I later realized, in other European countries) class differences are more entrenched. There is a marked difference between the bourgeoisie, the aristocracy, and the proletariat (working class), and rarely do class lines get crossed. Birth **is** destiny. In the United States there is more class fluidity, which was especially true in the 1950s. While today in America a growing U.S. hereditary elite and severe economic disparities make it less likely, it was more or less taken for granted back then that a person from a modest background could compose his or her own life scenario, at least given good health, an encouraging parent, an education, and a little luck. This fluidity, which exists alongside our unique political stability, is I think what makes for our particular energy and optimism. Would that all Americans could have had the opportunity to look back at their country from across the ocean in the early 1960s.

It was a magical time to be an American in France. During the Eisenhower presidency, the French had thought of us as gauche, too loud, too styleless: "ugly Americans." Now, with Kennedy and Jackie in the White House, everything seemed to have changed. The Kennedys brought us international esteem, and the Americans in Paris benefited from their popularity.

On November 22, I walked into the lobby of my hotel after a day's shooting on the Clément movie. Standing at the reception desk, telephone to his ear, was American actor Keir Dullea. His face was ashen. "Kennedy's been shot, they think he's dead," he told me. We stared at each other. I sat in the lobby, stunned, waiting to hear more news. A journalist came in to interview me for the French film magazine **Cahiers du Cinéma** and asked if I wanted to cancel. "No," I said. "I need to talk."

We went up to my hotel room, and after making a desultory attempt at conducting an interview, we both broke down.

Simone called. She was crying and said that I

shouldn't be alone on this night, that she wanted me to come over to their place. Sitting with Simone, Yves, and their friends that night, I realized that they mourned the loss of Kennedy as their own and shared a sense of terrible, unbelievable finality. For me a bubble had burst. The institutional world I grew up believing in was no longer stable. And it would get worse: The losses of Bobby and Martin were still to come.

I had come to France for work, yet I had been drawn there for more personal reasons. Maybe here I could begin to hear the sounds of my own voice, try to find out who I was, or at the very least find a more inter- esting persona than the one I inevitably slipped into back home.

I would end up staying in France six years. And at the hands of a man who was a master at polishing a woman's persona, I would start down a new path— as a female impersonator.

Our arms were linked as we solemnly followed his casket through the narrow, ochre-tinted streets of old Saint Tropez—Brigitte Bardot, Annette Stroy- berg, Catherine Schneider, Marie-Christine Bar- rault, and me. Of all Vadim's wives and companions, only Catherine Deneuve and Ann Biderman were missing. Our thirty-one-year-old daughter, Vanessa Vadim, carrying her infant son, Malcolm, and her half brother, Vania (Vadim's son with Catherine

Schneider), walked just in front of us. The streets were lined ten deep with fans, old friends, and onlookers who had come to pay their respects. It was two months into the new millennium.

The services in the small Episcopal church had been arranged by Catherine Schneider, whom he'd married after me. A Scottish minister, in a thick brogue, solemnly gave the sermon in French. An odd amalgam it was. Vadim's widow Marie-Christine Barrault, niece of fabled French actor Jean-Louis Barrault and the star of such films as **Cousin, Cousine,** was speaking of Vadim with the theatrics of high Greek tragedy when she was loudly interrupted by an unusually long fart, issuing forth from grandson Malcolm, bringing laughter to the assembled crowd, something Vadim would have appreciated. He was never one to shun laughter, especially if it meant interrupting a solemn occasion.

As we exited the church, we were surprised by three Russian violinists, in full costume, who began playing soulful Slavic music as they took their places behind the coffin. Brigitte had arranged this on her own as a surprise. I loved her for wanting to acknowledge Vadim's Russianness on this day, in this way. We broke off sprigs of mimosa along the route to the cemetery and laid them on his coffin as we walked past to say our good-byes.

Vadim and I had spent many happy times together in Saint Tropez, and whenever we'd pull his fancy Chris-Craft into the harbor after a day of island pic-

nicking or water-skiing, we'd look up to see this historic old cemetery, the one Vanessa referred to as the
"dead people's village," perched on the edge of the
cliff. Once, at about age five, Vanessa was walking
with her dad on the road that ran just above the
cemetery. She stopped and looked at the tall, lichen-
covered grave markers and began asking questions
about death and survival of the soul. Vadim wrote in
his autobiography **Memoirs of the Devil:**

> **She thought on the whole that there was
> probably some kind of existence after death,
> but was afraid there might not be any sensi-
> ble place where we could arrange to meet
> each other. Her face clouded over, and a few
> silent tears ran down her cheeks. Then, all
> of a sudden, her expression brightened.**
>
> **"We shall just have to die at the same
> time," she said.**
>
> **It is a very difficult promise to keep,
> but I gave my word I would live till I was
> very, very old so that I would wait for her.**

The two of them always had a profound relationship. He died with Vanessa lying beside him, her
head on his chest. He lived long enough to see her
grown into a remarkable woman and to know her little son, whom he referred to as Buddha.

When the funeral was over we drove to Catherine
Schneider's home and drank together and talked and

At Vadim's funeral: Brigitte Bardot, Annette Stroyberg, me,
Catherine Schneider, and Marie-Christine Barrault
in the foreground, out of focus.
(Nebinger/Niviere/Hadj/Niko/SIPA Press)

laughed, thinking how very Vadimesque it all was, all of us women together as friends, reminiscing about why we'd loved him. What we did **not** discuss that day were the reasons all of us had left him. In rereading Vadim's book **Bardot, Deneuve, Fonda,** I came upon something Catherine Deneuve said in an interview that may have been closer to the truth: "I wonder if it's not he who left [us]. **You know, you can leave someone by doing everything to make them leave you.**"

His full name was Roger Vadim Plemiannikov, and for years my passport listed me as "Jane Fonda Plemiannikov." **Plemiannikov** means "nephew," and the family is said to be descended from the nephews of the great Mongol conquerer Genghis Khan. That explains the exotic eyes that my daughter and grandson have inherited. In France, families must give their children an officially approved first name; hence "Roger" was tacked on, but everyone who knew him called him Vadim.

His formative years were spent during the Nazi occupation, and that must have had a profound impact on his character. In **Bardot, Deneuve, Fonda,** he wrote of the political hypocrisy he witnessed, the priests collaborating with the enemy, as well as acts of heroism:

> At sixteen, I had established a rule for myself: I was going to take the best from life. Its pleasures. The sea, nature, sports, Fer-

raris, friends and pals, art, nights of intoxication, the beauty of women, insolence and nose-thumbing at society. I kept my ideas on politics (I'm a liberal who is allergic to the words "fanaticism" and "intolerance"), but refused commitment in any form. I believed in man the individual, but had lost my faith in mankind at large.

As a young man he would work off and on as an assistant to film director Marc Allégret, writing scripts but essentially eschewing steady work. In **Memoirs of the Devil,** he wrote: "We rejected all occupations which would have deprived us of our liberty. . . ."

Liberty for him then meant being free for lovemaking, hanging out in Saint-Germain-des-Prés, where his acquaintances included André Gide, Jean Genet, Salvador Dalí, Edith Piaf, Jean Cocteau, Albert Camus, and Henry Miller. For a while he shared a mistress with Hemingway and would read aloud to French novelist Colette in her apartment on the rue de Beaujolais.

Vadim was always loyal and generous to his friends. If he had any money, he'd share it without hesitation, even if he was pinched himself. If he had a woman who was up for it, he'd share **her** as well.

After he and Brigitte, his first wife, had broken up and she was having an affair with Jean-Louis Trintignant, her co-star from . . . **And God Created Woman,**

Vadim stood outside the apartment they had shared, and was overcome by a jealousy so powerful it was almost suicidal. When he recovered, he vowed never to allow "this unknown demon [jealousy] to take possession of my body and soul again. I became immune to the virus forever." However, he also writes revealingly, "What you think you have buried lives on in you, feeding on you silently. Gnawing away. It is just that you do not realize it." I think of the pain my father felt as he stood beneath Margaret Sullavan's window while she made love to Jed Harris, and I think Vadim was right: You can appear to quash feelings of rage and jealousy, but those unacknowledged emotions can continue to play havoc with your heart, all the more so because they are unacknowledged.

Vadim abhorred jealousy, considering it petty, bourgeois, unworthy of him or of anyone he was with. As our marriage floundered, I often wished that he would fight harder to save it; demonstrate more concern—even including jealousy. Instead he would become almost passive, as if knowing that the ending had been fated long before—a stance I read as not caring. In **Bardot, Deneuve, Fonda,** Bardot is quoted as saying of their marriage (in an interview): "If only Vadim had been jealous, things might have worked out." People need to be wanted, and want to be needed.

I could write one version of my marriage to Vadim in which he would come across as a cruel, misogynistic, irresponsible wastrel. I could also write him as the most charming, lyrical, poetic, tender of men. Both versions would be true.

It was a month after Kennedy's assassination, December 21, my birthday, that Vadim reappeared on my horizon. He'd been invited to a party given for me by my French agent, Olga Horstig. We found ourselves sitting together most of the evening, talking. He wasn't at all as I had I remembered. He seemed funny and sweet in an offbeat, old-shoe kind of way. I've found that when you have a diabolical image of someone and he or she turns out to be a regular mortal, you then tend to elevate that person to an unrealistic place of perfection. Dangerous, that. A clear-eyed, balanced perspective is always the safest. As the evening wore on, he sang ribald French marching songs from the French-Algerian war and mispronounced English with irresistible charm. For example:

"Oh, Jane, you can't tell me alcoholeeesm is harry-di-tarry" (hereditary). "This chair is getting a leetle un-con-**fort**-eeble" (uncomfortable). "I see no ob-**stee**-cles" (obstacles . . . as in no obstacles to taking me home).

Okay, so you don't see that as especially charming? Ah, but you weren't looking into green, slanted eyes above high Slavic cheekbones, eyes that seemed filled with mystery and promise. My God, he was handsome. Not in some perfect way—his teeth were too big, face too long—but the way the whole came together was startlingly attractive. Besides, except for being tall, dark, and very slender, he didn't seem at all like my father.

The next encounter would be the deciding one. He had a meeting with his talented production designer Jean André at Studios Eclair, where we were filming with Delon. Word reached me that he was in the canteen, and as soon as we had a break, I ran straight from the scene to see him—scantily dressed in a teddy covered only by a trench coat, which managed to fly open as I entered the canteen, breathless, flushed, and clearly excited. That's what he needed, to see my excitement at seeing him. I was a fairly naïve, inexperienced twenty-six-year-old. He was ten years older, and a lot of water had flowed under his bridge.

When filming had wrapped for the day, he took me back to my hotel room and we began to make out passionately on the couch, but when we finally made it to the bed he was no longer aroused. I remember thinking it was my fault and feeling humiliated, but I didn't let on because I didn't want him to feel bad. Here was Vadim, renowned lover, unable to make it with me. Now I knew for sure there was something really wrong with me.

The situation went on for **three weeks,** with me feeling terrible, wanting to die, but I never let him know how I felt, because I didn't want to make matters worse. It never occurred to me to break it off. That would have been conceding defeat. **Make it**

better! I know I can make it better! The fact that he was impotent for that first period of our relationship, rather than turning me away, actually reassured me: He wasn't a superman, he was vulnerable, human.

When finally the curse was broken, we stayed in bed for two nights and a day and were together from then until I had to return to the States to promote **Sunday in New York.** Everything else in life seemed to come to a standstill. I ceased eating except for the crusts of his bread and the rinds of his Camembert. Every afternoon when I wasn't working, we would make love. Then I'd kiss him good-bye, and he would excuse himself to be with his three-year-old daughter, Nathalie, then living with her mother, Annette Stroyberg.

His lovemaking was imaginative, erotic, and tender. Though I couldn't understand all that he said (or maybe **because** I couldn't understand), his murmurings sounded to me like messages from some new planet. But what I found as irresistible about him as the sex was his attachment to his little daughter. **He must be a good man to love his daughter that way.**

There's no doubt that part of my attraction to him and his life was because it was so different from the repressed style in which I had been raised. Then there was a certain remote dignity about his person that belied his reputation. But what a reputation he had! In the first years of our relationship, walking down the Champs-Élysées, people would react to him as to a major movie star. I was also intrigued by his worldliness: He'd been through war, had risked his life, knew so many interesting people, and was so different from any man I'd known. He would wake up in the morning singing!

It was normal, I suppose, to pay no heed to the fact that we spent an inordinate amount of time in a club he belonged to, where we would drink and he'd go off to a side room to bet on a miniature electric car race, or that we were always driven by a chauffeur. Not even later, when he explained that he'd had his driver's license revoked for a year for having an accident while driving under the influence, did I think: Wait a minute. Nor did I make the connection later, when he told me that at the time of the accident he'd been driving Catherine Deneuve, who was pregnant with his child and almost miscarried. I paid no heed to the many red flags thrown up over those first months—the drinking, the gambling. Nor did I ask myself later, before committing myself to him "in sickness and in health," whether our respective weaknesses and strengths would complement one another; whether his vices together with my black-belt co-dependency (put up with everything— make it better) would bring us both grief; whether my emotional underdevelopment could surmount his "charming" addictions. Had I known enough to ask myself those questions, chances are I would have known enough to answer them—or known where to go to find the answers. But I didn't.

It certainly never occurred to me that this was not a man who could teach me intimacy, because I didn't know it was something I needed to learn. You can't look for something you don't know exists. Intimacy has a **feel** to it, and if you've never experienced it, you don't know that you miss it. In fact, if it's never been in your life and then it does come along, there's a chance it will make you feel extremely uncomfortable and that you'll run away from it.

Frankly, if I had it all to do over, knowing then what I know now, I would have plunged in just the same. I probably would have tried to get him to go to Alcoholics Anonymous meetings and whatever is offered for compulsive gambling. Being French, he would have refused (only in America do people self-identify as being "in recovery"), and I would have hung in anyway, maybe leaving a year or so sooner. Maybe not. I don't regret any of it. Well, at least not most of it.

I wanted to stay in Paris with Vadim, so—my earlier telegram from California be damned—I agreed to be in his film **La Ronde.** We moved out of my hotel and into a small, romantic walk-up apartment just around the corner, on the rue Seguier, while he was busy preparing the film. I knew that in addition to three-year-old Nathalie, his daughter with his ex-wife, he had a baby son with twenty-year-old Catherine Deneuve, but I assumed that having babies out of wedlock indicated a laissez-faire relationship, a lack of emotional commitment on both their parts.

So three months after coming to France, for the first time I found myself living full-out with a man— shopping, keeping house, cooking our meals: all in French (in which I was becoming quite fluent). Fortunately I'm a nester. Unfortunately I couldn't cook, and I also had food issues, which continued without Vadim knowing it.

I began to spend all my time reading cookbooks (food obsessions are not uncommon for people with eating disorders), everything from the old standby **The Joy of Cooking** to **The Alice B. Toklas Cookbook,** which included a notorious recipe for hash brownies. Never one to do things halfway, I would always attempt the most complicated recipes: Senegalese chicken soup, baked Alaska. This was presupermarket France, when shopping for food pretty much still meant going to one store for vegetables, another for fish, others for breads, diary products, and so on.

For one of our first home-cooked dinners, I decided I'd make minute steaks. I remembered watching Susan cook them when she was married to Dad. Seemed easy enough. About five minutes into the meal, Vadim stopped midbite, looked up bemusedly from his plate, and asked, "Where did you buy this meat?"

"At the butcher," I replied.

"Was there a horse's head over the door?"

"Actually, come to think of it . . ." Oh, my God, in a flash I realized what I'd done. It was horsemeat! I'd gone and cooked my favorite animal!

Then there was the time he announced he'd invited Bardot over for dinner. Yikes! I'd never met her. It was hard enough trying to banish from my mind the knowledge that he'd actually been married to her, held that body in his arms. Now I was going to have to be **in the same room, at the same table, with her!** I roamed the markets till I came upon something that seemed perfect for the occasion: **boudin noir,** blood sausage, big, fat, black, blood sausage. I'd never seen one before, much less cooked one, but it looked appropriately . . . Well, maybe she'd choke on it. Actually we got along fine. She was funny and down-to-earth and seemed to have no hidden agenda. She even complimented me on the meal—it turns out she couldn't cook, either.

CHAPTER TWELVE

THE MAGICIAN'S ASSISTANT

The magician's assistant is easy to spot
the way her arm curves
like a swan's neck as she points
To a favorite piece of furniture
for our inspection and approval,

The way her smile charms us into believing,
Disarming whatever might otherwise cut her in half.
Where does a magician find his assistant,

Such a beautiful woman (though we hardly notice her!)
who will smile at his side and give nothing away?
We assume she knows, of course, and imagine

that behind her perfect teeth, her mind
is haunted by the knowledge
of another, secret kingdom where a dove crouches
next to the heart-hammering hare
in a dark warren, waiting

To be abracadabred back
to the dovecote, to lapin reality.
In that country of lifted wallets,
colorfully endless handkerchiefs
and torn one-hundred-dollar bills
that heal themselves,

women, cut in half, seem to
dwell mindlessly under a spell,
play games with a marked deck
or recline in utter weightlessness,
suspended only by our wish
to believe in them.
—CHARLES DARLING,
"On Being Introduced at a Neighborhood Party
to a Magician's Assistant"

THE FILMING OF **La Ronde** (retitled **Circle of Love** in the United States) with Vadim was a happy time for us both. I loved the joining of our creative forces, and I discovered tremendous sexual excitement in having him place me in the positions he wanted, calling the shots—and in my exceeding his expectations. I have always liked being directed, not having to make the big decisions but having parameters set for me and then infusing life into the director's vision.

For an American I had a good accent, which meant people thought I was Swedish! In some ways speaking French acted as a mask for me, allowing me to be freer than I was in English. It slowed me down, softened me, and made my voice deeper and more nuanced.

Vadim's ex-wife, Annette, was in Morocco at this time, and three-year-old Nathalie had come to live with us. Remembering how important Susan had been in my life, I wanted to be as responsible as I could toward the little girl whom I had just started to know.

Our apartment on the rue Seguier was too small for Vadim, me, Nathalie, and her nanny. Lacking the money to rent a larger apartment, Vadim prevailed on his old friend Commander Paul-Louis Weiller, who had turned one of his many houses, the Hôtel des Ambassadeurs de Hollande, into a haven for friends and artists (and beautiful young women, for whom the old man had a penchant). Weiller gave us an apartment there. The hotel, a magnificent historic monument built in the sixteenth century, is on the rue Vieille-du-Temple, in Le Marais, one of the oldest sections of Paris. I was fortunate to have lived there at that time, before it became chic and recherché.

The rue Vieille-du-Temple, old, narrow, and cobblestoned, was lined by buildings so ancient that they leaned in toward each other like friends longing to touch. We lived in the attic—vaulted rooms where walls and ceilings were covered with maps of the world painted by sixteenth-century artists. Our bedroom window was directly opposite a school for

Vadim directing me in La Ronde.

cantors, and as we were at the top of the two leaning buildings, it was as though the singers were right in bed with us. On the first floor, Roland Petit, director of the Ballets de Paris, and his wife, prima ballerina Renée Jeanmaire, made their abode. There was an apartment reserved for Charlie Chaplin, though I don't remember ever seeing him there. This exotic atelier is where we made our home for several years and created a family.

Vadim wrote extensively about how, later, I spoke of having been "turned into a domestic slave" by him, as though this were a betrayal of woman-kind. I will admit to having made some pretty ex-tremist rhetorical statements during that period, but I doubt it was the domesticity I was objecting to. I have, in fact, always liked creating a home. My phys-ical surroundings are very important to me. I can't think straight if my surroundings are disorderly or dirty, and during times when we couldn't afford to have someone help out, I did the housework myself rather than live with the mess. During the years with Vadim it never crossed my mind to ask him to help with household chores. I saw it as women's work, even though it meant doing double duty, since I often left home for the studios before dawn and re-turned after dark, while he stayed home and wrote— or went fishing.

This acquiescence was, in part, due to the way we were all conditioned, and partly because I felt that being the perfect, unselfish housewife would make it impossible for him to leave me—just as my mother had thought about Dad. Interesting how we interpret the radical notion of bringing democracy into the home as selfishness! It wasn't that Vadim was mean or wanted to make my life hard. It's just that he didn't **notice.** He could live with dirty dishes stacked high in the sink for weeks. Now that I think of it, maybe **that** was what I railed about—his not noticing.

But there were other, more complicated problems that are much harder to write about. Vadim had created a view of life for himself, a view shared by all his friends, which held that any show of thrift, jealousy, or desire for organization and structure was a sign that you were bourgeois. God forbid! "Bourgeois" became the dreaded epithet, as horrifying as betrayal or dishonesty. There were even times when it was suggested that the French Communist Party had bourgeois tendencies.

I had inherited $150,000 from my mother. At the time, it was a nice sum, something I could fall back on if I stewarded it carefully. Vadim could not comprehend why I hesitated to give him large portions of it so that he could hire a friend to come with us to some vacation spot and work with him on a script. At first I was horrified and said so. But over time I began to feel that I was being petty and stingy. So I gave in. Only years later did I realize that Vadim was a compulsive gambler, that the locations for his films or vacations were often chosen for their proximity to a racetrack or casino. I had no idea that gambling was an addictive disease, as difficult to overcome as alcoholism, anorexia, and bulimia. Much of my mother's inheritance was simply gambled away.

Along with thriftiness, jealousy was a major no-

no. Why did women make so much fuss about the physical act of intercourse? Just because a husband or wife (though it always seemed to be the husband) had sex with someone else, that didn't represent betrayal—"It's **you** I love." Vadim would go on and on with his friends about how the sexual revolution of the sixties showed that people were finally beginning to see what they had always known: that middle-class morality needed to be discarded for sexual freedom and open marriage. (We weren't married . . . too bourgeois!) Maybe he'd smelled it on my skin when we'd first met—that I was malleable and insecure in my sexuality. In any event, I was vulnerable to him and felt that in order to keep him and be a good wife, I had to prove that I was, in fact, the queen of "nonbourgeoisness," the Oscar winner of wildness, generosity, and forgiveness.

As time went on, Vadim would fail to come home in the evenings. I'd have dinner ready and he wouldn't show. Often he wouldn't even call. I would usually eat all the food I'd prepared for us, go out and buy pastries and French glacé (not nearly as satisfying as our ice cream), devour all of it, throw it all up, and collapse into bed exhausted and angry. Sometimes he'd come home around midnight and fall into bed drunk. Sometimes he wouldn't show up till morning. I swallowed my anger (along with the ice cream), never really confronting him about this behavior. I didn't want to seem bourgeois. I didn't think I deserved better.

Then one night he brought home a beautiful

red-haired woman and took her into our bed with me. She was a high-class call girl employed by the well-known Madame Claude. It never occurred to me to object. I took my cues from him and threw myself into the threesome with the skill and enthusiasm of the actress that I am. If this was what he wanted, this was what I would give him—in spades. As feminist poet Robin Morgan wrote in **Saturday's Child** on the subject of threesomes, "If I was facing the avant-garde version of keeping up with the Joneses, by god I'd show 'em."

Sometimes there were three of us, sometimes more. Sometimes it was even I who did the soliciting. So adept was I at burying my real feelings and compartmentalizing myself that I eventually had myself convinced I enjoyed it.

I'll tell you what I did enjoy: the mornings after, when Vadim was gone and the woman and I would linger over our coffee and talk. For me it was a way to bring some humanity to the relationship, an antidote to objectification. I would ask her about herself, trying to understand her history and why she had agreed to share our bed (questions I never asked myself!) and, in the case of the call girls, what had brought her to make those choices. I was shocked by the cruelty and abuse many had suffered, saw how abuse had made them feel that sex was the only commodity they had to offer. But many were smart and could have succeeded in other careers. The hours spent with those women informed my later Oscar-winning performance of the call girl Bree Daniel in

Klute. Many of those women have since died from drug overdose or suicide. A few went on to marry high-level corporate leaders; some married into nobility. One, who remains a friend, recently told me that Vadim was jealous of her friendship with me, that he had said to her once, "You think Jane's smart, but she's not, she's dumb." Vadim often felt a need to denigrate my intelligence, as if it would take up his space. I would think that a man would **want** people to know he was married to a smart woman—unless he was insecure about his own intelligence. Or unless he didn't really love her.

As with my eating disorders, I believed I was the only one who betrayed myself by allowing other women into my bed when I didn't really want to, especially when there was no mitigating financial need. (I know many women who have no money and no job skills who do lots of things they don't want to do in order to keep their support, especially if they have children.) Then in 2001 I read **Saturday's Child,** the autobiography of Robin Morgan, cornerstone of the contemporary feminist movement, inventor of the feminist symbol, and editor of **Sisterhood Is Powerful** and its two sequels, **Sisterhood Is Global** and **Sisterhood Is Forever.** In her autobiography she writes of her own self-betrayal within marriage. She describes how she

> **bought into every sexual myth the guys could fling at me—about Bloomsbury, sexual liberation, not being a puritan; about keep-on-**

doing-what-you-don't-like-because-the-more-
you-do-it-the-more-you'll-like-it; about D. H.
Lawrence's ideal quartet (two women, two
men, all possible sexual permutations). I
never questioned **whose** needs and self-
interest these models served. . . .

I partly dissociated my consciousness in
order to survive them, an attempt to compartmentalize and contain the experience of
violation.

Until then I had not planned on writing about
my own experiences. I thought: There are enough
people who dislike me, I don't need to give them
even more ammunition. But when I read Robin's
book, it gave me courage to see that a woman like her
had had these experiences and written about them,
bravely and without salaciousness. I saw that if the
telling of my life's journey was to matter to other
women and to girls, I would, like Robin, have to be
honest about how far I've come and the meaning of
where I've been.

I got Robin's e-mail address from Gloria Steinem,
a friend, and wrote to her, telling her how important
her honesty had been to me. I asked, "How is it that
otherwise strong, independent women can do these
things?" She answered: "You'd be surprised how many
'otherwise strong, independent women' have done
these things."

In my public life, I am a strong, can-do woman.
How is it, then, that behind closed doors, in my

most intimate relations, I could voluntarily betray myself? The answer is this: If a woman has become disembodied from a lack of self-worth—**I'm not good enough**—or from abuse, she will neglect her own voice of desire and hear only the man's. This requires, as Robin Morgan says, compartmentalizing—disconnecting head and heart, body and soul. Overlay her silence with a man's sense of entitlement and inability (or unwillingness) to read his partner's subtle body signals, and you have the makings of a very angry woman, who will stuff her anger for the same reasons she silences her sexual voice.

Vadim was the first man I had ever loved, and in spite of the complexities (and in some part because of them), the love was real enough that for a long time my anger was only a background whisper. I loved that he was like a kaleidoscope and I could see the world through all his different prisms. He helped me rediscover my sexuality (and that of other women in the process), gave me an if-he-loves-me-I-must-be-okay kind of confidence, and helped move me out from under my father's shadow. I had a persona now. I was with a "real man," I ran his house, was a good stepmother to his daughter and to his son, Christian, when Catherine Deneuve agreed to let him visit us. Vadim's friends seemed to like me. What wasn't to like? I never complained, rarely scolded, worked hard, brought in the money, brought them their whiskeys at night, and made them their breakfast in the morning when they were hungover, and they knew I participated with Vadim in his sexual libertinism. I remember one of the group remarking, as I was leaving with a tray of glasses to be refilled, "Jane is something else, not like most women, more like one of us." I fairly purred with pleasure, as I had at age ten when someone had asked if I was a boy or a girl.

Unlike the magician's assistant in the poem at the start of this chapter, my functioning self did not know what was real, that there was another way to be, a "secret kingdom" of the embodied self that I could be Abracadabred to, authentic and whole. I had long since abandoned that self. I so needed to **not** know, in order to remain in the relationship. I transformed myself with Vadim's magic wand into the perfect sixties wife. I didn't need his money, so it wasn't an economic issue. It was the fear of losing the relationship, since it was the relationship that validated me. If someone had asked me to describe who I was then, I would have had a difficult time of it. But as film critic Philip Lopate once wrote: "Where identity is not fixed, performance becomes a floating anchor." And could I perform! Making the unreal seem real, the sad seem happy, hoping that somewhere along the way it would all work out, that I would discover who I was. Meantime I had an anchor.

I would often talk to Vadim about my insecurities, but he didn't really understand, though he tried in his own way to give me confidence. The problem was, he knew how to validate only my façade, and the façade worked so well that there seemed no pressing need to go deeper. "Deeper" might have meant my becoming more assertive, more opinionated, more who I was, and as Vadim said publicly (later, after I'd left him and become more . . . me), he liked his women "softer." At that time, if it was soft he wanted, I'd give him squooshy.

I made a list one day of what I considered my main faults: selfishness, stinginess, and being too judgmental were the top three. Then and there I decided that if I pretended to be generous and forgiving for a long enough time, maybe I would become those things. I remembered reading Aristotle in philosophy class at Vassar: "We become just by performing just actions, temperate by performing temperate actions, brave by performing brave actions." I had always felt that you become what you do—which is one reason I fretted so when I was asked to play silly young women like my characters in **Tall Story** and **Any Wednesday**. If you behave one-dimensionally day after day, you start to become one-dimensional, and after a while the ability to reach deeper becomes atrophied.

You could say that Vadim majored in vacations. His love of certain natural environments and talent for enjoying them was unbounded, and I was a beneficiary. He loved the sea and its shores. We would go not just to glamorous Saint Tropez, but to the rugged coast of Brittany on the Atlantic in the northern region of France and to the Bay of Arcachon on the southern Atlantic coast. We would pile into an out-board motorboat with Nathalie, Christian, and **grande** Nathalie (daughter of Vadim's sister, Helene) and go for picnics on some of the sand dunes that would emerge at low tide. **Grande** Nathalie was al-most ten years older than **petite** Nathalie and often accompanied us on our vacations.

Petite Nathalie was growing into a beautiful combination of her Danish mother and Franco-Slavic father, the same exotic eyes and dark hair, with legs that went on forever. She was a challenging child. Her stubbornness and moodiness were evi-dent; she kept her deeper self tucked away, and I never really knew what she felt—except for her love for her father. She and I were always battling over is-sues like brushing her teeth and doing her lessons, and I suspected she thought I was a nag. (Forty years later, she remains a member of my family.)

Often Vadim and I would go to Saint Tropez in the winter, my favorite time there. We'd stay in a small, not fancy hotel/restaurant called Tahiti Hôtel, right on Pampelonne Beach, the one that became fa-mous for its nude sunbathers in summertime (which is one reason I preferred winter). I loved the Mediter-ranean storms—the mistrals—that would bend the palm trees and send waves high onto the beach. Vadim and I would sit by a cozy fire, playing chess and watching nature rage.

Next to the sea, Vadim loved mountains best. He was an excellent skier and we often spent Christ-mas in Megève or Chamonix, two ski resorts in the

Beached in Arcachon, France, with Nathalie (in the boat with me) and Christian watching.

Vadim and me in Baja California on one of our many deep-sea-fishing trips.

French Alps. But just as I preferred Saint Tropez in the winter, I loved most when we would go to Chamonix in the summer. We'd always drive from Paris to the mountains with Nathalie, singing French songs and playing road games. We would rent a chalet in the little town of Argentière, adjacent to Chamonix, in the valley of the Mont Blanc.

It would be sunny, the air pure and brisk, the wildflowers just emerging. The sparkling, majestic Alps rose sharply on both sides of the valley, with Mont Blanc to the south lording it over them all. From time to time, an awesome rumble would echo down the valley as melting snow avalanched from the peaks. Once, at night, I saw the northern lights dancing in the sky, and sometimes, when the sun was at just the right angle, I could spy the faint blue of the glaciers. I took long walks along the creeks, watched the Lenten roses as they blushed open, and thought how I had never been happier in my life, so happy my heart felt like bursting. I learned that spring that I am molecularly suited to high altitudes. Fourteen thousand feet is as high as I've ever hiked, but up there where the air is thin and crisp and the tundra spongy, I feel transcendent.

On one of these alpine vacations, Vadim left me to go to Rome to fetch his baby son, Christian. I didn't know until I read Vadim's book **Bardot, Deneuve, Fonda** that he had had a passionate night with Catherine and that he thought "everything would work out with [her], that [his] relationship with [me] was only a dream, and that Christian would grow up living with a mother and father who loved each other." Reading that so many years later didn't hurt me, but I wondered how I could have been so naïve as to think his commitment to me was real.

I had no experience with the care and handling of infants, but I threw myself into it with enthusiasm when Vadim brought the baby to our chalet that spring. He was truly a hands-on father, comfortable with bottles and diapers. I remember Christian, Nathalie, and me taking our baths together in a tub much too small to accommodate us all. I didn't feel totally sure of myself as a stepmother, but I liked being with the children and having a family. Susan was never far from my heart at those times.

There are certain things you are not supposed to do if you are just becoming a star and want to survive in Hollywood. You don't go and live in an attic with a French director and refuse to come back unless you absolutely have to. But I never followed career rules. For better or worse, I didn't think of myself as a movie star with a real career. I was never fully vested in my celebrity. I felt I'd gotten into it by default, and I wouldn't die if I got out of it by default. I liked the work, the structure it gave my life, the challenges of different roles, and the pleasure I would sometimes derive from bringing a character to life. I also liked being financially independent. But the choices I made in relation to work were always connected to my relationships or, later, my politics.

In late spring I was offered the title role in **Cat Ballou** with Lee Marvin. It meant returning to Hollywood, but Vadim encouraged me to take it, saying he would come visit whenever he could. For reasons I don't recall, I was under a contract to Columbia Pictures, where **Cat Ballou** was to be made, and this was a way to fulfill part of it. The script was unusual, and I wasn't sure whether it was any good or not. I'm not sure Lee Marvin knew either. I remember him whispering to me one day during rehearsal that the only reason he and I were in the movie was that "we're under contract and they can get us cheap."

Cat Ballou was a relatively low-budget undertaking. It seemed we'd never do two takes unless the camera broke down. The producers had us working overtime day after day, until one morning Lee Marvin took me aside.

"Jane," he said, "we are the stars of this movie. If we let the producers walk all over us, if we don't stand up for ourselves, you know who suffers most? The crew. The guys who don't have the power we do to say, 'Shit, no, we're workin' too hard.' You have to get some backbone, girl. Learn to say no when they ask you to keep working."

I will always remember Lee for that important lesson. At least I was learning to say no in my **professional** life.

I have to admit, it wasn't until I saw the final cut of **Cat Ballou** that I realized we had a hit on our hands. I hadn't been around when they filmed Lee's horse, leaning cross-legged up against the barn in what's become a classic image, or the scenes when Lee tries to shoot the side of the barn. I didn't realize how director Elliot Silverstein would use the two troubadours, Nat "King" Cole and Stubby Kaye, like a Greek chorus. It would be my first genuine hit, though its success had very little to do with me. By the way, Nat "King" Cole was every bit as kind and wonderful as I had remembered him from my parents' parties after the war.

During the filming of **Cat Ballou** and the movie I did right afterward for Columbia, **The Chase**, Vadim, Nathalie, and I lived in a rented house in Malibu Colony, right on the beach. Like my father, Vadim loved to fish and would often do so from the shore, pulling in perch and sometimes halibut, which we'd have for dinner. Today, of course, you wouldn't dare eat fish from Santa Monica Bay even if you did manage to catch one, which is unlikely. The house we rented had belonged to Merle Oberon and was bright and cozy. We paid $200 a month for it, and I remember how astounded I was when the rent went up to $500. **What could they be thinking!** Today a house like that rents for closer to $10,000 a month or more. Back then, average folk who'd been there for decades could still afford to live among the millionaires. The powerful who did have homes there (usually second homes) were considered avant garde bohemians.

There were always friends hanging out with us: Marlon Brando; Brooke Hayward and her new husband, Dennis Hopper; my brother and his wife, Susan; Yvette Mimieux, who was dating a young

French director; Mia Farrow, who was dating Frank Sinatra; Julie Newmar; Viva, who would star in many Andy Warhol movies; Sally Kellerman; and Jack Nicholson. Every Sunday Larry Hagman would don a gorilla suit and march down the beach followed by a swarm of friends carrying banners.

It was an atmosphere the French would call **désinvolte**, friends casually hanging out, with good food and interesting conversation, what I had always been attracted to but was too shy to have initiated. Now I was learning to create that same ambiance, running a home and making things comfortable for people. We were always entertaining, and any French person who came to Los Angeles made a stopover at our home. Dad said in an interview around this time, "She's outgoing, not at all like me. . . . Look at the kind of home she's created, look at the life they lead out there in Malibu. People coming, people going, all day long, open house all the time, and Jane handling it all so beautifully, making people feel comfortable. . . ."

I was proud of that.

Dad was dating the woman who would be his last wife, a lovely, enthusiastic, pert woman named Shirlee Adams, only slightly older than me. They had taken a house just down the beach from us. Nathalie attended a nearby school, her English had become fluent as had my French, and we were quite a happy family. For Dad, the fact that Vadim was a fisherman created an affinity; besides, he was not immune to Vadim's charm.

Sam Spiegel, one of Hollywood's great producers, offered me a role in Lillian Hellman's **The Chase,** based on a novel by Horton Foote. **The Chase** was to be directed by Arthur Penn and to co-star Marlon Brando, Angie Dickinson, E. G. Marshall, Robert Duvall, and a relative newcomer, Robert Redford, who would play my husband. What a package, right? What I was to learn, however, was that even the best packaging and assembly of talent can't guarantee success. While the film did fairly well in Europe, it was a flop in the States. My performance certainly didn't help. It was a little like "Barbarella comes to small-town Texas." Maybe out of revenge for all those bad-hair years I'd endured, I was now playing second fiddle to a mane of hair that, as a friend recently said, should have had its own billing.

Two things happened that summer of 1965 that were especially important to me. Strangely enough, both involved parties.

I had a lot of time off during the filming of **The Chase** and decided I would throw a Fourth of July party on the beach. I had never given a big Hollywood party before, but as usual I took it on full bore. I asked my brother, who unlike me was into the new music scene, what band I should hire. The Byrds, he said without hesitation. The Byrds included David Crosby and Roger McGuinn, and there was an underground cult of Byrd Heads who followed them from gig to gig. They were just about to hit big with their version of Dylan's "Mr. Tambourine Man." Peter's instinct was right on target; they were perfect. We put up an enormous tent with a dance floor right on the beach. I invited Hollywood's old guard, and Peter, wanting to make sure there'd bc good dancing, got the word out to assorted Byrd Heads. Think "Big Sur Meets Jules Stein," "Dreadlocks Meets Crew Cut." Dad set up a spit, where he spent the evening roasting and basting an entire pig, glowing in the attention his unusual culinary skills brought him. I saw it as a big improvement for the shy man.

It was called "the Party of the Decade" and was talked about for a long time to come: the first coming together of old Hollywood and the new counterculture. I remember watching a barefoot flower child standing in the buffet line as she pulled out a breast and began nursing her baby—with George Cukor standing right behind her. This was clearly a first for Cukor, who didn't know whether to stare or pretend it wasn't happening. Next to him was Danny Kaye, pretending to **be** a baby who wanted to nurse. Darryl Zanuck, always one to appreciate beautiful women, looked apoplectic. Sam Spiegel, Jack Lemmon, Paul Newman, Tuesday Weld, novelist/diplomat Romain Gary and his wife, Jean Seberg, Peggy Lipton, Lauren Bacall, William Wyler, Gene Kelly, Sidney Poitier, Jules and Doris Stein, Ray Stark, Sharon Tate, Warren Beatty, Natalie Wood, Dennis Hopper, Brooke Hayward, Terry Southern, and all those Byrd Heads were floating out on the dance floor as the band played on. When dawn broke and the tents were coming down, Vadim took me in his arms and said, "You pulled it off, Fonda. Good for you."

Cat Ballou.
(Photofest)

The Chase.
(Photofest)

With Jason Robards in Any Wednesday.
(Photofest)

It **was** good for me.

That same summer I was invited to a fund-raiser for the Student Nonviolent Coordinating Committee (SNCC), hosted by Marlon Brando and Arthur Penn at Arthur's house. It was the first fund-raiser I had ever been to, and there was an astonishing array of heft in attendance. Two young people from SNCC spoke to us about the organization's efforts to register black voters in Mississippi. The national Voting Rights Act had just passed, but violent resistance from southern segregationists made getting blacks safely to the polls a dangerous undertaking. They painted a vivid picture of secret meetings at night, attack dogs, fire hoses, beatings, and shootings. They spoke of the reasons for SNCC's commitment to nonviolent protest; the courage of the southern blacks who worked with them. Many had been killed, black and white alike.

It wasn't just **what** the SNCC organizers said so much as **how they were** that struck me. There was the calm centeredness of people living beyond themselves. I didn't feel guilt-tripped, but I did feel like an outsider—as Ralph Waldo Emerson must have felt when he went to visit Henry David Thoreau, who was in jail for refusing to pay taxes to a government that supported slavery.

"Henry," said Emerson, "what are you doing in there?"

"Ralph, what are **you** doing out **there?**" Thoreau replied.

What was I doing out here?

A seed was sown. We were asked for money. No one had ever asked me to support a cause before. I gave what I could, but I also became a volunteer for the local SNCC group—writing letters, asking others for money. I was indefatigable. I didn't know how to do it very effectively and I was extremely naïve, but I learned an important lesson that evening: Never underestimate what might be lying dormant beneath the surface of a back-combed blonde wearing false eyelashes. All she might need is to be asked.

That summer I went to my second fund-raiser. All I remember is that Vanessa Redgrave was there, and during the question-and-answer period she raised her hand and, unlike all the others, stood up to speak, turning to look at everyone, owning her space. I will never forget my feelings of awe: Here was a woman who controlled her destiny!

Right after **The Chase** I made **Any Wednesday,** the first of the three films I would make with Jason Robards. Vadim was preparing our next picture in Paris, so I was alone most of the time. My brother would come over at night after work, and that's when I realized that while I had been adjusting to domesticity in France, he had been creating a niche for himself and was about to become the new generation's rebel star. It was a funny contrast: I'd have just come from work on the very conventional **Any Wednesday,** and he'd been shooting **The Wild Angels,** a low-budget Roger Corman film. I remember listening in shock while he described a scene where his biker gang had ridden right into a church and had an orgy in the pews. I was definitely an outsider looking in through Peter's eyes, at the new American counterculture. Usually these evenings would end with him pulling out his guitar, and we'd sing Everly Brothers songs in harmony.

Three years later, in 1969, my father, Vadim, and I sat in a private projection room and watched Peter's film **Easy Rider,** which hadn't been released yet. My father really didn't know what to make of it but was awed that his son had co-written and produced it. I loved parts of it, like Jack Nicholson getting turned on to pot around the campfire and the motorcycle odyssey across America. I thought it unbelievably audacious that they carried kilos of cocaine in their bikes and tripped on acid in a cemetery. But I secretly thought it would be too rough and far-out for most audiences. It was Vadim who understood that here was a no-holds-barred cinematic breakthrough that would resonate immediately and become a classic.

CHAPTER THIRTEEN

PUTTING DOWN ROOTS

I could be "**anything anybody wanted me to be**"—except that I still wasn't even **one** of the people doing the defining of who this latest-model Galatea would become.

—ROBIN MORGAN,
Saturday's Child

I WAS AN AMERICAN CITIZEN with a U.S. passport but had become a resident of France—except I **had** no residence. Vadim and I were not married, but we had been together almost three years and were still moving with Nathalie from one rented apartment to another, using furniture left behind by former wives. It was a nomadic lifestyle that suited Vadim, but I felt Nathalie needed more stability, and I needed to nest. I decided that Vadim and I needed a place that was truly ours. I found a very small piece of land thirty-seven miles west of Paris near Houdan. Once there, you meandered down a series of one-lane country roads, through villages hidden behind mossy stone walls, past farmyards and gently undulating fields of oats and barley, interspersed with forests of beech and oak, into and through the hamlet of Saint-Ouen-Marchefroy. Just beyond lay a flat, nondescript piece of land with an old stone farmhouse in great disrepair. I don't know why this was where I landed. Maybe it was the idea of living near a hamlet that appealed to me; maybe it was those stone walls and the proximity of the woods. Having been smitten with stone walls in Greenwich in my youth, I have remained susceptible all my life.

The hamlet of Saint-Ouen-Marchefroy was a ten-minute walk from the house, and I liked to stroll in at midday when folks were taking a break from their work, to get a sense of who my neighbors were. They had no idea that I was a movie star, and though I never asked, they probably wouldn't have known who Vadim was, either. I became friends with one woman who lived in the farm closest to ours. She liked to give me fruit tarts she'd bake. When I'd visit her, she was always at her sink or stove, and because her hands were wet or greasy, she'd bend her hand back and give me her wrist to shake, a gesture I encountered more than once in that hamlet, the shake of a farmer's wife. (I never got to use it in a movie, alas.) I enjoyed sharing such moments with my neighbors. I would sit in her kitchen, drinking her strong coffee and thinking how lucky I was; my friends back home would not likely get to do this.

Reluctantly I went to Hollywood for several months to make **Any Wednesday.** While there, I decided Vadim and I should get married—at least I think it was my idea. Like buying the farm, I felt marriage would make our commitment deeper, bring normalcy into our relationship, and be better for Nathalie. I think I also wanted to prove I could make it work and pull off something at which Dad had failed.

We arranged for a secret wedding in Las Vegas. Vadim flew up first to get the license. Then, after filming on a Friday, I flew up with my brother and his then wife, Susan; Brooke Hayward and Dennis Hopper; friend and journalist Oriana Fallaci (who was sworn not to write about it); Vadim's mother, Propi; and his best friend, Christian Marquand, with his wife, Tina Aumont. As the plane circled over Los Angeles, we looked down to see Watts in flames, an omen, though I didn't see it as such at the time.

The ceremony took place in our suite at the Dunes Hotel. The minister was disappointed that we'd forgotten to buy rings, claiming that reference to rings was the best part of his speech. So Christian lent Vadim his ring and Tina lent me hers; it was much too large for my skinny finger. I had to hold my finger upright throughout the ceremony, which created the impression that I was giving the whole proceeding the finger. The fact is, however, that I cried when we were pronounced man and wife. We

Vadim and me looking around the fixer-upper farm we bought outside of Paris, 1966.

Nathalie leading her pony, Gamin, with Christian and me riding and Vadim following. That's the stone wall I built behind us.
(© David Hurn/ Magnum Photos)

had been together for three years, but I hadn't realized how much formalizing our relationship would
mean to me.

After the ceremony, some in our small group
began enthusiastically renewing their relationship to
Chivas Regal, and by the time we got to dinner,
things were starting to feel sad. We ate in a cocktail
lounge, where a long buffet table with a massive glass
swan sculpture separated us from a stage on which a
striptease version of the French Revolution was
being performed. We watched as a topless woman
was "beheaded" on a guillotine to the strains of
Ravel's **Bolero.** I told Vadim I thought we should ad-
journ to our room. But Vadim disappeared into the
casino and I ended up sharing a bed with his mother.
I really was ignorant of the realities of compulsive
gambling, but it wouldn't have mattered. I was hurt
and angry, and as we flew back to Los Angeles the
next afternoon, I remember thinking, What have I
done? But, like I say, I'd learned to compartmentalize—bury the hurt and move on.

The following year we filmed **La Curée (The
Game Is Over)**, our second film together, and again
it was a happy experience for us both. Sharing a common goal, joining in a structured workday, gave
sense to our union that often seemed to be lacking
outside of work. During the filming of **La Curée,** I
received a letter from the Italian producer Dino De
Laurentiis asking me to play the title role in **Barbarella,** based on a French comic strip by Jean-
Claude Forest. Brigitte Bardot and Sophia Loren had

both been offered the role and turned it down, and this was my inclination as well. But Vadim was adamant that science fiction films would be the wave of the future, that this could be a terrific sci-fi comedy, that I should do it, and that he should direct.

Vadim had long been an aficionado of science fiction, and the added whimsy and sexiness of the story clearly played to his strengths. His passion for the idea convinced me to go along. As soon as **La Curée** wrapped, he began working on the script for **Barbarella** with satirist Terry Southern. Meanwhile, I returned to the United States to do the film **Hurry Sundown** with Otto Preminger, Michael Caine, Burgess Meredith, Beah Richards, Faye Dunaway, Robert Hooks, Diahann Carroll, Rex Ingram, Madeleine Sherwood, and John Phillip Law. It was shot in and around Baton Rouge, Louisiana, and while it was ultimately not very good, for me the experience was profound.

The entire cast, black and white alike, was housed in a motel in Baton Rouge, a small city about seventy-six miles from New Orleans. The motel had never been integrated before, and the first night we arrived, a cross was burned on the motel lawn. All the rooms opened onto a swimming pool, and the day Robert Hooks dove into that pool for the first time, locals peered from around corners as though they expected the pool to turn black. I was sure the reverberations were heard all the way to New Orleans. Diahann Carroll told me how concerned she was because as a black woman from New York, she'd

forgotten how to behave "down here in Klan country." She worried that without thinking she'd do
something that would be normal for her up north
but dangerous down here.

One day we were filming in the small county
seat of St. Francisville, in front of the courthouse,
when I looked down to see a cute little black boy of
about eight shyly watching the filming. I squatted
down to talk to him and then, as I was being called
back into the scene, I leaned over and gave him a
kiss. **Snap!**—someone took a picture of the kiss, and
it appeared on the front page of the local paper the
next day.

All hell broke loose. Shots were fired into the
production wagons, and threatening phone calls were
made to the production office about what would happen to us "nigger lovers" if we didn't get out of
town—which we did. I was shocked. I hadn't realized
what little progress toward desegregation had been
made. I'd been to an SNCC fund-raiser and had seen
Watts in flames, but I hadn't been paying enough attention. I was still using the term **Negro** while the
African-Americans in the cast were calling themselves
"black." I listened to conversations between Robert
Hooks, Beah Richards, and others following the
shooting incident: about a burgeoning "black nationalism"; about Stokely Carmichael calling for "black
power"; about a growing sense that blacks had only
themselves to depend on. I kept my mouth shut but
was disturbed and hurt—poor little me, a white do-
gooder, just beginning to feel I could get involved and

now being told I wouldn't be wanted by the new black movement they were describing.

For answers, I turned to a white cast member, Madeleine Sherwood. She was a close friend from the Actors Studio, and she'd been in **Invitation to a March** with me. Her longtime partner was black, and she had tried to get me involved in supporting the Freedom Rides. I'd gone to Big Sur instead. Madeleine helped me understand that in the years since I'd been living outside the United States, there had been a sea change in the civil rights movement. The nonviolent strategy that had been its foundation was based on the assumption that there was a latent conscience in America that, when appealed to, would step up and put an end to segregation. What had become apparent to blacks and to white civil rights workers alike was that neither the segregationist South nor the northern white liberal establishment was ready to integrate. Yes, laws had changed. But the new laws did little to alter the segregationists' pathological hatred of integration. The liberal establishment, with some exceptions, seemed to support the movement but refrained from taking strong enough action either to protect civil rights workers from violence or to uphold the law. Apparently the Democratic Party had been too dependent on racist Dixiecrats to dare to rock the boat seriously. But too much had happened and too much blood had been shed for the activists to settle for liberal tokenism. What was the good of new laws if the dismal reality of black lives didn't change? Blacks read the lack of decisive action as a signal that they had to go it alone. Hope had turned to cynicism. Peaceful protest was starting to look less viable than violent action.

I realized that I, who had sat out these turbulent years, never coming close to experiencing what black Americans endured, was in no position to judge the rise of black nationalism, though it was hard for me to comprehend how any group could achieve anything positive through separatism and violence. I thought of my father and his childhood story of the Omaha lynching, and of his hero, Abraham Lincoln—and I wondered how, in this democratic country of ours, we could have made so little real progress.

Vadim was able to visit only for a week or so during the shooting, because he was involved in preparations for **Barbarella.** But during his brief stay, while sitting around the motel pool, he saw the lean, tanned, blue-eyed John Phillip Law emerge from the water like a piece of sculpture—and he decided then and there that he was the one to play **Barbarella**'s Pygar, the blind angel who recovers his will to fly after he and Barbarella make love.

From **Hurry Sundown** I went almost immediately into **Barefoot in the Park,** which would turn out to be my first genuine hit—finally. How I ever survived so many bad films, I'll never know! Charles Bluhdorn, chairman and CEO of Gulf + Western, had just purchased Paramount Pictures, starting what became a wave of corporate buy-ups that would take American moviemaking out of the hands of impassioned, visionary individuals like Irving Thalberg, Jack Warner, Samuel Goldwyn, Harry Cohn, and Louis B. Mayer and turn the studios into corporate subsidiaries. I was informed that Bluhdorn had threatened to throw himself out of his New York skyscraper if I was cast in the female lead. I don't know why or what changed his mind, but once filming started we got along fine. I was very happy to be working with Bob Redford again and looking forward to our cuddling-in-the-cold-apartment scenes, something I hadn't gotten a chance to do in **The Chase.**

There's something about Bob that's impossible not to fall in love with. We've made three films together, and each time I was smitten, utterly twitterpated, couldn't wait to get to work, wouldn't even get mad when he was his habitual one to two hours late. He never knew it, of course. Nothing ever happened between us except that we always had a good time working together. I remember the first day he and I showed up in the Paramount administration building. As we walked down the corridors, secretaries stuck their heads out their office doors to watch him go by. **Ah,** I thought, **he's going to be a star.** But one of the things I love about him is that instead of puffing up his ego, this made him uncomfortable. I have never seen women react to a man the way they do to Bob: In Las Vegas once, when we were filming **The Electric Horseman,** a woman threw herself on the ground at his feet. He seems to want to disappear at times like this.

Of all the male stars I've worked with in my fifty films, Bob is the only one about whom women ask me, "What's it like to kiss him?" The answer I always give is, "Fabulous." The reality is a little different: fabulous for me, not so fabulous for him. He hates filming love scenes. He seems to want to get them over with as soon as possible. Damn it! Fortunately he has a sense of humor about this, and about most everything. Actually, he's a stitch. Besides his male attractiveness, I find a Hepburnesque quality about Bob: You feel that he is somehow better than most other mortals. You **want** Bob to like you, so you are loath to do or say anything that might make him think less of you. This is not someone you would want to gossip about. Maybe this is why, in a town known for gossip, no one tries to get into his business.

In between scenes on **Barefoot in the Park,** we shared stories about growing up in West Los Angeles in the forties, about living in Europe—where he'd also gone to study painting in the fifties (only **he** actually painted)—and about our shared love of horses. But mostly I remember Bob describing with great passion a piece of property he had bought outside of Provo, Utah, the home state of his then wife, Lola. They had designed an A-frame house that they had just built on the property, and Bob was full of excitement about the construction. Little did either of us imagine then that this property with its little A-frame would become first the Sundance ski resort (where my son, Troy, learned to ski) and later the Sundance Institute, which has made such significant contributions to independent filmmaking.

Goofing off with Bob Redford between takes on **Barefoot in the Park.**
(Photofest)

A scene in
Barefoot in the Park.
(Photofest)

Making **Barefoot** was a joy. First there was Bob; then we had that flawless script by Neil Simon; and Gene Saks was the perfect comedy director. Everyone in the cast was talented, nice, and fun to work with, especially Mildred Natwick, who'd been in children's theater and then the University Players with my dad.

It's not often that a comedy survives the passage of time, but I have seen **Barefoot in the Park** countless times and I find its appeal to be timeless. Bob's, too.

CHAPTER FOURTEEN

BARBARELLA

Hey! Nothing is what it seems.
—MADONNA

WHEN FILMING ON **Barefoot** wrapped, Vadim and I moved to Rome, where **Barbarella** was to be shot at the De Laurentiis studio. We rented a house on the outskirts of the city—part castle, part dungeon. There was a tower next to our bedroom that dated from the second century **before** Christ. At night we regularly heard scuffling and mewing coming from there. One evening during a dinner party in the cavernous living room below, there was a loud noise, some plaster fell from the ceiling, and an owl fell onto Gore Vidal's plate. It turns out that a family of large owls had been making the racket in the tower.

None of the special effects and optical techniques we take for granted today existed in 1967. Vadim and his collaborators had to invent everything, and sometimes the ideas worked and sometimes they didn't. The opening title sequence shows

Barbarella peeling off her "astronaut" suit as she floats topsy-turvy in her fur-lined space cabin. Much was made of this unusual scene, the first weightless striptease in movie history (and perhaps the last!). Claude Renoir, brilliant cinematographer and nephew of French film director Jean Renoir, came up with a way to film it while playing around in his hotel bathroom one evening. Here's how it worked: The set of the space cabin, instead of sitting like a normal room that you could walk in and out of, was turned upward so that it faced the ceiling of the enormous sound stage. A pane of thick glass was laid across the opening of the set, and the camera was hung from the rafters directly above it. I would have to climb up a ladder and onto the glass, so that from the camera's point of view the space cabin was behind me and I appeared to be suspended in space. Then I would begin slowly to remove my space outfit while a wind machine blew my hair and the discarded articles of clothing around as though they were floating with me in space. I was terrified that the glass would break; terrified of rolling around like that in the altogether; terrified of not being perfect. Once again, I just didn't think I could say no. But Vadim promised that the letters in the film credits would be placed judiciously to cover what needed to be covered—and they were.

The biggest challenge for us was figuring out how to film the sequences where Pygar, the blind angel, flies through space carrying Barbarella in his arms. A remote control specialist devised a scheme: A huge rotating steel pole stuck out horizontally from a cycloramic gray screen. The pole had large hooks and screws at the end, on which two metal corsets were attached. One corset had been made to fit John Phillip Law and one was for me, and they were skintight because our costumes had to fit over the metal and not look bulky.

We got all suited up, first the cold metal corsets, then the costumes, and then John's wings were strapped onto his back with wires running from the wings to a remote-control machine. Then a crane hoisted us up and we stood on the platform while John was hooked up to the end of the pole. Then my metal corset was screwed to the front of his, putting me into a position that made it look as though he were carrying me. After we had been suited up, hoisted up, and screwed up, the moment of truth arrived. The crane, which until then had been supporting us, was moved away, leaving us suspended in air, with the weight of our bodies jamming our hipbones and crotches into the metal corsets.

It was sheer, utter agony. And with all that, we had to remember our dialogue, look dreamy, and occasionally be funny. The muted sounds of misery I could hear from John (who was bearing the added weight of his wings) told me that his pain was worse than mine, and mine was nearly unbearable. No one had taken our poor crotches into consideration! John was convinced his sex life would be brought to a premature demise.

There we'd hang, while somewhere out in the

darkened sound stage the technician worked the remote controls, making the pole rotate this way and
that and making John's wings flap up and down.
While we hung there, rotating, a film of the sky with
clouds moving past (shot from an airplane) was projected onto the gray screen behind us. Nothing of
the sky and clouds could be seen on our faces or costumes, and you couldn't even see what was being
projected on the screen until the film had been developed. John and I weren't actually moving forward
through space, but the film was to make it appear
that way. That was the intention. This type of front
projection is common today, but back then it had
never been done before—we were the guinea pigs.
Lots of things had to work properly at the same time:
The steel pole had to rotate in sync with the moving
sky, the remote-control specialist had to make
Pygar's wings flap in the same way, and the projection onto the gray screen had to function properly.
This all took days and days to rig up, while John and
I hung there, our private parts growing progressively
numb.

I will never forget the first day we finally had
rushes to look at. Everyone was excited and anxious,
since flying without the help of wires had never been
done before and so much depended on the believ-
ability of the flying scenes. There was an entire aerial
battle that was critical to the story. The lights in the
screening room dimmed, the film began to roll
and . . . **Oh my God . . . we were flying backward!**
It was too funny not to laugh: The one most obvious

thing, what direction the clouds and landscape were moving, had been overlooked. But what was also apparent was that once they got us in sync with the background, it would work. It really did look like we were flying, like he was carrying me, like we weren't in pain, like the clouds and mountains were passing by—just going the wrong way.

It was a tough shoot, lots of scrapes and bruises. I was attacked by little mechanical dolls. I was shut into a tiny plastic box with hundreds of birds, flying, pecking, and pooping on my hair, arms, and face. I was constantly being asked to slide down clear plastic tubes or stand inside a cloud of noxious fumes. When I see what actors in action films have to do these days, however, I think I got off pretty light.

By today's standards **Barbarella** seems slow (it seemed slow to many critics back then as well). But I think the jerry-built quality of the effects and the offbeat, camp humor give it a unique charm. Pauline Kael, film critic for **The New Yorker,** wrote about my performance: "Her American-good-girl innocence makes her a marvellously apt heroine for pornographic comedy. . . . She is playfully and deliciously aware of the naughtiness of what she's doing, and that innocent's sense of naughtiness, of being a tarnished lady, keeps her from being just another naked actress."

"Just another naked actress" indeed! I can laugh about it now, but the tensions and insecurities that haunted me during the making of that film almost did me in. There I was, a young woman who hated

John Phillip Law as the blind
angle Pygar carrying Barbarella.
The agony doesn't show.
(Carlo Bavagnoli/Time & Life
Pictures/Getty Images)

Vadim making sure all the rips
are in the right places.
(© David Hurn/Magnum Photos)

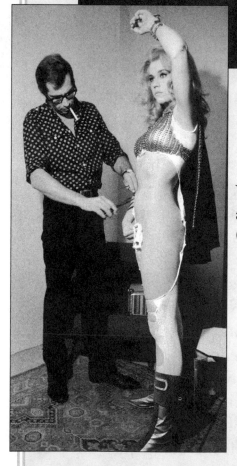

Pygar approaching his
nest, where we will make
love and he will get back
his will to fly.
(© David Hurn/Magnum
Photos)

her body and suffered from terrible bulimia, playing a scantily clad—sometimes naked—sexual heroine. Every morning I was sure that Vadim would wake up and realize he had made a terrible mistake—"Oh my God! She's not Bardot!"

At the same time, unwilling to let anyone know my real feelings and wanting, Girl Scoutishly, to do my best, I would pop a Dexedrine and plow onward. The "American-good-girl-innocence" that Pauline Kael described was really the Lone Ranger trying to "make it better."

Vadim's drinking had gotten much worse. He was a binge drinker: He would go for weeks and months without a drop (unfortunate, because it allowed him to feel he had the disease under control), but then things would seem to disintegrate. Partway through the shooting of **Barbarella** he started drinking at lunch, and we'd never know what to expect after that. He wasn't falling down, but his words would slur and his decisions about how to shoot scenes often seemed ill-considered. When I watch certain scenes from the movie now, I remember all too well how vulnerable I felt at the time. And more and more angry!

I was also growing more remote, feeling as if I were out on a limb (or a steel pole) by myself, that no one else seemed to care about what I cared about—like showing up to work sober and on time, getting a good night's sleep so you'd be prepared and creative the next day. But I still lacked the confidence to try to take charge when Vadim seemed particularly out of control.

Today **Barbarella**'s production costs would seem penny-ante, but for the time they were considerable. The cast and crew were large and multilingual, the technical challenges awesome, and too many things, including the script, hadn't been worked out sufficiently in advance. Often I would have to pretend to be sick so that the film's insurance would cover the cost of a shutdown for a day or two while Vadim, Terry Southern, and the others figured out script problems. One thing for sure, I never dreamed the film would become a cult classic and, in some circles, the picture Vadim and I would be best known for. It has taken me many decades to arrive at a place where I can understand why this is so and even share the enjoyment of the film's unique charms.

There was another feeling that began to nudge me. It was just a hint of something I could not yet name—the old feeling of being in the wrong place. But this time it wasn't the feeling there was a party going on that left me out. No. Now my life **was** the party—one long, unending party that I didn't especially want to be at. Rather, it was a feeling that something more important was going on out there and my life was being frittered away with whatnots and doodads. There were the struggles of blacks in the United States that I'd only just started to learn about. There was a growing anti–Vietnam War movement. But I hadn't followed the war news closely, and when Vadim's French friends criticized the U.S. involvement there, my reaction was usually defensive. I simply couldn't believe that America could be involved in a wrong cause, and I hated having foreigners criticize us. I was totally clueless about the nascent women's movement and would have felt deeply threatened by it had I been exposed to feminism.

It wasn't any specific alternative life I longed for, it was just a sense of growing malaise. I was a go-alonger, a passive participant, living "as if": **as if** I had a good marriage, **as if** I were happy and fully present. I was also trying not to be too serious about anything, because if you took things too seriously, it meant you were bourgeois and didn't have a sense of humor. There was a certain tyranny about Vadim's "don't take things too seriously" mandate, especially when it came to women.

When filming on **Barbarella** finished in the fall of 1967, it occurred to me that perhaps I could quiet the malaise and fill the empty place that seemed to be growing larger by having a baby. **Make it better.**

One of the things I liked most about Vadim was how he was as a father. Perhaps it was due to the fact that he'd never entirely grown up himself that he seemed able to inhabit a child's world. His lack of concern about punctuality and the doing of duties served him well when it came to his little children. Every night, after I'd badgered Nathalie into brushing her teeth and going to bed, Vadim would pick up the thread of some phantasmagoric tale he'd have concocted for her. Sometimes the story would go on for weeks. Usually there was an element of science fiction, always of whimsy, with little people turning

out to have wondrous big powers. Besides his stories, there were his paintings: Vadim had a unique
painting style—primitive, colorful, sensual, in many
ways the drawings of a child. Then there was his
patience and his generosity with his time—two
elements critical to good parenting: Vadim could
spend hours debating with his children the origins
of the universe, life after death, the meaning of gravity, the whys and wherefores of life, all with a charm
and attention that moved me deeply. He was totally
present, at least for his girls, at least when they were
little. Come to think of it, it was always true for our
Vanessa, too.

Like many people who feel their marriage dissolving, I thought that if I had a child, it would
bring us closer. But the desire for a baby wasn't only
to save a troubled marriage, it was a way to save **me**.
I thought that the experience of childbirth would
somehow make me right, that the pain of natural
childbirth would deliver me to myself. I still saw
myself as deeply flawed, unable to open my heart
and love enough to be truly happy.

Vadim thought that having a baby was a splen-
did idea, so I had my IUD removed, and a month
later, during Christmas vacation in Megève, a ski
resort in the French Alps—a week after my thirtieth
birthday, on December 28, 1967, to be exact—I
conceived. I knew the moment it happened and
told him so—there was a different resonance to our
lovemaking.

I had a whole round year ahead of me with no

commitments except to complete work on our farm, which included planting a garden and a forest. Though I have no conscious memory of my father transplanting the huge pines and fruit trees he brought onto our Tigertail property in the forties, I'm told that he did. I'll wager that way back then is when I got bitten by the tree-transplanting bug that is a trademark of mine. I'm not big on jewelry or fashion, but big trees—now, **that's** something I'll spend money on. I justify it now by pointing out that I'm too old for saplings.

I decided I wanted some very large hardwood trees in our front yard, maples, poplars, birch, catalpa, liquidambars. So I drove all over France to the largest nurseries with the tallest trees I could buy, so tall that they had to be transported at night and telephone lines had to be taken down to let them pass. A friend had given us her car, a 1937 Panhard Levasseur, a real collector's item—but since it no longer ran, I had a welder cut it in half and then solder it together around a newly planted plantain tree so that the tree was growing right through the car— a piece of yard sculpture.

It was in one of the nurseries, searching for trees, that I felt the first wave of nausea. It stopped me in my tracks. I knew exactly what it meant. I didn't need a pregnancy test to tell me. I broke into a cold sweat, returned to my car to sit down—and was overcome by a sense of dread! I felt I had to muster all my forces against an unknown terror that seemed to have invaded me. **Why? I wanted this!** Then tears came, then racking sobs. **What is happening? This isn't how I'm supposed to feel!**

And then I knew: The pregnancy was incontrovertible proof that I was actually a woman—which meant "victim," which meant that I would be destroyed, like my mother. It was one of those strange moments when I was feeling what I was feeling while simultaneously standing outside of myself analyzing the feeling—and being shocked by what it meant.

A month or more into the pregnancy, I began to bleed and was told I couldn't leave my bed for at least a month if I wanted to prevent miscarriage; I was given DES (diethylstilbestrol) to prevent miscarriage, a drug that has subsequently been linked to uterine cancer in daughters of mothers who've taken it. Then I came down with the mumps.

I saw these problems as a powerful sign that I was not meant to be a mother, and they provided me with a reasonable justification for backing out of the whole thing. Yet when my French gynecologist recommended I have an abortion because of the risk mumps posed to the fetus, I never for a moment considered that as an option (though I was grateful I had the choice). It's not that Vadim and I weren't concerned. But my attachment to motherhood was so tenuous that I felt if I aborted the fetus, I would never want to have another baby. It was a low point in my life, let me tell you: I had just turned thirty and was pregnant, bedridden, and risking a miscarriage; mumps had swollen my face to the size of a bowling ball; and to top off my misery, across the ocean Faye Dunaway had just created a sensation in **Bonnie and Clyde.** Not that I was competitive or anything.

I had just entered my second act, and as far as I could tell, my life had peaked and was on the decline.

ACT TWO

SEEKING

A hundred struggle and drown in the breakers. One discovers the new world. But rather, ten times rather, die in the surf, heralding the way to that new world, than stand idly on the shore!

— Florence Nightingale,
Cassandra

Maybe I can do somethin'. Maybe I can scrounge around and find out what's wrong and see if there ain't somethin' can be done about it.

— Tom Joad
in John Steinbeck's **The Grapes of Wrath**

I was always at meetings.

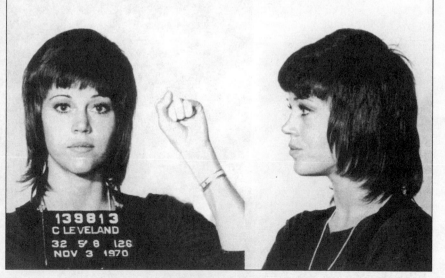

My mug shot.
(AP/Wide World Photos)

アサヒグラフ 12·31

反戦女優
ジェーン・フォンダ
（東京—沖縄）

政治を風刺する寸劇を演ずるジェーン・フォンダ（中央）右はドナルド・サザランド（東京・福生市民会館で）

中印国境の
秘境ラダク
（カシミール）

Rita Martinson,
Donald
Sutherland, and
me during the
FTA show.

Talking . . . always
talking to end the war.

At Laurel
Springs
with Tom,
Troy,
Vanessa,
and her
dog,
Manila.
(© Steve
Schapiro)

The night Tom won his race
for the assembly. Left to right:
Margot Kidder, Tom, me,
Shirlee.
(Barry E. Levine)

The Workout.
(Harry Langdon)

At the Oscars with Ted. At this point, he's the one in show business.
(Michel Bourquard/Stills/ Retna Ltd.)

Surveying the bison on Ted's ranch.

CHAPTER ONE

1968

> If a butterfly flaps its wings in Brazil, it might produce a tornado in Texas. Unlikely as it seems, the tiny currents that a butterfly creates travel across thousands of miles, jostling other breezes as they go and eventually changing the weather.
>
> —EDWARD LORENZ

OKAY, SO I WAS WRONG. My life didn't peak, nor was it on the decline. But like everything else in the world, it was about to go through major changes. Looking back, I believe it now seems fated that I began my second act in 1968, perhaps the most turbulent, tumultuous year of the century. I was thirty, pregnant, and ripe. Everything in me was poised, like a sprinter at the starting line, twitching to move forward.

Things had been brewing for a while: I needed

to make sense of life and feel I had a purpose. Filming **Barbarella** at a time when so much substantive
change was taking place in the world had acted as
yeast to my malaise. Who was I? What did I want
from life? I am carrying life—what does this mean
for me?

Change always holds an element of self-interest,
and mine was quite simply that I wanted to be a better person. To switch to a gardening metaphor, it's
possible that the seeds of my definition of "better"
were gathered and planted way back when I saw my
father's early movies: **The Grapes of Wrath, The Ox-
Bow Incident, Young Mr. Lincoln.** Stratified after
thirty years, they were now waiting to sprout. My
pregnancy during that fertile year—1968—created a
rich loam.

At first the evidence offered by my pregnancy (that
I was a woman, hence like my mother) had struck
terror in my heart, but as time went by, the fear gave
way to a strange peace. Peace was not something
with which I was familiar. Perhaps the hormones of
pregnancy were washing away my lifelong tendency
to depression. But I think it was more than that. I
believe that in facing and naming the terror I had felt
at the start of my pregnancy, a healing process had
been set in motion—a somatic realization that I was,
in fact, a normal female. My always troublesome
"down there" was doing what millennia of women's
down theres had done for them. I had conceived. In

a way, I was pregnant with a baby and also with my-self, connected by a primordial umbilical cord to other women—to all women past, present, and fu-ture; to the female spirit—interested in and needing to be with women more than men for the first time since adolescence. In fact, during my nine months of pregnancy I experienced being **in my body** for the first time since **pre**adolescent girlhood. I would not be capable of sustaining that embodiment after preg-nancy, but I would find it again later, in my third act.

I had never gone in much for watching television and was not one of the many Americans witness-ing the developing Vietnam War from their living rooms. What attention I did give to it allowed me to remain comfortable in the belief that it was an ac-ceptable cause—maybe not a "good war" like the one my father fought in; more of a fuzzy one, like the Korean War. But all that changed when the risk of miscarriage confined me to bed for the first three months of 1968. I saw images on French television showing damage caused by American bombers that, en route back to their aircraft carriers, unloaded bombs they hadn't already dropped, sometimes hit-ting schools, hospitals, and churches. I was stunned.

Then, beginning in January during the cele-bration of Tet, Vietnam's new year, the North Vietnamese and Vietcong launched a series of well-coordinated offensives in major cities throughout South Vietnam. It was shocking. For this to have been organized and carried out without the U.S. military and our allies having even a hint meant that the people we were calling the enemy was just about everybody. As I watched the Vietcong storm the grounds of the American embassy, it occurred to me that Vietnamese residents throughout Saigon must have participated: shopkeepers, peddlers, farmers, laundresses. Later it was discovered that guns, ammunition, and grenades had been smuggled into the city in laundry and flower baskets. The words of General William Westmoreland, commander of U.S. forces in Vietnam, claiming that he was close to ending the war, that he could see "a light at the end of the tunnel," echoed grotesquely in light of what we were seeing on television. We, supposedly the mightiest military force in the world, had so lost ground that even after four years of warfare the enemy was able to attack us in our own embassy.

The psychological impact of such images was devastating. Everything was turned upside down. Who was strong? What did "military might" mean? **Who were we as Americans?** As I lay in bed contemplating what I was seeing, I remembered a morning in Saint Tropez. Vadim and I were having a leisurely breakfast on the balcony of our room at the Tahiti Hôtel when he opened the newspaper.

"**Ce n'est pas possible! Mais ils sont fous ou quoi?**" he exploded, jabbing his fingers at the front page. "Look at this. Your Congress must be out of their minds!" It was August 8, 1964, and French headlines blasted the news that Congress had just passed the Tonkin Gulf Resolution. It gave President Johnson the power, for the first time ever, to bomb North Vietnam.

"There's no way you can win a war in Vietnam!" Vadim continued with uncharacteristic passion.

I wanted to ask, "Where **is** Vietnam?" but I was too ashamed. I also wondered why he was so certain the United States couldn't win, and I felt defensive. Sour grapes, I thought. Just because the French lost . . .

Now, with the grim reality of 1968 and the Tet offensive, it occurred to me that Vadim may have been right. But how could the United States lose to a country so small? And if a French filmmaker had known in 1964 that we couldn't win, why did the American government fail to get it? It would take me four more years before I really understood why Vadim had been so certain, and a few years after that to begin to grasp the most disturbing question of all: why five administrations, from Truman to Nixon, **did** see that we couldn't win and persisted anyway.

When the danger of miscarriage had passed, my sometime mentor Simone Signoret brought me with her to a huge antiwar rally in Paris. Jean-Paul Sartre and Simone de Beauvoir were among the speakers. For the first time I felt embarrassed for my country, and I also wanted to go home. It was too painful being in France, hearing the criticisms, and not doing anything.

But what to do? I didn't like criticizing America while I was in another country. I'm not a dabbler. If I was going to oppose the war, it would be in the streets of America with my fellow countrymen, who, I could see on French television, were marching in growing numbers in the States. The dilemma for me was that this could never happen in the context of my marriage to Vadim. (In years to come, he would publicly disparage me as a "Jane of Arc.") While personally opposed to the Vietnam War, he was too cynical to commit himself to any movement to end it. Then, too, I knew that if I threw myself heart and soul into the antiwar effort, a return to the permissive, indolent life I shared with Vadim would be unthinkable.

Around this time I had an experience that, oddly enough, would never have happened had my beloved former stepmother Susan not come to Paris to check up on me during my pregnancy. At dinner one evening, a friend of hers introduced me to a nineteen-year-old fresh-faced kid named Dick Perrin, who turned out to be a U.S. Army resister from the First Battalion of the Sixty-fourth Armored Brigade, stationed in West Germany. This was my first encounter with a U.S. serviceman who was actively opposed to the war, and it was my introduction to what within two years would become a major focus of my activism: GIs against the war.

Dick talked to us about an organization he and

other American army resisters had just formed, RITA (Resisters Inside the Army). RITA's goals were to spread anti–Vietnam War messages within the armed forces. Dick said that a soldier had the right, even the obligation, to dissociate himself from the military if he believed the war was wrong.

It seemed there was a growing underground network of American resisters and conscientious objectors in Europe. They were seeking employment and financial assistance. According to Dick in his book **G.I. Resister,** one of the "hideouts" for these resisters was a farmhouse southwest of Paris, near Tours. There Dick would drop off or pick up guys. He described how they sat at a fourteen-foot-long kitchen table where they could all eat together with the owner of the farm. This owner was a big, gentle American in bib overalls. Dick called him Sandy. Dick would gaze out the window onto the rolling farmland and see "crazy constructions that swung in the breeze and moved in nearly every direction." Dick said, "I had no name for them because I had never seen a mobile before, nor even heard of one."

Only later, sitting with his family in Canada watching "Sandy's" obituary being announced, did Perrin discover that their benefactor was none other than the great American sculptor Alexander Calder.

I had often been at that farmhouse with Sandy and his wife, but he never told me they were helping resisters, and I had never met one there.

After that dinner I saw Dick Perrin and several other GI resisters from time to time, helping them get dental care, passing on some of Vadim's clothes. I even invited them to a sneak screening of **Barbarella,** which would be released later that year. The young men with Dick described themselves as humanitarian rather than political and told how soldiers returning from Vietnam had joked about torturing Vietnamese prisoners. Yet, like me, they became defensive whenever a French person expressed criticism of America. At one of our encounters Dick gave me a book, **The Village of Ben Suc,** by Jonathan Schell. "Read this," he said, "and you'll understand." I went back to our farm and devoured the short book in one stunned sitting.

In it Schell described what happened in January 1967 during the largest U.S. military operation in Vietnam up to that time, Operation Cedar Falls. Having failed in its previous attempts to "pacify" the village of Ben Suc and the surrounding area known as the Iron Triangle, the American High Command had developed a new strategy: to bomb (including with B-52s) and shell the area for several days; then bring in ground troops, both American and our South Vietnamese allies from the Army of the Republic of Vietnam, to round up villagers and move them in trucks to a refugee camp. Bulldozers then leveled the village and the surrounding jungle, which was bombed again until no trace was left of what had once been a relatively prosperous farming village.

Perhaps it was the matter-of-factness of Schell's writing that made it so powerful. We learn with him how embedded the Vietcong were in the life of the

village, providing a full governmental structure and
protections and involving everyone in their programs; how the captive villagers deliberately allowed
the American soldiers to continue in their belief that
the VC were a "roving band of guerrillas" who occasionally appeared out of the jungle and then disappeared again, rather than the governing body they
clearly were. The reader comes to understand why
the goal of "winning the hearts and minds" of
refugees from Ben Suc was a grotesque joke. Schell
quotes American lieutenant colonel Kenneth J.
White, province representative for the Office of
Civilian Operations, exclaiming as he looks at the re-
settlement camp for the first time, "This is wonderful! I've never seen anything like it. It's the best
civilian project I've ever seen . . . you know, sometimes it just feels **right.**"

I was shocked at Schell's account of the smug-
ness of the high-level U.S. military officers who
seemed to revel in Operation Cedar Falls' massive
military destructiveness without seeming to consider
the effects on civilians. In response to a question
from Schell about civilian casualties of the bombing,
one sergeant said, "What does it matter? They're all
Vietnamese."

I closed the book. I knew that something fundamental in the general area of my heart had exploded
and blown me wide open. I'm not sure how I had
managed up until then to neatly compartmentalize
my generic, liberal opposition to war and avoid knowing more about the realities of this particular one.

I felt sickened. Part of my identity had been that I was a citizen of a country that, in spite of its internal paradoxes, represented moral integrity, justice, and a desire for peace. My father had fought in the Pacific, and when he returned wearing a Bronze Star, I had been filled with pride. I sometimes cried when I sang "The Star-Spangled Banner." I had been "Miss Army Recruiter" in 1959. I was a believer. Reading Schell's **The Village of Ben Suc,** I felt betrayed as an American, and the depth of my sense of betrayal was in direct proportion to my previous depth of certainty about the ultimate rightness of any U.S. mission. I began telling everyone I knew about the book, and I was shaken by the we've-known-this-for-years, what-are-you-so-bothered-about? reaction I received from most people (including Vadim). I found it difficult to understand how they had known this and not done more to end it. But they were **French.** They'd ended **their** war in Vietnam. Ending it this time was our job, as Americans.

As I began to read more—including reports from the International War Crimes Tribunal—I began to wonder: Why had I not paid more attention and taken action sooner? It wasn't that I was lazy or lacked curiosity. I think it had to do with giving up comfort—and I don't mean material comfort. I mean the comfort that ignorance provides. Once you connect with the painful truth of something, you then **own** the pain and must take responsibility for it through action. Of course, there are people who **see** and then choose to turn away, but then one becomes an accomplice. In **Galileo,** Bertolt Brecht wrote, "He who doesn't know is an ignoramus. He who knows and keeps quiet is a scoundrel." I'm a lot of things, but a scoundrel isn't one of them.

I wanted to act on what I was learning and feeling but didn't know what to do. I knew (without acknowledging to myself what I knew) that if I became involved, it would mean leaving Vadim; but I couldn't conceive of leaving him. Who would I be without him? I decided to go see Simone Signoret.

When I arrived at the bucolic country estate she and Yves Montand shared outside Paris, she was at the door to greet me. I could see in her face that she had been waiting for this to happen. Somehow, through all the silliness of my lifestyle, she had maintained a firm belief that what she loved about my father from his movie roles was waiting inside **me** to manifest itself through action. Sometimes I would catch her looking at me in such a deep way that I'd be tempted to look over my shoulder to see whom it was she was relating to—surely not me. It was her patience with me, the fact that she had never pushed or proselytized but had been content to put learning opportunities in my path, that told me I could trust her.

Bringing a bottle of fine cabernet and a platter of cheeses, she took me out to the back porch, where we ensconced ourselves in an arbor.

"I'm glad you read Schell's book. It's important," she said. She'd read it the previous year, when it had appeared as a series of articles in **The New Yorker.** I asked if she had been surprised by it.

"Yes and no," she answered. "We've known here for some time about your 'strategic hamlets' and the

bombardements de saturation [saturation bomb-
ing], but never in such detail. It was the details that
got to me. But remember, we were there before you,
we French, and the attitudes that Schell describes the
Americans having toward the Vietnamese—the total
disregard, as though they aren't human beings—
these were the same attitudes **les colonialistes Fran-
çais** had. The difference is that we didn't need to try
to hide it. Don't forget, back then most people still
believed it was all right to have colonies, whereas in
your country people need to believe you've been **invited** in to protect a democracy." And she cocked her
head at me and gave me a look that said "Who do
they think they're kidding!"

"Explain it to me, Simone," I asked, ashamed to
admit how much I didn't know.

"First of all, Jane, you need to know that at the
end of World War Two, when France had to go to
war to keep Vietnam as her colony, it was your country that paid most of our military expenses. **C'était
monstrueux, n'est-ce pas?** The U.S. was supposed to
be about independence, not colonialism."

"I didn't know this," I said quietly.

"Yes. The French couldn't have won alone, and
colonialism is a terrible thing, Jane." She described
how the French had manipulated the economy of
Vietnam to benefit themselves, how they gave
schooling only to the privileged but left most Vietnamese illiterate, how they had cultivated a bureaucracy of colonial wannabes from the Vietnamese
upper classes and gave privileges to Vietnamese who
agreed to convert to Catholicism.

"These are the kind of Vietnamese who support your so-called president Thieu right now," she said, "the same ones who supported **us** because they got power and privilege by identifying with the colonialists. Besides, they know there's a lot of money to be made off you Americans. Listen, Jane, these parasites are the people who allow you to believe that there are Vietnamese who want you there and who support Thieu. You had them during your own revolution. How did you call them?"

"Tories," I answered, beginning to understand things in a new way.

"Okay. You had Tories who supported the British. Did that make it a civil war?"

"No, it was a revolution."

"That's right. How can it be a civil war if one side is entirely paid for, trained by, and supported by a foreign nation?" She was getting worked up now. I liked Simone when she was worked up. "And you know who the Vietnamese revolutionaries thought of as the George Washington of their country? Ho Chi Minh. Americans are so blinded with anti-Communism that you don't even realize that most Vietnamese, including people who aren't Communists, still respect Ho as the founder of their country. He declared independence in 1945, for crying out loud! And when they had to fight France to keep their independence, Ho was certain he could count on the United States for help. You stood for national independence, that's what your wonderful father fought for in World War Two. Do you know that Ho petitioned and begged President Truman to help them get their independence from France, but each time he tried, they ignored him? Think about it: If your country had paid attention back then, none of this would have happened. There didn't need to be a war." She stopped to sip her wine and let this sink in. I took notes.

"This president of yours, how stupid! He's 'not going to be the first president of the United States to lose a war,' " she said in a mock macho voice. "But you can't win it any more than we did! Why can't they get it through their heads?"

I told her about Vadim's reaction in 1964 when he heard about the Tonkin Gulf Resolution. "Well, he was right. There's no way. All your presidents have thought they were fighting to stop the Soviets and China when they were really up against homegrown revolutionaries with a cause they're willing to die for. They've been fighting outsiders who've tried to take it away from them for centuries, and they always win sooner or later. Your GIs and those soldiers in Thieu's army, they don't want to fight because they have no cause to believe in." She leaned forward and looked hard at me.

"Dad voted for Johnson. He was sure he would end the war."

"Your dad and I have had many fights about this. I love him dearly, but he's too gullible when it comes to your liberal establishment."

"I had no idea it was all such a lie. I feel so angry and betrayed."

"As well you should, my darling girl. Your country has been betrayed by its leaders. What are you going to do about it?"

"I don't know what to do, Simone. I want to go back to America, but . . ."

I had to stop because I didn't want to cry. She was silent for a while, waiting to see if I would go on. Then: "It's hard to do much when you're here in France, I understand."

"But I can't ask Vadim to move to the U.S. We've just spent all this money on our farm, I'm having this baby . . ."

"You're in a difficult situation." Then she paused for a moment. "Do you love him?"

"Yes," I said, with a little too much certainty, as women do when they're not sure but don't know it.

The sun had gone down and a chill was setting in when we carried our wine and the remains of the cheese into her kitchen. "Do you want to stay for dinner? I'm alone tonight."

"Vadim's meeting me in Paris. I'm sorry, and I've taken so much of your time already." She put her arms around me. "I'm so glad we talked." Then, with her hands on my shoulders and holding me away from her, she looked into my eyes. "Jane, you will know what to do when the right time comes. Right now, you go and get ready for that baby."

I could see her standing in the doorway waving to me as I drove off. At dinner I didn't tell Vadim why I'd gone to see Simone, and he never asked.

In April Dr. Martin Luther King Jr. was assassinated in Memphis, and any hope that a nonviolent solution could be found to segregation and urban pov-

erty went down in tears. Violence and uprisings
were spreading around the world—from New York
and Mexico to Prague and West Germany. In May,
France's traditional month of demonstrations, students began a rebellion in Paris's Latin Quarter to
protest unpopular reforms in higher education. They
were met by police violence, and like a match to tin-
der, rebellion spread rapidly and unexpectedly
throughout Paris and then into the provinces,
launching what became known as Les Événements
de Mai, the Events of May. Ten thousand students
battled police for fourteen hours on May 6, turning
Paris into a city under siege. People poured into the
streets, barricades were erected, the CRS (the French
counterpart of the National Guard) responded with
shocking brutality.

Just prior to the start of the revolt, Vadim had
been elected president of the film technicians union,
and he was required to go to Paris for union meetings. I insisted on coming with him, not wanting to
be left barefoot and pregnant out on the farm while
history was being made. What I saw was astonishing.
Streets were being torn up, cars overturned and
burned, trees cut down for barricades. People were
bleeding from the blows of the police, from tear gas
and fires. Friends of ours were thrown in jail, and articles appeared daily about the brutality of the CRS.
Vadim's union meetings were filled to overflowing,
fractious, and passionate.

Then, a countrywide general strike brought
France to a virtual standstill. People, including me,

began stockpiling canned food in anticipation that the strike would continue. The French stock market was set ablaze by rioters. To appease the strikers and avert a potential civil war, de Gaulle called for a general election and raised the minimum wage by 33.3 percent. Along with the fear of being killed or hurt, there was a feeling of excitement and possibility in the air: Maybe this unlikely coalition between students and workers could actually topple the Gaullist government and achieve the reforms they sought; maybe change was possible; maybe people didn't have to be powerless. The stirrings were contagious. It seemed to be a worldwide phenomenon.

By now even loyalist American businessmen were publicly expressing concern about the deficit spending of the war and what it was doing to Johnson's vision of eradicating poverty. Bobby Kennedy had already taken the position publicly that the Vietcong should be included at the negotiating table. Now his presidential campaign was said to be bringing a brave, fresh sense of possibility to blacks, blue-collar workers, and youth, and to those committed to ending the war. Everything depended on his winning the critical California primary. Vadim and I were listening to the returns on the radio and the results slowly coming in showed that he was winning. But in the morning came the horrific news that he, too, had been shot. It felt like the Apocalypse was upon us.

I was six months pregnant by now, and Vadim wanted to get me out of the city, so with another couple we rented a house by the sea in Saint Tropez. The fact that the husband was an opium addict (and had a young girlfriend there as well as his wife) added to the alienation I was feeling. It probably wouldn't have affected me as much a year or two earlier. I would have shrugged it off as part of the dark side of life with Vadim. But now it caused me to retreat into my own world, encapsulated in the cocoon of my pregnancy. I spent most of my time floating on an inflatable raft in the pristine Mediterranean waters, my big belly curving toward the sun, reading (incongruously) **The Autobiography of Malcolm X.** It rocked me to my core. Malcolm's story opened a window onto a reality I had ignored. But the greatest revelation the book brought me was the possibility of profound human transformation. I was spellbound by his journey from the doped-up, numbers-running, woman-beating, street-hustling, pimping Malcolm Little to a proud, clean, literate, Muslim Malcolm X who taught that all white people were the Devil incarnate—to his final, spiritual transformation in Mecca. There he met white people from all over the world who received him as a brother, and he realized that "white," as he had been using the word, didn't mean skin color as much as it meant attitudes and actions some whites held toward nonwhites—but that not all whites were racist. At the time of his murder, he was anything but the hatemonger portrayed in the American press. Somehow, through the horrors that had been his life, he had become a spiritual leader. How had this been possible?

That summer in Saint Tropez I began to search my soul to see which kind of white person I was. While theoretically I didn't think I was racist, I hadn't had enough contact with black people to know with certainty. That would change. Malcolm had allowed me for the first time to have a glimpse into what racism feels like to a black man. What I was not ready to acknowledge was how the black **women** in his life were viewed as mostly irrelevant, voiceless, subservient. It's hardest to see what's wrong about what seems normal.

Those two books that I'd read within months of each other, **The Village of Ben Suc** and **The Autobiography of Malcolm X,** made me feel more uncertain than ever about lasting in Vadim's world. If someone like Malcolm could transform himself, so could I. I didn't want to die without making a difference. But still I could not see myself alone, without Vadim—not only because I was going to have a baby, but because I didn't feel I could survive on my own.

In July I was sent a script of **They Shoot Horses, Don't They?** It was based on a book of the same name by Horace McCoy. I was unfamiliar with the book, but Vadim had always loved it. The novel was a favorite among French leftists, who viewed it as the first true American existential novel. The script wasn't very good, but Vadim was adamant that I do it, saying it could be a very important movie. I accepted. It was to begin shooting three months after my September due date.

We returned to Paris at the end of August and

were invited to the American embassy to watch the
Democratic National Convention in Chicago nomi-
nate Hubert Humphrey for president. When it was
announced that Humphrey (who had not come out
in opposition to the war) had won the nomination,
Ambassador Sargent Shriver said, "They just put
Richard Nixon in the White House." Cutting away
from the vote proceedings, the television cameras
took us into the streets of Chicago, where thousands
of essentially peaceful protesters were being beaten
bloody and teargassed by Mayor Richard Daley's police; 668 people were arrested.

Little did I know that one of the leaders of the
protests, Tom Hayden, would one day be my husband.

I was due to give birth in a month. Wanting to
have a natural delivery, I had attended a number of
Lamaze classes in Paris but was unconvinced that the
rapid panting would succeed in alleviating the pain
of contractions, so I quit. In those days you couldn't
determine the child's sex beforehand, but I hoped it
would be a girl. I'd come up with a perfect girl name:
Vanessa. Vanessa Vadim. I liked the alliteration. I
also thought of the name because of my fascination
with Vanessa Redgrave—not just because she's a
transcendent actor, but because she is strong and
sure of herself and was the only actress I knew who
was a political activist, though I didn't know the par-
ticulars of her politics. I remember reading a magazine article about her that said she went to bed
studying Keynesian economic theory!

A room was reserved for me at a fashionable private clinic on the outskirts of Paris, where Catherine Deneuve had given birth to her son, Christian. I woke up at our farm at 5:00 on a morning close to my due date and thought I was dying. The pain was beyond anything I had imagined, and I assumed something was wrong: Where was the slow buildup, the water breaking, the slight contractions to signal it was time to go to the hospital? Vadim raced to the clinic with me writhing in agony and scared to death. We ran out of gas about a half mile before reaching the clinic, and Vadim had to carry me the rest of the way. By 6:00 A.M. I was on an operating table starting to efface, with a gas mask over my face. It felt like a rape. As I went under, I remember thinking that it wasn't supposed to be like this. Forceps were shoved up me, a man's voice came from far away, telling me to push, and then I was out. I was unconscious for my child's birth.

It was almost 8:00 A.M. when I came to, alone in the recovery room, groggy, hurting, wondering what had happened. I turned my head and saw a baby all wrapped up, lying in a bassinet alongside my bed. Was it my baby? Was it a boy or girl? I felt woozy and dozed back to sleep. Then the doctor came in and told me it was a girl. Vanessa. He was wearing riding jodhpurs (he'd been prepared to go fox-hunting when called to the hospital), and he showed me his finger, claiming I had bitten it hard during delivery. **Good!**

"Is the baby normal?"

"Yes," he assured me.

"Why did you give me gas?"

"Because you were in such pain," he answered defensively.

"But . . ." I wanted to tell him that he should have asked me first, and how much I had wanted to have a natural birth. It turns out that the hateful doctor in jodhpurs had really torn me up with the forceps, though later I was told by the nurses that forceps hadn't been necessary.

I asked to have the baby given to me, and for a long time I lay there looking at her. I felt exhausted, depressed, and angry. I was moved to a fancy room and nurses brought the baby to me when she was to be fed and then took her away somewhere. I asked if she could stay with me, and they told me no. Assuming the nurses knew better than I did, I never argued.

Vadim brought Nathalie to visit, but the nurses said they didn't allow children in the room because they "carried germs," so Nathalie had to stand outside with her little face pressed against my window peering in.

As it happened, September 28, Vanessa's birthday, was also Brigitte Bardot's birthday. Brigitte had predicted this would be the case and sent me a cabbage with a card that read, "In France, babies are delivered in cabbages, not by the stork." Some friends came to see me—and they're the ones who brought me germs, not Nathalie. I got sick and the nurses wouldn't let me breast-feed for a while, for fear I'd give whatever I had to Vanessa. I liked the feeling of milk coming into my breasts. I liked having breasts! I liked that, for a while, the first thing to go through a doorway wasn't my nose.

After several days I was able to get up. I wanted to lose the weight I'd gained in time for the upcoming film, so I started doing ballet pliés in the bathroom. But this caused me to hemorrhage, which meant I had to stay in the hospital for a week, seeing Vanessa only when they'd bring her to me to feed. **Stuck in a hospital. Sick, like my mother!** I was miserable. I did breast-feed a little, but the nurses were giving Vanessa supplements (without asking me), so it wasn't altogether successful—which made me feel I was already failing as a mother.

After a week Vadim came to take us home. There were paparazzi outside the clinic taking pictures, some of which I still have. I am looking down at the baby in my arms, and the uncertainty on my face reflects something that Adrienne Rich wrote in her book about motherhood, **Of Woman Born,** "Nothing could have prepared me for the realization that I **was** a mother . . . when I knew I was still in a state of uncreation myself."

A friend had recommended a cockney nanny named Dot Edwards, who had flown in from London and was waiting at the farm when we arrived. She took over the responsibilities of caring for Vanessa, just as nannies had cared for me and my brother. Wasn't it the way things were done? I went to bed and cried for a month (like my mother), not

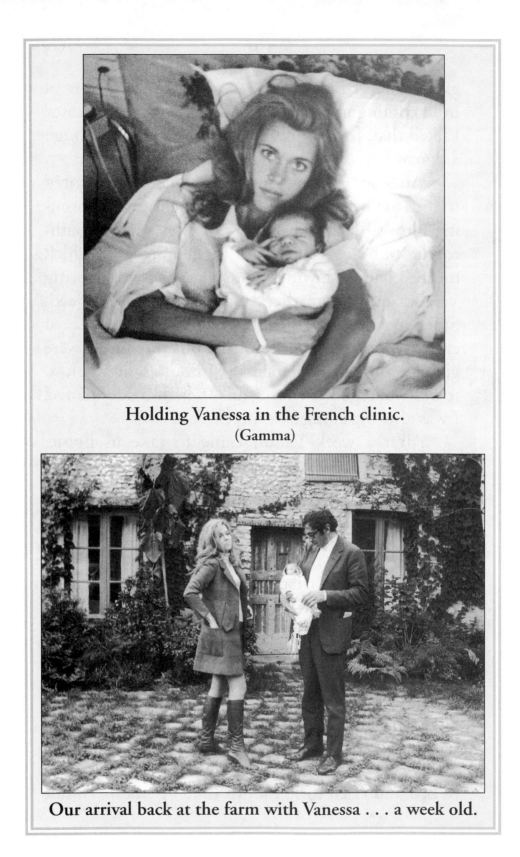

Holding Vanessa in the French clinic.
(Gamma)

Our arrival back at the farm with Vanessa . . . a week old.

knowing why. I felt that the floor had dropped out from under me. Vanessa knew it, I swear. She knew something was wrong and would cry whenever she was with me. Dot said it was colic, but I knew better.

In trying to understand my mother and how her state of mind at my birth might have affected me, I have learned a lot about postpartum depression: how, after the birth of a child, not just the body but the psyche is opened to the reliving of early, unresolved injuries; how these "memories" can penetrate to the deepest psychic fault line, causing profound grief. Perhaps after Vanessa's birth I was reexperiencing the sadness and aloneness I had felt as an infant. But, of course, nobody knew much of anything about PPD back then, so instead of seeing my depression as a not-so-unusual phenomenon (exacerbated by the horrid forceps), I just felt that I had failed—that nothing was turning out the way it was supposed to, not the birth, not the nursing, not my feelings for my child or (it seemed) hers for me. I don't know how women with PPD manage to cope when they can't afford the kind of help I had in Dot. I think this is partly why I would later find myself focusing on working with young, poor mothers and their children.

Unable to nurse successfully, I gave up and turned to Adelle Davis (the first mainstream health food proponent) for advice about what a baby should drink.

When Vanessa was three months old we went to Hollywood, where I began preparations for **They**

Shoot Horses, Don't They? I took my baby to a traditional pediatrician in Beverly Hills and told him that I was concerned because she was always throwing up.

"What formula are you giving her?" the doctor asked.

"Well, what Adelle Davis recommends," I answered. "Dessicated baby veal liver, cranberry juice concentrate, yeast, and goat's milk. Of course we have to make the holes in her bottle larger. . . ."

He was speechless for a moment, then he broke out laughing.

I switched to Similac formula, again feeling that I'd failed.

CHAPTER TWO

THEY SHOOT HORSES, DON'T THEY?

It is hard work to control the
workings of inclination and turn
the bent of nature; but that it may
be done, I know from experience.
God has given us, in a measure,
the power to make our own fate.
—CHARLOTTE BRONTË,
Jane Eyre

THE ORIGINAL WRITER/DIRECTOR OF
They Shoot Horses, Don't They? was fired
and replaced by a young director named Sydney
Pollack, who called to ask if he could come over
and discuss the script with me. I remember sitting

with Sydney at our house and his asking me what I thought the script problems were and would I read the original book carefully and then talk with him about what was missing in the adaptation. Wonderful Sydney had no idea what this meant to me. Naturally I had discussed script problems with Vadim on the movies we had made together, but this was different. This was a director who was actually **seeking** my input. It was a germinal moment. I began to study the book in ways I hadn't before—identifying moments that seemed essential not just to my character but to the movie as a whole, making sure everything I did contributed to the central theme. This was the first time in my life as an actor that I was working on a film about larger societal issues, and instead of my professional work feeling peripheral to life, it felt relevant.

They Shoot Horses was an existential story that used the marathon dances of the Depression era as a metaphor for the greed and manipulativeness of America's consumer society. The entire story took place in a ballroom on the Santa Monica Pier, a place that had been a part of my childhood, where marathon dances had actually been held. During the Depression contestants in the marathons, hoping to win prizes, would dance until they literally dropped from exhaustion, while crowds of people sitting on bleachers would cheer their favorite couples and thrill at the sight of dancers collapsing, hallucinating, going crazy—like spectators at the Roman Colosseum watching Christians being thrown to the lions.

From time to time there would be a race around the ballroom to wear the contestants down and speed up the eliminations. After several hours the dancers would get a ten-minute rest break, and then they'd go back out on the floor.

The ballroom had been re-created on a sound stage. Red Buttons would be my partner for several scenes. He and I decided to see what it felt like to dance on the set until we couldn't stand up, as we would in the movie. We were more or less fine for a day or so, then we got so tired we had to hold each other up as we shuffled around. Neither Red nor I could understand how people had gone on for weeks at a time. After two days I began hallucinating. My face was right up against Red's cheek, and when I opened my eyes I could see every pore of his skin; I realized that although he was a good deal older than me, his skin was remarkably young.

When we'd decided we'd had enough, that it was time to go home, I told him how impressed I was with his skin, and he told me it was due to a nutritionist, Dr. Walters, in the San Fernando Valley.

I promptly made an appointment to see the doctor, who gave me a thorough examination, which included taking samples of my hair and skin. A week or so later he put me on a complicated regimen of vitamin supplements, gave me a lot of little plastic jars to keep them in, and told me to mark each with "B," "L," and D," for breakfast, lunch, and dinner. (I tell you this because those little plastic jars will resurface and get me into a lot of trouble!)

**On the Ile de France in 1969. I'm wearing a wig, and
Dot is following just behind Vadim.**
(AFP/Getty Images)

As Gloria in They Shoot Horses, Don't They?
(Photofest)

Sydney Pollack directing **Horses**. Behind him, left to right: me, Red Buttons, and Susannah York in the lower-right-hand corner.

The film was a turning point for me, both professionally and personally. Sydney, having been an actor himself, is a wonderful actor's director, and with his guidance I probed deeper into the character and into myself than I had before, and I gained confidence as an actor.

But as I grew stronger I felt a parallel weakening of my marriage, a growing dissatisfaction, and less willingness to swallow the hurt that Vadim's drinking and gambling—not to mention the threesomes—caused me. But the idea of actually leaving him was still too hard to confront. I didn't want to be alone. I still felt that it was my relationship with him, however painful, that validated me. What will I be without him? I won't have any life. I had put so much into creating a life with him, fitting into **his** life, that I'd left myself behind. But who **was** "myself"? I wasn't sure. And now we had this little girl together, and there was Nathalie, and the home I'd created and all those trees I'd planted. In addition to everything else, a divorce felt like such an admission of—yes—failure. And I'd wanted so much to do better than my dad at marriage.

One day I was driving to the studio and, without noticing, ended up hours to the north, without knowing how I got there. I was having a mini breakdown, I think. Naturally I drew on my real-life anguish for all it was worth to feed my role as Gloria, the suicidal character in the movie who asks her dance partner to shoot her, the way they shoot horses with a broken leg.

I would spend days and nights living at the studio instead of going home to Malibu, partly because I wanted to enhance my identification with Gloria's hopelessness and partly because I just didn't want to go home to Vadim. I had a playpen set up in my dressing room and would have Dot bring Vanessa to me so I could feed her and sing to her. I knew only one lullaby from my own childhood, so I got a record of all the best lullabies and memorized them all. Then I would sing them one after the other to her (she sings them to her children now). In spite of my feelings of failure as a mother, giving birth—and to a **girl**—made me feel more connected to life and to femaleness in a way that was all my own, not a reflection of my husband. Even my body seemed to fall into a new, more graceful alignment.

One of the actors on the film was Al Lewis, who'd become famous as Grandpa in **The Munsters** on television. He would spend hours in my dressing room talking about social issues, and in particular about the Black Panther Party. Marlon Brando had taken up their cause and Al thought that I should, too. I remembered the conversations back in Baton Rouge, Louisiana, while filming **Hurry Sundown,** when I'd first learned about black militants. Al talked to me about the Panthers who'd been killed in Oakland, how others were being framed and put in jail with unreasonably high bail, and how Brando was helping to raise bail money and get lawyers.

I listened, storing things up. Making no moves. When the filming was over we went to New

Dad visiting us in Malibu during **Horses**. That's Dot
hovering in the background.
(Bob Willoughby/MPTV.net)

York, where I found my way to Vadim's hair stylist in the Village, Paul McGregor. There I had my first deep hair epiphany. Hair had ruled me for many years. Perhaps I used it to hide behind. The men in my life liked it long and blond, and I had been a blonde for so long that I didn't even know what my own color actually was. I simply said to Paul McGregor, "Do something," and he did. It was the haircut that became famous in **Klute,** the shag, and he dyed my hair darker, like what it really was. I didn't look as if I were trying to imitate Vadim's other wives any-more—I looked like me! I knew right away that I could do life differently with this hair.

Vadim sensed immediately that my cutting my hair was the first volley in my move for independence, though he did little more than grumble about it. It was during this time of making **They Shoot Horses** that director Alan Pakula sent me the script of **Klute** with a wonderful character named Bree Daniel. I immediately agreed to do it the following year.

My new haircut and I returned to France with Vadim and Vanessa. There I remained for the good part of a year, swinging with Vanessa in a hammock between two of the large trees I'd planted, trying to be a mother but not really knowing how. Parenting, I discovered, doesn't necessarily come naturally. I realized much later that I was parenting the way I'd been parented, taking care of all the externals but not countenancing the personhood of my baby. There is one especially powerful memory. It is late at night; I can't get Vanessa to sleep; I am despondent, again deep into the bulimia; I am lying on my back on the floor, with Vanessa lying on my chest. She lifts her head and looks straight into my eyes for what seems like an eternity. I feel she is looking into my soul, that she **knows** me, that she is my conscience. I get scared and have to look away. I don't want to be known.

I was at the country estate of my best girlfriend, Valarie Lalonde, when this happened. Part American, part British, ten years younger than me, Valarie was fun and smart and had a great giggle. She'd swing in the hammock with Vanessa and me and make Vadim mad because she was very pretty but liked me better than him. We have remained friends all these years, and recently I asked what her memories were of that time. Her first comment was that I was "upstairs a lot." Yes, of course I was—pretending to be sick so I could have time by myself. In addition, I was still actively bulimic, although no one knew. No one ever knew. It wasn't difficult to hide— especially since no one was really paying attention: I would simply leave the table, go upstairs, purge whatever I had eaten, and come back down again, all chipper and lively. Since the act of purging is somewhat orgasmic, the chipper part was easy. The difficulty would set in within twenty or thirty minutes, when a precipitous drop in blood sugar would flood me with fatigue and necessitate a physical and emotional withdrawal.

I watched how every minute of Vanessa's days seemed filled with discovery, as mine had been when

I was little. Time, the most valuable thing of all, where was it going? It was withering away, and I was becoming, not a grape of wrath—grapes are full and juicy. No, I was becoming a raisin of wrath, shriveled on the vine. I had to do **some**thing. So I did what I have always tended to do when confused and at a turning point: I go as far away from what's familiar as possible, in the belief that somehow the miraculous power of strange faces and foreign climes will reveal me to myself, force me to examine how much of my problem I brought with me and how much I can honestly blame on my current context.

A lot of people who seemed to be on a search for "inner truth" were going to India and coming back with what sounded like answers: Mia Farrow and the Beatles, for instance. So off I went with a small duffel bag to New Delhi.

I was shocked at what I encountered. Until then poverty was just a word to me. I had never before been to a third-world country. I soon realized that not everyone saw what I was seeing. When I told the young Americans I occasionally ran into how appalled I was by the poverty, they would say that I "just didn't understand India"; that I was bringing my bourgeois (there it was again) notions to a country where they weren't applicable; that I was missing the point if I thought the people were miserable; that their religion lifted them above "such things." Finally I met some Americans who were with the Peace Corps, digging wells, helping out. They understood my reaction—after all, that was why they were there, to help. I briefly considered joining them, but I was almost ten years older than them, and also I couldn't imagine bringing Vanessa to India while I worked with the Peace Corps.

Ultimately, in some ways my trip did "reveal me to myself." It taught me that I wasn't a hippie; that given a choice, I'd dig wells rather than go to an ashram or space out on dope. Hey, it's no secret that I've smoked pot. I've tried most everything that doesn't require piercing the skin. But except for alcohol, nothing has ever caught on with me. Basically I like life on the natch too much. Besides, it's not possible to **make things better** when you're spaced out.

I flew directly from New Delhi to Los Angeles, where I was scheduled to promote **They Shoot Horses, Don't They?** It was nighttime when I got to the room Vadim had reserved for us at the Beverly Wilshire Hotel. Talk about a rough transition!

I woke up in the morning with the cacophony of India still ringing in my ears, the odors of India still in my nose—and when I opened the curtains and looked out the window onto the quiet streets of Beverly Hills, I thought, My God, where is everybody? Has there been a plague? So clean. So empty. I had to struggle to remember that this was how it had always been, and it had seemed normal back then. But now I looked at the lavishness of the place with new eyes, and I was disturbed. How could we live this way when there were New Delhis in the world?

By now Vadim and I both knew that the woman

who showed up in that hotel room was no longer his wife. I had moved out psychically. And it was for good.

Marriages end in stages, and it has nothing to do with a piece of paper. Part of mine had ended years earlier, when we weren't even married yet, but I'd plowed along in deep denial. Denial can be a pathology or a survival mechanism—and sometimes it's both. I had felt I needed the structure of our marriage to keep me from . . . vaporizing. **I am with him, therefore I exist.** And the newness of our being together had still permitted passion and romance. Then there was the stage when I'd grown numb and abandoned my body—yet keeping up the routine was the only thing that seemed possible, since the alternative still had me falling down a dark hole. After six years I had begun to see a faint outline of a **me** without him. This had ushered in a feisty period, when I dipped my toes a few times into the uncertain waters of independence—cutting my hair, going to India, having a romance of my own. (In a rare fit of discretion I won't name him.) But by the time all this occurred, the marriage to Vadim was no longer emotionally viable, at least not for me. Vadim may have been able to continue with the status quo, but I couldn't. Yet I discovered that you have to watch out for extramarital romances. **You** are raw, and **he** is usually inappropriate. But the relationship can take on an unwarranted and intense place in your lonely heart simply because of its juxtaposition to your marriage. Fifteen years or so later, when Vadim gave me the manuscript of **Bardot, Deneuve, Fonda,** I was flabbergasted to find that he had portrayed himself as the faithful husband, cuckolded by **me** at the end of our marriage. I said, "Vadim, come on! How can you write that without saying what **you** had been doing all during our marriage! You're being hypocritical!" That did it. For Vadim, being called a hypocrite was almost as bad as being called bourgeois! He did some rewriting on his book, which acknowledged (barely) that he had regularly played around on me—but I was still made to look like the principal transgressor. I found this interesting, since Vadim never admitted to jealousy and would have sworn on his life that **he** didn't hold to a double standard.

Vanessa was only a year old when I told Vadim that I wasn't sure I could keep putting energy into trying to save what I suspected wasn't salvageable. A callus had formed around my heart, perhaps to protect me from feeling the pain of self-betrayal: betrayal of my own body (participating in threesomes in order to please him and show I wasn't a bourgeoise) and betrayal of my own heart (staying with him when I no longer respected him). But while my love for him had grown numb, new parts of me were waking and reaching for the light. Those were the instincts I wanted to follow.

In the winter of 1969, **They Shoot Horses, Don't They?** was released. Pauline Kael reviewed the film:

> **Jane Fonda . . . has been a charming, witty nudie cutie in recent years and now gets**

a chance at an archetypal character. . . .
Fonda goes all the way with it, as screen actresses rarely do once they become stars. . . .
Jane Fonda stands a good chance of person-
ifying American tensions and dominating
our movies in the seventies. . . .

This review of my professional work seemed to
be eerily emblematic of the changes that were rocking my personal life.

CHAPTER THREE

COMING HOME

It may be that the satisfaction I need
depends on my going away, so that when I've gone
and come back, I'll find it at home.
—RUMI,
"In Baghdad, Dreaming of Cairo:
In Cairo, Dreaming of Baghdad"

Though proportion is the final secret, to espouse it at
the outset is to ensure sterility.
—E. M. FORSTER,
Howards End

I T DIDN'T TAKE LONG for me to realize that
this was a new country, the America I'd come
home to, as different from the place I'd left as I was
from the me who used to live here.

Looking back, I see that it was more than America I was coming home to; I was coming **home.** It
wasn't a hotel or rented house I chose; I took Vanessa

and Dot and moved into the first-floor servants' quarters of my father's spacious Spanish colonial residence in Bel-Air. At the time I thought of it as a way to save money, but in retrospect I realize that it was more than that. I needed a safe haven, a place to regroup. Vadim's family—my ten-year-old stepdaughter, Nathalie; Vadim's mother; his sister, Hélène; his niece—they had been my family. Now, suddenly, I was alone but not emotionally anchored enough to be "out there," familyless. For a while, anyway, living in my father's home provided me with the roots I have always sought, a nest from which to fly and return. There I could figure out who I was now—post-Vadim.

Dad's way of relating to me, however, made this a little complicated. When I was married Dad treated me as a grown-up. Now that I was single again with no man to validate me, I became the little girl for whom he felt responsible and whom he seemed unable to respect or take seriously. In the months I was in his house we skirted each other politely, assessing the lay of each other's land, bumping up against each other on more than one occasion. Yet it was perfect. He provided a familiar landmark from which I could gauge how far I'd come from where I'd started.

In time I would discover a new "family" of people whose lives seemed to be motivated by the desire to create a better world. It would be a motley crew: black radicals, a former Green Beret, human-rights lawyers, soldiers, Native Americans. I wasn't always sure what they thought of me. But I wanted to learn from them and become someone who had my own narrative, my own direction.

They were, of course, all men.

Shirlee recently told me that Dad was happy when I became a mother. "Maybe now she'll see how hard it is to be a working parent," he'd told her during the time I was living with them. He hoped this would help me forgive him his parental shortcomings—which I have, many times over.

But it wasn't my being a "working parent" that caused me to be an inadequate mother. Had I been a stay-at-home mom, I might have been an even worse parent: I just didn't have it to give. I wasn't given it, I don't think my parents were, and I wasn't able to break that cycle of disconnect until later in my children's lives. What I **did** manage to do was marry men who were good fathers and provide surrogate adult support systems to fill in the gaps. Breaking the cycle requires that there be **someone**—the other parent, a grandmother, a loving nanny, a surrogate parent—who consistently gives unconditional love to the child. A child with even a modicum of this kind of loving will be better equipped to be a good parent to her or his own child and thus break the cycle. Today Vanessa is a remarkable parent to her two children. I attribute this to her father and to Catherine Schneider, the woman Vadim married after me. And as we went along, I learned some things that have made me a better mother and grandmother.

There is another way to break the pattern of parental disconnect, and that is to be taught **how** to parent. Relational skills are not static. They can be taught, especially during the super-receptive time when a woman is expecting; I know this because I have seen it happen. The gift of good parenting is something that the organization I founded in Georgia in 1995—the Georgia Campaign for Adolescent Pregnancy Prevention—teaches disadvantaged young mothers. I have seen how being a good mother is a transforming, empowering experience for a young woman—and how it gives her child a protective resiliency. **I'm proof that you teach what you need to learn.**

Having lived abroad for so many years, I had few close friends in California, and none with children Vanessa's age. I was lonely. Sometimes I would swim with her in my father's pool or I'd take her to the beach house that Vadim had rented and we'd play in the sand. When I was away (which would begin to happen more frequently as my activism increased), she and Dot would live at the beach with him. On weekends I would load Vanessa into my backpack and walk with Vadim along the ocean's edge. He was now seeing someone new, but we wanted to be friends and it wasn't difficult. I was happy to spend time with Vadim because he was almost always affable, and having him in my life gave me a sense of continuity.

But it wasn't only because the marriage was over

that I had come home. I was back because I felt compelled to join those who were working to end the war. En route to that joining, however, my attention was drawn to the recent Native American occupation of the island of Alcatraz, a former federal prison in San Francisco Bay no longer used by the government. The goal was to turn the island into an Indian cultural center and bring national media attention to the realities of Indian life: the high rates of unemployment, the low incomes, the high number of deaths from malnutrition and teen suicide; the short life expectancies.

I hadn't thought about Indians since my childhood days, when I incessantly played cowboys and Indians and asked God to give me an Indian brother. I decided I had some catching up to do and went straight to Alcatraz to find out what was going on. Altogether there must have been a hundred people from many different tribes on the island. Some were older, traditional Indians from reservations; some were student activists from the city. One student, La Nada Means Boyer, a twenty-two-year-old Bannock, became a friend and taught me much about what Native people were facing. She would visit me at Dad's house, where her two-year-old son, Daynon, played with Vanessa, and I brought her with me on a national talk show. I wanted more Americans to know what I was learning.

With the help of La Nada and other Indians I met along the way, I learned about the different strategies the federal government was using to rob

Vadim visiting Vanessa and me in my father's house. We had separated but were still good friends.
(© 1970 Julian Wasser)

Indians of the sovereign control that had been guaranteed them over the rich uranium, coal, oil, natural gas, timber, and other resources that lay beneath the ground within their fifty million acres of reservation. It was an important moment for me. Indians had leaped from the cobwebs of old myths and fantasies into a painful present that made me reexamine what my government was doing—much as the book **The Village of Ben Suc** had done two years earlier.

Alcatraz was also a watershed experience for Native people. There young Indians learned from indigenous leaders to value their traditional ways, to understand their lives in a historical context (which, I've subsequently discovered, is always a radicalizing experience for people who are oppressed). **It's not just me. It's the system.** A then young woman named Wilma Mankiller, for instance, described the Alcatraz experience as a personal turning point, saying that the leaders there "articulated principles and ideas I had pondered but could not express." Eventually this led her back to her people, the Cherokee, where in 1987 she was elected the first female principal chief in Cherokee history, serving three terms.*

One of the qualities that most attracts me to Native people is their attachment to the land. For them the earth is their mother, the sky their father. This has been kept alive in their collective memory through millennia by a tradition of oral history. Wilma Man-

---

*The Cherokee Nation is the largest tribal government in the U.S., with membership over 350,000.

killer told me that when a Navajo code talker from World War II was asked how he could help defend a country that had treated his people so badly, he answered, "It's the land. We are attached to this land."

Within weeks of my Alcatraz trip, I engaged in my first act of public protest. Several Indians I had met at Alcatraz asked me to come to Fort Lawton in Washington State, which they were planning to occupy. It too was closing, and it was being turned into a park, and inspired by Alcatraz, Indians wanted to make it into a cultural center. I felt I couldn't say no. I marched with 150 of them and was subsequently arrested, for the first time.

It was not a Vietnam War protest but my trips to Alcatraz and Fort Lawton that morphed me from a noun to a verb. A verb is active and less ego-oriented. Being a verb means being defined by action, not by title.

During these first few months in California, I also decided to act on my long-standing curiosity—piqued by Al Lewis on the set of **They Shoot Horses**—about the Black Panther party. I met some of the leadership, visited their free clinics and hot breakfast programs for children. (Little did I know that one day a girl who had benefited from the Panther program, the daughter of one of the party's Oakland members, would become a member of my family.) I tried to understand why the Panthers were an armed movement. I thought about how black children in the South had to be escorted to school by armed police. I remembered my father's childhood lynching story; the time we'd been shot at by white racists because I had been photographed kissing a little black boy. I remembered being told that black militancy had evolved out of the civil rights movement when attempts to end discrimination through nonviolent means seemed futile. I remembered John Kennedy's words: "Those who make peaceful revolution impossible will make violent revolution inevitable." We were reaping what we had sown.

While my natural inclination was to side with the underdog against the bullies, I couldn't espouse violence as a solution. Meeting state violence with citizen violence felt to me like a dead-end street, literally and figuratively.

My involvement with the Panther party appears in my FBI files as a major focus of the investigation they would soon launch of me, but in truth it was brief and consisted wholly of raising bail money. The party's FBI files, which I obtained under the Freedom of Information Act, would later show that many undercover agents infiltrated the party. I felt that if I was to be harassed or locked up, I wanted it to be for a group in which I was confident, not for the work of undercover agents. That said, the Panthers, like the American Indian Movement with Native people, helped many African-Americans see themselves within a political context rather than as individual victims. (It's not me, it's the system.)

I soon found myself plunged headfirst into what was about to become the focus of my antiwar ac-

tivism: the GI movement. I had met GI resisters in Paris, but I was unaware of the extent to which antiwar sentiment was growing among active-duty servicemen. I was planning a cross-country road trip when someone suggested I should visit GI coffeehouses along the way and meet antiwar soldiers. Coffeehouses, I was told, were off-base houses run by civilian activists where servicemen and -women could hang out and learn from visiting speakers about their rights as GIs and about the history of Vietnam.

I soon began meeting people who could give me a crash course in the military. Ken Cloke, a lawyer and history professor at Occidental College who specialized in military law, came to Dad's house with information about the Uniform Code of Military Justice. So did Master Sergeant Donald Duncan, a much decorated member of the special forces, the first enlisted man in Vietnam to be nominated for the Legion of Merit. Ken and Donald brought me newspaper articles about GI dissent and told stories about the ways servicemen were being denied their constitutional rights.

The U.S. Uniform Code of Military Justice, for instance, was created during the time of George Washington and today seems medieval: Your commanding officer can bring charges against you, appoint your military counsel, select the court-martial "jury," and even approve or disapprove of the verdict and sentence. A favorite saying in the GI movement back in the seventies was an old quote attributed to Clemenceau: "Military justice is to jus-

tice as military music is to music." Soldiers questioned why, once they put on a uniform, they were deprived of the rights they had been conscripted to defend—the rights to speak freely, petition, assemble, and publish—and that when they claimed those rights, unjust punishments were meted out with no legal recourse.

Attorney Mark Lane and his partner, Carolyn Mugar, were making a documentary about the GI movement, and from them I came to understand the class significance of the movement. While the civilian antiwar movement was primarily white and middle-class, the GI movement was made up of working-class kids, sons and daughters (ten thousand women were in the service at that time) of farmers and hard hats, kids who couldn't afford college deferments, and a preponderance of rural and urban poor, particularly blacks and Latinos.

I learned that while dissent within the military had started in the mid-sixties mainly as random, individual acts, after the Tet offensive, things began to change. Dissent was no longer a matter of individual acts. GIs began to organize, not just around the growing antiwar sentiment in the military ranks, but in response to the undemocratic nature of the military system itself.

The antiwar GIs represented a minority of our overall Vietnam-era troops. But there was a sizable enough minority of them by 1971 that the army reported an almost 400 percent increase in AWOLs in five years—enough that one military historian, re-

tired Marine Corps colonel Robert D. Heinl Jr., wrote in June in **Armed Forces Journal:**

> By every conceivable indicator, our army that now remains in Vietnam is in a state approaching collapse, with individual units avoiding or having refused combat, murdering their officers and non-commissioned officers, drug-ridden, and dispirited where not near-mutinous. . . .

We mustn't condemn the Vietnam-era soldiers for the things cited by Heinl. Clearly, when you ask soldiers to fight and perhaps die in a war they no longer believe in, you should expect terrible consequences. It would have been hard for the soldiers to believe in a war that by 1970 even moderate American papers and magazines like **The Wall Street Journal** and **The Saturday Evening Post** deemed a folly. When Walter Cronkite began urging a withdrawal, President Johnson said to his press secretary, "If I've lost Walter, I've lost Middle America." The GIs and their families **were** Middle America.

My first visit to a GI coffeehouse was near Fort Ord, a massive infantry training base in Monterey, California. I hadn't known what to expect or what was expected of me. I wondered if my recent Oscar nomination as Best Actress in **They Shoot Horses, Don't They?** would turn my visit into a circus, with GIs wanting my autograph and nothing more. As it turned out, the atmosphere was friendly but somber—no requests for autographs or pictures. They had more important things on their minds. We all sat on the floor, and some of the guys began to tell me about life in the military and their feelings about the war. Those who had seen combat in Vietnam were the quietest. I mostly listened. When I was getting ready to leave, a young man, twenty years old at the most and looking more like fifteen, came up to me wanting to say something but having trouble. I waited, leaning slightly in to him.

"Ahhh . . . I . . . kk . . . ahhh." I had to put my ear up against his mouth to hear him. He was shivering and there was sweat on his forehead.

"I . . . I . . . ah . . . I killed . . . ah . . ."

"It's okay, you can tell me," I said, putting my hand on his arm.

"I . . . k-killed a young . . . b . . . ," he whispered, and began to cry silently. Up to that moment I had thought only about what we were doing to the Vietnamese. Now, from his suffering, I glimpsed that the war had become an American tragedy as well. **What are we doing to our young men?**

P**oor Dad. He watched all of my comings and goings with increasing agitation. I wished I could discuss with him all the things I was learning and the questions I had, but the several times I did he'd explode in generalities about why I shouldn't have anything to do with these people. Maybe I should have asked him to talk to me in the character of Clarence Darrow or Tom Joad.

One day, for instance, we got into a heated argument about Angela Davis, the young black professor at the University of California at Los Angeles, who was a member of the American Communist Party. I said I didn't think she should have been fired from her teaching job at UCLA because she was a Communist, and he vehemently disagreed. Then he pointed his finger at me and said, "If I ever find out you're a Communist, Jane, I'll be the first person to turn you in."

"But Dad, I am **not** a Communist!" I shouted as I ran from him into my room and into my bed, the non-Communist Lone Ranger, pulling the sheets up over my head, desperate to blot out what his words implied. **He would turn me in? His own child?** I knew he had vivid memories of the days of HUAC and how Joseph McCarthy had ruined the lives and careers of people he knew. I knew he was afraid for me. But what about Tom Joad and Clarence Darrow and Abe Lincoln? I couldn't reconcile the father I thought I knew with the more conservative person I now saw him to be.

I can only imagine the confusion and anguish the changes I was going through must have caused my father, and now I am filled with love for his gruff attempts to remain connected to me, however tenuously. In time I could forgive him for not possessing the more radical courage I wanted him to have. Choosing what characters to play can reveal an **aspiration** on the part of an actor, not necessarily the actor's reality.

The march with Native
Americans at Fort
Lawton near Tacoma,
Washington. Janet
McCloud is next to
me. I was about to be
arrested for the first
time.
(Richard Heyza/Seattle
Times)

Me in the midst of a
welfare-rights march in
Las Vegas in 1970.
(Bill Ray/Time & Life
Pictures/Getty Images)

AN ASIDE

The activism upon which I embarked in 1970 changed me forever in terms of how I saw the world and my place in it. These changes remain to this day at the core of my being, though the way I express them has grown—fortunately, because in those first years back home there was hardly a mistake I **didn't** make when it came to public utterances.

I had heard and read things that threw into question everything I believed about my country. But what to do? I didn't know, but I felt I couldn't slow down while people's rights were being violated, while people were being killed, while the war continued. Everything (including my career) had to be put on hold till this was stopped.

Instead of reflection, what I did was talk—all the time, everywhere, on and on and on in a frantic voice tinged with the Ivy League. Press conferences became an almost biweekly occurrence. When I look back over that period I realize that I was not ready for so much antagonistic public exposure. I was angry enough going in because of all that I was learning, and when, increasingly, I felt reporters were coming after me and questioning my motives, I became even more defensive. In interviews I was humorless, talking too fast, in a voice that came from some elitist, out-in-space place, anger seething just beneath the surface. This was when I began to use radical jargon that rang shrill and false. **You try to prove what**

you're not sure of. I made it easy for the media and others to choose a dubious if not downright hostile lens through which to view me. There I was, up on my soapbox, pronouncing myself a "revolutionary woman," while **Barbarella** had just played in a theater around the corner.

In hindsight I should have listened more, talked less, taken it slower. I wish I had taken Vanessa with me on my cross-country travels. It would have been better for her, for me, for us. Shoulda, woulda, coulda. It makes me wince to think about it now.

Watching some taped interviews years later with my son, Troy (to whom I turn when I need support), I wanted to shout, "Will someone please tell her to shut up?" Troy, always a wise and generous soul, said, "Mom, listen, Taoist sages, when they were learning something new, would isolate themselves for a long time, until they had attained enlightenment and could teach. But you"—he shook his head and laughed—"you were out there in public before you had really made those issues your own. Your voice wasn't even your own. You weren't a complete person yet. You weren't **you.**"

The following is an explanation, and an explanation isn't an excuse. I have spent a lot of time trying to understand why I did what I did the **way** I did.

Partly it's the way I am. My instincts are good, but I am not by nature someone who goes slow. I get the picture quickly, and if something comes into my life and touches me and makes sense to me, I plunge in **jusqu'au bout,** right to the end. My life has been a series of gigantic leaps of faith, based almost always on intuition and emotion, not on calculation or ego—or ideology. As British playwright David Hare has said of himself, "I'm where I want to be before I can be bothered to go through the dreary business of getting there."

Then, too, it was the nature of the times. I returned to an America at war with itself in a manner and on a level I had not suspected. There was a visceral sense that everything was ready to blow up, that there could actually be a revolution. Having been in Paris the year before, I knew that it was not inconceivable that students, blacks, workers, and others who felt disenfranchised could bring down their government. What that would mean I hadn't a clue. That such a thing would (as ultimately it had in France) cause a backlash that might very well end in an even more oppressive state didn't occur to me. Certainly no one I knew was articulating any clear, more democratic alternative to what we had in the United States.

I wanted to be taken seriously, and I mistakenly thought that the more militant I appeared, the more seriously I'd be taken. I realized only later that my value was in being just who I was—a newcomer on a fast track seeing a lot of things that were rocking the foundations of my belief system; trying to put it all together; and most important, being a movie star whom servicemen and -women were eager to meet and talk to and from whom I was hearing truth I thought other Americans needed to hear.

What I wanted to be was better—and to **make it better.** I didn't think enough about how I was being perceived. I was too immersed in what I was learning, in trying to understand, and in day-to-day dramas. I would have gotten into a lot less trouble if I had been more self-conscious, more aware of my image, more concerned about how what I said or did might be interpreted or might affect my career. For better or worse, I still don't. It wasn't until **On Golden Pond,** when I got to know Katharine Hepburn, someone quintessentially conscious of her image, that I was forced to think about the extent to which I have **ignored** mine.

I wanted to be a repeater, like one of those tall radio transmitters at the tops of mountains that pick up signals too faint in the valleys and transmit them to a broader audience. In retrospect, and having survived to write about it, I don't regret having plunged in. Had I been more cautious, I might have become just another concerned observer. A character in E. M. Forster's **Howards End** says that the truth can be found only by exploring the extremes, and "though proportion is the final secret, to espouse it at the outset is to ensure sterility."

A persistent assumption about me is that I am a puppet, ready for a new man to pull my strings. There was some truth to this. Until age sixty I never had enough self-confidence to feel validated unless I was with a man, and the men I was with embodied something I felt would make me better than I thought I was. While each relationship did bring me new depth, I invariably ended up feeling: "Something's missing. This doesn't feel right anymore." I would then spend time on my own (though never more than a few years) and begin to identify what it was that was missing—and invariably an extraordinary man would come into my life who seemed to be the One who could help me get there. A puppet has no life without its puppeteer. A Svengali takes his Trilby and molds her into something **he** wants or needs, regardless of **her** potential. In my case, when I got into a committed relationship, I was always partway to where I was headed and my partner would help guide me further along on the journey. For me, this realization has been very important. It has shown me that I have always been, at the very least, the **co**-captain of my ship.

This aside is an attempt to address some of the controversial things said about me **personally.** I'll have more to say later on the subject of the **political** controversy that has surrounded me. If you haven't already, fasten your seat belts. It's going to be a bumpy ride.

CHAPTER FOUR

SNAPSHOTS FROM THE ROAD

There's something happening here
What it is ain't exactly clear
There's a man with a gun over there
Telling me I got to beware

I think it's time we stop, children, what's that sound
Everybody look what's going down
—STEPHEN STILLS,
"For What It's Worth," 1966

IN APRIL 1970, I went out to explore America. So much was new. This would mark the start of my needing to experience things firsthand. I can read and study, but to really "get it" I need to sit in people's homes, see their faces, hear their stories directly, find out what their lives are like. I wanted to put real faces to the troubling facts that I'd been hearing during my three first months back in the States—Native American faces, African-American faces, faces of men in uniform, Middle-American faces. Having lived exclusively on the coasts, what lay between was missing for me—a sandwich with no filling. Living in France had made me feel very American. Now I wanted to know what that meant—not just at the fancy edges but at the center, just as I was seeking my **own** center.

Film director Alan Pakula once said about me, "There seems in her some vast emotional need to find the center of life. Jane is the kind of lady who might have gone across the prairie in a covered wagon one hundred years ago." Instead I would rent a car and, like a pioneer in reverse, drive east across America.

I set out with Elisabeth Vailland, a friend from France, in a rented station wagon filled to the brim with sleeping bags, cameras, books, my guitar (David Crosby had been giving me lessons), and a cooler for my odd assortment of foods. I was in the anorexic phase of my food addiction, allowing myself only soft-boiled eggs, raw corn on the cob, and spinach. I was anxious that for two months I would not be taking my daily ballet classes—the longest danceless stretch since I was twenty. To compensate, I felt I had to exert rigid control over what I put in my stomach so as not to put on weight.

Almost from the get-go we were swept up in the

tumultuous events of 1970—the invasion of Cambodia, the killing of students at Kent State University in Ohio and Jackson State University in Mississippi, and a series of campus uprisings. Certain events from our trip stand out clearly for me, and like snapshots from the road, I will show them to you. But a lot was a blur of drama, danger, and stress. Fortunately both Elisabeth and I kept journals. Less fortunately there are tens of thousands of pages of FBI files on me, which were apparently begun within weeks of my starting the trip (I later obtained these files via the Freedom of Information Act, which was passed post-Watergate).

Elisabeth was handsome in a Georgia O'Keeffe way. In the press she would be described variously as my hairdresser, my public relations manager, and a Russian dancer. Not unexpectedly, there were hints that we were lovers. We weren't.

Elisabeth and her by then deceased husband, French novelist Roger Vailland, had shared Vadim's penchant for whiskey and ménages à trois, and Vadim hoped that my respect for their intelligence would validate his own sexual proclivities. In **Bardot, Deneuve, Fonda,** Vadim wrote about Roger Vailland: "He rejected, with equal rigor, Judeo-Christian puritanism and communist hypocrisy when it came to sex and man's right to pleasure"—**man's** being the operative word. The moral premise that Roger Vailland and Roger Vadim shared was that there could be no true love unless it was free from sexual jealousy and emotional possessiveness. Elisabeth not only was in agreement, but often introduced Roger to women she thought would please him. I had once asked Roger if he would be jealous if Elisabeth slept with another man. "That is absolutely forbidden!" he replied.

"Why?" I asked, stunned.

"Because she would stop loving me."

"That's right," added Elisabeth. "I wouldn't respect him anymore if he let me come in the arms of another man."

"That sounds more like hypocrisy than freedom to me," I said.

"But freedom is not always a mathematical equation," she answered in that way European intellectuals have, which always made me feel there was something I wasn't getting. Now I hoped that during our trip I would find out how Elisabeth really felt about her late husband's libertine ways, and I was prepared to be honest about my own experiences. She was the only person I felt I could discuss the subject with. In fact, I never did get clarity from Elisabeth on this subject, although I decided to broach it as we were driving through Yosemite National Park.

"Did you really not mind that Roger had other women?" I asked her. "Did you really enjoy bringing him other women?" Essentially she stuck to what she'd told me before, claiming that sexually and intellectually it pleased her to please him in that way:

"I knew he loved me and I knew that these other women didn't mean the same to him as I did."

"I guess I wasn't confident enough not to feel diminished by Vadim's philanderings. I never dared to tell him I wanted him to be monogamous, because I was afraid of being thought bourgeois. I thought that maybe if I were a participant, it wouldn't go on behind my back."

"Did you enjoy being with women?" she asks.

"I don't know. I thought I did at the time because I'm so good at becoming whatever my man wants me to be. I can convince myself of practically anything in the name of pleasing. But now that we're not together anymore, I have been trying to probe what was really going on in my body. In some ways I think I did enjoy it. I liked having an up-close view of the varied ways women express passion. But to go through with it, I'd always have to drink enough to be in an altered state. I always felt scared and competitive—not the best frame of mind to be in when you're having sex. And I always felt angry afterward, never at the women . . . at Vadim. I usually became chums with the women. It was the only way I could feel human under the circumstances, which made me feel used, not good enough, trampled over for **his** pleasure.

"What about you?" I asked Elisabeth. "Did you enjoy it?"

Elisabeth appeared to answer my question without really answering it. (At the end of that two-month trip, I still didn't know where she stood on

Vanessa, the plucky sprite, in front of Dad's house just as I was leaving for my first cross-country trip with Elisabeth.

1971.
On a quest for meaning.
(Billy Ray/Time & Life Pictures/Getty Images)

the subject of enjoyment.) I remember wishing I could be more . . . European, more opaque, like her. I suppose that's why Vadim used to say I lacked mystery.

The fact that I participated in threesomes with Vadim was one symptom of my disembodiment, my loss of voice. It's not as if he forced me to do it. Had I refused, he would have accepted that. I later discovered that his future wives didn't do it. I have written about it because I know that it is not uncommon for girls to accept another woman into their beds to keep a man.

Back to the trip. I loved not having a set itinerary. We would stop whenever we chose and always shared the cheapest motels we could find ($8 a night on average for a shared room), since I had borrowed money from my business manager to pay for the trip. My inheritance was long gone thanks to Vadim's gambling, and my film salary had been spent on the French farmhouse, which was now for sale.

No one recognized me. I didn't look the way I was supposed to anymore. Three months earlier I still wore the ultrashort miniskirts, revealing blouses, and makeup that had been my costume during my years with Vadim—all designed to attract men's attention.

It hadn't taken long for me to see that my appearance made it easier for people to objectify me and created a schism with other women. So I decided I wouldn't dress for men anymore. I would dress so that women weren't uncomfortable around me. My wardrobe was pared down to a few pairs of jeans, some drip-dry shirts, army boots, and a heavy navy pea jacket. I had stopped wearing makeup. I was often surprised by the **anger** this elicited from people—men, mostly—who I think saw it as a betrayal. Soon articles about "just plain Jane" began appearing, with William Buckley writing, "She must never look into the mirror anymore." That's right—I'd looked into the mirror altogether too much during my life.

One day I called a friend in New York, who told me that five thousand women in the city were demonstrating for the legalization of abortion. I wrote in my journal,

> **Don't understand the women's liberation movement. There are more important things to have a movement for, it seems to me. To focus on women's issues is diversionary when so much wrong is being done in the world. Each woman should take it upon herself to be liberated and show a man what that means.**

> **Did I write that?** Whew! I have included it here because I think it's important to see how far a person

can evolve. I've made it abundantly clear that I had not taken it upon myself to "be liberated" and show Vadim "what that meant." I didn't know yet that when part of the population is viewed as "less than"—culturally, economically, historically, politically, psychologically—it cannot be changed individual by individual. It takes the accumulated efforts of many, working in concert, for systemic change.

Long **after** I started identifying myself as a feminist, I still would not be brave enough to look within myself and identify the subtle ways in which I had internalized sexism—my willingness to forgo emotional intimacy with a man and betray my own body and soul **if** being honest and speaking my voice meant losing him. Put another way, I was the only person I could treat badly and consider that morally defensible.

We visited the Paiute Indian reservation, about forty-five minutes outside Reno, Nevada, to join a small protest against the U.S. Bureau of Reclamation. With permission of the U.S. Bureau of Indian Affairs (BIA), the Bureau of Reclamation was diverting water from the Truckee River and Pyramid Lake, on the reservation, to irrigate farmlands owned by white farmers. On the western rim of the lake were about twenty Indians. Some had brought little vials of water to symbolically pour into the lake.

My appearance at this mild protest was the first

item to appear in my FBI files. Their informant reported it this way:

> **The group with Fonda totaled about 200 people of which 40 were in Fonda's personal entourage. Her group of 40 dumped 20 Gallon jugs of water, brought from California, into Pyramid Lake. It was very peaceful, and no incidents occurred.**

. . . Lest we confuse intelligence with "intelligence."

While we sat waiting to order in the only restaurant on the reservation, several Indian men came in and invited us to sit at their table. One of them, a beefy guy with dark glasses, kept saying we should get some bombs and blow up the dam the white farmers had built—it was damaging the lake. My antenna went up immediately: **an agent provocateur.** The Panthers had warned me about this. We left immediately.

At the Shoshone reservation in Fort Hall, Idaho, we met up with La Nada, the Native woman I'd met at Alcatraz, and were taken to meet her family—my first time in a Native American home. Her father told us of his persistent suits against the government on behalf of the Shoshone Nation—to stop the stealing of their lands and water. He pulled out several worn cardboard shoeboxes and, with great reverence, showed us documents and letters that proved the tribal claims. He handled the papers as if they were sacred, never raising his voice or appearing angry as he told story after story of defeat and betrayal. Like all Native Americans, the family descended from a people for whom oral history had once sufficed. Experience had taught them that the white man wants proof in writing. So they'd saved the papers that carry their proof. Still no one had paid attention.

As we left Idaho I noted in my journal that indigenous people in the United States seemed to have all the characteristics of a colonized people: no power, no independence, no control over their own natural resources, and a carefully inflicted and fostered tendency to feel that it must be their own fault.

Years later I learned from my FBI files that a white woman who had met us on the Shoshone reservation was an FBI informant. She reported to the agency that Elisabeth and I had come there to "organize and indoctrinate" the local Indians. Wonder if the agency paid her? Wonder if American taxpayers would think it was money well spent, an informant watching us sit at the feet of an elderly gentleman holding shoe boxes? I remembered her because she had been disappointed that I didn't look like a movie star. She even admitted that she wanted to shout out to everyone that I was Jane Fonda and was angry that I didn't fulfill her fantasies.

I went back to California briefly and walked down the red carpet on Vadim's arm at the Academy

Awards. I had barely thought about my nomination for Best Actress (for my role in **They Shoot Horses, Don't They?**). Many friends had told me they thought I would win, but my instincts said that would not be the case, and I was right. The remarkable Maggie Smith won for her performance in **The Prime of Miss Jean Brodie.** I had attended the Oscars many times during the ten years of my career and had often been a presenter, but that night felt different—not just because I was a nominee, but because my life outside of movies was starting to interest me more than being an actor.

My first public act against the war was at a two-day fast in United Nations Square in the center of downtown Denver—one of many events planned by MOBE (Mobilization to End the War). Over one thousand people were there—all ages, including Vietnam veterans and Native Americans. It seemed to boost people's spirits to have a celebrity among them, and though it was cold and rainy, people stayed huddled together, joined in their commitment. On the final day of the fast, a group of hard hats working on a construction site opposite the square flashed us peace signs as they left work. Hard hats had been stereotyped as pro-war conservatives, just as antiwar activists had been branded as unpatriotic. I was glad to see the stereotypes were unfounded.

At the Home Front, a GI coffeehouse near Fort Carson in Colorado Springs, there were about thirty GIs and staff waiting, including a lawyer who had gotten the base commander to agree to meet with us to discuss a recent situation: A hundred soldiers had lined up in front of the medical dispensary flashing peace signs and saying they were sick—sick of the war. As a result, all of them had been put into the stockade, and it was rumored that they were being beaten. Given the potential media exposure that could result, it was hoped that my meeting the base commander would lead to the release of the soldier-protesters.

Surprisingly, the general took us on a tour of the stockade and let us talk to prisoners. If he hoped by this to show us that the GIs were being well treated, it backfired. We saw prisoners who seemed catatonic. One appeared to be schizophrenic. Some, who identified themselves as Black Panthers, said they had been beaten, and it appeared to be so. Perhaps the general had never been inside the stockade himself; perhaps he misjudged the effect it would have on me. In any case, the visit was abruptly called to an end and we were ushered out before I was able to determine which prisoners were the protesters.

Elisabeth pondered this paradox of our democracy: Men are punished for protesting the war, yet we are allowed to visit the stockade.

I received word that a psychiatrist from a nearby
military academy wanted to meet privately with me.
I was taken to a motel where the young doctor talked
to me about the training new recruits were being
made to undergo, training he said was horrifying,
turning the young men into "mechanical robots, de-
void of humanity, ready to kill anything."

I had brought dozens of books to give to GIs I met
along the way. They included copies of **The Village
of Ben Suc,** the abridged version of Bertrand Russell's **Against the Crime of Silence: Proceedings of
the International War Crimes Tribunal,** Robert
Sherrill's **Military Justice Is to Justice as Military
Music Is to Music,** and a collection of GI-movement
newspapers. Permission for me to reenter the base
had been denied following the visit to the stockade,
but several soldiers from the base offered to sneak us
on. They wanted me to see an on-base coffeehouse
that the brass had created, complete with girlie
shows, to keep the men from coming to the GI
movement coffeehouse.

We were smuggled onto the base in the trunk of
a soldier's car and managed to get to the on-base coffeehouse. It was a rather antiseptic room with a few
pinup posters and a small stage, where we quickly
distributed the books to the few soldiers who were
there (no time to try to get to the stockade). I told
them about the Home Front and why I had brought

the books. But no sooner had I finished than several MPs arrived and escorted us off the base. Later some soldiers told me that the general didn't make more of a stink about it because he didn't want any media attention, since it was active-duty servicemen who had smuggled us in. I realized that the higher-ups feared word getting out as to the breadth and depth of soldiers' antiwar feelings.

Later I learned that it was during my time in Denver that the FBI began its serious investigation of me—not just getting information from informants, but attempting to get me charged with sedition—which punishes anyone who "advises, counsels, urges, or in any manner causes or attempts to cause, insubordination, disloyalty, mutiny, or refusal of duty by any member of the military or naval forces of the United States." The FBI cannot investigate someone unless a criminal law has been violated, which was why the agency, soon joined by the United States Army, Secret Service, and National Security Agency, decided to cite sedition—and then set out to try to prove it. In this effort, the FBI questioned nine people who had been present at the time I was on base at Fort Carson.

The answers the FBI received were fairly similar to what they heard from other informants over the three years they pursued their investigation. The agent reported being told that I explicitly stated that deserting will not "help the cause for peace"; that nothing I said "could be construed to be undermining the U.S. government." Another informant said that I "did more listening than talking."

I began to be aware that I was followed constantly and took care not to drive over the speed limit. Nonetheless we were stopped numerous times on one pretext or another, and I had to show my driver's license and registration. I saw it as a form of harassment and realized that for the first time I had stepped across the line that allows upper-class white people, especially celebrities, never to have to experience what other people, especially people of color, face all the time—only far worse. There was a tightening in my stomach; I never knew what would happen next. I was aware of the possibility that I might be set up, but I also felt a deepening resolve to not turn back.

They're not going to scare me. I'm still the Lone Ranger, and my car is my horse.

One morning I stepped outside our motel room and there, stretching before me to the horizon, was Monument Valley—red, huge, humbling in its vastness. The monoliths towering up from the flat, timeless valley floor seemed divinely placed, like the vaulted domes of great cathedrals that carry our eyes and our hearts heavenward, a reminder of man's insignificance. I was dumbstruck. My heart filled with

Listening to soldiers at a GI coffeehouse.

Meeting with students during the road trip.
(Bill Ray/Time & Life Pictures/Getty Images)

love for this country, which I was getting to know. Right then I vowed to commit myself to ensuring that America's moral fiber remained as strong as its beauty.

As Elisabeth and I headed into Santa Fe, we heard on the radio the news that the United States had invaded Cambodia. Suddenly we shifted into emergency mode.

The motel we had checked into must have called the newspapers to say I was there, because several reporters showed up to get my reaction to the invasion. I was shaking with fury: Here was Nixon, elected by promising he would end the war, expanding it into another country! The American public did not yet know that the United States had been secretly bombing Cambodia since March 1969. Nor did we know that U.S. bombers, from 1964 through 1969, had secretly obliterated an entire civilization in the Plain of Jars in northeastern Laos. I would meet countless young people in years to come who cited the events of those days in May 1970 as their wake-up call to activism.

Before the United States bombed Cambodia, it was possible to view the war as President Johnson's "mistake" that President Nixon had inherited. After Cambodia we had to face the fact that the war was no president's mistake. Nixon was expanding the war under the pretext of ending it, despite the fact that by then at least half the Senate and most of the

American public viewed it as wrong! These were not actions a president made by mistake. It would be decades before I could see this as the curse of patriarchy—the fear of premature evacuation, of being called "soft."

A student leader at the University of New Mexico in Albuquerque invited me to speak on campus. He said the school had been apathetic about the war and he hoped my speech would get something going. I had never made a speech about the war before, and though I was nervous, I agreed. I called Donald Duncan to seek his advice. Donald had actually gone into Cambodia as a Green Beret and knew a great deal about the situation. I took careful notes and wrote out a serious, detailed speech.

The university auditorium was packed to overflowing, although we had not expected many people, given what the student leader had told us about campus apathy. People were hanging off the balcony and spilling into the corridors. I felt quite important and delivered my prepared, rather scholarly speech to an attentive but quiet audience.

When I finished, a drunken poet stumbled onto the stage demanding to know why I hadn't mentioned the four students who had just been killed by National Guardsmen at Kent State University. Oh my God! I hadn't heard the news. No **wonder** so many people had come to the auditorium! It had nothing to do with me. I was shocked by the news and felt like a fool. We were swept up in a mass of bodies marching toward the university president's home to demand he shut down the university as a way to mourn the Kent State deaths.

The rest of the trip was a blur of speeches, press conferences, and arrests—at Fort Hood, Fort Bragg, Fort Meade—for passing out antiwar leaflets. A few incidents stand out. At the Los Angeles press conference with Donald Duncan announcing plans for a GI movement demonstration on May 16, Armed Forces Day—the GIs were calling theirs Armed **Farces** Day—one reporter shouted, "Miss Fonda, why were you at the University of Albuquerque inciting the students to riot?" I should have said that he was giving me too much credit, and didn't he think the killing of the Kent State students might have caused the rioting? Instead, I got angry and defensive.

Donald wanted to open a GI office in Washington to act as ombudsman for soldiers—a place where GIs could call or write about what was happening to them, where acts of military injustice could be documented, and where doctors and lawyers could verify their claims and get information about it to the House and Senate for investigation. We decided on the spot that Donald would move to D.C. to head up the office and that I would raise money to fund it.

I had seen turmoil in Paris in 1968, but now in the United States it was happening nationwide. In May, 35,000 National Guardsmen were called out in sixteen states. Over a hundred demonstrators were wounded or killed. A third of the nation's colleges closed down. In early May, students were shot and killed by National Guardsmen at Kent State University. On May 14, police shot into a dormitory at Jackson State University, wounding twelve students and killing two. More than five hundred GIs were deserting every day.

I was refused rooms in two Albuquerque motels because my criticism of Nixon's invasion of Cambodia had appeared in the papers.

I met Terry Davis, an attractive brown-haired woman who was on the staff of another GI coffeehouse, the Oleo Strut, in Killeen, Texas, near Fort Hood. It was my first time experiencing a woman's leadership. This was so powerful for me that, when I think back over my 1970 trip, my time with Terry stands out above all else. Terry treated me not like a movie star but as a peer. She was interested in why I had become an activist and how I had gotten involved in the GI movement. She asked my opinion, included me in all decisions, and made sure I was comfortable. I saw this same sensitivity and compassion in the way she dealt with the GIs. With her, there was no hierarchy, only circle—everyone was valued, heard. It was a harbinger of the new world, a world of authenticity. This was the first time I had met an organizer who deeply embodied her politics, working toward true democracy in her own relationships.

It was at the Strut coffeehouse that I heard, for the first time, a speech about the women's movement. Terry had invited a feminist to speak to the GIs. I was impressed. Up until then I had been confused by women who identified themselves to me as feminists. Mostly, these women asked questions like "How did you feel doing **Barbarella?** Did you feel that you were being exploited?" I could tell that I was supposed to feel exploited, but secretly I thought: **No one forced me to make the film. I didn't enjoy it very much for lots of reasons, but I didn't feel exploited.** (Now I think that with a little tweaking, **Barbarella** could have been a feminist movie—and just as sexy.) The speaker that night, however, said that if there **were** true equality between women and men, it would be good for both sexes: men wouldn't feel that they alone have to carry the burden that has been placed on them by the patriarchal system. "It's not a matter of women taking a piece of your pie," she said to the gathered, attentive men, "it's about us sharing the pie and making it bigger."

My experience at the GI coffeehouse was what caused me to begin calling myself a feminist publicly—though it would be many more years before I had a true understanding of what the word and the politics really meant. It was much easier for me to organize on behalf of others—Vietnam veterans, Indians, blacks, and GIs—than it was to look at issues of gender. That would be hardest to face, because it meant questioning the foundation on which **my** identity as a woman had been built: Women are meant to please. They can rock all the boats there are **out there,** but they must do what's necessary to keep the man happy at home.

At the Oleo Strut, Elisabeth and I shared a queen-size mattress on the floor with just a quilt to cover us. This was new for me but, as I would learn, a common mode of sleeping among movement activists— one I would soon adopt out of financial necessity. For the first time I also saw wooden cable spools turned on end and serving as tables.

In Washington, D.C., at my first national antiwar rally, there were about one hundred thousand people. I saw white people chanting "Free Bobby Seale!" and many Vietnam veterans in uniform with peace signs on their caps. There were speakers representing all aspects of the antiwar movement. A black man named Al Hubbard spoke eloquently on behalf of Vietnam Veterans Against the War (VVAW). Shirley MacLaine was there, the only other Hollywood person I saw, and she was clearly far more experienced at public speaking than I was.

Being up there at the microphone before a sea of

upturned faces, hearing your voice echoing back at you when you're already on the next sentence—this took getting used to. My assignment was to talk about the GI movement and why the antiwar movement shouldn't view men in uniform as the enemy. I remember pointing to some uniformed men around the periphery of the crowd and saying, "Those men may very well have seen combat in Vietnam. They know better than any of us what this war is like. Don't assume they are against us for opposing the war." There was loud applause, and one of the men threw me a peace sign.

In Maryland I met with another military psychiatrist who told me about the mental problems he was seeing among many Vietnam veterans. He asked me to listen to a tape he had made of a few of his patients. This was a voice I had heard before, at Fort Ord—the whispering, tremulous voice of trauma.

The doctor stressed to me that the things the soldiers had done had been done in the presence of their officers, sometimes under orders. He himself was frightened of what might happen to him if his name was revealed. I felt heavy with the burden of all I was learning. I was also emotionally and physically exhausted, but it seemed unthinkable to take a break.

In Washington, D.C., Mark Lane and Carolyn Mugar joined us to identify legislators who would be

Representing the GI movement at the huge rally
in Washington, D.C., May 1970.
(Keystone/Getty Images)

Arrested at
Fort Bragg
military base,
with Mark
Lane and
Elisabeth.
(AP/Wide World
Photos)

interested in receiving information from the soon-to-open GI office. I had never set foot in the halls of Congress before, much less to lobby. The marble corridors and history-soaked chambers inspired awe and made it even more difficult for me to not feel like a little girl asking my father for something. But my presence caused a real stir. Everyone I met was friendly; some asked for my autograph. Arkansas senator James Fulbright liked the idea of the GI office, and my California senator, Alan Cranston, told us he was receiving eight thousand letters a day from constituents who opposed the war. The experience made me feel more optimistic than I had in a while.

On Memorial Day, right after another large demonstration in Central Park at which I spoke, Elisabeth flew home to Europe. I **was** home. I felt more American than I ever had. Elisabeth said to me before she left, "America is so alive and open. Your young people are not at all cynical the way they are in Europe." I felt this, too. During that two-month trip, I had experienced the best of America and the worst, and at the trip's end I felt certain that the best would prevail.

I am still baffled by those who feel that criticizing America is unpatriotic, a view increasingly being adopted in the United States since 9/11 as an excuse to render suspect what has always been an American right. An active, brave, outspoken (and **heard**) citizenry is essential to a healthy democracy.

CHAPTER FIVE

KLUTE

I was trying to get away from a world that I had known because I don't think that it was very good for me . . . and I found my-self looking up its ass . . . and I guess I just realized that I don't really give a damn, that what I would really like is to be faceless and bodiless . . . and be left alone.

—BREE DANIEL,
my character in **Klute**

I N 1970, before I left California to start filming **Klute** in New York City, I needed to line up a place to live when I returned in the fall, a place for Vanessa and me. I'd been living in my father's servants' quarters and I couldn't remain there any longer, especially now that my phone was being bugged. Since raising money was shaping up to be my main movement function, I thought I needed someplace not too expensive but large enough to hold fund-raisers. I found a house on top of a hill overlooking Hollywood, above the smog, and signed a rental agreement. Then I immediately set off, by myself this time, driving across America to New York, to start the film. But driving over the Rocky Mountains into Denver, I had an epiphany: I didn't want to be someone who lives on the top of a mountain and gives out money for people who live below. I wanted to be **with** the people below, to understand who they were, what their lives were like. This feeling welled up with an odd certainty. It was frightening because it meant I would have to change—give up things. Comfort and privilege are relative, of course. "Giving up things" for me might represent a state of comfort for someone else. It's also one thing to have an epiphany in the solitude of a car and another to go out and live it. **Can I really do this, or is it a momentary whim?** I wondered. **Can I be a movie star and at the same time not stand apart from others?** Then, as I came through the mountain pass, there, over Denver, clear as a bell, was the brightest double rainbow I have ever seen before or since. I took it for a sign. I called the real estate agent in California and canceled the lease on the mountaintop.

Mountaintops were about charity. I was about change.

I arrived in New York in time to spend two weeks researching my role as the call girl Bree Daniel. I had asked the director, Alan Pakula, to get his production assistant to line up some call girls and madams I could spend time with. Aside from that, I hadn't been thinking much about my role, and now that it was looming I was getting nervous. On my drive, I'd begun to wonder if it wasn't politically incorrect to play a call girl. Would a real feminist do that? I asked myself. **A real feminist wouldn't have to ask herself such a question.**

Before backing out, I decided to ask my friend the singer Barbara Dane to read the script and give me her advice. Barbara—a warm, wise, and talented blues singer spending most of her time those days singing for the GI movement—was, after all, an entertainer as well as an activist. I remember what she told me: "Jane, if you think you have room in this script to create a complex, multifaceted character, you should do it. It doesn't matter that she's a call girl, as long as she's real." Recently Barbara admitted to me that she hadn't been at all sure the script would allow for complexity, but she didn't know Alan Pakula—and she hadn't realized how ready I was for complexity.

I met different call girls or madams each night for about eight nights. Some were classy, some were strung out. The madams were high-class, though probably not on a level with Madame Claude in Paris (I had never met her, only heard about her). I went to a sleazy apartment one afternoon where a girl bought cocaine. I watched the dealer cut it up with a razor on a mirror, watched her snort it through a straw with an eagerness that chilled me. I had never seen anyone do cocaine before, and I disliked her helplessness in the presence of it, though it helped me understand the character of my girlfriend in the film: a fellow call girl junkie who disappears.

I asked one madam, "There's a scene in the script where I'm supposed to strip while I'm telling a sexy story to an old man who never touches me. Does that really happen?"

"Are you **kidding?**" She almost fell over laughing and proceeded to tell me about her favorite john. "He would be outside my door peeping through the keyhole while I stood on the other side playing with myself and talking dirty to him. Honey, that's the kind of john you dream for. Nobody touches nobody."

The women told me they had clients at all hours of the day: in the mornings fresh from home on their way to the office; during lunch breaks ("nooners," they were called); at cocktail hour, dinner hour, and after hours. "You wouldn't believe the men I service," one madam told me with a weary chuckle. "Senators, presidents of the biggest companies in the country, diplomats. And the more important they are, the kinkier they are."

She told me about one executive who always wanted hot wax dripped on his chest while having sex, another who liked a lot of girls together sticking pins in him. There was a story about a priest who insisted the call girl squat over a pan of cat litter; a

politician who kept a boa constrictor in his bathroom and could climax only when a terrified girl
would scream and come running out. (I spent too
much time pondering that one.)

Several times I went to after-hours clubs with
call girls, places they'd go to meet up with their
pimps and where pimps would bring new girls.
Never once during those evenings did a pimp even
try to solicit me. I interpreted their ignoring me as a
sign that I wasn't right for the character of Bree
Daniel. And while I knew there must be "whores
with hearts of gold" like those you read about and see
in the movies, the ones I met were, understandably,
hardened. I knew that if Bree was as cynical as these
women, with no inkling of something more underneath, the film wouldn't work. But how could I betray reality? That did it. I asked to meet with Alan
Pakula, my director.

"Alan, you've made a terrible mistake," I told
him. "I am all wrong for this character—there's no
way I can play her. Even the pimps know I'm not call
girl material." I proceeded to give him a list of the actresses who would be much better suited to the role,
starting with my friend Faye Dunaway.

"Alan, Faye would be perfect as Bree! Please let
me out of my contract. I just can't do it."

Alan just laughed at me and told me I was nuts.
He would go on to tell this story many times over the
years when speaking to acting students—I guess to
show how blinded actors can be by their insecurities.
My friend Sally Field once said to me that the anxi-

As Bree Daniel in Klute.
(Photofest)

Me in 1970.

ety and emotionalism just before starting a new role is part of the process of becoming raw and porous, so that the new character can inhabit you. Seen this way, the discomfort is a necessary stage in the morphing, when you are not quite **you** anymore but not quite someone new yet.

Vanessa and Dot were staying with me during the filming, and on weekends we made a habit of going to the Central Park Zoo and riding the carousel. Vanessa was a spunky, beautiful child with a husky, striking voice. Though only two, she was also more than able to let me know that she preferred her father, whose exotic eyes she shared. As a father preferrer myself, I couldn't blame her. Besides, I regret to say that I did not feel I had gotten better in the parenting department. It had nothing to do with my work. It was that when I **was** home, I still wasn't really present. Mother and Dad had been my models, but by now it was up to me, and I hadn't yet learned to leave my "stuff" at the door.

Since for better or worse I was going to go through with it, I began searching for a way to play a call girl differently—tough, angry, but not totally hardened—and this was when I drew on my experiences with some of the call girls I'd gotten to know in Paris with Vadim. There had been a few in whom I had seen glimmers of talent—and hope. That was it! Bree wouldn't be a call girl who wanted to be an actress or a model. She would be an actress, a talented one, whose life experiences, including early sexual abuse and a consequent need always to be in control, had led her to choose hooking as the way to pay for acting classes and rent. From that realization on, I turned a corner. Work on the film seemed to flow. Alan and I were so in sync that it was like having the perfect partner in a grand waltz. I loved him dearly.

I loved my co-star, Donald Sutherland, as well. I found his rangy, hangdog quality and droopy, pale blue eyes especially appealing. He also had something of the old-world gentleman about him. It was nice that through our mutual work as supporters and fund-raisers for the GI movement we had become friends months before beginning rehearsals.

Bree's apartment was built on a sound stage at a New York film studio, and Alan, at my request, made it possible for me to spend nights there, even going so far as installing a flushing toilet in the bathroom of the set. I would lie at night in Bree's bed in the eerie silence of the sound stage and slowly envision the items she would surround herself with. I had never seen books or pets in any of the apartments of call girls or madams. But I decided that Bree read, not Dostoyevsky, perhaps, but romance novels, how-to books, and the astrological then best-seller, **Sun Signs.** I decided Bree would have a cat, a loner like herself. I remembered an actress from Lee Strasberg's private classes who would be called down to Washington from time to time to pleasure President

Kennedy, so I decided Bree had done this and put a signed photo of Kennedy on the fridge. Bree, I realized, wouldn't do hard drugs—pot, maybe—but her control issue limited it to that.

In the script, Bree's psychiatrist was male. But early in rehearsals I realized that Bree would never reveal herself to a man, so I asked Alan to change the character to a woman. I didn't have to ask twice. I also requested that we wait until the end of shooting to film the scenes with the shrink, by which time I would have fully internalized Bree, and then I told Alan I wanted to improvise the scenes. He had given me several books on the psychology of prostitution, and together we talked a lot about the power/control issues that surround gender and the difficulties with trust and intimacy faced by women who have been sexually abused as children (mostly by family members or family friends). I understood how when Bree was with her johns, **she** was the one in control.

One of the scenes I most enjoyed filming was where I am with a john, having what appears to be a real orgasm and then sneaking a look at my watch over his shoulder. Women in the audience always howled at that scene. There was also a scene in which Bree is asked by Detective Klute to go with him to the morgue to see if her missing friend's picture is in the files of murdered women. At my request Alan arranged for me to visit the actual city morgue, where I was allowed to look through the case files. What I saw remains within me to this day: hundreds and hundreds of color photos of battered and bruised women who had been killed by husbands, lovers, johns. I had to excuse myself, go to the bathroom, and throw up. It's not that I hadn't known that violence against women was widespread, but the reality of it had not fully dawned on me until I saw face after face. This experience is what informed the scene toward the end of the film when Bree finds herself confronted by the murderer.

A well-dressed businessman, played terrifyingly by Charles Cioffi, sits across from me and begins to play a tape recording on which I can hear the voice of my missing friend talking to him in the come-on way call girls talk to johns when they first meet. Then the conversation takes a dark turn. I can hear fear rising in my friend's voice and I realize that the man sitting across from me had taped their conversation just before he murdered her and that he intends to kill me as well.

I had purposefully not done any preparation, wanting instead to let the raw impact of the scene carry me. Throughout the scene I was silent, just listening. But I'm a good listener, and I assumed I would be convincingly scared (although it's the most difficult emotion for me to play). But when the camera started rolling and I heard the fear in her voice, instead of fear for myself I was overwhelmed with an archetypal sadness. It was sadness for my friend, sadness for all the women who are victims of men's rage, sadness at our vulnerability. It felt . . . inevitable. I began to cry—for all the victims. Soon the tears came from my nose as well as my eyes. For an audience, it didn't matter what caused the tears. What mattered was that it was so unexpected, and the unexpected reality brought an electricity to the scene that wouldn't have been there had I simply been "scared." Lee Strasberg once said, "Don't plan. Be."

I knew when we finished the scene that my reaction would not have been the same had it not been for that cross-country trip with Elisabeth and the stirrings of a new feminist consciousness in me, locating an empathy toward women. I understood then that my expanding consciousness as an activist could broaden my understanding of people and why they behave as they do—from (rhetorical, but it's true) a purely Freudian, individualist perspective to one that includes historical, societal, economic, and gender-based factors—and that this in turn might make me more compassionate and my acting more intelligent.

Even now, when I watch **Klute** I admire everything about it. In these times of mega–special effects, when we've grown almost numb to what we used to find terrifying, Michael Small's ominous music track is still heart-stopping; Gordon Willis's photography, which caused him to be dubbed "the Prince of Darkness," sucks you in and then slams you with terror. Alan Pakula was alert to every nuance and knew just how to draw it out of me. As a result, a year later I would win my first Oscar, for my performance as Bree Daniel.

In retrospect I see the parallels between myself

and Bree, a woman who felt safer hooking than facing true intimacy.

I hadn't gotten used to being hated yet. Not that everyone had loved me up until then. What was to love—or hate, for that matter? I had occasionally been a bit outrageous in public statements, but generally I had come across as a slightly edgy, nonthreatening, fairly popular celebrity. So when the hate started, it took me by surprise, especially on the film set.

I'd always gone out of my way to be on time, know my lines, never behave like a diva. (I'd pulled that once in **Walk on the Wild Side**, when I was scared to go into a particular scene and kept having my makeup redone—as though different eyebrows and more rouge would somehow make things right. When I finally did show up on the set, I could feel people's anger and I froze. I learned then that if the on-set vibes toward me were negative, it was harder to do good work.) I needed the crew to respect me, to be rooting for me in the tough scenes. So when I came onto the set of **Klute** one morning early on and saw a huge American flag hanging over the doorway to Bree's apartment, I was taken aback. I didn't say anything to anyone, even Alan Pakula, because I didn't want people to know it had gotten to me, this sign that I was thought unpatriotic. Instead I remember sitting in my dressing room getting my makeup done, wanting to cry. But in the hour it took me to get ready, the other, more resilient part of me banished those feelings behind a high wall that (for many years to come) would shield me from feeling the pain of being a lightning rod for certain people's hostilities.

I knew that activism was right for me, that the killing in Vietnam needed to be stopped, and that using my celebrity to help people who were being bullied, deprived of safety and opportunity, was what I needed to do. So when I came out of that dressing room ready for the day's work, my attitude was very "Fuck you, guys, whoever you are." Since "Fuck you" was my character's general attitude about life, it worked for me on that film. Besides, I knew that the people who worked closest to me—Alan, Donald, Gordon Willis, and Michael Chapman, the camera operator—liked me. This was when disparity in people's feelings about me became a constant in my life. There was visceral hatred and there was something else I wasn't used to: admiration. I wasn't used to people throwing me high fives and peace signs. Fan letters were routine, but not letters filled with thanks for my having taken a stand, and when I went on TV talk shows, the audience response was different—as if people were rooting for me. That felt very good indeed.

Unbeknownst to me, during this time I had become the target of the government counterintelligence program known as COINTELPRO, a secret creation of J. Edgar Hoover, whose purpose was to disrupt and discredit members of the antiwar and militant black movements. This was done through infiltration, sabotage, intimidation, murder (directly assassinating or hiring rival groups to assassinate leaders), by framing activists for crimes the FBI committed, and through fake black propaganda—feeding journalists information through phony letters and inflammatory leaflets that slandered and discredited the targeted person. After extensive investigation of COINTELPRO, Senator Frank Church's Select Committee on Government Intelligence Activities pronounced it "a sophisticated vigilante program aimed squarely at preventing the exercise of First Amendment rights of speech and association." Seems the government felt it necessary to destroy democracy in order to save it. And look where it got us—Watergate and the first presidential resignation in U.S. history.

Richard Wallace Held was head of the Los Angeles section of COINTELPRO, and he specialized in black propaganda. In his 2002 book **The Last Editor** Jim Bellows says that in spring of 1970, while he was editor of the **Los Angeles Times,** Richard Held, with permission from J. Edgar Hoover, had planted a story with the **Los Angeles Times'** gossip columnist Joyce Haber saying that an actress who had recently appeared in a big musical film was now pregnant by a Black Panther. (Jean Seberg, a Panther Party supporter, had just starred in the musical **Paint Your Wagon** and was definitely pregnant, but by her husband, French novelist Romain Gary.)

In August an article appeared in **Newsweek** specifically naming Jean as the actress in question. In her seventh month of pregnancy, Jean attempted suicide and suffered a miscarriage as a consequence. She held an open-casket funeral in Paris so that her friends and family could see that her dead baby girl, whom she'd named Nina, was in fact white. Every year on the anniversary of Nina's death, Jean attempted suicide, until on September 8, 1979, she was found dead in her car in Paris. Also in September, the FBI admitted publicly to what it had done. Jean's husband shot himself several months later. Nice work, guys, and on taxpayers' money, too.

In June, soon after the first Seberg article had appeared, the same Richard Wallace Held received a memo from Hoover authorizing him to send a fictitious letter about me to Army Archerd, a columnist at **Daily Variety**. "It can be expected," emphasized Hoover's instructions to Held, "that Fonda's involvement with the BPP [Black Panther Party] cause could detract from her status with the general public if reported in a Hollywood 'gossip' column. . . . Ensure that mailing cannot be traced to the Bureau [FBI]." Held's subsequent letter read:

> **Dear Army,**
> I saw your article about Jane Fonda in "Daily Variety" last Thursday and happened to be present for Vadim's "Joan of Arc's" performance for the Black panthers Saturday night. I hadn't been confronted with this Panther phenomena [sic] before

but we were searched upon entering Embassy Auditorium, encouraged in revival-like fashion to contribute to defend jailed Panther leaders and buy guns for "the coming revolution," and led by Jane and one of the Panthers chaps in a "we will kill Richard Nixon, and any other M . . . F . . . who stands in our way" refrain. I think Jane has gotten in over her head as the whole atmosphere had the 1930's Munich beer-hall aura.

Army Archerd knew me, and to his credit, declined to print the letter. There would be more of the same to come.

One article, aiming to portray me as a rich hypocrite (though I can no longer remember where it was printed) said that I had been invited to speak at the University of Mexico but had insisted on having a limousine and on bringing my secretary and hairdresser. (Poor Elisabeth, there she was again.) Another reported that I had crashed a Nixon fund-raiser in New York, climbed onto a table, torn my blouse off, and shouted obscenities.

Starting in May 1970, the FBI, CIA, and counterintelligence branch of the Defense Intelligence Agency began monitoring me and eventually built up a file of some 20,000 pages. I would learn in 1975 that the National Security Agency had made transcripts of my 1970 phone calls and distributed them to Nixon, Kissinger, and other top government officials. One FBI informant reported at the time, "What Brezhnev and Jane Fonda said got about the same treatment." God help us!

It was through information given to my lawyers by columnist Jack Anderson that I learned the Morgan Guaranty Trust Company of New York and the City National Bank of Los Angeles had turned over my bank records to the FBI—without any subpoena. It turns out I was part of Group 1, which meant the documents about me could not automatically be declassified, and many were deemed top-secret. My "case" went by the code name "the Gamma Series," and I am variously referred to as a "subversive" and "anarchist"—although nothing in my files shows any proof as to why I was considered so dangerous.

Apart from government shenanigans, those were difficult times to be a newcomer to the movement scene. There was infighting on the Left, much debate about what the correct position was on this and that. For the radical left wing, the issue wasn't so much ending the Vietnam War as it was smashing U.S. imperialism. Sexism was rampant in the antiwar movement, and many women activists began to develop more feminist priorities. Then there were the yippies—and I wasn't sure **what** they were doing, although I spent a pleasant afternoon at the Central Park Zoo with Abbie Hoffman.

I was confused. Was it just limp, liberal politics to ask: "But what about all the American soldiers and Vietnamese dying . . . for a lie?" I had begun to feel there was no way I could possibly learn enough fast enough to understand why these ruptures were happening and what the radicals were all talking about.

This was a lonely time for me personally. Had I known at the start the hatred, scorn, and lies that would be unleashed at me, I would have gone ahead anyway; I was too immersed in this new world to turn back. What was lacking, I later realized, was a loving environment of fellow activists and friends with whom I could work. I didn't want to be the Lone Ranger anymore.

Then, in an amazing bit of synchronicity, I came upon an article in **Ramparts** written by the man who would within two years provide that loving environment for me: Tom Hayden. The article was titled "All for Vietnam," and it brought things into focus for me. Hayden wrote, "Most peace activists and radicals believe that Vietnam is a flaw—a terrible flaw—in the working of the American Empire. We should follow the war "not as a 'tragedy,' " he wrote, "but as a struggle in which humanity is making a stand so heroic that it should shatter the hardest cynicism."

That article confirmed and reenergized my commitment to ending the war, and I sensed that working with antiwar soldiers was the best way I could do that. The movement of active-duty soldiers and returned Vietnam veterans was potent, because these men and women were from America's heartland. They had enlisted as patriots; they returned as patriots. They had **been** there, and this made them more believable to Middle Americans than other groups in the antiwar movement. It was GI resisters, after all, who had brought **me** into the antiwar movement. I became even more committed to making these new heroes, the new warriors, the focus of my efforts.

CHAPTER SIX

REDEMPTION

I hear a lot of people say, "We know Vietnam veterans and they don't feel the way you do." My immediate reaction is, "Wait and see. If they are lucky, they will. If they are lucky, they will open up."
—Arthur Egendorf,
American Orthopsychiatric Association,
at a meeting in Washington, D.C.,
April 1971

I sincerely believe that we not only have the right to know what is good and what is evil; we have the duty to acquire that knowledge if we hope to assume responsibility for our own lives and those of our children. Only by knowing the truth can we be set free.
—Alice Miller,
The Truth Will Set You Free

I T WAS TO BE a war-crimes hearing, what has become known, famously, as the Winter Soldier investigation. The name Winter Soldier invoked Tom
Paine's reference to the revolutionary soldiers who,
through the terrible winter of 1777–1778, volunteered to remain at Valley Forge. Vietnam veterans
would testify about atrocities they had committed or
had witnessed while in Vietnam, as a way to let the
American public know the kind of war it was. Like
all information about the GIs and Vietnam veterans
who opposed the war (VVAW), with a Ramboesque
sleight of hand it has been disappeared, and history
has been conveniently rewritten. I want to help reverse this abracadabra.

The motivation for the Winter Soldier investigation was the My Lai massacre. When the story about
My Lai had broken in **The New York Times** in November 1969, it had staggered the public. What had
enraged a lot of Vietnam veterans, however, was the
way the government was scapegoating Lieutenant
William Calley and the men he commanded, calling
My Lai an "isolated incident of aberrant behavior."
To the membership of the Vietnam Veterans Against
the War (VVAW)—some 25,000 to 30,000 members
in 1970–71—the My Lai massacre was remarkable
only in the number of victims involved and the fact
that it became public.

The vets knew that atrocities were occurring as
an inevitable part of our Vietnam policies and that if
justice was to be served, the **architects** of those poli-

cies—from the president on down—needed to be held accountable, as had been the case at the Nuremberg trials following World War II.

Before the Winter Soldier investigation—the hearings were scheduled for early the following year, 1971—the VVAW, led by Al Hubbard, had organized an eighty-six-mile march from Morristown, New Jersey, to Valley Forge, Pennsylvania, where it would end in a Labor Day rally. Donald Sutherland and I spoke at that rally.

I will never forget it. The three-day march culminated as hundreds of the veterans swept up a hill, plastic AK-47 rifles held high, shouting, "Peace now!" Thousands of cheering people gathered to greet them. The most significant speaker that afternoon was a tall, handsome Silver Star winner, one Lieutenant John Kerry from Massachusetts. He had a charisma and an eloquence that immediately marked him as a natural leader. I was never introduced to him that day, although during the 2004 presidential campaign, photos doctored by George W. Bush supporters tried to malign Kerry by making it appear that he had stood next to me.

Getting ready for the Winter Soldier investigation required some hard, fast fund-raising and, not surprisingly, I volunteered to take it on, for which Al Hubbard made me VVAW's honorary national coordinator.

The moment we wrapped **Klute,** I hit the road

running. I went to people who had contributed to the GI office. I got my friends David Crosby and Graham Nash to do a benefit concert. But most of the money came from a grueling six-week speaking tour that took me to fifty-four college campuses across the country.

Whatever controversy I had experienced until then was nothing compared with what ensued on November 2, 1970, after my first speech in Ontario, Canada. Back in the United States, at Cleveland Hopkins International Airport, I was stopped by customs officials who, without explanation, demanded that my suitcase and purse be opened and searched. And what do you suppose they found? Little plastic bottles, 105 in all, each marked with "B," "L," or "D": the bottles that contained my array of vitamins.

That did it. They seized the bottles, my address book, and all my books and papers. I was taken to a room, held for three hours, and not allowed to make a phone call to my lawyer. When I tried to stand up, two hulking FBI chaps would shove me back in the chair. I said to them, "If there is a law that allows you to hold me here for no reason, that permits you to keep me from calling my lawyer, please show it to me and I'll be quiet." One of the agents answered, "You shut up! You're in my control. You take my word for it! I'm taking orders from Washington." I didn't yet know about COINTELPRO, but this news showed me that what was going on was serious. **Washington!**

I had just gotten my period, so after several

hours I desperately needed to go to the women's room. When the agent blocked my way and was rude, I tried to push him aside. As a result I was arrested for assaulting an officer—as well as for drug smuggling—though I didn't yet know the charges.

Early in the morning I was handcuffed and taken to the Cuyahoga County jail, where they fingerprinted me and took a mug shot. While I was being booked, a man who'd just been arrested asked me, "What are you in for?" I replied that I might be called a political prisoner.

"Well, they oughta throw you in jail," said he. "We don't want no Commies running around loose in this country."

"What are **you** in for?" I asked.

"Murder," he replied.

I was in a cell for ten hours. The next day I was brought from jail in handcuffs past a phalanx of TV cameras and photographers. As my hands are slender and double-jointed, I easily slipped out of one handcuff and threw a "power to the people" fist in the air, much to the chagrin of the guards. Leaving behind the cameras, I was taken to a courthouse, where I was surprised and relieved to see Mark Lane. He had heard the news of my arrest (TV was all over it and it had made the front page in many papers) and had flown in to defend me.

I refused to face the presiding judge but turned my back instead, as I felt the "system" had turned its back on me. Mark pleaded with me to turn around, but I wouldn't. I was released on $5,000 personal

Arrested at the Cleveland airport for "smuggling
drugs"—my vitamins.
(Reuters/Corbis)

bond on the drug charge and then booked on the local charge of assaulting the airport official, released on that charge on a $500 surety bond, and then booked for a hearing the following week.

Headlines across the country screamed the news that I'd been arrested for drug smuggling and assaulting an officer. Several months later one article tucked away on the back pages of **The New York Times** noted, "It was determined the pills she brought into the country from Canada were really vitamins, just as she said they were," and the charges of assault and drug smuggling were dropped. No headlines for **that.**

The day after my court appearance, I was back on the lecture circuit. Everywhere I went the surveillance had increased. At every airport there were at least two spooks in dark suits and shades (do they always operate in twos?), not even trying to pretend they weren't there to observe and intimidate me. Stress and fatigue began to get to me, but I was determined not to be cowed.

I was moving too fast. I was actively bulimic. I was depressed. I hadn't seen Vanessa and I felt anguish about that. I wasn't reading anymore. I was barely **thinking.** But I kept going. It never occurred to me not to. I was living in crisis mode. U.S. soldiers were willing to testify about the war—at potential personal risk—and I felt a responsibility to do everything I could to make that possible.

A few times the marquees announcing my appearances would say COME HEAR BARBARELLA SPEAK.

I began to feel like a sideshow and wondered if what I had to say about the war was getting through all the hoopla.

Mostly I traveled by myself with one small bag. I would arrive at the local airport, where the student in charge of the speakers' bureau would pick me up. En route to the campus, I'd try to get a sense from my host of what I needed to prepare myself for. Increasingly the atmosphere would be described as tense, which usually meant there would be a large turnout; most of the time the audience numbered in the many hundreds, if not thousands. I spoke about the war and the upcoming Winter Soldier hearings and said that I was contributing my speaker's fees to enable more veterans to attend. When I finished my speech, I would invite any vets in the audience to come up and give me their names and addresses if they were interested in participating, and as soon as I could get to a phone I would follow up with the VVAW's Detroit office.

Right up to the day the hearings began in January 1971, vets were showing up to see if they could testify, or at least attend. Most had never been part of any organized activity against the war; many had never before spoken to anyone about their war experiences.

It was critical for VVAW that all the men who were slated to testify were legitimate veterans with their DD-214 (discharge documents) in hand, and that they could prove they had been where they said they had been. The organizers did a remarkable job with this—which was fortunate, since the Nixon White House subsequently did all it could to prove the men weren't really combat veterans; and when they failed, they did the men the disservice of calling them "alleged vets" anyway, in an effort to discredit them and their testimony.

On January 31, hundreds of people from all over the country crammed into the large conference room in a Howard Johnson motel to witness this unprecedented event. Barbara Dane and Ken Cloke were there, Ken to review veterans' documents and offer legal help as it was needed. Another person who stopped by was Tom Hayden, author of the **Ramparts** article that had so influenced me.

I had never met him before, and he invited me to have coffee with him in the hotel's coffee shop. He was a bona fide movement "heavy" of whom I was in awe, and I was nervous and intimidated. I remember him talking mostly about the Red Family collective in Berkeley, California, of which he was a member. These groupings were springing up all over the country in the seventies. They were a way for longtime activists to overcome the depersonalization of the mass movements by creating close-knit, supportive families, models of a new way of living.

In his eloquent opening remarks at the Winter Soldier investigation, Lieutenant William Crandell,

Americal Division, an officer of VVAW, made it clear the investigation was not a mock trial. "There will be no phony indictments," he said. Instead the men would give straightforward testimony about "acts which are war crimes under international law. Acts which these men have seen and participated in. . . ." Civilian experts testified about different aspects of the war. For the first time, Bert Pfeiffer, a doctor from the University of Montana, discussed the toxic effects of a dioxin-laden 2,4,5-T herbicide known as Agent Orange, which the United States was spraying on the forests of Vietnam to kill trees and deprive the guerrilla soldiers of their cover. A message of support from family members and spouses of American prisoners of war was read.

I want to mention the presence of Staff Sergeant George Smith, the first U.S. POW from Vietnam I had ever met. He had served with Fifth Special Forces and had been a prisoner of the National Liberation Front in South Vietnam (Vietcong) from 1963 to 1965. George would later join me and others on a national tour.

The heart of the Winter Soldier investigation was the testimony from the veterans. They represented every branch of the U.S. military, officers as well as enlisted men. Sitting solemnly in front of microphones at a long table covered by white cloth, they made an unusual sight with their medals, uniforms, long hair, and beards. One by one they said who they were, where they had served, and what category of war crime they would testify about.

In voices sometimes choked with emotion, the men told how they and others had randomly killed Vietnamese civilians and tortured Vietnamese prisoners. They told of raping and mutilating women and girls; cutting off ears and heads; rounding up entire villages into concentration camps (called "new life hamlets" in the obscene war-speak that was being used to sugar-coat reality). They told of B-52 carpet bombing; throwing Vietcong suspects from helicopters; using white phosphorus (Willie Peter), which burned endlessly through a person's body. One pilot said:

> **Anywhere in North Vietnam basically is a free-fire zone. There were no forbidden targets. If you didn't find any particular targets that you wanted to hit, then normally you'd go ahead and just drop your bombs wherever you wanted to.**

All this, the vets repeated, was done in the presence of officers who said nothing, did nothing, to stop it. Some of the vets talked about getting hooked on drugs to numb themselves to what they did.

One of the many lies promulgated by the U.S. government came out at the hearings when five veterans revealed that the Third Marine Division had been in secret combat in Laos in 1969. They said the U.S. military refused to evacuate out any wounded or dead for fear the press would find out about the operation.

I was numb as I listened to speaker after speaker

describe these atrocities. I **heard** what was being said, but I couldn't get my heart to grasp it. Partly it had to do with my own emotional state. My nerves were shot. I couldn't sleep. Picketers outside the Howard Johnson hotel were brandishing signs saying I was a Communist. My father wasn't speaking to me and, because of the news reports about my arrest, probably thought I was a drug smuggler. My Hollywood connections feared I'd never work again. I felt my life was spinning out of control.

One of the few times I cried was over the "rabbit story." It was told by Sergeant Joe Bangert, First Marine Air Wing, about his last day at Camp Pendleton and reminded me of what I had heard about traumatic training from military psychologists:

> **You have a little lesson and it's called the rabbit lesson, where the staff NCO comes out and he has this rabbit and . . . then in a couple of seconds after just about everyone falls in love with it . . . he cracks it in the neck, skins it, disembowels it . . . and then they throw the guts out into the audience. You can get anything out of that you want, but that's your last lesson you catch in the United States before you leave for Vietnam. . . .**

Supporters of George W. Bush's administration, like those of Nixon at the time, have tried to portray the winter soldiers as frauds. The fact is, those soldiers were telling the truth. There is **no accurate**

refutation of any of the testimony given during the Winter Soldier investigation. Only one man (who did **not** testify) had falsified his military rank, and that was Al Hubbard himself. It turned out that Al had been not an air force captain, but an air force staff sergeant E-5. Al admitted on the **Today** show in 1971 that he had lied "because I recognize in this country that it's very important that one has an image."

A month or so later, while sitting in the projection room of Francis Ford Coppola's Zoetrope offices in San Francisco, watching a rough cut of the documentary **Winter Soldier** with other of the film's funders, I finally broke down. And once the tears came, they were unstoppable. Until then I had thought that what was important about the Winter Soldier investigation was its indictment of the U.S. government for sending men to fight a war whose very nature made atrocities inevitable. But something far more profound than the question of blame had transpired over those three days in Detroit.

A spiritual shift had occurred that signaled hope. These men, as they gave witness, were shedding the old, soul-destroying warrior ethic, emerging out of numbness, being reborn. They were pointing the way for all of us: If they, who had done and seen the unimaginable, could transform themselves by their collective truth telling, then couldn't we all? Today we do those who served in Vietnam a grave disservice to feign outrage at what these men said and did and to deny that any atrocities were committed by Americans **or to blame them.** They were not alone in revealing the horrors of the Vietnam War. In 2004 **The Blade** (Toledo) was awarded the Pulitzer Prize for its October 2003 series, **Buried Secrets, Brutal Truths,** which documented how the 101st Airborne Division's Tiger Force platoon went on a seven-month rampage through forty villages in the central highlands of Vietnam in 1967, killing scores of unarmed men, women, and children. The Pentagon undertook a full-scale investigation of the atrocities committed by Tiger Force and submitted it in 1975. It seems to have been "lost" at both the White House and the Pentagon when Richard Cheney was chief of staff and Donald Rumsfeld was secretary of defense.

What many people failed to do then (and continue to fail to do today) is admit what happened, understand the context, and make sure those circumstances never happen again. The winter soldiers showed us that redemption is possible when truth is spoken.

Nothing can change until we acknowledge what is—as I have learned over time.

CHAPTER SEVEN

INSURRECTION AND SEXUALITY

Nixon doesn't want to be the first
American president to lose a war
but he may be the first American
president to lose an army.
—DICK GREGORY

. . . Being the object of male desire
and the male gaze, that acknowledgment of personhood that, in
the conventional world, only a
man can bestow.
—CAROLYN HEILBRUN

B Y THE BEGINNING OF 1971—a year after
the release of **They Shoot Horses, Don't They?**
and while the Winter Soldier investigation was in
progress—I began thinking seriously about quitting
the film business. I didn't want to be a celebrity any-

more. I didn't want to be different. I wanted to join a film collective somewhere and just blend in.

Part of it was a desire to shed my celebrity, and part of it was that I needed a home, structure, a "family." While I have no problem now, at age sixty-seven, being by myself while I go through transitions, at age thirty-three I was adrift on every level. I needed anchoring.

I had become friends with Ken Cocheral, a charismatic black attorney in Detroit who was, among other things, lawyer for the League of Black Workers. I confided to him my desire to give up my career and he surprised me by saying, "Jane, there will always be people who can be in collectives. There is no one in the movement, no real activist, who is a movie star. Stay with it, we need you. Own your leadership."

Own my leadership? What leadership? I didn't see myself as a leader. I saw myself as a staunch lieutenant—give me my orders and I won't stop until I've carried them out. But his comment had an impact on me. It suggested that my career had broader implications beyond my own success or failure—that being successful at my work would give me more heft and a wider reach for what needed to be communicated. Maybe I could even figure out a way to make movies that themselves had something of value to say. But to be honest, the notion of having to step up to the plate and address my film career seriously felt overwhelming.

I moved back to Los Angeles and found a place

of my own. It was a rental in downtown Los Angeles just off the Hollywood Freeway, at the end of a cul-de-sac, crouched in a perpetual haze of smog. Vanessa and Dot were with me, and it was home base for most of the next eight months while Donald Sutherland and I worked on a film comedy called **Steelyard Blues.**

I had sold all my belongings, collected lovingly over the years in France when such things could be had for a price: the blond Biedermeier pieces, the pair of red lacquered Ruhlmann chairs from the 1930s, the Roy Lichtenstein rug—all gone. I wish I had them today, but I needed the cash. Now, instead of noteworthy furniture-cum–works of art, I did what others in the movement did back then: Wooden cable spools were my tables, mattresses on the floor served as beds and couches. They didn't look bad covered with the bright cotton fabrics I'd brought back from India. Some lamps and beanbag chairs from the nearest Salvation Army center rounded out the meager furnishings, and to tell you the truth, I was perfectly happy. The differences between the way I lived and the way those I worked with lived were beginning to disappear, and I was able to answer the question that had scared me during my Rocky Mountain epiphany: Yes! I can give "things" up; my desire to come down off the mountain was not a momentary whim.

My accountant, fearing the profits from the sale of the French farm and my furniture would disappear overnight into the coffers of some new movement organization or other, had encouraged me to hire someone to live with me and keep fiduciary control over my expenses. Ellen Lustbader was her name, and she was a five-foot-eleven blonde with a ready sense of humor, game for just about anything I threw at her. We called her Ruby Ellen, and I was grateful for her support and good company during those difficult in-between-husbands years.

Every morning I drove Vanessa to a preschool cooperative, and once a week I took my turn there as a parent-helper. I was still suffering with bulimia and probably didn't do a very good job. I was always tired.

On Vanessa's third birthday I baked a cake using a recipe from Adelle Davis's **Let's Cook It Right.** As I was carrying it into the living room, where a group of her schoolmates were eagerly gathered, the cake slid off the platter and broke into little pieces on the hardwood floor like a brick, which made the kids howl with laughter! Vanessa had a look that seemed to say "What's a kid to do with a mom like this?"

I felt I just couldn't get anything right when it came to mothering. For a while Vanessa took dance classes at UCLA, where children pirouetted around on tiptoes waving long, colorful streamers above their heads. Often she'd want to do encores in our living room for me, but she always refused to dance unless I promised to keep my eyes **closed.** She was a funny one—imaginative, feisty, unusually bright, with a tawny, tomboyish beauty. I loved her and hated the distance that remained between us. I didn't share the physical closeness she had with her father (to whom I was still legally married). Whenever a photo was taken of us together, there would be an I-don't-want-to-be-here expression on her beautiful little face—like me with my own mother. I needed to forgive my mother and to love myself more before I would learn how to be a better mother to Vanessa.

While I was living in the charmless house on the cul-de-sac, Donald and I launched a new organization in Hollywood aimed at harnessing the industry's powerful antiwar voice. We named it the Entertainment Industry for Peace and Justice (EIPJ) and invited everyone we knew in Hollywood to its launch in the grand ballroom of the Beverly Wilshire Hotel. Six hundred people from all walks of the industry turned out, including Barbra Streisand, Burt Lancaster, Tuesday Weld, Jennifer Jones, Richard Widmark, Don Johnson, Kent McCord—the sheer volume of star power was astonishing. The problem was that neither Donald nor I had ever started an organization before and weren't equipped to give leadership to this uniquely rambunctious group.

EIPJ should have made a big difference, but instead of focusing on how we could use the considerable talent and influence of this unique group of people to mobilize for ending the war, we got caught up in more divisive and diversionary issues—like whether or not film studios should be nationalized. Our meetings began to get longer and longer. It was easy to understand why most of the Hollywood folks drifted away after a time.

Today I can look back on the EIPJ experience with some forgiveness of my leadership failings. Leadership is complicated, especially for women. Men grow up in a culture that assumes their leadership. Even men who may not be true leaders are taught, explicitly or implicitly, what leadership looks like; it's passed down to men through generations.

Women were traditionally denied this generational fix on leadership, and this became evident in the early seventies. So we stumbled and groped. Now, as the women's movement has matured, we've made the delicious discovery that most women's style of leadership is very different from men's—more circular and inclusive than hierarchical and elite. For women it's not about having leadership **over.** It's about facilitating a process that evokes everyone's inherent leadership abilities. This isn't because women are morally better than men; we just don't have our masculinity to prove. Of course, there are some women (I won't name names) who are ventriloquists for the patriarchy, who try to get seats at the table by doing things the way men do them. But over the last decades we've discovered that despite our vaginas and breasts, if we do things the same old way, we're going to get the same old I-win-you-lose results, rather than win-win.

I **was** the leader within the Entertainment Industry for Peace and Justice organization, but because I lacked confidence, I didn't "own" my leadership and was always looking over my shoulder for someone who could take over and **really** lead.

I continue to be amazed at the number of women I consider strong leaders, who still worry about "taking up too much space in meetings," worry about being "too assertive" in expressing their ideas and needs, become little girls again in the presence of male "authority" figures. Once we women are able to **own** our leadership, to embody our power (and more and more women are—including myself), the world will be a better place indeed.

In June 1971, **The New York Times** began publishing articles based on secret government documents—the Pentagon Papers. It electrified the antiwar movement. Daniel Ellsberg, a Pentagon insider and ex-marine who had been one of the authors of the documents, together with a RAND Corporation researcher named Anthony Russo, had spent months copying and smuggling the documents out of RAND. As Ellsberg wrote in his 2002 book, **Secrets,** "What I had in my safe at RAND was seven thousand pages of documentary evidence of lying, by four presidents and their administrations over twenty-three years, to conceal plans and actions of mass murder. I decided I would stop concealing that myself. I would get it out somehow." Even Secretary of Defense Robert McNamara, when he read the study he had commissioned, said to a friend, "You know they could hang people for what's in here."

Of course the Nixon Justice Department freaked and issued an injunction against **The New York**

Times, ordering the paper to cease publication of the documents. But the Supreme Court ruled that the paper could continue publishing the articles. Nixon then got a federal grand jury in Los Angeles to indict Ellsberg and Russo for violating the Espionage Act and stealing government documents. All charges were eventually dropped against Ellsberg, for reasons of government misconduct against him.

No one knew it at the time, but the leaking of the Pentagon Papers was what led Nixon to create his team of "plumbers," so named because their job was to stop "leaks." Their first assignment was to burglarize Ellsberg's psychiatrist's office in the hope of finding something they could blackmail him with. The administration feared that Ellsberg knew that Nixon had began discussing the use of nuclear weapons in North Vietnam in 1969, and they wanted to silence him. The plumbers' Watergate assignment—well, that's history.

One day in the fall of 1970 while I was filming **Klute** and helping to plan the Winter Soldier investigation, a man named Howard Levy came to see me. He was a celebrity in the GI movement, a physician who had done prison time for refusing to train special forces going to Vietnam. He pitched an idea to Donald Sutherland and me: Why not put together an antiwar alternative to Bob Hope's traditional prowar entertainment? He even had a name for it: FTA.

Those letters formed a popular acronym among

GIs (Fuck the Army), but for us (publicly, at least) it meant Free the Army. Howard wanted us to try to bring the show to U.S. military bases both stateside and in the Pacific. I found the concept irresistible. Here was a way to support the GI movement—which I increasingly felt was the cutting edge of the peace movement—and to do so using my professional skills. Acting and activism—together at last!

At the time, Donald and I were planning **Steelyard Blues,** to be directed by Alan Myerson, who also agreed to direct the FTA show. Howard Hesseman, Garry Goodrow, and Peter Boyle (all of whom were going to co-star in **Steelyard Blues**) joined the FTA cast as well. FTA was political vaudeville with an antiwar, pro-soldier theme. It was written mainly by Jules Feiffer, Carl Gottlieb, Herb Gardner, Fred Gardner (no relation), and Barbara Garson. The show was intended not only to support the soldiers' antiwar sentiments but to call attention to the way soldiers were dehumanized in the military. Some may say that dehumanization is the only way the military can work, but if stripping young people of their rights and their feelings of empathy, and filling them with racist, sexist attitudes is the only way we can succeed in making them into good soldiers, then we have a problem.

Some high-ranking military officers share this view as well. I heard U.S. Army (ret.) general Claudia Kennedy say, for instance, that the military should be prepared to deal with "soft" issues like ethics and integrity, not just technology and weapons systems.

As Ken Cloke once said to me, "Defensive wars against oppressive regimes do not require dehumanization." The problem was that in Vietnam dehumanization was necessary, because rather than being a defensive war, it was a war of outside aggression (ours) against the popular will of the Vietnamese.

Dick Gregory and Barbara Dane joined Peter Boyle, Donald, and me for our first FTA performance on March 14, 1971, at the Haymarket Square coffeehouse near Fort Bragg in Fayetteville, North Carolina. JANE FONDA'S ANTIWAR SHOW SCORES HIT NEAR ARMY BASE, read next day's headlines in the **Los Angeles Times.** The article went on to say, "The soldiers roared time and again their desire for an end to the war."

We performed three times to packed houses in Fayetteville, even though the police used long-range infrared cameras to take pictures of all the soldiers as they entered and even announced there had been a bomb scare, which we ignored, to the delight of the soldiers.

We had assumed we'd be performing for the soldiers and sailors, but suddenly that spring, the air force erupted with antiwar sentiment—not surprising when you realize that Vietnamization was turning it into an air war.

The air force's desertion rate doubled; Travis Air Force Base in California, the primary embarkation point for flights to Vietnam, was in a state of siege for four days in May. The bachelor officers' quarters was burned, one man was killed, dozens injured, and 135 were arrested.

In June, Sheppard Air Force Base in Texas saw a revolt. In August, Chanute Air Force Base in Illinois saw a violent uprising, and that spring airmen and airwomen, with civilian support, turned an old theater into the first air force coffeehouse, the Covered Wagon. When we performed there, a local reporter asked me if we were urging servicemen to revolt. "No," I said, "they're ahead of us on that."

From the beginning, the intention had been to try to bring the FTA show to South Vietnam as an alternative to Bob Hope's pro-war, testosterone-driven tour. I wrote to President Nixon asking for permission to go to South Vietnam for Christmas. I wasn't holding my breath for a Dear-Jane-Sure-come-on-over-we'd-love-the-troops-to-see-you-Love-Dick letter, but I wanted to be able to say that I'd at least tried. The backup plan was to perform for GIs stationed in the Pacific en route to or from Vietnam. We also decided to make a documentary film of the tour, and a company called American International agreed to distribute it. By summer we had a new, more diverse cast. Besides Donald and me, there was singer Holly Near, poet Pamela Donegan, actor Michael Alaimo, singer Len Chandler, singer Rita Martinson, and comedian Paul Mooney. Francine Parker, a Hollywood producer, took over the directorial reins.

When I watch the film we made, I am impressed

by the extent to which we achieved a real ensemble.
Everyone had his or her own solo bit; no one stood
out more than the others. Donald, of course, was a
mainstay. He played President Nixon to my Pat:

> [Pat Nixon runs in breathlessly] "Mr.
> President, Mr. President . . ."
> "What is it, Pat?" asks Richard Nixon.
> "Mr. President, there is a massive
> demonstration going on outside."
> "There's a massive demonstration
> every day, Pat."
> "But this one is completely out of
> control!"
> "What are they asking for today?"
> "Free Angela Davis and all political
> prisoners, out of Vietnam now, and draft
> all federal employees."
> "All right, we have people to take care
> of that, Pat. Let them do their job, you do
> yours and I'll do mine."
> [Hysterical] "Richard, I don't think
> you understand. They're about to storm
> the White House."
> "Oh. Then I'd better call the army."
> "You can't, Richard."
> "Why not?"
> "It is the army!" [or air force or navy
> or marines]

We spent the fall touring the country performing for
some fifteen thousand GIs near major U.S. military

bases, and in November, after performing at Philharmonic Hall in New York, off we flew to Hawaii, where GIs were flooding in from Vietnam for R&R.

All told, we did twenty-one performances during the overseas tour, for an estimated sixty-four thousand soldiers, sailors, marines, and men and women in the air force. It was made extremely difficult for the servicemen to attend. They were photographed and risked getting harassed; the military authorities would put out misinformation about the time and place of the show in an effort to prevent the soldiers from getting there in time (we'd always wait for them). Also, those sixty-four thousand spread the word to countless others. Ken Cloke told me that when he'd gone to the Philippines and Japan to visit GI coffeehouses right after FTA had been there, bootlegged audiotapes of the show were "selling like hotcakes" among soldiers and were even circulated in Vietnam. He also told me that attendance at the coffeehouses increased dramatically following our tour.

One very important thing happened while the tour was in Japan. We filmed an interview with several men at Iwakuni Marine Base who told us that despite the agreement between Japan and the United States following World War II that stipulated nuclear weapons were never again to be brought onto the island, they themselves were moving nuclear weapons around the bases, **all in secret, all illegal.** They asked us to demand that a search be conducted to uncover the truth. We got nowhere.

On July 14, 1972, the FTA film opened in Washington, D.C., distributed by American International.

Some GIs were upset that I didn't live up to their fantasies. One soldier told Holly Near that they'd torn down my **Barbarella** poster in anger. I wasn't secure enough to let their disappointment roll off my back. So much of who I'd been had to do with what men wanted me to be; their admiring gaze was the "acknowledgment of my personhood." What would happen now? Would I ever be able to work again? Would anyone ever want to see me onscreen again? Yet another part of me knew I couldn't go back.

In years to come, as I approached fifty, I would again revert to that woman who needed to fulfill her man's fantasies. I was afraid that I'd never have the one, truly intimate relationship that I so wanted, and I thought it was only in that fantasy role that a man could love me.

Why does it have to take so long to heal?

I wish I could do the tour over again, as the person I am now. I would have gone onstage and said, "Hey, I know it must disappoint you to see me like this, not as sexy Barbarella, but as a regular person in jeans and no makeup. I could do the Barbarella bit, but

then I'd be in the Bob Hope show. And hey, I understand about sexy fantasies, but let me tell you something: When it's you having to live other people's
fantasies, it can be dehumanizing. 'Sexy' is great as
long as it doesn't require you to deny who you are—
well, that's what happened to me. I lost who I was.
Now I'm trying to get real and I hope you understand—and I love you."

Perhaps I could have found ways to equate how
the "Barbarella syndrome" affected **me** with how the
military was dehumanizing **them**. It could have
taken maybe four minutes at most; I could have said
it with humor; and I **know** most of the guys would
have gotten it and been there for me.

When I hear people today saying that anti–Vietnam War activists were antisoldier, I wish I could
rerelease that film. It wasn't a great piece of art—it
didn't **need** to be. Just the fact that we showed up in
support of the soldiers was important. What we did
was raw, unprecedented, outrageous, and, in today's
environment, totally unthinkable. We succeeded because the soldiers were ready and ripe with passionate antiwar, antimilitary feelings.

As soon as the FTA tour was over, I flew, on Christmas Day 1971, directly from Tokyo to Paris, where I
was to begin filming **Tout Va Bien** with Yves Montand—a movie I didn't want to make. I was homeless, structureless, loveless, and bulimic. Not a good
combination. My gray drizzle of a life felt as though

The FTA show. From left to right: Rita Martinson, me, Donald Sutherland, Michael Alaimo, Len Chandler.

Receiving my Academy Award for **Klute**.
(Bettmann/Corbis)

it was dissolving on some crucial level. There was the endlessly escalating war. Vanessa was having terrible, screaming nightmares every night; I was racked with guilt and didn't know what to do. Whenever I had a day off, I would play with her in the swank apartment Vadim was renting on the rue Trocadero or take her to the Jardins des Tuileries, where there was a wondrous variety of children's rides.

The director of **Tout Va Bien** was Jean-Luc Godard, the French avant-garde filmmaker who had become internationally known in the sixties with his movie **Breathless,** starring Jean Seberg and Jean-Paul Belmondo. Godard had offered me the role the previous summer without showing me a script, and I had accepted unquestioningly. After all, Godard was seen as a political filmmaker, and there weren't too many of those around. But when I received the script, I found it incomprehensible. It read like one long polemic. Godard, I learned, was a Maoist. I berated myself for having accepted the role with so little knowledge of its content, and through my agent I got word to Godard that I was backing out. I didn't want to be used by him to get financing for something with politics that seemed obscure and sectarian.

Probably his financing depended on my being in the film, and he wasn't about to take this lying down. All hell broke loose!

While I was visiting Vanessa in Megève with her father, a man who was close to Jean-Luc Godard arrived at Vadim's doorstep and threatened me with bodily harm if I didn't do the film. What was especially memorable about the encounter was how Vadim reacted. He shouted at this man: "**Sortez! Calviniste, vous êtes un sale Calviniste!**" ("Get out, you dirty Calvinist!") **Calvinist?** This was a new one on me, and I wasn't entirely certain what it meant to call this man, who was actually a Maoist, a Calvinist, but it sounded terrific and I loved Vadim for his lack of equivocation. Still, I went ahead and made the dreaded **Tout Va Bien.** I wasn't even thrilled that Yves was co-starring in it, because by now it was no secret that he was playing around on Simone (I was perhaps the last to know), and she was very unhappy. I spent time with her and hated to see her so down.

During the filming, I kept my head down, staying under the radar, showing up on time, and keeping to myself on the set to avert outright hostility between Godard and me.

In late February 1972, just as I was returning to California from Paris, I learned I had been nominated for a Best Actress Academy Award for my performance in **Klute.** For several weeks after my return I was a nomad, moving from place to place, sleeping on friends' couches. Desperate for a place where Vanessa could be with me, I borrowed $40,000 from my father and bought a home on a hillside above Studio City in the San Fernando Valley. Dad must have seen that this would afford me some needed stability, and I insisted on signing a promissory note to pay him back (which I did within the year). Dad had his own nonintimate ways of letting me know he was there for me.

As Oscar time drew near, everyone was telling me I would win, and this time I felt they were right. It was in the air. But what was I going to say when I accepted? Should I make a statement about the war? If I didn't, would it be irresponsible of me? I decided to ask Dad for his advice—Dad, who didn't believe in the whole awards business at all ("How can you pick between Laurence Olivier and Jack Lemmon? It's apples and oranges!"). But he came through. His verbal parsimony paid off: "Tell 'em there's a lot to say, but tonight isn't the time," was his recommendation—and the moment I heard it I knew he was right.

I was sick with the flu on the night of the awards. Donald Sutherland was my escort, and I wore a stark black wool Yves Saint Laurent pants suit I had purchased in Paris in 1968 soon after Vanessa's birth. My hair was still in the **Klute** shag, and I must have weighed all of one hundred pounds.

The Best Actress category is always third to last, followed by Best Actor and Best Picture. When my name was announced as winner, I somehow managed to make the endless march to the stage without falling, and as I arrived in front of the microphone, I was stunned by a feeling of love and support that emanated from the audience. I remember the booming silence as they waited for me to speak. I remember my fear that I would black out. I felt so small all alone on the stage looking out into the cavernous theater, seeing the upturned faces in the first few rows fixed on me, everyone holding their breath, their energy pushing toward me. I heard myself thanking the people who had voted for me and then: "There's a great deal to say, but I'm not going to say it tonight. Thank you"—just as Dad had suggested. There was an audible release of tension from the audience; they were grateful that I hadn't given a diatribe. I walked off with my Oscar as the applause erupted and walked right into a corner and sobbed, overcome with gratitude. **I am still a part of this industry!** Then, with disbelief, **How can this have happened to me when it hasn't happened to my father?** I skipped all the post-Oscar parties and got home to discover I had a raging fever.

Winning the Academy Award was a huge event for me as an actress; whatever else happened, I would always have that. But nothing really changed in my life—not that I expected it to. Yet there's always a vague hope that such acclaim will make everything else fall into place. It doesn't.

I was betwixt and between. Was I a celebrity? An actor? A mother? An activist? A "leader"? Who **was** I?

The Entertainment Industry for Peace and Justice, which Donald and I had launched a year earlier, was all but defunct. So much for my leadership. I still felt an urgent need to end the war, but I was unsure how to continue working with Vietnam Veterans Against the War (which was splintering into factions) or the GI movement (since most of the ground troops were home by now).

I managed to take Vanessa to school every morning, but basically I was functioning on automatic pilot.

CHAPTER EIGHT

TOM

Just when I thought I'd had enough
And all my tears were shed,
No promise left unbroken,
There were no painful words unsaid—
You came along and showed me
How to leave it all behind.
You opened up my heart again
And then much to my surprise,
I found love—love in the nick of time.
—BONNIE RAITT,
"Nick of Time"

HE APPEARED out of the darkness, an odd figure with a long braid, beaded headband, baggy
khaki pants, and rubber sandals of the type I'd been
told the Vietnamese made out of the tires of abandoned U.S. vehicles.

"Hi, I'm Tom Hayden . . . remember?"

I was dumbstruck. He didn't resemble the Tom
Hayden I'd met in Detroit the previous year at the
Winter Soldier investigation.

Thank God I hadn't known Tom Hayden would be coming to see the slide show I'd just given on the escalating U.S. air war; I'd have been too nervous. Tom was a movement icon, intelligent, courageous, and charismatic; one of the principal founders of Students for a Democratic Society (SDS), an author of its remarkably coherent and compelling Port Huron Statement and of the **Ramparts** article that had so influenced me.

The day after our meeting in Detroit, I had accompanied several people who were driving him to the airport. I was in the front seat, he was behind me. He said something that made me laugh, some irreverent remark. I was unused to laughter and turned to look at him. His eyes were sparkling and he was wearing an Irish wool cap that made him look rakish. Our eyes locked briefly, and he put his hat on my head. It felt nice, slightly flirtatious. I had not seen him since.

Now, more than a year later, here he was, exuding purposeful energy and needing, he said, to talk to me. Tom Hayden came here to talk to **me**! We found a place to sit in the dim backstage area and I told him that I was sorry to have missed him the previous summer when I'd visited the Red Family in Berkeley while filming **Steelyard Blues.** I felt him tense at the mention of the Red Family (I didn't know that he had been expelled from the collective). He was living in Venice now, teaching a class on Vietnam at Pitzer College in Claremont.

"You don't look like you did last year," I said to Tom. "What's with the braid and beads?"

Tom explained that he had just finished writing a book about how the Vietnam War paralleled our genocide against the Native Americans and that the experience had made him identify with the Indians. **Oh my God!** On top of everything, Tom Hayden identified with the Indians! But the reason he'd come to my slide show, he said, was to ask me to help him with a traveling display of posters and silkscreens about Vietnam and its people. He wanted to use art to show the Vietnamese as human beings, to understand what it was in their culture that enabled them to fight the way they did against a far superior military force.

Putting his hand on my knee, he said he'd also just finished his own slide show and that "I'd like to show it to you sometime"—at least I think that's what he said. An electric charge had gone right through me, and all I was thinking about at that moment was his hand on my knee. **Slide show?** "Sure, come on over anytime," I said, and gave him my phone number. It made sense: I'd shown him mine, now he'd show me his. . . .

I got home that night and told Ruby that I'd just met the man I was going to spend the rest of my life with. I was giddy with excitement. I wanted a man in my life I could love, but it had to be someone who could inspire me, teach me, lead me, not be afraid of me. Who better than Tom Hayden? Respected movement leader, passionate organizer, and strategist par excellence, **who was even into American Indians.** And he seemed so . . . grounded. I needed grounding.

So over he came early one spring evening shortly thereafter, carrying his slide projector. Vanessa was already asleep, but I introduced him to Ruby and showed him around the place, including the pool and the fruit trees I'd planted. I noticed how quiet he was during the tour. But a few days later as we were drinking coffee at the house, he said, "This is quite an operation you've got here." Then I realized that he didn't approve—of the grounds, or the pool, or the fact that I had an employee. I, of course, felt immediate guilt and wished I were still living in the smoggy house on the cul-de-sac. **Then** he would have seen I wasn't an elitist.

As we were heading back to the house, Tom asked if I was living with someone, meaning a live-in lover. I answered emphatically, "Oh no, never! I don't ever want to live with a man again!"

Tom laughed and said, "Oh," but his expression said **Whoa, lady! Why so defensive?** Good question. God forbid he should see I was lonely.

We went inside so he could do what he'd come for: show me his slide show. We sat on my living room floor, and there, on the paneled wall, unfolded a series of stunning images: children riding water buffalo, slender, reedlike women, graceful in their pastel **ao dais,** Buddhist temples with smiling roofs that curled at the corners, and always the rice fields stretching as far as the eye could see, dotted by Vietnamese in conical straw hats, waist-deep in an emerald vastness.

As the images flashed before me, Tom spoke of

things not apparent to the eye: how, for the Vietnamese, "growing rice is not just about raising food, it is part of a collective ritual that unites them with nature. Their dead are buried in these fields, their bones fertilize the rice that feeds their families and, thus, it is believed there is physical and spiritual continuity; the children inherit the strength of their ancestors." He didn't need to say that our saturation bombing was destroying not just crops and land but the connective tissue of their culture. It was clear, and more painful than any statistics could have been.

I wasn't prepared for **this.** Perhaps it was the very dryness of Tom's voice in contrast with the lyrical images and spiritual concepts that made the experience so compelling, but I could feel something shift within me.

Alongside the fresh and surprising cultural picture he was painting, Tom chose to effectively weave in quotes from the Pentagon Papers to highlight hard facts . . . such as that Vietnam was really one country divided artificially in 1954, at the end of France's war, into two separate entities, North and South, and was to have been **reunited** two years later.*

---

*When the division at the 17th Parallel was made in 1954 at the Geneva Conference, it was stated explicitly that the "demarcation is **provisional** and should **not in any way be interpreted as constituting a political or territorial boundary**" [PP Doc #15]. The division was to remain only until national elections were held two years later to determine which government would be chosen to represent the whole, united country. The United States pledged to adhere to these terms, yet almost immediately

Toward the end of the slide show there were devastating images that showed what had become of South Vietnam as a result of the U.S. presence there: GIs in Saigon brothels with Vietnamese girls in miniskirts with huge breasts and push-up bras; starving, hollow-eyed urban refugees living in fetid slums, the results of our "urbanization program," which aimed to drive the peasants away from their Vietcong-controlled land and into the cities that were controlled by the United States and the Thieu government, which we had installed. There was a large billboard advertising the services of an American doctor, a plastic surgeon, who could make Vietnamese eyes round and breasts bigger. Thousands of women were having this done, Tom said.

---

set out to try to destabilize the situation, including canceling the elections. President Dwight Eisenhower wrote in his memoirs that had elections been held, Ho Chi Minh would have won probably 80 percent of the votes. This is when the temporary line at the 17th Parallel began to be referred to as an "international boundary," the crossing of which was seen as "external aggression." This new concept, stated as it was in numerous public speeches by our leaders, became generally accepted, and by the time I became involved as an antiwar activist in 1970, Vietnam was being portrayed as two different countries, and Vietnamese coming down from the North, even if they had been born and had family in the South (which was frequently the case), were seen as outside aggressors. Imagine if the British had created a boundary at our Mississippi River, saying at first that it was temporary, then making it official and calling anyone who came across, whether to see family or to fight for reunification of their country, the "enemy."

I was speechless. Tom had brought to life for me an ancient culture that had survived foreign invasions, colonialism, torture, and war—and then shown how the United States was trying to overthrow that entire culture and replace it not with democracy but with a Western, consumer-driven, **Playboy** culture that was making Vietnamese women so ashamed of their slight Asian frames that they were willing to mutilate themselves to become westernized.

I began to cry—for them and for me. Tom has written about that moment in **Reunion**: "I was talking about the image of superficial sexiness she once promoted and was now trying to shake. I looked at her in a new way. Maybe I could love someone like this." I never could have imagined that in years to come I would mutilate my own body by getting breast implants, betraying what Tom saw in me that day—and betraying myself.

If Tom sensed that evening that perhaps I was someone he could fall in love with, I can tell you that I **did** fall in love with him—right then and there, head over heels. I know, it sounds so **seventies**—falling in love because of a political slide show. But of course it was Tom and his history of activism and the sensitivity I had seen with my own eyes that I fell in love with. I felt certain that he was someone with depth and soul, different from any man I had ever met.

We were making love on the living room floor when he heard Vanessa begin to rouse. Tom, with the agility of a leopard, managed to get himself up and

pulled together before she stumbled sleepily down
the hall and into the room. Tom knelt and introduced himself to her, asked her what her name was
and how old she was. I noticed that he spoke to her
not in the cloying, patronizing way some adults do
to children they're trying to butter up but with real
interest. Another good sign.

Tom and I began to spend more and more time together. I sat in on his classes and was captivated by
his brilliance as a teacher and how much his students
adored him. I was also awed by his strategic mind.
He had a historical perspective on most things, not
just the war. He was a powerful public speaker who
could capture people's seemingly disconnected, confused feelings and weave them into a coherent vision
they could identify with. In my living room, talking
with his longtime movement friends, I found many
political nuances hard to understand; it was almost
like being with Vadim before I spoke fluent French.

But there was more to the relationship than his
intellectual acuity. I loved his playfulness, the Irish
juiciness that brought welcomed moisture to what I
felt was my arid Protestant nature. Equally irresistible was his impish humor, his lithe body, and the
funny way his rubber-sandaled feet glided across the
ground while his upper body hunched forward as if
the weight of the world were on his shoulders. Then,
too, I had the sense that he really wanted to **know**
me. He has an ability to give that impression to

women, that he is—finally—the man who can delve into your psyche and understand you. Of course, I realize that I was projecting an impossible-to-live-up-to hero image onto Tom as surely as he had projected his slides onto my living room wall. For me he was the white knight who had arrived in my life just in the nick of time to set everything straight and save me from chaos. Poor Tom. How unfair projections are. No mortal man could possibly live up to that.

But there was something else I found fascinating about him: I had never been intimate with someone from his background—third-generation, midwestern, white-collar Irish-American . . . on both sides. He was never a Marxist or Maoist, as some critics liked to claim. One need only read the Port Huron Statement, SDS's founding document, which Tom co-authored, to see that his politics were always grounded solidly in democratic values.

His mother, Gene, was a sparrowlike woman who had been a librarian for twenty-five years, never missing a day's work. His father, Jack, was an accountant for the Chrysler Corporation. Both were natives of Wisconsin and during the Depression had moved to the Detroit suburb of Royal Oak, where for eight years Tom attended the Shrine of the Little Flower Church and parish school.

But things were far from picture perfect in Tom's childhood. Following World War II, his father began drinking heavily, and in time his parents divorced. Thereafter Gene devoted her life to Tom, never again remarrying or even seeing another man. Then, in the early sixties, Tom became a full-time activist in the civil rights movement, and his father, a conservative Republican, broke off all contact with him, his only child—for thirteen years! I had often pondered what kind of person my grandfather was to have refused to speak to my dad for six weeks because he was considering a career in acting—but thirteen years! Tom told me about this rupture with his dad in a matter-of-fact way, never in emotional terms. But I cannot fathom what an impact it must have had on him—growing up with a repressed, noncommunicative father who then cut off all relations and a mother who, though a fairly liberal Democrat, was frightened and confused by her child's activism and held a deep bitterness about life that I could never penetrate.

Perhaps this was why, like Vadim, Tom could cry easily about children, the war, animals, but couldn't show emotions in intimate areas like love, loss, and betrayal; he couldn't allow that degree of vulnerability. The sensitivity displayed in his slide show disguised Tom's lack of emotional availability. But I was so accustomed to the absence of emotionality in the men in my life that I thought Tom the most emotionally accessible human being I had ever met—and later I assumed that whatever problems we had in that area must be all my fault. (Of course, if Tom **had** possessed a real capacity for intimacy at that time, I probably would have fled in terror without knowing why. It's so much easier to stay with what's familiar.)

Others knew Tom differently. One day soon after we became lovers, a woman named Carol Kurtz arrived at my doorstep asking for Tom. I sensed she needed to be alone with him. I knew Carol a little; she and her husband were members of the Red Family collective. I told Tom she wanted to talk to him, but instead of asking her in, he stood just outside the front door for a few minutes, and when he came back in he was clearly angry. I went to say good-bye to Carol and found her sobbing. Carol wanted to repair the breach between them caused by his expulsion from the collective and maintain a friendship with Tom. He wanted no part of it. She said to me, "He has no heart, no emotions." I thought, She can't be referring to the Tom I know. Tom never spoke about what transpired between them that day, but I never forgot Carol's words, which so confused me.

Little by little I learned that after leaving the Red Family, Tom had migrated from Berkeley to Santa Monica, where he lived anonymously while writing his book about Native Americans and Vietnam. By the time he surfaced in my life that spring, he was sharing a small apartment with the brilliant, soft-spoken attorney Leonard Weinglass, who had represented Tom during the Chicago conspiracy trial. They lived on the ground floor of a house in Venice, a colorful coastal area just south of Santa Monica. In Tom, and in his circle, I felt I had at last found a haven from the storms of uncertainty buffeting me. I felt he would bring coherence, structure, and safety into my life . . . and in many ways he did just that. In some ways he didn't.

But if I thought the previous buffeting had been hard, nothing could compare with what was about to happen.

On May 8 President Nixon had ordered underwater explosive mines to be placed in the Haiphong harbor, something that had been rejected by previous administrations. Later that same month, a month after Tom and I had become lovers, reports began to come in from European scientists and diplomats that the dikes of the Red River Delta in North Vietnam were being targeted by U.S. planes. The Swedish ambassador to Vietnam, Jean-Christophe Oberg, reported to an American delegation in Hanoi that he had at first believed the bombing was accidental but now, having seen the dikes with his own eyes, he was convinced it was deliberate.

I might have missed the significance of these reports had Tom not shown me what the Pentagon Papers had to say on the subject: In 1966, assistant secretary of Defense John McNaughton, searching for some new means to bring Hanoi to its knees, had proposed destroying North Vietnam's system of locks and dams, which, he said, "if handled right, might . . . offer promise . . . such destruction does not kill or drown people. By shallow-flooding the rice, it leads after time to widespread starvation (more than a million?) unless food is provided— which we could offer to do 'at the conference table.' " President Johnson, to his credit, had not acted upon this option. Now, six years later, Richard Nixon appeared to have given orders to target the dikes—whether to actually destroy them or to demonstrate the threat of destruction, no one knew.

Tom explained that the Red River is North Vietnam's largest. Its delta is below sea level. Over centuries the Vietnamese people have constructed—by hand!—an intricate network of earthen dikes and dams to hold back the sea, a network 2,500 miles long! The stability of these dikes became especially critical as monsoon season approached and required an all-out effort to repair any damage from burrowing animals or from normal wear and tear. Now it was June, but this was no normal wear and tear they were facing. The Red River would begin to rise in July and August. Should there be flooding, the mining of the Haiphong harbor would prevent food from being imported. The bombing showed no signs of letting up, and there was little press coverage of the potential impending disaster. Something drastic had to be done.

The Nixon administration and its U.S. ambassador to the United Nations, George Herbert Walker Bush, would vehemently deny what was happening, but the following are excerpts from the April–May 1972 transcripts of conversations between President Nixon and top administration officials:

April 25, 1972

PRESIDENT NIXON: "... We've got to be thinking in terms of an all-out bombing attack [of North

Vietnam]. . . . Now by all-out bombing attack, I am thinking about things that go far beyond. . . . I'm thinking of the dikes, I'm thinking of the railroad, I'm thinking, of course, the docks. . . ."

KISSINGER: ". . . I agree with you."

PRESIDENT NIXON: ". . . And I still think we ought to take the dikes out now. Will that drown people?"

KISSINGER: "About two hundred thousand people."

PRESIDENT NIXON: ". . . No, no, no . . . I'd rather use the nuclear bomb. Have you got that, Henry?"

KISSINGER: "That, I think, would just be too much."

PRESIDENT NIXON: "The nuclear bomb, does that bother you? . . . I just want to think big, Henry, for chrissakes."

May 4, 1972

PRESIDENT NIXON TO KISSINGER, AL HAIG, JOHN CONNALLY: ". . . Vietnam: Here's those little cocksuckers right in there, here they are. [He thumps on his desk] Here we are. They're taking on the United States. Now, goddammit, we're gonna **do** it. We're going to cream them. . . .

"I'll see that the United States does not lose. . . . South Vietnam may lose. But the United States **cannot** lose. Which means, basically, I have made the decision. Whatever happens to South Vietnam, we are going to **cream** North Vietnam. . . .

"For once we've got to use the maximum power of this country . . . against this **shit-ass** little country: to win the war. We can't use the word '**win.**' But others can."

May 4, 1972

JOHN B. CONNALLY: ". . . Bomb for seriousness, not just as a signal. Railroads, ports, power stations, communication lines . . . and don't worry about killing civilians. Go ahead and kill 'em. . . . People think you are [killing civilians] now. So go ahead and give 'em some."

RICHARD NIXON: "That's right."

H. R. HALDEMAN: "There's pictures on the news of dead bodies every night. . . . A dead body is a dead body. Nobody knows whose bodies they are or who killed them."

RICHARD NIXON: "Henry [Kissinger] is overreacting on that . . . because they're going to charge us with it [killing civilians] anyway."

[Later in same conversation]

RICHARD NIXON: "We need to win the goddamned war . . . and . . . what that fella [?] said about taking out the goddamned dikes, all right, we'll take out the goddamned dikes. . . . If Henry's for that, I'm for it all the way."

H. R. HALDEMAN: "I don't know if he's for the dikes."

RICHARD NIXON: "No, I don't think he's for the dikes, but I am. I am for the Connally idea."

[Later in same conversation]

RICHARD NIXON: "I agree with Connally about civilians, too. I'm not going to worry about it."

So much for winding down the war. So much for our concern about civilian casualties and our "allies" in South Vietnam.

That May I received an invitation from the North Vietnamese in Paris to make the trip to Hanoi. Tom felt strongly that I should go. Perhaps it would take a different sort of celebrity to get people's attention. Heightened public attention—even if it took controversy to achieve it—was what was needed to confront the impending crisis with the dikes. I would take a camera and bring back photographic evidence (if such was to be found) of the bomb damage to the dikes we'd been hearing about.

I arranged the trip's logistics through the Vietnamese delegation at the Paris peace talks, bought myself a round-trip ticket, and stopped in New York. Since 1969 mail for the POWs had been brought in and out of North Vietnam every month by American visitors. This effort was coordinated by the Committee of Liaison with Families of Prisoners Detained in Vietnam. I picked up a packet of letters from families of POWs that I would deliver.

CHAPTER NINE

HANOI

Here is the true meaning and value of compassion and nonviolence, when it helps us to see the enemy's point of view, to hear his questions, to know his assessment of ourselves. For from his view we may indeed see the basic weakness of our own condition, and if we are mature, we may learn and grow and profit from the wisdom of the brothers who are called the opposition.

—DR. MARTIN LUTHER KING JR.,
Riverside Church, New York City, 1967

Love thine enemies.
—MATTHEW 5:44

I WENT ALONE. I'm not sure why. It can't be that we couldn't afford a plane ticket for Tom. Obviously Tom didn't think it was necessary for someone to accompany me to Hanoi. "They invited **you,**" he said recently when I put the question to him. "Besides," he added, "at the time, we weren't together publicly as a couple."

I didn't know how unusual it was for someone—especially a famous person, especially a woman—to go alone into a war zone. In spite of it, I do not regret that I went. My only regret about the trip was that I was photographed sitting in a North Vietnamese antiaircraft gun site. What that image suggested had no relationship whatsoever to what I was doing or thinking or feeling at the time, as I hope this chapter will show.

Beginning in 1965, over two hundred American citizens had traveled to North Vietnam, mostly in groups, to bring back eyewitness reports. They represented American peace and religious groups, Vietnam veterans, teachers, lawyers, and poets. Doctors and biologists from Harvard, Yale, and MIT had gone to assess the medical needs of the North Vietnamese. Tom had been one of the first to make the trip, in 1965, with historian Staughton Lynd and organizer Herbert Aptheker. He went again in 1967 and brought back the first three American POWs to be released.

All the travelers had returned with reports about extensive bombing of civilian targets, including churches, hospitals, and schools; reports that the morale of the North seemed undiminished, that the bombing was not having and would not have the desired effect of getting the North Vietnamese government to retreat at the negotiating table, and that the North Vietnamese were prepared to negotiate when the United States stopped bombing and withdrew its troops.

I am running full speed through Orly Airport in Paris. My flight from New York got in late and I am about to miss the plane to Moscow that will carry me to Vientiane, Laos, and on to Hanoi. As I round a corner, I slip on the polished floor and down I go. I know immediately that I have refractured the foot I broke the previous year. Bulimics have thin bones; I've had a lot of breaks. What to do? I have seconds to make up my mind: Should I use this as an excuse to turn around and go home, or should I keep going? For better or worse, I'm not the turnaround type. So I hobble to my plane, getting there just as the doors are about to close. I wrap some ice in a towel and strap it onto my foot, which the flight attendant kindly lets me elevate on the back of the passenger's headrest in front of me—the seat is empty. I wish Tom were here.

By the time we land in Moscow my foot is swollen and blue, and I know I must get it tended to. I have a four-hour layover till the next lap of the journey, so airport officials get me a taxi and instruct the driver to take me to the closest hospital on the outskirts of Moscow. After X-raying my foot, the doctors confirm it is a fracture, apply a plaster cast, give me a pair of crutches, and send me back to the airport.

What will my Vietnamese hosts think when

they see me get off the plane with crutches and a cast? They don't need the burden of a disabled American descending on them—and how am I going to climb over the earthen dikes that I am coming to film?

I decide to remain on board during the layover in Vientiane, in part because of my foot and in part because I am concerned that an American spook has been sent to nab me en route.

From my FBI files: A confidential cable from the American embassy in Vientiane to National Security Adviser Henry Kissinger in Washington, the U.S. delegation at the Paris peace talks, the commander in chief of Pacific forces, and the U.S. embassy in Saigon said:

> **Actress Jane Fonda arrived in Hanoi July 8 via Aeroflot from Moscow. Subject was not carried as passenger on Aeroflot manifesto deposited during Vientiane transit morning July 8 nor did she disembark to transit lounge.**

We finally take off for Hanoi after what has felt like an interminable layover. The plane is only partly filled, and I see that I am the sole woman among a burly assortment of what appear to be Russians and Eastern Europeans, with a Frenchman or two thrown in.

Soon we are over Vietnam. I begin to think of the country as a woman, her back nestled against Cambodia and Laos, her pregnant belly protruding into the South China Sea, so small and vulnerable that any superpower would feel certain it could call her bluff in no time flat. What a thin little slip of a country she is, much like the small, thin-boned people who inhabit her.

The flight is supposed to be short, but as we approach Hanoi, I look out my window and see the black silhouettes of eight American Phantom jet fighters circling above the city. I stiffen. Something about them tells my body what they are about even before my mind knows. In the journal I intend to keep of my trip, I write that they look like hawks circling their prey. An abrupt voice over the loudspeaker announces that the planes are bombing Hanoi and that we will have to turn around and go at least partway back to Vientiane (or all the way if we start to run low on gas) until the bombers finish their mission. (I have subsequently read that U.S. bombers took advantage of North Vietnam's unwillingness to fire at them when civilian aircraft were in range.)

I watch the planes recede from sight, riveted. My country's planes—bombing a city where I am about to be received as a welcomed guest. I hate the killing of and by American soldiers. I know that the way to support them is to end the war and get them home; that the people of this emerald country spread beneath me are fighting to defend their country from foreigners—and that we are now the foreigners.

I think of my childhood, when I would go with my mother to see Dad off at the air base in Burbank, California, during World War II. How beautiful the planes had looked all lined up under the camouflaged netting! How proud I had felt that they were there to protect us! Now our planes represent not protection from another mighty military power, but destruction of a peasant people who pose no threat to us.

We are flying into Hanoi. Has it been an hour? A day? As in a dream, time has lost its meaning. As we begin our descent to Gia Lam, the small, civilian airport, I see bomb craters dotting the surrounding landscape. A recent summer downpour has turned the craters into shimmering pink-and-blue pools reflecting the rose-tinted sky at dusk. Death and beauty, joined.

It is awkward getting down the plane's steps, because I am juggling the crutches and a purse, a camera, and a packet of letters from the families of POWs. I look up to see five Vietnamese walking toward me carrying flowers. They are the welcoming committee of the Vietnam Committee for Solidarity with the American People. The name sounds propagandistic to me, but the fullness of its meaning will soon be made clear in unusual, very human terms. As I'd anticipated, they look shocked and want to hand me the bouquet, but I can't hold it and the crutches at the same time. Standing on the tarmac, they hold a quick conference in Vietnamese with numerous glances at my cast. I understand their concern: These are the people who will be responsible for my well-being over the next two weeks. Clearly my condition is worrisome. I wonder whether this is a group of seasoned cadres whose job it is to manipulate me.

Some sort of a decision is reached: Suddenly they are all smiles. I am led into a reception room inside the airport, where we all sit on upholstered chairs and I am offered tea, bottles of carbonated water (which tastes rusty), and hard candy. I notice that the airport is very dilapidated: Paint is chipping, water from a roof leak has left stains on the walls. It is breathtakingly hot and humid. I hand over the packet of letters, then try to assure my hosts that my injury will not deter me from going into the countryside and photographing the dikes. I show them my small 8-millimeter film camera and my still camera and remind them that I was very clear in my pretrip letter that I am here primarily to photograph the damage to the dikes. Privately I am not certain how I will manage out in the countryside, especially if there is a bombing raid, as running for cover doesn't seem to be in the cards; but I say I don't want to change our plans, and everyone nods. Later I will discover that they tend to nod whether or not they agree with me. I suddenly feel very vulnerable.

In retrospect I wonder about my insistence at

continuing despite the danger. Yes, I was numb with exhaustion and pain. But more to the point is my character: To turn away out of fear is just about unthinkable.

My main interpreter, Quoc, briefly goes over the schedule for my visit. I notice that the trip to an antiaircraft installation is still on the agenda for the last day, despite my message from Los Angeles saying I was **not** interested in military installations. I tell them that I don't want to keep that visit on the agenda. Altering the plans appears to cause consternation. Decisions have been made. I am too tired to protest.

This is a lapse that I will live to regret.

I am relieved when Quoc suggests that they take me to my hotel. I am assured that I will soon get a good meal and that, after a night's sleep, I will be taken to a hospital to have my foot examined. (My head should have been examined as well!)

The hour-long drive into Hanoi is a shock. I was expecting desperation. Instead I see people, a lot of people, bustling about their business despite the fact that only an hour ago the city has been bombed. Battered old military jeeps and trucks pass us, covered with leafy camouflage. I see countless soldiers of both sexes in khaki uniforms, also with leaves on their helmets, and civilians, walking, riding, or pushing dilapidated bicycles through the mud and ruts of this much attacked highway. The civilians all wear conical straw hats, loose white tops, and black pajama-type pants, the traditional Vietnamese peasant attire.

Many have rolled up their pajama pants to keep them out of the mud and the bicycle gears, exposing universally sinewy legs and black rubber sandals like Tom's. Here and there I can see piles of rubble, houses without roofs, and more bomb craters.

In speeches back home I have said how outrageous it is that we are pounding this backward country with our unprecedented modern technology. Now that I am here, seeing how primitive it really is, it all becomes even more reprehensible. Were it not for the insights that Tom's slide show has given me—can it have only been three months earlier?—I could not comprehend how they are resisting.

The Long Binh Bridge, which crossed the Red River, has been destroyed, but next to it is a floating bamboo pontoon bridge permitting an uninterrupted flow of people, military jeeps, and trucks filled with soldiers to move in and out of the city. I have heard about the Vietnamese's ability to put up a bamboo bridge, take it down, and hide it away, all in a matter of minutes. Because the pontoon is narrow, all the traffic going in one direction is allowed to pass; then the traffic going the other way can proceed. We move slowly, with frequent stops, and I can feel the bridge swaying. It is so crowded I fear it will collapse. I am also acutely aware that should the bombers return, we are sitting ducks.

Sitting in the car, I cannot speak. I am too filled with emotions—sorrow and guilt at what my government is doing, admiration at the way these people are getting on with their lives, and disbelief: **This is not a dream, I am actually here—alone.** The enormity of it is washing over me. I feel that my hosts understand what is happening to me, since they remain quiet as well. I just sit and look out the car window, the lovely bouquet of fresh flowers lying in my lap, in ironic contrast to the reality outside.

It is one thing to refuse, in the abstract, my government's definition of "enemy." But being here with soldiers and trucks passing just outside the car window, I realize it is less simple. I am not afraid—it's not that. It's being here on the ground with people whose mission is to defeat us. Though I understand that they are fighting to defend themselves and that we are the aggressors, the "they" are right here at eye level, and the "us" is me. Everything seems upside down like in **Alice in Wonderland.**

It is dusk as we enter Hanoi, a sprawling, former colonial city shaped by French architects, with wide, tree-lined boulevards, parks, and lakes. I am told that the targets of the eight planes I saw earlier were a cigarette factory, a hospital, and a brickyard at the height of their working hours, all in Hanoi's outlying area.

We enter the old, colonial Thong Nhat Hotel through a rickety revolving door. There are quite a few Europeans and two American journalists sitting about the high-ceilinged lobby. I have been given an enormous room on an upper floor, with a ceiling fan and mosquito netting over the bed. Bed! My foot is throbbing terribly and I can't wait to lie down. A thermos of hot water, a can of tea, teapot, cups, candy, and individually folded pieces of thick brown toilet paper have been laid out for me, and I'm told there is plenty of hot water for a bath. I am too tired for a bath but grateful for the luxurious accommodations and relieved finally to be here.

Around midnight I am jolted from a deep sleep by shrill air raid sirens. A maid appears at my door carrying a helmet for me. She is there to escort me to the bomb shelter in the hotel's backyard. As I hobble down the back stairs and out into the darkened yard, I can see the hotel staff calmly going about their work. Later I am told that the maids double as militia and during alerts don their own helmets and go up onto the roof with rifles. I am led down a flight of stairs into a long, tunnel-like concrete bunker lined with benches. A dozen or so people are already there, all foreign visitors.

This is easier to take than seeing U.S. bombers from the air. John Sullivan, director of the American Friends Service Committee—the Quaker peace organization—is here. He doesn't recognize me—partly the cliché about seeing someone out of context (and this is about as out of context as it gets), but also because I don't look like me: I am without makeup, disheveled, and tired. I'm tempted to say, "I used to be Jane Fonda."

Sullivan asks when I arrived and why I've come. In his subsequent written report of the trip he will quote me as saying it was "vital that Americans speak out against this bombing because if they were silent, Nixon would ratchet up the damage as his peace plan was stripped of even the illusion of victory," that I didn't "believe that Nixon would accept a coalition government in Saigon," and that "Hanoi would never accept a Thieu government after American withdrawal." Not bad for someone who was still half-asleep and had a fractured foot, if I do say so!

There are two more air raids that night. Newly blasé, I stay in my bed for the third one.

Already up and outside the hotel at 5:30 in the morning, I am struck, as I was the previous evening, by the bustle of the place. I don't know if everyone seems to be hurrying because the bombing doesn't usually start until 9:00 A.M. or if hurrying is their custom (of course, the bombing has **become** their custom). There are no cars to be seen—I'm told that no one owns a private car—but there is dense bicycle and foot traffic everywhere and a sense of purposefulness. Blanketing the scene is a mellifluous female voice being broadcast from loudspeakers mounted on street corners. Impossible to know what she is saying: the morning news? political propaganda? a story about Vietnamese heroes and heroines from the past? The voice, I will discover, goes on till nightfall, interrupted occasionally by a song. After a while it loses some of its charm—especially when I learn that mostly it is spouting political propaganda. I learn to ignore it.

It is just dawn as we drive through the city to the Vietnam-Soviet Friendship Hospital, where I am to have my foot examined. I can see camouflaged vehicles coming and going, their lights off. At the hospital, two male Vietnamese doctors who have been briefed about my arrival lay me on a table to take an X-ray of my foot—or at least they try to. No sooner have I lain down than the air raid sirens blare and I have to be helped into the hospital's bomb shelter, essentially identical to the one at the hotel, only larger and now filling rapidly with doctors and those patients who can be moved.

I sense no panic; they seem to have grown accustomed to this ritual interruption of their daily lives. This is my first time sharing a bomb shelter with Vietnamese, and it makes the experience all the more surreal. I feel unspeakably guilty to be taking up space and the attention of two doctors while my country is attacking theirs. My interpreter for the day, Madame Chi, tells them I am American and this stirs up a lot of excitement. I search their eyes for some sign of hostility. There is none. Those unhostile eyes will stay with me long after the war ends.

The raid is over, and we return to the X-ray machine—only to be interrupted a second time by the sirens. Perhaps an hour goes by before the doctors are finally able to get the X-ray of my foot. Sure enough, there is a slight fracture across the arch. As they are removing the Soviet-made cast, they begin to laugh and chatter to each other. Madame Chi, who has remained by my side throughout, tells me they are laughing at the poor job the Soviets have done: They had neglected to put gauze between my skin and the plaster, and because it was mixed improperly, the plaster hasn't hardened on the inside . . . thank God! Had it hardened, my skin would have come off with the cast.

The doctors explain that they are going to strap a poultice made from chrysanthemum roots onto my foot and ankle. They tell me that it is so full of healing and strengthening elements that pregnant women in Vietnam drink tea brewed from the same roots. "Because of the war," one doctor says, "we have to rely on whatever we have, simple things, to meet our medical needs." (I wonder if Adelle Davis knows about this.)

The stuff is truly foul smelling, but the doctors tell me they are certain that within days my swelling will go away and the fracture will mend. Anything that smells this bad is bound to work! The irony of this whole episode is not lost on me: Here is this besieged, agrarian country accused by the United States of being a Soviet pawn when in mind, spirit, and medicine, at least, its people seem remarkably independent and to be "making do" just fine.

Driving through Hanoi, I notice that the streets are swept clean; I see no litter anywhere, no signs of poverty, no beggars, no homeless people—and few children. Most children, Madame Chi tells me, have long ago been evacuated to the countryside, where life continues. "We have moved our schools, the university, hospitals, and factories out of the city and rebuilt them in the countryside, sometimes underground and in caves." Flexibility and adaptability must be skills they honed during their war against the French colonialists—or maybe against the Japanese, or the Chinese, or the Mongols.

We attract a good deal of attention as we drive. I assume this is because there are so few cars to be seen, and ours signals the presence of a VIP. People wave and a few teenage boys run alongside, peering through the window to try to get a look at the passengers inside. When they see me, they shout something at the driver. Madame Chi tells me they are asking where I am from—am I Russian? The driver shouts, "She's an American," and they actually cheer!

"Why are they happy to see an American?" I ask Madame Chi, incredulous.

"You won't find any 'Yankee Go Home' slogans here," she replies. "Our people aren't anti-American. When we see a bomb crater we say 'Nixon's' or 'Johnson's,' not 'America's.' "

I find this incomprehensible. I wish Tom were here so we could ponder it together.

I am visiting the nine-hundred-bed Bach Mai Hospital, the largest in North Vietnam. Although it has been bombed on numerous occasions over the years, the hospital has continued to function. Some of the surgeons, still dressed in their blue hospital garb and masks, have come out to speak with me. I ask them how they continue their work. They describe how during bombing raids they carry patients into the shelter, where an operating room has been built.

It has been only two days, but I no longer need crutches and the swelling in my foot has almost disappeared. When I get home maybe I'll market chrysanthemum root for its healing properties!

I visit the Committee for Denunciation of U.S. War Crimes in Vietnam, run by Colonel Ha Van Lau, who will later be named Vietnamese ambassador to the United Nations. Colonel Lau guides me through the exhibit. There are the twelve-thousand-pound daisy cutters, the guava bombs, pineapple bombs, the Willie Peters, cluster bombs, pellet bombs—weaponry I had heard described by veterans at the Winter Soldier investigation. Sitting on the floor like a piece of metal sculpture is the casing of a three-thousand-pound "mother" bomb, the bearer of the little bomblets that are so devastating to humans because they float down and explode later. The smaller weapons are displayed on shelves inside glass cases with photographs next to them, showing the effects of the particular weapon on a human being or, in the case of the defoliants, an entire forest.

This is the true face of Vietnamization that President Nixon hopes Americans won't find out about: American soldiers may be coming home from war,

Walking gingerly over ruins in Vietnam.
(© G. Guillaume/Magnum Photos)

In Hanoi's War Crimes Museum photographing
a "mother" bomb.

Looking at photographic evidence of the effects of U.S. antipersonnel weapons and defoliation spraying.
(© G. Guillaume/Magnum Photos)

but the war is escalating and more Vietnamese are dying. Does he hope we've grown immune to the suffering of others? I resolve that no matter what, I will keep my heart open and try to communicate what I am seeing to other Americans back home.

Colonel Lau explains that since Nixon became president, the weapons have become even more sophisticated and damaging. "Before now," he says, "we were able surgically to remove the pellets. But now they have been made in such a way that they can't be removed without doing even more damage. Some of them now expand once inside the flesh." And he points to another X-ray. I am grateful for the colonel's air of detachment. Had he expressed anger, I would have disintegrated.

From the war crimes exhibit, I am taken to the Viet Duc Hospital. There I talk with Dr. Ton That Tung, who has begun research linking the U.S. chemical defoliant Agent Orange to birth defects in babies born to women in sprayed areas of South Vietnam.

"We are seeing more and more of these birth defects," he tells me. Then, as if reading my mind, he adds, "Yes, I fear you will soon be seeing these things among your own soldiers."

I know what I must do.

CHAPTER TEN

BAMBOO

Americans looked at photographs of the North and saw a poor country where life seemed drab and regimented and assumed that the regime was hated. There was hatred of the regime and opposition, but nothing similar to what existed in the South. The majority of the Northern population was loyal to its government. The photographs held a clue. . . . The clue was the absence of barbed wire. . . . The Vietnamese Communists were not afraid of their people.

—NEIL SHEEHAN,
A Bright Shining Lie

As WE STEP from the Viet Duc Hospital into the sunlight, I have made up my mind.

"I want to speak on your radio," I say to my hosts. "I want to try to tell U.S. pilots what I am seeing here on the ground."

I am used to talking with soldiers, and my work with VVAW and the FTA tour has given me some understanding of their realities. I know that a growing number of airmen have turned against the war, and I remember hearing that the maps they were given of their targets had no Vietnamese names on them—only numbers, remote, impersonal. They have never been in Vietnam, have never seen the faces of their victims. I feel I must try to make what I am seeing as personal an experience for them as it is for the soldiers on the ground in South Vietnam. I have come to bear witness, and while I have not planned this, I feel it as a moral imperative. I do not stop to consider that this will have consequences for me later—especially since I know that other American travelers to Hanoi have spoken on Radio Hanoi. Some will later accuse me of treason for urging soldiers to desert—something I do not do.

The first broadcast is done live. Others will be recorded over the next week.* Aside from a few notes

*For transcripts of my broadcasts in Hanoi, see **U.S. Congress House Committee on Internal Security, Travel to Hostile Areas,** HR 16742. Actually, there are two types of transcripts in

I have scribbled to myself, I speak extemporaneously, from my heart, about what I have witnessed and how it made me feel. (A CIA contract employee, Edward Hunter, was brought before the House Committee on Internal Security as an authority on Communist brainwashing techniques. He testified that my broadcasts were "so concise and professional a job" that he "most strongly doubt[ed] that [I] wrote them [myself. I] must have been working with the enemy." Committee chair Richard Ichord agreed. He was quoted as saying I "used a lot of military terms that wouldn't be within [my] knowledge." Obviously they were unaware of the time I had spent with soldiers.)

As I talk I see in my mind the faces of the air force pilots I have met. I feel as if I am talking to men I know and, eternal optimist that I am, I hope

---

HR 16742. The first (and most common) kind comes directly from my radio broadcasts. The CIA transcribers copied down what they heard me say in English. Nothing was translated. Some examples of these would be on pages 7645, 7646, etc. But HR 16742 has another kind of transcript that can be misleading. An example of these would be on page 7653 (top of the page) where the transcript reads: "Sister Fonda indignantly said, [first two sentences in English, fading into Vietnamese translation—recording] Melvin Laird the other day said that bombing of dikes may be taking place . . ." etc. In these transcripts, what I said was first translated into Vietnamese, broadcast in Vietnamese by a Vietnamese journalist, picked up by CIA listeners and translated back into English. Anything translated twice like that can end up far from the original and shouldn't be relied on.

that if they can see what I am seeing, they will feel as I do.

This is a transcript of a typical broadcast:

Eighty percent of the American people, according to a recent poll, have stopped believing in the war and think we should get out, think we should bring all of you [soldiers] home. The people back home are crying for you.

Tonight when you are alone, ask yourselves: What are you doing? Accept no ready answers fed to you by rote from basic training on up, but as men, as human beings, can you justify what you are doing? Do you know why you are flying these missions, collecting extra combat pay on Sunday?

The people beneath your planes have done us no harm. They want to live in peace. They want to rebuild their country. . . . Did you know that the antipersonnel bombs that are thrown from some of your planes were outlawed by the Hague Convention of 1907, of which the United States was a signatory? I think that if you knew what these bombs were doing, you would get very angry at the men who invented them. They cannot destroy bridges or factories. They cannot pierce steel or cement. Their only target is unprotected human flesh. The pellets now contain rough-edged plastic pellets, and your bosses, whose minds think in terms of statistics, not human lives, are proud of this new perfection. The plastic pellets don't show up on X rays and cannot be removed. The hospitals here are filled with babies and women and old people who will live for the rest of their lives in agony with these pellets embedded in them.

Can we fight this kind of war and continue to call ourselves Americans? Are these people so different from our own children, our mothers, or grandmothers? I don't think so, except that perhaps they have a surer sense of why they are living and what they are willing to die for.

I know that if you saw and if you knew the Vietnamese under peaceful conditions, you would hate the men who are sending you on bombing missions. I believe that in this age of remote-controlled push-button war, we must all try very, very hard to remain human beings.

A few days later I am driven south of Hanoi. Following us in a separate car is French filmmaker Gérard Guillaume and a small crew. He is in Hanoi to make a documentary and has decided to film some of my visit as well. Since my goal is to bear witness and get word out as broadly as possible, I welcome his being there.

All that is left of the city of Phu Ly, formerly a thriving industrial center, is the occasional frame of a building, a doorway, the steeple of a church lying on its side. The city has been flattened into rubble. I am seeing what our makers of war assume Americans will never see.

We are driving back to Hanoi through the township of Duc Giang when air raid sirens let us know we have to take shelter. We tumble from the car and hurry to a half-buried A-frame shelter that is filling up with local Vietnamese. The film crew stumbles in right behind us. Suddenly the roar of Vietnamese antiaircraft guns explodes all around us, drowning out the sound of the American planes. It is a sound beyond sound. Do GIs hear this noise from their own guns? How do they stand it? I can't fathom how anyone could ever grow accustomed to this devastation of sound. But still, except for their curiosity about who I am, the people in the shelter appear calm. Again someone asks if I am Russian, and when Quoc tells them I am an American actress they get very excited and seem inordinately pleased. Why? Why don't they shout at me? I want to shout at them, "Don't you understand it is my country that is bombing you!" Suddenly I feel claustrophobic, wanting to be out of there, to see firsthand what is going on, to film the planes that are bombing. Before Quoc can stop me, I grab my camera and bolt from the shelter.

(Thirty years later, over lunch in California, Quoc will remind me that he had pleaded with me to come back inside but that I refused. Poor Quoc. I should have obeyed him. He was, after all, the one responsible for my safety.)

The raid ends and a sudden, deafening silence descends. It all happened so fast. The planes are gone, none were hit, and at least in the immediate vicinity, I can see no signs of damage. Quoc takes me to a group of soldiers who are operating the closest gun installation. I am surprised to see that they are young women and that one of them is pregnant. Pregnant and fighting. I think that if she can have hope, so can I. Right then I determine to have a baby with Tom, as a testament to **our** country's future.

I have found that the few clothes I brought—a pair of blue jeans, khaki slacks—are too hot for the days when I am mostly outdoors, so Madame Chi takes me to a small shop near the hotel where I purchase a pair of loose black pants and rubber sandals.

I travel to visit schools in outlying rural areas. When I ask if the war has created obstacles to the children's schooling, I am told that on the contrary, they have succeeded in gaining widespread literacy in the north.

For a people who have gone directly from colonialism (which had left all but the privileged few illiterate) into war, it is an astonishing commitment to education.

I am taken to the Hanoi film studio, where I meet with a director and watch the most famous Vietnamese actor, Tra Giang, perform a scene in a film about a war heroine. I am surprised that they are continuing to make films despite the bombings. Tra Giang is from South Vietnam and about my age, with deep, sad eyes and an exquisite beauty. She is also pregnant. I will not forget her face.

Nguyen Dinh Thi is a well-known writer in Vietnam, and as he speaks fluent French, we can converse in the hotel gardens without a translator. As it happens, he is also very handsome, a Vietnamese cross between historian Howard Zinn and my dad: a long, lanky drink of water with expressive hands and black hair that flops over his forehead the way Dad's did in **Young Mr. Lincoln.** He is my favorite person to talk with, not only because of how he looks, but because of the way he has of capturing the essence of his country's struggle in brief metaphors, which he laughingly delivers like a gift on a tray, enjoying them as much as his listener does. He tells me, "We Vietnamese, because of our unique circumstances, have developed a deep sense of patience." He looks hard at me, making sure the words sink in, before continuing. "In our mountains here in the north there are huge limestone caves. We know these caves were not made by supernatural giants. No, they were made by little drops of water." And his grin stretches from ear to ear: It is the long-term, cumulative effects of seemingly weak things that achieve the impossible.

It is 3:00 in the morning as we leave the hotel in a camouflaged car to drive to Nam Sach forty miles east of Hanoi. We travel at night because of the danger of strafing by U.S. planes. Yesterday twenty foreign correspondents who had come to examine the damage done to the dikes three days earlier were witness to a second attack. Twelve Phantom jets and A-7s dove at the dike the journalists were standing on and released several bombs and rockets. The reporter from Agence France-Press wrote on July 11 that they "all felt the attack was clearly against the dike system."

This is what the United States is denying. This is what I have come to document.

The sky is beginning to lighten as we enter the province. Many people are already in the fields working. I am told they do a lot of work at night, when there is less danger of bombing. The whole area is protected from flooding by a complicated system of crisscrossing dikes.

The filmmakers are with us again. We walk

through the mud on the narrow paths that run between rice paddies. It is impossible to keep my poultice out of the mud, but at least I am walking and no longer need crutches. The sun is high overhead; sweat is running down my body. A flock of what appear to be starlings turns on a dime above us. Ahead I see my first dike, rising gradually eight or ten meters above the fields and built entirely of earth. Some men and women on bicycles and a few water buffalo pulling carts are moving along the top. Do they feel the heavy heat as I do or are they immune to it? On the other side is the Thai Binh River.

The particular spot that has been attacked for the second time just the previous morning is the most strategic, for here the dike must hold back the waters of six converging rivers. These rivers will be raging down the mountains in about two weeks. I am told that Nam Sach has been attacked by U.S. planes eight times since May 10 and the dikes have been hit four times. Although the planes are expected back, there are people all around, knee- and elbow-deep in mud, planting their rice and carrying huge baskets of earth to repair the dikes.

One of the committee members shouts to the people that I am an American actor, and this is greeted with smiles and waves. **Why?** Why don't they scream and shake their fists at me? That's what I would do in their place. Their lack of hostility seems passive and I feel the urge to grab their necks and shake some sense into them. **Get angry, dammit!**

As I stand on the dike, I look in all directions. I

see no visible military targets, no industry, no communication lines—just rice fields. Then I suddenly see the bomb craters on both sides of the dike—gaping holes, some ten meters across and eight meters deep. The crater bottoms, I am told, are two meters below sea level. The crater that had severed the dike is almost filled in again, but the main worry are the bombs that have fallen on the sides of the dike. They cause earthquakes that shatter the dike's foundation and make deep cracks that zigzag up the sides. Antipersonnel bombs have also been used; they enter the dike on an angle, lodging underneath and exploding later. This damage does not show up on aerial reconnaissance photographs. I am told that if these cracks aren't repaired in time, the pressure from the water—which will soon reach six or seven meters above the level of the fields—will cause the weakened dikes to give way and endanger the entire eastern region of the Red River Delta.

I am taken to another major dike in Nam Sach on the Kinh Thay River that was completely severed a few days before. Repair work is dangerous because of unexploded bombs. People in the province are preparing for the worst. I'm told everyone has a boat, that the top floors and roofs of homes have been reinforced, and that research is being done on crops that grow underwater.

A sulphur butterfly is resting on the lip of a bomb crater. Little things.

When I get back to Hanoi I make a radio broadcast about what I saw:

> Yesterday morning I went to the district of Nam Sach to see the damage that has been done to the dikes in that district. . . . Without these dikes fifteen million people's lives would be endangered and [people] would die by drowning and by starvation. . . . I beg you to consider what you are doing. In the area where I went yesterday it was easy to see that there are no military targets, there is no important highway, there is no communication network, there is no heavy industry. These are peasants. They grow rice and they rear pigs. . . . They are similar to the farmers in the Midwest many years ago in the United States. Perhaps your grandmothers and grandfathers would not be so different from these peasants. . . . Please think what you are doing. Are these people your enemy? What will you say to your children years from now who may ask you why you fought the war? What words will you be able to say to them?

I am driven south to the village of Nam Dinh, which had fifty bombs dropped on it on June 18, a raid that destroyed about 60 percent of the hamlet. People are hard at work rebuilding their homes, but Quoc says that the area is bombed almost daily. The Cuban ambassador in Hanoi told me the other day that a dozen or more Cubans, accustomed to working in the fields with the Vietnamese, collapsed after three hours of packing the earth into a dike. Maybe they should have drunk some chrysanthemum-root tea.

We are driving back to Hanoi down a tree-lined country road, past rice fields and hamlets. The driver suddenly stops the car and speaks urgently to Quoc in Vietnamese. "Quick," Quoc says, "there's a raid coming!" I hear nothing, but then my ears haven't been trained as theirs have in endless war.

Quoc makes me get out of the car and tells me to immediately get down into one of the "manholes" that line the road. These holes are everywhere in North Vietnam, dug into the sides of roads every fifty feet or so, each big enough for one person. In the cities, they are made of concrete and have concrete lids; in the countryside they are simply holes in the ground and the lids are made with thickly woven straw to protect people from the dreaded fragmentation pellets.

I am not yet able to run fast but am doing my best when suddenly I am grabbed from behind by a young Vietnamese girl with some books wrapped in a rubber belt slung over her shoulder. She pulls me down the road after her and motions for me to get into a hole directly in front of a thatched-roof house. No sooner have I climbed in than she wedges herself in with me, quickly covering us with the straw lid. This manhole is meant for one (small) Vietnamese body. But here we are, she and I, our bodies crushed together. One of her arms is around my waist; my hands are around her shoulders, my elbows pinned to my sides. Within seconds the ground begins vibrating with the noise of the bomber overhead, then **thud,** and another **thud,** and severe tremors that I assume come from bombs landing. It seems close, though it's hard to be certain. Then silence. The girl's cheek is pressed against mine. I can feel her eyelashes and her warm breath. **This cannot be happening. I am not jammed in a hole with a Vietnamese girl who has helped me escape American bombs. I know I am going to wake up and this will have been a dream.**

Instead I hear Quoc shouting to me that it is safe to come out (there are no sirens in the countryside). Then I feel the sun, warm on my head, as the girl moves the lid aside and climbs out. I see her little pile of schoolbooks with the black rubber belt around it sitting by the edge of the hole where she'd dropped it. Quoc helps me out. In the far distance I see plumes of smoke that tell me the bombs have not dropped as close to us as I thought.

I begin to cry, saying over and over to the girl, "I'm sorry, oh, I am so sorry, I'm so sorry." She stops me and begins speaking to me in Vietnamese, not angry, very calm. Quoc translates: "You shouldn't cry for us. We know why we are fighting. The sadness should be for your country, your soldiers. They don't know why they are fighting us." I stare at her. She looks back, right into my eyes. Solid. Certain.

I have thought about this experience many times over the last thirty years. Out of the blue some schoolgirl gives me this foxhole analysis about the war being our problem, not theirs? Unbelievable as it may seem, it really happened—and it could not have been staged. There was no way to know that our car would have to stop when it did because of the air raid, no way to have planted that girl right then.

As we drive back to Hanoi, I am wondering if Vietnam isn't some petri dish where God is developing a new, more evolved species of being. I am, as Daniel Berrigan once said about himself and all resisters, afflicted beyond remedy with idealism and glad of it. But I will soon discover that the extraordinary personal experiences I am encountering have nothing to do with divine intervention.

It is one of my last days here. I have been invited to a special performance by the Hanoi Drama Troupe of Arthur Miller's play **All My Sons**. Apparently they want me, an American actor, to critique the production. The play tells the story of an American factory owner (referred to as the "Capitalist") during World War II whose plant manufactures parts for bombers. He discovers that the parts are faulty and that there is a risk that planes will crash as a result, but he says nothing for fear of losing his lucrative government contract. He pays a price for this, however, when one of his sons, a pilot, is killed in a plane crash caused by mechanical failure. His other son, who knows the truth, condemns his father for the silence and greed that caused his brother's death.

I am told that the Hanoi Drama Troupe has been touring this play to villages that have been recently bombed. I am perplexed: Arthur Miller? In bombed Vietnamese villages?

The play is performed on a platform outside. I cannot assess the performance, nor am I interested in doing so. It is the **fact** of the performance, not its quality, that matters. Sitting next to me, the director leans over and asks, "Is that how the Capitalist is supposed to look? We don't know."

The actor playing the factory owner is wearing brown-and-white lace-up saddle shoes, yellow pants, and a bow tie . . . polka dot, if I remember correctly. "Yes," I say, "it's perfect." (Actually I do know a wealthy architect who dresses like that.)

The play ends and we all have our picture taken together. Then I ask the director why the troupe has chosen to take this particular play on tour. Here is his answer:

> This play shows that there are bad Americans and good Americans. We must help our people distinguish between the two. We are a small country. We cannot afford to let our people hate the American peo-

ple. One day the war will be over and we must be friends.

Again I am speechless. What is there to say in response to this most beautiful and utterly sophisticated answer? All I can do is put my arms around him. I have moved from the hallways of awe into its mansions. I finally understand why people have reacted to me the way they have and why all the Americans who have come back from Vietnam recount the same experiences of friendliness. This is no accident and this is not a race of superbeings. The development of their attitudes and worldview has taken a deliberate, strategic, and Herculean effort on the part of the North Vietnamese (Communist) government. This play is one example.

All My Sons is a play about betrayal, a father betraying his son. For me the war is a betrayal; the U.S. government has betrayed its people, its own sons. The Vietnamese are using the play to help their people forgive our government. Why is this harder for me to do?

It dawns on me that war is easy. Peace is harder. This sophisticated striving to build bridges is harder.

I am a novice. This is the first time I have ever been in a revolutionary situation. I don't yet know that, historically, revolutionaries are poetic during revolution and that when it's over, when bureaucracy sets in, things can get grim. But right now, here in Hanoi, I am certainly not looking ahead to protect my flank from whatever is to come once the war ends. All I know is what I am experiencing.

This does not mean I want my country to "lose" the war. Nor does it mean I want us to be killed. I just want us **out.**

Fast-forward to 2002. I am with Quoc again, this time in Little Saigon, an area in Orange County, California, where many Vietnamese have settled. He is elderly now, like me, but his eyes are still warm and his face, though rounder, is still pixieish. He is leading a delegation of young people who are visiting the States from Hanoi. Together with John McAuliff, an old friend from the war days, we talk over lunch.

"The young girl who took me into the manhole with her," I say. "How could she have been so . . . sophisticated . . . especially under those terrifying circumstances?"

"The girl was not so unusual," Quoc replies. "Many of our young people had this understanding. It just happened that she was the one who brought you this message that particular day. Our young people knew a lot about your country. They read Mark Twain and Hemingway and Jack London."

Back to Hanoi: This is the day when I am scheduled to meet seven American POWs, something many

American visitors before me have done. The men are driven from their camp, the Zoo, in a bus with blacked-out windows to the headquarters of the army film studio on the periphery of Hanoi, where the meeting is to take place. The French crew is also here to film the very beginning of the meeting, then they are ushered out. (I will show this footage at my press conference in Paris.) The POWs sit in a row, dressed in striped prison pajamas, and I sit facing them. In addition to the film crew there are several Vietnamese men present—guards, no doubt. The POWs appear to be healthy and fit. One of them has been a prisoner since 1967, one has been there since 1971, and the others were shot down this year (1972). All of them have called publicly for an end to the war and signed a powerful antiwar letter that they sent out with a previous American delegation to Hanoi.

I tell them the obvious: that I am against the war and that I decided to make the trip because of the reports of bomb damage to the dikes. They already know all of this because unbeknownst to me some of my radio broadcasts have been piped into their rooms over wall-mounted radios. A few of them tell me they, too, are against the war and want Nixon to be defeated in the upcoming elections. They express their fear that if he is reelected, the war will go on and on (they are right, it will) and that bombs might land on their prison. I have heard this fear before, from former POW George Smith and from POW families who have received letters. I am asked to con-

vey their hopes that their families will vote for
George McGovern.

I ask them if they feel they have been brain-
washed or tortured, and they laugh, indicating it was
not a part of their experiences. I do not mean to
imply that the atmosphere is relaxed. It isn't. It is self-
conscious and awkward for all the obvious reasons.
Besides, there is at least one guard present throughout. A few describe things that demonstrate to me
how much they have changed since being captured.
One man tells me that he read a book by the American Friends Service Committee and it helped him realize how much of his humanity had been lost
during his sixteen years of military service. Another,
marine lieutenant colonel Edison Miller, tells me
that he too has done a lot of reading in prison and is
writing a book about Vietnamese history.

A large, impressive man sitting in the middle
seat, navy captain David Hoffman, proudly raises his
arm up and down over his head and says, "Please,
when you go back, let my wife know that my arm
has healed." He tells me that the arm had been broken when he was ejected from his plane. I assure him
I will let his wife know (and I do, as soon as I get
back).

After twenty minutes or so, the seven are escorted out of the room. Though they seem genuine,
I realize that the men could have been lying to protect themselves, but I certainly see no signs in any of
the seven that they have been tortured, at least not
recently.

It is my last full day in North Vietnam. In spite of having made it clear to my hosts that I was not interested in visiting a military installation, I am going—and today is the day.

It is not unusual for Americans who visit North Vietnam to be taken to see Vietnamese military installations, and when they do they are always required to wear a helmet like the kind I have been given to wear during the air raids. I am driven to the site of the antiaircraft installation, somewhere on the outskirts of the city. There is a group of about a dozen young Vietnamese soldiers in uniform who greet me. There is also a horde of photographers and journalists—many more than I have seen all in one place in Hanoi. (I later learn some of them were Japanese.)

This should have been a red flag.

Quoc isn't with me today, but another translator tells me that the soldiers want to sing me a song. He stands close and recites the words in English as the soldiers sing. It is a song about the day "Uncle Ho" declared their country's independence in Hanoi's Ba Dinh Square. I hear these words: "All men are created equal. They are given certain rights; among these are life, liberty, and happiness." I begin to cry and clap. **These young men should not be our enemy. They celebrate the same words Americans do.** The song ends with a refrain about the soldiers vowing to keep the "blue skies above Ba Dinh" free from bombers.

The soldiers ask me to sing for them in return. I am prepared for just such a moment. Before leaving the United States, I had memorized a song called "Day Ma Di," written by students in South Vietnam who are against the war. I launch into it **con gusto,** feeling ridiculous but I don't care. Vietnamese is a difficult language for a foreigner to speak and I know I am slaughtering it, but everyone seems delighted that I am making the attempt. Everyone laughs and claps, including me. I am overcome on this, my last day.

What happens next is something I have turned over and over in my mind countless times since. Here is my best, honest recollection of what took place.

Someone (I don't remember who) leads me toward the gun, and I sit down, still laughing, still applauding. It all has nothing to do with **where** I am sitting. I hardly even think about where I am sitting. The cameras flash.

I get up, and as I start to walk back to the car with the translator, the implication of what has just happened hits me. **Oh my God. It's going to look like I was trying to shoot down U.S. planes!** I plead with him, "You have to be sure those photographs are not published. Please, you can't let them be published." I am assured it will be taken care of. I don't know what else to do.

It is possible that the Vietnamese had it all planned.

I will never know. If they did, can I really blame

Applauding soldiers who had sung for me at the
antiaircraft gun outside Hanoi.
(Tony Korody/Time & Life Pictures/Getty Images)

I am standing next to the antiaircraft gun,
singing a Vietnamese song back to the soldiers right
before I sit in the gun's seat.
(AP/Wide World Photos)

them? The buck stops here. If I was used, I allowed it to happen. It was my mistake, and I have paid and continue to pay a heavy price for it. A traveling companion, someone with a cooler head, would have kept me from taking that terrible seat. I would have known two minutes **before** sitting down what I didn't realize until two minutes **after**ward. That two-minute lapse of sanity will haunt me until I die. But the gun was inactive, there were no planes over-head—I simply wasn't **thinking** about what I was doing, only about what I was **feeling**—innocent of what the photo implies. Yet the photo exists, delivering its message, regardless of what I was really doing or feeling.

I realize that it is not just a U.S. citizen laughing and clapping on a Vietnamese antiaircraft gun: I am Henry Fonda's privileged daughter who appears to be thumbing my nose at the country that has provided me these privileges. More than that, I am a woman, which makes my sitting there even more of a betrayal. A gender betrayal. **And** I am a woman who is seen as Barbarella, a character existing on some subliminal level as an embodiment of men's fantasies; Barbarella has become their enemy. I have spent the last two years working with GIs and Vietnam veterans and have spoken before hundreds of thousands of antiwar protesters, telling them that our men in uniform **aren't** the enemy. I went to support them at their bases and overseas, and will, in years ahead, make **Coming Home** so that Americans can understand how the wounded were treated in

VA hospitals. Now by mistake I appear in a photograph to be their enemy. I carry this heavy in my heart. I always will.

The next day, departure day, Quoc says to me, "I think you need to prepare yourself. There are some U.S. congressmen who are asking that you be put on trial for treason." It is my broadcasts over Radio Hanoi that have triggered the charges. He shows me the transcripts of Reuters news reports. The photo on the antiaircraft gun isn't even the issue. It hasn't yet appeared.

I do not know if what I have seen is a true reflection of Vietnam's reality. I know that there is selfishness, bitterness, pettiness, and violence in that small nation, as in all nations. I can understand and sympathize with the very different perceptions that our soldiers and POWs bring back with them. I know that best feet were put forward for my benefit (though that still doesn't explain that schoolgirl, the Arthur Miller play, and the eyes of the peasants in bomb shelters even after learning I was American).

But I have seen the signposts; I have gained a new understanding of what strength is. Bamboo is the metaphor. Bamboo is deceptive. It is thin and willowy, it appears weak alongside the sturdy oak. But ultimately it is bamboo, with its flexibility, that is the stronger. For the Vietnamese, the symbol of

strength is the image of many bamboo poles tied together. Bamboo holds a forgiving, flexible, softer energy that can exist in men and women. Vietnam is
bamboo.

I am softening. Can it have been only two weeks?

In a screening room in Paris on July 25, I showed the
forty-minute film to the international press. It had
been roughly edited in Hanoi by Gérard Guillaume.
My central purpose for making this controversial trip
to Hanoi was to bring back documented evidence
that the dikes I visited had been bombed, a charge
the U.S. government was vehemently denying.

It seemed that every news service in the world
was in attendance. Simone Signoret was there as
well—my unique support system. The conference
was hosted by the well-known French photographer
Roger Pic. I do not recall if I carried the film out of
Vietnam myself or if Guillaume had it shipped from
Hanoi, but unfortunately, somewhere between
Hanoi and Paris the sound track was erased, so I had
to show it without sound.

I explained carefully how the antipersonnel
bombs entered the dikes at a slant and exploded inside the mud walls, doing damage that was invisible
in aerial photographs and difficult to repair. I explained that monsoon season was almost upon Vietnam and that if the weakened dikes should give way,
hundreds of thousands of people would drown or die
from starvation. It was all there on the screen: the

rubble of the cities and hamlets I'd visited, the damage to the dikes, the craters, the close-up of where an antipersonnel bomb had entered the side of the dikes, and the beginning of my meeting with the POWs.

I showed the silent film again at a press conference in New York City—and that was the last I saw of it. It has disappeared. All that is left now is a photo that appeared in a number of magazines, of me at the press conference with the image of some of the POWs visible on the screen behind me. I do not know if the footage was stolen by spooks or lost innocently.

I told the press that I hoped people would realize, as I and other foreign visitors had, that the repeated bombing of civilian targets and dikes was intentional and must be stopped, and how the damage was concentrated where the dikes were most strategic. I told them that the POWs had given me messages for people back home, saying that they were afraid of being bombed and asking their families to support George McGovern for president. (I carried a packet of letters from POWs back to the States with me.)

I was asked how I felt about being accused of treason. I tried to give a "bamboo"-type response and was quoted in the papers the next day saying, "What is a traitor? . . . I cried every day I was in Vietnam. I cried for America. The bombs are falling on Vietnam, but it is an American tragedy. . . . Given the things that America stands for, a war of

**At the Paris press conference, pointing to the film
showing two of the POWs I met with.**
(AP/Wide World Photos)

aggression against the Vietnamese people is a betrayal of the American people. That is where treason
lies . . . those who are doing all they can to end the
war are the real patriots."

Tom was waiting for me at the airport in New York
City when I landed. He whisked me downtown to
the Chelsea Hotel, where we holed up for the night
like two refugees. I needed rest. I needed to be held.

   Tom felt that because he had encouraged me to
go, he was responsible for the trouble I'd gotten into,
and he promised to try to make it up to me. Both of
us realized that it had been a mistake for me to go
alone. But I never felt that he was responsible. I hate
buck passers.

   As we lay in bed in our funky Chelsea Hotel
room, I told Tom that I wanted us to have a child together as a pledge of hope for the future. We held
each other and wept.

In the period of time right after my return, Repre-
sentatives Fletcher Thompson (R-Ga.) and Richard
Ichord (D-Mo.) accused me of treason. They said I
had urged American troops to disobey orders and
had given "aid and comfort to the enemy." Representative Thompson, who was running for the U.S.
Senate from Georgia, tried to subpoena me to testify
before the House Internal Security Council (the updated version of the House Un-American Activities

Committee made infamous in the fifties by Senator Joseph McCarthy), but his efforts were blocked. (He subsequently lost the election.) The committee issued me a subpoena, but when my lawyer, Leonard Weinglass, and I sent them a letter saying I was ready to appear, we were notified that they had adjourned the hearings and would contact us when a new date was set. We never heard from them again.

Soon thereafter, Vincent Albano Jr., chairman of the New York County Republican Committee, called for a boycott of my films.

I find it interesting that the government and news reporters knew that Americans before me had gone to North Vietnam **and** had spoken on Radio Hanoi. This was the first time, however, that the issue of treason was being raised.

The accusations about the bombing of the dikes that I along with others brought back from Vietnam caused an uproar within the administration. UN Secretary-General Kurt Waldheim held a press conference and said that he'd heard through private sources that the dikes had been bombed. Then Secretary of State William P. Rogers said: "These charges are part of a carefully planned campaign by the North Vietnamese and their supporters to give worldwide circulation to this falsehood." Meanwhile, Sergeant Lonnie D. Franks, an intelligence specialist stationed at Udorn Air Base in Thailand was due to testify before the Senate Armed Services

Committee about air force officers involved in bombing falsification of other targets. That investigation was eventually dropped, and only General John Lavelle, the commanding officer who had ordered (or overseen) the falsification, was held responsible.

While the United States may not have been waging an all-out bombing campaign to obliterate the dikes, they **were** targeting the dikes during the spring of 1972. The evidence that I, and many others, saw was incontrovertible. Perhaps this was done as a threat to get the North Vietnamese to cave in at the negotiating table. The massive B-52 bombing of Hanoi that would stun the world come Christmas was admittedly done to achieve this same thing. Both efforts would fail.

Despite the saber rattling, the Justice Department found I had violated no statutes, including those covering sedition. Attorney General Richard Kleindienst announced in San Francisco on August 14 that there would be no prosecutions. Later, when questioned about why he never prosecuted me under the charge of sedition, Kleindienst stated:

> **There was a real difficulty technically with respect to proof, but over and above that, I felt and I think most of us shared this view in the Administration, that the damage was slight and the interest in favor of free expression was very high. . . . I thought the interests in favor of free speech in an**

**election year far outweighed any specific
advantage of prosecuting a young girl like
that who was in Vietnam acting rather
foolish.**

Two months after my return from Hanoi, President
Nixon was informed in a daily briefing paper that
"according to excerpts being studied by Congress,
Fonda used her Hanoi radio time to pose questions
to the U.S. GIs, but limited her advice to pleas for
ending the bombing, and didn't urge defections."
The following month the FBI gave my files to three
of their own in-house reviewers, asking them to examine what the agency had on me and assess
whether or not the clandestine investigation should
be continued. All three determined that it should be
discontinued. One of the three reviewers, a Ms. Her-
wig, wrote to the FBI, "There are more dangerous
characters around needing our attention. Unless the
[Department of Justice] orders us to continue, these
investigations should be closed. The basis for investigation appears to be—pick someone you dislike and
start investigating."

More dangerous characters indeed. Five men
using funds from a secret Republican campaign fund
had recently been arrested trying to bug the offices of
the Democratic National Committee. One of them
was the security director for CREEP, the Committee
for the Re-Election of the President. At the end of
September it would be revealed that while serving

as attorney general, John Mitchell had controlled a slush fund used for illegal espionage and sabotage operations against the Democrats and other political opponents.

The bombing of the dikes stopped that August.

CHAPTER ELEVEN

FRAMED

We have not grown used to knavery, and to that species of untruth which lies so near to the truth as to be able to wear its clothing, and to turn upon the idealist its seductive and silencing countenance.

—DANIEL BERRIGAN,
Night Flight to Hanoi

MUCH HAS BEEN SAID about my actions against the Vietnam War, and you have just read about my controversial trip. I went because I wanted to expose the lies of the Nixon administration and help stop the killing on both sides. I believe the trip made it harder for Nixon to distract the public's attention from his escalation of the air war, and perhaps it helped end the bombing of the dikes. I wanted to speak to U.S. pilots as I had done on so many occasions during the FTA tour. I did not ask them to desert. I once read in a congressional report that A. William Olson, a representative of the Justice Department, said after studying transcripts of my broadcasts that I had asked the military "to do nothing other than to think." Nothing I did caused any POWs to be tortured. Torture in the prison camps of North Vietnam had stopped by 1969, three years before my trip.

I **do** regret that I allowed myself to get into a situation where I was photographed on an antiaircraft gun. I have explained how that happened and how it sent a message that was the opposite of what I was feeling and doing. I regret the angry remark I made when the POWs returned home that enabled apologists for the war to orchestrate the myth of "Hanoi Jane." I was framed and turned into a lightning rod for people's anger, frustration, misinformation, and confusion about the war.

The myth of "Hanoi Jane" lingers today; I would like to speak to the charges.

After I came back from North Vietnam, the trip wasn't a big story. While there was a brouhaha about it behind the scenes at the White House, publicly little fuss was made—nothing on television and one small article in **The New York Times.** After all, there had been almost three hundred Americans before me who had gone to Hanoi, and more than eighty broadcasts by Americans over Radio Hanoi had preceded mine. Once the Justice Department announced they had nothing to prosecute me for, what flap there was seemed to evaporate.

The mythmaking began in February 1973—after the U.S. POWs had returned home in a lavish "Operation Homecoming." No previous American POWs had ever received this type of welcome. The combat troops certainly didn't, and this made me angry. I saw that Nixon was using the event to create **something** that resembled victory. It was as close as he would come.

For four years the administration had seen to it that the issue of torture of U.S. POWs in North Vietnam was front-page news. There appears to be a reason for this, though no one knew it at the time. Starting in 1969, when the torture stories began to appear, Nixon had begun secret plans for an escalation of the war, including a major bombing offensive of North Vietnam, the mining of Haiphong harbor, and nuclear contingency plans. This would be a hard pill for the American public to swallow—unless the North Vietnamese could be demonized in a way that would resonate personally with Americans. Thus the torture of the POWs—and securing their release—became the justification for continuing and escalating the war.*

---

*It was at a press conference in May 1969 that Secretary of Defense Melvin Laird focused publicly on the issue of torture of U.S. prisoners in Hanoi. In his article "The P.O.W. Issue: A National Issue is Born," Dayton (Ohio) **Journal-Herald**, 13–18 Feb. 1971, Seymour Hersh, author and journalist who uncovered the My Lai massacre and the Abu Ghraib Prison scandal, reported that "Laird had, as many officials later acknowledged, somewhat overstated his case."

Once the POWs were home, the Pentagon and White House handpicked some of the highest-ranking POWs—senior officers—to travel the national media circuit, some of them telling of torture. These media stories were allowed to become the official narrative, the universal "POW story," giving the impression that **all** the men had been subjected to systematic torture—right up to the end—and that torture was the policy of the North Vietnamese government.

In particular, a Lieutenant Commander David Hoffman (who was among the POWs I met in Hanoi—the one who raised his arm above his head and asked me to tell his wife) was getting extensive media coverage with his story of torture. On national television he claimed that his meeting with me (and another one a week or so later with former attorney general Ramsey Clark) had **caused** him to be tortured—that is, he was tortured to force him to meet me and feign opposition to the war. I do not believe that this was so.

In Vietnam in 1973 Hoffman appeared **six times** at meetings with antiwar visitors, more than

---

"Solid evidence of systematic abuse of prisoners has always been missing," Hersh reported, and went on to say that when American families of POWs became alarmed at the reports of torture, they received letters from the Pentagon saying: "We are certain that you will not become unduly concerned over the [torture] briefing if you keep in mind the purpose for which it was tailored."

almost any other POW. Film footage taken by U.S. delegations at several of these meetings—footage I have actually reviewed—shows Hoffman appearing healthy and unusually verbal in his opposition to the war. He also signed antiwar statements. He has never claimed he was tortured to attend **those other** meetings or to sign those statements. But the visits with Ramsey Clark and with me were widely publicized, and I suppose he needed the allegation of torture to explain his attendance at them. Perhaps more important, the government needed a way to malign Ramsey Clark and me.*

According to books written by some POWs, conditions in the POW camps improved in the four years preceding their release—that is, from 1969 until 1973. They describe how the food got better, how they were given roommates and allowed time in the game room, how there was volleyball, Ping-Pong, and exercise. This explains why, upon their release, **Newsweek** magazine wrote, "The [torture] stories seemed incongruent with the men telling them—a trim, trig lot who, given a few pounds more flesh, might have stepped right out of a recruiting poster."

Lieutenant Colonel (ret.) Edison Miller, who was also among the POWs I met in Hanoi, was in the

---

*A handwritten note from President Nixon to H. R. Haldeman says that "the POW's need to have the worst quotes of R. Clark and Fonda" to use in their TV appearances, but this information "shouldn't come from the White House."

same camp as Hoffman. He says that about eighty to one hundred POWs were being held there.

"The visits with delegations were strictly volunteer," Miller told me recently. "I know of only two or three guys out of one hundred who didn't want to meet with you. At the least, it was a way to break up the boredom of the day." Hoffman's co-pilot and prison roommate, Norris Charles, agrees that there were more than enough POWs in the compound who wanted to meet with me and with Clark, and that he never saw or heard of any torture in his camp. Navy commander Walter Wilbur, who was also in the Zoo, has said the same thing. In the spring of 1973, before Hoffman made his claims of torture, Commander Wilbur was released and told the **Los Angeles Times** about my visit with the POWs, saying, "She could see that we were healthy and had not been tortured."

Hoffman's roommate said there was no torture; according to the POWs themselves, torture stopped in 1969. **Not that any torture is justified or that anyone who had been tortured should have been prevented from telling about it.** But the White House presented a distorted picture of what actually occurred.

In my anger at how the entire POW situation was being manipulated and how they were treated as opposed to the ground troops, I made a mistake I deeply regret. I said that the POWs claiming torture were liars, hypocrites, and pawns. I said, "I'm quite sure that there were incidents of torture. . . . But the pilots who are saying it was the policy of the Vietnamese and that it was systematic, I believe that that's a lie."

I firmly believe that the POWs I met with had not been tortured. But what I didn't know at the time was that prior to 1969 there had in fact been systematic torture of POWs. I found it difficult to believe, based on the Vietnamese I met during my visit, that torture would be approved—any more than I could have believed, prior to the Winter Soldier investigation or the Abu Ghraib and other Iraqi prison scandals, that GIs could commit atrocities. I was wrong and I am sorry.

My heart had always been with the soldiers, and I should have been clear that my anger was at the Nixon administration. It was the administration, in its cynical determination to keep hostilities alive, that tried to use the POWs. It was the deceitful blaming of me for torture, together with the Nixon administration's manipulation of the entire POW story and my unfortunate reaction to it, that was responsible for a dramatic upsurge of attacks against me. These, as well as a wave of inflammatory stories about my trip to Hanoi, are what launched the myth of "Hanoi Jane."

I became a lightning rod. People who defended the war saw me as antisoldier—something I am not and never have been, as I believe this book shows. Even though I knew the attacks on me were based on lies, my heart ached from them, because I never blamed the soldiers for the war or for any atrocities that were committed.

The attacks didn't let up. By the end of the nineties, truly grotesque lies were again circulated about me over the Internet (and continue as of this writing), although even former POW Captain Mike McGrath (USN ret.), president of the organization Nam-POW, says that the story circulated on the Internet is a hoax.

In spite of the efforts to demonize me, a 1976 **Redbook** magazine poll had me as one of the ten most admired women in America. In 1985, another poll—the **U.S. News**–Roper poll—showed that I was rated the number-one heroine of young Americans, and the **Ladies' Home Journal**–Roper poll that same year listed me as the fourth most admired woman in America. My books and videos continued to be best-sellers and my films, at least through the early eighties, were very successful. I tell you this not to boast but because I think it's important to show that the attacks and lies aimed at me seemed not to be sticking with a sizable number of Americans.

But the attacks didn't let up. In 1988, when it was announced that I would be filming **Stanley & Iris** with Robert De Niro in Waterbury, Connecticut, a furor was unleashed that raged for months and was reported widely in the press. The uproar was launched by ultraconservative elements in the area, led by Gaetano Russo, a World War II veteran and former chair of the local Republican Party committee who had been defeated in his campaigns both for mayor and for Congress. Russo formed the American Coalition Against Hanoi Jane, held town meetings, and tried to pass resolutions to bar me from Waterbury. He was joined in his efforts by the local Republican congressman, John G. Rowland, who later became governor of Connecticut and resigned in 2004 in the face of a federal corruption investigation and threats of impeachment.

No sooner was it announced that I would be filming in Waterbury than a Ku Klux Klan flag began to fly across the street from the Waterbury newspaper and several KKK members attended a meeting at the VFW hall in Naugatuck, trying to whip up the hostility against me. The Naugatuck Vietnam vets told the KKK to leave. But there was a large population of Vietnam veterans in the area and the controversy quickly caught on with them. As Rich Roland (retired First Marine Division, Seventh Marines) from Waterbury told me recently, "You were a lightning rod for the vets. A lot of guys had come back and didn't feel accepted as people. There were all those feelings of anger and frustration about our war experiences that had never been expressed and they all focused on you. After all, what could we say to the government?"

One afternoon Gaetano Russo organized a rally in Waterbury's Library Park, where I was hanged in effigy from a tree. Many people came out for the

event and it was decided they would try to get a resolution passed by the board of the city's aldermen to
bar me from coming.

Vietnam veteran Rich Roland was there to speak
in favor of the resolution and was shocked that only
eight Vietnam vets showed up. Where are all the
people? he asked himself. This is a joke. The resolution was overwhelmingly defeated.

My friend and publicist Stephen Rivers had
been monitoring the situation. I was in Mexico filming **Old Gringo** and Stephen kept me updated with
news clippings. I remember studying the pictures in
the papers that showed the faces of the veterans who
attended that town hall meeting. These were familiar
faces. I entertained guys like this with the FTA show.
I knew how to talk to them. Because of the time I
spent with the GI movement, I felt I was closer to
their experience than other people who weren't in
Vietnam.

I asked Stephen to try to organize a meeting
with the Waterbury vets—just the ones who were in
Vietnam.

When I arrived in Waterbury Stephen had
arranged for a local minister to host the meeting
with the vets in his church hall. I don't recall being
afraid as I went into the meeting room. If anything,
I felt relief that the time for the encounter had
come. I trusted the situation. I knew in my heart I
had never felt anything but compassion for the soldiers in Vietnam. I wasn't sure I would be able to
communicate this to all of them, but I was confi-

dent that, at least for some, this face-to-face would have a positive effect.

There were twenty-six veterans sitting in a large circle when I entered the room. Some of them were in uniform. A few wore buttons and hats reading HANOI JANE and TRAITOR. These men had been the ground troops, the grunts, as they called themselves.

I could tell they were surprised that I was alone, no escort, no bodyguards. Later one of them said to me, "You walked in, and I said to myself, Oh, she's so little. Just one little woman."

Rich Roland wore a camouflage jacket and had an ace of spades in his pocket, the "death card." When he went to Vietnam in 1969 he took with him an entire pack of aces of spades. His Marine Corps company was known as the Delta Death Dealers, and they would leave an ace of spades on each enemy corpse they killed.

"I intended to throw the card in your face if I wasn't happy with what happened in the meeting," Rich told me later, in 2003.

I took my place in the circle and suggested we go around the room and each tell our story. I began. I told them I wanted to put my trip to North Vietnam into context so that they would know why I went. I told them how concerned many people were at the time about the bombing of the dikes right before the monsoon season. I told them the government had denied the bombings. I told them many of the things I have written in these pages and about my previous work with active duty GIs and veterans. I told them how sorry I was that some of my actions had appeared callous with regard to U.S. soldiers and that that was the last thing I intended. I apologized for that and said that I would go to my grave regretting that pain and misunderstanding—but that I could not apologize for going to North Vietnam and doing everything I could to expose Nixon's lies and help end the war.

"I'm proud that I did that," I said, "just as you are proud of doing what you felt you had to do. No one has a corner on righteousness in this. We were all caught in the horror and did what we felt we had to do. All of us were affected. None of us will be the same. All of us were deceived."

Then we went around the room. It was raw, angry, and emotional. Many tears were shed. It felt like an exorcism. I had not realized how many families in that part of Connecticut were first-generation Americans. For these young men, serving their country in Vietnam was a rite of passage into true citizenship. One said to me, "There are two ways we can become truly American. One is to go to college—my sister has gone to college—and the other is to join the armed services. I joined. And I became American." The next man had also joined for this reason.

"But we're the first American soldiers to lose a war," he said, trying to stifle his emotions.

I was staggered. It had never occurred to me that our soldiers blamed themselves and thought they weren't good enough.

"But **you** didn't lose the war," I said. "It was not a war that could have been won—and Kennedy and

Johnson both **knew** that. It was the men who **sent** you there who were responsible for losing, not the soldiers!" I despaired at ever being able to convince them of this.

Some talked about things they had done out of hatred for me.

"Every time I go into a video store," one said, "I make a point of turning all your exercise videos around on the shelf." Another said, "I have never read a magazine that had an article about you."

Rich Roland had come into the meeting furious and was made more so when he heard me speak about the innocent Vietnamese civilians who had been killed by our smart bombs. "You tell me the difference between those dead civilians and a GI lying there with his dick stuck in his mouth," he demanded when it was his turn to speak.

I don't remember exactly what I said to him, but it wasn't my answer that was important for Rich; it was the fact that for the first time he had expressed some of what was inside of him. "Coming to the meeting in spite of my anger at you was positive. It was good for me to be able to vent my feelings. I heard you say you were sorry, and I was able to accept it," he told me recently.

The meeting lasted for about four hours. As we were winding down, Stephen Rivers came into the room and told me that word of the meeting had gotten out. I had wanted it to be confidential, but the local Channel 8 TV crew was outside wanting to talk to us. I told the assembled men about the situation and asked them how they wanted to handle it.

"Look, I'm not the one that went to the press," I said, "but they're here. What do you want to do? We can sneak out the back or we can invite them in and tell them what happened. It's up to you."

They wanted to invite the press in, and in they came, expecting, I suppose, to find an angry free-for-all. Instead they found us talking quietly, some of us hugging, a few of the men sitting silently. The reporters were clearly surprised to find so little tension in the room. Vietnam veteran Bob Genovese told the reporter (and it was broadcast on ABC's **20/20** the following week), "There was a lot of things that she talked about that I personally didn't know about before, and I don't think a lot of the men in the room knew before, and it helped to explain some of the reasons why she did some of the things she did back in 1972."

Instead of throwing his ace of spades in my face, Rich went out and threw it in the trash. "That was the beginning of my healing," he says.

The vets and I couldn't have started from two more wildly divergent places, but the fact of our being able to face one another for those four hours was important for all of us. I have come to feel that one reason healing doesn't happen more often is that the two sides don't allow themselves to really hear each other's narratives.

Empathy is the answer.

There must be a stepping back, a looking at the big picture. Stepping back is hard when your life has been traumatized and hatred has built up against the "enemy" and against those who opposed the war and seem to have sided with the enemy. This is why wars begun unnecessarily and for the wrong reasons—like the one we are fighting in Iraq as I write this—develop a momentum of revenge and justification. **We have to keep going. Our men and women can't have died in vain. The people on the other side are truly evil. If we pull out now, we'll lose our credibility. Better to continue to send Americans to fight and perhaps die than to say we made a mistake.**

After my meeting with the vets in that church hall, the energy seemed to drain out of the controversy. There were always a handful of demonstrators around whenever we filmed outdoors, but few of them were Vietnam veterans. During the worst of it, a dozen women from Waterbury sent me a videotape of themselves, one by one, expressing support for me, telling me they admired the way I lived my life, and thanking me for being a role model. They will never know how much that helped get me through those bruising times.

Later that summer Robert De Niro and I worked with a coalition of local Connecticut Vietnam veterans, including Rich Roland, to hold a fund-raising event at Lake Quassapaug. There were threats against us; we were warned that helicopters would fly over and drop things; local officials refused to take part. In spite of it all, on the evening of July 29 over two thousand people came. Thousands of dollars' worth of food was donated for the event and over one hundred volunteers, most of them Vietnam vets, worked hard to make it a success. Together we raised $27,000 for children who had birth defects as a result of their fathers' exposure to Agent Orange in Vietnam.

Supporting our troops has always been of great interest to me, partly because I have spent so much time listening to soldiers, veterans, and their families and have seen their issues up close and personal. I wonder how many Americans were as outraged as I was when—as soon as our soldiers had left for Iraq in 2003 with the Bush administration's "Support Our Troops" ringing in the air—Congress cut their benefits, and entire classes were frozen out of the VA system. Policies were proposed that would exclude some five hundred thousand veterans from the VA healthcare system. An attempt was made to increase fees and co-payments for medical services, which will drive another million veterans out of the system, and to cut 60 percent of federal education subsidies for soldiers' children. This is patriotism?

We create victims of new wars while not even taking care of the veterans of past wars.*

*Actually, when it comes to caring about the welfare of our soldiers, polls from the late 1970s published in congressional studies show that people who opposed the Vietnam War were much more sympathetic to the special needs of veterans than were those who supported the war.

CHAPTER TWELVE

ADIEU, LONE RANGER

The problem with the world is that we draw the circle
of our family too small.
—Mother Teresa

Funny, but despite our commitment to having a child, there never really was any discussion between Tom and me about the nature of our future together. Knowing the other women he'd been in relationships with, I have to assume he had had such conversations with them: **What do we want from this coupling? Where do you think this is going?** I assumed that the avoidance of explicit long-term commitment must have been my fault. After so long as a Lone Ranger I was ready to have someone in my corner and was just holding my breath, hoping things would evolve in a stable and loving direction, fearful that if I tried to make the future explicit, the bubble would burst. I didn't know how to ask for what I wanted, for fear of losing what I had. What we sensed (although this was never talked about, either) was that on the political level we made an unexpected and powerful duo—an odd couple in an odd time.

Tom was living with me by now and supporting himself writing and teaching. In June 1972, right before my trip to Vietnam, we had discussed putting together a national speaking tour for the fall aimed at exposing Nixon's escalation of the war and reenergizing the peace movement. Tom named it the Indochina Peace Campaign—IPC. The plan was to make a two-month, ninety-five-city speaking tour of unprecedented proportions. Joining us as full-time members of the tour were Holly Near and George Smith, who had been a prisoner of the National Liberation Front in South Vietnam for three years.

I vividly recall the day Tom sat on the edge of our bed while I cut off his long braid. The event had a ceremonial, rite-of-passage quality: We were leaving behind our counterculture trappings and reentering the mainstream; it wouldn't do if the way we looked turned people off to what we were saying. So I trimmed Tom's hair, bought him a suit and tie, exchanged his rubber sandals for brown leather, and got myself a couple of wrinkle-proof conservative outfits.

The tour began on Labor Day at the Ohio State

Fair, emblematic of our desire to appeal to Middle Americans. The 1972 tour was the most fulfilling experience of my life up to then. I was living full out, every neuron fired up, every bit of energy being tapped. I wasn't just speaking; I was watching and listening and learning every day, committing every ounce of everything I had to what I believed in, and doing it with someone I loved and admired, alongside scores of kindred spirits. Many of the people who were involved in the IPC tour became important influences in my life, and I want to name them: besides my roommates Carol and Jack (more about them later), there were Karen Nussbaum, Ira Arlook, Helen Williams, Jay Westbrook, Anne Froines, Shari Whitehead Lawson, Sam Hurst, Paul Ryder, Larry Levin, and Fred Branfman. I could write a whole chapter on each of them, but the book would be too long. They were my family in many ways and my role models. At last I had the political home I'd been missing. I no longer had to be the Lone Ranger.

For the most part we were received enthusiastically by huge crowds. I relied heavily on quotes from the Pentagon Papers, thinking that citing the government's own words would help people accept the truth. It was then that I first discovered it isn't enough to give the facts. Some people resist believing anything that might shatter their belief in their government—no matter how far from reality their misplaced belief takes them, no matter how many young lives might be squandered. This mass denial

was painfully demonstrated again in our 2004 elections.

Occasionally in interviews I would be questioned about the right of celebrities to speak out and
contradict officialdom. I believe in a democracy.
Everyone should be able to question and dissent.
When the public is being lied to, how else can the
truth be known? I think it is because celebrities command a wider audience when they speak that they
are attacked and infantilized so often by the Right:
"Who do these stars think they are?" We're involved
citizens who love our country and want to voice
views that might otherwise not be heard. What are
involved, informed citizens to **do** when presidents,
vice presidents, and secretaries of state give the public falsified evidence to justify war?

During the entire tour we had only one day off,
which Tom and I spent in bed and talking. I remember it well, because of all the questions Tom asked me
about myself—about my mother, my father, what
I thought about movies, how I thought being a
celebrity had affected me. After five months we were
still getting to know each other, but no one I had
been emotionally involved with before had ever asked
me these questions so intently. It made me realize
how doggedly I had plowed through life, and with little introspection. In the midst of our grueling schedule, we were trying to get pregnant. It happened one
cold October night somewhere near Buffalo, New
York. As had been the case with Vanessa's conception,
I knew immediately that **it** had happened.

During the tour Vanessa was living with her father in Paris. I had a perpetual knot in my stomach about her and would call two or three times a week to see how she was and let her know I was thinking about her. But in my heart I knew this long-distance stuff didn't hack it. It was what my father had done with my brother and me: absentee worrying in the hope that it would be interpreted as love. Was I shirking a more important duty than ending the war? Was this a ghost that would come to haunt me? (Yes.) At least my instincts about Vadim had been right. He was a good father to our daughter; he was assuming the role mothers usually play. But I would be criticized in ways fathers rarely are when they're away!

I have scattered visceral memories of the tour. In a drafty gymnasium somewhere in the Midwest, a young Vietnam veteran told the high school audience that he had personally raped and killed Vietnamese women. I could see him shaking as he spoke. The audience disbelief was palpable: How could this man, who seemed just like them, have done these things? Someone yelled at him to shut up. He stopped, looked around the gym, and then said quietly, "Listen, I have to live with this the rest of my life. The least you can do is know that it happened."

Sometimes things got rough. In Kensington, a working-class section of Philadelphia, a hundred angry men stormed the police barricade and attacked me, pulling out chunks of my hair. One man told an

Singing with Holly Near (on left) and a local organizer during the first IPC national tour.

Associated Press reporter, "She should be content to stay home and be a housewife."

Slowly, as I gained confidence, I was learning to speak more personally. I remember the first time I spoke of my journey, from **Barbarella** in 1968 to becoming an activist; of how empty my life had felt back then, that I hadn't thought a woman could change anything—except table settings or diapers. My message: "There was a time not so long ago when I didn't know where Vietnam was and I didn't want to believe what I was hearing about the war. Now I am a different person, and if I can change, so can you."

I could sense myself connecting with people better. This was a lesson that would serve me well in the future—once I had fully learned it. It took a while. Oddly, I had a hard time being personal in my speeches when Tom was present. His brilliance as a speaker intimidated me, and I worried that I wouldn't be "political" enough. Over his decades of activism Tom had grasped the big picture, one that allowed him to place the Vietnam War in the context of U.S. history and global history.

But it was **his** big picture.

Was there a big picture—a unifying narrative— that I could embrace as a woman? Not knowing the answer, I took shelter in Tom's narrative, which was compelling and enlightening. It would take me thirty years and then some to discover my own, gender-grounded narrative.

In spite of everything, Nixon won reelection in 1972 in a landslide. Ultraconservative presidential candidate George Wallace dropped from the race when he was shot and Nixon inherited his supporters. Right before the elections, Henry Kissinger had given his infamous "peace is at hand" speech, claiming that a peace agreement with the North Vietnamese had been reached in Paris. The war-weary American public fell for it. Our ally in South Vietnam, President Nguyen Van Thieu, hadn't agreed to the terms of the peace agreement, but the American people were never told that.

Nixon and Kissinger weren't the first to deceive the American public about the war. Lyndon Johnson, needing to escalate the war to avoid losing it (true for Nixon as well), had claimed that North Vietnamese boats had fired on U.S. ships in an unprovoked attack in the Gulf of Tonkin. Thus he got Congress to pass the Tonkin Gulf Resolution, which allowed him to begin bombing North Vietnam. It turned out the Tonkin Gulf incident was a hoax.* This terrible deceit aimed at justifying war has, I believe, been surpassed only by what the Bush II administration did to get Congress to authorize sending troops into Iraq.

Then came the final hoax of 1972: Despite

*In 1968, a reinvestigation by the Senate Foreign Relations Committee suggested that the "incident" of our ships being attacked was "imagined or invented."

Congress's clear mandate to end the war and Kissinger's pre-election promise of "peace at hand," saturation bombing of Hanoi and Haiphong began on December 17 and lasted into the first week of the new year. The North Vietnamese mounted an air defense that cost us heavily. It left ninety-nine airmen missing and thirty-one new POWs.

Feeling sickened and powerless, Tom and I went to a screening of **Last Tango in Paris** but had to walk out in the middle: With the bombing on our minds, anal copulation with butter didn't sit well.

Why would five administrations, Democratic **and** Republican, **knowing** (according to the Pentagon Papers) that we couldn't win militarily (short of annihilation), **knowing** they would have to keep escalating to avoid losing—**why** would they choose to postpone failure regardless of how many lives that cost?

Partly it was to get elected. President Kennedy told Arthur Schlesinger in November 1961 that if the United States ever went into war in Vietnam, we'd lose just like the French. But Kennedy was afraid the right wing would defeat him in the next election if he withdrew.

Mostly I believe it has to do with the perceived loss of manhood, the fear of being seen as soft—on anything, and especially Communism (or terrorism or whatever else seems to threaten). It is relevant to consider the views of Daniel Ellsberg, who has perhaps studied United States policy in Vietnam in more depth and for a longer time than most Americans.

"My best guess," Ellsberg said to **Salon** on November 19, 2002, "is that Lyndon Johnson psychologically did not want to be called weak on Communism. As he put it to Doris Kearns, he said he would be called an 'unmanly man' if he got out of Vietnam, a weakling, an appeaser. . . . Many Americans have died in the last fifty years, and maybe ten times as many Asians, because American politicians feared to be called unmanly."

Unfortunately, there are some so wedded to the notion of American omnipotence (manhood) that they claim the right to destroy any regime they don't like, scoff at the United Nations, and consider it, as reported recently in **The New York Times,** "reflexive submission" to adhere to international law. In his book **War and Gender,** Joshua Goldstein, a professor of international relations at American University, writes: "As war is gendered masculine, so peace is gendered feminine. Thus the manhood of men who oppose war becomes vulnerable to shaming." They are labeled wimps, pussies, or girlie men. (Beware of men who use words that relate pejoratively to females when describing the "other side.") For them, national omnipotence and their own potency are joined. They'd rather disappear from public life than be blamed for pulling out. The most dangerous leaders are those (usually, but not always, men) who were bullied and shamed by their parents (usually, but not always their fathers). War and the perpetuation of social inequities will be their way of proving themselves qualified to belong to the "manhood" club, which sees strength (violence, homophobia) and hierarchy (racism, misogyny, power **over**) as their ticket in. It is up to women—and men of conscience—to define a **democratic manhood** less susceptible to shaming because its virility is not dependent on dominance.

This has never been as apparent as during the last few years. Look at George W. Bush's macho posturing in relation to war, his "Bring it on" rhetoric, and his "Are you man enough?" challenge to John Kerry. Then there's Dick Cheney's implication that supporting the UN made Kerry effeminate or army lieutenant general William Boykin's "I knew that my God was bigger than his." The patriarchal mine's-bigger-than-yours paradigm and drive for control has the entire world tilted in dangerous imbalance, damaging not only individual women, men, and children, but entire peoples. In **Revolution from Within** Gloria Steinem wrote that we need to change patriarchal institutions "if we are to stop producing leaders whose unexamined early lives are then played out on a national and international stage." This is one reason why today, in my third act, I am committed to helping educate boys and girls against these arbitrary and destructive, violence-producing gender roles.

History shows us that nothing—no nation, no individual—remains number one forever. So remaining strong but also humble and empathic on your way up ensures that you will set a good example and not be a lonely ruin when you come down. A soft landing among friends is always preferable to a crash in hostile territory.

Enough of the Lone Ranger, in all his forms—even my own.

CHAPTER THIRTEEN

THE FINAL PUSH

We will fight you with all the joys / of a woman
in childbirth.
—VIETNAMESE POET TO RICHARD NIXON

I WAS BOTH IN LOVE with and in awe of Tom.
For me he was friend, mentor, lover, savior, pillar
of support, and example of what I hoped I could become. I saw him as a pure person who could not be
corrupted, someone who was on an eternal quest to
understand human nature. I loved watching him devour books and I loved watching him while his left
hand curled like a claw around his pen as he covered
page after page of the yellow legal-size pads he preferred.

I remember the day he called his mother, Gene,
to tell her I was pregnant. There was a long pause.

"What's the matter, Mom?" he asked, and then, with an occasional look to me, he just listened.

When he finally hung up he said, "Well, my mother wants to know if we're getting married. She says people won't like it if we have a child and aren't married. She said, 'What if you go on the Johnny Carson show to talk about the war and all he wants to know is why you aren't married? Is that a battle you want to have on top of all your other battles?' "

Right on target, Gene! I thought. I wanted to get married. I wanted to be with Tom forever. (I hadn't been that certain with Vadim.) But I had avoided bringing up the m-word with Tom and was elated his mother had jumped in. Perhaps Tom was, too, because it didn't take but a few minutes for the two of us to agree that marriage would be a good idea. But we couched it in political terms. Needing a political justification for everything was fast becoming a pattern of ours. I think it made Tom comfortable—and if he was comfortable, I was, too.

Vadim was friendly and funny when I called him to ask for a divorce in January 1973. We had been apart, really, for two years. I could tell we would have a better friendship as exes than we had had as marrieds. (I wasn't the only ex of his who felt this way.)

I was three months pregnant when Tom and I were married on January 19, 1973. The ceremony took place in the living room of my home with the two of us sitting on a brick ledge in front of the fireplace, my brother on one side, Holly Near next to him, the Episcopal minister on the other side. An eclectic group of about forty people sat facing us: Dad, holding four-year-old Vanessa on his lap, with his wife, Shirlee, next to him; and Tom's mother, Gene, who had flown in from Detroit. Holly and Peter sang us a wedding song that she'd written. As Tom said, it wasn't exactly Norman Rockwell, but then it was hard to find anything Rockwellian in those days. The marriage vows included a promise to maintain a sense of humor—only one of the promises we failed to keep.

My relationship with my father had been shifting subtly since Tom and I had gotten together. It was as if my being with a man again somehow made me okay—or at least not his responsibility—and it helped that Dad liked Tom. First of all, Tom, like Dad and Vadim, was a fisherman; second, Dad was impressed with how Tom could deliver an eloquent speech without notes; third, they both came from the middle of the country. In addition, Dad clearly wanted to mend fences and be there for me. Even today I am moved as I write this.

Tom and I wanted to find a name for our baby that was both American and Vietnamese, as a way to acknowledge what had brought us together and motivated us to have a child. The only name I could think of that met this criterion was Troy (Troi in Vietnamese). We also decided we didn't want to saddle our child with either of our surnames (both Fonda and Hayden carried too much baggage), so we chose Tom's mother's maiden name, Garity. The

Just after we wed, sitting in front of the fireplace. Left to right: Holly Near, Peter, me, Tom, and Reverend York.
(AP/Wide World Photos)

Pregnant in my purple poncho at a Claremont College antiwar rally with Ron Kovic, February 1973. This is when I heard Ron say, "I may have lost my body, but I've gained my mind."

middle name, Tom decided, would be O'Donovan, after the Irish national hero O'Donovan Rossa. Troy O'Donovan Garity. It felt right.

Not long after our wedding, former Nixon aides G. Gordon Liddy and James W. McCord Jr. were convicted of conspiracy, burglary, and wiretapping in the Watergate incident. Meanwhile the Indochina Peace Campaign had opened a national office in Ocean Park, the beach community just south of Santa Monica. One day while I was in the office working on the layout of our newly launched newspaper, **Indochina Focal Point,** I started to miscarry and was ordered to bed for a month, just as had happened at the end of my first trimester with Vanessa. Actually it was fortuitous: I needed downtime to reflect on my so-called career and what, if anything, I wanted to do about it. Tom or Ruby would bring me coffee in the morning and then drive Vanessa to school while I lay there and thought how slim the chances were that I would be offered the kinds of movies I wanted to make; in spite of the need for money, I couldn't conceive of spending three months (the average time for a feature film) doing something I didn't believe in when there was so much else to be done. But could I actually make my own movies? I knew I was not a businesswoman: I have always been numerically challenged. Faced with anything that has to do with numbers—costs, profits, distances, or bomb tonnage—my mind goes blank. Perhaps this is because my mother was always doing numbers on her adding machine and my father hated it. Whatever the reasons, I was at a disadvantage as a producer. What I thought I could be good at, however, was conceiving a story.

The week before being sent to bed, I had shared a platform at an antiwar rally in Claremont, California, with Vietnam veteran Ron Kovic, a highly decorated Vietnam marine now in a wheelchair, paralyzed from the waist down from a shrapnel wound to his spine. In time everyone would know Ron's story: Tom Cruise would play him in the film based on his autobiography, **Born on the Fourth of July.** I can still see Ron on the speaker's platform, ferocious in his wheelchair, insistent, articulate, telling how he had been a believer, had enlisted and reenlisted, how he'd been wounded and paralyzed, and how, on his journey back from war through rat-infested, understaffed VA hospitals, he realized that he'd been used and discarded. This had got him thinking about the entire nature of the war and the macho ethic behind it, the realization, he said, that had saved him. Then he added: "I may have lost my body, but I've gained my mind."

As I lay in bed, this sentence haunted me. It echoed the redemptive journeys I'd seen the Winter Soldier veterans take. Could a movie be built around Ron's sentence?

I began to imagine a story: Two men, both believers, go to Vietnam; one returns like Ron, angry but able to shed the old warrior ethos and free his mind; the other returns brittle and empty, unable to let go of the militaristic myths of what a man should be. I didn't know where to fit in a role for me, but I didn't really care. It was about the two men and the transformation and salvation of one of them.

I mentioned the idea to my friend Bruce Gilbert, an IPC staffer who was a film buff and dreamed of becoming a producer. We had often talked about the kind of movie we'd like to see made about the Vietnam War. We decided Bruce would try to develop a story draft based on Ron Kovic's sentence, and I insisted that screenwriter Nancy Dowd work on it as well, to ensure a woman's perspective.

Nancy and Bruce went to work for hardly any money, since we had no studio to put up development funding. With the help of my lawyer and my agent, Mike Medavoy, we got Bruce a job as a script reader with an independent movie production company so he could start learning about scripts. He was there for a year, and because he was able to get copies of early drafts of masterpieces like **Chinatown,** he had opportunities to learn the ways in which scripts evolve, as directors and actors become attached. Bruce came to me one day and said that he'd rather be a partner than an employee of mine, and instead of seeing this as a brash move by an inexperienced young man, I made a leap of faith. I figured someone who could organize rallies the way he could, with meticulous attention to detail, could probably be just the partner I needed. So we formed a production company and called it IPC Films, in honor of the Indochina Peace Campaign, the organization that had brought us together (we didn't tell outsiders what the initials stood for).

Nearly six years later, **Coming Home** won Academy Awards for Jon Voight, me, and screenwriters Nancy Dowd, Waldo Salt, and Robert Jones. But I'm getting ahead of myself.

While I was still bedridden, Tom convinced me that we needed to relocate our home closer to the IPC office in Ocean Park, where he had lived before moving in with me. Sell my house? That I'd had only one year? I loved my house. But more than anything I wanted to do what Tom thought was right. Though he never said so outright, I believe Tom felt that how you lived reflected whether you were pure in your politics (read: "one of the people") or just an armchair liberal (read: "bourgeois"). Given my Rocky Mountain epiphany three years earlier, I held this perspective myself, so I was ready to be challenged by whatever Tom offered up. Several days later he came back and told me he'd found a place, one block from the beach, for $45,000. We bought it without my even seeing it.

The Ocean Park of today is gentrified with swank restaurants and clothing stores. Later, I heard that in 2003 our $45,000 house was sold for $2 million. But back in the seventies Ocean Park consisted primarily of seedy bars and thrift shops, and it was redlined, meaning that banks considered it a poor investment and refused to make any loans for community development.

When the danger of my miscarrying had passed and I was able to get up again, Tom took me to see the new house he had chosen for us. It sat on the south side of a narrow, one-way, one-block-long street called Wadsworth Avenue, which ran almost to the beach. All the little streets were lined with wooden houses built side by side in the 1920s as summer homes for wealthier folks, who would take the famous red trolley from Los Angeles down San Vicente Boulevard to the beach. In their time the houses must have been charming, but now most, including ours, had been converted into duplexes and were run-down, with thin, uninsulated walls and floors vaguely slanted from sinking into the sand over the years.

The residents of Ocean Park were an interesting mix of blue-collar, radical, and counterculture. In a one-story house next to us lived a conservative Catholic family: a burly night watchman, his wife, and their many children, one of whom was Vanessa's age. Next to them was a two-story building; on the ground floor lived a Maoist writer and his bright, redheaded son, also Vanessa's age. Across the street lived a group of women activists Tom knew. With few exceptions there were no driveways or garages, so we all had to park on the street.

I recall the first time I walked into the house. It was dark and dampish. I had to swallow hard, but I was determined to show I could make the move with no complaints, though it would mean saying good-bye to Ruby Ellen, who had been my faithful friend and assistant for almost three years. On top of that, Tom felt we didn't need the entire house for ourselves, so to save money Jack Nichol and Carol Kurtz, both with IPC, moved in on the ground floor. This was a good thing, actually. During the times of increased controversy that were about to roll over me, Carol in particular was a pillar of support, stability, and tenderness. She was a lanky, handsome woman ten years my junior, with soft brown hair and a ready giggle. Both Carol and Jack had been part of the Red Family collective, had reconciled with Tom (Carol was the woman who cried on my doorstep that Tom had no emotions), were intelligent, committed activists, and were the parents of a ten-month-old boy named Corey—the only other couple we worked with who had started a family.

Jack and Carol had the bedroom, dining room, and kitchen on the ground floor, and we shared the living room. Tom had persuaded Fred Branfman, a writer and researcher who had developed outreach materials for the IPC tour, to move from Washington, D.C., into a small room on one side of our front porch, where he slept on a straw mat with his diminutive Vietnamese wife, Thoa. Fred stands about six feet five, and when I would come down in the mornings to take Vanessa to school, I would risk tripping over his feet, which always stuck out past the door.

Off the other side of the porch, a separate door led up a narrow flight of stairs to the second floor, where we lived. It consisted of a bedroom that looked out onto the street with a minute closet and a small bedroom opposite ours for Vanessa and Corey. The kitchen was tiny, with no vent, and when I turned on the stove cockroaches would sometimes run out. I just plowed on, always thinking I'd deal with it later.

There was little privacy. The walls were made of tongue-and-groove slats so thin that if I put a nail in a wall to hang a picture, it would stick right through to the other side (lovemaking was subdued). My father, only half joking, called the house "the shack."

We didn't have a dishwasher or a washing machine, so twice a week I would take our clothes to the nearby laundromat. One day, when I'd stepped next door for coffee, someone stole all my clothes, including the silk pajamas I'd worn in North Vietnam.

I set to work brightening up the place with a pregnant woman's nesting intensity, and in spite of the downside I actually loved being there. This was community living of a kind I had never experienced. Because the streets were so short and the houses so close (and all had porches), all the neighbors knew one another and would exchange sugar, coffee, and gossip. There were kids for Vanessa to play with, and the beach with swings and slides was a block away. Because I could always hear the sound of breaking surf and smell the salt air, living in our home on Wadsworth Avenue felt like a return to the summers of my childhood. We would stay there for close to ten years.

When celebrity friends would visit, they'd usually ask if the lack of privacy and security bothered me. There were several reasons I liked being so accessible: The first had to do with the issue of "coming down from the mountaintop." Then, when my children came of school age, both went to public schools, and we didn't want their friends who came over to play to find that we lived differently from them.

Furthermore, my relationship to my profession had changed. I was beginning to feel I could be in control of the content of my films, and this made me care more and want to go deeper as an actress. How can an artist plumb reality if he or she lives in the clouds? Of course, the fact of my being a movie star created an inevitable separation; most people have a hard time overcoming their intimidation around celebrities. But you'd be amazed how much this separation can be minimized, and I really worked at it. It wasn't that difficult. I've always had a high tolerance for what other celebrities might call inconvenience or discomfort.

Also, for me, the security and privacy issue that so concerned some of my more famous friends was not about being accessible to fans. It was the **government** that was the problem. The first year we were in the house (during the Nixon administration), our home was broken into, drawers turned upside down, all our files and papers strewn about, and our phone tapped, and one day an FBI undercover agent posing as a reporter came to interview me in order to confirm that I had been three months pregnant at the time of our marriage. How do I know this? Because I later read it in my FBI files.

In retrospect I wouldn't have given up the Wadsworth experience for anything, but I no longer believe that it is necessary to prove your political purity by living in a manner that makes your teeth clench. If you can afford to hire someone to help run a comfortable, attractive home, there is nothing wrong with that, as long as you pay a decent wage with benefits and as long as materialism doesn't become your focus in life.

During my pregnancy, I spent a lot of time doing research for the film that Bruce and Nancy were developing. I traveled to San Diego to interview wives of Vietnam veterans. One told me, "I talk to my husband now, but it's as if there's no one there. He's empty. It's like I can hear my voice echoing inside him." A character was beginning to emerge for me to play: My husband goes to war while I remain at home and go through my own changes because of a relationship with a paralyzed vet I meet in the hospital.

I learned a lot from a Vietnam vet named Shad Meshad, who had been a psych officer in Vietnam. He was a friend of Ron Kovic's, equally charismatic and fearless, and had an intuitive way with troubled vets, who were flooding to the warm climes of Southern California. When I met him he had become an important member of the staff of the largest psychiatric facility for vets in the country, at the Wadsworth VA Hospital in Brentwood, California,

one zip code up from Santa Monica. Back then doctors didn't have a diagnosis for the symptoms Vietnam vets were presenting. It would be several more
years before posttraumatic stress disorder (PTSD)
would be recognized by the medical establishment as
a complex of symptoms and a specific diagnosis—
and only then thanks to the tireless and empathic
work of Drs. Robert Lifton, Leonard Neff, Chaim
Shatan, and Sarah Haley and Vietnam veterans
themselves. But guys identified with Shad. He had
established rap (discussion) groups in Venice, Santa
Monica, Watts, and the barrio and helped put Bruce
and Nancy in contact with many of them.

Ron Kovic invited me to come to a meeting of
the Patients' Rights Committee at the Long Beach
Veterans Hospital, where he was currently a patient. He wanted me to hear from other guys about
the poor conditions there. It was midday when several hundred people, the majority on gurneys or in
wheelchairs, gathered on the lawn behind the paraplegic ward. Ron and another ex-marine, Bill
Unger, had had a leaflet distributed announcing
that I would be there. In protest there was a coun-
terdemonstration of World War II and Korean War
vets, waving flags and singing patriotic songs to try
to drown us out.

I don't remember what I said to the vets that
day, but I do recall being totally shocked at what they
said to me. The guys from the paraplegic ward told
me how their urine bags weren't emptied and were
always overflowing onto the floor; how patients were

left lying in their own excrement and would develop festering bedsores; how call buttons weren't answered and when patients protested they'd be put in the psych ward, given Thorazine, or even lobotomized. Ron had been rolling his gurney around the different wards with a hidden tape recorder, gathering evidence, and journalist Richard Boyle verified these stories while researching an article for the **Los Angeles Free Press.** I immediately arranged for Nancy Dowd and Bruce Gilbert to come down and see for themselves, and everything we heard and saw found its way into the film **Coming Home.**

As it turned out, the final push to end the war coincided with the birth of Troy. It was 1973. Friends of ours, Jon Voight and his wife, Marcheline, had just had a baby boy, James, and they recommended we take birthing classes with the woman who had coached them, Femmy DeLyser, who lived just south of us in Ocean Park.

My water broke one morning while I was standing on the porch with Carol. This time I was ready, and this time the birthing was different. For one thing, I was an empowered participant; Femmy had seen to that. No doctor was going to give me drugs unless I wanted them; no nurse was going to make me feel she knew more than I did about how it should go. I was awake, Femmy was there with me along with Tom and Carol, and though I begged for pain relief just before I was being wheeled into the delivery room, Troy was born before it took effect, so for all intents and purposes it was a natural birth.

Tom lifted the baby out of me, and I saw immediately in the overhead mirror that it was a boy. They laid Troy O'Donovan Garity on my chest, and I noted with groggy astonishment that he didn't cry. Tom was crying. I was crying. But not Troy. I'd never heard of a newborn not crying, and I saw this as a sign that his journey through life would be blessed.

During the first few weeks I was very resistant to letting Tom hold or change Troy. I think this was because I was defending my domain as the one who knew what she was doing. This was one area where I, who had already had a child, knew more than Tom—and I wasn't about to let this go. When I finally did let go, however, I was terribly moved by how tender Tom was with his son and how touched by fatherhood. He would lie naked in bed with Troy on his stomach for hours, just cooing to him. In his autobiography Tom wrote, "Then and there . . . I made a pledge: I would build my life around this little boy until he became a man." I don't believe anything in Tom's life softened his heart the way Troy did. Although Tom and I would divorce sixteen years later, he kept this pledge to his son and has always been a present and involved father.

Almost until the day I delivered, I had continued making speeches against the war on campuses all over California. With my protruding belly, usually draped in a bright purple knit poncho, I looked like the defiant prow of a ship. Within days after Troy's

Tom holding Troy.

On our front porch
with Troy.
(John Rose)

birth I returned to meetings and speeches, bringing him with me everywhere. I handled the experience so differently from the way I had with Vanessa. A lot of this change was because of Tom: He would not have tolerated leaving Troy, he was against nannies, and neither of us was about to stop what we were doing—so by necessity I had a different relationship with my son than I had had with Vanessa. I was, perhaps for the first time, really showing up for someone.

Troy would nurse and our eyes would lock as he gazed at me across my breast for many minutes at a time. I realized that I was imprinting him with love and that my touch and this prolonged gaze between us were important. I know that for many mothers these things come naturally, but they hadn't for me—partly because of my own early childhood. As I have learned more about parenting over the years, I see that sometimes when you haven't healed your own wounds, as I hadn't, it is painful as a parent to open your heart to a child and you avoid it. My way of avoiding it was to stay busy. I was at the beginning of the process of healing when Troy was born, and the bittersweet part was my awareness and sadness that I was giving Troy something I had not given enough of to Vanessa. She was nearly five years old when Troy was born, and during the first years afterward, she moved back and forth between our home in Ocean Park and her dad's place in Paris.

The escalating scandal surrounding Watergate (many of Nixon's staffers had been forced to resign) was weakening the administration, which offered us a strategic opportunity to mobilize the antiwar forces IPC had built the previous year. When Troy was three months old, we embarked on a three-month tour. The goal was to put pressure on Congress to cut funding of the Thieu regime in South Vietnam. Troy would sleep in dresser drawers that I padded with blankets and set on the floor by our beds. When I'd make a speech, someone would hold him in the wings until I was through, and occasionally I'd be in the middle of a speech when my milk would let down, and I'd have to hand the microphone to Tom and step into the wings to nurse.

Following the tour, I made my second trip to North Vietnam, this time with Troy and Tom. The purpose was to make a documentary film, **Introduction to the Enemy,** aimed at showing a human side of Vietnam, a view of the people's lives and stories very few Americans would otherwise ever see or hear. We wanted it to be not about death and destruction but about rebirth and reconstruction. Haskell Wexler, the brilliant American cinematographer whose credits included **Medium Cool** and **Who's Afraid of Virginia Woolf?**, filmed it for us.

It was very different this time. Not only had the bombing of the North stopped, but having Tom there to buffer and support allowed me to relax. It had been what I had learned about hope, on my first trip to Hanoi, that had motivated me to have another child. Now here was Troy, actually in Hanoi, a little bundle of manifested hope.

We went directly from North Vietnam, that spring of 1974, to six weeks of around-the-clock lobbying in Washington, D.C., to persuade Congress to stop funding the Thieu government. We found that the lobbying effort we had helped mount during the tour was generating thousands of letters and phone calls to congressional offices. One congressman was so inundated with mail that he pleaded, "Please call your people off. I'm voting with you, okay?"

In 1973 I had filed a lawsuit against the Nixon administration to compel the various government agencies to admit they had been carrying on a campaign of harassment and intimidation in an attempt to silence and impugn me. I wanted them to acknowledge that this was improper and to cease and desist. One afternoon that spring of 1974, I went with my friend and attorney, Leonard Weinglass, to take the deposition of former White House special counsel Charles Colson. Before, we met off the record with David Shapiro, Colson's law partner and chief legal adviser for Watergate matters. Tom was with us.

Shapiro told us it was Attorney General John Mitchell who ordered the Watergate break-in and also admitted that "my client [Colson] is not cleaner than driven snow. He heads the list of the biggest sons of bitches in town and they say everything points in his direction . . . but he has committed no crimes." His was merely "peanuts and popcorn politics," said Shapiro of Colson, who was in charge of compiling the White House enemies list and of destroying Nixon's opponents (who included not simply activists but antiwar Democrats, heads of major corporations, newspaper editors, labor leaders, and presidential candidates).

After thirty minutes Colson came in with a stenographer and the formal deposition began. I recall staring at an enormous cross that hung around Colson's neck and rested atop his potbelly. That's right, I thought, he has a cross to bear. It was an odd experience sitting in that posh office in the presence of this well-groomed, well-heeled, cross-bearing man who had been so involved in subverting American democracy. Colson admitted there were memos on me in the White House files but said they came from John Dean. He denied any official ties with the government other than his publicly known job and said he knew nothing about the enemies list. Nonetheless Mr. Colson was indicted on March 1, 1974, on one count of conspiracy to obstruct justice and one count of obstruction of justice.*

*Final Report (October 1975) of the Watergate Special Prosecution Force in the Watergate cover-up case, U.S. v. Mitchell et al. This indictment was dismissed by the government on June 3, 1974, after Colson pled guilty in the case relating to the Nixon White House sponsored break-in at Daniel

My lawsuit against the Nixon administration was settled in 1979. The FBI admitted that I had been under surveillance from 1970 to 1973; that they had used counterintelligence techniques, in violation of my constitutional rights, to "neutralize" me and "impair my personal and professional standing"; that they had seized without subpoena my bank records during that time and had made pretext calls and visits to my home and office to determine where I was.

In addition, the CIA admitted to opening my mail. I am told this was the first time the Agency had ever acknowledged conducting a mail-opening campaign in the United States against an American citizen. The suit also revealed that the State Department, IRS, Treasury Department, and White House all kept files on me. By then new guidelines and laws had been put in place by Congress and the new attorney general that prohibited all of these activities without judicial process.

Ellsberg's psychiatrist's office, **U.S. v. Ehrlichman et al.**, where Mr. Colson had been charged with conspiracy to violate civil rights. That indictment was also dismissed when Colson pled guilty to obstruction of justice in connection with the prosecution of Dan Ellsberg, a case that was dismissed by the federal judge because of government misconduct. Colson was sentenced on June 21, 1974, to serve one to three years in prison and fined $5,000. (His actual sentence, however, only ran from July 8, 1974, until January 31, 1975.)

In 2001 the Bush administration got Congress to pass the Patriot Act, which has rolled back the post-Watergate protections of our constitutional rights, expanding the government's authority to conduct wiretaps and allowing a noncitizen suspected of associating with terrorists to be detained without a warrant and without the right to consult an attorney. Even more Big Brotherish, the Patriot Act gives the FBI broad power to require libraries and bookstores to identify individuals who read or purchase books the government deems suspect; and the law provides that such individuals may not be notified that they and their reading habits are being investigated.

In the spring of 1974 Nixon's supplemental aid bill for Thieu was roundly defeated. In August impeachment proceedings began in Congress. That week Nixon became the first president in American history to resign from office. In addition to the Watergate crimes, the Senate Armed Services Committee had developed evidence suggesting Nixon had violated the law by permitting secret ground operations in Laos and Cambodia. But in the end it was for the narrower issues of illegal cover-ups in response to antiwar dissent, not because of the war itself, that Nixon was finally forced to resign. In the wake of the Watergate scandals, when asked what I thought of it all, I replied, "I'm still here. The last government's in jail."

Gerald Ford became president, pardoned Nixon one month later, and by attempting to reinstate funding for Thieu proved that the United States was still unwilling to give up its corrupt South Vietnamese ally and leave Indochina to the Indochinese. But in the spring of 1975, after more than ten years of war, the North Vietnamese and their supporters in the South entered Saigon. The war was over.

It was hard to believe. There was joy that it was over, but there was sadness, too, as we watched the scenes unfold on television: helicopters lifting out embassy personnel, Vietnamese allies of the United States clinging to the skids. It didn't need to end this way. All along the Vietnamese had offered olive branches, believing that we who had fought our own war of national independence would understand them. So many wasted, lost lives on both sides. So much land and forest destroyed for no reason.

I have not returned to Vietnam since the war ended thirty years ago, and not all that I have heard about the situation there makes me happy. In North Vietnam the "hard-liners" won out over more moderate leaders, and they were heavy-handed and disconnected from the people in the southern cities when they set about trying to bring order out of chaos. Thousands of former Saigon administrators and military officials were put into reeducation camps with no rights of appeal. Economic reforms were rigidly instituted without sensitivity to what people wanted and needed in the South. The Hanoi government went about imposing a centralized economy and social order ill suited to local conditions, with almost the same sense of entitlement that had allowed the United States to try to reorganize South Vietnamese society according to **our** westernized concept: an urban consumer culture. Still, none of this justifies what the United States did—and none of it seems to be keeping American tourists from spending their holidays there or U.S. corporations from investing there.

The Vietnamese were expecting the United States to honor its agreement to provide reconstruction aid. Instead the economic embargo of the North was extended throughout the country, all Vietnamese assets in the United States were frozen, and the United States blocked Vietnam's entry into the United Nations. The country was in desperate need of aid. Without it terrible hardships were imposed on South Vietnam, where years of war had taken the hardest toll, where hundreds of thousands of refugees were crowded into cities. The North Vietnamese hard-liners had to deal alone and ineptly with severe problems. On top of this there was a massive exodus from Vietnam. Mostly the ethnic Chinese (Hoa) fled the country in makeshift boats; tens of thousands died at sea. U.S. officials claimed that the "boat people" were victims of massive political persecution, and the crisis became the new "See? I told you so" justification of the war.*

Whatever hardships were foisted on the Vietnamese people by the new Communist regime, the widespread publicity put out by the Pentagon that, should they take over, the Communists would murder hundreds of thousands, even millions, of people turned out to be propaganda to manipulate American public opinion—like Iraq's "weapons of mass destruction" in 2003.

There have been plenty of people who accused me of romanticizing the Vietnamese. Well, yes. They were easy to romanticize during the war, as they battled the mighty U.S. military power. The David and Goliath legend hasn't survived the centuries for nothing. Do you know anyone who roots for Go-

---

*But congressional delegations who went to Vietnam and visited refugee camps in Indonesia in the late 1970s disputed this, saying the exodus was more due to historic hatreds and economic devastation exacerbated by the U.S. embargo. When antiwar activists were asked to sign public petitions about the boat people, aimed at the North Vietnamese, I refused. I felt it was the U.S. government that should have been petitioned to live up to its treaty obligations and help alleviate hardships we had brought about. Unfortunately, it would take another whole decade for the Clinton administration to normalize relations and lift the trade embargo.

liath (except maybe those who want something from him)? It's the Davids who touch our hearts.

A FINAL WORD

There are still many Americans who believe the United States could have won the war had we "gone all out." Because of this, I cannot conclude the Vietnam chapters of this book without addressing this question.

The U.S. military did everything that General William Westmoreland, commander of U.S. forces in Vietnam, and his successor, Creighton Abrams, asked for: bombing Laos and Cambodia to cut the Ho Chi Minh Trail, mining Haiphong harbor and imposing a naval blockade, dropping more bomb tonnage on Vietnam than we did on **all** of Europe during World War II, pummeling Hanoi and Haiphong with B-52 bombers, and waging an all-out air assault against the rest of North Vietnam.

We could win battles, and did. Our soldiers fought bravely and well. But we couldn't win the war, at least not by conventional means. Of course, we could have dropped a nuclear bomb on them, and Nixon was threatening to do so. In other words, if we couldn't defeat them, we could at least have annihilated them. But if the mighty United States had had to annihilate a country of rice farmers and fishermen in order to win, wouldn't that have cost us our national soul? I'm sure there are those men—Henry Kissinger and Dick Cheney most likely among them—who think that mentioning "soul" shows we're soft, unmanly. If you feel this way, then forget about soul and think more pragmatically about the issue of global capitalism—apparently not an invalid reason to send our boys to die. But from an investment point of view we never had to fight a war there at all: Since way back in the 1940s Ho Chi Minh had said he would turn Vietnam into a "fertile field for American capital and enterprise." He even suggested he might offer the United States a naval base at Cam Ranh Bay if we helped his country stay independent from the French.

Today—fifty-eight thousand American lives and millions of Indochinese lives later—even with the "enemy" running the country, the United States has more than $1 billion invested in Vietnam; trade between the two countries has reached $6 billion a year; the United States is Vietnam's largest export market. In the fall of 2003 Vietnam's defense minister, Pham Van Tra, was received in our nation's capital with full honor guard at the Pentagon. All the dominoes are still standing. Vietnam is considered one of the safest havens for tourism and business.

The real question isn't how we prosecuted the war but whether the entire United States enterprise in Vietnam was wrong from the get-go. We sent our men to die there **not** to help the Vietnamese gain freedom, but to destroy an indigenous nationalist movement because it threatened U.S. influence and control over the country and because we needed to maintain our "credibility as an ally," to quote the Pentagon Papers. This was a betrayal of what we stand for. In a battle that pits bamboo against B-52, the victory for bamboo symbolizes hope for the planet.

The U.S. loss represented our nation's chance for redemption. But we did not learn the lesson, and then we tried to rewrite history to blame it all on the very people who tried to stop it.

CHAPTER FOURTEEN

I'M BAAAAAACK!!

> The world changes according to the way people see it,
> and if you alter, even by a millimeter, the way . . .
> people look at reality, then you can change it.
> —JAMES BALDWIN

ONCE THE WAR WAS OVER, I returned to filmmaking and Tom began to investigate the pros and cons of running for the U.S. Senate. Although I did not see it at the time, in hindsight I realize that this marked the beginning of a less harmonious time in our marriage. For three years we had been joined together, at the heart and hip, in our effort to end the war. Now I was resuming a career that would have more impact on our lives than either of us anticipated—an impact that would both please and dismay Tom.

Because of the profound changes I'd experienced over the previous five years, I had a new sense of the possibility of personal transformation, and I wanted to use films as a catalyst for this process. Movies like my brother and Dennis Hopper's **Easy Rider,** as well as **Five Easy Pieces** and **Midnight Cowboy,** show the revolutionary changes that were rocking American filmmaking in the 1960s and 1970s. I, however, subscribe to what British playwright David Hare says: "The best place to be radical is at the center." I wanted to make films that were stylistically mainstream, films Middle America could relate to: about ordinary people going through personal transformation. Though it was inchoate at the time, I was also beginning to view transformation from a perspective of gender: What is man? What is woman? What makes them do what they do the way they do it?

I saw the fledgling film that Bruce Gilbert, Nancy Dowd, and I had been developing as a way to help redefine masculinity.

Our story had a marine, my husband, with full use of his body (including his penis), who wanted above all to prove his manhood by being a "hero." But because he was neither sensitive nor spontaneous, he was not a good lover. The paraplegic I met in the VA hospital, on the other hand, did **not** have a functioning penis, and all he wanted was to be human. His willingness to reexamine long held beliefs, along with his physical incapacity, made him sensitive to another's needs. His pleasure came through giving pleasure—at least that was my intention, and thus the film could potentially illuminate a sexuality beyond genitalia.

We needed to take the project to the next stage, where we could pitch it to a studio, and veteran screenwriter Waldo Salt, writer of **Midnight Cowboy,** was the one we wanted. My agent told us he would be impossible to get: "Forget it, there is no way. There's no studio attached and it isn't a commercial project." Not to be discouraged, Bruce got Waldo's phone number in Connecticut and called him cold. To our surprise Waldo said, "Sounds interesting. Send me what you have."

Waldo agreed to come onto the project but wanted to start from scratch and bring in the team with whom he had done **Midnight Cowboy** and **The Day of the Locust:** British director John Schlesinger and producer Jerry Hellman. I had great respect for Schlesinger, who had come from the world of documentaries and whose films had an unusual, gritty realism that would be perfect for us. Jerry Hellman's experience, taste, and enthusiasm for the fragile project made me optimistic that we might actually get it made. Though it was not an easy pill for Bruce to swallow after the work he had put into it, he agreed to be associate producer. We both knew we needed all the experience and heft we could get (as well as a new script) if the film was to get made. Studios weren't exactly clamoring for stories about Vietnam vets in wheelchairs, and the few Vietnam-based stories that had been released hadn't done well.

In a grand gesture of commitment and generosity, Waldo and Jerry did something very rare: They agreed to work on spec until we had something that would convince a studio to give us development money. Jerry got us an office at MGM (where United Artists was then headquartered). Bruce quit his job, and thus began the second phase of our project's development.

Waldo Salt was an old lefty, one of the Hollywood writers who had been blacklisted in the fifties. He had a heart of gold and a great talent for capturing the subtext of a scene. With Bruce and Jerry's help he threw himself into his research with the gusto one would expect from a man with his history, visiting VA hospitals, talking with vets. (It was Waldo who encouraged Ron Kovic to write **his** memoir, **Born on the Fourth of July.**) Jerry financed the research from his own pocket and came up with the film's title, **Coming Home.**

Waldo's script maintained the original triangular story, turning my husband into a marine officer and me into a traditional officer's wife, waiting for her husband to come home from Vietnam in the late sixties. He had me getting my own apartment and volunteering (against my husband's wishes) in the VA hospital, where I meet a man who has already come home from Vietnam and needs to heal—body **and** soul—from the physical and psychic wounds of the war.

On the strength of Waldo's lengthy treatment, the heads of United Artists agreed to finance the development of a full screenplay. We were off and running, but we would soon learn how much time goes into producing original material. I would have two other films under my belt—**Julia** and **Fun with Dick and Jane**—before **Coming Home** would be ready to shoot. Before that happened, only seven weeks before our intended start date, Waldo suffered a massive heart attack and was unable to continue working. Then John Schlesinger bowed out with these memorable words: "Jane, you don't need a British fag on this one." I loved him for his forthrightness but was beginning to wonder if, in the face of such setbacks, victory could be pulled from the jaws of defeat.

Meanwhile Tom's interest in running for office grew, stemming from the fact that in the wake of the Vietnam War and Watergate, new political forces had been unleashed, which he labeled "progressive populism." Jimmy Carter was running for president, Jerry Brown was the new governor of California, and a whole new class of congressmen and women like Bella Abzug, Tim Wirth, Andy Young, and Pat Schroeder were in office, making their strength felt.

Tom had spent six months traveling the state, meeting with people, testing the waters, debating whether or not to run for the U.S. Senate. The meeting I remember most vividly during that time was with César Chávez, the internationally respected founder and leader of the United Farm Workers union. It was the first time I had met César, who like Martin Luther King Jr. was a devout fol-

lower of Gandhi's principles of nonviolent resistance, not just as a tactic but as a governing philosophy. I was mesmerized by his soft eyes and quiet
wisdom. The meeting was especially moving because my father's film **The Grapes of Wrath** had so
personalized for me the plight of migrant farmworkers, whether they were "Okie" refugees from
the Dust Bowl or Mexicans.

When Tom asked César what he thought about
the idea of his running for the U.S. Senate, César answered, "We've seen many candidates come and go.
It would be a waste of time and money unless you
build something lasting, like a machine. Not like
Mayor Daley has, but a machine for people. **That**
would interest us."

Meanwhile a woman came into my life who would
become a pivotal friend. A year or two before the war
ended I had received a call from film producer Hannah Weinstein in New York, asking if I would help
her daughter, Paula, get a job in Hollywood. Back in
1971 Hannah had been the first person to give me a
generous contribution for the GI office; I remembered well how warm and encouraging she had been
to me at the time, and though I didn't know Paula, I
wanted to return Hannah's favor.

Paula was a tall brunette with sexy brown eyes
and a dry sense of humor. A recent graduate from
Columbia University, where she had been involved
in student antiwar protests, she now wanted to fol-

low in her mother's footsteps and become a film producer. I was impressed with her guts and obvious intelligence. As soon as our lunch was over I walked across the street and asked my agent, Mike Medavoy, to hire Paula. He did—as a script reader. It didn't take long for the agency to recognize talent, and soon thereafter, when Mike left to become an executive at United Artists Pictures, Paula became my agent—and to this day she remains one of my most cherished friends. Our lives are intertwined personally and professionally. I am godmother to her daughter Hannah, she was one of the producers of the most recent movie I made, **Monster-in-Law** (fifteen years after my retirement), and we always have each other's backs.

As my agent, Paula did something for me that no one had ever done: She fought a passionate and personal battle to win me the role of Lillian Hellman in **Julia**. Lillian, the author of such plays as **The Little Foxes** and **Toys in the Attic,** happened to also be Paula's godmother.

Julia takes place in the 1930s during the rise of Nazism in Europe and is the story of the relationship between Lillian and her childhood friend Julia. Julia goes off to Vienna and becomes involved in the anti-Fascist movement, trying to get help to Jews inside Nazi-occupied Austria and Poland. Though they have not seen each other for years, Julia seeks help from her friend Lillian, asking her to smuggle money (sewn into the lining of a fashionable fur hat) through customs into Poland, where she arranges to

Speaking at a rally with César Chávez, founder and leader of the United Farm Workers union.
(AP/Wide World Photos)

meet her. Their last, memorable, terribly moving scene together, which is both a reunion and farewell, takes place in a restaurant in Warsaw where Lillian surreptitiously passes the hat with the hidden money to Julia under the table. Years later Lillian learns that her friend has been murdered by Nazis.

The film provided me with a multidimensional, dramatic role in what has become a film classic and brought me my third Oscar nomination for Best Actress. It also gave me the chance to work with the great director Fred Zinnemann—who had made **From Here to Eternity, High Noon,** and **A Man for All Seasons**—and my professional idol Vanessa Redgrave. There is a quality about Vanessa that makes me feel as if she resides in a netherworld of mystery that eludes the rest of us mortals. Her voice seems to come from some deep place that knows all suffering and all secrets. Watching her work is like seeing through layers of glass, each layer painted in mythic watercolor images, layer after layer, until it becomes dark—but even then you know you haven't come to the bottom of it.

Vanessa was perfect as Julia, who Lillian knows is braver, stronger, and more committed than she is herself, and I benefited from the memory that I held in my bones of my own brave childhood friend Sue Sally, whose lead I had always been ready to follow, just as Lillian tried to follow Julia's. When we worked together I recall never being sure where Vanessa was drawing her inspiration from, what choices she was working off of, and this invariably threw me slightly

As Lillian Hellman in **Julia**. (Eva Sereny/ Camera Press/ Retna Ltd.)

With Vanessa Redgrave in a scene from **Julia**. (Photofest)

off balance—which worked in the film. The only other time I had experienced this with an actor was with Marlon Brando in **The Chase** (written, by the way, by Lillian Hellman). Like Vanessa, he always seemed to be in another reality, working off some secret, magnetic, inner rhythm that made me have to adjust to **him** rather than maintaining my own integrity in the scene. I suppose I didn't **have** to; but maybe that's just who I was back then.

Among the members of the cast of **Julia** was a newcomer playing the role of the bitchy black-haired Anne Marie. I remember the first time I saw rushes in which she appeared; it was the scene where Lillian comes into Sardi's restaurant following the smash opening of her Broadway play **The Little Foxes.** I am seen making my way through the crowd of well-wishers, and as I walk offscreen the camera lingers on Anne Marie's face: With a slight hand gesture to her mouth and an indefinable look in her eyes, the young actress revealed an entire character. I think my own hand must have come to my mouth at that moment, and as soon as rushes were over I ran to a phone to call Bruce in California. "Bruce," I said, quite out of breath, "listen carefully. There's this young actress with a really strange name, Meryl Streep. Yes, M-e-r-y-l, with a 'y.' I haven't seen an actress so amazing since Geraldine Page. I'm telling you, she's going to become a huge star. We have to try right away to get her for the other woman's part in **Coming Home.**" As it turned out, Meryl was committed to a play and unavailable. But I feel lucky to have had that early glimpse of her unique talent.

Another wonderful thing about **Julia** was the chance to work again with Jason Robards. We had done a silly comedy back in the sixties, **Any Wednesday.** But in **Julia** he was perfect as Lillian's gruff, leave-no-prisoners partner, Dashiell Hammett, author of **The Thin Man.**

Tom brought Troy to Europe twice, for ten days each, during the three-and-a-half-month shoot. Years later he told me how hard these long separations were for him. I accepted the fact that he had to remain in California to take care of organizational matters. I didn't want to face the possibility that he was angry—or that **I** was angry that he and Troy didn't visit more.

Before leaving, I had hired a baby-sitter to help Tom out. She was a nice, attractive young woman; I thought she was sexy and told Tom so. One night in Paris during his visit, he told me he wanted to talk to me about something; it was about the baby-sitter, he said. He reminded me that I thought she was sexy, and from the way he then hesitated, I sensed what was coming and told him not to say any more. "I don't want to hear it," I said. I assumed he was going to tell me he had slept with her. I was going to have to be by myself for another month once he was gone, and I didn't want to be angry and do something I would regret. Since we didn't even talk about far easier subjects, it should be no surprise that we never discussed the issue of monogamy or what I expected from him when I was away for so long. Because I hadn't worked a lot during our first years together, it took him by surprise when I began to be absent for work. I'd done **A Doll's House** in Norway and then another film in Leningrad, **Blue Bird,** directed by George Cukor, and now **Julia.** This was new for him. It was usually Tom who did the coming and going. Perhaps he was used to having a more "open relationship" with other women, but my experience with Vadim had taught me that it didn't work, at least not for me. I take full responsibility for cutting Tom off from what might have been an important conversation for the good of our relationship. But neither one of us ever broached the subject of infidelity again. I never did find out what, if anything, had happened between Tom and the baby-sitter.

Vanessa was now seven years old. I told Vadim I didn't think it was good for her to keep breaking up her school year between California and Paris. At least partially because of this, when he and Catherine Schneider divorced, Vadim moved to his old haunt on Malibu Beach and remained in California for a good part of the next five years, later moving into a house in Ocean Park a few minutes from us.

Three years had elapsed since we had begun work on **Coming Home,** but the script still wasn't quite ready when **Julia** wrapped. By now, at the instigation of Jerry Hellman and to our great good fortune, Hal Ashby had come on board as our director. Hal, an offbeat, aging hippie of a man, with glasses, long wispy gray hair, and a full beard, had directed some of my favorite films: **Harold and Maude, The Last Detail,** and **Shampoo.** He appeared to be very laid-back but in reality was wired and tough as a bull. When Waldo Salt had the heart attack, Hal brought in his longtime friend, editor and screenwriter Robert Jones, to complete the script. Working overtime and selflessly, Jones crafted a script from Waldo's first draft and many notes, but the script remained a work in progress during the entire shooting. Haskell Wexler, who had filmed **Introduction to the Enemy** with Tom and me in North Vietnam and **Bound for Glory** with Hal, was our cinematographer. Jon Voight had been offered the role of my husband, the rigid marine officer, but he worked tirelessly to convince us all that he was the man to play Luke, the paraplegic role inspired by Ron Kovic. Jon participated actively in much of the research with the vets, and finally his passion and commitment persuaded us to go with him. Bruce Dern, my old pal from **They Shoot Horses** days, would end up being wonderful as my husband.

While Jones was working on the script, out of the blue I got a script from my friend Max Palevsky and his producing partner, Peter Bart, called **Fun with Dick and Jane.** It was serendipity—a social satire about an overconsuming, middle-class, keep-up-with-the-Joneses couple (Dick was played by George Segal) and how they deal with his sudden layoff from an executive position at an aerospace company. Despite all the trappings of the American dream (mainly for the neighbors' benefit), they own nothing and have saved nothing. All they have are mortgages and credit card debts. As soon as word of his firing gets out, all the creditors show up to repossess everything. Faced with the hard realities of people on food stamps and welfare, they turn to crime. I couldn't believe my luck—a quick shoot that didn't require me to leave home, in a comedy with something to say, in which I could show I was still funny and could still look good. The film would be released before **Julia** and be my "she's back" film, proving to the studio heads that I was still a bankable star.

Fun with Dick and Jane was an easy film from an acting point of view, which was fortunate because I spent every second I wasn't on camera raising money for Tom's Senate race. I organized an auction that brought together Steve Allen, Jayne Meadows, Groucho Marx, Lucille Ball, Red Buttons, Danny Kaye, and my dad in support of Tom. I got Linda Ronstadt, Jackson Browne, Arlo Guthrie, Bonnie Raitt, Maria Muldaur, the Doobie Brothers, Little Feat, Chicago, Boz Scaggs, Taj Mahal, James Taylor, and many others to do benefits; I got Dad to do paintings I could auction off (I bought them all myself). I was a whirlwind of activity on Tom's behalf, and when **Fun with Dick and Jane** was finished, I traveled the state, building support and putting hundreds of thousands of dollars into the campaign war chest. In the end he didn't win, but he got 36.8 percent of the vote—1.2 million Californians had cast their votes for a New Left radical, cofounder of SDS,

Multitasking during a lunch break on **Fun with Dick and Jane**—fund-raising for Tom's U.S. Senate campaign. (Michael Dobo/ www.dobophoto.com)

Me and Troy in our campaign T-shirts. (Star Black)

Campaigning with Tom. (Anne Marie Staas)

and co-conspirator of Chicago. This was unprecedented in recent political history.

But we lost. I think I took it harder than Tom did. I felt it as **my** failure—not an unusual response, I have discovered, for women whose sense of self is tied to their husbands' public life. Does this surprise you? Me, with my financial independence and career? But there you have it. A woman can be powerful professionally, socially, and financially, but it is what goes on behind the closed doors of her most intimate relationship and within her own heart that tells the story. And like Vadim, Tom defined me to myself: If brilliant, articulate Tom was with me, then I couldn't be all bad.

Tom kept his promise to César Chávez and morphed his Senate campaign structure into a statewide grassroots organization called the Campaign for Economic Democracy (CED), which focused on economic issues. The average American family was earning less then than a decade earlier; inflation, largely the result of the Vietnam War, was robbing them of their savings; and unemployment was rising sharply as more corporations automated or took jobs overseas to cheap labor markets. We also took on the nation's reliance on foreign oil and the use of nuclear energy (we pushed the use of alternative energy sources like solar and wind); we supported small farmers against agribusiness; and we fought for the rights of workers, including office workers. Many of CED's concerns found their way into the movies I would subsequently make.

As soon as **Dick and Jane** wrapped, we began shooting **Coming Home,** even though many of the key scenes still weren't locked in. In fact, we had no ending everyone was happy with, and Hal and I disagreed about the nature of the critical love scene between Luke and my character, Sally Hyde. There were always vets in wheelchairs all around us as we filmed, and a few had their girlfriends with them. Some were quadriplegic, which means the injury is high up on the spine and paralysis is from the neck down; some were paraplegic, which means the wound is lower on the spine and paralysis is from the waist down (for a man, the lower down the wound, the less the penis is affected). I remember one quadriplegic in particular, whose really cute girlfriend would sort of flip him over, fold him up, and sit on him playfully. There was a vibe about them that was utterly trusting and deeply sexual. Since I needed to find out as much as I could about what sex was like for a couple in their situation, I talked to them quite a bit. I learned that the girl had been brutalized by a previous boyfriend who had once thrown her from a moving train. This in itself was illuminating: It made sense that a victim of abuse would be attracted to a man who couldn't hurt her physically. When it came to sex they said they never knew when he would have an erection; it was not connected to anything she did or said. "It can happen anytime—when we're driving past a gas station or looking at a daisy. But when it happens it can last for hours . . . one time for four hours," she said with a sexy, knowing look to him. I had to go off by myself and think about that for a while till my palms stopped sweating.

Anyway, until the dramatic "four hour" revelation, genital penetration was not something I had considered possible between my character and Jon's, and this to me was a powerful aspect of the story—a dramatic way to redefine manhood beyond the traditional, goal-oriented reliance on the phallus to a new shared intimacy and pleasure my character had never experienced with her husband. But Hal didn't see it that way. He too knew the "four-hour story," and penetration was definitely where he was headed with the scene.

There were a number of things Hal and I didn't agree on (like my character's husband's suicide at the end), but I tried to make my points as clearly as I could and then let go and leave it up to him. I had neither the confidence nor desire to fight with Hal, whom I respected enormously as a director. The one exception was the Battle of Penetration. Both of us knew that the scene had to be really hot—not as arbitrary sex but as the centerpiece of their relationship, emblematic of her transformation and—for me, anyway—of a masculinity sans erection. Jon agreed with me, by the way, and there were endless, very funny on-set discussions about it between us: "Where **can** he feel something?" I would ask Jon. And, "Are his nipples sensitive?" That sort of thing. As the time approached to film the pivotal scene, we all agreed that Hal should not be limited in what he shot, that it should include total nudity, at least the semblance of oral sex, and anything else he might need to create a groundbreaking love scene. I knew I could not do that myself. I may have been **thought** of as a wild sex symbol for a period of time, but it was more the art of suggestion than anything overt. So I suggested a body double be hired to do all the long shots. We decided Hal would shoot those first, so we'd know what shots we'd need to match when we came in for the close-ups. I stayed away while they spent all day filming with the double, and when I saw the footage the next day it was evident from the way the actress was moving on top of Jon that Hal had won the first round of the Penetration Battle.

"Hal," I said, "she can't be riding him that way; he can't get an erection. I thought we had agreed!" Hal, however, was not about to throw out the footage and concede to me. So I thought, Ah-ha, when the time comes for me to match my close-ups to the body double's, I'll just make sure I don't move like that, and he won't be able to intercut the footage.

Finally the day came for shooting the love scene. Large sheets were hung around the area of the bed and the set was closed to everyone except the camera operator, Haskell, and Hal. Jon and I spent most of the day in bed, naked under the sheets, being filmed from various angles. It's a strange experience doing this kind of scene: There is a sexy, electric charge in the air, and everyone overcompensates by becoming very businesslike. You appear to be doing the most intimate things together, naked, skin against skin, pretending ecstasy, while signaling to your body, **Hush now, this is just a job.** Then the director says, "Cut," and you stop and move away in bed because you want to show that it **was** only acting—but not moving **too** far or **too** fast, so as not to hurt the other actor's feelings, all the while working on getting your breathing back to normal. I remember feeling grateful for Jon's trust and happy that we could giggle together between takes, that we both had a commitment to our friendship above and beyond the scene. He was as much Tom's friend as mine, after all.

Hal had saved the key shot for last, the one with me/Sally sitting on top of Jon/Luke with the camera framing me from my shoulders up. For me, Sally was experiencing oral sex, and I was moving and reacting accordingly when Jon suddenly whispered, "Jane, Hal's yelling at us!"

From far away behind the hanging sheets, I heard Hal's voice, "Ride him! Dammit! Ride him!" I froze, refused to move. I was not going to give up my concept of what was happening. The cameras kept rolling, Hal kept shouting, "Move your body, goddammit!" but I wouldn't. Finally he gave up and stormed off the set. I felt bad. I'd never seen Hal mad; he was usually so mellow.

Hal ended up using both shots, even though the long shot of the body double didn't match what I did in the close-up. In the end, I think audiences read into the scene whatever they wanted. God knows everyone had a strong reaction to it, though com-

With Jon Voight
in a scene from
Coming Home.
(Steve Schapiro)

Accepting my sec-
ond Academy
Award (Best Actress
in **Coming Home**)
in sign language.
(© Motion Picture
Academy of Arts
and Sciences/Long
Photography)

pared with today's love scenes it seems pretty tame. Of course, in my opinion what made it especially hot was the sexual tension that had built up between the characters in the preceding scenes. Just as in life, the buildup of desire **beforehand,** especially when it is withheld, is what makes the act itself explosive.

To be truthful, Jon and I didn't know up until we saw the final version of the film if it all really worked. Hal and Jerry showed a very rough cut for an invited audience of about fifty people in a United Artists projection room. These events are always fraught with anxiety, which was compounded by the personal, emotional investment I had made in the film. When the lights came back on, Tom got up and walked right past me without saying a word. As he went out the door, he turned and said to Bruce, Jon, and me, "Nice try." The coldness of his response was devastating for all of us. It took me weeks to recover.

Tom was not used to seeing rough cuts, and it was true that the film was too long and had problems; but it also had powerful moments, even at that early stage. Yet Tom chose to dismiss all our work outright. I came to believe that the explicit love scene shook him more than I had anticipated, though he claims it was the film's "watered-down politics." This was the first time I had shot a love scene since Tom and I had married. I knew it was just pretend, and I hadn't anticipated that my husband would get upset. Maybe I was too used to Vadim, who was famous for **liking** to put his wives in explicit scenes. Maybe it was an eruption of the unexpressed anger we both felt toward each other.

In the end, there were many aspects that made the completed film work. One was Hal's style of directing: He had started off in the business as a film editor. Unlike other directors with whom I had worked, he would do thirty or forty takes of each scene, not saying very much to the actors about what they should do differently each time—and **he'd print all of them.** Then, in the solitude of the editing room, his brilliance would shine like that of a sculptor with clay. He would take a glance here, a sigh from me there, a slight turn of Jon's head, and would edit them together in a way we hadn't expected—or in some cases hadn't intended.

Then there was the way Haskell shot the movie, using long lenses and natural light, which gave the scenes a sense of beauty and voyeurism, as though the audience were looking through a keyhole at something intensely private and real. The improvisational nature of our acting added to this feeling of cinema verité. Then there was the music, which was all Hal. He wallpapered the film with the essential music of the sixties, and all of us who had lived through it were transported back to the rage, the existential angst, the desperate idealism of that time.

There was also the heartful attention and care with which Jerry Hellman attended to every detail of the project. By the time the film was completed, all the senior executives at UA had left to form Orion Pictures and Jerry had the unenviable task of, in his

words, "delivering it to a skeptical group of new executives who had had little or no involvement in the
project, and hence, no particular emotional commitment to it." But he kept the film safe from the va-
garies of Hollywood. All of our tenacity paid off
when, in April 1979—six years after its inception in
my bedridden head—**Coming Home** received Academy Awards for Best Screenplay for Nancy, Waldo,
and Robert; Best Actor for Jon; Best Actress for me,
and nominations for Best Picture, Best Director,
Best Film Editing, Best Supporting Actor, and Best
Supporting Actress. Tom, Vanessa, and Troy were
with me at the ceremony; I wore a dress that a supporter of Tom's designed for me, and I accepted my
Oscar in sign language, to acknowledge GLAD, an
advocacy organization for the deaf and hearing im-
paired that supported Tom. I had learned from them
that the ceremony wasn't made accessible to the deaf
in the United States. It was one of the happiest nights
of my life. Besides, Ron Kovic told me later that the
film had improved his sex life immeasurably.

In 1980 a Veterans Administration poll asked
Vietnam veterans which feature films portrayed
them most favorably. The highest ratings went to
John Wayne's **Green Berets**—and **Coming Home.**

One day during the filming of **Coming Home**
actor/producer Michael Douglas sent Bruce and me
a script called **The China Syndrome,** about a near
meltdown at a California nuclear power plant that

company executives try to cover up. Everything about
the script rang with authenticity, owing to the fact
that it was written by Michael Gray, who had studied
to become a nuclear engineer, was extremely knowl-
edgeable about all that had gone wrong with nuclear
technology in various plants over the years, and had
consulted closely with three former nuclear engineers
who'd resigned from General Electric over safety concerns. Gray had fashioned a taut, low-budget thriller
about a nuclear engineer and a radical crew of documentary filmmakers. The only drawback was that
there was no woman's role. Jack Lemmon, a passionately vocal opponent of nuclear energy, had agreed
to star in the film, with Michael producing as well
as starring. The third star, Richard Dreyfuss, had
dropped out.

Bruce Gilbert and I had been developing a film
about the nuclear industry inspired by what happened to Karen Silkwood, a worker in a Texas
County, Oklahoma, nuclear power plant who was
killed under mysterious circumstances when she was
on her way to deliver evidence of defective welds in
the plant's core. We had considered having me play a
television reporter who gets involved in a nuclear
story. The research we had done showed us that local
news was undergoing a disturbing change: In an effort to boost ratings, news consultants had recommended to station heads that they develop a new
format where a racially balanced team of slickly attractive men and women would deliver "news lite,"
lacing their stories with "happy talk."

We were developing our story for Columbia Pictures and, it turned out that Michael Douglas had brought **The China Syndrome** to the same studio. A studio executive, Roz Heller, suggested we combine our efforts, and that was when Michael came to us to see if the Dreyfuss role could be rewritten for me—with Bruce as executive producer this time.

We wanted Jim Bridges, best known at the time for **The Paper Chase** (and later for **Urban Cowboy**), to rework the script and direct. He excelled at character-driven stories, and he did not see our nuclear thriller as something that suited his particular talents. While Michael was working on the film **Coma** and I was in Colorado filming **Comes a Horseman,** Bruce kept coming back to Bridges in an effort to get him excited about the idea of creating a parallel story to the nuclear accident: the morphing of TV news into infotainment, with a female TV reporter who is trapped between pressure from her bureau chief (who wants to bury the nuclear story) and her growing commitment to getting it told. The reporter, Kimberly Wells, is ambitious and doesn't want to rock the boat, yet she resents being assigned fluff stuff and being told how to look. I told Jim the story of my early experiences in Hollywood, when Jack Warner wanted me to wear falsies and Josh Logan suggested I have my jaw broken and reset so that my cheeks would sink in. These were personal issues to me. Again, as with **Coming Home,** we were able to bring an added gender dimension to a story that hadn't started out that way. After turning us down four times, Jim finally saw his way into the story and its potential character dynamics—not just between Kimberly and her bureau chief, but between Kimberly and her more radical cameraman, played by Michael Douglas.

Jim and I talked by phone about the developing character of Kimberly. One day I announced to him that I wanted Kimberly to have flaming red hair. It was a way to tip my hat to a childhood heroine of mine, Brenda Starr, the gorgeous redheaded newspaper reporter in the comic strip of the same name. Jim had liked what I did with the Bree Daniel character in **Klute** when she was alone in her apartment and asked me how I thought Kimberly would be when she came home from work. Did she have a pet? How was her place decorated? I told him that she hadn't even gotten around to unpacking from her move six months earlier from the San Francisco TV station to Los Angeles. Everything was still in boxes. In **Klute** I had decided Bree had a cat, and in one scene I licked the fork after I'd scraped some tuna fish into her bowl. Kimberly, I said, should have a giant turtle as a pet, something she'd had as a girl, and she talks to it every night when she carries it indoors with her to get it some lettuce (which Kimberly eats before handing it over to her turtle). In Bree's apartment there was a signed photo of President Kennedy that seemed out of context and made audiences wonder about its significance to Bree. In the same way I wanted Kimberly to have a reproduction of the famous Andy Warhol silkscreen painting of Marilyn

Monroe. Like a lot of women, I felt Kimberly would
have a special thing for Marilyn because of the tensions she symbolized between humanity and ambi-
tion, strength and malleability. No small number of
people over the years have asked me about both the
turtle and that image of Marilyn. It doesn't matter
that they don't know **why** Kimberly has these things;
it gives her specificity and interest as a person. Jim
and I loved throwing in these sorts of odd, conspira-
torial tidbits. There was nothing but creative chemistry between us as we worked long-distance to create
my role.

The reason it was long-distance was that no
sooner did I wrap **Coming Home** than I was off to
Colorado to film **Comes a Horseman,** a story about
a small Montana rancher just after World War II
fighting to save her land from land barons and oil
companies. James Caan was the co-star and Jason
Robards played the land baron. But the big draws for
me on this film were that Alan Pakula, who had directed me in **Klute,** was the director (with Gordon
Willis once again the director of photography). It
was also a great summer location where Tom, Troy,
Vanessa, and I could be together; and I would be reunited with horses in a role that resembled a grown-
up version of my childhood friend Sue Sally: a
weathered, tough woman who ran her cattle ranch
all by herself. It had been more than thirty years since
I had been in a saddle, except for filming **Cat Ballou**
in 1964, the only other western I'd ever done and it
was of an entirely different nature.

Frankly, I was unsure whether I could really play the part of this crusty woman, but Alan again gave me the courage to try. I knew that to do it properly I would have to become like the wranglers who rustle cattle and work the horses on western films. It wasn't the riding that would be the challenge; like sex and bicycles, that comes right back. But I needed to learn to throw a lasso, rope a calf, round up cattle, and brand and castrate male calves. Not that I had to do all of that in the film, but I needed the wranglers to know that, like my character Ella, I **could** do it all if asked, that I wasn't a city slicker. The wranglers' belief in me would give **me** belief in myself—as Ella.

I was working steadily, without a break, and my career was going full speed. I think about this when I hear admonitions from the powers that be warning outspoken actors to remember "what happened to Jane Fonda back in the seventies." This has me scratching my head: **And that would be?** The suggestion is that because of my actions against the war my career had been destroyed and that this will happen to them if they don't get with the program. But the truth is that my career, far from being destroyed after the war, flourished with a vigor it had not previously enjoyed.

It was during this period that Tom and I did one of the best things we did together: We bought two hundred acres north of Santa Barbara (two hours from our home) and created a performing arts summer camp for kids called Laurel Springs. Though I didn't recognize it at the time, what I learned at Laurel Springs laid the foundation for my third-act activism.

We wanted it to be a place where our friends could send their children—but we had an unusually diverse group of friends, ranging from people in the United Farm Workers union to city council and school board members to former Black Panthers to directors of community-based organizations to movie stars and heads of major studios. These were the varied backgrounds of the children who came to camp, and this diversity was what made it a unique and transformative summer experience that ran for fourteen years, from 1977 until 1991. Girls who had always had maids making their beds shared a cabin with girls who had never had a room of their own. Macho Latino gang member wannabes shared a bunkroom with a pale blond boy who suffered from muscular dystrophy and had to be carried everywhere. His courage in the face of his disability helped the other boys redefine the meaning of being a "real man."

I learned that even in a short period of time, a camp experience can transform a bully into a brother, a shy girl into someone unafraid to express herself, an urban kid who had been afraid of long grass into a real outdoorsman. I was surprised to see how exposure to nature could be terrifying for an

I learned to rope
for my role in
**Comes a Horse-
man**—here with
James Caan.
(© Steve Schapiro)

At Laurel Springs
Ranch with Tom,
Troy, and our Ger-
man shepard,
Geronimo.
(© Steve Schapiro)

The first group of campers at Laurel Springs. Vanessa is in the second row, directly behind the boy holding the camp sign, staring straight into the camera. Troy is way down in the front on the right. Tom is in the hat, back row, right.

Vanessa, age eleven.

urban youngster who had never seen a night sky filled with stars or felt mud oozing between his toes. Camp gave kids an opportunity to try on new identities. At home and in school, children often get tagged as being the "troublemaker," the "fast girl," the "macho boy," the "nerd." Camp allowed them to become a tabula rasa, a clean slate, where they could start over and discover other parts of themselves. It always surprised me when parents would tell me, as they dropped off their children for the new camp season, how the effects of last year's two weeks had remained with their child all year long. As Michael Carrera of the Children's Aid Society has written, "Young people may forget what you say or what you do, but they will never forget how you made them feel."

This is the age when youngsters are going through intense changes and too often have no one to go to for help in working through the complicated maze of adolescence. The counselors at Laurel Springs heard a lot of "I have these feelings when I'm around her, like in my body, something happens. What is that?" This gave the counselors the opportunity to explain puberty, what menstruation signifies, or how the boy's body was changing and new feelings were coming up; that this was totally normal and beautiful; but that having the feelings doesn't mean he or she has to act on them. (The kinds of things my parents never discussed with me, nor I with my children—to my deep regret.) Campers came to our counselors to talk about their parents' addictions, about divorce, about death. I learned how important it is for children who've lacked physical affection to be held, to feel a warm, loving human touch **without** sexual overtones. Girls who have never had the loving arms of a father in which to safely rehearse tenderness will tend to go straight to sexuality in an attempt to get the craved contact. I learned how transformative it is for children to set goals and achieve them, be witnessed and acknowledged for it. I learned the extent to which deprivation can exist among children of the rich and the emotional richness that can exist among the very poor. I learned the importance of exposing children who have everything to children who have very little, and vice versa. I learned, to my amazement, that approximately one-fourth of the girls at camp had been sexually abused.

Vanessa went to camp from age eight until fourteen and feels it was an important influence. She liked being physically challenged (with the older campers she climbed Mount Whitney) and spending time in the wilderness.

Troy says, "Camp was sort of my great social learning experience. I came to know children of farmworkers, children from all walks of life, through emotional, caring relationships. Regardless of what material possessions you had in the 'real' world, at camp people interacted with each other based on your character, not your possessions."

Troy grew up with the camp, starting out as its mascot when he was too young to attend officially and becoming an assistant counselor by the end. I watched him come into his own over the summers, developing crushes, learning the pleasures of slow dancing. One day when he was about fifteen, I came face-to-face with the realization that he possessed an unusual acting ability. I was watching him rehearse a play in which he played a gay tango dancer. His choices were so brave and free, so much more comedic and physical than mine (or his grandfather's, for that matter) had ever been. Right then and there I decided to do the opposite of what my father had done with my brother and me. I went up to Troy after the rehearsal and said, "Son, you have real talent. If you decide one day that this is a profession you want to go into, I will totally support you in that decision." Some years later, that is exactly what happened.

There was a beautiful eleven-year-old black girl from Oakland named Lulu. Everyone loved her. She had a laugh like a cascade of wind chimes. Her parents had been members of the Black Panther party, and her uncle worked with Tom. Lulu came for two years running, and then for several years we saw no more of her. When she returned at age fourteen, she had changed. She slept all day, couldn't tolerate being in a crowd, rarely spoke, and had terrible nightmares every night. At the end of the camp session, she confided to a counselor that she had been brutally molested by a man over a prolonged period of time. She had told no one because the man threatened to kill her and her family if she did.

Lulu was suffering from severe posttraumatic stress disorder, sleeping most of the time (as PTSD sufferers are prone to do), and getting D's and F's in school despite her innate intelligence. She had come back to camp because she needed to tell someone. I made a deal with her that if she brought her grades up to B's by the end of the school year, I would get her into a school in Santa Monica and she could stay with us.

Lulu was fourteen when she came into our home and had been with us for about a month when one morning she came up to me as I was washing breakfast dishes and said, "I need to say something, but I'm a little ashamed."

"It's okay, Lulu, go ahead."

"I never knew till being here that all mothers don't beat their children."

I realized that simply allowing this young woman to be in a home where children disagreed with their parents and weren't beaten for it, where people sat at the table and talked together, was opening up a new world to her. Frankly I often wonder which of us has learned more from the other, Lulu or me.

I asked her once why the camp was an important experience for her. She hesitated for a moment before answering. "It's the first time I've been with people who think about the future."

That stopped me short, and coming to terms with what it implied has framed the way I see my work today with children and families in Georgia. There's a saying: "The rich plan for generations; the poor plan for Saturday nights." Middle-class folks take for granted that we have a future that requires planning for. To never think about the future means you live without hope.

One day while we were driving back from Laurel Springs, Lulu announced to me that she wanted to have a child.

"Why?" I asked, taken aback.

"I want something that belongs to me," she answered simply and honestly.

"Get a dog!" was my reply. Then I went on to talk with her about what would happen to her life if she had a child to care for before she was an adult woman. Having a child has few consequences if you don't see a future for yourself. When I once heard Marian Wright Edelman, president of the Children's Defense Fund, say, "Hope is the best contraception," I knew because of Lulu how true these words were in relation not just to early pregnancy, but to drugs, violence, and a host of other behaviors that are indicators of hopelessness.

Lulu did not have a child. She went on to graduate from college, got herself into graduate school in public health at Boston University (with no help from me), and has developed into a remarkable success story. Filled with intellectual curiosity and commitment to justice, she remains a member of my family. Early in her life Lulu had received just enough love from her mother to instill resilience in her, which is what enabled her to survive—spirit intact—later difficulties, of which her sexual molestation was but one example. Lulu also attributes her resilience to the Black Panther party in Oakland.

"I grew up with the Panther programs—their hot breakfasts and the things they did for kids. They were like my family."

Sometimes I feel as though I have a magnet on my skin and when I walk through the world the relevant input I need for my journey jumps out from the hurly-burly and sticks to me. That's the way it was at Laurel Springs. I needed the lessons the camp taught over those fourteen years.

My children had their own learning experiences. Both Vanessa and Troy grew up feeling different from others their age. Vanessa lived in two countries, spoke two languages, experienced two styles of parenting. "I liked having two lives—being different," she says. "I still do."

Troy's sense of difference didn't start until he entered a public junior high school and students would ask him why he wasn't driven to school in a limousine since his mother was a movie star. "This made me uncomfortable because it made me feel I was being looked at as a material object. I had never before had any awareness of material things or of the paradoxes of my life—living simply the way we did, yet you being famous. I began to feel like a misfit. But the best thing about being a misfit is that it attracts you to other misfits. And they're usually the most interesting people."

One area in which Troy realized there were differences with his friends had to do with the nature of his extended family. "Whereas my friends had aunts, older sisters, grandmothers, to assist in raising them," he told me recently, "I had au pairs, nannies, political organizers, and your assistants. You were my 'core mother,' and then you had tentacles. Dad would be one. Laurel Springs was another."

For Vanessa and Troy, camp provided a safe setting for many firsts: first kiss, slow dancing, wilderness. For Lulu, it provided a future.

Troy, age six.

Lulu, age thirteen.

Singing hymns with Tom and Mignon McCarthy at our annual Easter bash at the ranch. I was always the Easter bunny. I miss that.

CHAPTER FIFTEEN

THE WORKOUT

There are no gains without pains.
—BENJAMIN FRANKLIN

Great ideas originate in the muscles.
—THOMAS EDISON

I**T WAS EXPENSIVE** running a statewide non-profit organization like CED in a state as big and diverse as California, and the weakness in the economy was making it increasingly difficult to raise the necessary funds. I was making one or more movies a year by now—**Julia, Coming Home, Fun with Dick and Jane, The China Syndrome, Comes a Horseman, California Suite**—most quite successful, and every premiere would be a benefit for CED. Still, we worried about being able to sustain the work.

Then I read an article about Lyndon LaRouche, founder of the National Caucus of Labor Committees. (You may remember back in the late seventies seeing people standing in major airports with signs saying things like "Jane Fonda Leaks More Than Nuclear Power Plants" or "Feed Fonda to the Whales." Those people had ties to LaRouche, as did some of the goons who went into bars to beat with chains people they suspected of being gay.) This article said that LaRouche's organization was financed, at least in part, by his computer business. That set Tom and me thinking: Why not start a business that would fund CED? For a while we considered going into the restaurant business, and we actually spent a month or so driving around looking for one to buy, asking people what went into running a successful restaurant. We also toyed with the idea of an auto repair shop where people wouldn't be ripped off.

One day John Maher, charismatic co-founder of Delancey Street, an entrepreneurial halfway house for addicts, said to me, "Never go into a business you don't understand." That was about the best business advice I have ever received, but it not only ruled out the restaurant and car repair ideas, it seemed to narrow our options to zero. What did I know about **any** business?

As it turned out, plenty. I just had to see what was staring me in the face.

In 1978, while filming **The China Syndrome,** I again fractured my foot, so ballet became impossible for me, at least for the foreseeable future. For more than twenty years ballet, with its strict classical structure and music, had been my haven, my way of staying in shape and keeping at least a tenuous connection to my body. What to do? I had to get into shape for my next movie, **California Suite,** in which I had to appear in a bikini. Understanding my urgency, my stepmother Shirlee suggested that when the foot was sufficiently healed (where was that Vietnamese chrysanthemum poultice when I really needed it?), I should check out a class at the Gilda Marx studio in Century City, California. The instructor was marvelous, Shirlee said. Her name was Leni Cazden.

Leni was in her early thirties, about five feet five, with short copper-colored hair, green eyes, narrow hips, and an enigmatic combination of aloofness and availability. Her class was a revelation. I entered so-called adult life at a time when challenging physical exercise was not offered to women. We weren't supposed to sweat or have muscles. Now, along with forty other women, I found myself moving nonstop for an hour and a half in entirely new ways.

Leni's class wasn't what would soon become known as aerobics. For something to be aerobic it needs to get your large muscle groups—your thigh, hip, or upper body muscles—working steadily so as to increase your heart rate for at least twenty min-

Lyndon LaRouche fielded these folks in major airports around the country back in the late seventies. It was hard to walk by with Vanessa and Troy and maintain my composure. (Anne Marie Staas)

On Malibu beach between scenes in **California Suite** with director Herbert Ross. (Photofest)

utes. This is the form of exercise that burns fat calo-
ries and strengthens the heart. But Leni, I would discover later, was a smoker and aerobic activity wasn't
for her. Instead her routine was more about strengthening and toning through the use of an interesting
combination of repetitive movements that included,
to my great pleasure, a surprising amount of ballet,
which Leni had learned during her early days as a
competitive ice-skater.

Another thing that made the class special was
Leni's choice of music. This was the beginning of the
disco craze, and most other types of classes relied on
this high-volume, repetitive beat to drive the class
forward. Not Leni. The music she brought in was Al
Green, Kenny Loggins, Fleetwood Mac, Teddy Pen-
dergass, Stevie Wonder, and Marvin Gaye.

Up until then I had known next to nothing
about current popular music. If I listened to the
radio, it was to NPR for the news. Now these new
sounds entered my life. I began to move to a different rhythm, becoming one of those people you see
through their car windows singing and grooving to
music only they can hear. I never did go back to
ballet.

I had ceased bingeing and purging the year before (more about that later) but was still a recovering
food addict and way too compulsive when it came to
exercise. I hated to miss even a day, and when there
were no scheduled classes, I would hire Leni to teach
me privately.

One day an idea hit me: Leni and I could go

into the exercise business together! It was perfect. Here was **one** thing that I **understood** in my gut: how exercise could affect a woman's body and mind. I knew it myself from ballet and now was learning another way from Leni. Helping women get fit was a business I could understand and respect. If it was successful, it could help finance CED!

Leni liked the idea. We searched for names for the business and decided on Jane and Leni's Workout.

During this time, I began to teach the routine myself in St. George, Utah, where I was on location with **The Electric Horseman,** my third film with Bob Redford. At night after work women of all ages and a few men from the film crew came from miles around to take the class, which I held in the basement of a small spa. The experience of teaching such a diverse group opened my eyes to a much broader array of the benefits of exercise than I had ever expected. One woman said she'd stopped needing sleeping pills. People told me they felt less stressed. Most profound, though, were the testimonials that showed how women were starting to feel differently about themselves—empowered. Clearly we were on to something that mattered more than just how a person looked, and no one was really talking about that beyond the vanity stuff.

Leni and I began to interview teachers to hire for a studio. We found a space in Beverly Hills, on Robertson Boulevard, and I hired an architect to begin renovation plans. I wanted to offer ballet, jazz, and stretch classes and felt we needed some easier and shorter classes in addition to Leni's marathon routine. Then the time came to set up the actual business structure and draw up contracts. What happened then is painful to write about.

My primary goal in going into this business was to raise money for CED. My lawyer at the time persuaded me that the best way to do the contract from a tax perspective was to have CED own the business. What would Leni's role be, then? Leni was no more a businesswoman than I was, and it was clear that neither of us could actually **run** the Workout. I would have to hire someone to do that job. Yet if we were going into the business together, she couldn't be just one of the teachers; it was **her** routine that would be the foundation for the business. But if she was a partner in the usual sense, how could we square that with CED owning the business? No one, least of all me, ever imagined that the Workout could become as successful as it did. So round and round we went, me with the lawyer. What to do about Leni?

Looking back, I see so clearly that the answer to "What to do about Leni?" was to **talk to her,** find out what she wanted and what it would take to make us both feel that our needs were addressed. Instead I let the lawyer frame the debate, putting Leni into the position of adversary who (we were sure) would fight against CED owning the business. (I was to take no money at all for myself out of the business.) Then one day Leni told me that she had met and was going to marry a wealthy man, and they were planning a round-the-world trip for two years on a sailboat they had built. But I doubt that she would have done this had she felt able to sit down with me and work out a fair deal for herself.

The Workout went on to become a worldwide phenomenon, beyond anything any of us had ever imagined. For those of you who came to one of the Workout studios and did the advanced Workout class, that was a somewhat easier version of Leni's original routine. The one-and-a-half-hour video called **Workout Challenge** was a replica of the class I took with Leni. It is important that I tell this story—and that Leni finally get the credit due her for her original routine.

Many years elapsed. Leni found herself training my then-husband, Ted Turner, at a gym in West Los Angeles. That's how she and I reconnected and became friends. And that's when I learned that because of a growing-up as traumatic as any I have ever heard about, Leni had been robbed of the ability to speak up on her own behalf. The word **no** was not part of her vocabulary, and she had felt powerless earlier to negotiate with me and the lawyer. Had we been able to sit face-to-face as women—Leni owning her voice and me not ceding mine to the lawyer—things could have been worked out. At least I've tried over the intervening years to make it up to Leni.

We weren't at all prepared for the huge success. The Workout was very small, with only three studios and bathroom facilities suited to the modest mom-and-pop-type business I had envisioned. But from the minute we opened our doors in 1979 it was like an avalanche, without our once having to pay for advertising. Talk show hosts Merv Griffin and Barbara Walters **asked** to come and film classes. People flocked from all over the country. It became a "must visit" site for tourists from other **countries.**

I hired a woman activist from CED, the only person I knew with an MBA, to run the studio. We learned as we went, and it was never easy. We often had upward of two thousand clients a day—seventy thousand a year—working out in three small classrooms. In summer the air-conditioning wasn't up to the task, the bathrooms weren't large enough, clients would get into fights if someone took their accustomed place in front of the mirror, and teachers bridled at having to start and end on time and follow a set routine. Yet the clients kept coming, filling just about every class. There were beginning, middle, and advanced Workout classes, and stretch classes.

My friend and birthing coach Femmy DeLyser became director of the Pregnancy, Birth, and Recovery Workout classes, which were immensely popular. I'd regretted having to give up all exercise both times I'd been pregnant and felt committed to providing a safe, effective way for women to stay fit while waiting for their deliveries. It was Femmy's inspired idea to also have classes for the moms **recovering** from childbirth. The babies would come with them and were often incorporated into the exercises—lying on their mothers' bellies during ab-

The Workout.
(Kelvin Jones)

I traveled the country raising money for Tom's campaigns by teaching huge workout classes like these.

dominal work, for instance—and the classes would end with lessons in baby massage. These classes proved wonderful on many levels, not least of which was their social value: The women enjoyed comparing notes about their birthing experiences while they nursed and discussing how others were dealing with new-mother issues. Later Femmy and I did a pregnancy, birth, and recovery book and video, using pregnant women from the class, including actress Jane Seymour. Women who had just given birth demonstrated recovery exercises and baby massage. It was the first of its kind.

Two years later (1981), I wrote my first **Jane Fonda's Workout Book.** It was number one on **The New York Times** Bestseller List for a record twenty-four months (that was before they put such books in their separate How-To books section) and was translated into over fifty languages. It was while writing the book that I realized I needed to study physiology to more deeply understand what was happening during exercise. For instance, I had learned from personal experience that an exercise was more effective if I worked hard enough to cause a burning sensation in the muscle, but I didn't know why. I knew what aerobic meant—sort of—but not really. So I began to research sports physiology and talk to doctors, like Dr. James Garrick at Saint Francis Memorial Hospital in San Francisco, with whom I did a sports medicine video. I did the same with nutrition—discovering, for instance, why complex carbohydrates give more lasting energy than simple carbs, why having a healthy breakfast and a light dinner was advisable, and why some fat is healthier than others. My bedtime reading changed from books like **The Wealth of Nations** to **Gray's Anatomy.** I studied the process of aging and menopause and co-wrote a book with another CED activist, Mignon McCarthy, called **Women Coming of Age,** which also became a best-seller.

Less than a year into the business, a man named Stuart Karl came into my life. Stuart was the father of how-to home videos, having made the very first of the home improvement types. His wife, Debbie, read the Workout book and told her husband he should get me to do it as a video. When I got the call I remember thinking, Home video? What's that? Like most people back then, I didn't own a VCR. I'm an actor, I thought. It would look foolish for me to be exercising on camera. I gave Karl a firm no. But he kept coming back until finally I relented, thinking, **It won't take long and it will bring some additional income into CED.** I certainly never saw it as a big moneymaker. No one I knew had ever bought a videotape.

I remember writing out the shooting script for the first Workout video in pencil on the floor. Despite protestations from Sid Galanty, a friend who became the producer and director of the first wave of my videos, I decided that to reduce the cost of the production we wouldn't use hair or makeup people or teleprompters. I'd just wing it. I never imagined how hard it would be. First of all, because everything on the video would be reversed for the viewer, every time I wanted them to move right I'd have to say left, and all this while executing the moves correctly and trying not to seem breathless—on a concrete studio floor never designed for aerobics.

As it turned out, it didn't really matter **how** we did the video. We had no competition (**that** would soon change), and we could have all been painted purple and covered with sequins. All that mattered was that people could follow what we were doing. The crucial thing about creating a successful business, I have subsequently realized, is timing—giving people something they really want that they can't yet get anywhere else. But at the time I was not aware of how serendipitous our timing was, or that there was a budding video industry poised to explode.

That first video, the original **Jane Fonda's Workout** (1982), remains to this day the biggest-selling home video of all time (seventeen million copies). In addition, it helped create the home video industry. Up until then people weren't buying videos, because they didn't own the necessary hardware—a VCR player, which was expensive—and there weren't any videos that people felt they had to have for repeat use that would justify the cost of the hardware. But once the Workout videos arrived, people were suddenly buying VCRs like crazy. This is why I am the first person in the "Talent" category to have been inducted into the Video Hall of Fame, an honor usually reserved for inventors and marketers of hardware. I am extremely proud of this and appear to be boasting (well, maybe I **am** boasting), but remember, all this success happened in spite of me. **Who knew?** Well, Debbie Karl knew. And her husband, Stuart, was smart enough to listen to his smart wife.

Letters began coming in by the basketful from women who were "doing Jane," as they called it, all over the world. They were touching, handwritten letters I have kept to this day, usually starting with how they had never written to a celebrity before and were sure I wouldn't actually read their letter myself. Some were about my Workout book, some about the videotapes or the audiotape version. These women poured their hearts out, about weight they had lost, self-esteem they had gained, how they were finally able to stand up to their boss or recover from a mastectomy, asthma, respiratory failure, diabetes. One woman described how, brushing her teeth one morning, she was stunned to see arm muscles in the mirror for the first time. A Peace Corps volunteer wrote me about how she "did Jane" using the audiotape every day in her mud hut in Guatemala. Another told how a group of nine women in Lesotho in southern Africa would get together three times a week to "do Jane" and had discovered that the social aspect of these sessions was as rewarding as the exercising. Here's a quote from a thirty-eight-year-old woman who had lost eighty pounds using my book and video:

> I couldn't begin to put in a letter how my life has changed. It's incredible. I'm a per-

son I've never been before. I've started a
cleaning business, set my own hours, asked
for a raise, and got it. This may not sound
like much to someone as strong as you, but
I used to be so ashamed of myself I never
even wanted to go outside. Now I like myself, I'm strong, I'm confident, I feel so
wonderful I can't describe it!

Something new was starting to happen to me as
well: When your voice and image are coming into
someone's living room (or mud hut) every day, via
video or on a record, you become part of people's
lives in a personal way, different from movie stars on
the big screen, and this was affecting how people reacted to me. **They felt they knew me.** Often I would
come into a store to buy something, and when someone heard my voice, even if their backs were turned,
they knew who I was—and would want to tell me
stories about which tape they used, whom they "did
Jane" with, how it had affected them. Once a woman
got down on the floor of a drugstore to ask if she was
doing her pelvic tilts correctly. Husbands would say,
"I wake up to your voice every morning 'cause my
wife does you in the living room."

I didn't know whether to say thank you or to
apologize.

I'd been used to celebrity, but this was a new
world, and I began to think, Hey, wait a minute.
What about me as an actor? What about the causes I
am fighting for? What's with the pelvic tilts already?

The Workout phenomenon, it seemed, had super-
seded everything else about me, and while I loved
knowing I was making a positive difference in wom-
en's lives, it made me uneasy. I didn't want pelvic
tilts to define me. Still, I was becoming fascinated
with the business itself—and not only the money it
was bringing in.

I found that making the business a success was a
creative process. I wanted to see it make a difference—
not just for wealthy women in Beverly Hills but,
through the videos, for senior citizens, kids, and employed women who had little disposable income and
even less time. I did focus groups to better understand
what women wanted. I would be riveted listening to
the thoughts of these secretaries, small-business owners, wives, students, women in real estate—Middle-
American women—as they expressed their wants and
needs in the area of exercise. They spoke of their difficulty finding time to go to a gym and affording baby-
sitters, and they all expressed gratitude to the Workout
for creating our home videos.

I sometimes taught classes myself, especially at
the beginning, so that I could learn what worked.
During filming on **9 to 5** in Los Angeles, I taught a
5:00 A.M. class three times a week before going to
work. Dolly Parton thought I was mad as a hatter
coming in all sweaty and red as I did.

I soon opened a second studio in Encino, a small
city in the San Fernando Valley, and then a third in
San Francisco. Business consultants were advising me
to franchise the Workout, and that was when I knew

I had to engage an executive search firm to help me find an experienced businesswoman to run it.

I interviewed fifteen women. I never considered hiring a man, because so much of my business was made up of women and because I felt I would be more comfortable with a woman partner. I chose the woman I did for three reasons: First, she was from the Midwest; because of Dad, I see midwesterners as hardworking, frugal, and honest. Second, she told me she cried when she heard "The Star-Spangled Banner." Third, she had married her high school sweetheart. The last two told me she was bedrock and loyal. I was not mistaken. (Actually there was a fourth reason: Her name was Julie Lafond and Lafonda made a great name for our partnership.)

The first vital piece of advice Julie gave me was to close down the two newest studios and not franchise. "You don't want to be in bricks and mortar," she said. "It's the tapes and books that will be your main source of money (and fewer headaches), and the Beverly Hills Workout will be the laboratory where you try out new classes and keep your finger on the pulse of the people we serve—what works for them and what doesn't."

Two years after Julie arrived, I decided to separate the Workout from CED. I wanted to grow the business but could not because all the income was being paid out in dividends to the organization. By that time (the mid-1980s), the Workout had brought $17 million into CED, and I felt we had more than fulfilled our original mission of providing it with a solid finan-

Julie Lafond, director of the Jane Fonda Workout, is on the right. Jeanne Ernst, a lead instructor, is between us.
(Lynn Houston Photography)

cial base. As long as I owned the Workout business, I could grow it while continuing to donate money to CED as needed.

By now Tom had been elected to the California State Assembly and others were running CED day to day. But from the get-go Tom had hated the Workout, seeing it as an exercise in vanity. He told me once that he felt the problems in our marriage began with the Workout. Maybe. My time was certainly taken up more and more with the business, but whenever he made disparaging remarks about it, I would just think, Okay, I'm vain, call it what you will, but it sure makes a lot of women feel better. Besides, where else would you have gotten $17 million?

In the end Julie and I produced five books, twelve audio programs, and twenty-three videotapes—everything from the basic Workout to yoga and step aerobics; some short, easy ones for older people; and two for kids called **Funhouse Fitness**. By now competition had become fierce, which forced us to spend more money on our productions and marketing. But we got it down to a science and could shoot a video in five days (though we would spend from six months to a year developing each one). I was adamant that there be a variety of people performing on the videos with me, so that home viewers would feel represented: We had racial diversity and men as well as women, some young, some older, some slim, and some not so slim.

I had fun coming up with innovative ideas. For instance, instead of the traditional disco workout beat, we used Scottish jigs, Latin, country, and bluegrass, and we would choreograph accordingly. I would usually do the choreography myself. That way I could be sure it was something that I—a good decade or more older than the other dancers—was able to do. In one video I came up with the idea of having teacher Jeanne Ernst and myself perform part of the routine in front of a screen, on which a film appropriate to the music was projected. I used these tapes myself and knew how important it was to keep them interesting. On another tape I had thought it would be funny to have a guy seem to crash the class, just sort of come in late and insert himself into the back row and then act very crazy. To this day people refer to "that tape with the crazy guy." In one of the aerobics videos we did, **Lean Routine Workout**, I wanted an urban feel, so our set was the roof of a city tenement building at night.

Right after making that video, I met Ted Turner, and I never had time after that to do a full ensemble aerobics video (which took months of creating, weeks of rehearsing, and a week of shooting). But the business did continue under Julie Lafond's guidance for a number of years, during which I put out Workout videos with me alone (much easier to do). Together Julie and I also created a second Workout book and a cookbook, **Cooking for Healthy Living.** Julie helped me develop a self-generating treadmill we sold that didn't need to be plugged in (appealing to my desire for energy efficiency), plus a host of other Workout paraphernalia that was also very lucrative.

Julie and some of the Workout teachers became

close friends—Jeanne Ernst and Laurel Sparks in particular. We would go on marathon bike rides and hikes together. Troy and Vanessa came with us on one wild and woolly three-day bike trip through Napa Valley. That was when I saw how naturally strong and fit both my children are . . . without even trying!

I came to depend a lot on my friendships with many of the teachers at the Workout. In retrospect I see they were like a safety valve, allowing a suppressed part of me to surface. I remember a journalist friend of mine coming to the set one day while we were taping the **Lean Routine** video. He hung around for a while and later said to me, "I can't believe how different you were around those women. I've never seen this laughing, joking side of you before."

It isn't easy for me to accept the fact that many young people, if they know me at all, know me as "the woman in the exercise video their mother used." Yet I am proud that the Workout got so many women feeling better about themselves and their bodies.*

---

*I am releasing several new exercise DVDs featuring my most popular workouts. Two to three complete workout programs will be combined on one DVD. The Personal Trainer series—three complete programs in one DVD—focuses on distinct body parts. **The Complete Workout and Stress Reduction** DVD combines my Complete Workout program with a unique low-impact stress-reduction program. In recognition of the growing childhood obesity trend in the United States, I'm re-releasing my two successful Funhouse Fitness kids exercise programs on one DVD, called **Jane Fonda Presents: Funhouse Fitness for Kids.**

Working out can mean different things depending on where a person is at a given time in her life. Working out can be narrowly about armoring ourselves in muscle or about striving for toxic, elusive perfection. But it can also, for a more conscious person, be about breathing energy and life into the core of the body, building chi, communicating on a deep level with your cells. For me it started off in the former categories and later developed into the latter as I began moving more frequently out of the gym and into nature, climbing mountains, biking, doing meditation and yoga. That's when I began adding working **in** to my working **out**.

I know now that, for me, the moving to the music, the endorphins, the sweating, led me into the long, slow process of accepting my own body. (It would also help me remain intact during the dark times that lay ahead.)

CHAPTER SIXTEEN

GHOST

A body without a spirit is a corpse,
and a spirit without a body is a ghost.
—ABRAHAM JOSHUA HESCHEL

WHEN I MET TOM, my attention had been focused almost entirely away from my film career, and there was no reason to assume I would ever be a major star again. While I had been active in the antiwar movement for two years before meeting him, Tom's unique, decade-long experience as an organizer made it natural for me to follow his lead. This created a power balance between us that offset the inordinate celebrity that accrues to movie stars. So when **Fun with Dick and Jane** came out, followed closely by **Julia**, then **Coming Home** and a second Oscar, it created tensions.

Soon after **Coming Home** opened with all the attendant fanfare, magazine covers, and press junkets, Tom asked Bruce and Paula to come up to Laurel Springs, where the four of us were to have what we

thought was a criticism/self-criticism encounter—
where we would discuss our shortcomings, hear one
another out, clear the air. Neither Paula, Bruce, nor I
was entirely sure what the air needed to be cleared of,
but these sorts of meetings were not unusual among
movement people back then, so we all assumed it
would be constructive.

Soon after the meeting began, Tom turned on
me, accusing me of hogging the limelight and not
giving Bruce the attention and credit he was due for
Coming Home. But it soon became clear to all three
of us that Bruce was only an excuse for Tom to express his own barely suppressed rage over what he
viewed as the injustice of a movie star receiving so
much attention when the "real" people—who risk
their lives every day and work hard to change the balance of power in the world—never get public credit.
They, Tom said, are the unsung heroes, and it's not
fair. Which is largely true, I suppose. On the one
hand, films can put out powerful images and messages that have a deep impact on people; on the other
hand, they are only images, not actions in themselves. There's something fundamentally superficial
surrounding the profession—not the art of it but the
celebrity, the self-promotion, the rarefied atmosphere. I'd had it all my life, first through my father,
then on my own, so I hardly noticed it. But to Tom
it was deeply disturbing.

Ultimately the discussion played right to my
Achilles' heel, making me feel that what I did wasn't
worth a damn, that I and it were superficial and pe-

ripheral to what was really important. Paula and
Bruce still have vivid memories of the experience,
and as Bruce said later, "The level of his anger at you
surprised me. It was personalized, intense, and designed to hurt." But instead of dealing with things
personally and saying, "What's happening with the
renewal of your career is hard for me to handle" or "I
am not happy in this marriage," Tom couched everything in political terms: "Is this behavior correct or
incorrect?" I recently came upon an interview done
with the two of us in 1973, the year of our marriage,
which is another illustration of this: Writer Leroy
Aarons asked what had brought us together, and
Tom's answer was, "The degree to which Jane had
changed and the mutual strategic outlook was exactly right." Gone were the days, it seemed, when a
man would say, "Because I fell in love with her," or,
"Because I love her and her commitment to things I
also believe in."

When I read the article at the time it came out,
the coldness of Tom's reply didn't register, possibly
because I too had learned to set aside or hide personal emotions in favor of a more "politically correct" stance. We were becoming mirror images of
each other.

When I fell in love with Tom, I thought he was
someone whose sense of himself was so secure that
my celebrity would pose no threat; someone who
could be gentle, with whom I could begin to unwind
and open up. I was wrong. I don't think it was purposeful on his part, but Tom's emotional coldness re-

flected my father's, and Tom also played on my insecurities, making me feel stupid and superficial when
I was with him.

In spite of my theoretical identification with
feminism, I was passive with Tom, still assuming that
whatever was wrong was **my** fault. If he didn't like
one of my women friends (and generally he didn't), I
assumed he saw flaws I couldn't see. I rarely disagreed
with him about where the family should go for vacations, what we should do, or (as you now know)
where and how we should live. I simply didn't think
that my ideas or feelings were as credible or important as his. Anger had started to roil up in my body
during lovemaking, blotting out intimacy. It's hard to
enjoy lovemaking when you're mad. It confused and
scared me, because I didn't **know** I was angry, or why.
Such is the power of denial when you need to keep a
marriage, a family, together. I read somewhere, probably **Cosmopolitan,** that women are supposed to ask
for what they want. Ask! I'd rather die.

**What if he won't or can't give me what I want?
Then he'll feel bad and I'll feel worse, and I don't
want to make him feel bad because then he won't
like me even more, and what if he is opposed on
some moral or political grounds to giving me what
I want? Then I'll just be left with my anger. It's easier on everyone if I just don't say what I want. No
one will notice, and anyway I've learned to do without. Does everyone else ask? Am I the only one
whose communication lines have been permanently severed?**

So I postponed the pain I feared would come if I truly communicated, figuring it would go away. Years went by and I'd think, **Well, that's in the past, why raise it now?** But pain and anger **stay** there and accumulate; together they fester and create distance. Someone once said that under the bell jar of compliance, the only thing that blooms is rage.

I wanted the marriage to work and so chose not to see what I later learned was evident to all our friends: that Tom constantly put me down. In her autobiography, the late Katharine Graham writes how after her husband, Phil Graham, had left her, women friends told her how shocked they had been at the nasty way he often treated her. This took her by surprise. "I always viewed it as a joke," she wrote, "and thus didn't see the comments and behavior as put-downs." It was oddly comforting to learn that even a woman as bright and successful as Kay Graham—publisher of **The Washington Post**—could choose not to see what her friends saw. Eleanor Roosevelt, another strong woman with her own experiences in such things, once said, "No one can make you feel inferior without your permission." That's right. By choosing denial, I had permitted inferiority. It would take another passage through another marriage, to Ted Turner, for me to fully emerge, popping up like a periscope to look around and say, "Hey, wait a minute! This is who I am! I need you to deal with it."

I don't know when it started, the change from the cozy comradeship Tom and I had shared early in our relationship to something that resembled a business arrangement—except one in which I was still expected to remain sexual and desirous, although I didn't want to be. Widening the chasm was Tom's addiction to alcohol. Because neither of us would 'fess up and deal with it, our disconnectedness grew. But at the time I was still so into my own addiction to food that I didn't even see his. Or maybe it was one more thing I didn't want to see. **He's Irish after all . . . it's a cultural thing, right?**

In the swirl of interesting activity that was our life, it wasn't hard for me to sweep things under the rug with the false certainty that just around the corner everything would change. A part of me thought that perhaps this was what marriage was meant to be like. I'd had no training in intimacy—but I'm getting ahead of myself.

I knew that a big part of the problem was the eating disorder that had been with me since age fifteen, hovering darkly over my life, and especially over my relationships—a secret that no one knew. I haven't continually brought it into this narrative, but it was always there, as you know. Anyone reading this who has an addiction knows that you carry the secret demon within you and it colors everything you do, at certain times more than others. That's the thing about addictions: They occasionally take phony leaves of absence, which trick you into believing you have it all under control, only to return and whack you across the back of your knees. And down you go. No one sees this, of course. It's the soft **inner** you that's been brought down, not the perfect, efficient, in-charge, outer container that seems to manage life so well.

By the time I hit my forties, though, I was living on sheer willpower. The effort it took to keep the outer me together left the inner me exhausted for longer and longer stretches of time. Sometimes it took a whole week to recover from a binge and purge. Author/poet Robin Morgan once told me about a translucent third eyelid, called the nictitating membrane, beneath the lower lids of the eyes of some animals like cats and owls. The eyelid isn't closed, but it isn't open either; it's just gray. That was me in the periods following a binge and purge. A nictitating membrane would settle over my being. My husband and children were so accustomed to this veil that they thought it **was** me, and they would have been shocked if it had suddenly disappeared. It's impossible to connect in a real way with your intimates when you are living with an addiction.

I realized I had to make a choice between life and a living death. I had to move toward the light or succumb to the darkness. I had an unusually full, interesting, demanding life that was important to me: my family, my films, my political work. I was going a mile a minute, developing films, winning awards, raising money. People were depending on me. Plus, I wanted to make a difference, and that's hard when you're under a nictitating membrane. It wasn't worth it, blowing my life.

One morning I woke up and knew that I would

have to quit—cold turkey. I couldn't keep going. It was like going into a battle that lasted for several years. I gave up the excitement, the fast-beating heart, the momentary pleasure—and the insufferable guilt, depression, and sense of worthlessness that followed. Still, it was not until about five years or more after I quit that I could sit down for a meal and not feel my heart pounding, not wish I could just banish food from the house the way you can banish alcohol or drugs. But I couldn't. I had a family to feed.

I was like a dry drunk who'd stopped drinking but had left unexplored the reasons for her addiction. The dark, empty place at my core was still there. It never occurred to me to consider working the twelve-step program for addictions. That might have led me to open myself so that a higher power, a holy Spirit, or whatever one wants to call it could enter me and soften the hard, empty place. But I didn't see myself as the spirit type, not then. I was living entirely in my head, certain that if I was smart enough—and as "pure" as I felt Tom to be—we would be together forever.

I still needed a man to validate me. Sometimes that came from the waist down, sometimes it came from the neck up. I believed that Vadim had seen me from the neck down, as a physical object who appealed to him and whom he enjoyed displaying. I didn't want that ever again. I wanted Tom to see me from the neck up, to respect me. I didn't realize how dangerous this body/mind split can be to relationships.

My food addiction had represented a misguided search for perfection and nurture, to fill the emptiness and to "get into" my body. I quit the bingeing and purging but the need remained, a need to connect with my body and break out of the rigid container of false control I had built around myself.

I replaced food with sex. I had an affair.

It was wonderful, and traumatic. I lived with the constant sense that I would be struck down for my transgression, and at the same time I felt joyously liberated. Being with someone for the sole purpose of pleasure, for whom I was not "wife" (hence under no obligation to be "good"), brought me back to a part of myself that had gone dead. Though my marriage actually improved during this time, after a while I could no longer tolerate the duality of my existence, so I had to put an end to the affair. It was excruciatingly difficult to give up that part of myself. I had been miserable in the lie and I was miserable without it. But I knew I had to end it. Above all I did not want to destroy our family. I never spoke of this to Tom, nor did I know that he himself was seeking solace elsewhere. We simply continued in our unusual, seemingly successful partnership.

I often think of alternative how-it-could-have-gone scenarios about events in my past that didn't go right. In the case of my marriage to Tom, I should have taken his face in my hands, looked into his eyes, and said, "I want us to work this out. If you do, too, then let's each admit our addiction and try to heal, and get help with 'us.' I think the issues go deep and I am frightened to do it alone. I am very angry and I don't know why. We need a referee. Let's look for a caring professional who can help us work this through." Instead I would say, "I think we should see a therapist," and he would say, "No," and I'd fall silent. Like the magician's assistant, with body cut in two, I took up permanent residence in my head and ventured out only when in the company of women friends or while exercising, dancing, or getting massaged.

But there are many truths in any relationship. Tom and I shared many interests, and we continued for eight more years after the affair to have an exciting life. When we were working together on a project or a tour and were hitting on all fours, I could forget what was missing. He brought structure to my life, depth of field to my vision, and a sense of how change can happen. Above all, there's our wondrous son.

I loved Tom's passion for baseball, how he coached Troy's Little League team and never missed a game, not once. I always learned so much from him. It was Tom who brought fascinating thinkers like Desmond Tutu, Alvin Toffler, and Howard Zinn into our home; Tom who initiated incredible family vacations that took us to faraway lands like Israel and South Africa, where we would spend time with the keenest minds in a given country. He opened up whole new vistas of ideas for me, and I am very grateful.

CHAPTER SEVENTEEN

SYNCHRONICITY

> Do not leave the theatre satisfied
>
> Do not be reconciled. . . .
>
> You cannot live on our wax fruit
> Leave the theatre hungry
> For change
> —FROM EDWARD BOND,
> On Leaving the Theatre

IN MANY WAYS, I was starting to come into my own as I found ways to move the social issues that Tom and I were organizing around into mainstream Hollywood films. I found this synchronicity exciting, almost miraculous.

No sooner had I wrapped **Comes a Horseman** with Jason Robards and James Caan than I began filming **The China Syndrome**. It was exciting to once again be working on a project that I felt passionately about with people who shared the passion. **The China Syndrome** dovetailed perfectly with what the

Campaign for Economic Democracy was all about: blowing the whistle on large corporations that were willing to risk the public's welfare to protect their profits.

As Jim Bridges had developed it, **The China Syndrome** told of a Los Angeles TV reporter who is filming with her crew at a nuclear power plant near Los Angeles when something causes panic in the control room. Unbeknownst to her, her cameraman (played by Michael Douglas) films what is going on, but the TV station refuses to air the footage. The cameraman steals the film and shows it to a physicist, who says, "You're lucky to be alive—and so is the rest of Southern California." The expert explains that what we have captured on film was a near core meltdown: when a reactor loses its cooling water and the heat of the radioactive fuel becomes intense enough to melt the reactor core—and the steel and concrete of the containment building beneath it, sinking through the earth all the way to China (hence the term **China syndrome**). When the fuel meltdown hits groundwater, clouds of radioactive steam are sent into the atmosphere, potentially killing many thousands of people and contaminating many square miles of land. The plant's supervisor (Jack Lemmon) refuses to be mollified by the power company's assurances that nothing important went wrong. He begins his own investigation and discovers structural hazards at the core of the plant's reactor. He is in the process of seizing control of the reactor when a SWAT team enters the control room and guns him down.

The China Syndrome had been playing in theaters for about two weeks, with great box office success. Conservative columnist George Will had called us irresponsible for making a thriller that would scare people about nuclear power because, he said, it was based on fantasy, not fact. Then, on March 30, 1979, while I was in St. George, Utah, filming **The Electric Horseman,** the Nuclear Regulatory Commission announced that high levels of radiation were leaking from inside the reactor of the Three Mile Island atomic power plant near Harrisburg, Pennsylvania. Radioactive steam clouds were escaping. The commission admitted there was "the ultimate risk of a meltdown," and Pennsylvania's governor, Dick Thornburgh, asked that children and pregnant women within a five-mile radius of the Three Mile Island facility evacuate the area.

It was beyond belief, the most shocking synchronicity between real-life catastrophe and movie fiction ever to have occurred. The film had been doing brisk business, but once Three Mile Island happened it became a blockbuster—not just in the United States but all over the world. People went to see it to understand what had happened in Pennsylvania.

Immediately after finishing **The Electric Horseman,** Tom and I went on our third national tour, the first since the end of the Vietnam War, this time focusing on economic democracy, the perils of nuclear

With Jack Lemmon in **The China Syndrome.**

Vanessa visiting
me on the set
of **The China
Syndrome.**

energy, and the benefits of energy alternatives like solar and wind. We received a lot of media coverage, mostly due to Three Mile Island.

Along the way it was women who really stood out for me—women like Lois Gibbs at Love Canal, who organized other women to fight against the toxic wastes buried beneath the community and causing serious, even fatal, health problems. There were others like her, housewives who had looked over their shoulders to see who would come to the rescue, only to find it would have to be themselves— and discovering **they** were true leaders.

Karen Nussbaum, my friend from the antiwar days, had gotten me interested in office workers. Karen told me about sexual harassment, about women being on the job fifteen years and seeing men they trained get promoted right past them and made their supervisors, and about clerical workers at some of the wealthiest banks who were paid so little they were eligible for food stamps. This was what got me thinking about making a movie on the subject. During the tour we did events in eight cities to promote 9to5, the national clerical workers organization that Karen started, and when I talked about the idea of a film to the thousands of office workers who attended these events, their excitement was palpable.

We did not see it as a comedy at first. What's funny about working fifteen-hour days and getting paid for forty hours' work a week?

Back in Los Angeles I went to see Lily Tomlin in Jane Wagner's one-woman play, **Appearing Nitely** (later titled **The Search for Signs of Intelligent Life in the Universe**), and fell head over heels for this woman and her unique, spectacular talent. Driving home from the theater that night, I turned on the radio and Dolly Parton was singing "Two Doors Down." Bingo! Lily, Dolly, and Jane!

Bruce and I knew that to get Lily and Dolly to agree to be in the film meant my taking the least interesting role, whichever one that turned out to be. Paula Weinstein, my friend and former agent, was now a production executive at Twentieth Century–Fox, and she steered us to writer/director Colin Higgins.

Bruce and I brought Colin to Ohio, to the offices of Cleveland Women Working,* which was being run by my former housemate Carol Kurtz. She had assembled a diverse group of about forty women who took turns telling their office stories while Colin took notes. Just as veterans in the VA had told us of experiences that ended up in **Coming Home,** so it was with the secretaries. When every woman in the circle had had her say, Colin asked a question that took me by surprise: "Have any of you ever fantasized about what you'd like to do to your boss?" The women looked at one another and burst out laughing. **Fantasize? You want to know what we fantasize?** Shazaaam! We had the central idea for our movie—secretaries' fantasies about doing away with their bosses.

---

*It was also the central office of 9to5, the National Association of Working Women, which grew out of Nussbaum's Working Women Organizing Project in Boston.

During the IPC tour, walking the gauntlet
at the L.A. airport with Vanessa.
(Michael Dobo/www.dobophoto.com)

Within weeks of our return, Colin wrote the script and Dolly and Lily agreed to be in the picture. We filmed in the winter of 1980, and the entire experience was a joy from start to finish.

Dolly thought that when shooting began she had to have memorized the entire script and astounded us by doing just that. With great comedians the work seems just to flow spontaneously, but I learned from watching Lily that it's not like that. I once had to co-introduce someone with Steve Martin at a fund-raising function, and he reworked and rehearsed "Hello, this is . . ." for at least ten minutes before we went onstage, turning it around in his mouth, trying out different timings. I was awed. Lily's like that—never sure it's good enough, always wanting to do it one more time with a slightly different twist. Henry Miller once said, "Art teaches nothing except the significance of life." To me, this sums up the work Lily does in partnership with Jane Wagner. Through her quirky and always identifiable characters, she reveals truths that lie just outside our consciousness; she wakes us up.

I had never met anyone like Dolly. She always had a wisecrack, usually high raunch, that would break us all up. My son, Troy, who was around seven, loved coming to the set just to look at her. One day Dolly asked him if he knew why her feet were so small. He turned bright red and shook his head. "Well, Troy, it's because things don't grow big in the shade." He was too young to get it right away, but the rest of us doubled over laughing.

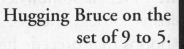
Hugging Bruce on the set of 9 to 5.

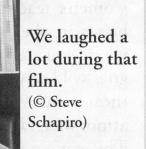
We laughed a lot during that film.
(© Steve Schapiro)

Dolly invited all the women who worked on 9 to 5 to come to the recording studio and sing the chorus with her for the album. That's Lily to the left of Dolly and way to the right (in the white shirt) is Dot, Vanessa's former nanny, who was my dresser on the film.
(© Steve Schapiro)

Dolly specializes in laughter. Hers is somewhere between a girl's giggle, an explosive shriek, and a cascade of little bells. It's not her boobs that precede her through a door, it's her laughter. Between that and the clicking of her spike heels, we could always hear her coming.

Karen Nussbaum says she's seen the movie five times or more and always loved to watch the women's reaction to various scenes. "I remember being in the theater one time and in the scene where you are working on the Xerox machine and it goes wild, a woman stood up in the middle of the theater and yelled out, 'Push the star button!' The atmosphere in the theaters was always the same: The women went wild, shouted back to the screen, and applauded at the end. Men liked the movie but were quiet; they knew something dangerous might be happening."

Karen, who remains an important figure in the labor movement within the AFL-CIO, says she always considered **9 to 5** the perfect example of popular culture moving a public debate forward, something that can really happen, she says, only "when there is a social basis, a nascent movement which can benefit from and exploit a popular expression. The way I saw it," she explains, "was that before the movie we had to argue that women's work was plagued by discrimination. The movie put an end to that debate . . . the audiences recognized it and laughed at it. Now the debate could shift to what we should do about it." Immediately after the movie was released Karen traveled to twenty cities across the country, building what she called "the movement behind the movie." Very soon 9to5 grew to include twenty staffed chapters, and that was when they began to lay the groundwork for their national union, District 925 of the Service Employees International Union.

The movie was a blockbuster.

Dolly wrote "9 to 5," the film's theme song, and got all the women in the cast and crew to record the chorus with her. The song "9 to 5" won every music award and sold over a million copies. It was the perfect movement anthem for working women.*

During the filming of **9 to 5** Dolly would tell me stories about growing up in the mountains of Tennessee in a tarpaper shack with eleven brothers and sisters, how they made their own soap and candles, how hard their life was, yet how much joy they had. I also learned that besides her gift for laughter Dolly was an intuitive and savvy businesswoman—mountain savvy, I call it.

There was a project I had been developing for almost a decade, based on a magnificent novel by Harriette Arnow called **The Dollmaker.** My charac-

---

*It was nominated for a Best Song Academy Award and became an RIAA Gold record. The film was one of the top-grossing films of that year. What most amazed Bruce and me was that it appealed almost equally to men. Bruce attributes this to the fact that everyone has, at one time or another, worked for a hellacious boss and had their ideas ripped off or been passed over for promotion, so the theme of employees getting even was appealing across the board.

ter was a powerful, creative woman from the Appalachian Mountains of Kentucky—what we call a hillbilly—who runs her farm, raises her five children, and carves wooden toys for them. She was as far from me as any character I had ever played. I knew I would need to do a lot of research to prepare for her—and here, in the person of Dolly Parton, was my opportunity. Dolly was the only hillbilly I had ever met (until then). Though the script for **The Dollmaker** wasn't right yet, I was already learning to whittle, and every day I would bring my knife and pieces of wood to the set of **9 to 5** so I could practice between shots. If you could tell where Dolly was by her laughter, you could tell where I'd been by the blood and shavings I'd leave behind.

Dolly, along with everyone else on the set, was wondering about my carving. One day over lunch I gave her **The Dollmaker** to read and asked if she would consider helping me find a real mountain woman to spend time with. Dolly immediately understood what I needed and also knew that her part of the country was not easy for outsiders to access. She agreed that when **9 to 5** wrapped she would have me come down to Nashville and together, on her touring bus, we would travel through parts of Appalachia and she would introduce me to her people, mountain people.

When I arrived in Nashville it became immediately clear that Dolly had put a great deal of time and attention into planning our trip, making sure I visited all the people and places that might help with my research for **The Dollmaker.** This moved me deeply. Dolly was and is an enormous star, a busy woman, and despite her amazing ability to be open and accessible in public, she is actually a very private person who does not easily or often open her personal life—her friends and family—to an outsider. I saw it as her way of thanking me for **9 to 5.**

Five of us loaded onto Dolly's touring bus. The back end of the bus was where Dolly had her stateroom and the rest of us slept in narrow bunk beds that lined both sides of the middle part of the bus. During the day we all gathered together up front. In all of those seven days not once did I see Dolly without her wig and makeup. She would appear in the morning looking like a million bucks and looked that way when she disappeared into her room at night. Usually when a woman is that accoutred it is because she is trying to hide some defect, but in Dolly's case (and I've spent enough time with her to be able to say this with certainty) if you peeled it all away, what you'd be left with is a true beauty—something, by the way, that runs in her family.

We wound our way through the Smoky Mountains of Tennessee and the Ozarks in Missouri and Arkansas, taking the bus as far as the big vehicle could go and then meeting up with various friends of Dolly's from her early days in radio. Up until then I had supposed that Dolly's ability to tell a good tale was a gift unique to her. Now I was seeing that just about everyone we met on the trip had the storytelling and laughter gift.

Dolly would introduce me and explain that "Jane's wantin' to do a movie 'bout folk like us" and ask if they wouldn't mind talking with me awhile. Usually this ended up with Dolly and me sitting inside a little one-room home without plumbing or electricity. I remember that the walls inside one of the cabins were covered with newspapers to keep out the cold air. There was usually a color print of Jesus hanging somewhere, some plastic flowers, maybe a faded photo of a man in uniform, and usually an old shoebox would be brought out filled with photos and other memorabilia. The folks were invariably in their seventies or eighties and had lots of memories of the Depression times when the mines had closed and many families had to move away, just the way it was for my character in **The Dollmaker.**

There was a town in the Ozarks where Dolly had relatives. They put us up for the night and, as we were pulling out the next morning, presented us with a big ceramic jug of white lightning. "Passed three times," Dolly explained proudly. "It don't git any purer." I learned that each time the homemade alcohol is passed through a gauze filter more impurities are removed, until what's left is on a par with the finest eau-de-vie to be found anywhere in France. I also learned how to hook my thumb through the handle and tip the heavy jug to my lips by balancing it on my arm. We did a lot of tipping during that trip, and though the volume of laughter increased accordingly, I was not aware of being inebriated and never awoke with a hangover. (Though once home it took me a week to recover!)

It was in the Ozarks that I saw my first bottle trees and other startling signs of creative affirmation from people whose art comes not from schools or galleries, but from an inner need to beautify their surroundings with whatever lies within reach, unencumbered by concerns about how others might judge them. There was the home in which every single thing, from tables and chairs to floors and icebox, had been painted with polka dots; another in which the recently deceased owner had covered every piece of furniture in the house with the tinfoil from gum wrappers. A dead and leafless tree in one yard had been readorned with countless milk of magnesia bottles, resplendent as the sun made magic with their unique blueness. Another tree was hung with years' worth of empty beer cans.

In Arkansas we drove to the home of music historian Jimmy Driftwood, known for, among other things, his song "The Battle of New Orleans." After hearing what I had come to Appalachia for, Jimmy decided he had just the people I needed to meet, whereupon we all piled into someone's car and drove through the mountains till we came to a small hamlet known as Mountain View, and ten minutes or so from there, down a dirt road that wound through the forest, we arrived at a log cabin covered with clematis. There was what appeared to be a zebra in the yard (turned out to be a very striped mule that pulled the family's plow) and several peacocks on the roof. I was sure I'd arrived in the magical kingdom of Oz. Lucy and Waco Johnson, an elderly couple in their seventies, came out to greet us. Lucy was a big-boned woman with short brown hair, thick glasses, and proud new dentures. She carved apple dolls (faces carved into apples that when dry shrivel into interesting weathered expressions). She also carded wool from her own sheep and colored it with dye she made from the vegetables and flowers she grew in abundance. She would then weave lovely small rugs and placemats that she sold at fairs. Like my character in **The Dollmaker,** Lucy was an artist who did not consider herself such. "Busywork" was what she said she did. She was the woman I'd been looking for.

As we prepared to leave I said to Lucy and Waco, "If we ever get the movie script right, I'd like to come back and spend time with you." They nodded, expecting never to see me again.

Three and a half years later I returned. The moment Bruce and I had a good script and a date set for filming, I had written asking if I could come stay with them for two weeks, "but only if you let me work for you and not tell anyone who I am." They were surprised but agreed to the arrangement.

It was Easter and bitter cold in Mountain View. Waco, now seventy-eight, had been chopping wood, the fireplace being their only source of heat, and on my first day there I insisted he let me take over the job. I had never chopped wood in my life, but I figured, Heck, he's in his seventies and I'm the fitness queen. No sweat. I awoke the next morning unable to move my hands, much less lift my arms. I developed boundless admiration for Waco and realized the depth of the problem that faced folks like them:

What would happen when Waco got too old to chop wood? Their children, like most of the young people from the mountains, had moved away to cities and towns. This was a way of life that would soon disappear before most Americans would even know what it had been.

Having proved I was not strong enough to do what old Waco did every day, I moved on to other chores. I milked their cow every morning, collected eggs from the free-roaming chickens, and learned to churn butter in an old wooden churn like the one my mother had made into a floor lamp back on Tigertail Road. I went with Waco into the woods, where he shot a possum and showed me how to skin it. Lucy told me how to find a sassafras tree and use the bark to season the possum, which I cooked for dinner on the wood-burning stove. (I didn't like it. It was greasy and had too many tiny bones.) Lucy also taught me to make scratch biscuits (biscuits from scratch) and cook them in the fireplace in a heavy iron Dutch oven. I learned about sorghum and how you could slather it on bread, what a back log was (the largest log that you'd put at the back of the fire), how to carve apple dolls, and how a late spring frost could wipe out the garden and leave them short of food.

We all slept in the same room with sheets hung on wires between the beds for privacy. They were iron beds with old, sagging springs and lightweight feather mattresses so thick that I had a hard time crawling out in the morning. Every evening after supper we would sit on their well-worn sofa in front of the huge stone fireplace and they would tell stories and jokes and sometimes play their instruments and sing. It dawned on me (duh!) why everyone we'd met told great stories and played at least one instrument. Without electricity there was no radio or television to entertain them. They had only each other, and especially on those cold mountain nights, the arts of storytelling and music were precious as gold. I wondered: Was this special art of talking to one another every day in danger of extinction for those of us "blessed" with electricity?

On Easter Sunday Lucy and Waco brought me with them to church. It was a one-room whitewashed structure heated by a woodstove. The preacher stared intently at me over its rusty top. He wore denim overalls and his hands showed he was a hardworking farmer like Waco. Suddenly he said, "You know, you look mighty like Jane Fonda. Anyone ever tell you that?" I ducked my head and mumbled something, praying that Lucy wouldn't tell and that he wouldn't say something nasty. Instead he said, "Well, I don't know what you think, but I think she's a brave lady." I nodded in silent agreement and wanted to hug him.

During the service there was a good deal of back-and-forthing between the preacher and the congregation—the men in the congregation, that is. No woman said a word. When I asked Lucy about this later, she told me that women were forbidden to play any role in the service. She also told me that just down the way was another church where people drank arsenic and handled live rattlesnakes.

I felt privileged to have been permitted for a time to know this world and its people . . . a world that as late as 1984 was probably not so different from that of my pioneer ancestors. I was saddened by the thought that in a few decades it might all be developed, hooked up to "civilization."

CHAPTER EIGHTEEN

ON GOLDEN POND

*Sometimes you have to look very hard at a person
and remember he's doing the best he can.*
—Ethel Thayer,
On Golden Pond

I DON'T LIKE YOU!" said Katharine Hepburn, pointing her finger straight at my face, her anger making the famous voice and classic head, which quivered at the best of times, shake with tsunamic tremors. I had never met the legendary actor before, and it was a terrible moment, coming within minutes of my arrival with Bruce at her Forty-ninth Street town house—terrible not only because someone only a notch below God was damning me, but also because in less than two weeks she was supposed to travel to New Hampshire to begin rehearsing **On Golden Pond** with my father and me.

Katharine Hepburn was critical to the financing of this film. No American studio thought anyone would want to see a movie about two old people and a kid. On top of that, my father was suffering from heart disease that was serious enough to keep us from getting insurance coverage for the film. Everything depended on all of us working for far less than our usual salaries, and if we lost Katharine Hepburn, the whole project would be doomed.

It was difficult for me to know exactly what was at the root of her anger with me. She was famously liberal, so I knew it had nothing to do with my politics. It seemed to have something to do with my not having been present at her first encounter with my father (my having chosen instead to make the bus trip with Dolly). Despite their decades in the same profession, knowing many of the same people, Hepburn and Fonda had never met until now, and though my company was producing the film, it had never dawned on me that my presence at this coming together of two Hollywood icons was necessary. For better or worse, the need for homage had never reared its head in my twenty-five years in the business. It never dawned on me that Katharine Hepburn would perceive my absence at the meeting as a lack of respect.

There was another factor at play: The seventy-three-year-old Ms. Hepburn had dislocated her rotator cuff and torn a tendon in her shoulder while playing tennis. Our visit was in order to ascertain whether or not she would be able to begin filming on schedule.

Shortly on the heels of "I don't like you" came "I'm afraid I'm not going to be able to do this film, Jane," announced with the certainty of a New England Brahmin. "I don't think my shoulder will get well fast enough to do it, and there are those scenes where I'd have to lug wood and carry the canoe into the water. So you'd just better go ahead and get Geraldine Page or someone to take over." She reminded me of myself with Alan Pakula before starting **Klute.**

But then suddenly she was on to film credits—whose name would be above whose. I was relieved, because it meant she was still seeing herself in the movie; but I couldn't fathom why she would see the credits as a problem. I just assumed she and my father would get top billing and that my name, as a supporting actress, would run beneath theirs. Then it hit me. She suspected that I might want billing above hers. **Oh my God!** It never would have occurred to me to feel competitive with Katharine Hepburn or to expect any special treatment because of my producing role! Film credits and such things that serve as outward proof of one's standing had never been especially important to me: You do a good job and people take notice is the way I see it. But maybe this competitiveness is what separates the legends from the mere movie stars. I was more like my father, comfortable in an egalitarian context, and I've always tended to forget that everyone is not like this. I realized that this whole meeting, for her, was a testing of the waters to determine whether I knew my place . . . and, if not, to put me in it.

Once I realized this I could see how vulnerable she felt. She was a legend, yes. But I was the younger actress who because of youth was currently more of a box office draw—and I was only one Oscar behind her. (This was on her mind, as will become clear.) She was used to being in charge; but my company was producing the film as a vehicle for my father, and I was in the driver's seat. Moreover I had not conformed to her need for approbation. Now, with her injury, she probably thought I might want to replace her. I quickly realized that her opening salvo had been her instinctive way to put me on the defensive—**I don't like you!**—and by announcing she wasn't going to be in the film, she was assuming the offensive, getting out before I replaced her, scoping out where she stood in the delicate balance of power and protocol. From the moment I sensed what was really going on, it was easy to open my heart to her.

I apologized for not being there when she and Dad met and said that under no circumstances would we replace her, that she was critical to the film (which was true), and that we would do whatever was necessary in terms of schedule to ensure that she had time to heal.

"Geraldine Page is a brilliant actress, Ms. Hepburn. I've worked with her. But what will make this film magic is the pairing of you and my dad—

and that's what we will make happen, whatever it takes."

When she began offering ideas about how the scene with the canoe could be rigged to ease the burden on her shoulder, I knew that she had never been ready to leave the project. She was just testing us.

No sooner was the issue of her being in the movie put to rest than she issued another challenge: "Are you going to do the backflip yourself, Jane?" She looked at me and I think I saw a twinkle in her eyes.

In the film, the backflip plays an important role in my character's relationship with her father. She hadn't been able to do it as a youngster because according to him she was too fat. But this summer, as a grown and newly married woman, she decides to prove to him that she is now able. But holy s——! I had no intention of doing the dive **myself.** A stunt double was already lined up to do it for me. For one thing, I have a phobia about going over backward, and for another, I hate cold water. But the moment the question left Ms. Hepburn's mouth, the image of **her** doing that perfect dive in **The Philadelphia Story** came into my mind, and I knew what my answer would have to be.

"Of course I am going to do the dive myself, Ms. Hepburn. But I'll have to learn how because I've never done one." I'd be damned before I'd let on that I was scared.

The meeting ended with friendly embraces all around. Ms. Hepburn announced that ten days

**Chelsea, Norman, and Ethel Thayer
in On Golden Pond.**

(© Steve Schapiro)

hence she and her companion and employee, Phyllis Wilbourn, would be driving up to Squam Lake to choose a house for themselves, and we arranged to meet them when they arrived.

Once Phyllis had shown us out the front door and we'd exited the wrought-iron gate to the side-walk, I walked far enough away from her windows so there was no risk of Ms. Hepburn seeing me and sat on the curb, right there on Forty-ninth Street. I was dazed. Within the space of one hour we'd gone from "I hate you" and "I'm not going to be in the movie" to "I'm going up to choose my house." I'd been given a preview of what clearly would be a complicated and challenging relationship with our leading lady. I had my work cut out for me.

"Bruce, take me somewhere, I need a stiff drink."

W anting to check out the housing situation before Ms. Hepburn got there, I went to Squam Lake, a wild, pristine body of water, big and irregularly shaped, with small islands scattered about that made it impossible to see from one end to the other.

Bruce and his wife were already settled into a pleasant camp (that's what homes on Squam Lake are called) on the far side of the lake and had lined up a number of summer rentals for me to look at. Over the course of the three months we would be there, Vanessa, Troy, Tom, and our German shepherd, Geronimo, would be living with me, and plans had been made for CED's entire steering committee, all ten of them, to come up for some strategy sessions. I needed a large house.

Shirlee had already picked out a place for herself and Dad. It was a guest house close to a spacious two-story, eight-bedroom, brick main house that sat on a hill with a wide lawn that swooped down to the lake. The main house was perfect for my considerable needs, and besides, it was right next to Dad. There was another camp to the north, much smaller but cozy, with a beautiful bay window overlooking the water and a number of small outlying rustic cabins—perfect, I thought, for Ms. Hepburn and the ever attentive Phyllis.

At the appointed time Bruce and I drove to the parking lot of the restaurant where we had arranged to rendezvous with them. Within minutes their station wagon pulled up, and Ms. Hepburn got out and came over to me.

"Well, have you picked your house yet, Jane?" In that instant I knew that I had to throw out my assumptions about who would take which house.

"I have seen a number of houses, Ms. Hepburn, but you make your choice first and I'll take what's left."

"Now you're talking!" she said with a big grin, knowing I'd learned my lesson and wasn't about to make the same mistake again. Whew! It had been a close call. Ms. Hepburn and Phyllis in a cozy little cabin? What **could** I have been thinking? She chose the eight-bedroom mansion.

Let me provide a little backstory: For years I had wanted to do a movie in which all the Fondas—Henry, Peter, and I—could act together. When Bruce saw the play **On Golden Pond** in New York he wanted to buy it right away, as time was of the essence: Dad had been increasingly in and out of hospitals with heart disease and a variety of complications that resulted from it, and I knew there wasn't a lot of time left for us to work together. Even though there was no role for Peter and mine was very much a supporting one, I believed that in the role of Norman Thayer, Dad would win the Oscar that had eluded him for so long. I wanted to make that happen for him.

Mark Rydell had agreed to direct the film, and Ernest Thompson, the young author of the play, would rework it for the screen.

The film tells of an elderly couple who have summered for decades on a lake in Maine called Golden Pond. Norman, a moody curmudgeon played by my father, is about to turn eighty, and his daughter, Chelsea, en route to Europe with her fiancé, has planned to stop by the lake for his birthday party. Along with them is the fiancé's thirteen-year-old son, Billy, whom they hope to leave with Chelsea's parents for a month while they travel. Chelsea, a real estate agent who lives in California, has had a troubled, distant relationship with her father all her life and has made a point of not visiting her parents because of it—something that has hurt her father, though she doesn't even realize he cares.

Young Billy is angry, feeling as though he's been dumped someplace boring with a couple of "old poops"; but in the course of the summer Norman and Billy bond as Norman never has with his own daughter. He teaches Billy to fish and to execute a fine backflip (the dive Chelsea was never able to accomplish), and Billy teaches Norman such expressions as "cruisin' chicks," "suck face," and "San Fran–tastic." We can feel Norman's heart soften because of this relationship with Billy, and when Chelsea returns from Europe to fetch the boy, she sees this and gets jealous. With her mother's encouragement Chelsea is finally able to muster the courage to confront her father, telling him she wants them to be friends, and he is able to show his love for her for the first time. The main fabric of the story is the touching fifty-year-long relationship between Norman and his wife, Ethel, played by Hepburn. It is deeply touching when he loses his way in the woods while trying to pick strawberries and comes running home to her. So is the scene when he suffers acute angina and she tells him how scared she is of losing him. The two of them bring a rare poignancy to these scenes, and I for one cannot watch them without sobbing uncontrollably.

Time was of the essence. Because of my father's failing health, we all knew it was this summer or never.

On Golden Pond is a summer story, and we had to get it done by early fall, when the deciduous hardwood tress so characteristic of that part of New England would begin to turn their fall colors.

Cinematographer Billy Williams had insisted on finding a lake that ran east to west, because it would give him a certain kind of light he felt was essential. Our location scout visited over one hundred lakes from the Carolinas to Maine, but Squam was apparently the only one on the East Coast that met this requirement. Then there was the unusual fact that while almost all other lakes were rimmed with summer homes, Squam seemed frozen in time. It was hard to believe that a place so beautiful was so undeveloped (until someone introduced me to the term **conservation by exclusion:** All the land bordering the lake is owned by wealthy families who intend to keep it undeveloped).

So we were working against time: the season changing, Ms. Hepburn's injured rotator cuff, and my father's health. Also, an actors strike was looming against the Motion Picture Association of America (MPAA) and it threatened to shut down all productions. We hoped that if we had actually started shooting before the strike began, they wouldn't ask us to stop. We were wrong. The actors struck, and we got the call to shut down. Bruce spent three desperate days arguing that because we were with ITC, a British independent company, not an MPAA studio, we didn't fall under their jurisdiction. He was successful in getting a waiver that allowed us to continue. Had that not occurred, **On Golden Pond** would never have been made.

Once rehearsals had begun, Ms. Hepburn would invite me over to her house for tea. We'd sit in the comfortable white wicker chairs that were scattered about her glassed-in porch and she would tell me how I should play my role. I'm serious—and so was she. Ms. Hepburn would have me read her part and she'd read mine and give me line readings. Though I was stunned by this, I never let on that I found it . . . well, strange. I did not want to offend her.

I never tired of looking at her. Though in her mid-seventies, she was still magnificent. It was part attitude and part bone structure. I realized that if the architecture of a face is upward reaching (those cheekbones!) and properly proportioned, as hers was, it mattered not if the skin that was draped over the scaffolding was wrinkled and blotched . . . the essential beauty held. Aging takes more of a toll on less structured faces.

Though she told me once that she thought the two of us were very much alike—both strong, independent, liberal-minded women—she also let me know what she saw as our differences. For one thing, she thought I should be more involved on a day-to-day basis with the film production, which of course is how she was in her heyday—involved in all the details from casting to lighting. She has been quoted as saying, "Acting was all I ever wanted to do," but I wasn't like that. I loved acting, especially once I began producing my own pictures, but it was one important part of my life among others. I had my children, my ongoing political work with CED, the new Workout business to help fund it all . . . and a dog. (Ms. Hepburn wasn't big on pets, either.) But I know Ms. Hepburn looked askance at all of this; she simply didn't understand the concept of having a working partner like Bruce, of having a business unrelated to my profession, and of putting as much or more time into political work as I did into my career. Ms. Hepburn was livid that CED's steering committee were all there, living at our camp (the smaller one, which I'd thought appropriate for Ms. Hepburn and Phyllis) in cabins and tents. She thought it was unpardonable for me not to be 100 percent concentrated on the film. We had to wait for a day when we were utterly certain Ms. Hepburn would not be coming to the set before we could invite the CED organizers to pay a visit and watch the shooting.

Of course, the idea of an actor having children was anathema to her. She told me that she had never wanted children because she thought she was too selfish. "If I'd had a child," she said, "and the child got sick and was crying just as I had to leave for the theater, where hundreds of people were waiting for me to perform, and I had to make a choice—the play or the child—well, I'd smother the child to death and go on with the show. You just can't have both," she said with frightening certainty, "a career **and** children."

I don't think she was right, at least not for me. Maybe for her she was: To have had the career she wanted perhaps required 100 percent attention. I do know that I felt terrible after these conversations. They played to my tendency to feel that I should be handling my life differently, more like . . . I don't know. There was always a roster of women whose lives seemed more sensible than mine, just as there was always a list of actresses who could do my part better than I. I stayed awake many a night fretting about this, feeling sure that she was right, that my kids would be totally screwed up because of me.

But guess what. They aren't. In fact, my kids have grown up to be amazing, talented, well-balanced, lovable people. Not that I can take credit for it all, but still. Anyway, I am what I am. In a 1978 interview in **Rolling Stone**, Donald Katz wrote about me, "No one else has ever stepped out to such a band of new drummers in the movie world and maintained a career."

On more than one occasion during those teatime conversations, Ms. Hepburn talked of her relationship with actresses Constance Collier and Ethel Barrymore, both elders with whom she seemed to have assigned herself the role of acolyte. She described how when Barrymore was hospitalized toward the end of her life, Hepburn would visit her regularly. She told me about this so often that I began to wonder if she was hoping for a younger actress who would befriend her—and whether perhaps the actress she had in mind was me. I was never sure. But she was more comfortable with people who had no other attachments, not even pets.

She talked a lot about the importance of her parents in her life, always speaking of them as the most wonderful, fascinating parents anyone could have and crediting them with making her what she was. Apparently her habit of swimming every morning when she was at her country house in Connecticut, even in winter, had been developed at an early age. She told me that her father had insisted all his children take baths in a tub filled with ice every morning before school. When I suggested that this might be considered child abuse, she said, "Oh no, that is what builds character; and that is why I have such a strong constitution and never get sick." I wasn't convinced but kept my mouth shut.

She told me that every morning in the city she would get up at 5:00 A.M., have breakfast in bed, and write about her life's experiences. One chapter, she said, was called "Failure" and described her monumental failure in a Broadway play called **The Lake**.

"One reviewer said, 'Go see Katharine Hepburn run the gamut of emotions from A to B,' " she said with a snort. "I'm writing about how you learn more from failure than you ever do from success." On that one I agree with her.

Having learned my lesson, I was not about to miss a second historic event, so I was present on the first day of shooting, even though I was not in the scene. Ms. Hepburn was all made up and waiting for my father on the front steps of the house in which we were filming. She had a twinkle in her eye and we could tell she was hiding something behind her back. As soon as Dad arrived, she walked up to him and said, "Here, Hank. This was Spence's favorite hat. I want you to have it for this film." Dad was clearly moved by this gesture from his leading lady, as were we all. In the course of the film he wore three different hats and Spencer Tracy's was one of them. When the film ended, he made a painting of the three hats, so real that you could feel their texture; he had lithograph copies made and presented one to every member of the cast and crew.

My first day of filming was the scene of my arrival at my parents' summer home with my fiancé and his son. Ms. Hepburn had not seen me in costume and makeup. She took one look at my high-heeled shoes and disappeared, returning a few minutes later in a pair of her old platform shoes from the thirties, which increased her height by at least two inches. That's when I remembered that height was important to her. (I'd read that she'd brought it up in her first encounter with Spencer Tracy, telling him, "You're not as tall as I expected." This prompted producer Joseph Mankiewicz's famous comment, "Don't worry, Kate, he'll soon cut you down to size.") I suppose that for her, height established dominance. She'd be damned if she'd let me tower over her.

That same day, between takes, I was standing in front of the mirror that hung near the front door where Norman's hats were hung when Ms. Hepburn surprised me by coming up behind me. She reached around and took a chunk of my cheek between her fingers.

"What does this mean to you?" she asked, pulling on my cheek.

"What do you mean?"

"Your image. What do you want your image to be?" She gave my cheek another little tug. "This is your package. We all have our package, what presents us to the world. What do you want your package to say about you?"

"I have no idea," I answered.

But I thought a lot about this for days afterward and still do today. (That's the thing about Ms. Hepburn: She got under my skin and stirred things up.) I think I now know why she asked me the question. She thought I needed to be more self-conscious about my image. That's what she felt movie stars needed to do—God knows she did. She had a persona, a style particular to her that will live on in the minds of her public, and she never wavered from it. I, on the other hand, was a hodgepodge, still searching for who I was, lacking self-consciousness about my persona, and this bothered her. She didn't want me to be this way; it was one more thing about me that she didn't approve of. We tend to think of the term **self-consciousness** as meaning something bad, as being awkward or uncomfortable with oneself. But the way I am using it it means something rather different—a **consciousness of self**, the impact our presence has on other people. The only other person I have known as self-conscious is Ted Turner. And, as it was with Hepburn, it's part of his charm.

Everything about our summer on Squam Lake was magical. Even nature wanted to get in on the act. Take the loon, for instance. The loon is a wondrous bird about the size of a small goose, with dramatic black-and-white markings and a haunting cry that resembles the trill of distant laughter. It dives underwater to catch fish and nests in the lake-rich areas of the northern regions. In the winter it migrates to warmer climes. Loons mate for life, the males and females share in the rearing of their children, and for all of us they became emblematic of the film's couple, Ethel and Norman Thayer. Loons are shy, wary of humans. One rarely gets the opportunity to watch them up close, but one day some crew members were eating lunch down by the lake's edge and one of them suddenly came running, calling us to come down. A family of loons, mama, papa, and several babies, were just a few feet offshore and seemed to want to stay there. The camera operator grabbed the camera and filmed them, and they hung out there for several days, as though knowing that this film would be wonderful and wanting to be a part of it. They are the first image you see in the film.

From the moment I arrived in New Hampshire, I began taking backflip lessons from the University of Maine's swimming coach, who summered near Squam Lake. I started with a belt around my waist, hooked up to a rope that assisted me in the flip, with a mattress to cushion the fall. After a week or so I graduated to the coach's diving board, and Troy would sit poolside and watch his mother's pathetic attempts to get herself all the way around, which generally ended with me landing on my back. I was terrified, always on the verge of tossing in the towel. After a month of this I moved to the float, the one in the movie, in front of the house, out in Squam Lake. It was the beginning of July, and I had less than a month to get it right. Every day when I wasn't needed on the set I would be out there, diving backward, over and over again, my body slapping against the water as I failed to make it around.

Then one day about three weeks into this ordeal on the lake, I finally got it right. Nothing to write home about, but I had managed to flip far enough over to have time to straighten my legs and enter the water headfirst. I wasn't sure I'd ever be able to do it again, but at least I'd done it **once**. As I crawled, battered and bruised, onto the shore, out of the nearby bushes appeared Ms. Hepburn. She must have been hiding there, watching me practice. She walked over to where I was standing and said in her shaky, nasal, God-is-a-New-Englander voice, "Don't you feel good?"

"Terrific," I answered. And it was true.

"You've taught me to respect you, Jane. You faced your fear. Everyone should know that feeling of overcoming fear and mastering something. People who aren't taught that become soggy."

Thank you, Lord! I'd been redeemed. God knows the last thing in the world I wanted to be was soggy, certainly not in the eyes of Ms. Hepburn, a living testament to nonsogginess. It was odd. In the film the backflip was to prove myself to my father. In real life I had proved myself to Ms. Hepburn. Dad probably couldn't have cared less if I'd done the dive myself or used a stunt double.

We finally shot the diving scene in the third week of July. I managed a fairly good dive and was relieved to have it out of the way. Wrong, wrong, wrong, as Ms. Hepburn would say. A few days later we learned that the footage of the scene had somehow been damaged in the lab and I would have to do it all again. As though that weren't bad enough, when we finally got around to reshooting, it was mid-September and the water was numbingly cold. I will never forget having to walk out on the diving board, all wet and shivering, while the crew sat in the camera boat in their down parkas. I was out of practice and too cold to execute the dive as well as I had the first time. When I came to the surface and said, "I did it! It was lousy, but at least I did it," those were my own words, spontaneous and totally true.

There is a scene where Dad and Ms. Hepburn are playing Parcheesi and I'm sitting on the couch reading a magazine. Dad makes a remark about my not wanting to play because I'm afraid to lose. I respond, "Why do you like playing games? You seem to like beating people. I wonder why." After we shot the master and the crew had finished lighting for my close-up, I got into place and realized that there were so many lights on me that I couldn't see Dad's eyes, which would hinder my playing of this brief, hostile exchange. It was easy to fix; I just asked the cameraman to throw a little light onto his face. That done, it was time for Dad's close-up, and just before we were set to go, I asked, "Is it okay, Dad? Can you see my eyes?"

"I don't need to see your eyes," he answered dismissively, "I'm not that kind of actor."

Whoa. His words pierced me to my core. It felt like such a put-down. Forget that I had made this project happen for him. Forget my two Academy Awards, that I was the mother of two children, forget all of that. I was suddenly reduced to a quivering, insecure fat girl, in the same way my character is. As Chelsea says to her mother in another scene, "I act like a big person everywhere else. In California I'm in charge of things . . . yet I get back here with him and I'm just a fat little girl again!" I could relate to that.

And yet—and this is what makes life so interesting for actors; hell, maybe it is why some of us **become** actors—while one part of me was in emotional agony because of his comment, the other half of me was saying, **Oh my God—this is so great. This is exactly the way I'm supposed to feel. This is just perfect for the character.**

When the scene was over and everyone had prepared to go home for the day, I remained on the couch, unable to move but sure that no one was aware how Dad's words had hurt me.

To my surprise Ms. Hepburn came over and sat next to me, put her arms around me, and whispered in my ear, "I know just how you feel, Jane. Spence used to do things like that to me all the time. He'd tell me to go home after I'd done my close-up, say that he didn't need me to be around, he could do his lines just as well to the script girl. Please don't feel badly. Your dad has no idea that his words hurt you. He didn't mean to. He's just like Spence." I was deeply grateful for her understanding and compassion. It showed me it hadn't all been my imagination. I had a witness; I wasn't alone.

Speaking about her experience on the movie, Ms. Hepburn told her friend and biographer A. Scott Berg, "It was strange. . . . There was certainly a whole layer of drama going on in the scenes between her [me] and Hank, and I think she came by to watch every scene he and I had together. There was a feeling of longing about her." She was right about the longing. I longed for him to love me and see me as an able grown-up. And for me to do so, too!

On Golden Pond is an archetypal story of love and loyalty, but it's also about the difficulty of resolving generational differences when a parent is withholding and a child is angry because of it. Of all the films I have made, none seems to have resonated so profoundly with so many people as this one. I realize the universality of the dilemma, because people—men and women—to this day go out of their way to tell me how their relationships with their fathers resemble Chelsea and Norman's. In many cases, they tell me that it was taking their fathers to see the movie that enabled a breakthrough to occur.

Isn't one of the difficulties knowing who should make the first move? The child is angry because the parent hasn't been what he or she should have been, and the child waits for the deficient parent to admit he or she was terrible and to ask forgiveness. But it's harder to change when you are older. You know you've made mistakes, but you don't understand this new generation and you're stuck in your ways (unless you keep working on yourself to not get stuck). Playing Chelsea in On Golden Pond and paying attention to the advice her mother gives her allowed me to see that it has to be the child who makes the move toward forgiveness and that if it is done from a loving place, the parent will almost always be there to receive. One important caveat that Ethel gives Chelsea: "Sometimes you have to look very hard at a person and remember he's doing the best he can."

Everyone on the set was sensitive to the fact that

my father and I had had a complex relationship and that this film in many ways mirrored real life—but with a resolution at the end. I hoped that somehow the resolution between father and daughter in the film would lap over to Dad and me. He always said that acting gave him a mask that allowed him to reveal emotions he did not feel safe revealing in real life. Maybe showing his emotion about his daughter in the film would release the real ones.

There is a scene with the mother when Chelsea comes back from Europe to pick up Billy. She is hurt that her father has developed such a close relationship with the boy, and her mother is trying to get her to realize that underneath the gruff exterior her father loves her, that she just needs to talk to him and pay close attention.

"I'm afraid of him," says Chelsea.

"Well, he's afraid of you. The two of you should get along just fine."

"I don't even know him," Chelsea says plaintively.

"Chelsea," the mother admonishes, "Norman is eighty years old. He has heart palpitations and trouble remembering things. Just exactly **when** do you expect this friendship to begin?"

The scene that follows is my key scene in the movie, the one where I confront my father. I wade into the water by the dock as Norman and Billy pull up from their fishing trip. "Norman, I want to talk to you."

"Oh yeah, what about?" he says dismissively.

"I think maybe you and I should have the kind of relationship we're supposed to have."

"What kind of relationship is that?" Norman snaps.

"You know, like a father and daughter. . . ."

"Worried about the will, are you? Well, I'm leaving everything to you except what I'm taking with me."

Chelsea begins to choke up. She fears her attempt at contact will end just like all the others. "I don't want anything. . . . It's just . . . it seems you and I have been mad at each other for so long."

"I didn't think we were mad. I just didn't think we liked each other."

Chelsea is stunned by this cruelty but persists. "I want to be your friend." And she places her hand on his arm.

From the first, every time I read the script I would come to that scene and tears would pour down my cheeks. In rehearsals I was so emotional that it was hard to speak the lines. Finally the day of reckoning came. I woke up and ran to the bathroom to vomit, more scared than I had ever been before a scene and knowing it was because I had to say intimate words to my father that I had never been able to say in real life. We blocked the scene for the camera and lighting crew, he in the boat, me waist-deep in the water. Even then I was nearly overcome with emotion.

We began with the wide shot that included the two of us, the boat, and the pier. Though I knew a scene like this was ultimately going to play in close-up, I was unable to hold back my emotions. Next we shot over my shoulder onto Dad, and still I gave it my all, partly because I couldn't help myself and partly because I wanted him to be emotional, too. As I have written in an earlier chapter, I waited until his last shot to touch his arm as I tell him I want to be his friend—I wanted to take him by surprise. It worked. Tears welled in his eyes and he ducked his head, not wanting it to show. But it did. I was so happy.

Then the camera swung around for my close-up. We did a rehearsal for the camera and . . . **oh, no,** the actor's ultimate nightmare: I was bone dry, spent, unable to call up any emotions. No one knew it, of course, because this was just a rehearsal, but I panicked. What to do? It wasn't that I had to be overtly emotional in the scene, but I needed to **feel** emotional and then stifle it. I tried to relax, as Strasberg would have wanted. I tried all the sense-memories I had, sang my old song that always made me cry, everything. But nothing seemed to work. As I was pacing around onshore waiting for the camera to be ready (dreading that the camera would be ready), up came Ms. Hepburn. She wasn't even sup-posed to be on set that day, but there she was. She looked at me.

"How are you?" she asked, sensing something.

"I'm in trouble. I've gone dry. Please don't tell Dad," I answered weakly, and then I was called to the set. The time of reckoning had come.

Ethel telling Chelsea to talk to her father.
(© Steve Schapiro)

I've just brought Dad his Academy Award. Left to right:
Bridget Fonda, Amy Fonda, Tom, me, Vanessa, Shirlee,
and Troy with his back to the camera.
(© John Bryson, 1982)

Hoping that some last-minute miracle would unleash my heart, I said to Mark, "I'm going to turn my back to the camera while I prepare, and when I turn around, it means that I'm ready for you to roll." He understood.

I turned away to prepare, though I had no idea what to do, and as I was staring at the shore, trying to relax and bring myself into the scene, there was Hepburn, crouching in the bushes just within my line of vision. Nobody could see her but me. She fixed me intensely with her eyes, and slowly she raised her clenched fists and shook them as if to say "Do it! Go ahead. You can do this!" She was willing me into the scene: Katharine Hepburn to Jane Fonda; mother to daughter; older actress, who'd been there and knew about drying up, to younger actress. It was all those layers of things and more. **Do it! Do it! You can! I know it.** With her energy she literally **gave** me the scene, gave it to me with her fists, her eyes, and her generosity, and I will never, ever forget it.

That night I asked Dad and Shirlee if I could come over to dinner. The scene had been so utterly personal for me, so intimate in a way that he and I had never been. I was raw and felt so close to him, and I needed to acknowledge it and see if he felt the same. I wanted to tell him how terrifying it had been to dry up like I did, and to ask if this had ever happened to him—at least, you know, share some actor's talk. But mostly I wanted to know if he had changed in any way as a result of the intimacy.

I told him about drying up and asked if such a thing had ever happened to him.

"Nope."

I couldn't believe it. "Never? Not once in your whole career?"

"Nope."

My heart sank. That was it, just "Nope." Why did these things happen to me and not to him? What was I doing wrong? Moreover it was all too clear that he was no more open or forthcoming now than he'd been before the scene. I was so sad. I felt like a dope for getting all soft and fuzzy over what to him was obviously just a scene.

Katharine Hepburn told Scott Berg, "Hank Fonda was the hardest nut I ever tried to crack. But I didn't know any more about him after we had made the picture than I did at the beginning. Cold. Cold. Cold."

Yup.

On the set one day, Ms. Hepburn told our unit publicist that she thought it was the duty of a star to be fascinating. There is no denying that the lady worked hard to do her duty and as a result was one of the two most fascinating people I have known (the other being Ted Turner). But despite this and despite my father's coldness, in the genetic scheme of things I am glad I am my father's daughter. I never loved him more than when I watched him, day after day, as he sat on the set between takes in his canvas chair with his name printed on the back panel, waiting to be called before the cameras: quiet, demanding little, **not** looking to fascinate. He was what he was.

On **Golden Pond** was the largest-grossing film of 1981. The studios were wrong: People **did** want to see this movie about old folks . . . because it spoke of universal issues with pathos and humor. Never has a movie of mine had such a profound personal impact on people; never have people crossed the street just to hug me and tell me that seeing it, and then bringing their fathers to see it, had altered their relationships forever. This has moved me and gladdened me greatly over the years.

The film received **ten** Academy Award nominations, among them Best Picture, Best Actor, Best Actress, Best Supporting Actress, and Best Screenplay. Dad was too ill to attend the ceremony, and given his lifelong antipathy for awards and competition, I'm not sure he would have gone even if he had been well enough. But he intended to watch the proceedings with Shirlee from his bed. Ms. Hepburn did not attend, either. The first one of us to win (for Best Writing, Screenplay Based on Material from Another Medium) was Ernest Thompson, who actually leapt with joy as he crossed the stage. I did not win Best Supporting Actress (losing to the remarkable Maureen Stapleton playing the radical Emma Goldman in **Reds**). Eight-year-old Troy was sitting next to me, and as the names of the nominees for Best Actress were being read, I saw him drop his head and squeeze his eyes tight. When Katharine Hepburn's name was announced as the winner (for an unprecedented fourth time), Troy tugged excitedly on my arm and whispered, "Mom, I prayed she'd win and my prayer was answered."

Then Sissy Spacek came out to present the award for Best Actor. For all his great performances, Dad had been nominated only once before, for Tom Joad in **The Grapes of Wrath.** This time he had stiff competition: Warren Beatty, Burt Lancaster, Dudley Moore, and Paul Newman. There was nothing I wanted more in life than for him to finally win. This was my fervent prayer. When Sissy opened the envelope and announced his name, the theater erupted in applause and cheering; I went up onstage to claim the Oscar on his behalf, as he had asked me to in the event he won. It was the happiest moment of my life.

Tom, Troy, Vanessa, and I left the ceremony immediately, along with Amy (the daughter Susan and Dad had adopted at birth) and my niece, Bridget Fonda, to carry the statue to him. He was sitting in his wheelchair next to the bed when we arrived.

Shirlee was right next to him, as always.

Watching his face closely, I could see he was pleased. When I asked him how he felt, all he said was, "I'm so happy for Kate."

The next morning I called Ms. Hepburn to congratulate her and her first words to me were, "You'll never catch me now!"

It took a moment for me to understand what she

was talking about, and then it hit me. Of course—if she **hadn't** won and I **had,** we'd be tied with three Oscars each. Now she had four, and I had only two. No way I'd catch up. I had to laugh. We were still operating on different wavelengths, but how could I not love her spunk?

Dad died five months later.

CHAPTER NINETEEN

CLOSURE

Maybe a fella hasn't got a soul of his own,
just a piece of a big soul—the one big soul
that belongs to everybody.
—TOM JOAD IN JOHN STEINBECK'S
The Grapes of Wrath

THE END CAME SLOWLY. Following the filming of **On Golden Pond** and before its release, I visited Dad's home in Bel-Air as often as I could. There he'd be, sitting in the kitchen in his wheelchair or, more and more frequently, in his bed. Shirlee worked hard to make him look dignified for these visits, dressing him in natty cashmere cardigans. He would be awake but remote, already gone from us on some level. At such times I would sit with Shirlee and make small talk, glancing over at him occasionally, hoping that the inner world into which he seemed to have retreated was filled with curtain calls, tumultuous applause, and visions of the kites that he and Jimmy Stewart had flown as youths.

During this time I enjoyed being able to please him in little ways. I would cook him pork roast and bring him crisp, tart pears from an old pear tree we had at the ranch, things I knew he loved. It's a strange pleasure—when a parent you have always feared, who has never seemed to need you, becomes old and weak and you are finally able to do for him. Being able to give him the nurture he had not given me filled me with an almost spiritual satisfaction. I wished he were poor and needed me more.

One day I was allowed into the intensive care unit at Cedars-Sinai Medical Center, where he had been rushed during a close call. It was the first time I had seen him like that, all hooked up to IVs and monitors, sunken and pale, with dark bruising on his arms and hands from the needles. He seemed to be asleep, so I pulled up a chair, sat at the end of his bed, lifted the ends of the sheets, and began rubbing his feet. Dad had suffered with painful gout in his feet for as long as I could remember, and I knew gentle massage helped relieve it. I loved being able to touch him like that, even though he was unaware. It created an intimacy, albeit one-way, we'd never had. I must have sat there massaging his beautiful, long, pale feet for twenty minutes; then, fearing I'd overstayed my time, I stood up and got halfway to the door when a weak voice that seemed to come from far away said: "Don't stop." He had been awake all along!

There were the times I'd sit by his bedside looking at him, his eyes closed, wondering if he was

Dad blowing out his seventy-seventh-birthday candles at home. Left to right: me, Tom, Shirlee, Troy, and Vanessa.
(© Suzanne Tenner)

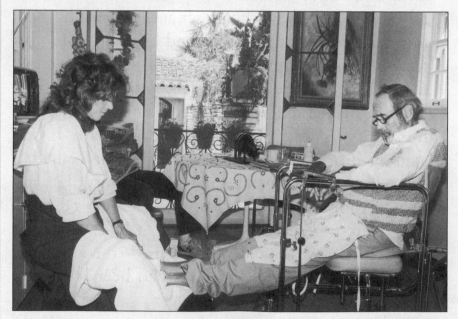

Dad loved me to rub his feet.
(© Suzanne Tenner)

asleep or just avoiding talking to me. I wanted to ask him if he was in pain, if he'd seen any angels yet, if he could see to the other side, if he was scared. I never did. Shirlee hadn't allowed any of us to admit he wasn't going to get better, so we all went around pretending he'd be up and about in no time. I hated it. It all rang so false, but I felt I had to honor her wishes; it was she, after all, who was living through this with him night and day, being the loving caretaker. But I often wondered if it was Dad who needed to believe this or Shirlee. Personally I'd rather know when the jig is almost up so as to be intentional about that last kiss, that final "I love you." But that's just me.

Perhaps it didn't matter and my desire to communicate with him was futile. After all, how could I expect him to do something he'd never done, be someone he'd never been, now at the end? How could I talk to him about feelings now, when it was almost over? Yet I knew he had feelings. I'd seen him laugh hard when he was with his men friends or when he'd had a drink or two. I saw him cry, once—the day Roosevelt died. He was standing in his vegetable garden, and I was very little, and he never saw me there watching.

Another day I went to his home and found him sitting in a chair in his room with a lap rug over his knees. He had been moved into the same downstairs back room where I had lived during the time when I was morphing from Barbarella into an activist, causing him so much angst. From the window he could look out onto his beloved vegetable garden. Shirlee was away on an errand, and I realized that I might not get another chance to tell him how I felt.

I sat at his feet and told him that I loved him very much; that although things had not always been good or easy between us, I knew he had done his best to be a good father; that I loved him for it and was sorry for things I had done that had hurt him. I also told him how much I appreciated the way Shirlee looked after him—above and beyond the call of duty; all the nurses said they'd never seen a wife like her—and that no matter what, we would always consider her a part of our family and would keep her close. I don't remember him saying anything, but he began to cry. I didn't know if it meant he was moved because I had spoken of love and forgiveness or if my words showed him that I knew he was dying and that perhaps this was the first time anyone had said these closure words to him.

There is a saying that we all repeat often to explain our family members' readiness to tear up over silly things: "Fondas cry at a good steak." It's one thing to get teary over a good steak and another to weep from the depths of your heart—that display of emotion was what my father always hated, because he felt it showed weakness. Except for when Roosevelt died, I had not seen him cry from that deep place, and I hurt for him and was scared of this display of his pain and sadness. I stayed for a while in an effort to comfort him but then had to leave because I could sense that he hated to be crying in front of me. Shirlee told me that when she got home a little later she found him still in the chair, sobbing.

Then one morning Shirlee called me to come quickly to the hospital. I prayed I would get there while he was still alive, but he had died three minutes before. It doesn't matter how long a loved one has been near death, when it finally comes you never feel prepared. I wanted to sit by his bed and look at him for a long time. I **needed** to look at what there was, now that his soul had left, and to think about that. I needed closure. But the nurse officiously asked us all to leave the room so they could clean him up.

I went home and picked up Tom and the kids and we all drove to Dad's house to be with Shirlee. The press was already gathered outside their Bel-Air driveway, interviewing friends as they came to pay their respects. Slowly they gathered: Jimmy Stewart, Eva Marie Saint, Mel Ferrer, Dad's very first leading lady from Omaha, Dorothy McGuire, Joel Grey, James Garner, Lucille Ball, Barbara Stanwyck. My brother and his wife, Becky, came, with his daughter, Bridget, and son, Justin.

That first afternoon, when the house was crowded and everyone was in deep shock trying to wrap their minds around the reality that he was gone from us, I remember sitting in the study across from Jimmy Stewart. On his way in he had told the press, "I've just lost my best friend." He had been sitting across from me with his head hanging down for several hours, without saying a word, when a movement from his direction caught my attention. Jimmy was

The faces of my father that I loved: center is Norman
Thayer, clockwise from bottom left: Abraham Lincoln,
Tom Joad, Gil Carter (**Ox-Bow Incident**), **Mr. Roberts,**
Juror #8 (**12 Angry Men**), Clarence Darrow.
(Photofest)

lifting his arms up over his head and it dawned on me that he was remembering the kite that he and my dad had once made together, and he was trying to describe its enormity. I remembered Dad telling us the story of this kite when he and Jimmy were in their late twenties in California. Jimmy didn't seem to be talking to anyone in particular; he wasn't even paying attention to see if anyone was listening. He was just totally wrapped up in his memory: "It was so big . . . this big"—his arms went higher and his hands wider—"and . . . and"—Jimmy was always a stammerer—"when it caught the wind, it pulled me off the ground." He smiled. Then his arms came down and he was again silent. Those of us in the room looked at one another, understanding what a unique and deep loss this was for Jimmy. He seemed to enjoy it when I got him to reminisce about the days in New York during the Depression when the two of them had lived on rice.

I sat for a while next to the man who had been Dad's makeup artist for many years. He told me how much Dad talked about me, worried about me. "You can't imagine how much he talked about you."

Funny, I thought, how Dad talked to others **about** me but never directly **to** me, unless there was a problem. And I wondered if maybe I wasn't guilty of this with regard to my own children.

Not having been able to mourn my mother's death, and never again wanting to have internal tears that can't come out, I made a conscious decision that I would allow myself to experience fully Dad's passing. I moved into the house with Shirlee and did not leave for a week. For days people kept coming by to pay their respects. We'd sit together and watch his eulogies on television—all week they went on. It hit me that this wasn't just my loss, the family's loss. It was a national loss. Dad was a public figure, a hero, who didn't belong just to us. Dad lived out these quintessential American values. He represented things that we all want to be and that the **country** wanted to be. He often said he was attracted to certain kinds of roles—the working poor, powerless people, and the men who helped them get some power for themselves—because somehow their characters might rub off on him and he would become a better person. But now I saw that there had been a dialectic; he **did** have many of those qualities.

One of the things I learned during that time was how courtesies matter. I had often not written to people I knew when they had lost a loved one, because I didn't really know what to say. Now I was seeing that just getting a letter, whether articulate or not, matters; it lets you know that the person is mourning with you, countenancing your pain. There were two letters especially important to me; one was from Carl Dean, Dolly Parton's husband, who wrote movingly of his admiration for my father; the other was from Gary Cooper's daughter, Maria, who spoke of the complexities of dealing with the loss of a father who was also a national hero.

I spent a lot of time in Dad's garden during those days of mourning, sitting under one of his fruit trees sorting out my feelings. While I still had a long way to go, in hindsight I see that this was a first step in my learning to be still, to **be** and not to **do**. I was grateful for having had **On Golden Pond** with him and that I'd managed to tell him I loved him before it was too late. I could feel myself making peace with the fact that though he hadn't given me all I had needed from him, he'd given me plenty. I somehow sensed that now that he was gone, some part of me would be able to come into its own, though I couldn't quite put my finger on what it would be. I was sad that at his request there would be no memorial service, that he would be cremated but never buried. I like graves, always have. They give a tangible presence to the spiritual realm. I knew that there would be times when having a gravestone to sit by and touch would make it easier to remember and communicate with him. But it wasn't my decision to make. This was when I decided I wanted to be buried with a gravestone, where my kids and grandkids could come and lay down their heads.

I don't think we can fully live until we have come to terms with our mortality. My friend Fred Branfman calls it "life-affirming death awareness." There's something far worse than death, I think, and that is to not really **live**.

I learned from watching Dad die that it is not death I fear as much as it is dying with unresolved regrets about things not done. This realization is determining how I am living my third act. If I want Vanessa to have sweet dreams, I have to work on that now, and I am. If I want to leave my family stronger for my having lived, that is also something I have to work on—now.

It is possible that the words I quoted at the start of this chapter, spoken by my father in **The Grapes of Wrath,** are what determined early on my feelings about an afterlife. Flesh and bone are temporal, but I believe that our souls, the twenty-one grams of weight we are said to lose the moment we die, become part of the "one big soul that belongs to everybody." Our energy is born into the future, in the bodies of our children and loved ones. I have felt it. My father has come to me in dreams, stepping out from behind a bush, radiantly happy, to tell me not to worry about him. I see him in Vanessa's talent at composting and growing things. I have watched Troy onstage turn and say a line with a certain inflection, and I realize it is my father—yet Dad died when Troy was a little boy. I see it in the commitment my children and I have to justice. In these ways my father lives on.

CHAPTER TWENTY

MAKING MOVIES

A lawyer and the doctor **practice** their callings. The plumber and the carpenter **know** what they will be called upon to do. They do not have to spin their work out of themselves, discover its laws, and then present themselves turned inside out to the public gaze.

—ANNE TRUITT,
Daybook, the Journal of an Artist

Grandma, what a great job you have! You get paid for using your imagination.

—JOHN R. SEYDEL,
my eleven-year-old stepgrandson

PLAYING DRUNK had always frightened me. If there was even a short scene in a movie where I had to be tipsy, I dreaded it. That's why I decided to do **The Morning After,** a murder mystery about a heavy drinker who blacks out and finds a dead body in her bed. For that role I had to be perpetually drunk. Well, I thought, at this stage in my life why not try to do the things I fear the most? Mustn't get soggy. Besides, we got Sidney Lumet to direct and the superb Jeff Bridges to co-star. Bruce produced **The Morning After,** and the associate producer was Lois Bonfiglio, who would soon become my new partner.

As I write this I realize that I've done a good deal of thinking about acting in the fifteen-year hiatus I have taken, and I'd like to try to give you a sense of what it's like, at least for me.

In most films there is a scene when the main character is going through a critical transition or defining event. Whether or not the story works often depends on the success of that scene. Sometimes the director will want to shoot it in one long take, with the camera following you as you move from place to place, hitting your marks, all the while making the emotional transitions. This delicate balance between technical and emotional demands is the hallmark of movie acting.

I would usually wake up the morning of the critical scene feeling queasy, with a knot in my belly. I'd arrive at the studio for makeup and hair, and at some point I'd be asked to stop what I was doing and come to the set for rehearsal. **Should I give it my all?** There is the risk that if I do, I won't have anything left when the real time comes (as was the case in my big scene in **On Golden Pond**). On the other hand, the purpose of rehearsal is to discover what my moves will be so that the lights can be set and the camera will know where to follow me; and if I don't dip fairly deep into the emotional waters during rehearsal, how will I know where I'm apt to go? So I rehearse and pray that I've given just enough, but not too much.

Rehearsal now over, I go back to my trailer to finish hair and makeup and then wait while the crew lights the set and practices camera moves with my stand-in. It can be a thirty-minute wait or an hour or, if it's a complicated setup, three hours. What to do? Do I read a book or get into a conversation that might risk taking me too far away from where my emotions are meant to be? Do I just sit here and think about the scene and risk getting too much into my head? The challenge is knowing myself well enough to calibrate correctly the balance between physical relaxation and emotional alertness that will most benefit me during the one- to three-hour wait. But it's hard not to feel like a balloon from which air is slowly leaking.

Then the moment comes. The knock on the door: "We're ready, Miss Fonda." Truthfully some small part of me (which I would try to ignore) has hoped that the sound stage would catch fire or the director would have a breakdown so that this moment could be postponed—for a year, maybe. But, no, there's the knock. No going back now. So I step out of my trailer and begin the endless walk to where everyone is waiting, all one hundred people who work on a film on any given day. As I run the gauntlet, the issue of my salary comes to mind. **Why didn't I agree to do the damn thing for free? I know there are people on the set who are just waiting to see if I'm worth all that dough, like that guy over there on the ladder reading the** Sports Illustrated **swimsuit issue.** I remember being told that shooting on an average Hollywood film costs in the neighborhood of $100,000 a day. **If this goes badly, maybe I can offer to deduct it from my salary; otherwise I may never get hired again. Please let me stay relaxed, help me stay in my truth, tell my muse to be with me now.** I arrive on the set that just a short while ago during rehearsal was a place of forgiving shadows. Now it's a pitiless glare of light under which my possible disintegration will be exposed for all to see. **Breathe deeply, Jane. Get out of your head and into your body . . . quiet the demon voice that is trying to tell you that today is the day you'll be exposed as an overpaid fraud.**

This is the part of film acting that I was only too happy to leave behind, the part that became more agonizing as time went on. Yet you have to go through those terrifying times if you are ever to have the magic ones, the times when it all works—and to be truthful, those I have missed. There were perhaps only eight or nine of them out of forty-five films, but they were the times when I stepped into my light and my muse **was** with me, all my channels were open, the creative flow coursed through my body, and I **became.** Whether the scene was sad or funny, tragic or triumphant, never mattered. When it worked it was like being enveloped in love and light, as I danced the intricate dance between technique and emotion, fully inside the scene while simultaneously a separate part of me observed and enjoyed the unfolding.

Ah, but just because it has happened once doesn't mean it will again! Each time is starting new, raw; it's a crapshoot—you just never know. Which is why this profession is so great for the heart—and so hard on the nerves.

I always assumed that the more you did something the easier it would get, but in the case of my career I found the opposite to be true. Every year the work seemed to get harder and my fear more paralyzing. Once, on the set of **Old Gringo,** I watched Gregory Peck late in his career doing a long, very difficult scene over and over again all day long. I saw that he too was scared. I went up to him afterward and hugged him and told him how beautiful and transparent he had been.

"But, Greg," I asked, "why do we do this to ourselves? Especially you. You've had a long and incredible career. You could easily retire. Why are you still willing to be scared?"

Greg sat for a moment, rubbing his chin. Then

At the Cannes
Film Festival for
Old Gringo with
Gregory Peck.

With Kris Kristofferson
in **Rollover**.
(Photofest)

he said, "Well, Jane, maybe it's like my friend Walter Matthau says. His biggest thrill in life is to be gambling and losing a bit more than he can afford and then have one chance to win it all back. That's what you live for—that moment. The crapshoot. If it's easy, what's the point?"

Looking back, I sometimes think I enjoyed the story meetings more than the acting. With acting you're on your own; with script meetings you're part of a group. I never liked being number one. Co–number one worked for me; but when the burden of creativity rested exclusively on my shoulders, I would freeze—and echoes of the doors of creativity clanging shut were almost audible. What I like best is working with a group of people who share a vision and are able to set aside their egos—people you trust, who respect one another. I hated it when I thought that just because I was the star people were kowtowing, telling me my ideas were good even if they weren't. With Bruce, and later with Lois Bonfiglio and most of the writers and directors we worked with, I felt free to express an idea, knowing that if it wasn't good, they would let me know and we'd move on. I remember exhilarating script meetings when one person would have an idea, and that in turn would stimulate another idea from someone else, and that might lead to a sudden breakthrough in a scene, with everyone having placed a building block in the process but with no one having an overweening ego stake in any of it; it was the final product that mattered. I would have missed this sort of creative collaboration, except that I have found it in my life as an activist.

Actually it's not unusual for actors to suffer from self-doubt. Our profession feeds insecurity. Success and fame can come so fast and in this business can go just as fast. It takes stability and maturity to handle it. It's not like most other professions, where you go to college and then medical school, for instance, then years of internship—and at the end you're a doctor and no one can take those years away from you. There is no license or diploma that certifies that you are a for-real actor with the talent to bring a character to life. If you make it as an actor, suddenly there you are—and you don't exactly know why; why you and not her?

I tried never to get too used to the perks because I knew they might not last. But it was hard because the perks are addictive. There's the comfort of knowing that when you wake up you will roll into a waiting car and be driven to a predetermined place. Then you go into a trailer or a dressing room where someone puts on your makeup, someone else does your hair, and yet a third person lays out the clothes you are to wear that day. You don't have to make any choices. Your **identity** is all taken care of, what you're supposed to think, feel, and say that day are determined by the pages you are given, and your only responsibility is to bring them to life (that's the hard part—the part you're paid for). At the day's end you take it all off, get driven back home, and are usually forgiven for being so tired that you collapse into bed—only to do it all again the next day.

For three months you are absolved of all responsibility except to bring your character alive. But then suddenly the shooting ends and it's **Who am I? Oh God, I have to start making decisions.** It's like morphing backward, like a film running in reverse. We step outside the circle of light and move from whoever we have temporarily become into the shadowy persona of who we were **before**—the "real" **us,** the one who has dogs that crap on the floor, kids that let her know her time-out is over and that she'd better show up for them and make up for lost time, and has a husband who doesn't say it but leaks resentment at her exciting absences. It's hard; at least it was for me. I was always an emotional noodle after a film, feeling as if I needed a halfway house where I could exhale all the accumulated **stuff** from three months of living in a protective bubble. But there is no such place if you have a family. You **have** to try to reconnect with husband and kids and pick up life where you left off: straightening up, doing laundry, driving kids to school, sitting in the bleachers watching Little League games with other moms, buying the groceries—the mechanical stuff. After a while the normalcy of the daily routine itself would get me back on track. Routine is what I cling to when the abyss beckons. But the pendulum swing from fantasy to everyday reality is dizzying, and it takes a healthy, grounded spirit to do it well.

In 1980 Tom launched a fierce, expensive two-year campaign for the California State Assembly. My last film before I took a hiatus to work on the campaign and grow the Workout business was **Rollover,** another project that Bruce and I undertook together. Inspired by the book **The Crash of '79,** the story told of secret financial manipulations between an American banker and the Saudis, ending with the collapse of the U.S. economy. The late seventies, when we began to develop the script, was a time when the price of Arab oil was so high, the OPEC alliance so powerful, and our dependence on Saudi oil so great that economic blackmail—moving oil overnight from a dollar-denominated commodity to a gold-denominated commodity—was a possibility. We wanted to call attention to the perils of U.S. dependency on Arab oil, and it dovetailed with our organizational work to shift America's sources of energy to alternatives like solar and wind. With **9 to 5** we had cloaked the tough issues that office workers faced in comedy's softening mantle; with **Coming Home** we used a love story; **The China Syndrome** was a thriller; and **Rollover** was a combination murder mystery/love story. It was my third film with director Alan Pakula. My co-star was the chiseled, gravel-voiced actor/singer/songwriter Kris Kristofferson. I have to chuckle at the thought that Kris and I played important figures in the world of high finance. I can barely read a profit-and-loss statement, and Kris . . . well, let's just say that a man who hitchhiked across the country in the 1960s with Janis Joplin and wrote "freedom's just another word for nothing left to lose" is not by nature someone who wants to cozy up to mezzanine financing or interest rate swaps. An interesting, complicated man, Kris— a onetime Rhodes Scholar who worked on an oil rig off the coast of Texas, who cares deeply about injustice, and who captured angst the way few other songwriters ever have. It was fun working with someone who, like me, had a life beyond movies.

This was when Nathalie Vadim came back into my life. She was working as a script supervisor in Paris, but I sensed that she needed a change of scenery so I arranged for her to work on **Rollover** as the third assistant director. By then Nathalie was twenty-one years old, lean and lanky, with an appealing, gaminlike beauty; she took to her new job with a professionalism and presence that impressed everyone. The assistant director liked her so much that he hired her for many of his subsequent films and she quickly moved up to second assistant and for the next ten years had a solid career in Hollywood.

In 1982 Tom won his election for the California State Assembly with a healthy nine-point margin. He served his district with integrity for seventeen years—working on behalf of working women and mothers, for child care, workplace safety, and affordable housing; against pollution; to improve the public education system. He spearheaded the Proposition 65 campaign to keep toxins out of California's drinking water, and I assembled busloads of celebrity warriors who helped with the tough but ultimately successful battle. Prop 65 continues today as a substantial safeguard for Californians.

With the campaign over, I returned to acting in a role that is one of my favorites: Gertie Nevels, in **The Dollmaker,** the one Dolly Parton helped me prepare for. If you think of emotions as muscles, then approaching a new role is like entering a new sport: You bring to it the muscles you use habitually. **Anger? Oh yeah, I know what that muscle feels like**—but not everyone expresses anger the same way. The truth is, all during the eleven years Bruce and I fought to bring **The Dollmaker** to life there was a small, scared part of me that hoped it wouldn't happen, because I doubted I had the right muscles to inhabit her. What would Gertie's anger look like? If you are lucky enough to have a good director, he or she gets you to shift to a new set of "anger" muscles, often ones you didn't know you had. It feels awkward at first; you get sore, but then you fall into it as if it's what you've always done.

For me **The Dollmaker** is an archetypal fable that tells of Gertie, her husband, and their five children as they live a hard but value-rich life on a farm in the Appalachian Mountains of Kentucky, where her husband works in the coal mine. In contrast with the fundamentalist, fire-and-brimstone fear-based Christianity of her mother (played by Geraldine Page), Gertie sees Christ as a joyous, forgiving, laughing figure. She wants to carve his laughing face into a block of cherrywood. The family is uprooted when the mines close and is forced to move to the squalid, consumer-driven, buy-on-credit world of wartime Detroit, where men like her husband hope to find jobs in the factories. In the tacky workers' housing, in the shadow of a steel mill, Gertie finds consolation carving her Jesus on the block of cherrywood.

We developed **The Dollmaker** for television, and I was fascinated by the differences between film and television. For one thing television is a writer's medium, whereas film is a director's medium. With film you sit in a darkened theater with nothing else going on, looking up at the huge screen, moved as much by evocative images and camera angles as by the words. Often in films the essence of the story is conveyed visually. Television, on the other hand, is a cozy medium. You're at home in your living room or in bed, looking at a little box, far less aware of the visual impact than you are the dialogue. This is why, often in television, the writers are also the producers—and have more power than they do in movies. And since with television you don't have to wait for just the right cloud formation or the perfect lighting effect to fill a huge screen, a TV movie can be shot in a matter of weeks, whereas a feature film usually takes three months. This came as a shock to me when we began shooting **The Dollmaker.** Scenes I had imagined and labored over for years—like the opening, where Gertie, riding a mule and carrying

The star-studded Clean Water Caravan in support of Proposition 65, with Dweezil Zappa, Linda Gray, Bobby Walden, Victoria Principal, Ed Begley, Jr., Joanna Kerns, Patricia Duff, LeVar Burton, Charlie Haid, Tyne Daly, Georg Stanford Brown, Troy, Moon Zappa, Bonnie Bedelia, Shari Belafonte, Linda Evans, Daphne Zuniga, among others.
(© 1986 Michael Jacobs/MJP)

As Gertie Nevels in
The Dollmaker.
(© Steve Schapiro)

her ill infant son, stops a car and performs a tracheotomy on him in the glare of the car's headlights on the side of the road—would take a week to complete in a film. We shot it in a day!

This didn't keep **The Dollmaker** from being one of the most joyous acting experiences of my career. Our director—the nurturing, supportive, sensitive Dan Petrie—hovered like an angel over it all.

Petrie once told a film class of his that after my last shot he turned to me and said, "Well, Miss Fonda, it's a wrap," and I broke down and sobbed for a long time while he held me.

"I tried to analyze later why those tears," Dan told the class. "Why racking sobs? It was because of the death of the character, of somebody that she had invested so much time in and lavished so much love on." Yes, I had tapped into the Gertie part of me and it was hard to let go. I loved her so.

I think most of us have many personas inside us at the outset, but over time we lean to the one that is dominant and the others atrophy for lack of use. The difference with actors is that we are paid to **become** all the people inside us and to bring **into** us all the people we may have met along the way. Thus we remain instinctively aware of, unsettled by, curious about, empathetic toward, and eager to display all those potential beings we carry. Of all these, the empathy part is the most important and is, I believe, why actors—the good ones—tend to be open, progressive creatures: We are asked to get inside the skin of "other," to feel with "other," to understand "other." Being able to see from this "other" point of view gives actors compassion. Is that why artists have little tolerance for dictators, even those disguised as patriots? Because dictators abhor the variables in human nature, the very things artists cherish.

The Dollmaker aired on ABC on Mother's Day 1984, and I learned something else about television that day: I knew exactly what time my film would show, and as the time approached I found myself wanting to go up to everyone I saw on the street and say, "What are you doing? You should be going home to watch this movie." Lots of people did see it, and for many it is their favorite of my films. I won an Emmy for it.

By the mid-eighties Tom was in the state legislature and I was in emotional limbo, plowing through life by sheer force of will (of which I have an abundance), but willpower can be anathema to creativity. Creativity requires a looseness, a letting go, an openness that allows the psyche to plumb the moist depths where the stuff of dreams and myths percolate. On the other hand, the I-will-get-that-done-I-will-remain-married-I-will-be-perfect-I-will-not-express-my-needs mode of living means existing in a contracted body with shallow breath and nothing to nourish the spirit—"No wild and unheard-of melodies / No tunes that rise from the blood / no blood calling from the deep places," as poet Rainer Maria Rilke put it.

Without "blood calling from the deep places," my work that followed **The Dollmaker—Agnes of God, The Morning After, Old Gringo,** and finally **Stanley and Iris**—became harder and harder, although there were moments in all of them that I cherish.

I just didn't want to be doing it anymore. It was too agonizing. I was experiencing creative disintegration, and I didn't understand that my inability to be honest about the disintegration of my long marriage, the shutting down of my body, **and** my feeling totally responsible for it all was slowly draining me of life. I remember sitting in my hotel room in Toronto, where I was making **Stanley and Iris,** and thinking, What will I do with my life? What is there for me? I saw only a joyless road ahead, and I couldn't admit that it was because there was no future in the marriage. It was inconceivable to me that my couplehood with Tom wasn't going to be forever. Leaving would be a sign of defeat, and defeat was not an option. Besides, without Tom what would I be?

He asked, "Do you love me?" and when I answered, "Yes," he asked me to write him a letter telling why. Once I'd finished the part about his being a wonderful father, I got stuck. Why couldn't I think of reasons for loving him? Why did my hand want to write only the anger?

My wonderful, loyal, always intelligent body kept desperately sending me signals by repeatedly attracting mishaps the way abandoned bodies do: **Pay attention to me, listen to me.** This hadn't happened

Jimmy Smits,
Gregory Peck,
and me in **Old
Gringo.**
(Mary Ellen Mark)

**With director
Sidney Lumet
on the set of
The Morning
After.**

to me since my injury-prone days in Greenwich when my mother and father's marriage was delaminating. When I ignored my body's signals I was paid back in broken bones: fingers, ribs, feet. On his desk Tom kept a photo of me that he'd taken when I broke my collarbone. When I broke my nose in a biking spill during the filming of **Stanley and Iris** he wanted a photo of that as well. Maybe he liked me better broken.

I **was** broken—sexless and fallow. I think it is when people have lost touch with their spirit, their life force, that they become most vulnerable to consumer culture and the toxic drive for perfection. Instead of dealing with my crisis in a real way, I got breast implants. I am ashamed of this, but I understand why I did it at the time. I somehow believed that if I **looked** more womanly, I would **become** more womanly. So much of my life had become a façade; what did it matter if I added my body to the list of falsehoods?

It was for **me** that I did it. In fairness, Tom was adamantly opposed. Here was the woman who had once impressed him by crying in empathy for the Vietnamese women who had mutilated their bodies to conform to a **Playboy** image of femininity and now she was doing the same thing to herself. I knew when I did it that I was betraying myself, but my self had shrunk to the size of a thimble.

With Robert De Niro in Stanley and Iris.
(© Steve Schapiro)

CHAPTER TWENTY-ONE

THE GIFT OF PAIN

No phoenix can arise from no ashes.
—MARION WOODMAN,
Leaving My Father's House

O N   T H E   N I G H T I turned fifty-one Tom announced to me that he was in love with another woman.

The bottom dropped out of life with a devastation so abrupt and severe that my very existence appeared as a foreign landscape. I felt as though I had
just learned I was adopted. Oddly enough I hadn't
seen it coming.

It happened during Christmas 1988. We were all
in Aspen, Colorado: Troy, Vanessa, Lulu, Nathalie,
Tom, and me, sharing a small rented condo. I didn't
want to spoil everyone's vacation, so I said nothing—
stiff upper lip and all that. So as not to let on there

was trouble, I'd wait till everyone had gone to bed and then I'd lie on the living room couch alternately sobbing and reading a novel by Amos Oz.

Never in my life could I have imagined surviving such emotional pain or known that it would assume an **actual physical presence.** I felt blood oozing through the pores of my skin; the pain of a dagger being turned in my heart that now weighed a hundred pounds—allowing me for the first time to understand the meaning of "heavy heart." I was unable to speak above a whisper for almost a month, or to move swiftly or to swallow food. My throat closed in on itself. Back in Los Angeles, my friend Paula offered me a massage but I fled from the table, unable to stand being touched, unworthy of pleasure. I had been nothing'd.

Given what I have written about the deterioration of our marriage and our lack of communication, you may be wondering why Tom's blurted admission affected me so deeply. It opened some old, primal rupture, exposing me to an onslaught of pain and grief that went way beyond the end of a troubled marriage.

I don't think Tom expected it to be the end. I think he believed, as did others, that I had known all along of his infidelities and didn't really mind. Maybe some part of me **did** know. Maybe that's why anger would well up when we made love.

I felt overwhelming shame. I didn't tell anyone for several weeks, not even Paula. When I finally did tell her, she took me in. For more than a week I lived with her and her husband, Mark Rosenberg, in their house on Wadsworth Avenue, right down from where Tom and I had spent over ten years. I didn't have the strength to ask Tom to move out.

When I finally did decide to call it quits months later, I went back to my house, gathered all of Tom's belongings into large plastic bags, and threw them out the window into the garden. That helped . . . a little.

But not much. This was so new for me. I had always been the strong one, the Lone Ranger, never blindsided by a pain so profound that my customary arsenal of self-protection was rendered inoperable. The terrain was so unfamiliar that I was unhinged from all my moorings. I would set out for the market and have to pull off the road because my body would be so racked with sobs that I couldn't drive. I would step outside and wonder why the sun was shining, astonished by this undeniable proof of nature's indifference. The robin's-egg-blue sky, unchanged from yesterday, gave an acute sense of permanence to the idea of going forward alone. Death loomed so vividly that I remember insisting it be stipulated in my divorce settlement that Tom not be allowed to speak at my funeral. (I was convinced that he would opportunistically try to do so and couldn't imagine that we would ever again be close enough friends to justify it.)

It wasn't **him** I missed as much as an amorphous **us**, the "usness" that celebrated every Easter at the ranch with two hundred of our friends, me dressed up as the Easter bunny, the egg hunts, hay rides, hymn singing, and square dancing; the "usness" that went to Dodgers games with Troy and his buddies from Little League; the "usness" that had, I felt, helped end the war. Usness was gone. And I was fifty-one years old.

Later I realized that both Troy and Vanessa had known the marriage was troubled; but if Tom and I were unable to talk to each other about what was happening, we certainly weren't able to talk to the children, and they didn't feel able to initiate the discussion. Vanessa would try to open a dialogue through her anger, but when she did I would shut down. Troy was fifteen and Vanessa twenty when we told them we were separating.

Vanessa was in Africa, working together with Nathalie on a television movie that Vadim was directing. She was acting as language coach, still photographer, and assistant director. I wasn't sure what to do. I was unaccustomed to reaching out and asking for help. I didn't want to burden her or disrupt her work, and I also felt so ashamed. Here I'd gone and failed again. But as soon as I told Paula what had happened, she said, "You have to call Vanessa right away. She absolutely needs to know." Her saying this allowed me to acknowledge how desperately I needed Vanessa with me. Within days she was home, and this meant more to me than she will ever know.

Vanessa had never particularly liked Tom—or rather she didn't like what she saw me becoming with Tom: giving up myself to suit him (they have subsequently become good friends). Confronted with my sadness, however, I remember her saying (mostly to herself), "Be careful what you wish for." It was her way of expressing both her own long held hopes that I would leave him and her empathy for me.

She also said, "Maybe now you can spend more time with your women friends who Tom chased away."

"He did?" I asked, wanting now to know truths that I'd not been able to receive before.

"Mom," Vanessa said, rolling her eyes heavenward in disdain at my inability to see what everyone knew. "Lois, Julie, Paula—why do you think they haven't come around much? Tom doesn't like them and they know it. He was always putting you down, too, but **you** didn't know it."

Tom moved to Santa Monica into a rented apartment with a room for Troy, and that's where Troy mostly stayed. This struck terror in my heart: Was he choosing Tom over me? Was I going to lose my son? But today he explains his decision: "I could see that Dad needed me more than you did. He was in bad shape." He was right.

I remember asking a friend what I should say to Troy about the breakup and being told, "Say what you feel."

Say what I feel! If nothing else, I knew I couldn't do that. Think of every angry, damning, never-to-be-forgotten word you could call somebody you wanted to murder, and that will give you some idea of what I **felt**. I couldn't foist that onto my son. A small voice inside was telling me that when the roller-coaster ride was over, my anger would subside and I'd see it was for the best and be grateful that Tom had been the catalyst to end it (which **is** what happened, but it took two years). I spent a lot of time thinking how awful it is for children to become the battleground between warring ex-spouses and how much self-control and maturity it takes to keep a lid on things. Yet I didn't want to do what my parents had done and what I'd done with Nathalie when I left her father—not show emotion, not encourage a discussion of what was happening that would create a space for them to express their feelings. The trick was to try to do it without anger. Sadness, yes, but not anger.

So I allowed Troy and Vanessa to see me cry, but at the same time I made sure to let them know that a split was a two-way street and that I was partly to blame, which I knew to be true. I talked to them about the primary lesson I was learning from it all: the need to communicate, to recognize feelings, and to express them. Tom and I really didn't let each other know what we were feeling. Maybe he didn't try hard enough, or maybe I didn't try hard enough or didn't want to hear, or maybe the marriage was meant to be resonant only for a certain period of time (it was—for seven years) and unintentionally we were both looking for ways out.

The comedy **The Seven Year Itch** was onto something, and it's about much more than sex. According to science, all our cells change every seven years. The Bible is also full of significant sevens ("**On the seventh day . . .**"). And it seems that people go through major psychic transitions every seven or so years and therein lies the rub: What if a couple's transitions don't mesh? That's when choices have to be made: We can part, we can remain together on different wavelengths and do our best, or we can try to understand each other's transitions and work to make them compatible. Tom's and my wavelengths had grown too distant. After sixteen years, not knowing how to make our differences compatible, we parted.

My friends told me to stay busy. I knew that was wrong for me. Busy was what I'd been—busy and inside my own head. Now for the first time I was in a situation where **who** I was and **how** I was used to functioning were no longer valid. Therefore I had to allow everything to reorganize, not on a cognitive level (since I was, quite literally, out of my mind) but somatically, on a cellular level. For this to happen, I knew unconsciously that I needed to be very still and allow myself to witness what was happening and **feel** it.

I surrounded myself with loving women friends and classical music. My home became a haven. I knew that I needed all the endorphins my body could muster, so I forced myself to keep working out and took marathon bike rides and hikes with women friends.

Through the pain I could tell that something new was happening to me. Trauma was creating an opening in my psyche. I needed to pay attention, to be ready to step through and descend into it, whatever **it** was. **It** felt archetypal. Something in me was being slain in the fires of pain so that some new thing could be born. I knew it and went with it, and in the alchemy of my pain, like flowers whose seeds open only in the presence of fire, tendrils of something new began to sprout. Pain for me was a Trojan horse, penetrating the protective walls I'd erected around my heart, bearing within it hints of a future I might never have awakened to had I tried to numb myself with busyness.

One day I heard myself say out loud, "If God wanted me to suffer like this, there must be a reason." God? I looked around. **Did I just say God?** Never had such a thought come into my head. I'm an atheist, right? But the moment I said it, the texture of my pain changed ever so slightly. It became easier to be patient, giving myself over to . . . what? I didn't know, but I was so weakened that it was easy to let myself go limp and just **be**.

Ever so slowly, over the months, a membrane began to cover the heart wound, and I could tentatively begin to cross the abyss without falling in. In psychologist Marion Woodman's **Leaving My Father's House** I read: "When humans suffer they are vulnerable. Within this vulnerability lives the humility that allows flesh to soften into the sounds of the soul." Maybe this was what was happening to me. I felt lighter, as if a space had been cleared around me allowing coincidences (**God's way of remaining**

anonymous) to manifest. Maybe these coincidences had been happening all along and I just hadn't been open to them. Now it was as though I were being led to them.

For example, there was the way I came to find a therapist. While Tom and I were still living in Ocean Park, at the end of our little street a house was torn down and rebuilt. This was the house that Paula and her husband, Mark, moved into. Then one day about two weeks after Tom and I split up, I was bike riding along the beach with Julie Lafond, and as we passed Wadsworth she pointed to that very house and said, "The therapist who saved my marriage owns that house and has her office in the basement."

Well, thought I, who was holding back from going into therapy because I worried I wouldn't find "the right one," **This may be a sign: I've just been staying there with my best friend, I saw it being built, it's on my old street, and the therapist who owns it saved my other friend's marriage.** I called up that very afternoon and made an appointment.

It was a fortuitous coincidence that led me to a female professional I would talk to once a week over the ensuing two years. She set me on a path of self-reflection and, after retiring, referred me to the therapist who would make a life-altering difference.

Then there was the psychic (hey, therapists, psychics—why not cover all bases?) who told me I would begin writing: "Writing and writing—and what you write will be important to women." That's when I began the journal writing that has helped with this book.

Over the following months, awash in what felt like miracles, surrounded by the love of my children and women friends, I could feel myself growing stronger. The sense of being led remained. The dark, empty space inside was beginning to fill with Spirit. I was entering my body, and I could feel a quickening.

CHAPTER TWENTY-TWO

PHOENIX ON HOLD

For everything there is a season
And a time for every matter under heaven:
A time to be born, and a time to die

—ECCLESIASTES 3:1–2

IT WASN'T TIME YET. The ashes were there, the Phoenix was beginning to rise, the Spirit was beginning to fill me. But my ego wasn't strong enough yet to contain it. A large part of me still panicked at going forward without a man.

The day after my divorce was announced in the papers, the phone rang. Someone yelled, "Jane, there's a Ted Turner on the phone for you." Ted Turner? I'd met him once with Tom at a screening of a documentary about child abuse that his Turner Broadcasting System was going to run. He's probably calling to offer me a job, I thought as I picked up the phone.

Suddenly a voice boomed through the phone so loudly that I had to hold the receiver away from my ear.

"Is it true?"

"Is what true?" I thought it was an odd way to start a phone conversation with a virtual stranger.

"Are you and Hayden really getting a divorce?"

"Yes." I was still in the throes of depression and unable to speak above a whisper.

"Well then, would you like to go out with me?"

I was dumbstruck. Dating was the furthest thing from my mind. "To tell you the truth, I can't even think about dating right now. I can hardly even speak. I think I'm having an emotional breakdown. Why don't you call me back in three months?"

"Hey, I know just how you feel." I could tell he was trying to modulate his voice to approximate compassion and that this was hard for him. "I just broke up with my mistress," he went on. "I wrecked my whole family and my marriage two years ago to go and live with her, so now I'm having a hard time myself."

It occurred to me that this was just about the most inappropriate thing a man could say to a woman who had just been dumped by her husband of sixteen years for **his** mistress. Didn't it occur to him that it would be his **wife** I'd identify with, not **him? This is one strange guy,** I thought.

But what I said to him was, "Call back in three months, when I'm feeling better. Okay?" He said he would do that, and we hung up. Whatever would come of it, the call in and of itself made me feel better. So did calls from friends like Warren Beatty and Quincy Jones, who wanted to check in to see how I was doing.

"Chin up now, cuz," Quincy said lovingly. (He'd recently had his genealogy traced by the Mormons and it showed that we were distant cousins.) "Don't let yourself get too down now, cuz. This is your time to play, have fun."

Ted called back almost three months to the day. I'd all but forgotten about his promise and was surprised and flattered that he had remembered. I realized I didn't know enough about this man who would be my first date in seventeen years. I knew about CNN but had never watched it. I got my news from the papers and National Public Radio. Besides, this was pre–Tiananmen Square, pre–Gulf War days, and CNN was still referred to occasionally as "Chicken Noodle News." Nor was I familiar with the world of sailing and the fact that he'd won the prestigious America's Cup. So as time approached for the date, I hurried to find out everything I could.

It wasn't encouraging. Someone gave me an article about his life that revealed he probably had a drinking problem. Not what I needed—again. A friend of one of his children whom I happened to know told me he liked only younger women and if he was interested in me, it would only be as a notch in his belt. Of course there were lots of positives as well: his environmentalism, his global vision, his work for peace. My brother, the sailor in the family, filled me in on **that** facet.

"Oh, sis, this is really exciting! He's the **real** Captain America" (unlike the bro, I guess, who had had a different take on Captain America in **Easy Rider**). "Ted won the America's Cup!" He couldn't believe I didn't know this and went on breathlessly to tell me the whole saga of the Bubba from the South who stormed into Newport, home of the blue-blazered bluebloods, wearing an old engineer's cap; how at first nobody in the race took him seriously; and how he kicked their asses.

"You gotta understand—he's a hero!" Peter's voice gets high when he's excited. It was contagious. But as I said to my kids right before the date, "Don't worry, this is just a way to get my feet wet, practice how to do the dating thing again. This isn't going anywhere. Trust me."

Actually I had come down with a bad cold the day before the date but decided not to cancel on him, given how long he'd waited. When he called to get directions to my house, I told him I was sick and would have to make it an early evening. It didn't seem to faze him. But I was nervous! I'd gathered the clan around me for support: Peter, Nathalie, Troy, Vanessa, Lulu, and my assistant, Debbie Karolewski.

I may not have been invested in this date "going anywhere," but I wanted to be sure it wouldn't be because **he** didn't want it to. So I wore a very short black leather miniskirt, a tight black halter top, black hose, and spike black heels. A few studs and I could have passed for a dominatrix.

I remember being up in my room putting on last-minute touches when Ted arrived. I could hear when Peter opened the door and Ted burst through, his over-the-top voice booming out, "Hey, Montana! Gimme five!" Peter lives in Montana and, as I learned later, Ted had just bought a ranch there and was excited that they had this in common.

A few minutes later I came down the stairs and Ted swung around to watch me. "Wow," he said in a husky voice, devouring me like so much eye candy with an unabashed lust so palpable that I could feel it on my skin. I also saw he was nervous, and I found that endearing. He shouted good-bye to my family (they seemed subdued, as in the wake of a tornado), ushered me quickly out the door, and helped me into a hired sedan with a driver he introduced by name (which impressed me).

"I have friends who are Communists," he offered eagerly as soon as we were seated. He said it like a little boy bringing home good grades. "I've been to the Soviet Union several times because of the Goodwill Games. Gorbachev is my buddy and so is Castro. I've been to Cuba two times. We go hunting and fishing together."

I had to laugh. I didn't know if it was because he really thought I was a Communist and wanted to let me know that wouldn't stand between us or if he thought it was something I'd find endearing. I did. It was the second time in a matter of minutes that the word **endearing** had come to mind—not what I had been expecting. Before we'd even gotten to the restaurant, he pulled another stunner:

"I don't know much about you, see, so . . .

1984, with Vanessa.
(© Suzanne Tenner)

ahhh . . . I got CNN to do a printout of your archives and I read through it. The stack was about a foot tall. So . . . ahhh . . . then I had them do a printout of my files and mine is about three feet tall." Pause. "Mine's bigger than yours! Pretty cute, huh?"

I was astonished—by his comparing our files, by his telling me about it, and by his favorable editorializing . . . **Pretty cute, huh?** All I could do was shake my head and laugh, telling him that I hadn't known much about him, either, and had done my own, far less extensive research. He was bowling me over and my whole body was abuzz.

"I need a driver when I'm out here," he explained, " 'cause I don't know my way around even though I actually owned a Hollywood studio . . . did you know I bought MGM?"

"Yes," I replied. "I read that."

"But I didn't get to keep it for long. They ran me out of town in a barrel. I didn't even get to use the casting couch. Kept the library, though. I own thirty-five percent of the greatest movie classics of all time, and I'm colorizing 'em. Young people these days don't want to watch black-and-white movies. What's your position on colorizing?"

"I don't know. I haven't thought about it."

"Scorsese's against it. But, hey, women put on makeup and nobody gives a hoot. I think it's gonna bring in a whole new audience." During the brief pauses he seemed to hoover me up with his eyes. It was hard keeping my breathing steady.

I had made a reservation at a small dark Italian restaurant in a neighborhood where I knew we would not run into reporters. As soon as we were seated I apologized for not feeling well, reminding him that I would need to go home right after dinner, whereupon he excused himself, saying he had to use the john. I naturally assumed he was calling some Hollywood starlet to make a late date now that he knew he wouldn't be scoring with me.

As soon as he returned to the table he launched into a long speech about how he had been raised by his father to be a male chauvinist pig (his words); how his father always told him that women were like a bus ("If you missed one, another would always come along"); how his father drank a lot, had lots of women, and would come in late at night, wake up his young son, and recount the details of his evening's exploits.

"I just think you should know that . . . ahhh . . . well, from a feminist perspective you'd say I was a sexist because of how my father raised me. But my mistress, the one I just broke up with—"

"The blond pilot?" I interrupted, wanting to be sure we were on the same page mistresswise.

"Yeah, that one, J.J. She's . . . ahh . . . a feminist and she's helped me to see things differently. I was actually . . . ahhh . . . magn . . . ahhh . . . mong . . . ahhh . . . magnanimous with her."

"Are you trying to say 'monogamous'?" I asked, this time laughing for real. **Oh my God! He can't even get the word out of his mouth!**

Then he gave me a recap of his credentials, always punctuating his sentences with a drawn-out "ahhh": how he was an environmentalist, how he'd gotten his network to pay for and broadcast all of Jacques Cousteau's documentaries and National Geographic's and Audubon's.

He told me that he had become an environmentalist growing up on his father's plantations in the South; how he'd had a pretty unhappy childhood, always moving; how every time he'd come home from school his father would have bought a new place in a new state.

"So I never had many permanent friends and I sort of found solace in nature. I was always outside and I notice things other people don't see. That's because I pay attention, and besides, I'm a hunter. Hunters are real environmentalists—they're the first ones to notice how things are changing. For instance, I noticed early on that there were fewer and fewer ducks migrating up and down the flyway every year. Are you against hunting?"

"No, but I've never done any."

"Hmmm. Well, the real problem is too many people . . . too many damn people. We have to stop people from having so many kids. I have five myself, but that's because I didn't know better back then. Excuse me, I have to tighten my skates," he said, getting up to go to the bathroom again. It was a journey he'd make four more times during the dinner. Could he be having difficulty getting a late date? "Tighten his skates"? Yeah, sure! What'd he take me for, a fool?

I'm certain I must have said **something** during

the dinner. Surely he asked me questions about my-self (besides if I was opposed to hunting), but I don't recall anything coming from me, only what was coming **at** me in that boyish, irrepressible flood of information.

No sooner was he back at the table than with an involuntary sideways glance at my breasts, he asked, "Have you had . . ." and immediately stopped him-self, flustered. "Never mind. It's . . . ahhh, nothing," he stammered, dropping his gaze to a neutral place on the tablecloth and arranging his face in an appro-priate expression somewhere between contrition and gravity. I realized that he had been about to ask if I had breast implants (I chose not to satisfy his curios-ity). What I didn't realize was that I had just wit-nessed a historic moment, perhaps the only such: Ted Turner had actually decided not to say what was on his mind. Not knowing this, I couldn't appreciate and be flattered by the Herculean effort at self-censorship it represented.

As he walked me to my door following dinner, he asked, "Can I hug you?" and when I nodded, he gave me a sweet, long hug. Then, as I opened the door, he said, "I'm smitten. . . . Ahh . . . listen, can I call you tomorrow?" I nodded and disappeared into the house. Smitten. So was I.

He called first thing in the morning. "I didn't wake you up, did I?"

"No, I'm an early riser."

"Hey, that's terrific. Me too. That's a good sign. Listen, I really like you. Do you think you can come spend a weekend at my ranch in Montana?"

"I really like you, too, Ted, and I'd like to get to know you better. But . . . I'm . . . well, to be honest, I'm not ready to have an affair. And I have to assume you'd expect us to sleep together if I went up there for the weekend. I'm still kind of shaky. So, no. I don't think I should come." There was a brief silence on the other end—a first.

"Well, okay." He sounded like a Boy Scout. "We don't have to sleep together. I have an extra guest room where you can stay. I . . . ahhh . . . promise I won't touch you. Aw, come on. You'll love it. Heck, your brother lives in Montana. It's a great place."

"I know, I've been there many times."

"Well then, come on. We'll drive around and I'll show you all the critters. I've got elk and deer and eagles and . . ." He was relentless. Of course I caved.

"Okay. I'll come. But I can't until June, 'cause I'm going to the Cannes Film Festival with a film of mine and I'm real busy with promotions and stuff."

"No kidding? Well . . . but that's two weeks from now!"

"Yeah, that's right, but that's as good as I can do." He reluctantly agreed, and we set a date for early June.

Flying to Ted's Montana ranch, I had no idea what to expect. Would he fetch me in a chauffeured limousine? Would his be one of those marble-floored faux ranches with a huge staff? I needn't have worried. He was driving a small Jeep, and the ranch, when we finally got there over an hour later, was a very modest log cabin. Ted, I would learn, is frugal when it comes to spending money on personal comforts.

During the drive I couldn't help noticing that Ted was exceedingly agitated, and I asked him why. For you to understand why his answer appeared to me as a miraculous coincidence, I must give some backstory: Following in the footsteps of the Mel Gibson movies **The Road Warrior** and **Mad Max** had been other films that gave a dark, apocalyptic view of the future, and this had made me want to make a film that went against all these grim projections, one that showed what might happen if we avoided Armageddon and did things right. "People need to be able to envision what the world we're working for will look like," I had told my new producing partner, Lois Bonfiglio. I had actually begun researching it. So imagine my astonishment when in answer to my question about his agitation, Ted replied:

"I'm so excited about this idea I have. I've decided to launch a worldwide contest with a cash reward for the best story that gives a positive vision of the future. I'm going to call it the Turner Tomorrow Award."

"I don't believe this! I've had the same idea, Ted, only I've thought of doing it as a movie." I knew I was in a psychically susceptible state, but this seemed amazing. (Two years later the Turner prize was awarded to the now cult classic **Ishmael.** But no movie ever ensued, from either of us. By then I'd retired from filmmaking.)

Bouncing over rugged dirt roads, thirty minutes after entering his property, we finally arrived at the small house where we'd be staying. As soon as he'd put my suitcase in the (basement) guest room, Ted asked me to watch a videotaped speech he'd made at a recent National Abortion Rights Action League dinner defending a woman's right to reproductive choice.

No sooner was that over than he dropped dramatically on one knee and recited, " 'At the feet of Hannibal / Then like a ripe plum Rome once lay / Oft he put the time of conquest / To a later, better day.' . . . I wrote that myself, in high school. Pretty strong, huh? I was a classics major at Brown. Thucydides? Have you read him? I know his **History of the Peloponnesian War** and everything about Alexander the Great. He was my hero until I switched from war to peace. Martin Luther King and Gandhi are my heroes now. . . . Whaddaya think, huh?"

"Pretty cute," I replied.

I may have descended the basement stairs alone that night, but I had a dizzying head full of Turner to take to bed with me—he'd made sure of that. Like one of those male birds in a nature documentary that puffs and struts and fans his plumage in a wild mating dance, Ted had, it seemed, decided to conquer me. His efforts were endearing.

The sun was barely up the next morning when he yelled down for me to get dressed so we could have breakfast and go for an early drive. "Do you mind making breakfast?"

"No, of course not," I answered, grateful to have something to do while acting as audience.

In the daylight I could see that we were situated at the bottom of a long, narrow valley surrounded by rocky cliffs. Sixteenmile Creek, the creator of the valley, meandered close by, looking far more riverlike than the word **creek** implied. I asked him how he had discovered this place, and over breakfast he recounted how the previous summer he had been a guest of a longtime friend at a ranch in Wyoming.

"I love fishing," he explained, "but it's been mostly bass. I'd never fly-fished before and I really liked it, and when I saw the views . . ." Of course. This man from the piney flatlands of the South had encountered vistas to match his expansive vision. Before even leaving Wyoming, he had called his friend's real estate broker and the very next day he flew to Montana and purchased this "starter ranch," as I would later refer to it.

"At first I couldn't think of a good name for the place," Ted went on, "but I thought it was the best ranch bar none, so that's what I call it, the Bar None Ranch." The place has more than quadrupled in size since then, but at three thousand acres it was the largest piece of private property I'd ever visited as a guest. When singer Michael Jackson told me he had bought a two-thousand-acre spread near my ranch in California, I thought it was sinful—one person owning that much land. What to make, then, of this acquisitive man who already owned one of the barrier islands off the coast of South Carolina near Hilton Head, an old rice plantation in the same state, a quail-hunting plantation in north Florida, and a one-hundred-acre farm outside Atlanta?

After breakfast we took off in the Jeep, bouncing over miles of old logging roads that switch-backed from one pine-covered mountain to the next through breathtaking terrain. Elk and mule deer were everywhere, just as he'd promised. Even a black bear and a bald eagle managed to make an appearance, as if called up by Ted. At one point he leaned out the car window and pointed to a bird flying in silhouette high overhead. "See that?" he asked. "That's a ferruginous hawk." Another time it was a red-tailed hawk. I'd never known anyone who could recognize birds on the wing in silhouette. I was duly impressed.

"How can you tell?" I asked.

"By how their wings move. I know a lot about birds. I'm sort of an ornithologist. You know that songbirds are becoming extinct? You know there used to be so many passenger pigeons that the sky would be darkened when they flew over? There are none left. We wiped them all out. And squirrels used to be able to travel through treetops from the East Coast to the Mississippi River without ever touching ground. Can't do that now. The trees are gone." I was mesmerized, thinking how much I could learn from this man.

"I gotta stop for a second and tighten my skates."

And with that he left the motor running, jumped out, and peed off the side of the road, his back barely turned.

In fact, nature called Mr. Turner every ten minutes or so. After several of these stops I had to laugh. "When you kept going to the bathroom during our dinner date," I confessed to him, "I had assumed you were arranging a late date with a starlet, but I see it was just paranoia on my part."

"Yep. When I'm nervous I have to pee a lot."

"Am I making you nervous?"

"Yeah. Like I said, I'm smitten with you." Then, realizing where we were, he abruptly stopped the Jeep. "Come on, I want to show you something," he said excitedly as he hopped out and motioned for me to follow him. We climbed a small rise alongside the road and he pointed proudly to a shallow cave that ran vertically from the ground up the side of the cliff. I peered closer into its vaginalike opening and saw it was a shiny, purplish vein of rock crystal.

"Pretty cute, huh? My very own crystal mine." He broke off a small crystal and handed it to me. "Here," he said, "a memento." Then suddenly he kissed me and I . . . well, I had a mini meltdown. Warm lips on my lips. Whew! Hadn't realized how much fervor was bottled up. We got back in the car and continued silently on our way. My heart was pounding.

It turned out that Ted didn't know the back roads of his ranch all that well, which wasn't surprising given how many there were. We got seriously

lost. In a place like that, getting lost is an I-wonder-
if-someone-will-find-our-bodies-months-from-now
kind of experience. But the most memorable part of
the drive was the conversation . . . well, "monologue" is a more appropriate word, with Ted all the
while chewing and spitting Red Man tobacco juice
into a small Styrofoam cup as he urged me to sit
closer to him. "Come on, move over here. I want to
feel you against me. Put your hand on my knee."

"Where did you grow up, Ted?" I asked.

"I lived in Cincinnati to begin with . . . a Yankee. I loved being outside collecting bugs and butterflies. I'm told my first word was **pretty**. I loved to
draw, especially pictures of birds, animals, and boats,
and I wrote poetry. My dad had a billboard business.
He was a real conservative. He thought Roosevelt
was a Commie."

"Roosevelt was my dad's hero. The only time I
ever saw Dad cry was when Roosevelt died."

"Yeah . . . well . . . But still, you and I have a lot
in common. My father killed himself when I was in
my twenties—shot himself. Your mother committed
suicide, too. Right?"

"Right."

"So see? That's probably why we're both overachievers." He told me that his father had suffered
from depression and emphysema, had taken barbitu-
rates, and had secretly sold his failing billboard company right before he took his life. "He was the one I
wanted to prove myself to, and he wasn't there to see
me make it," Ted said sadly. "He was something.

Women loved him and he loved them. Couldn't get enough. He thought it was a sign of true manhood to play around. He thought mongo . . . magno . . ."

"Monogamy?" I offered.

"Yeah, that's it. He thought that was for sissies." Ted went on to describe how when he'd come home from boarding school at age twelve, he was put to work on a labor crew erecting roadside billboards for his father's business. He earned $50 a week and had to pay $25 of that for room and board in his own house. His father told him that if he found a better deal, he could go somewhere else to live. Apparently Ed Turner was a dapper, theatrical, charismatic, heavy-drinking, womanizing manic-depressive who believed that sparing the rod would spoil the child. Judy Nye, who was married to Ted for two years when they were both in their early twenties, once said of Ed Turner, "He believed that insecurity bred greatness." Ted's aunt Lucy told me that even when Ted was an infant his father would pass by his crib and snap his fingers against his son's cheek. "Think about that," Lucy said, wanting me to understand why Ted was the way he was.

That day, as we drove through his ranch, Ted talked with utter dispassion about the beatings he had taken from his father, all the while assuring me that his father loved him and was his best friend. He spoke of the belts and straightened wire hangers used for the beatings; of refusing to cry; of his mother pounding on the bedroom door, pleading for her husband to stop; of the time his father lay down on

Ted's bed and made his son beat **him** with a razor strap.

But of all the stories he told me that day, the one that seemed to hold the deepest pain happened to him at age five—the critical age developmentally for a boy—when his father placed him in a boarding school and went off to the navy with his mother and younger sister.

"There wasn't even any grass in the playground," Ted said wistfully, "only pebbles. I was all alone. The only place I could go for comfort was the floor proctor. She was young and pretty, and she would hold me on her lap and rock me at night. Otherwise I would have died. I guess that's why I can't be alone. I have a real fear of abandonment. But I'm working on it. J.J. [the not-so-former mistress] has given me books on how to learn to be okay with solitude. She said she felt inundated by me. . . ."

"Ted," I exclaimed to him as we drove together that first day. "This was child abuse! It's so sad."

He seemed stunned that I had started crying. "No, you don't understand. My father really loved me. It was for my own good. It made me strong," he protested. "Come on, why don't we make love? Huh? How long's it been?"

"Six months," I replied, wondering if that entitled me to claim secondary virginity.

"Wait too long, it'll grow over," he said with just enough good humor to render it benign.

I drew a deep breath . . . I needed time before

surfacing. Was I being arbitrary? Prudish? What's to be gained by refusing? Why not celebrate my return to pleasure by accepting Ted Turner's once-in-a-lifetime offer, a quick dip in the waters of bliss? After all, it was hard to refuse this wounded child-man so in need of care and nurturing.

"Okay," I said, finally breaking the surface.

"Hot dog!" He put foot to gas and back to the cabin we sped.

I would love to write a lyrical passage or two about what it was like. I described it later to friends as Versailles with all the spectacular lit-up fountains. Ted is a wonderful, thorough lover, and I was captivated (as well as relieved that everything still worked). After a nap—he's the napper; I just lay there, too much all-of-a-sudden feeling, too much to think about—he said he wanted to show me another ranch he was thinking of buying a few hours south of where we were. "It's a hundred twenty-five thousand acres. We can spend tonight there. It's closer to the airport. Whaddaya say?"

"Fine. Sure. Whatever." **Why would anyone want another, bigger ranch when they had this one?** I wondered as we drove out the long, bumpy road.

An hour later we entered the western edge of the new property that began at Madison River and stretched twenty-five miles to the east, where it ended at the Gallatin River. Two hundred square miles of utter beauty.

"Whaddya think? Should I buy this place? It's still in escrow."

"No," I replied. "Why would you want two big ranches? Wouldn't the Bar None be enough?"

He pondered this briefly, and I realized his had been a rhetorical question; he'd already made up his mind. "The fishing here is easier," he replied. "This is like elementary school, then I graduate to the Bar None . . . high school. Besides, I want to bring it back to the way it was before the white man came here. Bison are the grazing animals that were here originally till we wiped them out in our attempt to deprive the Indians of their source of food and clothing." Fine. Great. Weird. Tom was also fascinated by bison . . . and how about Ted's interest in Indians!

Somewhere along in there, Ted pulled out a small calling card entitled "Ten Voluntary Initiatives."

"The problem with the Ten Commandments," he explained, "is that nowadays people don't like to be commanded, so I've rewritten them as voluntary initiatives."

"You rewrote the Ten Commandments?!" I asked, astonished.

"Yep. Moses had no way of knowing about the environmental crisis mankind is facing, the dangers of nuclear war, and overpopulation, so I've brought the Commandments up-to-date. Take a look. Pretty strong, huh?"

I glanced down the list: I promise to care for planet Earth and all living things thereon . . . to treat all persons everywhere with dignity, respect, and friendliness . . . to have no more than one or two children . . . to contribute to those less fortunate, to help them become self-sufficient . . . I reject the use of force, in particular military force, and I support United Nations arbitration of international disputes. . . . Pretty good list, I thought.

"What do you do with these cards?" I asked, the organizer part of me wondering if he really believed he could change anything with a list.

"I give them out to people. I read them when I make speeches. I made a lot of speeches last year to all kinds of groups. Sometimes it's for business, but I really like to speak on college campuses. Right now I'm trying to beat Bob Hope's record in doctoral degrees."

The Turner loquacity was unending. My innate shyness with people I didn't know well usually made me uncomfortable, feeling I wouldn't know how to fill in the silences. With Ted, this was no problem, for there were no silences. I wondered that his brain didn't just empty out.

"I think you're perfect for me," he said suddenly. "We care about the same issues, we're both overachievers, we're both in the entertainment business, and you need someone who is as successful as you—and I'm **more** successful than you, which is good. Those last two movies you did were real dogs—let's face it." I was dizzy with overstimulation and taken aback at his lack of self-censorship. "In fact," he went on, "there's only one negative as far as I'm concerned . . . your age." Wow! And here I was under the impression I was looking pretty good. **Doesn't this guy keep anything to himself?**

"So, describe your former life to me," he asked suddenly. I began, feeling ever so pedestrian and boring next to him, by telling him about my family, my children, about the times I spent away on movie locations.

"I wouldn't have put up with it," he interrupted. "I would have gone crazy if you had been in a love scene with another man and I'd have to watch it on the screen. I wouldn't have allowed you to go away for three months at a time. It must have been absolute hell for Tom." Long silence, then: "If this is going to work, you'll have to give up your career." **This guy is crazy! Doesn't he know anything about process?**

"Hey, you know that song 'Ballerina'? It's about a dancer who lost her one true love because she wouldn't give up her career?" And before I could respond, he began singing it:

> Once you said his love must wait its turn
> You wanted fame instead.
> I guess that's your concern,
> We live and learn.
> And love is gone, ballerina, gone
> So on with your career, you can't afford a
> backward glance.
> Dance on and on and on. . . .
> Ballerina, dance, dance.

"That's not what you want, is it?" And then he abruptly went on, "I just realized . . . you're not going to give up your career . . . not until you have an Oscar."

"Ted," I said, "I've got two of them. One for **Klute** and one for **Coming Home**."

"Oh . . . really?"

So there! It felt really good.

We arrived at the almost-previous owner's house as the sun was going down in a poinsettia-red blaze with orange trim in a navy blue sky. Ted swirled around me like a dervish as I prepared dinner, singing romantic songs, reciting more of his boyhood poetry (always from bended knee, always in iambic pentameter, like my first boyfriend, Goey), telling me how hard it was—with all his many properties, the clothes he had to keep straight in all the different locations, all the traveling—to do without a wife to help him out. "Get a maid," I replied, laughing at this rapscallion, whose words tumbled uncensored and unexamined from his mouth.

That night we shared a bed, and I told him more than I should have about my previous experiences in the sex department, even my childhood fantasies, subjects that for me had been traumatic but for him . . . well, they convinced him that I was what he was looking for. Anyone who'd had **those** fantasies and done **those** things, well. . . .

The "bed" is different things to different people. To some it's a proving ground; to others a battleground; for still others a playground. For me, bed has been so fraught with theatrics over the years that I've found I need to know someone **prebed** for bed to be more than genital pleasure. For me, sex needed to be total anonymity or soulful connection.

I was in a deep sleep when I heard a voice: "Gore Vidal is writing something for Turner Films." It took me a moment to surface and realize it wasn't a dream, that it was morning and that he'd actually started the day with such an out-of-the-blue boast.

"Do you always start your day in sprint mode?" I asked groggily.

"I really like Gore Vidal," he said.

"Me too," I answered. "One time an owl fell in his soup at my house in Rome."

"What?" That got his attention.

"Never mind." It was too early and I was too sleepy to explain.

After breakfast Ted pulled a calendar out of his briefcase—or rather, it was a huge sheet of folded paper that when opened showed the entire year, month by month: so linear, so different from my own circular view of a year, that I found it hard to follow.

"Let's block out the times when we can get together this summer, okay? You got a calendar?"

"Not really, but it's okay." I quickly ran my mind down the left curve of my year—July, August, September . . . nothing. "I really don't have much planned."

Before there could be any more discussion, Ted had penciled me in for one or two weekends every

month for the next four months, the follow-up coming just three weeks hence at his place in Big Sur.
Yep. In addition to all the other properties, Ted apparently owned a place that jutted into the Pacific
right above Pfeiffer Beach.

"Ted, this is kind of fast, don't you think? I
mean, don't we need time to get to know each other
before we lock in all these dates?" I didn't know him.
I didn't understand that he needed to know way in
advance who he was going to be with so he wouldn't
be caught alone, God forbid, even for one night.
Over his shoulder I could see up to September. Most
of the days were already penciled in.

By the time we got to the Bozeman airport, I was a
noodle, limp from overstimulation. If the super-
stupendous performance (I swear, it felt as if a 3-D
stereophonic Shakespearean-level, sound-and-light
show had rolled over me) I had been privy to over the
last thirty-some hours had been designed to knock
my socks off, it had succeeded. My socks, my nerves,
and my tongue were knocked. Over and out. On top
of it all, he dropped me off at the airport two hours
early, because he had to go to the private airport next
door, where his jet was waiting to take him to Atlanta, where he was going to a fiftieth-anniversary
celebration of **Gone with the Wind** (he owned it)—
with a girlfriend who'd rented a Scarlett O'Hara
gown just for the occasion. He was, of course (could
I have doubted it?), going as Rhett Butler. He didn't

want to be late. Okay, so we left it there. It felt bad. So much performing and then this. Off to the next one. I thought, Well, I had a lot of fun with this guy. He's totally amazing, and I definitely have a crush, but I must have bored him to death. I didn't say anything interesting.

When I got home, I talked with my therapist and did a lot of deep breathing. Something about Ted felt . . . dangerous, and I didn't want my heart broken again. I ended by writing him a letter thanking him for the weekend, telling him that he was a national treasure that deserved to be nurtured and preserved and that I'd had a lot of fun—but that I didn't feel good about the way he'd left me at the airport and I really wasn't sure all those dates we'd made were appropriate. The chemistry between Ted and me had been powerful, and I was fascinated by his put-everything-on-the-table forthrightness, but I think I was afraid of how vulnerable I'd be if I actually allowed myself to fall in love with him. Instead I fell into lust with a tall, dark, handsome Italian seventeen years younger than me, who made me feel like a girl again.

I called Ted to tell him I had fallen in love with someone and that I wouldn't be coming to Big Sur.

"Oh no!" I had to hold the receiver away from my ear. "I knew I should never have left you for this long. I was afraid this would happen. Dammit! Oh, come on . . . just for one weekend. You can't end it like this. We just started. You gotta give me another chance."

"No, I can't, Ted. I'm sorry, but I am in love with someone else."

"Well, I'm coming out there. You're going to have to tell me to my face. I'll be there in three days. Make a reservation at that same place where we had dinner that first time."

Three days later, when the waiter asked Ted for his dinner order, he replied, "I'll just eat crow and some humble pie for dessert." I marveled at his humor and resiliency, given that he kept insisting this was an utter tragedy for him. But then he began reciting other tragedies, like the time when he was in his early twenties and had come home from school for a vacation to learn that his girlfriend Nancy, the love of his life, had fallen in love with someone else. He'd sat on a high-up hotel window ledge and contemplated suicide until he remembered his father's words: "Women are like buses. If you miss one, another'll always come along." That did it. He vowed never to let himself be that vulnerable again. (Shades of Vadim . . . and Dad . . . and Tom. Hmm.)

I sat back and tried to decipher what was going on in the head of this unusual man. Was he convincing himself that I was, after all, just another bus? Was he really upset? I didn't quite get it yet—that with Ted what you see is what you get, no hidden agenda. All I had to do was listen **carefully**. It was all right there, like it or not. Full (though involuntary) disclosure.

I recall telling him that I was looking for intimacy with a man and that I thought I would find it with my Italian boyfriend. "This is what has eluded me so far. Before I die I want to know intimacy, and intimacy may be the one thing I don't think you're good at."

Three months later I went to visit my brother and his wife, Becky, and take a week of classes at the Orvis Fly Fishing School in Bozeman. I had booked the classes in early May, a month before I ever met Ted. In fact, I told Johnny Carson on his show in early spring that every important man in my life had been a fisherman—deep-sea, bass, everything but fly-fishing. I told Johnny that I intended to learn fly-fishing so I'd be ready for the next one.

Somehow Ted found out that the classes were taking place in the old railroad station–turned-hotel a mere twenty minutes from his ranch (The Flying D, the big one that had been in escrow in June) and he showed up one afternoon, nervous and talkative, to suggest I take the final "exam" on his Cherry Creek and stay for dinner.

When I arrived the day of my exam, Ted hovered about, insisting on driving me to the creek himself with the fishing instructor following in his truck. Once more I was impressed at his sense of humor: "I know you're looking for intimacy, so I've started taking intimacy pills." And later: "Enough of this stuff with younger men. What about older men's rights?" And in a quiet moment he turned to me and said, "It would be a shame if we were eighty by the time we finally get together."

Dinner that night was strained. The Scarlett

O'Hara girlfriend was there with him, and Ted made no effort to disguise his interest in me. I can't imagine how three's-a-crowdish she must have felt. My brother, always there for me when I need support, was with me. As we drove away I could hear Ted calling to me, "I'll take Italian lessons," "I'll get myself stretched to six feet five" (the height of my Italian boyfriend). Total charm. But I am basically a serial monogamist, so that was that.

CHAPTER TWENTY-THREE

TED

All I know is I get what I want.
Maybe because I want things more than others do.
—TED TURNER

> . . . Let's see
>   what I am in here
>   when I squeeze past
>   the easy cage of bone.
> Let's see
>   what I am out here,
>   making, crafting,
>   plotting
>   at my new geography.
> —IMTIAZ DHARKER,
> from "Honour Killing"

THE ITALIAN STALLION IS GONE." That's all the postcard said. Unbeknownst to me, my sister-in-law, Becky, a loyal Ted supporter and CNN junkie who was rooting for our coupling, had decided to alert him the moment I was single again. So when Ted's call came early one morning, I was surprised.

"Hey, I hear you've broken up with the Italian. Wanna come up to Big Sur for that weekend we never had?"

"You're really something, Ted," I said, again impressed at his persistence.

This time he picked me up at Santa Monica Airport in his jet and we flew to Big Sur together. I was excited to see him and struck by his handsomeness and candor. Once airborne, he asked me if I was a member of the mile-high club.

"What's the mile-high club?" I asked.

"You know, when you've made love in a plane—a mile up in the sky?"

"No, I haven't done that," I replied, feeling quite square.

"Wanna do it right now?" he asked with boyish exuberance, and before I could inquire about the logistics, a fully-made-up double bed materialized where just minutes before there had been a row of seats.

"Oh boy! Playtime," he said gleefully.

Thus began my initiation into the mile-high club.

Driving from Monterey airport in a small Jeep identical to the one he had in Montana, he talked about how he had an okay thing going with a woman in Atlanta and needed to know if I would commit to being his girlfriend, because if not, he didn't want to blow what he already had.

"But, Ted, I can't do that till we know each other. How can we know if this will work? Why don't we just go with the flow . . . see how things work out?" It wasn't the definitive answer he was looking for, but "go with the flow" became his mantra for two years.

Ted's Big Sur house is tiny and mostly glass. It sits atop a narrow mountain ridge that juts out into the azure blue Pacific, Pfeiffer Beach on one side and on the other a heart-stopping, southern view down the rugged coast. I was familiar with this view, having often stayed in the Big Sur Hot Springs Lodge in the early 1960s, before it became the famous Esalen Institute, a center of the "human potential" movement. Vanessa had even lived and worked there for a time.

Big Sur is an intense place, all about edges. When edges of things meet, energy is ratcheted up. There is a mysterious altering of molecules in the air, and those who live at the edges are caught up in it. Mary Catherine Bateson writes that it's at the edges where disciplines meet that thinking becomes most creative: "Where lines are blurred, it is easier to imagine that the world might be different." Maybe that's why some people prefer edges. In Big Sur's offshore waters, the warm Pacific currents converge with the cold arctic waters and this, coupled with Big Sur's savage topography, creates wild clashings of extremes. Of course Ted would love Big Sur—he's a man made to live on edges. Brave, brash, **edgy.**

Surrounding the house is a terraced garden, wild

and tangled, the kind I like, and a wooden hot tub built on a ledge with the view of the coastline.

"Pretty great, huh?" he said as he walked me around the garden. "Ted Turner actually owning all this . . . the most beautiful spot in Big Sur."

I was discovering that Ted is, in the words of novelist Pearl Cleage, a man who enjoys "creating a perfect moment but can't let you enjoy it for reminding you how perfect it really is." I could barely contain the desire to say, "Well, actually, Ted, there's a place up Limekiln Creek that's more beautiful," but I bit my tongue. Standing out on this knee of seacoast, looking down onto Pfeiffer Beach, I told Ted about my long-standing feelings for Big Sur, but while he said, "Oh, that's great," I could tell he wasn't really interested. I remember feeling a shiver when it dawned on me that being with Ted would mean being divorced from my own history.

During dinner I again noticed that my words lay like droplets on an oil slick, never penetrating his surface. This vague indifference to what was not himself left me feeling unseen. The next morning I told him, "I don't think this will work, Ted. I'm sorry. You want to push me into some sort of commitment. But something doesn't feel right and I don't want you to blow that other relationship. I think I'd better go home."

Over the following months I dated other men. I fell asleep on a date with a real estate developer from Laguna Beach. A Beverly Hills doctor took me out several times, but when he told me that he'd gone to South Africa with Frank Sinatra and become convinced that Zulu tribal leader Mangosuthu Buthelasi was the true nonviolent peacemaker there, not Nelson Mandela, I stopped seeing him. Ted called fairly regularly, and there was a constant niggling inside my gut telling me I'd blown my best chance at having the relationship I was searching for, that the problems I'd sensed were really my own, not Ted's.

Ted was funny, quick, complicated, smart. Unlike the doctor, he understood the significance of Mandela. We had a common interest in the environment and peace and a commitment to **make things better.** The chemistry between us crackled. And he was a terrific lover. **What's not to fall for?** I couldn't say for sure . . . just that something didn't feel right. Yet I was miserable, feeling that cowardice (fear of intimacy, fear of being hurt) had made me blow what might well have been the love of my life.

Then my friend the singer Bonnie Raitt called to tell me she was opening for the Grateful Dead's annual New Year's Eve concert in Oakland and invited me. I remember the famous concert promoter Bill Graham making his traditional slow descent from the stadium rafters dressed as a chicken; the Dead Heads tripping in their straight-from-the-sixties tie-dyed shirts and beads; my feeling old and out of it. And I remember how happy Bonnie seemed, more at peace and centered than I had ever seen her. We had known each other and shared intimacies for a number of years and it was no secret that relationships and commitments had been challenges for her. Now here she was with actor Michael O'Keefe and enjoying the heck out of it. Somehow her happiness gave me courage. I thought, Gosh, if she can do it, maybe I can, too, and the very next morning, January 1, 1990, I called Ted and asked if we could try again. Again I was amazed that he was not only willing, but fairly ecstatic. He was always so sweet that I had to ask myself if my trepidations weren't my own demons trying to undermine me.

That was when we began "going steady," as we described it, which I thought was rather charming for two fifty-somethings. Vanessa was in college, but Troy was still in high school. Being away from home for too long made me anxious, so when Ted had to be in Atlanta, I stayed in Santa Monica, even though he was honest about spending those nights with the other woman (or two). I didn't like it. It confused me, but I wasn't ready to lay down ultimatums. I wanted, as I told Ted, to go with the flow, see how things went.

At those times we would talk on the phone for hours. Often he would say, "I need 'fonda-ling. . . .'" He found it hard to believe that he was the only one who had ever made this pun on my name. He would tell me he felt himself shrinking when he wasn't with me, and at first I took it as a compliment. Later I realized that it wasn't so much his need to be with me as it was his fear of being alone. Sad to say, Ted doesn't hold his well-being

The Fondas being inducted into the Hollywood
Entertainment Museum. Here I am with Peter,
his children Bridget and Justin Fonda, Shirlee, and Troy.
(Alan Berliner © Berliner Studio/BE Images)

within himself (something we had in common for a while). It has to come from the outside: from a woman, from applause, from achievements and good deeds. It took several years before I began to understand the profound ramifications this would have on me and our relationship. But I had fallen head over heels in love with him—still am in many ways—and I wanted to hang in and try to make it better for this lovable, fascinating man-child, who was just enough **not** like my father that I wanted to crawl inside his skin and know him.

Despite the oddities, being courted by Ted was heady business. Here was a man who shared my commitment to making things better but wasn't so perpetually preoccupied with that that he couldn't shift gears and give equal and talented attention to what can be communicated only through the body. **Above the neck and below the neck, together at last!** One-stop shopping. You want the sex, romance, laughs, shared values, intellectual stimulation, companionship, eroticism, friendship. You want it all, and he seemed to have it all. Besides, everyone close to me liked him: Debbie, my assistant, Lois, Paula, Troy, Nathalie, Lulu, Vanessa—well, actually things weren't so cut-and-dried with Vanessa. From her vantage point here I was giving myself over to another man again, and she was angry.

The first time Ted invited me to Atlanta, he met me at the airport in his modest Ford Taurus and we drove straight to the CNN Center. Oh my! Walking into the huge glass-domed atrium, looking up at the building rising fourteen floors all around me, CNN and TURNER everywhere, every nation's flag flying, even that of the United Nations, testifying to Ted's commitment to a global network. **My boyfriend made this all happen!** I was surprised to discover that this building was also his residence when he was in Atlanta (which was as infrequently as he could get away with). For years after leaving his second wife he had lived in his office and slept on a Murphy bed, until his mistress had complained. Recently, he'd punched through the ceiling of some storage rooms on the fourteenth-floor and built a tiny (seven-hundred-square-foot) penthouse that you reached by going up a narrow wrought-iron take-your-life-in-your-hands spiral staircase. For the ten years Ted and I were together, that penthouse was my home base, making me the only woman in the world who had to walk through a sports-marketing department to get to her front door.

The way he introduced me to everyone in Atlanta made me realize that despite his unquestionable importance in the world, Ted was like a kid, so proud to have me on his arm. This was new for me. So much was new: I had never before been with a businessman, not to mention a very wealthy one, and this one also had the heart of a rebel and social values that didn't put money first. Ted understands money, but he's not **about** money. He's also a playful renegade, an outsider, impolite, impolitic, with grand dreams of changing the world for the better. He put me on a pedestal, clearly needed me, and wasn't afraid to show it. In many ways he was simply irresistible.

I began to get to know Ted's business associates, many of whom had been with him since the very beginning. They told me that since we started dating they had never seen Ted so happy and how much easier he was to work with. The many people who loved him deeply had been growing concerned about his state of mind, partly because of his father's history and partly because of his uncertainties in the relationship department. So they gratefully embraced me as "the woman who had come to the rescue." As one of his sailing buddies said, "Well, it appears Le Capitan is finally in good hands." Of the people around him, only one, his executive assistant, Dee Woods, had something worrisome to tell me (though she loved him dearly): "Jane," she said, "he's a male chauvinist pig and he always will be." She laughed when she said it, and I chose to think she was being funny—sort of. I stored it away.

Ted's adoration for me made me feel good about myself. **Good about myself.** I have to stay with that one for a moment. He told me, so generously and frequently, that he loved me, that he thought I was smart and beautiful, the love of his life, that it began to chip away at my low self-esteem: **Ted Turner thinks I'm great and smart and beautiful, and he's no dummy.** What's touching is that while I was feeling this, Ted was feeling: **Wow, if Jane Fonda loves me, I can't be all bad.** Much as some people might find it hard to believe, we were two people with fragile egos who could make each other feel stronger.

Yet for more than a year there were times when I would feel myself falling into a dark hole. I was learning to listen to my body more, to pay attention to my feelings, and something just didn't feel right. I was certain that he loved me, but then he would say or do something that made me feel his antennae were still up, that my position in his life was permanent, perhaps, but not solo.

We talked about it a lot. He would say, "We're looking at the same canvas and you are seeing one thing and I am seeing another," and he would assure me that my paranoia was unfounded. He began to tell me that the problem was that I was scared of intimacy. **True.** Why else had I twice before chosen men who were not capable of intimacy? I was, I would remind myself, the daughter of my parents: They were two people who lacked emotional attunement.

Perhaps you think that by **intimacy** I mean sex, so allow me to clarify. Sex can be intimate but isn't necessarily so; sometimes it's just the pleasurable stimulation of genitalia. By **intimacy** I mean an attunement between two people who, despite each other's evident flaws, open their hearts fully to each other. This openness makes them vulnerable, so trust is key. So is **self**-love: It's impossible to be truly intimate with someone if you don't like yourself.

On at least four occasions I told Ted that I didn't feel he was really there for me and that I would have to leave. Each time, he would become so palpably miserable that it would convince me to stay. "Jane," he said to me one night, "I need to know I can depend on you. You can't keep threatening to leave me, or this won't work."

And suddenly . . . **whack**! The thought slams into me how easily I could blow it because of fears about things that might only be my imaginings. Why am I not allowing myself to be happy? It's so much easier to hold on to those old ghosts, the hurts and grievances, to knead and nurse them. It's comforting because they are what's familiar, not these new feelings of happiness. Mustn't trust them . . . they're too fickle.

But, Jane old girl, this isn't some rehearsal where you'll get notes afterward and a chance to do it better. No, this is but a few years away from the beginning of the last act of your life. Every day counts; every chance to make peace with the old ghosts must be seized. They're not your friends— they're your jail keepers who have outlived their usefulness. They won't keep you warm on a cold night in Montana. Humor and love and the understanding of your new partner will keep them at bay. He'll do that for you and you'll do that for him.

One day Ted asked me, "What do you want out of this relationship?" I liked the question and knew that I needed to take my time and really think before I answered. Ted is a negotiator, and whatever my answer was, I would be held to it as to a contract.

"Give me twenty-four hours to think about it," I said.

And then I pondered: What **do** I want? Trust. Happiness. Love. To be seen, countenanced. I had begun to notice how when those things are not present, when I feel scared or am doing something I don't want to be doing, my breathing gets shallow and my muscles tense and I don't feel good.

"What I want out of this relationship," I told him the next evening, "is to feel good."

"Great! Me too. I want to feel good. Oh boy, party time."

"No, Ted," I interrupted, laughing at his take, which I should have expected. "I don't mean feeling good that way. I mean feeling good the way people do when they feel safe: seen, heard, fully loved."

"Oh yeah . . . okay. That's fine. I get it. Me too."

Only then, a good year into the relationship, did I tell him that I needed him to be monogamous. He agreed.

For all intents and purposes, I had decided to stop acting and producing by the time I met Ted, but once I committed to the relationship, it became a done deal. Ted made that abundantly clear. I was convinced that my career (and the long absences from home that it required) had been a big problem in my marriage to Tom, and I wasn't going to let that happen again; but the feelings that this new reality brought up in me were tough to handle. I had worked from the time I was twenty-two. It was in many ways who I was, though I never quite realized this until I decided to stop working. It wasn't about money. I had enough money to pay my own bills, buy my own clothes, and support my children, all of which I continued to do while I was with Ted. Financial independence was of fundamental importance to me. This fact, I believe, was what created a semblance of a balance of power between us. The anxiety that arose with my retirement was more about giving up what had been my personal, creative outlet and about being subsumed into Ted's orbit.

While Vanessa, never one to steer away from confrontation, expressed outright anger about my subsumation, Troy simply said one morning while he was visiting Ted and me, "I don't want a mom who doesn't work," which, I think, translated into his not wanting me to be merely "wife of." Both of them sensed that some part of me wouldn't be able to flourish. Lulu took to Ted immediately. He was the father figure she'd never had. Nathalie seemed to sense that Ted made me happier than she'd ever seen me, and that was enough for her. But I don't want to minimize the impact that my decision to take up a full-time relationship with Ted had on Vanessa and Troy. They saw me leave behind their home base, as well as my identity as an actress, producer, businesswoman, and political activist, to enter the constantly moving, glitzy life of the corporate media world and on the arm of a former Goldwater Republican. But it wasn't as though they were waiting for me to come home. Troy would soon head to the University of Colorado in Boulder; Vanessa was in her last year at Brown University and had taken a year off to help build a village school in Nicaragua and work with her father in Zaire. Nathalie had a flourishing career as an assistant film director; Lulu was a graduate student at Boston University.

Once again I seemed to have become someone new because of a man. But beneath the surface I felt a continuity in core values. With Ted I felt I could achieve the true, deep soul connection that had eluded me. Ted was not intimidated by me. I loved him. I loved his smell, his skin, his playfulness, his worldview, his transparency—and I knew that I was finally ready to do the needed work on myself to overcome my fear of intimacy. I wanted this to work and I was prepared to put some parts of myself (moviemaking, mostly) to bed, believing that other parts (my heart) would be waking up. Ultimately I was right, though it didn't end up the way I thought it would.

My fear of intimacy had yet to be conquered, so I wasn't able to see that Ted himself wasn't capable of really showing up in a relationship. I didn't even notice his absence until I began to heal myself. Still, I **did** heal, and I learned so much from Ted on so many levels that I don't regret throwing myself wholeheartedly into trying to make it succeed. Even so, there were days when I was overcome with the feeling that I was making a big mistake and could lose my children and my life.

Nonetheless, I sold my home in Santa Monica as well as Laurel Springs Ranch, packed my belongings, moved all my furniture into Ted's various houses, and migrated south.

I'd never been in the South long enough to get to know it, and immediately I was struck by people's friendliness. Never in all my travels had I been in a place where people came up and said, "Welcome, we're so glad you're here." I knew, of course, about the political conservatism. And some of Ted's acquaintances were less than happy about my appearance on the scene. Ted would say, "Jane was right about Vietnam. I was wrong." He was ready to stand beside me.

The South took some adjusting to. It forced me to slow down, shift gears, and pay close attention. There were so many otherances: the yes-ma'am-no-sir culture, for instance.

My women friends in the West had been feminists; their relationships with their partners were democratic—shared child care, housekeeping, and cooking, working outside the home, holding independent political opinions. Therefore I was surprised at what I first perceived as subservience, a high importance placed on tradition and propriety among many southern white women. (I found this **not** true of most of the black women I met, perhaps because, from childhood, many black women have been taught that they have to take care of themselves.) As I got to know them, however, southern white women turned out to have plenty of starch in their spines, much more than had been apparent at first blush, and I have, over time, given much thought to why there is that misleading first impression.

The South was an agrarian culture for much longer than the industrialized North: Families lived on farms, some on plantations; it was a culture of property, including humans **as** property. The institution of slavery condoned one **race**-based group of humans serving as commodities to enhance the social and economic power of the other. This made the **gender**-based subservience **within** the patriarchal family seem more normal and acceptable. Add to this the fact of living in isolated rural communities, where it was difficult for women to know there was any other way and no place to go to if they were cast out because of their uppity behavior. Church life was the South's central social outlet, and there, too, hierarchy and conformity rule. Seeing it from this historical perspective made it easier for me to embrace my less uppity southern women friends.

One more obvious difference: **church.** In California, the only people I knew who regularly went to religious services were my Jewish friends. Now, suddenly, I was getting to know—and like—smart, progressive, funny, not-uptight practicing Christians. Some were not famous; some were—President Jimmy and Rosalynn Carter, Ambassador Andy Young, and others with whom my relationship with Ted brought me in regular contact.

I was still experiencing a feeling of being "led"— watched over—but I viewed it as a secular phenomenon, and the deep faith of my new friends was a source of fascination to me. **Could it be,** I wondered, **that what is leading them is what is leading me?**

Whenever I was with my Christian friends, I would always ask them questions about their faith.

Not since my early years in Greenwich, Connecticut, had racial issues been so much in evidence as when I moved south, though I don't know to this day whether there actually **is** more racism in the South. It may just be more hidden elsewhere. Early on, Lulu (who is dark-skinned) made me aware of differences in **how** racism in the South has been internalized by African-Americans. Asked how she felt about living in Atlanta (where she moved a few years after I did), she said, "I have felt more discriminated against by **blacks,** especially light-skinned blacks, down here than I ever did by whites in the North."

An important part of the new world that I stepped into were Ted's five children: Jennie, the youngest, was a student at Georgia State; Beauregard (Beau), the youngest of the three boys, was in his second year at the Citadel in South Carolina; Rhett, the first child from Ted's second marriage, to Janie Smith, was a cameraman with CNN in Tokyo; Teddy, the eldest son from Ted's first marriage, to Judy Nye, was working with a country music cable network; and Laura, the firstborn, ran her own clothing store in Atlanta's fashionable Buckhead district and had just started dating a man with the wonderfully southern name Rutherford—Rutherford Seydel II—whom

Side by side with President Jimmy Carter at a Habitat
for Humanity blitz in Americus, Georgia.
(Julie Lopez/Habitat for Humanity International)

Janice Crystal took this picture of Ted and me at
the Flying D while she and Billy were visiting.
(Billy and Janice Crystal)

she would soon marry. I'm glad that I came into Ted's life in time to see two of the children graduate, all of them marry, have babies, and grow into adulthood.

Like their father, they are survivors of complicated childhoods, and I grew to admire and love each of them for how they have coped and matured.

Because of the important role Susan had played in my adolescence, I knew how to be a stepmother, and saw right away that one important thing I could do was help bring Ted closer with the children. The five of them love and admire their father and embrace his values.

Ted embraces differences; he believes in putting his arms around everyone, including people with whom he doesn't agree. He would say to me, "You catch more bees with honey than with vinegar." I watched him practice what he preached and saw people change as a result. I changed as a result. I have met and become friends with conservative Republicans and Christians I would never otherwise have taken the time to get to know; I would thus have missed seeing the common humanity beneath the surface differences.

I'm someone who loves learning new things and facing challenges, and there were plenty of those in the new life I'd chosen. Besides Ted's humor, sex appeal, and intelligence, he was offering me Paradise. Most of our time together, especially in the beginning, was spent on his various properties, riding, fishing, hiking, and exploring. Back then the proper-

ties numbered five, not counting Atlanta, and just as you start a jigsaw puzzle with the corners and edges, his "starter properties" ranged from his coastal island off South Carolina to Big Sur on the other edge, with Montana at the top. By our third year together, he had begun filling in the middle—two more in Montana, three in the Sand Hills of Nebraska, two in South Dakota, and three in New Mexico, one of which includes an entire mountain range, the Fra Cristobal just to the east of Elephant Butte Reservoir. Vermejo Park Ranch, on the northern border of New Mexico near Raton and overlapping into Colorado, comprises almost 600,000 acres—the largest privately owned, contiguous piece of property in the United States, nearly as large as Rhode Island (it starts in the Rockies and ends in the Great Plains). Besides these, Ted has two spectacular properties in Patagonia and one in Tierra del Fuego, for a total of something in the neighborhood of 1.7 million acres.

Once he got started with his bison, Ted decided to grow his herd for commercial purposes, knowing that this once almost endangered animal would never become more than an exotic trophy species in the United States unless it had market value. To grow a herd, you need to buy more land, and that was the underlying reason for most of his purchases of western ranches. At last count he had thirty-seven thousand head of bison, 10 percent of the entire U.S. herd.

The flagship ranch was and still is the Flying D, the one in Montana I told him not to buy. One

afternoon Ted blindfolded me, drove me into the hills, led me out of the car, took off the blindfold, and said, "This is where we'll build our home." He pointed to a valley with a tiny stream running through it. "Right down there I'm going to create a lake that will reflect the Spanish Peaks. It will be our Golden Pond." And that's exactly what he did. He did the lake and I did the house. I wanted us to have at least **one** home that reflected me, with a ceiling under which no one before me had made love with him.

Hardly a day went by that Ted and I weren't riding over the Flying D's wide expanse of rolling green hills, through forests of aspens and herds of elk, hundreds at a time. By now I had brought my three horses from Laurel Springs Ranch: two Arabians and a palomino. I like riding Arabs—they're hot-blooded, all nerves, heart, and endurance, like Ted. You can feel their spirit under you.

Then there was fly-fishing. The sport is so hard to master; my week at the Orvis Fly Fishing School notwithstanding, I often ended a day in despair, throwing myself screaming onto the banks. But since Ted was spending an average of a hundred days a year wetting a line, I felt I had to get good at it.

Fly-fishing is endlessly humbling. Every time I thought I'd graduated to the next level, Ted would buy a new ranch with harder-, faster-flowing water and smarter, bigger fish. But I learned why the sport is so important to him: It requires total Zenlike focus, and it is silent. You won't catch much if you

Left to right: Lois Bonfiglio (my producing partner after Bruce), Paula Weinstein, me, and Becky Fonda—visiting me on the Bar None Ranch.

Troy and Lulu bass fishing at Avalon Plantation.

don't want to be there or if you have other things on your mind. For Ted—who doesn't handle stress well and is hard of hearing—fly-fishing is a balm. The sport requires you to be fully tuned in to every aspect of the natural world around you: the insects that may (or may not) be rising over the water, the position of the sun, where your shadow is being cast. Then there's the underwater world you have to try to penetrate.

There's something sensual about this world. In his book **Fly Fishing Through the Midlife Crisis,** Howell Raines describes its magic this way: "Imagine that cells scattered throughout the bone marrow— and particularly in the area of the elbows—are having subtle but prolonged orgasms and sending out little neural whispers about these events." Maybe **that's** why Ted loves the sport so much!

Within a few years Ted had four ranches in Montana within two-hour drives of one another, each offering a different fishing experience. It was not unusual in the summers for us to have breakfast and early morning fishing at one, then drive two hours to another, where we'd have lunch and afternoon fishing, then drive to the third for dinner and evening fishing. My dear friend Karen Averitt, who had run one of my Workout studios in California and then my health spa at Laurel Springs Ranch (and then married Jim, my ranch hand/musician), had now, at my urging, moved with her family to Montana to cook and look after Ted's houses. For those long summer months I marveled at how Karen managed to pack and unpack coolers, load them into her truck, and have the three meals ready in three different places—all in one day. It's still going on, I might add. When Ted and I separated, Karen came to me and said, "Jane, you know I love you and always will, but Ted needs me more." No kidding!

By the way, if you eat at one of Ted's Montana Grills around the country (which I strongly recommend), you'll see items like Karen's "Flyin' D" Bison Chili on the menu.

Some of the most precious memories I have of my time with Ted are those of the predawn hours, rowing with our dogs out to a duck blind in the ACE Basin of South Carolina, past the falling-down old rice mill and cabins from the days of rice plantations and slavery; waiting in the blind for the sun to come up; listening to the dogs' teeth chatter, partly from cold and partly from excitement; the sounds of the forest coming to life behind us; the gray mists lingering in the tall pines; and the pale pinks and mauves of dawn reflected in the shallow marsh waters. I remember during morning quail hunts in the woods at Avalon how the sun shone through the beads of dew that hung on spiderwebs, turning them into glimmering tiaras and the sulphur butterflies fanning the velvet air and alighting briefly on spires of lespedeza; Ted rowing me slowly through the Tai Tai canal through the swamps at Hope Plantation in South Carolina's ACE Basin, where the swampy, brackish water was so dark and still that in my photographs I couldn't tell which was real and which was the reflection of reality; Ted knowing that the orange streak that had just gone by was a summer tanager; Ted knowing where the pair of bald eagles was nesting (he had a pair on every property, it seemed).

It was as though all the critters knew that the land was in the hands of someone who cared about them, so they came. A pair of sandhill cranes made their nest on an island Ted had created in the lake in front of our house on the Flying D Ranch. One morning we woke to a shrill cry and immediately Ted sat up in bed and said, "It's the crane! Her egg has hatched." He was right, and I loved him for his knowing. He knew his animals, especially his birds. No matter which part of the country we were in, Ted could always recognize every bird on the wing—and he knew their mating and nesting habits. He wasn't as conversant in wildflowers, so I decided I would become the expert in that field. I spent our first years together with eyes focused earthward or with my nose in one of my many flower books, picking, pressing, and identifying every new one I found. Within three years I had hundreds of them mounted, some very rare, and as we rode our horses through the ever changing landscapes I relished being able to identify them for him. I had found a wonderful way to do "my thing" within the context of Ted's life.

Another creative project I took up was photographing his properties. I wanted to become deeply familiar with all of them, so I decided I would try to capture the essence of each one and then create albums called **Homes Sweet Homes** for Ted and each of his children. Within a few years, as the properties began to expand in number, what I thought would be a one-album-per-person job became a five-album-per-person travail.

Every one of my projects caused friction with Ted. He felt abandoned, said it was a way for me to avoid intimacy (he was partly right), and called me a workaholic—while I thought of myself as needing a creative outlet and felt, as Mark Twain once said, that "really a man's own work is play and not work at all." I tried hard to understand Ted's neediness, so I'd reluctantly cut back. But I refused to give up my pastimes entirely, especially since (unbeknownst to him, or to me at the time), I had given up things far more important. Like my voice.

Ted is the only person I know who has had to apologize more than I have. He has apologized to Christians, Catholics, Jews, African-Americans, the antichoice people, and the pope. He's an equal opportunity offender. He can't help himself; like a child, he often seems at the mercy of his impulses. It's a rare occurrence when something enters his head that doesn't come out of his mouth.

Like the time he was making a very important appearance at the National Press Club in Washington, D.C. Time Warner was represented on the Turner board of directors and was preventing Ted from buying a major broadcast network to add to his cable empire, and he felt this would keep him from competing with other media conglomerates like Rupert Murdoch's News Corp, Disney, and Viacom. At the same time he was in major negotiations on a TBS merger with Time Warner: One false move and everything could fall apart. I was too nervous to sleep the night before. Not Ted. As usual, he hadn't prepared and had made no notes; but like his hero Alexander the Great, he always slept well on the eve of battle.

On the day of the speech all the journalists who packed the hall were aware that it was a precarious time. So imagine their shock (and mine) when in the midst of the speech he said, "Millions of women have their clitorises cut off before they are ten or twelve years old, so they can't have fun in sex. . . . Between fifty percent and eighty percent of Egyptian girls have their clits cut off. . . . Talk about barbaric mutilation . . . I'm being clitorized by Time Warner." Some people laughed; others were too stunned. Many looked over at me. I simply slid down in my seat. **Hey, it wasn't my idea.**

Several years later Ted would give an unprecedented $1 billion to establish the United Nations Foundation. Over the years many large grants from the foundation have gone to stop FGM (female genital mutilation). You can't say he doesn't put his money where his mouth is.

Certainly the most public part of my new life with Ted was our attendance at the Braves games. In the fall of 1991, right before we got married, the Atlanta Braves played in their first World Series. I can't remember ever being on such a protracted adrenaline high or so superstitious: If I had a Band-Aid on my index finger during a winning game, I'd make sure it was there for the next one. Same with underwear, earrings, and caps. I began a personal collection of winning Braves caps that people gave me, and for the Braves' victorious 1995 World Series, I was wearing my all-time good-luck black-and-white coat made from bison hair. Plenty of things he'd done in his life justified his celebrity, but none guaranteed Ted's standing as folk hero to Atlantans like his having stuck with the Braves and brought home a winner.

During the first year of our going steady, besides traveling with the team during baseball season, we crisscrossed the globe constantly, visiting the Soviet Union, Europe, Asia, and Greece as Ted's various undertakings demanded his presence. I had been in many of the places before and had had my own experiences there, but being on the arm of Ted Turner made it different. With a few noticeable exceptions the spotlight was always on him. He was the one who did the speaking and was feted and celebrated, and although people at CNN used to say that I was the first woman in Ted's life who had a talking role, it was definitely a supporting one. Sometimes I would feel invisible and frustrated, as when he would give a speech about something that was important to

Ted getting carried away during "Auld Lang Syne" at the start of a Braves game. Left to right: Nancy McGuirk, Ted, me, President Carter, Jennie Turner, over the president's shoulder, and Rosalynn Carter with her back turned.
(AP/Wide World Photos)

1995 in San Francisco at the State of the World Forum with President Mikhail and Raisa Gorbachev.
(AP/Wide World Photos)

both of us without having prepared and would, in my opinion, end up rambling.

Occasionally, though, the tables were turned, like the time we met with President Mikhail Gorbachev in his office in the Kremlin. During the half hour the three of us spent together, the president spent a good chunk of our time talking to me. As we left Ted whispered, "You know, that was a very unusual situation for me."

"It's not easy, is it?" I replied. "I know. I feel like a tagalong all the time these days and I'm not used to it, either. I'm willing to settle into this new role, but it must be hard when it happens to you, too."

Fortunately we were getting better at talking about our feelings, so instead of pouting or pretending it hadn't happened, Ted was able to regale listeners with the story of how he had spent twenty-eight minutes staring at Gorbachev's back.

I was learning a valuable lesson: When you confront problems and work them through, what might have been a rupture becomes stronger at the broken place. It is analogous to bodybuilding: When you lift weights to build muscle, you cause microscopic tears to occur in the muscle tissue, and when the tears heal (it takes forty-eight hours) the torn places become stronger. Still, much of me remained a handmaiden to my insecurities. My long-standing fear of not being good enough kept me feeling that if he knew me fully, he couldn't possibly love me. What this meant was that I was willing to forfeit **my** authenticity to be in a relationship with **him**.

Often at business receptions I would stand silently by Ted's side, listening to men in the highest echelons of power discuss how much better things were in, say, Brazil or some other less-developed country I had visited, and I would think, Haven't they seen the favelas? The slums? People see what they need and want to see. I realized that these men, these makers of policy, designers of structural adjustments, and rationalizers for conflict, cannot allow themselves to see any consequences of their policies that might shake their certainty that they are doing the right thing. The bar girls, the boys and girls who prostitute themselves to feed their families, the women who earn $1 a day in U.S. maquiladoras in Mexico, the desperate gangs of youth, the garbage pickers, the displaced farmers—these brutal realities pass under the radar of liberal academe, of the economists and social scientists who sip their champagne and praise themselves about the great job they've done in Central and South America, or wherever.

Were it not for Ted, I wouldn't have been at such gatherings. They gave me indigestion. But because they involved Ted's businesses I never felt I could say, "But people have been really harmed by those policies you are praising. Don't you see that?" Afterward I would often tell Ted about my discomfort, but he would never fully engage. There's a Horatio Alger side to Ted: **Anyone can pull themselves up by their own bootstraps** (making those who don't feel that it's their own fault). I think it pains him too deeply to countenance the possibility that while there are Horatio Alger–type successes in the United States, they

aren't frequent enough to matter. Structural inequities are too ingrained and too invisible.

While traveling the world with Ted, I realized
the historic importance of what he had done, how
his revolutionary vision for twenty-four-hour news
had transformed the planet into Marshall McLuhan's
global village and changed news reporting forever—
rather remarkable for a man who hadn't liked watching the news because he found it depressing. I
learned that all the big news companies had researched whether or not a twenty-four-hour news
channel would work. Their research said it wouldn't.
As usual, Ted plunged ahead, sans polls or research,
relying only on instinct.

It amazed me how in America people bemoaned
television as a passive medium for so long, yet when
a swashbuckler from Atlanta—a romantic renegade
with a global vision—turned the passive medium
into a more democratic and empowering one, people
had difficulty with it. We forget how it was at the beginning with CNN. Maybe it was easier for audiences when news was predigested and all the seeds
and stems were disposed of; maybe having news as
raw material made them work too hard.

It's strangely analogous to what I had seen happening in Eastern Europe in 1990 when I visited
there right after the fall of the Berlin Wall and after
the Velvet Revolution in Czechoslovakia. Under the
Communist system, people had had everything decided for them by the government- and by state-run
institutions, and when the possibility of democracy
came along, forcing them to participate and make

choices, they didn't have such an easy time adjusting. I remember meeting a lyricist in Prague who said to me, "I've spent my life writing words for people who have grown adept at reading between the lines. Now we can write clearly and I'm not sure I know how."

When Desert Storm, the first Gulf War, began in 1991, Ted's dreams for world peace received a blow. He got physically sick. Like so many Americans, both of us had hoped that the winding down of the cold war would see a commensurate cutting of the military budget, freeing up funds for domestic and peacetime needs. It was a sad time, yet it was exciting to watch Ted's responses to crises.

Tom Johnson, former publisher of the **Los Angeles Times,** had just become president of CNN. The second day he was on the job, we were at the Flying D when Tom phoned from Atlanta to say that he had just gotten three calls—from President George H. W. Bush, Joint Chiefs of Staff chairman Colin Powell, and press secretary Marlin Fitzwater—asking him to order the CNN reporters out of Baghdad "immediately." It was clear, Tom went on, that Operation Desert Storm was about to begin. From what he had been told, Tom was convinced that Bernard Shaw, John Holliman, and Peter Arnett were in imminent danger, and he wanted them out. He explained what he knew to Ted, who replied, "Tom, those who want to stay [in Baghdad] will stay. Those who want to come out can come out." Then, shouting into the phone, he said, "Tom, you will not overturn me on this, pal. You understand me? I will take complete responsibility for this decision. If they die, it will be on my conscience, not yours." Ted and Tom had to resist very strong pressure from Washington, but if Peter Arnett had not stayed in Baghdad, the alternate (and real) view of the war—which represented a total revolution in TV war coverage and was certainly the defining moment for CNN—would never have occurred.

This gave me a bird's-eye view of how good Ted is in tough times. He has an easy, confident feel for when and how much to risk. It's not that he's unafraid. The bravest soldiers aren't unafraid, but they're the ones who are able to harness their fear on behalf of courage. In the years that I was with him, I saw numerous circumstances when Ted was able to mobilize courage, weigh priorities, and then make the winning decision. He's often played it close to the edge. I guess it's similar to sailing close to the wind. I wasn't with Ted when he sailed competitively, but I'm told that whenever he'd take the helm he'd find a way to go just a little faster, cut it a little closer, although his competitors were hours (or even days) behind him.

"Hope for the best and prepare for the worst" is a homily very much at the center of how Ted lives his life. It's why he would have made a great general. His troops would have followed him into any battle, as his sailing crews did, because they would know that no **foolish** risks would be taken; everything would have been thought through, every option weighed, and he would never ask his men to do something that he himself wasn't willing to do. I think that it was his studies of the classics, which teach clear, strategic thinking; his familiarity with the major battles of history; and his competitive sailing that honed these skills so finely. Ted was a sailor of large boats. This is important. Smaller boats require brawn. Big boats require brains: knowing how to build a winning team and how to empower them; how to envision all the things that could happen and to be prepared for any eventuality.

When his company merged with Time Warner in 1995, I watched Ted begin to create an alternate life for himself. He had already started down that path, but now he was far more intentional about building his bison herd, increasing his landholdings and his philanthropy, and not wanting his future to be totally circumscribed by Turner Broadcasting in the event that his new boss, Gerald Levin, decided to drive him out of his own company. When his worst fears materialized, everything was already in place for him to be a full-time rancher, philanthropist, and restaurateur. Ted's Montana Grill, where his bison meat is the star attraction, is providing this entrepreneur with a whole new arena in which to work his magic.

What I **didn't** anticipate was how Ted's "hope for the best, prepare for the worst" dictum could apply to our marriage. That would come later. Seven years later, to be exact.

CHAPTER TWENTY-FOUR

A CALLING

Where we had thought to travel
outward, we shall come to the center of our own existence; where we
had thought to be alone, we shall
be with all the world.

—JOSEPH CAMPBELL,
Hero with a Thousand Faces

Any single path truly taken leads
to all the others. Even then, you
will find that outward and inward
become the same direction. The
center of the wheel is everywhere.

—ROBIN MORGAN,
The Burning Time

IT STARTED BECAUSE I wanted to be a responsible trustee of Ted's family foundation. It resulted
in my discovering my calling.

I had been with Ted only a short time when he decided to create the Turner Foundation and focus its grant making on protecting the environment and reducing population growth: Growing numbers of people on a small planet with finite resources spells trouble, not just for the environment but for the human species as well, since a healthy environment is our life support system.

While I understood environmental issues, the population part was a little fuzzy—not the **reason** it is a problem, but what to **do** about it. Whenever he spoke publicly (and privately), Ted hammered away relentlessly about how population growth was the central problem of our time. He would recite statistics: 840 million people go hungry every night and 2 billion are chronically malnourished; 1 billion people try to live on less than $1 a day and another billion on less than $2; more than 2 billion people lack basic sanitation; 1 billion do not have access to clean water, adequate housing, or rudimentary health care. This was his mantra.

Often, when I had pounded away about an issue, the press would label me strident and shrill. "Nag, Nag, Nag" was the title of one **Life** magazine article about me. Ted, it seemed, was simply considered "passionate." He was, and is, and his passion led me to study the issue of population in earnest to try to figure out a strategy. As I delved deeper I saw that population growth was a more complicated and divisive issue than I had realized: On the one extreme were those who thought the problem was not the number of human beings but inequitable distribution of resources; there were those who believed that technological breakthroughs would mitigate against growth in population; there were those who were concerned because they foresaw a world where people of color would dominate white people; and there were those who approached the issue solely from an environmental standpoint and favored setting quotas. I was confused by the argument from feminist groups that the population problem was, at its core, a gender issue. To be honest, in my heart of hearts I still saw gender issues as a distraction. All this was about to change.

It was 1994. I was asked to be a goodwill ambassador to the United Nations Population Fund (UNFPA) and to speak at the upcoming Conference on Population and Development in Cairo, Egypt. The challenge gave me an impetus for studying harder. I had never participated in a United Nations conference before, although two years before, I had gone to the Earth Summit in Rio with Ted. There I saw that women attendees had been relegated to the beachfront, where all the nongovernmental organizations (NGOs) were holding a separate People's Forum far away from the official conference (where the "real work" was being done). Apparently women, like NGOs, were viewed as a "special interest group" with no real place at the table. Within the year I would come to believe that women are not factions, afterthoughts, or an ancillary issue to be addressed after everything else is taken care of. Women **are** the issue—the **core** issue. They are the majority of humanity, whose rights are **human rights.** An attempt to solve **any** problem—poverty, peace, sustainable development, environment, health—by making an end run around women will fail.

Bella Abzug was there on the beach in Rio and under her phenomenal leadership women had begun to study how the UN works, where the institutional cracks and crevices are and how we might widen them and next time get inside, where we belong.

"Next time" was the Cairo conference at which I was speaking, and its purpose was to figure out how to stabilize population growth to enable sustainable development (economic progress that doesn't destroy the ecosystem). The previous population conferences (they take place every ten years) had resulted in plans of action written mostly by men and had focused on contraception (or the **withholding** of it—then, as now, ideology took precedence over evidence) and setting quotas. This time would be different.

Bill Clinton was president; Bella was on the official delegation, not simply at the NGO forum. Thanks in large part to Bella, former Colorado senator Tim Wirth (now president of Ted's United Nations Foundation), and other powerful organizers and advocates, the United States had a strong and determined contingent. This time women were **at** the table, actually drafting the plan of action. For them, population growth was not just a demographic issue or simply a health issue. These were frontline workers, experiential experts (as women usually are). No one knew better than they why the number of humans was climbing, and what to do about it.

The conference halls were filled to overflowing with women from around the world, striking and proud in their colorful robes, saris, and tunics. They were Buddhist, Catholic, Hindu, Muslim, black, brown, red, yellow, white. This was my first time on my own at one of these international gatherings, and I felt both exhilarated and intimidated.

But as I went from workshop to workshop and listened to the speakers, a new understanding washed over me. Gender was not the "distracting feminist issue" I had thought. It was the very crux of the matter. It was, in fact, the conceptual framework of the entire conference. Here, essentially, is what I was discovering: If you want to eradicate poverty, stabilize population growth, and create sustainable development, you—the World Bank, International Monetary Fund, Agency for International Development, and all other governmental and nongovernmental agencies—have to view everything through a gender lens. Does your project help women and girls? Does it make their lives easier? Does it empower them? Is your structural adjustment scheme going to make it harder for women to get loans to start their own businesses? Is your proposed dam going to make it harder for girls to fetch water for their families? Because everywhere in the so-called developing world, also known as the Global South, it is women and girls who plant the seeds, till the land, harvest the crops, fetch the water, cook the food, tend the livestock, bear the children, take charge of the family's health, find money for school fees, and spend whatever pennies they can scrape up on the family's well-being.

They are already stretched to their human limits and beyond. Make it worse for them and **everything** gets worse. Make it easier for them and virtually everything important in the family environment—education, income, community stability, and health—gets better.

I learned that if you want to reduce population growth, you have to increase the supply of contraceptives, but that this must be done in a culturally sensitive, nonjudgmental manner, and women must be offered a **choice** of methods. But more is needed. In some countries, if a woman tries to use contraception, she risks being beaten by her partner. In some cultures she needs all the children she can bear in order to have any status at all or to have enough hands to do the needed work. So if you want to **really** reduce population growth, **try educating girls.** Educated girls marry later, want smaller families, have more power within their marriages to bargain for the use of contraceptives, and practice child spacing. Try helping girls and women start businesses, become wage earners, access financial resources, be recognized and engaged as citizens. Such investments yield great benefits to the individual girls but also give girls a vision of their lives apart from simply marriage and rapid childbearing.

The conference had a special focus on adolescent reproductive health and sexuality. Girls, I discovered, are the strategic focus for reducing world population growth. The earlier a girl begins having children, the more children she will have during her childbearing years and the more generations are compacted. Adolescent pregnancy was of special interest to me because Georgia had the highest rate in the United States.

To do something about this, I learned, meant changing the way things were done. This is never easy. Family-planning clinics often exclude adolescents, formally or informally, through inconvenient hours, the high cost of services, and government- or state-mandated absence of confidentiality. Young people need time to develop trust with a potential service provider. They have lots of questions about feelings and about how to know when a relationship is right. Answering them takes time and attention and sensitivity. I remembered all too well my own positive first experience with a gynecologist and how different my life might have been had that **not** been the case. If young women feel judged by someone on a clinic staff or they are frightened at the prospect of a pelvic exam, they might not come back.

As I listened to the conference speakers, suddenly the "Just Say No" mantra of conservatives back home seemed so simplistic. The problem, I could see, wasn't the "no" part of it—it was the "just." It ignores the complex reasons that many women and girls have no choice about when they engage in sex (because of rape, early sexual abuse, low self-esteem, or economic considerations). "Just" makes it seem so easy, so black-and-white.

During the conference I wasn't just discovering strategies to reduce population growth; I began to see that my own experiences—of vulnerability to pressure from men around **their** sexual pleasure, around acquiescence and needing to be "acceptable"—were universal issues for women: in "developed" as well as "developing" countries! I kept thinking, If I am vulnerable to these pressures and fears, how can poor women—with little or no legal recourse, social status, financial independence, education, and knowledge of human rights—possibly stand up and say, "Sorry, I don't want any more children and I intend to use contraception"?

Then came a serendipitous experience that brought it all together, allowing me to see in practice the layered approach needed to bring girls hope and reduce early parenthood. I was taken to visit a community of impoverished Coptic Christians, the Zabaleen (garbage collectors) people of the Mokattam community, deep in the heart of Cairo at the bottom of a rock quarry. With me were my stepson Rhett Turner and Peter Bahouth, then executive director of the Turner Foundation. We had come to see a project funded by the Egyptian government, several NGOs, and the World Bank that was transforming the lives of the girls in the community through education, employment, and delayed childbirth. As we entered the community, we saw garbage-filled wagons with very young children sitting on them. Directly at the center of the community was a yawning compost pit perhaps sixty feet deep and more than half a football stadium long filled with garbage and pig excrement, which was composted. When the car door opened I was assaulted by a stench thicker and more unbearable than anything I could have imagined. I had to force myself out of the car and had to breathe through my mouth just to keep from getting sick. I could not believe that people lived their whole lives breathing this air.

Marie Assaad, a Catholic sister who chairs the Mokattam Committee for Health and Development, greeted us, and as we walked with her she pointed out the "homes" people lived in—dark, doorless structures with dirt floors, and garbage piled high in some places.

"It's hard to see all the way through to the back," Sister Marie explained, "but that's where each family keeps its pigs. The pigs eat much of the garbage, and then the excrement is taken and dumped into that pit you see over there, where it composts and is sold as fertilizer."

Children, mostly older girls, were sorting through the garbage, removing anything that wouldn't compost, and setting aside all paper materials for recycling. Marie Assaad told us that during part of the day some of the boys attended school but that until the project we'd come to visit had been started, girls never did. "There is no reason for parents to invest in the education of their daughters," Marie told us, and she went on to explain that girls are used, as their mothers were before them, as servants—to sort garbage, take care of siblings, cook food. Though responsible in large part for the family's health needs, they can't read prescriptions the doctor might give them and aren't accustomed to discussing things with (male) doctors.

When girls enter puberty they are married, fre-

quently earlier than Egyptian law permits (age sixteen). A girl may be married off to someone she
didn't choose or to someone many years older who
may have numerous partners, putting the girl at
risk of HIV/AIDS. Once married, a girl moves to
her husband's house to work as a servant for her
mother-in-law and other older women in the new
household.

Girls marry, leave home, and begin having babies sometimes right after menarche. Boys marry and
bring a new wife (fresh labor) into the family. This
was why parents invested in sons but not daughters.
And this was how the crippling cycle of deeply ingrained gender bias got repeated generation after
generation, driving up fertility rates and poor health.

But, slowly, things were changing. We entered a
small new school poised on the edge of the compost
pit. There I saw girls as well as boys sitting at desks,
studying. Sister Marie explained that to counter the
historic parental resistance to sending girls to school,
the organizers had taken a more holistic approach—
education and salaried work. She then led us to a
concrete building on the side of a hill. The rooms
were filled with huge looms, sewing machines, and
paper-pressing machines. In contrast with the rest of
the community, everything here was very clean. The
girls were using recycled paper from the garbage and
making it into stationery and cards that they embroidered and sold. Other girls were at looms, weav-
ing recycled bits of fabric into rugs. In another room
girls sat around a table sorting pieces of colored fabric, leftovers donated by Cairo's textile shops. They

were cutting them into squares, rectangles, triangles, applying what they'd learned in the school—math, fractions—to create symmetrical designs they sewed into beautiful quilts. While they worked they were taught health concepts, including reproductive health, contraception, and the dangers of early marriage and closely spaced births. Some of them were also trained as health outreach workers.

Marie Assaad told us that up to one-sixth of the girls in the community were engaged in these income-generating projects, which paid them (at the time) roughly $17 a month. It may be hard for us to imagine that $17 could be profoundly transformative, but this is the effect it had. Girls had achieved a goal, on their own, and had been rewarded for it; their sense of self was changed: "I **am** somebody." They could read. They could earn. They could, just maybe, break out of the cycle of servitude and despair.

Mothers and fathers began to view their girls in a new way. Now that the girls had developed income-generating skills, there was less resistance to educating them. Smart enough to read and to earn, they were becoming valuable assets. Mothers often identified with their daughters' new pride in themselves.

Family health had begun to improve as girls learned to read and grew less timid about moving about in public spaces, seeking information and services, talking with doctors. Another innovative part of this program was the creation of rewards to girls for delaying marriage, which gave them leverage and

Standing before a quilt made by girls in the Mokattam community—part of the nonprofit development project I visited while in Cairo, Egypt, at the UN Conference on Population and Development.
(Rhett Turner)

To Jane — who brings intelligence, a caring heart and discipline to the world's most vulnerable people.
With great admiration and thanks
[signature]

At the 1996 UN Women's Conference in Beijing, China. Left to right, standing: Tim Wirth, Barbara Pyle, Donna Shalala, Geraldine Ferraro, Sarah Kovner. I am seated next to Bella Abzug.

bargaining power with their families. Girls were offered 500 Egyptian pounds ($80) if they waited until after the age of eighteen and it was known that the marriage was freely chosen.

The example of Mokattam proved to me in the most human terms that in poor countries, if you changed the lives of girls by educating them and allowing them the opportunity to become wage earners, to participate in public life, it meant a twofold gain: You expanded human capital while simultaneously improving reproductive health and slowing population growth. Giving girls the chance to delay marriage until a later age meant that they postponed the first child's birth, resulting in a smaller family overall.

The Cairo conference was a turning point for me. I returned to Atlanta pondering how I could apply what I had learned.

When Ted was preoccupied with business and wouldn't mind my absence, Peter Bahouth and I traveled to different parts of the state to meet with America's frontline workers and to examine the realities of adolescent life at home. Although far less severe, adolescent girls (especially poor girls) in Georgia have things in common with the girls in Mokattam: limited identities apart from their sexuality; no bright future to motivate them to remain pregnancy-free and in school. There are high rates of child sexual abuse and domestic violence and few job opportunities.

I will never forget the day I was touring the maternity ward of a small county hospital near Albany,

Georgia, and was taken to a cubicle where a four-teen-year-old girl was in labor with her second child. Before I went in the nurse told me that the girl lived in a shack with no indoor plumbing. I looked down into her dark, expressionless eyes, which were looking straight at me. I prayed she saw no judgment in mine. I wish I had kissed her. She needed someone to take her in their arms and not let go for about twenty years. I wondered if anyone ever had, except for during sex. What could "Just Say No" mean to this girl? It was right about then that I read a quote from Marian Wright Edelman, founder and president of the Children's Defense Fund: "Hope is the best contraceptive." That was when I understood that those fifteen years of the Laurel Springs children's camp, along with what my daughter Lulu had taught me, had provided me with an experiential foundation for understanding what young people need in order to grow up healthy and productive. The Cairo conference had provided the conceptual framework.

I believe Ted and I made a unique and potent duo in the arena of population stabilization. We complemented each other perfectly. **We made it better:** he with his passionate, contagious, macro vision of the problem, his money, and his generosity; and I with my micro, on-the-ground, hands-on view (what specific factors cause individual women in different cultures to have large families). Both views are needed, but evidence shows that unless we address women's and girls' specific realities and to deliver high-quality services in a respectful, sensitive manner, all the contraception in the world won't make enough of a difference.

The following year, 1995, I founded the Georgia Campaign for Adolescent Pregnancy Prevention (G-CAPP) with the help and generous ongoing support of the Turner family and its foundation. Laura Turner Seydel in particular has been tremendous in helping fund-raise for G-CAPP. All the Turners have embraced this effort. While the organization's strategies have evolved, what I learned at the Cairo conference remains at its heart: a holistic approach that addresses "above-the-waist" issues—**hope**—as much as or more than the traditional "below-the-waist" ones.

The Georgia Campaign for Adolescent Pregnancy Prevention has been active in Georgia for ten years, and each year we have probed deeper into the lives of adolescents to discover what factors impel them to have babies when they are not yet **themselves.** We have learned that small things—like being rocked, held, and gazed at—can enable a child to remain resilient even in the face of unspeakable abuse and neglect. I learned from Lulu and Leni that a child who has received this kind of nurture will, as an adolescent, be less likely to become a parent too soon. That's why G-CAPP works with pregnant young women and mothers to assure they will know how to do this. I know from my own mothering experience that these skills don't always come naturally but that they can be learned.

Child sexual abuse, we have learned, is very

much connected to adolescent pregnancy and parenthood. That is one reason G-CAPP and the Jane Fonda Center at the Emory University School of Medicine, which opened in 2001, work with emergency room doctors and nurses, pediatricians, juvenile court justices, and mental health experts to enable more frontline workers to identify and learn how to get appropriate treatment for sexual abuse. Studies have estimated that one out of four American females has been sexually abused. Four in ten women who have sex before age fifteen report that their first sexual experience was coerced. Sexual abuse survivors often begin voluntary sexual relationships earlier and are more likely to become pregnant before the age of eighteen. One study found that one-half to two-thirds of pregnant teens reported sexual abuse histories.

Sexual abuse is more than physical: It is a form of brainwashing. The message emblazoned on the mind of an abuse victim is that her only worth **is** her sex, that her body doesn't belong to her, that saying no means nothing. She is stricken with what Oprah Winfrey, herself a victim of abuse, calls the "disease to please." Sexual abuse eradicates the very skills that are needed for girls to protect themselves from pregnancy, STDs, and HIV/AIDS. Knowing my mother's history with abuse, I found that this knowledge helped me immeasurably to understand and forgive her—and to want to help others heal. And, naturally, I also feel great passion for the work I do now because these issues have been at the center of my own life.

Friends come to Atlanta to support the work of G-CAPP. Here are Dolly, Lily, and me. (Erik S. Lesser/ Getty Images)

The following year Bob Redford and Peter came to help. (© 2004 Ashley Walsh)

In 2000, Oprah was our knock-'em-dead keynote speaker at G-CAPP's annual conference. (Mark Randelle King/Millennium Entertainment, Inc.)

CHAPTER TWENTY-FIVE

YEARNINGS

Being unfaithful is like the outside of a fruit peeling.
It's dry and bitter because it's facing away from the
  center.
Being faithful is like the inside of the peeling,
wet and sweet. But the place for peelings
is the fire. The real inside is beyond "sweet"
and "bitter." It's the source of deliciousness.

—RUMI

I YEARNED FOR the "source of deliciousness," in Rumi's words, which for me means emotional intimacy and soul connection. We got there on occasion, Ted and I (I remember each time vividly, when he would look deeply into my eyes and I felt we were truly connecting), and sometimes when that happened I swear he'd get scared. It was as though emotional intimacy (as opposed to needy longings) had to be kept in check. Still, there were the lovemaking times when we would lock eyes and melt into one. There were the times when something would set us to laughing so hard we'd sink to the floor, like the night when our guffaws collapsed us at the foot of the **Gone with the Wind** staircase at his Avalon plantation and we had to crawl up to bed on hands and knees.

We had been going steady for almost two years when in 1991 we got married at Avalon on my fifty-fourth, winter solstice, birthday. Troy gave me away, and Vanessa was maid of honor.

A week later Ted was **Time** magazine's Person of the Year.

A month later I discovered he was sleeping with someone else.

Life had taught me that men, at least those I tended to go for, operate by the **Fornicato, ergo sum** (I f——, therefore I exist) principle, but since there'd been plenty of Versailles moments of lovemaking with Ted and me, I'd rarely be away from him for more than a few hours, and since I knew he loved me, why?

The discovery was pure fluke. I was sitting in our car in the motor lobby of the CNN Center waiting to go to the airport with him. I saw a woman step up to valet parking. I'd seen her from behind, walking into the hotel two hours earlier. This time I saw her face and realized I knew her, but when I called out her name, she foolishly hid behind a pillar. I knew. In my gut, I knew. I called Ted's office on the car phone, and when his assistant, Dee Woods, answered I put it to her straight: "He pulled a nooner today, didn't he." (This was Ted's term for lunchtime dalliances.) She stammered and denied it (probably thinking, Hey, Fonda, didn't I warn you?). She told me Ted was on his way down to meet me.

I remember sitting there, my heart pounding, my mind imploding. Ted was ashen when he got into the car, behind the wheel. That's when I began hitting him about the head and shoulders with the car phone. Simultaneously, part of me was thinking that I'd never seen anyone do this in a movie and what a good scene it would make. (Is it only actors who think this way?) Then I poured my water bottle over his head and, crying and shaking, said, "I sure hope it was a great f——, because you just blew it with me. I'm outta here." Hitting someone is not my style. But it also occurred to me that I'd never cared enough before to express this kind of balls-out rage. "Why did you do it? Haven't things been great with us?"

He stopped at a red light and put his face into his hands. "Yes. Yes. I love you madly and our sex is great. I don't know. I guess it's . . . it's like a tic"— that's actually the word he used—"something I've gotten used to doing. I've always needed a backup in case something happens between us." **Hope for the best, but prepare for the worst.**

"Well, you've succeeded in making sure something would happen and now you'll be stuck with your backup. I hope you're happy."

That evening I flew to Los Angeles, booked myself into the always calming Hotel Bel-Air, and holed up there for two weeks, telling no one where I was except Leni, the woman who had taught me the

Workout and who had become my friend. Leni was Ted's gym trainer when we were in California. She knew him, and given her street smarts I intuited that she would be the one to best midwife me through the anguish, which was just what she did. She would come to my room every day, sit by the bed, give me hard Coffee Nips candies ("They're comforting"), and hold my hand while I cried and kvetched.

Ted suspected that Leni would know where I was and kept calling her, asking her to convince me to take him back. For two weeks I was determined that it was over. Then one day Leni came to my hotel room and said, "Think about it, Jane. If you don't give him a second chance, someday you may see him happy, with another woman on his arm, and you'll always wonder if that woman could have been you. He really wants you back. He says he'll do anything."

I called my former therapist (who was retired by then) and she recommended the people who had trained her, Beverly Kitaen Morse and Jack Rosenberg, who work with couples. I immediately made an appointment with them for a few days hence and asked Leni to arrange for Ted to come to Los Angeles and meet me in her apartment.

He flew from Atlanta the next day and came crawling into her living room on bended knee (which wasn't saying much, since this was his supplicant gesture of choice whenever he had apologies to make, often combined with kissing of shoe and/or head in hands).

"Oh, get up, for heaven's sake," I said. "You look foolish and I know that doesn't mean anything anyway. Half your business associates have seen you in that position at one time or another." I then told him I would give him another chance on three conditions: that he would never betray me again, would never see the woman again, and would go into counseling with me. He agreed to all of it, and the next day we spent six consecutive, life-altering hours with Jack and Beverly and continued to see them off and on for eight years whenever we were in Los Angeles. **Make it better.**

For seven of those years (there's that seven again) Ted kept his promise and never betrayed my trust, never went behind my back to exercise his "tic" (except for our last nine months together, when he sensed the marriage was doomed and was looking for a substitute). In fact, the day came when he said to someone who had heaped praise on him for something he'd done, "Stop, you're being too monogamous."

"Ted," I said, "don't you mean 'magnanimous'?"

"Oh yes," he replied proudly. "I didn't use to be able to say the word **monogamous** at all, but now I use it so much, I say it by mistake. Pretty cute, huh?"

Before this early crisis in our relationship, I would feel Ted leave me energetically if an especially inviting woman came around. At those moments I would imagine the testosterone washing through his frontal lobe and obliterating all else. After the crisis, I swear I could feel his antennae retracting.

Over the years, Ted and I were given many tools that helped smooth things out in our relationship. We developed better communication skills; we learned the importance of "skin time"—when we would lie together quietly, skin to skin, and have it not be about performing. I discovered that Ted abhorred being presented with faits accomplis, so I tried vigilantly to avoid presenting them. But, sadly, I learned that this was easier said than done. It was easy to consult and discuss things before doing them when the things were relatively insignificant and external, like moving a painting, changing dinnertime, buying a new saddle. But when later in the marriage they were decisions of critical importance to me—having to do with spiritual faith or with spending time with Vanessa when she was about to give birth—I would simply arrange to do what I felt I needed to do. I was accustomed to not having my feelings and needs respected by the men in my life, and I feared that if I opened up such decisions for discussion, I would be bullied out of them or they would be denied me outright—or love would be taken away. (As it turned out, my fears were well-founded.) Those times were very infrequent, but they ended up playing a role in the dissolution of our marriage.

While it was Ted's dalliance that brought us into the therapists' offices, I decided that in addition to our couples counseling, I wanted to work separately on my own issues. I sensed that my relationship with Ted, with all its challenges, was my opportunity to heal, and because I so wanted the marriage to work, I was willing to do the needed work on myself. Ted never did the same. Still, given how he was raised, it is extraordinary that he was willing to do as much as he did.

For those of us who harbor old ghosts (doesn't everybody?), it is in our relationships that they surface, and then we are confronted with a choice: Either we learn to manage the ghosts or we settle for distance or instability. Some can learn the managing part on their own; some, like me, need the help of a trained professional to put the pieces back together.

I believe that the moment I met Ted, I intuited that this man was the one my heart could finally, fully, open to. I thought that all the elements were there for the kind of deep soul-to-soul love that I had never really had with anyone before. Ironically, this was why I fled from him at first and was so skittish when we started going together: I was frightened of the vulnerability that comes with the heart's opening and was scared of being hurt and steamrolled. With Ted I was determined to put this fear behind me. I wanted us to be two fully authentic people meeting in mutual affection, communication, affirmation, and respect—and I assumed that's what he wanted as well. After all, he was constantly talking about wanting intimacy and reminding me that I was afraid of it. It never occurred to me that he was too . . . well, not afraid of it so much as incapable of it.

The crisis with Ted was actually a blessing, because it had brought me to Beverly Morse, who turned out to be the perfect guide for the next part of my journey to . . . what shall I call it? Wholeness. Heartfulness. Authenticity. Integration? I had been living for so long in my head. What was essential for me now was to get back into my body, where I hadn't

On the steps of Avalon Plantation just after the wedding.
(© Barbara Pyle)

Our Hollywood wedding party given for us by
(left to right) Barry and Carole Hirsch and
Paula Weinstein and her husband, Mark Rosenberg.

been since adolescence—to be reembodied. I have discovered that there are different degrees of embodiment, and certainly, with Ted's love, I made major forays in that direction. But Beverly's method of using breathing techniques and bodywork—"somatic therapy"—took me to a deeper level. Over the years, with her help and a lot of hard work on my part, I was able to gain confidence. I learned to forgive my mother and so was able to forgive myself for my shortcomings; to know that I had done the best I could with what I had at any given time, just as my mother had; that I was no longer the woman with little love to give. I was learning to love myself. Baby steps at first, a beginning.

When I look back now over the landscape of my ten years with Ted, on the one hand I am struck by how happy I was much of the time, growing stronger and more confident every year. In part this was due to the personal work I was doing on myself, and in part it was because of the positive, centering role I knew I played in Ted's life. Yet alongside this, behind the closed doors of the most intimate parts of our relationship, I still deafened myself to the signals from my body telling me how **not**-good I felt about many things he did that hurt me and about things I agreed to do to please him even if it went against my own well-being. I would drink to get numb and stuff my feelings in order to be sure Ted felt good. I would accommodate his needs (even when he didn't ask me directly) out of fear of not being loved. I thought I had gotten over this "disease to please" with the ending of my marriage to Vadim. And, again, when the marriage to Tom ended, I thought, Well, I'll never do **that** again. But this burying, this betraying, of myself was such an ingrained part of my modus operandi that in each new relationship I repeated the pattern, managed hardly to notice, and convinced myself that somehow the problems would just fade away. Besides, life with Ted was full and interesting, and denial was relatively easy.

I tried my best to understand and comply with his need to fill empty spaces with movement, activity, or the planning thereof. After all, it wasn't as if I were a stay-at-home slouch myself. Actually we were rather well-balanced when it came to levels of energy. I still loved winging back and forth among his beautiful properties and being privy to the exciting events that swirled around us. I knew that together we were making a difference. I still found myself smiling when I heard him coming through the door. There were still times of rapture and melting. But the rigidity of our schedules and the constant moving had begun to empty me out.

We would no sooner arrive and settle into one of the Nebraska ranches, for example, than two days later we'd be off to the next one. Every time we'd walk into a new place, Ted would kiss me and say, "Welcome home," a ritual that I found charming. And God knows I worked hard to make every place feel like home. But I felt homeless. Homeless with twenty houses—weird. When saleswomen would ask if the two dozen panties I'd just bought should be wrapped as gifts, I'd laugh. They were all for me, to be spread out among the different places.

We both got a kick out of the extremes of our life, from muddy jeans and waders to tuxedos and gowns and back again within less than twenty-four hours. But with all the yawing between extremes, there was little time to put down the roots I have always yearned for. Nor was I able to spend time on things that mattered deeply to me, like reading, working on the fledgling Georgia Campaign for Adolescent Pregnancy Prevention, or, most important, spending time with my children. If I wanted to see them, I had to ask them to arrange to meet us somewhere along our travel route. I felt their disappointment acutely, and it pained me because I knew they were right in feeling that I was again losing myself, and them, just to make the marriage work. I would have liked Ted to understand and support such needs of mine. And he tried—but only when my needs didn't interfere with his own. It's not that I didn't **know** what I needed to do; it was that I didn't have the courage to go ahead and **do** it. I was not ready to enter an authentic relationship with **myself** if it meant risking my marriage.

Have you noticed how we are presented with the same lessons, over and over and over, before a tipping point is reached? The lessons we need to learn circle round us, closing in, until finally we are ready to take them in. **Take them in.** Those are the words that matter, because until I had **embodied** the lessons I was supposed to learn, absorbed them into the warp and woof of my being, they didn't "take"; they remained a head trip and didn't lead to changes in my behavior.

We'd been together eight years, married for six. Behaviors destructive to the relationship had gone unchallenged and become sacrosanct, like squatter's rights. When I became resentful and would turn inward, he would fragment and yell that I was abandoning him. I had learned not to argue, not to say a word, just to let him vent. It was his safety valve. In spite of this, on Ted's scale of one to ten (he always rated things numerically), life hovered around six . . . in other words, more good than bad.

To complicate matters, I could feel myself yearning for spirituality in my life, something I had to keep to myself because of Ted's hostility to anything metaphysical. I found myself increasingly interested in questions about God. What is God? What is it I feel is "leading" me? One day in south Georgia a conservative Christian asked me if I had been saved. He was not coming from a friendly place, and feeling his hostility, I chose not to engage. I let him know that I felt myself to be a spiritual person. But his question stuck with me.

I went to my friend Andrew Young, civil rights leader, former UN ambassador, and minister, and asked him if he thought I should be saved.

"You don't need to," he replied. "You're already saved." And he went on to tell me that the original

Greek meaning of the word **saved** meant that a person was whole.

Then I asked my friend Nancy McGuirk the same question about being saved. Nancy is married to a top executive at Turner Broadcasting, and over the years we had spent countless hours at business receptions off in a corner talking about religion. Nancy, a Presbyterian, teaches a weekly Bible class to hundreds of women.

"Well," said Nancy, "I'll tell you what being saved did for me—it took me to the next step." Now, for a champion take-it-to-the-next-stepper like me, that was hard to resist. Yet I knew all too well that Ted would disapprove. Christians were one of the groups he'd apologized to after he'd said that Christianity was a religion for losers. I wasn't ready to take him on yet.

One day around the time I turned fifty-nine, I was participating in the annual bison roundup on one of Ted's New Mexico ranches. It was an awesome experience: thousands of the animals stretching out before me in a line so long that it disappeared over the side of the mesa, reappearing miles ahead, lumbering across the valley floor and up the side of the distant mesa. Bison move silently, no mooing like cattle, just the soft thudding of hooves and a deep, purring breath that you must listen for carefully to hear. My horse Geronimo was a black-and-white paint, and I am convinced that the painted ponies

Indians often rode during their hunting forays must have been imprinted on the collective memory of the bison, because often one would suddenly charge from the center of the line and rush me full speed while the old cowboys, like the seventy-year-old Till twins, Emmett and Emory, on their plain brown horses would laugh and shout at me for getting too close.

At day's end I would pile into the back of someone's pickup with four or five of the cowboys, pop a beer, wedge myself between the old tires so as not to get too jostled on the twenty-some miles of rough roads back to headquarters, sink back against some hay bales, and gaze at the sky, deeply happy. You know the feeling, when you are exactly where you want to be in the world? I thought about how I had played a cowboy in **Comes a Horseman** and about the childhood question I'd once put to my brother: "Peter, who could round up buffalo better, Sue Sally or me?" And here I was coming full circle to where I'd been in my girlhood, only it wasn't a fantasy or a movie role.

It dawned on me that in one year I would turn sixty. That was when the whole notion of my third act came to me with a jolt that wasn't a bump in the road. **Oh my God! This will be a biggie. How do I want to handle it? I need to figure out what my life has meant up until now in order to know what I need to do with what lies ahead.**

As I wrote in the preface, "Know thine enemy" is one of my rules: Confront head-on the things that scare me and become deeply familiar with them. This is why, knowing that sixty would be a difficult threshold to cross, I decided that the best way was for me to make a short video of my life to discover its different themes. I had all the makings: My father had been a home movie buff, so I had access to more than the average amount of footage and photos of myself as an infant and toddler. Plus there were the archives of interviews, movies, and press clips from when my life became public. All the raw material was there for me to resurrect the forgotten moments of my girlhood. It would be up to me to decipher the clues it held, to identify the patterns—and to be brave enough to name them.

I wanted to do it mainly for myself and for Vanessa, and it would also be for Troy, Lulu, Nathalie, and Ted's daughters, Laura and Jennie. I had a sense that if I did it right, the notion of confronting the third act in this manner—intentionally working to address what my regrets might be— would resonate with my friends, especially my women friends. I then decided I would have a big party to celebrate the start of my third act and offer the movie as my gift to the guests.

Vanessa is a documentary filmmaker and editor, so I invited her to help me put it together. Her answer, albeit prickly, pointed to one of the central issues I would have to deal with. She said, "Why don't you just get a chameleon and let it crawl across the screen?" Ouch. This was the rap on me: I've had so many personae over my lifetime that it's easy to think, Who is she, anyway? Is there a "there there"?—to quote Dorothy Parker describing Oakland, California. When I looked at photos of myself over the years and matched them up with my husband of the time, I couldn't help feeling that maybe it was true—maybe I simply become whatever the man I am with wants me to be: "sex kitten," "controversial activist," "ladylike wife on the arm of corporate mogul." Vanessa had exposed one of my central issues: **Was** I just a chameleon, and if so, how was it that a seemingly strong woman could so thoroughly and repeatedly lose herself? **Or had I really lost myself?** I also hoped that exploring my past would help me define the next thirty years so that the ending, when it came, would be as free of regrets as possible. That was the promise I had made to myself as I had watched my father die almost two decades earlier.

Over the summer of 1996, as I researched my journey, a trail began to appear. But to make sense of the emerging patterns, I had to concentrate hard on remembering how I **felt** each step of the way: how I felt sitting on Sue Sally's mother's lap as she reprimanded me for using bad language; how I felt when Pedro tried to hump Pancho; how I felt when Susan asked me how I felt about Mother's death; how I felt when Sydney Pollack asked me my opinion of the script of **They Shoot Horses, Don't They?**

I knew that by watching my films—all forty-nine of them (at the time)—and by reading through my old interviews (many of which I had pasted into albums over the years), a sense of who I was back then would come to me and help me understand the ways in which I had changed. This process caused me much wincing, and much looking over my shoulder to make sure no one else was watching. Trust me, there's something to be said for having your various utterances disappear into obscurity rather than linger in print or on film to haunt you.

All this research was done rather sporadically. I had to search for air pockets in the frantic life I shared with Ted. It was done mostly during the spring and summer while we were in Montana, and it wasn't easy. Whenever my personal extracurricular activities (which, by the way, kept my head above water) would take time away from Ted, he would suffer abandonment anxieties. So to work on the "script" of my life, I would often "fake it": I would drive out to the river with Ted and we'd separate, each to fish different stretches; then, instead of fishing I'd park myself under a tree and read, write, or think. Sometimes I'd sneak my laptop into the back pouch of my fishing vest and pull that out to write on it until the battery died. Then I would fish like crazy in order to have something to report when we hooked back up again. Occasionally I'd pretend to not feel well and send Ted off with other guests to fish or hunt while I worked.

As it turned out, what I was doing intuitively by choosing to prepare for my sixtieth the way I did was preparing myself for **myself**—starting at the very beginning.

ACT THREE

BEGINNING

We shall not cease from exploration
And the end of all our exploring
Will be to arrive where we started
And know the place for the first time
—T. S. Eliot,
"Little Gidding," **Four Quartets**

At the end of every road you meet yourself.
—S. N. Behrman

With Vanessa and Malcolm (around age two).

In Rome with Troy for a V-Day summit meeting.
(©Joyce Tenneson)

In Juarez, with Eve Ensler, far left, and Sally Field, right.
(Jorge Uzon/AFP/Getty Images)

March 2004, in Mumbai, India, where I did **The Vagina Monologues** with Eve Ensler, Marisa Tomei, and Indian and Pakistani actresses.

Girls are at the core of G-CAPP's work.
(Courtesy G-CAPP)

Christmas 2004 in Atlanta with Lulu, Malcolm on my lap, Viva on Vanessa's lap, and Nathalie.
(Matt Arnett)

CHAPTER ONE

SIXTY

We are commanded to love our neighbors as ourselves, and I believe that to love ourselves means to extend to those various selves that we have been along the way the same degree of compassion and concern that we would extend to anyone else. If to do so is unseemly, then so much for seemliness.

—FREDERICK BUECHNER,
Telling Secrets

Silence is the first thing within
the power of the enslaved to shatter.
From that shattering,
everything else spills forth.
—ROBIN MORGAN,
Demon Lover: The Roots of Terrorism

ON DECEMBER 21, 1997, the curtain went up on my third act. Ted threw me a wonderful sixtieth birthday party. Vanessa designed the invitation: On the front was a yellow road sign reading WORK IN PROGRESS, and it accordioned out into a series of photos of me in various phases of my life, ending with "to be continued." Our families and friends were there—three hundred in all—and it was probably the most diverse group Atlanta had ever seen.

Keeping a secret is near to impossible for Ted, but he managed not to tell me what he was giving me as a gift, only teasing me by saying it was "a gift that would keep on giving." That night he stood up and told the guests about how I had often said I thought he was smart to have set up his family foundation, because it guaranteed that all his children would be together with him at least four times a year.

"So for your sixtieth birthday, Jane, I'm giving you a ten-million-dollar family foundation."

I thought I'd heard wrong. He asked me to come to the stage, and when I stood my knees buckled. I would have gone down had it not been for Max Cleland, one of Georgia's U.S. senators and a triple Vietnam amputee, who was next to me in his wheelchair. When I got to the stage, I threw my arms around Ted, kissed him, and said to the guests, "He told me he was giving me a gift that would keep on giving . . . but, oh my God! I had no idea."

With the help of my friend the editor Nick Boxer, I had finished the twenty-minute video of my life, and later in the evening I showed it to the guests. Although they seemed interested, even moved by it—especially my women friends—it was of necessity done in such broad strokes that when I look at it today it seems quite superficial. I now realize it couldn't possibly have had the impact on others that making it had on me, for it changed me in ways that would become apparent only as my third act began to unfold, and in ways I did not necessarily intend.

Toward the end of the video, over images of my life with Ted, I explained in a voice-over how eight years earlier I had decided to leave my life in California and commit to him because I wanted to accept the challenge of intimacy. I talked about how frightening this had been for me; how Katharine Hepburn's advice to never get soggy had come back to me. And then I said, "Suddenly it hit me: This was what I was supposed to face, my biggest fear—intimacy, the one thing that had eluded me, a true, lasting, intimate relationship with a life partner. If I didn't make a leap of faith, this would be the thing at the end of my life that was left undone; the big 'if only.' "

I was sixty. I had done the hard work needed for intimacy to become a reality, at least on my end. The work was bearing fruit: I was beginning to sense what my marriage could be like if Ted and I really showed up for each other. Working on my birthday video had allowed me to see that there **was** a "there there" within me after all. It exposed for me the threads of continuity, like suspension bridges, that had spanned the canyons of change in my life. I

Dancing with Ted at my sixtieth birthday party.

Peter and Nathalie at the birthday party.

The birthday party: Jon Voight cracking up the Fonda
cousins (all women) from out west.

could see that the main thread was courage in everything **except** my personal life.

As the weeks went by following my birthday, I
became aware of feeling more like **me,** a whole being,
standing next to but no longer overlapping into
the being that was Ted. I was ready. But I knew it
wouldn't happen unless Ted was willing to make
some changes in the way he regarded our relationship. Unfortunately, his tendency was to like things
just the way they were, and despite my growing self-
esteem I **still** wasn't able to come right out and ask
for what I wanted—even after I had realized that
there could be no truly intimate relationship between
us unless I spoke my truth. **I still felt I had to please
him at the expense of myself.** The subtle power of
sexist roles and their inherent inequality has been
deeply imprinted in all of us raised under them.

More and more frequently I'd send him subtle
signals about how I was feeling, and when the signals
weren't received, I would drink to numb myself until
the anger had passed. If he'd bothered to look closely,
Ted could have seen the silent me, like a trout swimming out from behind a rock and coming closer to
the surface. But Ted is not a close looker, especially if
what he might find would risk muddying his waters,
and I—accomplice that I was—wasn't willing to
break the surface. One voice was telling me, **Jane,
you can't go on this way,** while another (very strong)
voice was whispering, **Maybe you shouldn't rock the
boat. Things are okay. It's an interesting life. He's a
wonderful man.**

Out of love and respect for Ted and his children, I will not go into specifics about what was not working in our relationship. Quite honestly it is not necessary, and I have already given you a sense of the issues. What I **can** write about (and what is important because of its universality) is how in spite of everything I remained paralyzed when it came to actually speaking up for myself in ways I feared might end the relationship. And I **can** write about how it took two more years for me to get up the courage to do it. I had been unafraid to travel to North Vietnam in an effort to help end the war; to place myself in harm's way; to risk public censure; to stand up to the government when I thought what they were doing was wrong. But when it came to a relationship with a man, I still could not raise my voice. **And I wasn't even dependent on him financially!**

One specific problem that increasingly wore me down was all the traveling. While it had seemed relatively easy and fun at first, I hadn't realized that it would never end, that we would be continually on the move, like migrating birds, always packing, never totally unpacking. First there was one place in Argentina, and we'd go there for a restful week or ten days of fishing when it was winter in North America. But then Ted added two more properties in Argentina, so that even when we were there we were shuttling from one place to another.

Guilt was beginning to set in when I didn't want to fish every single day, when I didn't want every hour programmed. Some days I wanted to do noth-

ing . . . just read, think. I wanted to acknowledge to
Ted that I was on a journey and invite him to join
me, but it required slowing down to what psychologist Marion Woodman calls "soulspeed," and for the
driven, soulspeed feels like death. Quincy Jones put
it well in his autobiography, **Q:**

> I was always running, but every time I ran
> I kept crashing into myself coming from
> the opposite direction, and he didn't know
> where he was going either. I ran because
> there was nothing behind me to hold me
> up. I ran because I thought that was all
> there was to do. I thought that to stay in
> one place meant to die.

I thought it was a male thing, until I read **Miss
America by Day,** by former Miss America Marilyn
Van Derbur, whose father had committed incest
with her from age five until eighteen. She writes
movingly about how often victims of early abuse
(sexual, physical, or psychological) must stay busy,
keep moving, so as to avoid feelings that might otherwise arise. Ted had to keep moving so that his
demons wouldn't catch up with him. I felt empathy
for him, but I was becoming aware that there was no
deepening to our life, just a lateral repetition of
scheduled activities. Now that I had started my last
act, I wanted to stop all the **doing** and start **being**—
to slow down and show up. Ted couldn't. When it
came right down to it, I think he was scared.

I began to descend into quiet desolation, disappearing into sleep much of the time. Ted, I was discovering, thought that intimacy meant to tell his innermost thoughts to his significant other, which was odd since he told his innermost thoughts to everyone. But **listening**, in turn, **to** that other? No. I was becoming aware of how nearly impossible it was to have a two-way conversation with Ted, unless I was talking about something he could easily recognize as relevant to himself. There just wasn't room in his brain for words other than his own. It's not as if I hadn't seen the warning signs.

Time was fleeting; color was beginning to drain out of things; the nictitating membrane was settling in; increasingly I found myself engaging in angry mind rehearsals with Ted and venting to my closest women friends. I would think, I don't want to live laterally anymore, skimming over the surface. Vertical is how I need to live. Moving so fast through life leaves no time for the spirit, for mystery, for the existential.

I asked him, "Who are you, Ted? Beneath your worldly successes and the applause and clamor of the crowd, who are you?" I tried to explain by using myself as an example: "I have been an award-winning actor, but that's just what I **did,** that's not who I **am.** If that was who I am, I'd have been miserable leaving it all behind." I tried to tell him who I felt I was: a woman in the last act of her life who wanted to be authentic, whole, to deepen my life, to embody the soul I felt hovering around me, asking to be invited in.

I love Ted and always will, and I knew that it wasn't for lack of intelligence that he didn't understand me. Well, yes, in a way it was—lack of emotional intelligence, the result of his traumatic childhood.

Perhaps I could have handled the constant traveling if it hadn't been for the other things that hurt me; if I had been allowed more time on my own every now and then; if I had been able to spend more time with my emotionally accessible women friends, my children, my organization. Perhaps I would have been able to return to him better able to accept not only his drivenness but his enmeshment. He fears if no one is there to witness him, he will no longer exist.

Then something quite unexpected was thrown into this unsettled mix: the magic of grandmotherhood. Vanessa told me she was pregnant, and I knew that I wanted and needed to be there for her in whatever ways I could. Ted had always generously gone out of his way to help Vanessa and me grow closer, inviting her to travel with us, even offering her a job at Avalon Plantation doing what she does so well— organic farming. But when I told him she was going to have a baby and that I wanted to be there for her as much as possible, he exploded in rage. I think he sensed that my energy would be drawn away from him for a while. But frankly I was stunned and disturbed by his reaction.

As the time of the birth approached, I told Ted I wanted to be with Vanessa for the ten days surrounding her due date. Although by now he had gotten over his anger, he wasn't happy about my going. But there was no question that this was where I had to be, and Ted even surprised us by showing up as Vanessa went into labor.

It was a home birth at Ted's farm outside Atlanta, with a midwife in attendance. Theoretically we parents know when our children are grown-ups, yet a part of us is still awed when circumstances force us to see that they've grown **beyond** us. I was impressed by Vanessa's decision to have a home birth, how she had gone about finding a midwife (home births are not legally sanctioned in Georgia) and prepared herself for all eventualities. I read books she gave me on home birthing, and together we watched videos of actual home births. I realized sadly how I, like many women, had relinquished to doctors my ownership of this ultimate metamorphic experience. This had been true when I gave birth to Vanessa, but now I was watching her do it right—not in the sense that everyone must have a home birth, but "right" in being intentional, fully in charge, informed. In case it might be needed, we preregistered at a hospital and practiced driving there. She carefully prepared a birth plan (instructions the mother gives to the doctors and nurses about what she wants and doesn't want to happen to her and her newborn). For instance, Vanessa was adamant about having natural childbirth, and she specified that the baby not be taken from her or given any bottles.

I stayed with Vanessa and Malcolm for four days after he was born. I was so proud of the brave way she handled the birth and grateful that I could be there to help her with him. I would sit in a rocking chair for hours at a time while she slept, holding Malcolm against my chest, singing the lullabies I had sung to Vanessa thirty years earlier. A May breeze would gently lift the slipcovers on the porch furniture, and as I gazed out over the freshly blooming dogwood, the wild azaleas, and the lake where two swans held court, I felt that life could never get any better. No one had prepared me for the feelings that arose when I held this little boy, Vanessa's child. I was utterly broken open in ways I had never been before. Malcolm had enabled me to discover the combination to the safe where the soft part of my heart had been shut away for so long. Depths of feeling washed over me, cleansing me, carrying me too far down the new path of intimacy for me to ever want to turn back. Perhaps Ted knew it would be this way and that's why he had gotten so upset at the news I would be a grandmother.

With the birth of Malcolm, the Phoenix that had been on hold for ten years had risen: I also was being born anew. I knew now that I had to muster the courage to ask for what I needed in my relationship with Ted. At the time, these things seemed huge and difficult to me, but looking back, I see that I was asking for reasonable, bread-and-butter, emotional things. I knew that if I didn't speak up, I would end my life married, yes, but filled with longings and regrets— just what I'd vowed I would not do. Deception is a lousy foundation for intimacy, and sustainability in a relationship is as critical as it is in the environment.

Then one day when Ted's business brought us to Los Angeles, I went to see my therapist. She said,

"Jane, the choice is yours. You like challenges, so I am throwing the gauntlet at your feet. Take the challenge. Be brave in your relationship, whatever the outcome will be. Ask him to join you."

I was acutely aware that there was more time behind me than in front of me and that I had to shake myself awake. Maybe Ted would also like to jolt himself onto a new path but didn't know how. **Maybe I'm supposed to do this . . . for both of us. I love him enough to try.**

It was June. We were up early at his ranch in Montana. The sun had barely risen above the Spanish Peaks, yet a sultry air shimmered across the sleeping fields, signaling the hot day ahead. It had taken me two years to muster the courage for this crucial moment.

We gathered our fishing gear, and as we were driving over the bumpy dirt road to his favorite part of Cherry Creek, I said, "Ted, I am scared. I feel myself going numb. I need us to try to do some things differently in our marriage, because otherwise I'm not sure I can show up for you the way you want me to." And I spelled out what I hoped would happen. I don't remember what he said, only that a rush of discordant, confused emotions suddenly sucked up all the air in the car. He was angry, that much I knew.

When we got to the creek he said, "Let's go fishing and we'll discuss this later."

As usual we went to separate stretches of water and for several hours I attempted to fish, but my heart was pounding with dread. Oh my God, I thought. What if he actually refuses to try? For almost nine years I've made a core part of myself invisible in order to be "good enough," and now I've put it out there. What if . . . No, it's too awful to countenance. For a moment I imagined our marriage going under, like my grasshopper fly disappearing under a riffle.

From the moment we got back in the car, I knew things were not going to be as I had hoped. He had not calmed down; anger was boiling. He was fragmented into little pieces, and I could get no traction anywhere to slow him down and explain my feelings in any depth. I should not have been surprised. As is typical of people who don't speak up, I had overwhelmed him by dumping everything on him all at once—he, who can't handle change. When we got back to the ranch, all he could do was bang the walls with his fists and his head. I was stunned by his reaction, but I watched him with detachment. **I did what I had to do, and for once I am not going to "fix it" by backtracking.** That morning I stepped outside the framework that had held me in thrall most of my life and I could not go back. There was detachment but also a sense of free fall, similar to the limbo an actor feels when he or she is morphing into a new character. Only this **was my life,** and I had no road map.

Over the ensuing months I tried to find ways of making Ted understand my point of view. But it was as though something had snapped, as if he had been hijacked by his emotions and was incapable of hearing me. I was dumbfounded, because I knew he loved me and that our life together was more important to him than the few things I had asked him to

try—**try!** I hadn't even demanded a "never again."
Yet our life seemed to be crumbling before my eyes.
**Was it possible that his male identity was so inex-
tricably bound up with things as they were that he
would risk losing me to avoid change?**

There was another factor that, understandably,
compounded his fragmentation and convinced him
I had lost my mind: He learned that I had become a
Christian. Remember Ted's abhorrence of decisions
made without his consultation? Well, this was about
as major a one as can be imagined.

Several months earlier my friend Nancy Mc-
Guirk had taken me to my "next step." I hadn't told
Ted beforehand, because by then I didn't feel we were
on the same team. Alongside the frantic life we
shared, I was living a parallel inner life, where I took
care of my own needs. I was used to doing this.

I also knew if I had discussed with him my need
for spirituality, he would have either asked me to
choose between him and it or bullied me out of it. It
was too new. I was too raw. Besides, it was not for
nothing that he'd been captain of the debating team
at Brown University. If I had discussed it with him
beforehand, there was no way I could have held up
under what I knew would be his blistering attack on
Christianity, most of which I actually agreed with.
**Don't you know that Christianity, just like Islam,
Judaism, and Hinduism, says women are inferior?
What do you think the Garden of Eden myth
means, anyway? Woman was an afterthought, made
from Adam's rib to serve him, and then was blamed**

for man's fall from grace. And what about the witch burnings, the Crusades, and the Inquisition? He had it all at his fingertips. He knew the Bible far better than I did; he'd read it twice, cover to cover, had been "saved" seven times (including once by the Reverend Billy Graham). He had even considered joining the ministry as a young man, in the years before his younger sister died a terrible, prolonged death from lupus and he had turned from God.

In hindsight I realize that not telling him was a wildly unfair thing for me to do. But I felt lost and empty. I needed to be filled. An inner life had been emerging for some time, and I needed to name it. I named it "Christian," because that is my culture. I began to pray every day, out loud, on my knees, and it was like being hooked up to the power of the Mystery that had been leading me for the last decade. It wasn't so much a **learning** about the existence of God, because learning implies use of intellect. It was more an experiencing of His presence, a psychic lucidity, that was allowing me access to something beyond consciousness.

It wasn't long, however, before I found myself bumping up against certain literal, patriarchal aspects of Christian orthodoxy that I found difficult to embrace. I will address this in the next chapter. But I discovered that alienation from dogma doesn't have to mean a loss of faith.

Ted's level of rage and stress in the six months following my speaking up almost incapacitated him.

Marilyn Van Derbur gave me an insight when she wrote in **Miss America by Day** that her early trauma "had literally hard-wired my brain so that my stress level on a scale of one to ten was fifty. If someone humiliated me, I had no way to accommodate the additional stress, so I would go into a kind of craziness." There had been too much stress, abuse, and instability in Ted's early life. Anyone who knows him knows that he reacts to stress almost like someone suffering from posttraumatic stress disorder. I had blindsided him with my need to renegotiate our marriage **and** with my becoming a Christian—and this double whammy acted as a trigger to rage over which he had no control.

Ted insisted that it wasn't normal to change after sixty. I told him I thought it was dangerous **not** to. While I had become stronger, Ted had not, and my speaking up for myself was a blow from which he could not allow himself to recover. Maybe he was too invested in his projection of me as someone who expressed her needs only if they didn't threaten his and who would never place another love—for self, for children, grandchildren, friends, or Jesus—above, or even on a par with, her love for him.

I had started out hopefully. I knew that other very successful alpha males can, after a certain age, when testosterone levels drop, make the shift, slow down, open their hearts, and reduce the need to perform. I felt that he loved me enough to at least **try**. In fact, he did say at one point that he would try to do what I had asked in the marriage. For many months I was ecstatic. I no longer wanted to leave myself behind; I

Sitting down to lunch at a UN Foundation meeting in
Capetown, South Africa. Left to right: Tim Wirth, the
foundation president; board member Graca Machel; her
husband, Nelson Mandela; Carolyn Young, whose husband,
Ambassador Andy Young, is a board member. I had just
come from a tour of Robbin Island prison, where Mandela
had been jailed for twenty-five years.

wanted sexuality to come out of **relationship**—eye-to-eye, soul-to-soul pleasure, where everything wasn't all planned out to a fare-thee-well. He was happy with sexuality that came out of performance. The very thing I had feared the most—that I would gain my voice and lose my man—was actually happening. It wasn't how I thought the story would end. You see what you need to see in another person, and when your needs change you try to see different things. The problem comes when what you need and what you see isn't seen or needed by your partner. It doesn't mean your partner is bad; it just means that she or he wants something else in life. My happiness was short-lived, for I could see Ted withering before my eyes. Clearly he wasn't going to be able (or willing) to make the journey with me. We agreed to separate.

It was only after we separated that I discovered that while Ted was telling me he would try to do things differently he had turned to his old adage: "Hope for the best, but prepare for the worst." He had spent our last year together looking for my replacement. That was why he seemed to be graying before my eyes: It was killing him to be dishonest with me. The day we parted, three days after the millennium, he flew to Atlanta to drop me off. As I drove from the airport to Vanessa's home in a rental car, my replacement was waiting in the hangar to board his plane. My seat was still warm.

CHAPTER TWO

MOVING ON

It begins with the vision to recognize when a job, a lifestage, a relationship, is over—and let it go.

It involves a sense of the future, a belief that every exit line is an entry, that we are moving on, rather than out.

—ELLEN GOODMAN

AT AGE SIXTY-TWO I found myself alone, living in my daughter's guest room. I was acutely aware of how different I felt this time from the way I'd felt after my breakup with Tom eleven years earlier. I didn't feel alone, because I wasn't. I was with myself, for the first time, and proud that I hadn't capitulated out of fear. So what if it had taken so long? What matters is that I got there.

For two weeks I was alone in the house with my golden retriever, Roxy. Vanessa had gone to Paris with eight-month-old Malcolm to be with Vadim, who had been battling cancer for three years. Her pain and concern were palpable, and I was glad my new circumstances made me available should she need me.

Neither Roxy nor I was accustomed to stillness. The absence of Ted's booming voice and constant activity left a deafening silence. I had wanted stillness. Here it was. My friends wondered if I would experience "luxurium tremens" (as singer James Taylor calls the sudden loss of luxury). I didn't. In fact, I found the smallness of my surroundings humorous: I had gone from twenty-three kingdom-size properties and a private plane that could sleep six to a small guest room with no closet in a modest house in a charming but not quite gentrified section of Atlanta.

I experienced mourning rather than anger— mourning not so much for the relationship as it was as for the loss of what I had hoped it might become. The anger rose somewhat later, when in agonizing drips and drops, I began to find out about Ted's quests for my replacement during the year I was rejoicing in what I thought was his concession to monogamy. For about a month I would write him letters venting my rage and hurt; fortunately I never mailed them. (Time and understanding take the edge off anger. Best not leave everlasting proof of your temporary insanity.)

Vanessa and Malcolm returned to Atlanta for a while, and in the quiet of her home we talked about fathers and husbands, marriage and divorce. But when it became clear that Vadim hadn't much longer to live, she hurried back to him while I re-

mained in Atlanta with Malcolm. I felt bonded to
this little boy in a way I never had with anyone before. He was showing me how to love. I would lie in
bed with his sleeping body draped across me (his position of choice), his nose in my right ear, his toes in
my left, and feel utterly complete. Later, Malcolm
would take my face in his hands and say, "I yuv you,
Gamma."

It was a painful time for Vanessa. Not only was
the father she adored dying, but she was separated
from her son. She had been breast-feeding, and by
the time I brought him back to her in Paris, that precious window had closed. I stayed in France for a
while, wanting to see Vadim one last time and to
help Vanessa with Malcolm. She spent her days at
her father's bedside, alternating shifts with Vadim's
sister, Hélène, and greeting friends, family members,
and former wives and companions as they came and
went. It felt synchronous that my separation from
Ted had made it possible for me to be totally available when I was needed, and to reconnect with my
family from my first marriage.

I remembered something Katharine Hepburn
said to me during the filming of **On Golden Pond:**
"Make no mistake, Jane, women choose their men
and not the other way around." If this is true (and I'd
like to think it is), then in spite of everything, I feel
that I chose well. I learned and grew with Vadim,
Tom, and Ted (sometimes because of them, sometimes in spite of them), and I feel grateful for that. I
also have to say that in hindsight, each divorce,
painful though it may have been at the time, marked

a step forward, an opportunity for self-redefinition rather than a failure—almost like repotting a plant when the roots don't fit anymore. Of course, I wish I'd found just one husband, also capable of redefinition, to make the whole journey with, but self-redefinition is harder for most men, especially since in a patriarchy they are not supposed to need it. Given my parents' difficulties with relationships, and my personal evolution, choosing right for the long haul just hasn't been in the cards. I comfort myself in knowing that should I choose again, the haul will be shorter.

Often during periods of transition in my life people or books have appeared, like miracles, to teach me what I need to learn. During my final months with Ted, as I struggled to make sense out of the impending separation from a man I loved, I began reading **In a Different Voice,** by feminist psychologist Carol Gilligan. In the very first pages, Gilligan wrote that women "often sensed that it was dangerous to say or even to know what they wanted or thought—upsetting to others and therefore carrying with it the threat of abandonment. . . ." **Exactly what I had been facing.** Gilligan went on to describe the damage that this does to women: "The justification of these psychological processes [of silencing the self] in the name of love or relationships is equivalent to the justifications of violence and violation in the name of morality."

If I'd been a cartoon character, the balloons over

my head would have read: "Oh my God!"; "Now I understand"; "So that's why!" I saw that the issues I had been wrestling with in my marriage were not just **my** struggles; they were **other women's** struggles, and they were important enough for a psychologist like Gilligan (and the many others I subsequently read) to study. I had had revelations before with books—**The Village of Ben Suc** and **The Autobiography of Malcolm X**, for example—but this time the book was speaking to **my own life experiences.** I was like a nearsighted person suddenly given corrective lenses (or having the old lenses, distorted by patriarchy, suddenly removed). The whole world looked different to me now—so many elements in my life and my mother's life began to make sense. I don't know if another woman would have the same visceral response to Gilligan's book, but the time was right for me. I was ready. Earlier I could not have taken in the full implications of what she wrote. I would have been more worried about rocking Ted's boat than captaining my own.

On the second page of Gilligan's book I read:

> **Women's choices not to speak or rather to dissociate themselves from what they themselves are saying can be deliberate or unwitting, consciously chosen or enacted through the body by narrowing the passages that connect the voice with the breath and sound, by keeping the voice high in the head so that it does not carry the depths of human feelings. . . .**

When I read this it hit me so forcefully that I cried out, remembering my early years as a young movie star—**Sunday in New York, Any Wednesday, Tall Story**—when my voice was high and thin. Alone in Vanessa's home, I watched videos of my films chronologically and was able to track my growth as a woman by noting when my voice began to drop. It started with **Klute,** which was when I began to define myself as a feminist; it was also when I won my first Oscar. My acting had improved as my voice deepened, because I was beginning to inhabit myself.

Change can come from the inside out or the outside in. I got a call late one night in early 2000, when Vanessa was still in Paris. It was Paula Weinstein in California. Richard and Lili Fini Zanuck, producers of the Academy Awards show that year, wanted me to be a presenter.

"I can't, Paula," I said. "I'm not in the business anymore."

"Do it anyway," said my dearest friend, who can't seem to remember that she's not my agent anymore. "It'll be good for you."

She wouldn't take no for an answer. Finally I said, "Oh, okay, I'll do it. I have a dress that I bought four years ago that's really pretty that I can wear."

"Jane," Paula shrieked, "no way. Vera Wang is going to design you a dress, and you're going to get your hair cut by Sally Hirschberger, and that's that! I don't want any arguments."

Isn't it great to have persistent friends?

Psychologist Marion Woodman has said: "Changing your hair is a reflection of a shift in thinking." Well, thanks to Paula, I had new hair to go with my new thinking.

Within months of my singlehood, another germinal event took place: My close friend Pat Mitchell asked me to perform one of the pieces in Eve Ensler's **The Vagina Monologues.** I had gotten to know Pat during the years she was president of CNN Productions and Time Inc. (Pat had just been named president and CEO of PBS.)

I had not acted in eleven years and had little desire to do so again, but I asked Pat to send me the script. I read one page of the monologue they wanted me to perform (it was titled "Cunt") and called Pat.

"No, Pat," I said. "I have enough problems. Hanoi Jane saying 'cunt' in Atlanta? I don't think so." But as is her way, Pat wouldn't let up—not necessarily pressuring me to perform, just asking me to meet Eve Ensler. She told me that Eve was in New York performing the monologues and insisted that I go and see it for myself. "Trust me, Jane. You have to do this."

So I did.

I had no idea what to expect, but as I sat there listening to Eve enact the monologues she'd written based on interviews she'd done with women about their vaginas, I felt something happening to me. I don't remember ever laughing so hard or crying so hard in the theater, but it must have been during the laughter part, when I wasn't paying attention, that my feminist consciousness slipped out of my head and took up residence in my body—where it has lived ever since.

Up until then I had been a feminist in the sense that I supported women, brought gender issues into my movie roles, helped women make their bodies strong, read all the books: I had it in my head. I thought I had it in my heart—in my body—but I didn't; not really. I couldn't. It was too scary, like stepping off a cliff without knowing if there was a trampoline below. It meant doing **life** differently.

Fans of Robert Heinlein's science fiction masterpiece **Stranger in a Strange Land** know what the word **grok** means: to understand something so thoroughly on every level—spiritually, intellectually, bodily, psychically—that you become one with what you have observed or grasped; you merge with it. My experience upon seeing **The Vagina Monologues** (as with reading **In a Different Voice**) can only be described as "grokking" feminism.

Eve Ensler has remained a beloved presence in my life ever since that night. Beaten and subjected to incest for years by her father, she is a force of nature, a person who with lots of work has risen, burnished and purified, from the fires of violence and pain, and her vision of ending violence against women is contagious. She has turned her play into a global cam-

As a presenter at the Oscars in 2000 with
my new haircut and Vera Wang dress.
(Catuffe/SIPA Press)

paign, and as of this writing her organization, V-Day: Until the Violence Stops, has raised over $26 million in support of local efforts to stop violence against women around the world, more than the total amount that the United States government has spent on this pandemic. I serve on her organization's V-Council and have traveled to many countries with Eve to help build this global movement.

Vaginal epiphanies and Oscar presentation notwithstanding, life was ratcheting down to soulspeed, just as I had wanted. My daughter's home had become a womb in which I was pregnant with myself, entering what Dr. Susan Blumenthal described to me as "the infancy of my second adulthood." It felt right, like when you hit a tennis ball on the "sweet spot" of the racket. It took place in small, incremental, cumulative steps that I might not have noticed, **except that I was paying attention**—becoming intentional. I also know that, manless (and not afraid of that) and surrounded by vibrant, brave, emotionally available women friends, I was able to remove the blinders and see things, which necessitated my rethinking fundamentals I couldn't see before—like how differently most women "do" life. We listen with our hearts; we try to mirror the other's humanity.

It's not that I was entirely conscious of what was happening to me. It was like a slow letting go at the very center of myself. My relationships with people began to shift. I wasn't reactive anymore (amazing, if reactive is what you've been most of your life). I was detached, yet my heart had opened. The space between me and other people seemed filled with a new, vibrating energy that grew exponentially more intense when I felt connected to other women. In the "old days," I would go to a party and wonder, **Will they like me? Will I be pretty enough? Interesting enough?** Now I was coming into a party thinking, Do I really want to be here? Is there anyone I want to connect with?

After a month or two Vanessa made it clear that I needed to start thinking about moving out. I no longer had a home of my own, having sold it in order to make my home (homes) with Ted. When it dawned on me that we were splitting up, I had to think about where I was going to live. It took me about three seconds to realize I wanted to stay in Atlanta. This decision had been so sudden and certain, it took me by surprise. (It certainly took many of my New York and California friends by surprise.) There comes a time in life when you have to put down roots. Why not Atlanta? I was sixty-two; Vanessa, Malcolm, and Lulu were all living there now; I had made many good friends in Georgia; I was committed to the important work my organization, the Georgia Campaign for Adolescent Pregnancy Prevention, was doing with our school-based programs for girls and boys and with young mothers and fathers, and I longed to be more hands-on. Enough moving around! Besides, I like the Chekhovian nature of the South: a slowness, a love of talk for its

With Eve Ensler, having just performed the final monologue in **The Vagina Monologues** at Madison Square Garden. I had been so scared beforehand that I prayed I'd be sideswiped by a taxi—not killed, just hospitalized—so that I wouldn't have to go through with my first acting in fifteen years. It went well—the whole event was memorable— and gave me courage.
(Mark Abrahams/German Vogue)

Left to right: Actress Tantoo Cardinal, Karen Artichoker, me, Suzanne Blue Star Boy, and Eve Ensler at a V-Day event in Rapid City, South Dakota, to raise funds for a women's shelter on the Pine Ridge Reservation. I've come full circle.

As a fund-raiser for G-CAPP, I lived a lifelong
dream and, with ten fit friends, made the
five-day trek to the ancient Inca city
of Machu Picchu. I was single now
and could do these things.

own sake, the friendliness and humor; the jokes, like heirlooms, passed back and forth and savored as though for the first time; an acceptance of people's idiosyncrasies. And where else can you hear expressions like "frog strangler" (for a heavy rain) and "lower than a pregnant duck" (when you're depressed)?

But there is something else that contributes to my love of the South. Most of my life I had lived in sophisticated, relatively privileged coastal cities like Los Angeles and New York. I had grown weary of criticism about people in those places being elitists, out of touch with the American mainstream. Just as it had taken my going to France to begin to understand America, so it had taken my move to Georgia to show me that the criticisms were at least partly true. With this had come a realization that appealed to the activist in me: If you can effect change in the South, you can effect change anywhere. There's a sense of reality—things aren't as prettified and above the fray as in Hollywood. History is closer to the surface, possibly because our Civil War bloodied the soils and souls of this southern land in ways that can never be entirely wiped away or understood by northerners or West Coast folk.

So out I set on a new life as a solo, short-haired southerner, not entirely certain where my less traveled road would lead me, but sure that my choice was right.

CHAPTER THREE

LEAVING MY FATHER'S HOUSE

Oh this is the animal that never was.
They hadn't seen one; but just the same, they loved
its graceful movements, and the way it stood
looking at them calmly, with clear eyes.

It had not **been.** But for them, it appeared
in all its purity. They left space enough.
And in the space hollowed out by their love
it stood up all at once and didn't need
existence. They nourished it, not with grain,
but with the mere possibility of being.
And finally this gave it so much power
that from its forehead a horn grew. One horn.
It drew near to a virgin, white, gleaming—
and was, inside the mirror and in her.
> —RAINER MARIA RILKE,
> from The Sonnets to Orpheus, II, 4

ALL MY LIFE I had been a father's daughter, trapped in a Greek drama, like Athena, who sprang fully formed from the head of her father, Zeus—disciplined, driven. Starting in childhood, I learned that love was earned through perfection. In adolescence, my feelings of imperfection centered on my physical being, and I abandoned my poor, loyal body and took up residence in my head. Whether you are male or female, that split between body/heart and mind is the fatal one when it comes to being a fully realized person. Your soul becomes homeless. In the house of the Fathers, there is no room for soul.

I am referring here to "father" not in the biological sense but metaphorically, to the house of the Fathers, the patriarchs—to a way of existing by seeing myself through the eyes of men and accommodating them on the deepest, invisible level (while seeming to do the contrary) and, in so doing, delivering a part of myself to a world that bifurcates head and heart, renders empathy (for oneself or for others) impossible, and makes both men and women, boys and girls, less human than they inherently are.

Don't get me wrong—I love men. One reason I didn't become a feminist sooner is that I erroneously thought it required male bashing. In fact, the more I have come to understand the nature of the Fathers' house, the **more** I love men, because I see how patriarchy's toxic cloistering has dehumanized them as well.

For me, the journey from the house of the Fathers has been a long time coming. I didn't know, when I started writing this book almost five years ago, that I would arrive at this place, nor did I know exactly what "place" I hoped to get to.

There have been (and will continue to be) many course corrections on this path to enable my whole embodied spirit, the unicorn in Rilke's poem, to manifest itself. For me, as Rilke describes, the journey had to start with "the space hollowed out by . . . love"—self-love—despite the absence of perfection. That love allowed me to accept myself and imagine going beyond where I'd been as a disembodied, male-identified woman, to arrive at a belief so strong in "the mere possibility of being" that the unicorn— my embodied spirit—"stood up all at once and didn't need existence." Because the transformative experiences we go through over our lives are so elusive, their essence can sometimes best be captured through metaphor.

Two very nonpoetic impediments at the start of this third part of my journey were my breasts. It's hard to squeeze through the door of the Fathers' house with breast implants. Soon after my separation from Ted, I began to feel an urgent need to have those implants removed, because I now saw these false appendages as sad, misguided reminders of a woman who didn't own her womanhood.

A series of male doctors assured me that the procedure could not be reversed successfully, but finally a friend of mine, a woman my age who had had it done, referred me to her female surgeon. This doctor told me that it is not uncommon for women of a certain age—when they have developed an authentic self and no longer need to define themselves by what shows on the outside—to want the implants removed.

When he first saw me postremoval, Troy said, "Mom! You're back in proportion again!" Yes, in more ways than one.

Psychologist Marion Woodman says the body is our "chalice for Spirit" and if there is no Spirit, we may try to fill its emptiness with addictions. In my forties I had stopped bingeing and purging, but I wasn't really healed; I was the way a dry drunk is in relationship to alcohol. Now I feel I have found spiritual food to fill what was always spiritual hunger, so I am no longer a dry drunk in relation to my eating disorder. Along the way I have also stopped drinking alcohol. Since this is my last act, I sure as hell want to try to do it on the natch—replacing spirits with Spirit.

Perhaps you are wondering how I can talk about leaving the patriarchal, hierarchal structures of the Fathers' house only to turn around and slip into the patriarchal, hierarchal structure of Christianity. This is exactly the conundrum I have been facing.

Always one to give my all to whatever I undertake, when I began this part of my journey—the soul's journey—I committed myself to what was presented to me. But as I diligently slogged through my weekly Bible classes, I felt the reverence slipping away, and I began to get scared. How to get back what had begun as an intense personal experience? I met some inspiring, extraordinary Christians who clearly lived their faith. Yet others came at me, fingers pointing: "How could you have spoken at that pro-choice rally?" They demanded to know my position on this or that issue. When I commented to one Christian columnist about the difficulty I was having with the belief that all non-Christians would go to hell, he replied, "Uh-oh, you sound like a Universalist!" Hey, that sounded about right. Given all the bloodshed and persecution that has gone on through the ages in the name of religion, shouldn't we start practicing tolerance? Claiming that Jesus was the **only** way to salvation felt like Christian imperialism. **Maybe this isn't the spiritual home I seek.**

For me, religion is not so much about a belief in dogmas and traditions. It must be a spiritual **experience,** and I find it impossible to have that experience when I cannot reconcile myself to the Judeo-Christian assumption that man was God's principal creation, with woman (Eve, fashioned from Adam's rib) a mere derivative afterthought. Nor can I accept woman as the cause of man's downfall, an assumption that has permitted men through the ages to regard women with suspicion and misogyny. (The best bumper sticker I ever saw read, EVE GOT A BUM RAP.)

Women were anything **but** an afterthought for the Jesus I believe in. His acceptance of and friendship with women was truly revolutionary at a time when the male-dominated status quo had severed religion's connection to the prepatriarchal ancient goddess and to nature. There was a reason why women were among Jesus' most ardent followers: They responded to his revolutionary message of compassion, love, and **equality.**

The outlawed Christian communities that spread into the desert to worship in secret after Jesus died included more women than men, by a margin of two to one. Women were among the early Roman Christians who met clandestinely in their homes, preached, converted men, and performed the Eucharist.

I am moved and inspired by those early Christians—like those in the Gospel of Thomas, the Secret Gospel of Mark, and the Book of John—who saw themselves as seekers more than believers; who felt that **experiencing** the divine was more important than mere **belief** in the divine. According to them, Jesus preached that each individual has the potential to **embody** God (embodiment again). Perhaps this is one reason these teachings were outlawed and excised from Christian dogma back in the fourth century: They meant there was no need for priests or bishops—or hierarchy. By erasing these early interpretations of the founding myths of Judeo-Christian civilization, the fathers of patriarchy (in this case bishops) caused a potentially fatal split between mind and body, Spirit and matter. This split is the essential cornerstone of patriarchy—of the Fathers' house. I have lived this split alongside my (biological) father and my three husbands. This split is more evident in men (which is what gives it toxic heft, since men currently run things), but it exists to varying degrees in women as well—as my story shows. If our civilization hadn't been built on devaluing, fearing, and denigrating women, men wouldn't split head from heart and distance themselves from their emotions, which are supposed to be the domain of women.

I am only at the start of my soul journey, but with my discovery of the early Christian interpretations and having found a community of feminist Christians, reverence is humming back to me.

Sometimes the open wounds left by regret can become fertile ground for the seeds of restitution. My regrets are that I wasn't a better parent and that I have had to wait so long to feel like a whole person. People often ask me why have I chosen to work on issues of adolescent pregnancy, sexuality, and parenting. These are the issues that call to me, asking me to try to prevent young people from having to wait as long as I did to respect, honor, and be themselves.

To know what needs to happen to make children resilient and healthy, and to avoid early pregnancy, I can draw on my research, travels, and interviews with parents and youths around the world. But I can also think back on what did or didn't happen in my own and my children's early years. The parent—especially the mother (or mother figure), especially in the formative years when the brain isn't yet hardwired—is the critical factor. And if the mother, for whatever reason (depression, addiction, violence, abuse), can't show up for her child, another caring, nurturing adult must be found to provide the necessary bond. Fathers, if they are warm and loving, can be crucial to a child's resilience. The safety of a father's loving (nonsexual) embrace can help ensure that a daughter won't seek a man's love in the wrong places. A son can be inoculated against the toxic effects of patriarchy if his father (or another consistent, loving male) models emotional expressiveness and caring. For girls and boys, being fatherless is less damaging than having a rigid, abusive father.

But whether we are parents, grandparents, aunts, uncles, neighbors, teachers, ministers, or athletic coaches, we all have a responsibility. This means, through our example, showing "perfection" to the door and helping girls respect themselves whether or not they conform to society's current aesthetic norms; talking to them about feelings, relationships, and sexuality; and, most important, listening to and **hearing** them.

I have talked more about women and girls because . . . well, because I am one of the former and I used to be one of the latter. But over the last number of years I have seen how boys are affected by the

In 2000 I went to Nigeria with staff of the International Women's Health Coalition to make a documentary about three unique and highly successful programs for girls. Here I am squatting amid a group of schoolgirls in Lagos.

same things as girls, only it manifests earlier and differently in boys. I have some very personal reasons for needing to understand boys as well as girls. I have a brother, a son, a grandson, and (more recently) a granddaughter for whom I hope one day there will be an empathetic partner to love. I know that lack of empathy is systemic in the patriarchal culture—one reason my heart goes out to men.

Psychologist Carol Gilligan has three sons and has done extensive research on the development of boys. Her research shows that whereas girls lose relationship with themselves at the start of adolescence (as I did), boys experience this loss roughly between the ages of five and seven, when they start formal schooling. This is when boys can begin to shut down and show signs of emotional stress (depression, learning disorders, speech impediments) and out-of-control behavior. Obviously not all boys experience this. It seems that warm, loving, but structured home and school environments act as vaccines against gender stereotypes.

When little boys begin to go out into the world, they internalize the message of what it takes to be a "real man." Sometimes it comes through their father, who beats it into them: **Don't be a sissy.** Or it can be a mother who won't or can't respect a child's real feelings. Sometimes it comes because our culture rips boys from their mothers: **Don't be a mama's boy.** Sometimes it's the "manhood" messages from teachers and the media. It can be a specific trauma that shuts them down, like what happened to Ted at five, when he was sent to boarding school. Think about all the men you know who are oddly divorced from their emotions. This isn't just a question of "Boys will be boys." It goes way beyond male/female differences in brain chemistry, and it has had an impact on all of us. Fear of being considered unmanly is so deeply ingrained that I believe a series of U.S. presidents refused to withdraw from Vietnam because they were afraid of being called soft. How many lives have been lost because leaders needed to prove they were "real men"? (And it is usually the poor who are sacrificed on the altar of our leaders' insecure manhood.)

For their own good, and for the good of every other living thing on the planet, men should join women in leaving the Fathers' house.

EPILOGUE

"It doesn't happen all at once," said the Skin Horse. "You become. It takes a long time. That's why it doesn't often happen to people who break easily, or have sharp edges, or who have to be carefully kept. Generally, by the time you are Real, most of your hair has been loved off, and your eyes drop out and you get loose in the joints and very shabby. But these things don't matter at all, because once you are Real you can't be ugly, except to people who don't understand."

—MARGERY WILLIAMS,
The Velveteen Rabbit

I am, gratefully, still a work in progress. I have part of one act to go in which to practice conscious living, be there as fully as I can for my children and grandchildren, contribute in whatever ways I can to healing the planet. If I can do these things, I'll be able to die gracefully and without regrets. We'll see.

In three years I will be seventy—which leaves me a little more than twenty years, if I'm lucky. I've worked hard to get where I am, and I can tell you with utmost certainty that entering my third act the way I did made all the difference, because it has forced me—every day—to show up, to remember that this is not a rehearsal and that I have promised myself to do what was needed so I wouldn't have regrets. Things change when you become intentional.

Bit by bit I have learned to love and respect my body. I may have betrayed my body, but my body has never betrayed me. Maybe in our Western culture you have to be a certain age for this to happen: to have lived long enough to love your hips for having enabled you to bear children, your shoulders to bear burdens, your legs to have carried you where you needed to go.

I have known failures. Those I have run from taught me nothing. Those I got to know intimately permitted me quantum leaps forward. The failures are what deliver us to ourselves. You don't get Real by playing it safe.

In 2004, after fifteen years in "retirement," I made another film, **Monster-in-Law.** I did it for two reasons: I needed money to create endowments that will ensure the future of the adolescent reproductive health programs and services I helped start in Georgia, as well as professionals to run them. I also recognized that I am a very different woman today than I

As Viola Fields in **Monster-in-Law**, my first film in fifteen years. It was fun. (© MMV, NewLine Productions, Inc. All rights reserved. Photo by Melissa Moseley.)

On the set of **Monster-in-Law** with Paula, one of its producers. (© MMV, New-Line Productions, Inc. All rights reserved. Photo by Melissa Moseley.)

was fifteen years ago—at once lighter and heavier—
and I wanted to see if this would change my acting
experience. It did! Unlike fifteen years ago, I felt confident, playful. As of this writing, I haven't seen the
movie, but the process was joyful both in the acting
and in the relationships with cast and crew. It didn't
hurt that my beloved friend Paula Weinstein was a
producer of the movie and that it was filmed entirely
in Los Angeles, where Troy could spend hours on the
set watching me work and giving me great acting
tips.

Vanessa has long since graduated with honors
from Brown University, went on to study English
and creative writing at NYU's graduate school and
then to its Tisch School of the Arts to study film. She
is a fine documentary filmmaker with two advocacy
documentaries under her belt—one, **Fire in Our
House,** made with Rory Kennedy (Robert and
Ethel's youngest child), about the effectiveness of
needle exchange as a harm-reduction strategy, and
The Quilts of Gee's Bend. A granddaughter, Viva,
has arrived—as bright and beautiful as a dream. I
watch in awe as Vanessa mothers Malcolm and Viva
with intention, intelligence, and unconditional love.
Vanessa has grown into a woman with strong values,
a discerning mind, and a desire to **make it better.** My
in-house Jiminy Cricket, she continues to teach me.
When I asked her to describe what she does, she said
she was "one of the spiders on the web of life, pulling
threads between elements—activists, organizations,
funding—to create a more cohesive and sustainable

Vanessa with her daughter, Viva.

Troy went to Afghanistan with Eve Ensler in 2002. He is standing in a metal box that had been riddled with bullets.
(Paulo Netto)

Lulu with retired NBA player Manute Bol and one of her Lost Boys, Valentino Achak Deng.

whole." In Atlanta, she is developing a nationally replicable model of an environmental curriculum for preschoolers. She walks her talk.

Troy studied acting at the American Academy of Dramatic Arts and has become a fine actor, brave, with a range and style all his own. I had the surreal joy of walking down the red carpet on his arm when he was nominated for a Golden Globe for his lead role in Showtime's powerful **Soldier's Girl**. Then there was the thrill of someone walking right past me in a mall to ask him for his autograph. But beyond his creative talents, Troy is a beautiful, deep soul, a political activist who works to end youth violence, particularly our gang epidemic. When Eve Ensler asked me for a quote about how the world would be different if violence against women stopped, I said, "More men would be like my son."

Lulu lives in Atlanta, where she established the Lost Boys Foundation, which grants scholarships to young men who fled Sudan's civil war. She is also the director of the Atlanta Thrashers Foundation and their community development. She has grown into a confident woman with an insatiable intellectual curiosity.

Nathalie left the film business, graduated magna cum laude from Brown University as a cultural anthropologist, and lives in Maine, where she started a shelter for victims of domestic violence.

Thanks to Ted's generosity, the five of us continue our work with our family foundation, each with our own unique focus.

Ted and I are close friends and see each other regularly. His children are thriving. Beau runs his father's wildlife programs; Teddy owns a boatyard in Charleston, South Carolina; Rhett is a fine documentary filmmaker and photographer; Jennie raises children and horses in Virginia. They are all environmentalists and philanthropists. Laura sits on the boards of numerous environmental organizations and is a progressive force to be reckoned with. Their children call me Grandma.

Tom and his wife, the actor and singer Barbara Williams, are also friends of mine. Their five-year-old son, Liam, is Malcolm's uncle and Troy's brother. Families come in all configurations.

As for me, I feel myself being drawn forward along a path shaped by my new understandings of gender and of faith. I don't know where it will lead me, but I do know that my energies will be devoted to helping make things better.

We face a shrinking, congested planet with diminishing resources and no vast, conquerable frontier to escape and expand into. Globalization may be creating one sort of unified world, but for it to be a peaceful, just, sustainable form of unity, our consciousness needs to catch up to it.

The new reality **demands** internationalism, multilateralism, humility, and compassion. But these approaches are considered "effeminate" by the men who currently run our country. If Christ returned today, would he be labeled "effeminate" by these same people?—**those disciples, that emphasis on**

2004, in Santa Monica with Tom; his wife, actress/singer Barbara Williams; their son, Liam; me, Vanessa, Viva, and Malcolm.

forgiveness, that suspicious identification with women and with the poor!

There's a lot of work ahead. But the longest, darkest night of the year—the winter solstice, my birthday—is also, in the Southern Hemisphere, the summer solstice, the longest, brightest **day** of the year. It all depends on your perspective.

From **my** perspective, what we are seeing are the final paroxysms, the flailing, dangerous death throes, of the old, no longer workable, no longer justifiable patriarchal paradigm. I believe that just beneath the surface a great tectonic shift is occurring. I don't know if you've ever been to Yellowstone National Park. Yellowstone is one of the places where the earth's crust is thinnest and where thermal activity is closest to the surface (the famous geyser Old Faithful is but the most dramatic evidence of this activity). If you walk or drive through the forests and meadows, you can see steam and puddles of hot mud bubbling up through cracks in the earth's surface. I have witnessed the equivalent of that steam and hot mud bubbling up all around the world—in the form of women and men who are ripening the time for the bubbling to become volcanic. I am one of them.

My arms and heart are flung wide—welcoming more transformation, wherever it leads. I am filled, rich with an inheritance of memories and lessons: Not only my mother's lovely, doomed butterflies and my father's final silent tears. Not only my cherished blood family and chosen family and the men I've loved and my trusted women friends. But also Susan

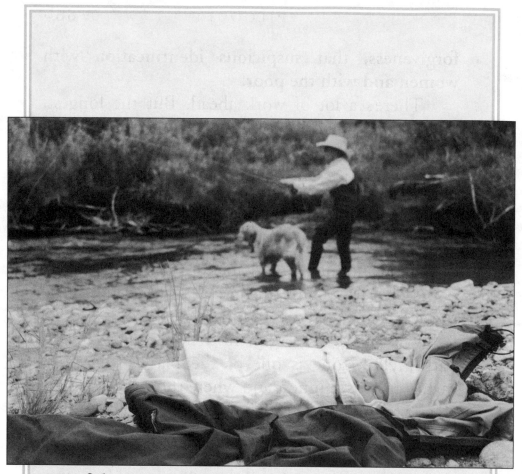

**2000, fishing on Ted's Flying D ranch, Roxy at my side and
Malcolm sleeping on the shore. Life is good.**
(Vanessa Vadim)

and Sue Sally, and Ms. Hepburn's evocative challenge: "Don't get soggy!" Hope smiling in the eyes of a schoolgirl in a bombed Vietnamese shelter hole, and pain brimming in the eyes of veterans. Girls in clean dresses making stationery from garbage. Every character I've played onscreen/onstage **and** every role I found myself playing in my personal life. All the trees I've planted and animals I've loved. Some pretty terrific fountains-of-Versailles-and-fireworks sex! The conversations and books—including this one—that changed my life; the lessons of pain; the healing anger that shatters silence; the courage to scrape oneself up off the floor and try **again**—and then **again.** The moments I've glimpsed of searing epiphany and simple grace.

Every earned line on my skin and scar on my heart—I can own them now. I can affirm every **imperfection** as my share of our mutual, flawed, fragile humanity.

Each story and individual, each metamorphosis—they live in me now, and celebrate being here, being useful.

Deep in my blood, brain, heart, and soul— they've all come back to live in me.

And, finally, so have I.

FILMOGRAPHY

2005   **Monster-In-Law**

1990   **Stanley & Iris**

1989   **The Old Gringo**

1987   **Retour**

1986   **The Morning After**

1985   **Agnes of God**

1984   **The Dollmaker**

1981   **On Golden Pond**

1981   **Rollover**

1980   **9 to 5**

1979   **The Electric Horseman**

1979   **The China Syndrome**

1978   **Comes a Horseman**

1978   **Coming Home**

1978   **California Suite**

1977   **Julia**

1977   **Fun with Dick and Jane**

1976   **The Blue Bird**

1974   **Introduction to the Enemy** (documentary)

1973   **A Doll's House**

1973   **Steelyard Blues**

1972   **Tout Va Bien**

1972   **F.T.A.** (documentary)

1971   **Klute**

1969   **They Shoot Horses, Don't They?**

1968   **Tre Passi nel Delirio**

1968   **Barbarella**

1967   **Barefoot in the Park**

1967   **Hurry Sundown**

1966 La Curée
1966 Any Wednesday
1966 The Chase
1965 Cat Ballou
1964 La Ronde
1964 Les Félins
1963 Sunday in New York
1963 In the Cool of the Day

1962 The Chapman Report
1962 Walk on the Wild Side
1962 Period of Adjustment
1960 Tall Story

ACKNOWLEDGMENTS

I am indebted to my editor, Kate Medina, who gracefully persuaded me that less is more and whose creative diplomacy allowed me to feel that all the "contouring" was my idea.

I am forever grateful to Robin Morgan, the "angel on my shoulder," whose sisterhood and attention allowed me to sleep at night.

And to Eve Ensler, who has enveloped me in protective love and inspiration these last five years.

I want to acknowledge my children: Vanessa, my conscience, for keeping me honest; Troy, my soul, for drawing me always toward the light; Lulu and Nathalie, for reminding me to search deeper for the love in my marriages.

My thanks to Laura Turner Seydel, Teddy Turner, Rhett Turner, Beau Turner, and Jennie Garlington Turner for their righteous critiques; and to

Tom Hayden and Ted Turner for vetting their chapters in my life.

I must acknowledge my wonderful researchers, Suzanne McCormack, Frankie Jones, and Sarah Shoenfeld.

I am grateful to the gang at Random House: Gina Centrello, Dennis Ambrose, Benjamin Dreyer, Richard Elman, Lisa Feuer, Laura Goldin, Margaret Gorenstein, Carole Lowenstein, Elizabeth McGuire, Timothy Mennel, Gene Mydlowski, Tom Perry, Danielle Posen, Carol Poticny, Robin Rolewicz, Allison Saltzman, Carol Schneider, Sona Vogel, and Veronica Windholz. Your support has meant the world to me.

To each and every one of the following people I give thanks for their generous and ready input, encouragement, and advice: Joe Bangert, Hannah Bergen, Susan Blanchard, Dr. Susan Blumenthal, Fred Branfman, Thoa Branfman, Judith Bruce, Leni Cazden, Laura Clark, Ken Cloke, Cyndi Fonda Dabney, John Dean, Donald Duncan, Diana Dunn, John Echohawk, Dan Ellsberg, Tod Ensign, Peter Fonda, Shirlee Fonda, Roger Friedman, Lois Gibbs, Bruce Gilbert, Carol Gilligan, Jim Gilligan, Jerry Hellman, Mary Hershberger, David Hilliard, David Hodges, Dr. Marion Howard, Al Hubbard, Henry Jaglom, Maria Cooper Janis, Tom Johnson, Beverly Kitaen-Morse, Carol Kurtz-Nichol, Julie Lafond, Valarie Lalonde, Robin Laughlin, Laurel Lyle, John McAuliffe, LaNada Means, Edison Miller, Gordon Miller, Pat Mitchell, Bob Mulholland, Karen Nussbaum, Francine Parker, Dolly Parton, Dick Perrin, Hélène Plemiannikov, Bonnie Raitt, Terry Real, Sil Reynolds, Stephen Rivers, Rich Roland, Catherine Schneider, Olga Seham, Jim Skelly, Gloria Steinem, Lily Tomlin, Mike Uhl, Vania Vadim, Jon Voight, Leonard Weinglass, Paula Weinstein, Jay Westbrooke, Corinne Whitaker, Helen Williams, Marion Woodman, and Ambassador Andrew Young.

If life continued to run smoothly these past five years it's thanks to the inestimable assistance of Steven Bennett. Cindy Imlay has been a constant help throughout, and Carole and Tommy Mitchell have provided essential support as well.

My love and thanks to you all.

INDEX

Abzug, Bella, 550, 780
Academy Awards, 641,
    658
  for Chaplin, 96
  and **Coming Home**,
    524, 570, 609, 734
  and Henry Fonda,
    419, 646, 667–68
  JF as presenter at, 841
  and **Julia**, 554
  and **Klute**, 379,
    419–20, 734, 841
  and **9 to 5**, 629n
  and **On Golden Pond**,
    646, 667–68
  and **They Shoot
    Horses, Don't
    They?**, 333, 353

Actors Studio, 166, 179,
    199, 255
Agnes of God (film),
    697
Alaimo, Michael, 411
Algren, Nelson, 198
All My Sons (play),
    470–72, 480
Allen, Steve, 560
American Academy of
    Dramatic Arts, 178,
    865
**And God Created
    Woman** (film),
    155, 158, 201, 213
Any Wednesday (film),
    234, 246, 250, 557,
    841

Aptheker, Herbert, 438
Archerd, Army, 382–83
Ashby, Hal, 558, 563, 564–66, 569
Assaad, Marie, 785–87
Astaire, Fred, 67
Atkinson, Brooks, 196
Atlanta Braves, 180, 770
Averitt, Karen, 764–65

Bacall, Lauren, 95, 162, 243
Bahouth, Peter, 784, 789
Baker, Carroll, 173
Baldwin, James, 546
Ball, Lucille, 95, 560, 675
Bancroft, Anne, 166
Barbarella (film), 192, 242, 253, 256, 261–65, 267–68, 269, 282, 288, 338, 363, 393, 414, 479, 511, 673
Bardot, Brigitte, 155, 158, 201, 208, 209, 213, 221, 252, 302
Barefoot in the Park (film), 256–60, 261
Barrault, Marie-Christine, 208, 209
Bateson, Mary Catherine, 743

Beatty, Warren, 197, 243, 668, 713
Bentley, Carol, 122, 124, 138, 142, 147, 148
Berg, A. Scott, 659, 666
Berrigan, Daniel, 470, 489
Blanchard, Susan (stepmother), 98, 103, 107, 109–17, 118, 122, 132, 133, 135, 136, 137, 141, 142, 145, 156, 159, 220, 224, 238, 286, 668, 760, 809, 869
Blue Bird (film), 558
Blumenthal, Susan, 59, 100–1, 845
Bogart, Humphrey, 95
Bonfiglio, Lois, 682, 687, 705, 748
Bonnie and Clyde (film), 273
Born on the Fourth of July (film), 522, 549
Boyer, La Nada Means, 326
Brando, Marlon, 48, 242, 245, 313, 556
Branfman, Fred, 507, 526, 679
Bridges, Jeff, 682

Bridges, Jim, 572–74, 620

Brokaw, George, 30, 39–40

Brokaw, Pan (Frances) (half-sister), 7, 13, 14, 19, 22, 30, 34, 40, 58, 60, 70, 79

Browne, Jackson, 560

Bush, George H.W., 433, 774

Bush, George W., 389, 398, 512, 515, 539

Buttons, Red, 309, 560

The Byrds, 242–43

Caan, James, 574, 619

Cairo, Egypt, U.N. conference about population in, 779, 780–87, 789–90, 791

California Suite (film), 587, 589–608

Campaign for Economic Democracy (CED), 562, 587–88, 592, 593, 595, 598, 603, 605, 620, 644–45, 650

Carroll, Diahann, 253–54

Carson, Johnny, 739

Carter, Jimmy, 550, 757

Carter, Rosalynn, 757

Cat Ballou (film), 239, 240, 574

Cazden, Leni, 589, 591, 592, 594, 791, 796–97

Chandler, Len, 411

Chapin, Eulalia, 22, 33, 39

Chaplin, Charlie, 96, 152, 226

The Chase (film), 240, 242, 246, 257

Chávez, César, 550–51, 562

Cheney, Richard, 400, 515, 544

Chi, Madame, 449–50, 451, 462

The China Syndrome (film), 570–73, 587, 589, 619–21, 690

Circle of Love (film), see La Ronde

Clarence Darrow (film), 47, 97, 335

Clark, Laura Pyzel, 28–32, 40

Clark, Ramsey, 492, 493n, 494

Cleage, Pearl, 744
Cleland, Max, 818
Clément, René, 201, 203, 207
Cleveland Women Working, 624
Clinton, Bill, 542n, 780
Cloke, Ken, 331, 395, 410, 413
Coca, Imogene, 52
Cocteau, Jean, 152, 213
Cole, Nat "King," 240
Colson, Charles, 536–37, 537n
Comes a Horseman (film), 572, 574–75, 587, 619, 807
Coming Home (film), 479, 521, 524, 529, 549–50, 556, 558–60, 563–66, 569–70, 572, 574, 587, 609, 610, 624, 690, 734
Cooking for Healthy Living (Lafond and JF), 606
Cooper, Gary, 95, 120, 678
Cooper, Maria, 678
Coppola, Francis Ford, 399

Corman, Roger, 246
Costa-Gavras, Constantin, 203
Crosby, David, 242, 390
Cukor, George, 243, 558

Dane, Barbara, 370, 395, 410
Davis, Adelle, 306, 404, 450
Davis, Angela, 335, 412
Davis, Bette, 57
de Beauvoir, Simone, 204–5, 285
De Laurentiis, Dino, 252, 261
De Niro, Robert, 496, 503
Delon, Alain, 201, 216
DeLyser, Femmy, 531, 595, 597
Deneuve, Catherine, 208, 212, 218, 219, 232, 237, 301
Dern, Bruce, 559
Dickinson, Angie, 186, 242
The Dollmaker (TV film), 629–36, 692, 693–96
A Doll's House (film), 558
Donegan, Pamela, 411

Douglas, Michael, 570, 572, 620

Dowd, Nancy, 523, 524, 529, 531, 547, 570

Dreyfuss, Richard, 571, 572

Dullea, Keir, 207

Dunaway, Faye, 253, 273, 372

Duncan, Donald, 331, 360, 361

Dunn, Diana, 21, 26, 89–91, 103

Duvall, Robert, 242

Easy Rider (film), 247, 547, 714

Edelman, Marian Wright, 583, 790

Edwards, Dot, 303, 305, 313, 323, 325, 374, 403

The Electric Horseman (film), 257, 592, 621

Ellsberg, Daniel, 407–8, 513, 538n

Emma Willard Boarding School, 45, 121, 127–29, 134–41

Emmy Awards, 696

Ensler, Eve, 130, 842–43, 845, 866

Entertainment Industry for Peace and Justice (EIPJ), 405–6, 420

Ernst, Jeanne, 606, 607

Farrow, Mia, 241, 317

The FBI Story (film), 169

feminism, 370, 378, 384, 612, 623, 756–57, 780, 840–41, 843, 851, 856
    See also women's movement

Field, Sally, 166, 179, 372

Fire in Our House (documentary), 864

First Monday in October (play), 29

Fisher, Carrie, 145, 147

Fonda, Afdera (stepmother), 142, 145, 151, 152, 154, 155–56, 160, 161, 203

Fonda, Becky (Peter's wife), 675, 739, 741

Fonda, Bridget (niece), 178, 669, 675

Fonda, Frances Seymour
(mother), 8–14,
16–25, 51, 52–55,
59–61, 64–65,
67–68, 69–72,
79–81, 83, 84, 86,
87, 92, 114, 130,
227, 348, 374, 405,
442, 579, 700, 792,
802, 839, 869
birth of, 35–36
childhood/youth of,
36–37, 39, 41
death/suicide of,
21–27, 29, 99–103,
106, 110, 119, 677,
809
divorce of, 18, 20–21,
26–27, 90
family background of,
34–37, 39, 45, 58
and JF's birth, 58
Fonda, Harriet (aunt),
46–47, 142, 149
Fonda, Henry (father),
19–21, 32, 55, 60,
64, 69–70, 90,
91–92, 103, 104–5,
110, 111, 115–16,
117, 120, 131–33,
135, 145, 151–52,
155, 161, 214, 226,
241, 247, 250, 271,
282, 312, 323, 324,
325, 334–35, 368,
374, 398, 463–64,
508, 519, 527, 551,
560, 579, 581,
665–66, 670–71,
673, 678–79, 680,
700, 738, 748,
808–9, 839, 869
and Academy Awards,
418–20, 646,
667–69
Broadway career of,
13–14, 25, 29, 52,
85, 86–87, 109,
133, 160, 183
as celebrity, 113, 134,
140, 203–4, 291,
610
childhood/youth of,
47–48, 53
death of, 669, 675,
677–80, 809
early jobs/film career
of, 47–52, 178,
430, 677
family background of,
42, 45–47, 603
Hollywood career of,
47–48, 51–52, 57,
71, 96, 141, 142,

165, 169, 181–82,
203–4
Hollywood images of,
204
and JF as actress, 142,
169, 175, 176, 178,
179–81, 183, 192,
201
and JF's birth, 57–58
and JF's California
childhood/youth,
67–68, 70–72,
84–85
and JF's Connecticut
childhood/youth,
9–11, 12–14,
16–18, 23–26, 87
and **On Golden Pond**,
638–39, 642, 645,
646, 648, 653,
657–63
and "the Party of the
Decade," 243
and politics, 93, 95
and race issues, 47,
97, 256
and religion, 129
views about acting of,
47–48, 141, 142
and World War II, 14,
31–32, 68, 72–73,
83–84, 442

Fonda, Herberta
(grandmother), 46,
48
Fonda, Jane
birth of, 52, 56–57,
57–58, 60
California
childhood/youth of,
11, 13, 31–32, 64,
67, 70–72, 73, 75,
77–81, 83–85,
442
Connecticut
childhood/youth of,
7–14, 16–27,
86–93, 95–106,
807
early film career of,
142–45, 160,
163–64, 172–82,
185–99
education of, 13, 21,
45, 121, 125,
127–29, 134–41,
142–43, 148,
150–51, 234
and Frances-Henry
divorce, 18, 20
and mother's
death/suicide,
23–27, 99–103,
109–10, 119

Fonda, Jane (**cont'd**):
　at sixty, 807–8, 810,
　　817–19
　spirituality of, 805–6,
　　831–33, 853–56
Fonda, Jayne (aunt), 46,
　48
Fonda, Justin (nephew),
　675
Fonda, Peter (brother),
　8, 10, 12, 14,
　16–27, 30, 51,
　59, 60–61, 68, 71,
　75, 86, 87–88, 91,
　96, 104–6, 107,
　109–17, 121, 131,
　133, 142, 145,
　148–50, 240, 243,
　246–47, 250, 303,
　509, 519, 547, 581,
　646, 674, 714–15,
　739, 740, 807
Fonda, Shirlee Adams
　(stepmother), 241,
　324, 519, 589, 645,
　665, 667, 668, 670,
　673, 674–75, 678
Fonda, Susan (Peter's
　wife), 240, 250
Fonda, William Brace
　(grandfather), 46,
　47–49, 116, 430
Ford, Eileen, 170, 172

Ford Modeling Agency,
　170, 172
Fort Carson, Colorado,
　354–56
Fort Lawton,
　Washington, 329
France
　communism in,
　　204–6, 227
　demonstrations/
　　protests in, 284–85,
　　296
　intelligentsia in,
　　204–5, 268
　strikes in, 296–97
　and Vietnam,
　　284–85, 291–95,
　　296, 544
　See also specific
　　person
Franciscus, James
　"Goey," 143–45,
　147–48, 150,
　154–55, 734
Franks, Lonnie D., 485
Freedom Rides, 255
FTA (Free the Army)
　shows, 408–15,
　457, 489, 498
Fun with Dick and Jane
　(film), 550,
　559–60, 562–63,
　587, 609

Garbo, Greta, 67, 152–53
Gardner, Herb, 409
Garfield, John, 95
Garity, Troy (son), 163, 166, 178, 258, 338, 519, 521, 528, 531–32, 534–36, 557, 570, 574, 581–82, 584–85, 607, 618, 626, 644, 656, 667–68, 675, 680, 701, 704–6, 714, 746, 748, 754–55, 795, 804, 808, 853, 864, 866–67
Garland, Judy, 67
Garner, James, 675
Gary, Romain, 243, 381–82
Gazzara, Ben, 166
Georgia Campaign for Adolescent Pregnancy Prevention (G-CAPP), 325, 582, 781–87, 789–90, 791–92, 804, 847, 849, 856–57, 859–60, 862
GI movement, 331–34, 354–56, 361,
362–63, 365, 370, 375, 385–86, 388–90, 408–9, 420, 479, 498, 551
Gilbert, Bruce, 523, 529–31, 547–49, 556, 568, 569–72, 609–10, 611, 624, 629n, 638, 644–45, 646, 648–50, 682, 687, 692
Gilligan, Carol, 839–40, 859
GLAD, 570
Godard, Jean-Luc, 201, 417–18
Golden Globe Awards, 866
Gorbachev, Mikhail, 715, 771
Graham, Katharine, 613
Grant, Cary, 67
The Grapes of Wrath (film), 97, 116, 203, 282, 334, 551, 668, 670, 680
Greenwich Academy, 13, 21, 89, 91, 96
Gregory, Dick, 401, 410
Grey, Joel, 675
Griffin, Merv, 595
Group Theatre, 179

Guillaume, Gérard, 460–61, 481
Guthrie, Arlo, 560

Haber, Joyce, 381
Hagman, Larry, 241
Haig, Alexander, 434
Haldeman, H. R., 435, 493n
Hammerstein, Oscar, 98, 103
Hare, David, 339, 547
Harris, Jed, 50, 214
Harris, Julie, 166
Harris, Radie, 17
Harvey, Laurence, 199
Hayden, Gene, 429, 517–18, 519
Hayden, Liam, 867
Hayden, Tom, 424–25, 427–28, 436, 432–33, 437, 439, 451, 484, 505–9, 511, 513, 517–19, 521, 524–29, 535, 536, 557–59, 562, 568, 570, 574, 575–76, 585, 587–88, 609–18, 621, 644, 668, 675, 700, 733, 738, 753, 867

childhood and youth of, 429–30
and 1968 elections, 300
JF's first meeting with, 395, 421–23
JF's separation/divorce from, 532, 701–10, 712, 803, 836–49
political career of, 546, 550–51, 562, 605, 690, 691–92, 696
and Troy's birth, 532, 534
writings of, 385–86, 395, 422, 427, 431
Hayward, Bill, 67, 96
Hayward, Bridget, 68, 96, 198
Hayward, Brooke, 21, 67, 85, 96, 97–98, 99–100, 101–2, 106, 132, 148, 193, 198, 240, 243, 250
Hayward, Leland, 52, 67, 85
Heatherton, Joey, 192
Heilbrun, Carolyn, 401
Held, Richard Wallace, 381, 382

Hellman, Jerry, 548–49, 558, 568, 569–70

Hellman, Lillian, 242, 556–57

Hemingway, Ernest, 152, 213

Hepburn, Audrey, 141

Hepburn, Katharine, 340, 638–42, 644, 663, 665–66, 667–68, 669, 819, 838, 871

Hersh, Seymour, 491n

Higgins, Colin, 624, 625–26

Hoffman, Abbie, 384

Hoffman, David, 475, 492–94

Hollywood Ten, 95–96

Hooks, Robert, 253–54

Hopper, Dennis, 240, 243, 250, 547

House Committee on Internal Security, 458, 484–85

House Un-American Activities Committee (HUAC), 93, 95–96, 335, 384–85

Hubbard, Al, 364, 389, 399

Hurry Sundown (film), 253–54, 256, 313

Huston, John, 95

Ichord, Richard, 458, 484

In the Cool of the Day (film), 199

India, JF in, 317–18

Indochina Peace Campaign (IPC), 506–7, 511, 521, 523, 526

Introduction to the Enemy (film), 535–36, 559

Invitation to a March (play), 198, 255

Jackson State University, 344, 362

Johnson, Lucy and Waco, 633–37

Johnson, Lyndon B., 285, 297, 333, 359, 432, 451, 501, 512–14

Jones, Chipper, 180

Jones, Dean, 193

Jones, Jennifer, 132–33, 405

Jones, Mrs. (Sue Sally's mother), 77, 87, 90, 809

Jones, Quincy, 713, 824

Jones, Robert, 524, 559, 570

Jones, Sue Sally, 75, 77, 87, 90, 554, 574, 807, 809, 871

Joplin, Janis, 691

Jorgensen, Christine, 129, 138

Julia (film), 550, 552, 554, 556–58, 560, 587, 609

Justice Department, U.S., 407, 486, 490

Kael, Pauline, 264, 267, 320

Karl, Debbie, 598, 600

Karl, Stuart, 598, 600

Karolewski, Debbie, 714, 748

Kaye, Danny, 95, 243, 560

Kazan, Elia, 165, 173, 197

Kellerman, Sally, 241

Kelly, Gene, 243

Kelly, Grace, 154

Kennedy, Claudia, 409

Kennedy, Jacqueline, 152, 207

Kennedy, John F., 152, 204, 207, 215, 330, 375–76, 500, 513, 573

Kennedy, Robert, 208, 297

Kennedy, Rory, 864

Kent State University, 344, 361, 362

Kerry, John, 389, 515

King, Martin Luther, Jr., 97, 208, 295, 437, 550, 723

King, Yolanda, 97

Kissinger, Henry, 383, 434–35, 440, 512, 544

Kleindienst, Richard, 486–87

Klute (film), 128, 192, 230, 315, 368–72, 374–86, 389, 408, 418–20, 573–74, 640, 734, 841

Kovic, Ron, 522–23, 529, 530, 549, 559, 570

Kristofferson, Kris, 690–91
Kurtz, Carol, 430–31, 507, 526, 531, 624

La Curée (The Game Is Over) (film), 252
La Ronde (film), 200, 219, 223
Lafond, Julie, 603, 605, 606, 705, 709
Lalonde, Valarie, 318
Lancaster, Burt, 405, 668
Lane, Mark, 332, 365, 391
LaRouche, Lyndon, 588
Lau, Ha Van, 452, 455
Laurel Springs Ranch/Camp, 576, 577, 579–84, 609–10, 755, 762, 764
Laurents, Arthur, 198
Law, John Phillip, 253, 256, 263–64
Lemmon, Jack, 167, 169, 243, 571, 620
LeRoy, Mervyn, 169
Les Félins (film), 203
Lewis, Al, 313, 329

life video, 808–10, 818–19
Lifton, Robert J., 530
Logan, Joshua, 50, 85, 185, 188, 193, 195–96, 198, 572
Loren, Sophia, 252
Lulu, 581–84, 701, 714, 748, 754–55, 758, 791, 808, 846, 866
Lumet, Sidney, 142, 165, 682
Lustbader, Ellen "Ruby Ellen," 404, 423, 424, 521, 525–26

MacLaine, Shirley, 364
Maddux, Greg, 180
Malcolm X, 298, 840
Mandela, Nelson, 745
Mankiewicz, Joseph, 653
Mankiller, Wilma, 328
Marquand, Christian, 157, 250
Martin, Steve, 626
Marvin, Lee, 239
Matthau, Walter, 687
Maxwell, Elsa, 152
Mayer, Louis B., 257
McCarthy, Joseph, 93, 95, 335, 485

McCord, James W., Jr., 521

McGovern, George, 475, 482

McGuire, Dorothy, 113, 675

McGuirk, Nancy, 806, 831

Meadows, Jayne, 560

Medavoy, Mike, 523, 552

Meredith, Burgess, 253

Meshad, Shad, 529–30

Midnight Cowboy (film), 547, 548

Miller, Alice, 54, 387

Miller, Arthur, 470–71, 480

Miller, Edison, 475, 493–94

Miller, Henry, 213, 626

Mister Roberts (film/musical), 13–14, 25, 85, 86–87, 97, 109, 169

Mitchell, Pat, 842

MOBE (Mobilization to End the War), 353

Monroe, Marilyn, 167–68, 173–74, 180, 186, 199, 574–75

Monster-in-Law (film), 552, 862

Montand, Yves, 203, 204, 208, 291, 415, 418

Morgan, Robin, 229, 230–31, 248, 615, 777

The Morning After (film), 682, 697

Morse, Beverly Kitaen, 525, 797–98, 800–2

Mugar, Carolyn, 332, 365

Nat, Marie-José, 157

National Association of Working Women, 624n

National Caucus of Labor Committees, 588

Native Americans, 326, 328–29, 350–52, 423, 431

Natwick, Mildred, 260

Near, Holly, 411, 414, 506, 518

New York Drama Critics' Circle, 196

Newman, Paul, 166, 243, 668

Nichol, Jack, 507, 526

Nicholson, Jack, 241,
247
9 to 5 (film), 602,
623–24, 426,
428–29, 629n,
630–31, 690
Nixon, Richard M., 95,
285, 300, 359, 362,
383, 395, 398, 407,
412, 432–36, 448,
451, 455, 474, 487,
489, 491, 493n,
495, 500, 506, 512,
517, 521, 528,
537–38, 539–40,
543
Nussbaum, Karen, 507,
623, 624n, 628
Nye, Judy, 728, 759

Old Gringo (film), 498,
685, 697
On Golden Pond (film),
183, 340, 638–69,
670, 679, 683, 838
Onassis, Aristotle, 152
The Ox-Bow Incident
(film), 47, 97, 282

Pacino, Al, 128, 164,
166
Page, Geraldine, 166,
556, 640, 641, 692

Pakula, Alan, 128, 315,
343, 369, 372, 373,
375, 378, 574, 575,
640, 690
Parton, Dolly, 602, 624,
626, 629, 630–32,
639, 678, 692
"the Party of the
Decade," 243
Peck, Gregory, 685,
686–87
Penn, Arthur, 242,
245
Pentagon Papers, 407–8,
425, 432, 507, 513,
545
Period of Adjustment
(film), 199
Perkins, Anthony, 185
Poitier, Sidney, 243
Pollack, Sydney, 307–8,
312, 809
population issues, 719,
778–79, 780–87,
789–91
Powell, Colin, 774
Preminger, Otto, 253

**The Quilts of Gee's
Bend**
(documentary), 864
Quoc, 461, 468–70,
473, 476

race issues, 47, 97,
253–56, 757, 759
Raines, Howell, 764
Raitt, Bonnie, 421, 560,
745
Reagan, Ronald, 95
Real, Terrence, 116, 149
Redford, Robert, 242,
257, 258, 260, 592
Redgrave, Vanessa, 246,
300, 554, 556
Reiner, Michelle, 64
Reiner, Rob, 64
religion/spirituality, 81,
97, 128, 757, 804,
831–32, 853–56
Rich, Adrienne, 303
Richards, Beah, 253, 254
Rilke, Rainer Maria, 28,
69, 107, 696, 850,
852
RITA (Resisters Inside
the Army), 287–88
Rivers, Stephen, 498,
501
Robards, Jason, 246,
557, 574, 619
Rocky Mountain
epiphany, 369, 524
Rogers, Ginger, 67
Roland, Rich, 497, 499,
501, 502

Rollover (film), 690
Roosevelt, Eleanor, 613
Roosevelt, Franklin D.,
51, 57, 72, 96, 673,
727
Rosenberg, Mark, 703,
709
Rowland, John G., 497
Rumi, 322, 794
Rumsfeld, Donald, 400
Russo, Gaetano, 497
Rydell, Mark, 646, 665

Saint, Eva Marie, 675
Saks, Gene, 260
Salt, Waldo, 524, 548,
549, 559, 570
Sartre, Jean-Paul, 204,
285
Schary, Dore, 64
Schell, Jonathan,
288–92, 299, 328,
355, 840
Schlesinger, John, 548,
550
Schneider, Catherine,
208, 209, 212, 324,
558
Seberg, Jean, 243,
381–82, 417
Segal, George, 559
Selznick, Danny, 132

Selznick, David O., 132
Senate Armed Services
    Committee, 485,
    532
Senate Select Committee
    on Government
    Intelligence
    Activities, 380
September 11, 2001,
    367
Seydel, John R.
    (stepgrandson), 681
Seydel, Rutherford II,
    758
Seymour, Ford
    (grandfather),
    34–37, 60
Seymour, Sophie Bowen
    (grandmother), 11,
    20–21, 23, 24, 26,
    35–37, 38, 40, 58,
    59, 60, 64, 70, 90,
    102, 103, 107, 111
Shaw, Bernard, 774
Sheehan, Neil, 456
Sherrill, Robert, 355
Sherwood, Madeleine,
    253, 255
Signoret, Simone, 201,
    205, 208, 285,
    292–95, 418, 481
Silkwood, Karen, 571

Simon, Neil, 260
Sinatra, Frank, 241,
    745
sixtieth birthday, JF's,
    807–8, 810, 818
Smith, George, 396,
    474, 506
Soldier's Girl (TV film),
    865
Some Like It Hot (film),
    166–68
Southern, Terry, 243,
    253, 268
Spiegel, Sam, 241, 243
Stanislavsky, Konstantin,
    165
Stanley & Iris (film),
    496–97, 697, 700
Stanwyck, Barbara, 198,
    675
Stark, Ray, 198, 243
Steelyard Blues (film),
    403, 409, 422
Stein, Doris, 170, 243
Stein, Jules, 113, 170,
    243
Stein, Susan, 170
Steinem, Gloria, 231,
    515
Stewart, Jimmy, 51, 67,
    93, 95, 169, 670,
    675, 676

Strasberg, Lee, 164–66, 169, 170, 173–75, 179–82, 189–90, 196, 203, 375, 378

Strasberg, Paula, 166, 168

Strasberg, Susan, 165, 166, 170

Streep, Meryl, 556

Streisand, Barbra, 405

Stroyberg, Annette, 158, 208, 217, 224

Student Nonviolent Coordinating Committee (SNCC), 245–46, 254

Students for a Democratic Society (SDS), 422, 429, 560

Sullavan, Margaret, 49, 67, 193, 214

Sunday in New York (film), 217, 841

Sutherland, Donald, 375, 380, 389, 403, 405, 408–10, 412, 419, 420

Tall Story (film), 185, 188–89, 192, 198, 234, 841

Taradash, Daniel, 192, 196

Tate, Sharon, 243

Taylor, James, 560, 837

Taylor, Robert, 95

Teichmann, Howard, 19, 51, 112, 141

Thalberg, Irving, 257

There Was a Little Girl (film), 192, 196

They Shoot Horses, Don't They? (film), 299, 305–6, 307, 312, 315, 318, 320, 329, 333, 353, 401, 809

Thompson, Ernest, 646, 667

Three Mile Island, 621

Tiger Force, 400

Tigertail (JF's California home), 69–70, 87, 271

Till, Emmett, 807

Tomlin, Lily, 623, 626

Torn, Rip, 166

Tout Va Bien (film), 415, 417

Tracy, Spencer, 653, 659

Trintignant, Jean-Louis, 213

Truffaut, François, 201
Truman, Harry S., 93, 285, 293
Turbell, Susan, 99
Turner, Beauregard, 758, 867
Turner, Jennie, 758, 808, 867
Turner, Laura, 758, 791, 808, 867
Turner, Lucy, 728
Turner, Rhett, 758, 784, 867
Turner, Ted, 20, 64, 147, 594, 666, 711–15, 717, 719–40, 741–79, 789–91, 794–810, 818–19, 822–33, 835, 866–67
  childhood/youth of, 147, 180
  family background of, 718, 727–31, 750, 826
  JF first meets, 606
  JF's separation/divorce from, 765, 835, 836–49
  "Ten Voluntary Initiatives" of, 731
Turner, Teddy, 758, 867

Turner Broadcasting, 776
Turner Family Foundation, 778, 784, 791, 818, 866
Turner Tomorrow Award, 722
Tutu, Desmond, 618
12 Angry Men (film), 47, 142, 203
20/20 (ABC-TV), 131, 502

United Farm Workers, 550, 576
United Nations, 485, 515, 541, 732, 749, 779, 780–89, 790–92
United Nations Foundation, 768, 780
University of New Mexico, 360–61
University Players, 50, 193, 260

Vadim, Christian, 232, 235, 237, 301
Vadim, Hélène, 235, 323, 838

Vadim, Malcolm
    (grandson), 208,
    209, 212, 828,
    836, 838, 847,
    864, 867
Vadim, Nathalie, 217,
    219, 224, 232, 235,
    238, 240, 241, 248,
    250, 269, 302, 312,
    323, 691, 701, 706,
    714, 748, 754, 755,
    808, 866
Vadim, Propi, 250, 252,
    323
Vadim, Roger, 211,
    216–17, 220,
    225–235, 239–40,
    248–49, 269–70,
    282–83, 284, 286,
    288, 291, 295–99,
    301–3, 308, 312,
    315, 344, 345, 348,
    350, 352, 374, 404,
    417, 428, 430, 509,
    518, 558, 562, 568,
    616, 758
  death of, 208–9, 210,
    836, 837
  as director, 201, 203,
    703
  early life of, 147,
    212–13

films of, 155, 157,
    201, 203, 213, 219,
    223, 246, 252, 256,
    261–65, 268, 382
  JF's first encounter
    with, 157–58, 201
  JF's separation/divorce
    from, 319–20,
    322–25, 518, 705,
    800, 838
  and "the Party of the
    Decade," 244
  writings of, 147, 210,
    212, 215, 237, 320,
    344
Vadim, Vanessa
    (daughter), 208,
    210, 212, 270,
    301–2, 305, 313,
    315, 316, 320, 323,
    324, 325, 326, 338,
    374, 393, 403, 404,
    417, 418, 420, 424,
    427, 509, 519, 521,
    525, 527, 528, 529,
    534, 558, 570, 574,
    580, 584, 607, 644,
    608, 675, 679, 680,
    701, 704, 706, 714,
    743, 746, 748,
    754–55, 795, 799,
    804, 808, 818,

826–28, 835, 836, 837–38, 846, 864, 866

Vadim, Vania, 208–9

The Vagina Monologues, JF's performance of, 130, 842–43, 845

Vailland, Elisabeth, 344–45, 346, 352, 354, 359, 364, 367, 378, 383

Van Derbur, Marilyn, 824, 833

Vassar College, 45, 125, 139–40, 142, 148, 150–51, 234

Vidal, Gore, 261, 735

Vietnam, 437–55, 456–84, 487–88, 491–92, 499–500, 535–36, 541–42, 542**n**, 823
  bombings in, 432–36, 485, 491, 512, 543
  end of war in, 512, 540
  and France, 284–86, 292–94, 296, 544
  and French intelligentsia, 205, 268
  and Tonkin Gulf Resolution, 512
  and winning the war, 500–1, 543–45

Vietnam Veterans Against the War (VVAW), 364, 388, 390, 394–96, 420, 457

The Village of Ben Suc (Schell), 288–90, 291, 299, 328, 355, 840

Voight, Jon, 524, 531, 559, 564–69, 570

Wade, Joe, 32–33, 83

Wagner, Jane, 623, 626

Wahl, Teddy, 12, 21, 90, 98

Walk on the Wild Side (film), 198, 379

Walters, Barbara, 131, 595

Warhol, Andy, 241, 573

Warner, Jack, 188, 257, 572

Wasserman, Lew, 113

Wayne, John, 93, 95, 570

Weinglass, Leonard, 431, 485, 536

Weinstein, Hannah, 551
Weinstein, Paula,
    551–52, 609, 611,
    624, 702, 709, 748,
    841, 864
Wexler, Haskell, 535,
    559, 565, 569
Widmark, Richard, 405
Wilbourn, Phyllis, 644,
    645, 650
Wilbur, Walter, 494
The Wild Angels (film),
    246
Wilder, Billy, 167, 169
Williams, Barbara, 867
Willis, Gordon, 378–80,
    574
Winfrey, Oprah, 792
Winter Soldier
    Investigation,
    388–91, 394–400,
    401, 408, 452, 495,
    522
Women Coming of Age
    (McCarthy and JF),
    598

women's movement,
    349–50, 362–64,
    406–7
    See also feminism; 9
    to 5 (film)
Wood, Natalie, 186,
    197, 243
Woodman, Marion,
    121n, 126, 701,
    708, 824, 841, 853
Woods, Dee, 750, 795
Woodward, Joanne, 166
Workout Program, 192,
    589–608, 650, 690,
    764
Wyler, William, 243

Young, Andrew, 550,
    757, 805
Young Mr. Lincoln
    (film), 47, 97, 203,
    282, 335, 463

Zabaleen people (Cairo,
    Egypt), 784–89
Zinn, Howard, 463, 618

CREDITS AND PERMISSIONS

Grateful acknowledgment is given to the following:

Bloodaxe Books: From "Honour Killing" from **I Speak for the Devil** by Imtiaz Dharker (Bloodaxe Books, 2001). Reprinted by permission of the publisher.

Charles Darling: "The Magician's Assistant" by Charles Darling is reprinted by permission of Professor Charles Darling, Capital Community College, Hartford, Conn.

Egmont Books Ltd.: From **The Velveteen Rabbit**. Copyright © 1922 The Estate of Margery Williams. Published by Egmont Books Ltd., London, and used with permission.

Farrar, Straus & Giroux, LLC: "Ah, as we prayed for human help" from **Uncollected Poems** by Rainer

Maria Rilke, trans. by Edward Snow. Translation copyright © 1996 by Edward Snow. Reprinted by permission of North Point Press, a division of Farrar, Straus and Giroux, LLC.

HarperCollins Publishers Inc.: From "I am too alone in the world . . ." and from "The Ashantis" from **Selected Poems of Rainer Maria Rilke**, ed. and trans. by Robert Bly. Copyright © 1981 by Robert Bly. Reprinted by permission of HarperCollins Publishers Inc.

Kokomo Music: From "Nick of Time" written by Bonnie Raitt, copyright © 1989 Kokomo Music. All Rights Reserved. International Copyright Secured. Used by permission.

Majorsongs, Co. and Harrison Music: "Ballerina" written by Carl Sigman and Bob Russell. Published by Majorsongs, Co. (ASCAP)/Administered by Bug Music Inc. (BMI). Published by Harrison Music. All Rights Reserved. Used by permission.

Methuen: From "On Leaving the Theatre" by Edward Bond used by permission of the publisher, Methuen and Casarotto Ramsay & Associates Ltd.

Robin Morgan: An excerpt from **The Burning Time** by Robin Morgan and an e-mail written by Robin Morgan are reprinted with the permission of Robin Morgan.

New Directions Publishing Corporation: From "Relearning the Alphabet" by Denise Levertov from

ABOUT THE AUTHOR

JANE FONDA was born in New York City in 1937. She attended the Emma Willard School in Troy, New York, and Vassar College. Fonda later studied with renowned acting coach Lee Strasberg and became a member of the Actors Studio in New York. Her subsequent work on stage and screen earned numerous honors, including two Best Actress Academy Awards—**Klute** (1971) and **Coming Home** (1978)—and an Emmy Award for her performance in **The Dollmaker.** Fonda was also a successful producer, whose credits include **The China Syndrome** (executive producer), **9 to 5, On Golden Pond,** and **The Morning After.**

Fonda revolutionized the fitness industry with the release of **Jane Fonda's Workout** in 1982, which remains the top grossing home video of all time. She then produced twenty-three home exercise videos, thirteen audio recordings, and five best-selling books—altogether selling sixteen million copies.

She now focuses her time and energy on activism and philanthropy, in such areas as adolescent reproductive health, pregnancy prevention, and building resiliency in girls and boys by addressing destructive gender stereotypes. In 1995 she founded the Georgia Campaign for Adolescent Pregnancy Prevention (G-CAPP), which she chairs, and opened the Jane Fonda Center at the Emory School of Medicine. She lives in Atlanta.